Sex Crimes and Offenders

THEORY AND PRACTICE IN CRIMINAL JUSTICE SERIES

Series Editor

Kimberly A. McCabe, University of Lynchburg, mccabe@lynchburg.edu

Theory and Practice in Criminal Justice provides professors with textbooks that cover popular criminal justice topics. This series of textbooks are comprehensible to students, while also having direct coverage and case examples. Each textbook in the series includes both core textbooks and supplemental textbooks, with complementing formats to allow instructors to utilize them together for the same course. Finally, the authorship of this series incorporates an academic and practitioner perspective that brings scholarship and real-life experiences to the student for a better preparation in the classroom and to the field.

Books in the Series

Acts of Violence in the School Setting: National and International Responses, By Kimberly A. McCabe—With Brianna Egan and Toy D. Eagle

Child Abuse, Child Exploitation, and Criminal Justice Responses, By Daniel G. Murphy and April G. Rasmussen

Sex Crimes and Offenders: Exploring Questions of Character and Culture, By Mary Clifford and Alison Feigh

Sex Crimes and Offenders

Exploring Questions of Character and Culture

◆ ◆ ◆

Mary Clifford
St. Cloud State University

Alison Feigh
Jacob Wetterling Resource Center

ROWMAN & LITTLEFIELD
Lanham • Boulder • New York • London

Acquisitions Editor: Kathryn Knigge
Sales and Marketing Inquiries: textbooks@rowman.com

Credits and acknowledgments for material borrowed from other sources, and reproduced with permission, appear on the appropriate pages within the text.

Published by Rowman & Littlefield
An imprint of The Rowman & Littlefield Publishing Group, Inc.
4501 Forbes Boulevard, Suite 200, Lanham, Maryland 20706
www.rowman.com

86–90 Paul Street, London EC2A 4NE, United Kingdom

British Library Cataloguing in Publication Information Available

Library of Congress Control Number: 2019918303

ISBN: 978-1-5381-2516-8 (cloth)
ISBN: 978-1-5381-2517-5 (pbk)
ISBN: 978-1-5381-2518-2 (electronic)

∞™ The paper used in this publication meets the minimum requirements of American National Standard for Information Sciences—Permanence of Paper for Printed Library Materials, ANSI/NISO Z39.48-1992.

Contents

◆ ◆ ◆

Foreword

Kimberly A. McCabe, PhD
Professor of Criminology
University of Lynchburg

◆ ◆ ◆

SEX CRIMES AND OFFENDERS: Exploring Questions of Character and Culture, written by Mary Clifford and Alison Feigh, is a necessary textbook for courses that focus on victims of violence, children's legal services, or criminal justice policy. This textbook, with its broad focus on gender-based violence, introduces the dynamics of sexual violence as a precursor to discussions on sex offenders to include the many challenges of response from a collective community.

Through their approach, Clifford and Feigh remove the myths in the idea of the sex offender to the reality of violence and trauma throughout history. The authors, both knowledgeable about crimes of sexual violence within the practical and research communities, provide the reader practical approaches to discussions on sex crimes and explanations of cultural responses.

Within this book, sex crimes are discussed within the context of national and international settings. Because technology now facilitates many of these crimes and connects victims and offenders across police jurisdictions, these authors assert the need for international policies and practices as related to rules of law and personhood rights.

Central to the themes of this book are insights into the label of sex offender, the reality of sex crimes and offenders, and the need for cooperation among all parties to address these crimes of violence. In addition, this book expands on the conflicting policies and practices by the law enforcement community and the court systems.

From a professor who teaches courses on victimology, it is my opinion that this book would be an excellent addition to numerous criminal justice courses. In addition, this book is recommended for many subject areas within the academic discipline of criminal justice as well as being applicable to subjects within the disciplines of sociology and social work.

Introduction

Listening to the Silence Surrounding
Sexual Health and Harms

Before the child ever gets to school it will have received crucial, almost irrevocable sex education and this will have been taught by the parents, who are not aware of what they are doing.

—Mary S. Calderone, MD and (1954) co-founder of the Sex Information and Education Council of the United States (SIECUS)[1]

What is peculiar to modern societies, in fact, is not that they consigned sex to a shadow existence, but that they dedicated themselves to talking about it *ad infinitum*, while exploiting it as *the* secret.

—Michel Foucault, *The History of Sexuality*[2]

The very first part in healing is shattering the silence.

—Erin Merryn, *Living for Today*[3]

A bill that defines sexual consent and sparked national controversy passed the Utah House of Representatives on Tuesday, after an awkward silence on the House floor. No lawmakers wanted to talk about Rep. Angela Romero's House Bill 74, which changes Utah's sexual consent law to state that an unconscious person cannot consent to sex.

—FOX13 Salt Lake City, February 10, 2015[4]

#metoo

—Tarana Burke, 2006, community organizer and activist

CONVERSATIONS ABOUT SEXUAL VIOLENCE and related harms are moving out from a kind of shadowy silence and into the light of a progressively more

1

vocalized world. Questions about the boundaries of sexual health and sexual harm continue to represent ongoing curiosities for people of all ages, raising a myriad of ongoing social and political controversies along the way. Lessons about appropriate and inappropriate social behaviors typically come in the form of praise and prohibitions, often outlined by adults or deciphered by watching others conform to or challenge existing social boundaries. Silent, nonverbal cues say a great deal, especially when conversations about sex that do happen are whispered in stilted or hushed exchanges or used as a punchline for a laugh. In reality, what a younger person might *see* regarding the parameters of socially acceptable behavior can sometimes compete with what they might be *told* about socially appropriate boundaries, and, when the topic is sex, this can be extremely confusing, particularly in the age of Google.

Be they religious, political, social, economic, cultural, or any other form of a social collective, various groups have long sought to both informally and formally regulate certain sexual acts or forms of behavior defined as sexual. At different times and places in history the following acts have been characterized as sexually deviant and or criminal:

> exhibitionism, voyeurism, abortion, bestiality, masturbation, contraception, consensual sadomasochistic activity, sexual relations with a person of a different race, homosexual relationships between consenting adults (male or female), heterosexual relationships between men and women not legally married to each other, and the practice of miscellaneous positions or techniques, with even marriage providing no defense against prosecution for consensual oral or anal sex.[5]

In some cases these crimes were deemed so injurious to the collective social body, the penalty for the perpetrator was death. With historical distance, some of these same acts have come to be legally protected, if not socially supported, while others remain prohibited. These and other shifts regarding the boundaries of what is identified as criminal activity illustrate at least some of the reasons why ongoing social conversations about sex crimes are important for people of all ages.

In a surface review, the lines separating sex crime classifications and the socially determined parameters of sexual health, disease, deviance, and sexual harm are not as clearly delineated as they might at first appear. Consider, for example, the existence of well documented, even notorious, acts of sexual violence and related harms throughout history, such as a notorious serial rapist or abuse by a teacher or a leader within a well-respected faith community. Few would dispute the abuse; however, it was seen as an isolated, even rare, incident. More recently, however, questions are being raised regarding other kinds of less prominent but potentially hurtful sexualized behaviors traditionally overlooked. Harassing behaviors argued to be accepted as "normal" or something "to be expected" are being challenged and called out.

A bright light against the more shadowy backdrop, the 2018 arrest of internationally known film producer Harvey Weinstein on sexual assault charges came eight months after national stories broke, documenting claims from victims going back decades[6] and exploding the once local **#MeToo** community effort into a viral movement and a national statement to "find entry points for individual healing and galvanizing a broad base of survivors to disrupt the systems that allow for the global proliferation of sexual violence."[7] Allegations against several other prominent men promptly followed, as did the high-profile conviction of comedian Bill Cosby for sexual assault.[8]

Linked to a long history of controversial public and private practices, an increasing number of people are asking, *How is it possible such harmful actions linger in the shadows, or worse, exist openly with little or no collective social or legal responses to stop them from happening or to prevent them from happening in the first place, and what can be done about it?* In addition, they are demanding healthy change. The layers of analysis regarding the impacts of sexually harmful behaviors are many. Questions about sexual violence and sexual violence prevention require the preference for individual and social conversation, critical reflection, and well-researched information over silence or whispers.

The information presented throughout the text is designed and organized to be a great place to come to learn about a broad range of dynamics related to any given discussion on sex crimes. For some, the content can sometimes be difficult to take in, however, and the material or one's individual response may be more emotionally charged than anticipated while reading about a given subject. Therefore, after a brief review of the format of the text, this introduction presents six themes to reflect on, particularly for those new to this area of study: (1) The "Silent" Sex Talk; (2) Consent, Compliance, Coercion, and Continuums; (3) The Bully and the Bystander; (4) The Media; (5) Self-Care; and (6) Creating Space for Ongoing Personal Reflections.

INDIVIDUAL CHARACTERS AND CULTURES: A BRIEF PRELUDE TO THEORY AND PRACTICE

Focused and intentional efforts to reduce or eliminate sexual harms within a given society require intentional and informed action be taken by as many people as possible within that given society. What researchers have come to know and are continuing to learn about sex offenses and offenders could fill countless pages in countless numbers of books. It seems almost impossible to include everything needed for this conversation here, social theories, psychological theories, crime theories, prevention theories, and all kinds of research and theories. While researchers are exploring theories, practitioners are developing ways to put those theories to work, and then researchers study whether and to what degree the ideas translate from theories and papers to real-world application. That is a lot of research and a lot of teaching and learning.

And yet, as much as research is teaching us, what remains unknown looms larger. The truth is, studying sex crimes and incidents that cause some of the most intimate kinds of human harms is not easy. One way to think about this is to imagine a constant state of reflecting forward. Usually, a person reflects backward, on something that has already happened. Here, as researchers, practitioners, or life-livers, difficult and life-altering incidents can surprise you, even when you think you are ready for the worst . . . of the worst. Here, studying sexualized harms requires police officers, social workers, health and human services personnel, educators, and health care professionals to be alert, to be ready and aware. And yet preparing those who work in the helping professions is not nearly enough. Here, we know sexual violence often happens in the most intimate of social circles. Here, we know preventing sexual harms—and developing better responses to those harms—requires all of us: friends, families, neighborhoods, faith communities, daycare providers, coaches, and scout leaders. Here, the offenders violate a kind of sacred trust. As researchers and helping professionals, moms and dads, friends and family, we must all be, at some level, a sexual violence prevention practitioner.

The entire body of theories used to study sex crimes and offenders includes focused attention on both the individual actor and the possible influences of larger social systems and structures. Questions are raised here about the individual characteristics of a person who would commit a sex crime, but these individual actors also move through a particular social existence. To the degree that researchers and observers understand those dynamics, between the individual and their choice and social experiences, is the degree to which solutions emerge, evolve, are clarified and modified for the best possible responses to very difficult crime experiences. This is why the text includes themes on individual character as well as culture.

The primary goal of the text is to explore contemporary research and related occupational practice to best illustrate and overview a range of sexually harmful behaviors and the social responses to this particular kind of crime and criminal. The goal is to reduce, if not eliminate, sexual violence and related harms. In an effort to build a bridge between the day-to-day practitioners responding to sexual violence or assisting those who have been harmed and the newly recruited prevention practitioners mentioned above (all of the rest of us), the parameters for the content presented start with a review of sexual health and sexual deviance. Studying sex crimes without having at least considered what society generally identifies as healthy or deviant sexual practice might feel a bit like trying to find the ground from midair. You'll get there eventually, but it may be a bit of a jolt. Definitely better to have a solid footing first. Reviews of historical traditions and landmark events follow, with a broad review of what steps researchers, practitioners, and policy makers have taken to address the issues related to sex crimes and related harms. The information presented explores individual treatment efforts as well as the social and political responses designed to hold perpetrators accountable and help support victims. Finally, the book concludes by shining a light on the efforts each of us can take to identify, reduce, and work toward eliminating sexual violence and harms. Please note that several terms are introduced in this overview with very brief definitions but more complete definitions and discussions are provided in subsequent chapters. Content is divided into five sections, each with a primary question as its predominant theme. Chapters in each section are organized to address the larger section theme and are briefly reviewed below. Together, these are questions about the role of character and the role of culture and the role of each of us in learning about how to work toward eliminating sexual violence and related harms.

Section I: Is it possible to agree about the parameters of healthy, deviant, and criminal sexual behaviors?

Like in many places around the world, open discussions of sexual behaviors in the United States have been considered inappropriate among certain segments of the population. Although researchers and social critics had been talking about the study of human sexuality in Europe by the end of the nineteenth century, **Dr. Alfred Kinsey** and a team of research assistants from the **Institute for Sex Research**, founded in 1947 at Indiana University, did some of the earliest work studying and discussing sex more publicly in the United States. Their efforts to collect and document the self-reported sexual histories of "average Americans" was praised in some circles but rigorously challenged academically, socially, and politically after their findings were presented in the 1948 publication of *Sexual Behavior in the Human Male* and the follow-up volume, *Sexual Behavior in the Human Female* in 1953.[9] Beginning in the late 1960s, interest in and attention to particular medical knowledge about human sexuality was present in the US mainstream with medical research from **Masters and Johnson**. Section I explores these questions about sexual health and outlines enquiries related to classifications of deviance.

The dialogue about sexual health established a foothold in various fields, primarily medicine and psychology, and more recently in the emerging field of **sexology**, the interdisciplinary study of sex. The related crime classification discussions have traditionally fallen under the purview of the political system and are then transferred to the criminal justice system for identification, investigation, prosecution, and punishment. Sometimes, policy makers require a working knowledge of research that can at times be technical because it comes from a range of social, medical, and psychological sciences. The fact that *The Joy of Sex* (1972) spent more than a year on the bestseller list seemingly suggests at least some shifts in popular attitudes of openness about sex, and yet as late as 2008 some communities across the country found the book too controversial for public libraries and were forced through legal action to make them available.[10] If society, as a rule, cannot agree about what is healthy, it seems that making laws about what is deemed unhealthy or inappropriate will be almost impossible.

Section II: How does history continue to shape understandings of sexual health, harm, and definitions of sexual violence today?

In the United States, history offers a seemingly unlimited number of cases involving allegations of sexual harm that circumvented any formal proceedings or were ignored more broadly. Such has been the case with many incidents of incest or rape of a marital partner, forced sex within the institution of slavery, or abuse by priests, as examples. To pave the way to a better understanding of the complexities associated with sexual harms committed today, questions of how violence is identified, acknowledged, and defined; who perpetrates violence; who is victimized; and how to better understand the conditions that surround victimization are among the essential and powerful historical themes under review in section II. In the case of incest, for example, the social taboo has existed for thousands of years across many countries, yet people in the United States had rarely spoken about incest or child sexual abuse before the 1970s. Why? Further back in history, sexual abuses of slaves and indentured servants went virtually unrestricted and, when confronted, were seldom punished. Why? The full extent of sexual abuse of First Nation and indigenous children in church and state-run boarding schools in both Canada and United States remains unknown to this day while indigenous women are increasingly acknowledged as representing the highest rates of sexual violence victimization in any given demographic.[11] Targeted abuse of people who identify as or are suspected of being LGBTQI continues. A compilation of historical themes and markers is presented in an effort to better understand aspects of sexual violence today.

Section III: What do researchers and practitioners know about sex offenders and the people they harm?

Perhaps one of the most confounding realities in the study of sexual harms is the behavior of the offender. In spite of targeted research, no single profile has emerged to provide a clear indication of who might be a sex offender or what causes someone to offend against another in a sexual way.[12] Add to that multiple studies suggesting that as many as 93% of people who are victimized know the perpetrator, and it becomes clear why it is so important to get good information out to expand effective prevention. Incomplete understandings of who might "look like" an offender make efforts to define suitable punishments difficult. While research continues, comparatively little is known about offenders, and widespread but erroneous assumptions are often made about victims. The effects of an incident of sexual harm are different for every victim/survivor, and for some they can be extremely traumatic. Section III addresses what researchers and practitioners know about both offenders and the people they offend against. Traditionally, many people who have been offended against have not been squarely acknowledged or identified or supported through what can be a terrifying experience. Research on the victimization experience is reviewed. Additional attention is given to how offenders behave leading up to an assault, with a focus on how to educate ourselves and others about prevention when and where it is possible.

Section IV: In what ways is the criminal justice system addressing the issue of sex crimes and allegations of sexual violence?

The topics of child sexual abuse, domestic violence, and intimate partner violence offer a window into some of the complex dynamics that can be involved in addressing sexualized harms when the victim and the offender not only know each other but are family members or marital or domestic partners or live or work together in some other relationship. In 2005, researcher **Karl Hanson**, well known for his work on sex offender treatment and recidivism research, highlighted a general trend suggesting that 40% of kids molested by strangers report the abuse but only 10% do so if they are molested by someone they know.[13] This is particularly unsettling; if the majority of offenses go unaccounted for in the larger criminal justice system response because the offense never gets reported, then offenders never get identified, charged, prosecuted, convicted, sentenced, or punished. Section IV will address the social response to allegations of sexual harms for those who are taken into the criminal justice system and includes a review of several laws and policies governing the process, the police, the courts, and the correctional management of offenders.

Section IV will also review issues related to legislation, social policy, and the criminal justice system process. Significant questions have been raised about whether the design of the legal process imposes additional burdens or injury on victims.[14] The variety and severity of problems is receiving significant attention. In September 2010 the US Senate Judiciary Committee held public hearings on the chronic failure of the criminal justice system to successfully investigate and prosecute sex crimes.[15] That hearing was credited, at least in part, for producing a new (2012) federal definition of rape to ensure these crimes will be more accurately reported and charged by police.[16] Yet another 2010 report found sexual misconduct to be the second most frequently reported form of police misconduct, after excessive force,[17] and in 2016 a National Institute of Justice study found that half of police arrests for sexual misconduct made were for incidents involving minors.[18] In 2018, separate incidents in several states prompted the passage of legislation making it illegal for police officers to have sex with someone being detained in police custody. Examples of how the system falls short, particularly for victims, can be found at every stage in the process.

The trial process is also a momentous event as offenders are prosecuted. A 1925 New York divorce trial became famous when Alice Jones married the son of a wealthy New York family. Under pressure from his family, the young man sought an annulment of the marriage when it was reported in the press that her father was of mixed race. Accused of attempting to "pass" as white, the judge famously made her display portions of her body to the all-male, all-white jury in the judge's chamber in an effort to "prove" she was "colored." Although the annulment request was denied and the marriage upheld, the actions in the courtroom were unprecedented.[19]

In a well-known 1989 case, famously referred to as the **Glen Ridge rape case**, a woman with cognitive disabilities[20] who had been brutally gang-raped by four high school football players was characterized at trial as a seductress and then referred to by defense attorneys as "not credible" when her testimony had omissions and inconsistencies.[21] Among the many details of the trial at issue was whether she understood or could agree to sex, but her treatment by defense counsel in the courtroom was seen as shocking. More recently, Montana's judicial system made headlines when in one case a judge made comments from the bench that seemed to blame a 14-year-old who was raped by a teacher and then handed down an inexplicably light sentence.[22] In another Montana case, the judge departed from legal requirements when he handed down a 30-year suspended sentence to a father who pled guilty to raping his 12-year-old daughter.[23] Both cases resulted in significant public outcry and again raise questions about the treatment and protection of victims of sexual assault in the legal proceedings.

In perhaps one of the most surreal court proceedings, a 2011 Florida rape trial, the accused rapist acted as his own attorney. For two hours he cross-examined the person he was accused of raping, asking questions like "Were you wearing underwear on the night of the alleged attack?" After receiving numerous admonishments from the judge and having significant difficulty throughout the court proceedings, he then asked the judge to grant a mistrial claiming he had received inadequate legal representation. After the judge denied his request, he reinstated his attorney but was found guilty and sentenced to life in prison.[24] Although the offender was within his legal rights to serve as his own defense counsel, imagine the burden of this legal involvement for the victim, who was forced to confront the person on trial for raping her in such a prominent role at trial.[25]

Section V: What can be done to help identify, address, and prevent sexual harm?

In a research area where the most extreme examples make the headlines, it is perhaps easy to forget—and important to remember—that, for every case that hits the press and catches fire on social media, other victims and offenders proceed quietly through a system after the events that bring them there have likely changed their lives in dramatic ways. Sentences for sex-related crimes vary dramatically from state to state, and few sex offenders will spend the rest of their lives in prison. Eventually, most offenders sentenced to prison are released back into the community. How the community reacts to offenders coming out of prison can create layers of challenges for victims and, more broadly, the community.

Questions about the efficacy of individual and/or community efforts to protect against sexual harms remain a central, controversial, and essential subject for refining ongoing prevention and response efforts. Treatment options for offenders and programs that offer support for both victims and offenders will largely depend on local community resources, goals, and priorities. The fifth and final section is focused on prevention. Emphasizing the need for individuals to explore the communities close to home, by the time readers get to the end of the larger discussion, it is important to talk about how individuals and communities are coming together to respond to both the perpetrators of sexual harms and the people they have hurt. Ultimately, it takes everyone to expand prevention efforts.

Supplemental Materials: Media messages, myths and facts, and appendices

Each of the five sections closes with a brief piece on the media, offering points for consideration related to issues from the preceding section. The role and reach of media and emerging technologies will help explore how people learn about sex; the messages they get from movies, TV, and the internet; and for developing interpersonal relationships. The use of media is explored to better understand how people interact with information used to advise if not create overarching understandings when people have questions about healthy sex, sexual deviance, and sexual harms as well as exploring sexual offenders and sexual offending. Supplemental and updated materials will also be provided on the textbook website.

Because sex offenders and sexual violence is likely one of the most misunderstood areas of research and the ideas people have about sexual violence and sexual offenses and offenders has been steeped heavily in cultural lore and myths, a collection of some of the most common myths and evidence supporting the research-supported reality is offered in appendix A. Appendix B includes various national resources for protection and prevention.

People learn about their social and sexual reality from various places. Some people live in smaller community groups or belong to active communities with well-developed sex education programs. Whether based in the family, school, faith communities, neighborhoods, or friendship groups or on TV, social conversations about sexual attitudes, healthy sex, definitions and parameters of deviant sex, and the legal boundaries of inappropriate sex come from all over. Making sure the information sources used to educate individual and social attitudes while fostering critical thinking and reflection is an important part of making sure to encourage dialogue, evidence-based data collection, and successful policy development.

A final note about terms. The terms **sexual violence** and **sexual harm** are used here and through the book in an effort to navigate between different perceptions as well as researcher definitions of what is identified as "violent" and what is identified as "harm." Technically, a sex "crime" is an act defined and addressed by the legal system, but an act that is technically legal can also cause harm. Because issues of violence and harm are not neatly enveloped in the term "sex crime," the terms *sexual violence* and *sexual harm* are used to distinguish the legal status of an act from the harm caused. Sexual violence will refer to the act of aggression, and sexual harm will refer to the impact of an act, even if that action was not intended to cause harm. More detail is provided about these and related terms in section I.

THE "SILENT" SEX TALK

A great deal of what children and young people learn comes to them by watching and listening. Cartoons and other media images, friends, older kids, and family members inform the messages kids receive about healthy and hurtful interactions. Social interactions can be seen from various levels: at the level of the individual, in relationship with another person, from within a social group (such as a family, faith community, neighborhood, or school), and from within larger groups even still (such as a city, region, state, or nation). Messages about sex are no different. One of the goals for this project is to explore and critically review the elements of the larger social conversations about sex that happen publicly *while also including* parts of the conversations that go underground, remaining more secretive and hidden.

Anyone undertaking a serious study of sex crimes will undoubtedly confront confounding or contradictory information as they research any given area of study. Certainly, the material being compiled for consideration in each chapter could be expanded into an entire book on its own. Research is ongoing and updating regularly, as are social attitudes about sexual behaviors and practices. Sadly, few will experience life completely free from this kind of violence, and, increasingly, individuals and communities are seeking out solutions and creating ways to improve current approaches and responses. Individual conversations and experiences blend into larger social conversations while people create and sometimes complicate intense desires to minimize hurt and prevent future harms. To be sure, well-intentioned people approach this goal in various and diverse ways, sometimes, complicating the prevention and protection efforts further.

As recently as the late 1970s, French philosopher and social critic **Michel Foucault** famously published the first in a multivolume exploration on the social discourse of human sexuality, *The History of Sexuality*, volumes 1, 2, and 3 (1979).[26] The reflections on sexuality were used to explore, at least in part, the idea of **social discourse**, or subjects of ongoing social dialogue. Questions are raised about how these decisions are made. Who has the power to effect change or direct the larger conversation? On the subject of sexuality, a particularly interesting question focused on asking how sexuality can be an ever-present theme simultaneously identified and discussed as something secret or hidden. Said differently, *How can sex be described as a taboo topic while at the same time people talk incessantly about the appropriateness and inappropriateness of social rules directing sexual behavior and the related punishments for violation of socially accepted sexual rules?*

Children observe when their parents shift uncomfortably during certain scenes in a movie or turn the channel quickly when something they identify as inappropriate comes on the screen. Researchers collectively work to clarify the number of children and young people who are vulnerable to being abused sexually, but in reality that number is not known. Statistics suggest a smaller percentage of these offenses against children result in death. These acts, in whatever form they come, affect in ways similar to others' social interactions: on individuals and their friends, families, and other social groups and on the larger communities. The degree to which the family and friends of the victim and/or the family and friends of the offender are affected by the event must not be overlooked in the larger conversation.

One point of analysis focuses on the individual experiences—the need to support victims, prevent future victims, and hold offenders accountable. On the other end of this range of conversations about sex crimes, researchers and social critics are asking the larger community to reflect on their role in creating sexually harmful messages between those two points—the individual and the larger community. What messages exist in the social interactions among friends at school, at church, and in the neighborhood who work to enhance awareness and prevention? Questions about unspoken ideas, intangibles, and things that might be hard to identify or measure must be included.

Things Said

What should children be told about sex and when, and who should decide what is said to them? One long-standing political battle is around determining the role schools are to play in teaching children and young people about sex. Does teaching kids about sex make them want to have sex or help them prevent becoming victims? **Abstinence only education** has been a popular conversation regarding sex education for years and refers in general to the idea of teaching young people to wait until marriage to have sex. Although still popular in some circles, another idea is **comprehensive sex education** in which discussions about sex are presented starting early and in age-appropriate ways. Reflecting a bit of the political nature this has taken on over the years, in 2010 District Attorney Scott Southworth in Juneau County Wisconsin warned teachers against teaching aspects of the new comprehensive sex education law that had just been passed in the state, threatening teachers who tell students how to use condoms and other contraceptives with the criminal charge of "contributing to the delinquency of a minor."[27]

Without question, contemporary US society remains riveted, somewhere between perplexed and animated, by the ongoing efforts to establish appropriate legal and social limits of regulating sexual behavior. For example, social media platforms are providing investigators with an evidence trail they didn't have in the past, and in May 2018 as many as five teachers were in the Ohio court system.[28] These cases demonstrate the community's lack of tolerance for illegal and inappropriate sexual behavior in people in positions of trust with children. What of cases of sexual deviance that are not the most gruesome but are still identified as illegal or problematic? In a 2006 Texas case, an art teacher was fired for taking her art class on a school-approved field trip to an art museum that displayed nude images of the human body. A student told her parents about the trip, the parents complained to the school, and the teacher was suspended and then later fired.[29]

In 2003, Joanne Webb, a 43-year-old former school teacher and mother of three, made national news when she was arrested by two undercover Texas law enforcement officers and charged with violating the state's obscenity law after hosting a "passion party," where women over 18 get together for a Tupperware-style party and shop for lotions, lingerie, and sex toys "designed to enhance their sex lives."[30] The case got extensive media coverage. The misdemeanor charges, threatening up to a year in jail with a $4,000 fine, were later dropped. But companies in the industry sued, and in 2008 a federal appeals court overturned the Texas sex toy ban, citing the Fourteenth Amendment, right to privacy.[31] Are sex toy laws outdated, or should they be included with other efforts to outlaw certain types of sexual behaviors?

In January 2018 a 14-year-old girl was charged with felony distribution of child pornography when she sent an explicit Snapchat to a boy she liked.[32] Without her permission, he sent the picture on to other students. This circumstance makes her both the perpetrator and a victim. Even if she pleads to a lesser charge, she faces 10 years on probation and must register as a sex offender. Young people who take naked or semi-naked pictures of themselves and either send the pictures to other people or receive a picture and send it on to others are committing a serious felony-level crime. More is discussed on this in section IV on criminal justice, particularly chapter 11, on laws and policies. The laws in this area are shifting; however, questions are still being raised about whether these young people are appropriately classified as sex offenders.

Undoubtedly, individuals who abuse other people in the most horrible of ways are a significant social concern that needs to be addressed. People who maliciously bully or attempt to humiliate people by forwarding images or uploading sex tapes without the person's consent might be seen as less significant offenders, but how should they be treated? Should they be treated differently from in-person sexual aggressors? It is clear the definitions of sexual harm and violence are developed differently by different social groups, exposing them as **social constructs**, or ideas created by social groups. The social construction of crime has been well documented.[33] The more laws that are passed to increasingly regulate nuances of sexual behavior and make them illegal, the more people will be arrested, charged, and convicted and the more sex offenders there will be to police, arrest, convict, treat, and/or punish. Said differently, and perhaps more obviously, the more sex acts that are made illegal, the more violations of the law there will be and the more arrests and prosecutions and convictions for sex offenses will follow. What role do less-formal social sanctions play in regulating sexual behaviors?

When such extreme degrees of difference exist between people's attitudes about sex and the boundaries between healthy sex and sexual harm are unclear, the idea of identifying or labeling everyone who violates a sex law as a "sex offender" requires additional and expanded reflection. As an example, as far back as 1998, *Moral Panic* documented the historical trend of social groups, legislators, media outlets, sociologists, psychologists, criminologists, and legal professionals lumping together anyone with any kind of sex offense in one large pool collectively called "sex offenders." In the past, the terms used to identify this population included pervert, pedophile, molester, defiler, psychopath, and predator.[34]

Yet the most extreme conceptualization of a "sex offender" typically is assigned to the perpetrator of any variety of related sex crimes. The most atrocious crimes represent only a small percentage of homicides and sex offenses in general. **David Finkelhor**, director of the **Crimes Against Children Research Center** at the University of New Hampshire, said that, of the 60,000 to 70,000 arrests each year for sex crimes against children, about 40 to 50 involve homicides.[35] Concerns are raised about how effective the related social policies are and how far they go toward addressing a reduction in sexual harm and crime.[36] When new laws and regulations are hastily passed, people criticize them as being something that makes people feel better but do not actually effectively reduce sexual harm.[37]

When the larger community conversation overtakes the informed conversation or people talk about sex offenders in a generic way without a full understanding about the breadth of sex crimes and the related legal system, things said dramatically affect efforts to expand awareness and educate more broadly. Loud demands for immediate action surrounding the social focus on sexual offenses have also produced laws facing strong public backlash amid claims of unfair treatment of convicted sex offenders.[38] A critical focus is spending time thinking about how what is said about sex crimes helps or hinders the process that is intended to protect society from sexual violence and sexual harm.

Things Left Unsaid

When complex social issues are discussed, it is often difficult to state flat out what is not known. Sometimes, research cannot point out a specific number, or people do not have the interest to read about a subject in detail. Related to the things people say about offenders, information is often presented about what an offender might look like. In reality, conversations about how offenders behave and how they make initial contacts with people they intend to harm need to be had. So, while attention must be given to what people say, information and critical dialogue must be shared regarding what is not typically known or talked about.

As suggested above, the inability to identify sex offenders who evade capture but who may continue to abuse if they are not stopped creates a significant concern. The **dark figure of crime** refers to the number of crimes committed that remain unknown to law enforcement. For decades sexual violence has been described as an **epidemic** in the United States, but, more recently, that idea has been challenged. An *epidemic* is a *trend that has a spike, a period of time when the event under study goes up and then comes down*. But the statistics on sexual harm, including child abuse, rape, and domestic violence, have never peaked; they have stayed at steady levels across various measures over decades of data collection.[39] In this way, sexual violence has increasingly been described as **endemic**, *an event prevalent in or peculiar to a specific locality*. For years researchers and social observers of violence and abuse have watched a consistent level of incidents throughout the United States. Is this abuse a widespread and socially pervasive feature of life in the United States, which many are so used to seeing that it not only goes unreported but also unnoticed?[40] If it is noticed, why are there not more efforts to stop it?

When important issues are confounding, a future course of action is difficult to determine. For many, simple is "better," which makes complicated "worse." To this end, a kind of **ideological dualism** provides an effective conversational tool: simple/complicated, better/worse, healthy/unhealthy, criminal/noncriminal, or right/wrong. Separating complex ideas into two competing parts seems to make things simpler, but it also leaves a lot of things unsaid. Sex crime classifications are not simple. Assessing which pervasive features of the social fabric need mending might seem easy in a dualistic way when a politician or a concerned citizen says "the system needs to work better" or "laws need to be tougher." Who would disagree? Yet structuring the exploration or framing such a complex issue as a dualistic, or yes/no, dynamic makes it possible to miss things. When looking for people who seem to be boldly taking refuge in the dark figure of crime from within a structure and a system that seems to provide them the cover they need to remain undetected, the idea of leaving things unsaid seems to work to the advantage of the undetected offender.

All of these ideas are complicated quickly when relevant research confirms that, in between 85% and, in more recent studies, 93% of cases of child sexual abuse, the child knows his or her abuser.[41] Parents are shocked to discover that teachers, priests, coaches, and other people close to the family whom they trusted are abusing their children. And, rather than making things simpler, which all of us would prefer, when the abuse comes from within the family, an already confusing dynamic is further complicated. Young people are taught to trust their coaches, teachers, parents, and family members. As a result, adults who actively seek to protect children often learn incomplete and erroneous messages by thinking they need to learn what an offender *looks* like when the better question is, what does a sex offender *act* like? If there is no chaos-producing abduction, the parent may falsely assume things are OK. Even when a child does tell, which is extremely uncommon, the person is in such close and consistent contact with the family that parents simply cannot believe what their child is telling them. Parents want to believe that the adults they choose to trust their children to would not harm them. In these cases, way too much gets left unsaid.

Also true is that a mere allegation of a sexual offense can produce a vicious social reaction. A 1958 case, which still regularly captures the attention of social media, is the story of a 7- or 8-year-old white girl who was playing with two young black boys, aged 7 and 9, and later told her mother she kissed them on their cheeks. The parents called local law enforcement. The boys were accused of rape, unlawfully detained in the local jail, beaten, refused legal counsel or visits from their parents, and then convicted of molestation and sentenced to reform school until the age of 21. Intense international attention to the case eventually produced a pardon from the governor of North Carolina, and the boys were released after three months.[42]

Certain high-profile cases of sexual violence seem to manufacture desire for a high-profile style of justice system response. Yet children are abused and mothers and wives beaten or killed in their own homes with little or no social response or little or no action taken; no community rallies; and, in too many cases, nothing is said at all.

CONSENT, COMPLIANCE, COERCION, AND CONTINUUMS

Young people may agree to have sex with other young people who have not yet reached the legal age when having sex is allowed by law (discussed below and throughout the book). The age at which the law says it is OK to have sex is referred to as the age of **consent**. Having sex with someone who has not yet reached the age of consent is a crime.

Conversations about sexual health and sexual harm require a clear understanding of the terms *consent* and *coercion*. Conversations about sexual health and sexual harm will produce various points of departure, and the act of securing consent, an agreement to have sex that is freely given, is a critical factor for distinguishing between what is identified as sexually healthy and sexually harmful. *The idea of consent,* the agreement to have sex that is given freely, *is an essential* constant *required for a healthy sexual encounter.* Much of the assessment of healthy sex and sexual harm is linked to the presence or absence of consent. If an individual does not consent to sexual contact, there is no line to be erased, relocated, or discussed as appropriate or inappropriate by classmates or friends. The decision about consent is personal and is to be respected and left alone. It is not one to be discussed or mediated. Consent is one of those instances when what a person says goes.

Consent is given or denied from within the context of a range of socially acceptable sexual behaviors. **Coercion,** on the other hand, refers to occasions when a measure of force is used to influence a person's decision. The goal, of course, is to be mindful of one's own behavior when considering the behavior and attitude of others. When reflecting on comparisons, a continuum can be a useful tool for assessing social and individual attitudes about various sexual themes, such as those presented for consideration throughout this book. One way to talk about abstract sexual behaviors in a concrete way is to think about them in the context of a continuum of acceptable and unacceptable behaviors. This can be done in referencing attitudes at the individual level, referring to what an individual might see as acceptable and/or appropriate for their own personal choices, and in referencing social attitudes, assessing individually or as a group what perceptions are held about current social attitudes. Examples of several continuums are provided for consideration in appendix A. While it is the intention here and throughout the book to solidify the idea that consent is freely given and freely taken back at any time during any sexual encounter, many actions or behaviors can demonstrate a sexually charged or sexually aggressive tone with or without it being the sender's intention.

Sometimes, people mix signals, and, sometimes, people intentionally push up against someone else's stated preferences, resulting in harm. Remember, too, the idea of being touched is also an individual and personal decision, which might become confusing. Touch is an essential part of the human condition, but it can also be exploited. Consider the Touch Continuum presented in Text Box Intro.1.

Text Box Intro 1. The Continuum of Touchy Behaviors
© C. Anderson, 2000

Lack	Nurturing	Confusing	Exploitative
Boundaries	**Helpful**		**Hurtful**
Deprivation	**Safe**	**(???)**	**Harmful**
	Good		**Not safe**
			"Bad"

Touch is confusing when:

* the receiver is not use to the touch
* the receiver is not sure about the intent of the giver
* there are double messages about the touch
* all touch is equated with sex
* what was learned to date is that all touch is bad
* the touch feels good but there is something "secret" or not safe about it
* the touch changes from something that was OK to something that is unclear or not OK

Confusing touch is not clearly positive/safe or negative/not safe. We all need skills to identify and talk about each type of touch. When touch is confusing, the person who is confused has the right to say something like "Stop," "I'm not sure about this," or "Something about this is confusing for me," and the person doing the touch should respect that and not coerce.

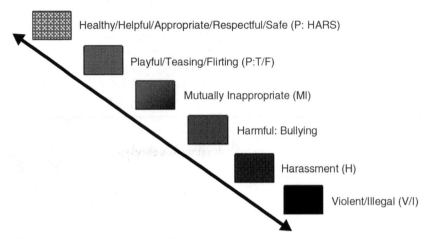

Figure Intro 1   The Sexual Behavior Continuum

© 2002 Developed by Cordelia Anderson, Sensibilities, Inc.

Cordelia Anderson of Sensibilities, Inc., developed a **continuum of sexual behavior** to further illustrate this idea (Figure Intro.1). In part these continuums are offered because much of the information presented throughout this text is based on there being degrees of difference in attitudes about sexually related acts, events, and ideas. One term, **consent**, is presented as a definitive, nonnegotiable idea. *Consent* is essential for assuring an affirming and healthy sexual encounter.

The concept of consent also includes a legal distinction to reflect the *minimum* age someone must be to legally agree to have sex. The age required to legally consent to sex in the United States is set by each state. Most states have established the age of consent to be 16, although selected states are 17 or 18; the age of consent can be lower with parental permission. The legal age of consent is important because a person who has sex with someone younger than the legal age of consent can be charged with **statutory rape** because the other individual cannot legally consent. Statutory rape is defined as unlawful sex with someone below the age of consent and can be punishable by prison time.[43]

Beyond the time when the legal age of consent has been reached, the focus in sexual encounters distinguishing healthy from harmful remains on consent. Some scholars and social critics suggest young girls are especially vulnerable to the idea of coercion because they feel pressured to have sex as they begin exploring relationships. In this way the use of the term **sexual compliance** is also helpful.[44] Talking about compliance is important when exploring the sometimes murky area between consent and coercion. To further expand this idea, compliance may also be seen as a stepping-stone to the outer edge of coercion, particularly when a person agrees to have sex because they believe they will be harmed in some way or socially ostracized. The act of someone putting a gun to a person's head and demanding sex is clearly an act of violent coercion. What about a girl whose boyfriend says he will break up with her if she does not have sex with him? Is this consensual? Who decides whether consent was freely given?

Partners may participate in unwanted sexual acts because they feel like they will lose the relationship if they don't consent to sex, or they may incorrectly think they have no choice.[45] Sometimes, young couples will struggle with the balance between consent and coercion if, for example, one partner wants to have sex and the other is not ready or, within a long-term relationship, one person is under significant stress or is tired but agrees to have sex with their partner anyway. More research on coercion and compliance and how those cases are handled in the criminal justice system is presented in chapter 11. In this review of the material here in the introduction, the central idea that *sex without consent is rape* seems very clear, yet some examples illustrate a blurring of those lines in some people's minds during the course of a sexual encounter.

THE BULLY AND THE BYSTANDER

The final segment is focused on introducing the role of the **bystander** in sexual violence prevention conversations. If victims and their experiences are on one side of the issue and offenders and their experiences are on the other side of the issue, what of the third group, the bystander? The *bystander*, also referred to as the witness, may not perceive a direct connection to the problem of sexual assault but may be confronted with the role they play when a significant other discloses abuse or they witness an angry boyfriend refusing to let go of his girlfriend's hand. When confronted with any behavior on the sexual violence continuum, the bystander witness has a choice to find a way to get involved or keep on walking.

Unfortunately the topic of sexual crimes is incomplete without discussing those people who are victims of these sexual crimes. Traditionally, attention was given only to the victim and the offender. As awareness and research developed in the field, it became clear that sexual assault advocates (more on advocates is presented in chapter 14) serve a critical role in providing services and support to victims, survivors, the criminal justice system, and the surrounding community. More recently, attention has been given to the conceptualization of **sexual bullying**. Pulled from the language of bullying presented in public schools, the idea about sexual bullying requires people to understand that harassing someone until they have sex with you is coercion. Saying you won't date someone unless they have sex with you is bullying behavior.

In addition to thinking and talking about the bully, attention has also been given to what is being referred to as the bystander. The idea of the bystander is more fully discussed in chapter 14 in terms of how people are desensitized to violence; the effect of watching violence between others, particularly family members or friends; and how being an active bystander can be an effective tool for preventing sexual harm.

THE MEDIA

Since the advent of television, the media and related industries have been on the receiving end of some pretty scathing critiques from a variety of social sectors. Entire new disciplines have been built around studying popular culture and media messaging, including advertisers; TV; movies; news; computer games; and, more recently, the internet, pornography, and social media platforms and their influence on mainstream culture. Related to the work here, the media have been challenged for their narrow representation of women and girls and equally restricted representation of masculinity among men and boys. Jean Kilbourne was among some of the first researchers to focus directly on sexualized and potentially harmful messaging in advertising in her 1979 documentary, *Killing Us Softly 4: Advertising's Image of Women*.[46] Questions about the impact of the media on communal sexual health and harm are only a subset of larger questions raised about media influences more broadly on relationships. Parents blame producers for making violent programs and messaging, and producers blame consumers for buying the violent programming while legislators and the courts often point to the First Amendment and free speech as a justification for not restricting parameters of violence on TV and other media programming outlets.[47] Sexual choices and related decisions are believed to be extremely personal, yet political leaders and governments often have much to say regarding the regulation of sexual behaviors and choices. Reflections on how the media are connected back to the particular chapter subjects will be more directly discussed after each section.

Researchers work to offer more detailed understandings of the influence of media and associated ranges of violent messaging. Questions are raised, for example, as to whether youth who watch violence act out in more aggressive ways, whether people are more afraid because they assume their communities are more violent than they really are, or whether people are becoming immune to the effects of violence, which makes them less likely to act when someone is actually being harmed.[48] Direct relationships between media and violence are difficult to establish, but those concerned about these issues are watching closely and digging deeper.

Whether or not appropriate, the media have assumed a central role in keeping communities informed about events happening locally and around the world. In the internet age, communities are being defined quite differently from the geographic focus of previous generations. A 2018 request for Facebook founder and CEO Mark Zuckerberg to appear before Congress resulted after a significant data privacy breach created an international scandal at the company.[49] Emerging online communities, such as the extremist groups converging around the idea of "involuntary celibacy," known as "incels," are described in the national presses as an online community of men who are angry they can't convince women to have sex with them.[50] How information is shared, what individuals learn about complex social subjects and where, and what people think the government can and should do is being affected by media platforms.

When the issue is healthy sexuality and sexual appropriateness, people change their attitudes throughout their lives, but to what degree, if at all, does the media have in these shifts? What messaging is offered regarding the links modern-day attitudes have to history and to the past harm done? How does the presentation of news stories on victims and sex offenders play to a popular cultural mythology or present accurate well-researched information? Because rape and other kinds of sexual violence can be traumatic for those harmed, the media coverage of particularly difficult traumas and harms can be retraumatizing to a victim or the victim's family. As a result, much is being written about responsible coverage of sensitive stories and what that might look like.[51] Can the justice system be a focus of accurate assessment and reflection as issues of sexualized violence are emphasized, and what role would the media play in sharing the results of such a targeted focus with a national readership? Would only those individuals who sought out to study sexualized violence prevention get the necessary information for advancing prevention information?

SELF-CARE

In healthy relationships, the ability to listen for and learn from the social cues of others is balanced with the need to be able to state one's thoughts and feelings directly about a given topic or event. Yet to discuss specific topics or to ask certain questions in many social settings is seen as socially awkward or inappropriate. Traditionally, this has been especially true about sexually explicit topics. In mainstream society, statistics and research findings reflect a social reality where just about everyone is affected by sexual harms to varying degrees. For this reason, the introduction here would not be complete without a conversation about the importance of assessing personal needs and inviting opportunities for self-care when moving through the material included throughout the text. Consideration is given to ideas about what self-care and social support might look like if or when the material becomes challenging at any point along the way.

A caution must be given here. For some people, the study of violent crimes, especially violent sex crimes, warrants care and short recesses after being exposed to the material at length. Subjective and relativistic language about bodies, feelings, emotions, and relationships makes room in the conversation for acknowledging the profound role of the human spirit in what may be a difficult conversation about physical violence and harm. The consequences of these harms can be felt not only in the body but also in the spirit of a person. Language is used to express the possibility of devastating sadness or intense anger, for example, and feelings of hurt can accompany related words about various kinds of sexual harm, to one's self or to another.

Every victim of sexual violence experiences that harm differently, just as every witness to or perpetrator of a sexual harm acts or reacts differently. Not everyone who experiences the consequences of sexual harm or knows someone who has been harmed or who has *caused* harm reacts to the event in the same way or at the same time throughout the event timeline. Targeted and executed violence not only harms individuals; it harms friends and families and can extend that damage to communities and countries. For some people, it is easy to separate themselves from the topic on the page. For others, the harm committed against them or someone else has a **somatic resonance**, like PTSD, and is deeply held in the body at an energetic level, which can be **triggered**, or activated, as they bear witness to the harm of others or are reminded of their own hurts or traumas represented by the stories from the text.[52] For these reasons, before beginning the primary content to be covered, a variety of thoughts on the topic of self-care are offered with a review of resource and outreach options available in most communities.

Moving through examples can sometimes trigger difficult memories. In our experience, as researchers and educators, people who come to this material casually, thinking it will be an interesting topic to learn more about, can also have unexamined events come to the surface during their review of the material. A student shares part of a classroom conversation with roommates or friends, but one of those friends reveals they have been abused or a girlfriend of six months feels like she knows her partner well enough to tell that person about a sexual abuse experience. These conversations can bring about life-changing results and realizations. Whatever the situation, whether about one's own personal experience or the experience of a good friend or partner, the emotional and physical response can be very personal and require focused attention outside the classroom.

Students may not realize they have any background in addressing these concerns until a topic appears before them in an assigned chapter and the material starts to sound familiar. Or a student will describe what it was like to find out that a close friend was abused by someone whom they never reported but see regularly because they have friends in common or they run into them at the mall. Some of the questions posed throughout the book won't really have one right answer. How any given person responds to the issues of sexual harm depends on them and on their religious, familial, social, and cultural backgrounds and the support they have. This book is not structured to provide counsel; however, it is highly recommended that everyone reading the book *take a minute to learn more about resources in the community that might offer information and support should more specialized questions arise*. In this way, be your own best friend and become your own best advocate; if you are not sure you can process through some of the information on your own, find trusted people or reliable resources to make sure you get good support so you can respond to your needs in the healthiest way possible. Remember, being your own advocate may require finding someone with specialized or professional training who can meet your specific needs.

Another important component in self-care is to assure yourself that *your* opinion on this topic *does* matter. Regardless of your gender, it is important to find reasons for staying engaged. It can be tempting, for example, for men to disengage from this topic for fear that they will be accused of being out of touch or insensitive to what have traditionally been defined as "women's issues." Yet consider this: statistically, men are the most likely to commit sex crimes at rates of approximately 96%.[53] If men are the most likely to commit sexual assaults, the involvement of men is likely to help create even more solutions for addressing and preventing sexual violence. In fact, author Jackson Katz suggests the number of male perpetrators demonstrates violence against women is a men's issue.[54] Certainly, some men find humor in telling jokes that are derogatory to women. There are men who, rather than looking at the part they play in the issue of sexualized violence, choose to identify other men as the source of the problem—leaving their own behavior unexamined. Whether men are aware and attentive or lack awareness and contribute to the problem, sexual abuse is not exclusively a woman's problem; it is a human problem. Research has verified that a few offenders are known to commit a large proportion of sex crimes and *most men do not rape*.[55] Reductions in violence and harm will happen sooner if all sexually healthy people feel comfortable participating freely and engaging fully in the goal of reducing sexualized violence and enhancing gender equality.

Finally, while most conversations about sexual violence center on men as perpetrators and women as victims, *not all offenders are men and not all targets are female*. While it is typical to consider male perpetrators when discussing sexual abuse, young boys are also abused by men, and females may offend against others. For some uninformed or uneducated people, sexual violence can be seen as "normal" behavior or even behavior that is identified by a given group as behavior that must be adopted to be socially accepted or included. Be careful when doing this work to make sure *all* victims, regardless of gender or sexual identity, be acknowledged and accepted to help avoid feelings of exclusion or perceptions suggesting disinterest in the experiences of all people who have experienced these and related harms. It is essential that *all* victims be heard and their experiences acknowledged.

Because the topics covered here are so far reaching, this book will undoubtedly leave many questions unanswered and will almost certainly require the reader to develop a set of answers that makes sense within their own understanding, education, and experiences. It is the nature of the topic to realize some related areas of study will not cause a great amount of debate, while others may create unanticipated conflict among students or even within the heart and mind of a solitary reader. *Please be gentle with yourself and others as you move through these sometimes difficult discussions.* Align yourselves with advocates for information and resources. If the information doesn't make sense, give yourself permission to learn more and find out what fits for you; just be careful to use reputable resources. Please be sure to locate resources in your area so you know where they are if you or someone you care about needs them.

Text Box Intro 2.   Common Community Resources for Help with Sexual Abuse

- Emergency 911 police response or campus public safety
- Domestic violence shelter for women and children
- Sexual assault community center (sometimes, a county program) or gender violence resource center, where a person can get information and personal support and have a place to visit and meet groups of people addressing various issues and finding support working through the issue together
- Community-based resource clinic or medical facility will have staff or resources for addressing the issue of sexual violence.
- Campus communities almost always have a gender violence resource center, a women's center, or an advocacy program. Any of these groups can help provide direction.
- Campus communities typically also have counseling services for students, male and female. They have professional counselors trained to address a multiplicity of issues raised by clients.
- Excellent resources about sexual harm and sexual violence are offered online:

  For Minnesota, examples include

  ○ Minnesota Coalition Against Sexual Assault: https://www.mncasa.org/
  ○ Central Minnesota Sexual Assault Center: https://cmsac.org/

  National online organizations and resources include

  ○ Rape, Abuse, and Incest National Network (RAINN): https://www.rainn.org/
  ○ An Abuse, Rape, and Domestic Violence Aid and Resource Collection: http://www.aardvarc.org/

CREATING SPACE FOR ONGOING PERSONAL REFLECTIONS

The final segment in the introduction, before the notes section, is structured to get people thinking about the process ahead. Each of us brings our own social and cultural attitudes to the conversation. Depending on the groups involved in these discussions, it might make sense to simply check in with each other and see about working together to critically reflect on the issues and perhaps challenge each other but, most importantly, to challenge ourselves to see what part we might play in perpetuating or reducing sexual harm in our everyday interactions.

Reflection #1: In the United States, any individual interested in understanding the dynamics of sexual behavior, from discussions about sexual health to assessments about sexual deviance, sexual harm, and classifications of sex crimes, will undoubtedly uncover varying degrees of outrage amid what can also be an awkward silence. Sex is used in many ways in modern American society—as a weapon, as advertising, as a sense of connection, as a punch line, as a pleasurable experience, as a commodity to be bought and sold, as a money maker, as a way to prove to yourself you are lovable or loved, as a form of blackmail, or as a way to enhance your self-esteem. The list seems endless.

- What do you see as the difference between how sex is used and how sex is expressed?
- How do you see things said about sex from where you live as similar to and different from what you see about sex on TV and in other places around the United States?
- Do you know people who use sex as a weapon?

Reflection #2: Some of the most offensive words in the English language are sexually charged words but are also sometimes thrown around quite casually. For example, the "F" word is described in a popular YouTube parody as the most versatile word in the English language because it can be used as a noun, a pronoun, a verb, an adverb, or even as a stand-alone sentence.[56] Comedians have been known to use the "F" word as the centerpiece in comedy routines, somehow making what in other social settings could easily be offensive into something actually quite laughable. For some people, the use of sexually explicit terms becomes a way to express a heightened degree of hostility in a frustrating situation or is directed toward a particular person, while others easily exclude the word because they think it's offensive or they use such terms only in specific settings among close friends, for example, but certainly not around parents or grandparents. An arguably infinite list outlining how sex or sexualized terms are used also hints at how sex is said to be *mis*used. Perceptions of power and control can merge in ugly ways with conscious and perhaps subconscious cultural ideas about superiority, dominance, humiliation, and exploitation, themes that clash directly with popular notions of romantic love, healthy relationships, and views about what healthy human interactions actually look like. Thoughts? Why do we hurl sexually charged language at each other as the worst kind of thing to say to someone?

Reflection #3: The history of sex-related public policy in the United States suggests a fairly constant conversation about different aspects of sexually appropriate and sexually inappropriate behaviors. On one hand, protests and rallies demonstrate a desire for change. Communities turn out in huge numbers to search for missing children. As a nation, the United States continues to generate harsher penalties for sex offenders who get caught. On the other hand, emphasis about the need to protect against stranger assaults has overshadowed the truth that most sexual offenses are not perpetrated by strangers but by people who are known to the victim (see more on this in chapter 3). We watch, literally, with what certainly passes as silent acceptance while sexualized images and violence are being merged in video games marketed to young people (particularly young boys) in popular movies, in music lyrics and music videos, and as violent, body-punishing pornography finds its way into community video rental stores, or pop-up screens on the internet, or in hotels and motels across the country. How is it that something said to be so special and intimate and personal and beautiful, an essential part of generating new life within the human condition, is also the same thing identified as vulgar or degrading and in its abusive forms can damage lives irreparably?

Reflection #4: Often, upon discovering that a family member, friend, or loved one has been sexually assaulted, we are shocked and outraged. When a sex offender is released from prison, an outraged community demands accountability. When a child goes missing, outrage leads to decisive, intentional, and directed action. When a collective and public rape chant by a group of young men at prestigious Yale University is so outrageous that it results in a lawsuit, a federal Title IX investigation, and a statement from the Department of Education delivered by the vice president of the United States to all educational institutions receiving federal funding, it is clear that more than a few people are outraged by aggressive, potentially threatening, sexually charged behavior.

Reflection #5: Ironically, silence seems to be the alternative to outrage. Scandalous news stories of abductions and kidnappings sometimes overshadow the equally serious realities of a young girl afraid and ashamed to tell her parents she was attacked in her own home by boys from her neighborhood. An adolescent boy wakes to abuse by a friend's dad after passing out drunk from alcohol given freely by the same adult. Instead of being certain of support, he is filled with questions and fears. Will people believe him? Who else knows? Will people who hear about this think he is gay? How will people react when they find out what happened? Will they make fun of him? What will his parents say if he tells them? These are harsh realities facing any sexual assault victim, and sometimes survivors choose to confront their situation alone rather than risk being met with further harm in the form of being challenged, confronted, or minimized if they do decide to share their story.

Reflection #6: Instead of creating a safe place for victims of violence, some victims choose instead to live with silence. Given a number of factors, including a fear of retaliation or further abuse, a decision to remain silent may make the most sense and be the safest choice for a victim. An unfortunate consequence of silence is the reduced likelihood of perpetrators being held accountable and prosecuted, but, as is discussed in chapter 24, it is best when a victim defines their own pathway for recovery.

Reflection #7: A sad reality of sexual violence is that it happens every day and often goes unnoticed. Occasionally, the actions are so egregious that the event stands out. In October 2009 a 15-year-old girl was brutally raped for two and a half hours by an estimated 10 young men during a homecoming dance. While the vicious assault was reported to have left the community stunned, equally shocking was the fact that an estimated 20 people were said to have watched the assault as it was happening. Although some observers took pictures and filmed the incident, no one called the police.[57] The victim was injured so severely she had to be airlifted to the hospital. Certainly, many questions are brought to mind in the wake of such an act of sexual aggression and sexual violence, but the decision to remain quiet has almost everyone who learns of the event scratching their heads and asking why.

Reflection #8: For the past decade and earlier, people across the country have been asking how arguably the largest religious institution in the world, steadfastly promoting the idea of celibacy, could be so deeply involved in sexual abuse scandals that the extent of those abuses is still being uncovered decades later? Initial reports of those abuses were met with individual and institutional silence. To victims, silence can seem like a blanket of protection, a way to keep what happened locked away from the judgments or accusations of others. For sexual offenders, social and political silence can be used to mask anything from a lack of appropriate boundaries and social awareness to the commission of deliberate and intentionally malicious acts.

CHAPTER SUMMARY AND MOVING FORWARD

While some things are left unsaid, other matters related to sexual behaviors are discussed as inappropriate or deviant but remain visible in the most accessible of places. Few people know what someone else brings to a conversation about sexual health, definitions of deviance, or personal attitudes and distinctions between sexual harms and sexual crimes. Assessments or decisions about if or how social influences appropriately affect or restrict personal choices and whether specific restrictions are extremely invasive are different for everyone. One of the motivating forces for putting this book together came from a collection experiences in the classroom and in community forums listening to people of all ages describe stumbling into their own understandings about sexually charged themes while attempting to make sense of the many contradictory words and behaviors they saw all around them. In so many instances, people refer to events in their lives where opportunities for dialogue came and went, with important things being left unsaid. High school students are notorious for struggling with a curiosity about sex and confronting adult restrictions about sexually related conversations or comprehensive education.

College students often tell stories about having their parents cover their eyes and ears at certain parts of movies or buying them a book about sex and telling them that, if they have any questions about sex, the information is in the book but not really making time to talk with them about sex and relationships face-to-face. Students talk about getting a sex education, but they also talk about the fact that what they experienced is not the kind of sex education they would want for their kids. As they got older, they wished they had been given the freedom to ask questions that were then carefully and respectfully answered.[58]

The authors have come to see opportunities for future conversations about sexual health and sexual harm in everyday moments between the outrage and the silence. Sometimes, sexual images are screaming out of songs or movies or video gaming systems so loudly that other important information is overlooked or missed. Not only is it important to discover what people are saying about sex but also what messages people are hearing. Are people saying one thing in public and doing something else in private? Social science research, newspapers, books, and TV shows seem to suggest that, as a nation, we *are* talking about sex. Important aspects of this conversation can offer opportunities for prevention if everyone chooses to "listen a little louder" to those subtle statements about sexual harm.

If modern social stories and media do not reflect individual attitudes around healthy sex and harmful sex, how is it possible for adults as well as young people to determine appropriate boundaries and definitions and practices to live by? If, on the other hand, modern social stories and media *do* reflect individual attitudes about definitions and distinctions between healthy sex and sexual harm, do the events in communities around the country verify the fact that we have, as a nation, simply achieved a level of sexual violence we find acceptable? How much of what is happening in hurtful ways is due to ignorance and how much is a premeditated, purposeful act intended to inflict harm on another person?

Young people are certainly watching, listening, and making their own decisions about what constitutes sexual health and sexual harm. A conversation about healthy sexuality might seem like a strange place to start a conversation about sex crimes and sex offenders. But before beginning a trudge through the muck of all of the ways sex has been harmful, it is essential to bring up the fact that sex can be, without question, a positive, life-affirming, healthy act. In other words, before listing all of the ways sex has gone horribly wrong, it is important to stop to remember that there are plenty of times when sex has "gone right." In the same way sexual assault advocates are encouraged to surround themselves with reminders of the good in the world, we would like to anchor this book in images that show healthy sex to be a positive act for creating bonds that go beyond words.

The building blocks of self-care, messages about healthy sexuality, and being aware of the sources of your existing opinions and perspectives about sex are important first steps to cover before moving forward. These steps will help create an environment for learning that will allow you to better process this difficult material. Ultimately, this book is organized around some tough conversations about sex, sexual deviance, sex crime classifications, punishment, and assault prevention. Human history depicts a violent history. Nowhere is this more evident than in the examples of sexual harm discussed throughout these pages. One of the overarching goals of this work is to support sexual violence prevention efforts, but prevention work is not possible unless people begin to understand how any given issue relates to them in their daily lives. It is not possible to address the issue fully if certain acts of violence and abuse are systematically overlooked or ignored. Really looking at how sexual harm affects each of us and the people we love takes courage because it requires looking at something unpleasant, and, in some cases, it requires taking responsibility for the harm we cause or part we play in perpetuating the systems of violence.

Even though the content of the text is focused on some gruesome aspects of the human condition, the goal for the book is much more aspirational. The intent is to offer a place to consider sexual violence and sexual harm as a range of behaviors and then emphasize the part each of us can play in reducing these kinds of harms. To a certain degree, sexual violence is preventable. Therefore, a bigger goal is to help raise awareness and provide information and education as a means for assessing our own behavior and the behavior of others in everyday life to reduce the likelihood of victimization and increase the objections to any form of sexualized violence or harm. The ability to eliminate victimization is, unfortunately, not always possible. For those who are sexually abused, the hope is that they quickly find the support they need to best meet their needs for healing the harm.

Certainly, this book provides reflections on research and the current state of sex-offending treatment practices and responses in the United States today. In some ways, this book is also about more than what each of us knows or comes here to learn. It is also about what you *do* in response to what you learn. It is about action. Bystander conversations invite important questions about the role each of us plays in either reducing violence or perpetuating violence in our everyday interactions. If readers of this book are anything like students in our classes and community meetings, for some, the content of this text will produce individual activism among both men and women. But this is not necessarily about marching in rallies or joining organizations, although it certainly can take that form. Many students talk about how their relationships with their fiancé changed as a result of the conversations they had or the way they interact with friends. Choosing to make self-supporting individual choices can change lives. Everyone will have their own response to the material covered in the book. *We hope everyone who reads the book comes to see themselves as a part of the solution: to prevent, reduce, and eliminate sexual violence and sexual harm.*

Text Box Intro 3.   MEDIA MESSAGES SECTION I: Is It Possible to Agree about the Parameters of Healthy Sexuality?

Section overview: Media messages about healthy sexuality can be wickedly diverse and loaded with confusing messages. Showering with AXE body wash makes you irresistible to women, and women don't need a sex partner if they shower and wash their hair with Herbal Essence shampoo and cream rinse. Consider a few of the media issues raised here about the themes of healthy sexuality, sexual deviance, and child sexual abuse. Spend some time reflecting on how the conversations about healthy sex, definitions of deviance, and the range of harmful sexualized actions might affect young children as they grow and mature.

KEY TERMS

#MeToo
abstinence only education
bystander
coercion
comprehensive sex education
consent
continuum of sexual behavior
Crimes Against Children Research Center
dark figure of crime
David Finkelhor
Dr. Alfred Kinsey
endemic
epidemic
Glen Ridge rape case
ideological dualism

Institute for Sex Research
Karl Hanson
Masters and Johnson
Michel Foucault
sexology
sexual bullying
sexual compliance
sexual harm
sexual violence
social constructs
social discourse
somatic resonance
statutory rape
triggered

REVIEW QUESTIONS

1. What is the definition of *criminalize* and how does it represent a social process involving the justice system?

2. Identify the six themes the authors presented as important for a discussion on sexual violence and harm.

3. What does the author refer to in the section "Silent Sex Talk"?

4. What is the difference between consent, compliance, and coercion with regard to sex acts?

5. What is the dark figure of crime and how is it related to sexual violence?

DISCUSSION QUESTIONS

1. Consider Foucault's theme in the *History of Sexuality* as both ever-present and secret or hidden. Does this message play out in the world today? What are some examples of how sex is ever-present but hidden?

2. The following questions are introduced to help review and understand the authors' position that sexual violence is discussed as both an individual act and a cultural condition. What questions would you add?

    Section I: Is it possible to agree about the parameters of healthy sexuality?
    Section II: How does history (continue to) shape modern understandings of sexual harms and sexualized violence?
    Section III: What do experts say about sex offenders? More specifically, what does a sex offender *act* like?

Section IV: In what ways is the justice system addressing the issue of sexual harm?

Section V: What can be done to help promote sexual health and prevent sexual harm?

3. The author suggests that the real-life lived consequences of sex crimes are often lost in the media crush of a highly sexualized culture that doesn't want to talk about sex but spends a lot of time talking about how to regulate sexual behaviors. Discuss what you think this means and how it relates to your understanding of both healthy sexuality and deviant or sex crimes.

4. The text outlines various places where social conversations about sexual attitudes might take place in local communities. As examples, these places include in families, in schools, in faith communities, in neighborhoods, in friendship groups, on TV, and in social conversations. Where do you think most people get their information about sex, whether healthy or unhealthy information?

5. Why do you think a space for personal reflections was offered at the close of the introduction?

NOTES

1. Mary Vespa, "America's Biggest Problem? Fearless Dr. Mary Calderone Says It's 'Fear of Sex,'" *People*, January 21, 1980, accessed June 8, 2015, http://www.people.com/people/archive/article/0,,20075651,00.html.

2. Michel Foucault, *The History of Sexuality*, vol. 1: *An Introduction* (New York: Pantheon Books, 1978), 35.

3. Erin Merryn, *Living for Today* (Deerfield Beach, FL: Health Communications, Inc., 2009).

4. Ben Winslow, "After an Awkward Silence, Sexual Consent Bill Passes in the Utah House," FOX13 Salt Lake City, February 10, 2015, accessed March 22, 2015, https://fox13now.com/2015/02/10/after-an-awkward-silence-sexual-consent-bill-passes-in-the-utah-house/.

5. Philip Jenkins, *Moral Panic: Changing Concepts of the Child Molester in Modern America* (New Haven, CT: Yale University Press, 2004), 13.

6. "The *New York Times*, for Reporting Led by Jodi Kantor and Megan Twohey, and *The New Yorker*, for Reporting by Ronan Farrow," https://www.pulitzer.org/winners/new-york-times-reporting-led-jodi-kantor-and-megan-twohey-and-new-yorker-reporting-ronan. In 2019, as this book was in final editing, Kantor and Twohey published *She Said: Breaking the Sexual Harassment Story That Helped Ignite a Movement* (Penguin Random House, 2019). Farrow published *Catch and Kill* (Little, Brown and Co., 2019) as the story of his experiences at NBC, and he produced a three-part series for *The New Yorker* titled *The Black Cube Chronicles* (https://www.newyorker.com/news/annals-of-espionage/the-black-cube-chronicles-the-private-investigators), all relating to the story of Weinstein and related workplace harassment and efforts to cover up abuse by high-profile men.

7. Me Too Movement, "About: History and Vision," para 3, https://metoomvmt.org/about/.

8. Eric Levenson and Aaron Cooper, "Bill Cosby Sentenced to 3 to 10 Years in Prison for Sexual Assault, CNN, September 26, 2018, https://www.cnn.com/2018/09/25/us/bill-cosby-sentence-assault/index.html.

9. Alfred C. Kinsey, Wardell B. Pomeroy, and Clyde E. Martin, *Sexual Behavior in the Human Male* (W.B. Saunders, 1948); and Alfred C. Kinsey, Wardell B. Pomeroy, Clyde E. Martin, and Paul H. Gebhard, *Sexual Behavior in the Human Female* (W.B. Saunders, 1953).

10. Kristin Rodine, "Nampa Board Restores *Joy of Sex* Books," *American Libraries* 39, no. 10 (2008). © American Library Association. COPYRIGHT 2008 Gale Group.

11. "Maze of Injustice: The failure to protect Indigenous women from sexual violence in the USA," Amnesty International, 2007, accessed August 13, 2019, https://www.amnestyusa .org/pdfs/mazeofinjustice.pdf; Sarah Deer, *The Beginning and End of Rape* (University of Minnesota Press, 2015).

12. This subject is discussed in greater detail in chapter 7.

13. Wendy Koch, "Despite High-Profile Cases, Sex-Offense Crimes Decline," *USA Today*, August 24, 2005, accessed November 10, 2013, http://usatoday30.usatoday.com/news/ nation/2005-08-24-sex-crimes-cover_x.htm.

14. This subject is discussed in greater detail in chapter 11 on police, courts, and advocacy.

15. US Congress, Senate, Committee on the Judiciary, *Rape in the United States: The Chronic Failure to Report and Investigate Rape Cases*, 111th Cong., 2nd sess., 2010, accessed August 13, 2019, https://www.gpo.gov/fdsys/pkg/CHRG-111shrg64687/html/ CHRG-111shrg64687.htm.

16. US Department of Justice, "An Updated Definition of Rape," January 6, 2012, accessed August 13, 2019, https://www.justice.gov/archives/opa/blog/updated-definition-rape.

17. Andrea J. Ritchie, "How Some Cops Use the Badge to Commit Sex Crimes," *Washington Post*, January 12, 2018, sec. Outlook, accessed August 13, 2019, https://www.washingtonpost .com/outlook/how-some-cops-use-the-badge-to-commit-sex-crimes/2018/01/11/5606fb26 -eff3-11e7-b390-a36dc3fa2842_story.html?noredirect=on&utm_term=.2f9b47325178.

18. Philip Matthew Stinson Sr., John Liederbach, Steven P. Lab, and Steven L. Brewer Jr., "Police Integrity Lost: A Study of Law Enforcement Officers Arrested," January 2016, accessed August 13, 2019, https://www.ncjrs.gov/pdffiles1/nij/grants/249850.pdf.

19. Nadine Ehlers, "Hidden in Plain Sight: Defying Juridical Racialization in *Rhinelander v. Rhinelander*," *Communication and Critical/Cultural Studies* 1, no. 4 (2004): 313–34, accessed August 13, 2019, http://www.ingentaconnect.com/content/routledg/rccc/ 2004/00000001/00000004/art00002.

20. She had an IQ estimated at 67 (an average IQ is within a range of 90 to 110).

21. Robert Hanley, "Defense Cross-Examines Woman in Assault Case," *New York Times*, December 11, 1992, accessed November 11, 2013, http://www.nytimes.com/1992/12/11/ nyregion/defense-cross-examines-woman-in-assault-case.html?srcpm.

22. "Montana Judge Who Partly Blamed Teen Rape Victim Censured," NBC News, July 22, 2014, accessed August 14, 2019, https://www.nbcnews.com/news/us-news/montana -judge-who-partly-blamed-teen-rape-victim-censured-n162621.

23. "Montana Judge Sparks Outrage with Light Sentence for Man Who Raped 12-Year-Old Daughter," *Chicago Tribune*, sec. Nation/World, October 21, 2015, accessed August 14, 2019, http://www.chicagotribune.com/news/nationworld/ct-montana-judge-rape-sentence -20161021-story.html.

24. Laura Byrne, "Convicted 'Bayshore Rapist' Gets Life in Prison," 10News, February 17, 2011, accessed June 8, 2015, http://highlandscounty.wtsp.com/news/news/47702-convicted -bayshore-rapist-gets-life-prison.

25. Jessica Hopper, "Accused Rapist Cross-Examines Alleged Victim during Trial," ABC News, January 12, 2011, accessed November 10, 2013, http://abcnews.go.com/US/ accused-rapist-cross-examines-alleged-victim-florida-courtroom/story?id=12600166# .T4BAzoH4JMR.

26. Michel Foucault, *The History of Sexuality*, vol. 1, *An Introduction* (New York: Vintage Books, 1990); Michel Foucault, *The History of Sexuality*, vol. 2, *The Use of Pleasure* (New

York: Vintage Books, 1990); Michel Foucault, *The History of Sexuality*, vol. 3, *The Care of the Self* (New York: Vintage Books, 1988).

27. Patrick Marley, "Juneau County DA Warns District on Sex Ed Law: Teaching Curriculum Could Lead to Criminal Charges against Teachers, He Writes," *Journal Sentinel*, April 6, 2010, accessed November 10, 2013, http://www.jsonline.com/news/statepolitics/90020507.html; Bill Novak, "Gov. Doyle Signs Controversial Sex Ed Law," *The Cap Times*, February 24, 2010, accessed October 20, 2019, https://madison.com/ct/news/local/health_med_fit/gov-doyle-signs-controversial-sex-ed-law/article_329c9068-2172-11df-9299-001cc4c002e0.html; ACLU Editor, "ACLU of Wisconsin Respond to Juneau County District Attorney's Attack on New Comprehensive Sexuality Education Law," https://www.aclu-wi.org/en/news/aclu-wisconsin-responds-juneau-county-district-attorneys-attack-new-comprehensive-sexuality-0.

28. Nick Blizzard and Mark Gokavi, "Local Teacher Sex Cases: 'Evidence Trail' Leads to Plea Deals," *Dayton Daily News*, May 27, 2018, accessed August 14, 2019, https://www.mydaytondailynews.com/news/local-teacher-sex-cases-evidence-trail-leads-plea-deals/R529OCDnhbSUCDtSL3JMhP/.

29. Ralph Blumenthal, "Museum Field Trip Deemed Too Revealing," *New York Times*, September 30, 2006, accessed November 10, 2013, http://www.nytimes.com/2006/09/30/education/30teacher.html.

30. Mireya Navarro, "Arrest Startles Saleswomen of Sex Toys," *New York Times*, January 20, 2004, accessed June 8, 2015, http://www.nytimes.com/2004/01/20/us/arrest-startles-saleswomen-of-sex-toys.html; "Texas Mom Faces Trial for Selling Sex Toys," CNN, February 11, 2004, accessed June 8, 2015, http://www.cnn.com/2004/LAW/02/11/obscenity.trial.reut/.

31. "Federal Appeals Court Overturns Texas Sex Toys Ban," KTBS3, February 13, 2008, accessed August 14, 2019, https://www.ktbs.com/news/federal-appeals-court-overturns-texas-sex-toys-ban/article_4e9be8c2-abe5-5a48-9ea9-9c0e72c37682.html.

32. Teresa Nelson, "Minnesota Prosecutor Charges Sexting Teenage Girl with Child Pornography," ACLU, January 5, 2018, accessed August 14, 2019, https://www.aclu.org/blog/juvenile-justice/minnesota-prosecutor-charges-sexting-teenage-girl-child-pornography.

33. See, for example, Peter L. Berger and Thomas Luckmann, *The Social Construction of Reality: a Treatise in the Sociology of Knowledge* (Garden City, NY: Anchor, 1967); F. Heidensohn, "The Social Construction of Crime," in *Crime and Society* (London: Palgrave, 1989), doi.org/10.1007/978-1-349-19763-7_1; Imogene Moyer, *Criminological Theories: Traditional and Justice Nontraditional Voices and Themes* (Sage, 2001); D. Polizzi, *A Philosophy of the Social Construction of Crime* (Policy Press, 2016).

34. Philip Jenkins, *Moral Panic: Changing Concepts of the Child Molester in Modern America* (New Haven, CT: Yale University Press, 1998), xi.

35. David Finkelhor, "Current Information on the Scope and Nature of Child Sexual Abuse," *The Future of Children* 4, no. 2 (1994): 31–53; Wendy Koch, "Despite High-Profile Cases, Sex Crimes against Kids Fall," *USA Today*, August 25, 2005, p. 1A.

36. See, for example, questions raised in Jenkins, *Moral Panic*; Zilney and Zilney, *Perverts and Predator: The Making of Sexual Offending Laws* (Rowman & Littlefield, 2009); and *Reconsidering Sex Crimes and Offenders: Prosecution or Persecution?* (Praeger, 2009).

37. See, for example, Human Rights Watch, *No Easy Answers: Sex Offender Laws in the United States*, September 11, 2007, https://www.hrw.org/report/2007/09/11/no-easy-answers/sex-offender-laws-us.

38. See, for example, Jenkins, *Moral Panic*; Janus, *Failure to Protect*; "USA Today Investigative Report: Imprisoned for Crimes They Might Commit," *USA Today*, March 19, 2012, A-1, https://www.pressreader.com/usa/usa-today-us-edition/20120319/288943926526471.

39. Roni Caryn Rabin, "Nearly 1 in 5 Women in U.S. Survey Say They Have Been Sexually Assaulted," *New York Times*, December 14, 2011, accessed June 8, 2015, http://www.nytimes.com/2011/12/15/health/nearly-1-in-5-women-in-us-survey-report-sexual-assault.html; Susan Nicole Rayment-McHugh, Stephen Smallbone, and Nick Tilley, "Endemic Sexual Violence

and Abuse: Contexts and Dispositions," *International Journal for Crime, Justice and Social Democracy* 4, no. 2 (2015): 111–24. doi:10.5204/ijcjsd.v4i2.233; Diana E. H. Russell and Rebecca M. Bolen, *The Epidemic of Rape and Child Sexual Abuse in the United States* (Los Angeles, CA, 2000).

40. Rabin, "Nearly 1 in 5 Women in U.S. Survey Say They Have Been Sexually Assaulted"; Martha Chamallas, "Feminist Legal Theory and Tort Law" (Ohio State Public Law Working Paper No. 448, 2018).

41. "The Scope of Child Sexual Abuse," Stop It Now, accessed October 20, 2019, https://www.stopitnow.org/node/1874#xiv; E. Douglas and D. Finkelhor, "Childhood Sexual Abuse Fact Sheet," May 2005, http://www.unh.edu/ccrc/factsheet/pdf/childhoodSexualAbuseFact Sheet.pdf.

42. "'The Kissing Case' and the Lives It Shattered," NPR, April 29, 2011, accessed August 14, 2019, https://www.npr.org/2011/04/29/135815465/the-kissing-case-and-the-lives-it-shattered.

43. David M. Bierie and Kristen M. Budd, "Romeo, Juliet, and Statutory Rape," *Sexual Abuse* 30, no. 3 (2018), https://doi.org/10.1177/1079063216658451.

44. See, for example, Jennifer Katz and Vanessa Tirone, "Going Along with It: Sexually Coercive Partner Behavior Predicts Dating Women's Compliance with Unwanted Sex," *Violence Against Women* 16, no. 7 (2010): 730–42. https://doi.org/10.1177/1077801210374867l Emily Impett and Letitia Peplau, "Sexual Compliance: Gender, Motivational, and Relationship Perspective," *The Journal of Sex Research* 40, no. 1 (2003): 87–100; and Eric Grollman, "Is It Just a Matter of Consent? Compliance in Sexual Relationships," *Kinsey Confidential*, November 16, 2010, accessed June 8, 2015, http://kinseyconfidential.org/matter-consent-compliance-sexual-relationships.

45. David Knox and Caroline Schacht, *Choices in Relationships: An Introduction to Marriage and the Family*, 11th ed. (Belmont, CA: Wadsworth Publishing, 2012), 272.

46. *Killing Us Softly 4: Advertising's Image of Women*, video, 44:59, posted February 7, 2018, by openedmieyez, accessed August 15, 2019, https://www.youtube.com/watch?v=xnAY6S4_m5I.

47. Christian Science Monitor, *Safe-Guarding the Children: Urgent Needs, Practical Steps, Spiritual Solutions* (Boston: Christian Science Publishing Society, 1997).

48. Ibid., 56.

49. Julia Carrie Wong and Sabrina Siddiqui, "Mark Zuckerberg Agrees to Testify Before Congress over Data Scandal," *The Guardian*, News sec., March 27, 2018, accessed August 15, 2019, https://www.theguardian.com/technology/2018/mar/27/mark-zuckerberg-testify -congress-cambridge-analytica-data-scandal.

50. Sam Louie, "The Incel Movement: The Sexual, Social, Recreational, and Racial Implications," *Psychology Today*, April 25, 2018, accessed August 15, 2019, https://www .psychologytoday.com/us/blog/minority-report/201804/the-incel-movement; and Zoe Williams, "'Raw hatred': Why the 'incel' movement targets and terrorises women," *The Guardian*, News sec., April 25, 2018, accessed August 15, 2019, https://www.theguardian.com/ world/2018/apr/25/raw-hatred-why-incel-movement-targets-terrorises-women.

51. "Victim Media Advocacy: How to Facilitate Sensitive and Respectful Treatment of Crime Victims," Justice Solutions, accessed March 3, 2012, http://www.victimprovidersme diaguide.com.

52. Rachel Kimerling and Karen S. Calhoun, "Somatic Symptoms, Social Support, and Treatment Seeking among Sexual Assault Victims," *Journal of Consulting and Clinical Psychology* 62, no. 2 (1994): 333–40. See also, for example, B. Van Der Kolk, *The Body Keeps the Score: Brain, Mind, and Body in the Healing of Trauma* (Penguin Books, 2015); Wendy Maltz, *The Sexual Healing Journey: A Guide for Survivors of Sexual Abuse*, updated edition (William Morrow Paperbacks, 2012); Staci K. Haines, *Healing Sex: A Mind-Body Approach to Healing Sexual Trauma* (Cleis Press, 2007); Maggie Scarf, *Secrets, Lies, Betrayals: The Body/Mind Connection* (Random House, 2004).

53. Howard N. Snyder, "Sexual Assault of Young Children as Reported to Law Enforcement: Victim, Incident, and Offender Characteristics," Bureau of Justice Statistics (2000), 11, accessed June 8, 2015, http://bjs.ojp.usdoj.gov/content/pub/pdf/saycrle.pdf.

54. Jackson Katz, *The Macho Paradox: Why Some Men Hurt Women and How All Men Can Help* (Naperville, IL: Sourcebooks, 2006); and Jackson Katz, "Violence Against Women: It's a Men's Issue," video, 17:37, TEDxFiDiWomen, November 2012, http://www.ted.com/talks/jackson_katz_violence_against_women_it_s_a_men_s_issue?language=en).

55. David Lesak and Paul Miller, "Childhood Trauma, Posttraumatic Stress Disorder, Substance Abuse, and Violence," in *Trauma and Substance Abuse: Causes, Consequences, and Treatment of Comorbid Disorders,* ed. Paige Ouimette and Pamela Brown (Washington, DC: American Psychological Association, 2003), 73–87.

56. "The Word Fuck," YouTube video, 2:33, posted by "wickedwildabeast666," September 23, 2007, https://www.youtube.com/watch?v=26UA578yQ5g.

57. Sarah Netter, "No One Called Cops during Gang Rape, But Some Took Pictures," ABC News, October 27, 2009, accessed June 8, 2015, http://abcnews.go.com/WN/high-school-gang-rape-stuns-california-community/story?id=8925672; Radha Chitale, "How Could People Watch Alleged Gang Rape 'Like an Exhibit'?," ABC News, October 30, 2009, accessed June 8, 2015, http://abcnews.go.com/Health/MindMoodNews/bystanders-teen-raped/story?id=8948465.

58. The stories presented here are from Dr. Clifford's experience working with students in the college classroom.

1

Talking about the "Healthy Sex" Talk

◆ ◆ ◆

Each person should have the right to *choose* between pink and blue tinted gender categories, as well as all the other hues of the palette. At this moment in time, that right is denied to us. But together, we could make it a reality.

—Leslie Feiberg[1]

Sexuality is much more than sex. Healthy sexuality is emotional, social, cultural, and physical. It includes our values, attitudes, feelings, interactions and behaviors.

—National Sexual Violence Resource Center[2]

EACH MAY THE FAMOUS GALLUP ORGANIZATION measures American's views on the moral acceptability of a variety of social issues in an effort to track attitudinal changes in the United States over time.[3] Their annual "Values and Beliefs" survey asks about various sex-related issues, including abortion, out-of-wedlock births, gay and lesbian relations, extramarital affairs, premarital sex, the use of pornography, and divorce. Closing in on the end of the 2000s, the numbers suggest attitudes about divorce and premarital sex were increasingly seen as morally acceptable, whereas attitudes about abortion and having a baby out of wedlock remained more controversial. A whopping 91 percent of Americans find birth control morally acceptable, with ten of the nineteen moral and social issues they measure showing the most permissive views to date.[4] A majority of respondents identified sex between unmarried people as morally acceptable (69 percent) and attitudes about premarital sex, gay and lesbian relationships, and the use of pornography differed significantly by age, with younger respondents more likely to see these behaviors as morally acceptable.[5] Attitudes about the issue of pornography and sexual relations outside of marriage represented some of the biggest divides between the generations.[6]

On any given day, people in the United States display dramatically divergent attitudes about sex and sexuality. The elements selected for Gallup's "Values and Belief" poll remind us that attitudes often differ by age and change over time. The poll also highlights a long-standing cultural reality in the United States. For Americans, sexual and moral questions have historically been inextricably linked. Religion has played a significant role in determining how sex, particularly healthy sex, is discussed in the United States. Ironically, and perhaps arguably, it was the exposure of sexual abuses in the Catholic Church that played a significant role in bringing about a more intensified conversation and study of sexual abuses not only in the United States but around the world. After years of denial and intentional obfuscation, focus on abuse in the Church shifted. A plethora of lawsuits followed, as did years of negotiation. In the spring of 2018, the Minnesota Archdiocese agreed to pay $210 million for 450 victims of clergy sexual abuse,[7] second only to the 2007 settlement with the Archdiocese of Los Angeles for $660 million settlement with 508 victims who had come forward.[8]

While questions about sex may be an awkward or uncomfortable idea for some, it is also a social reality. In fact, the United States has had a variety of awkwardly public social incidents where issues of sexual morality and sexual abuse have taken center stage. In addition to the international church scandals, the nation watched a presidential affair and subsequent impeachment, governors and state senators have offered resignations, professional and collegiate sports figures have come forward as victims, police practices have been challenged to protect victims, and sexual abuse between teachers and students—even at the elementary grade school levels—present a smattering of cases with what is a surprising if not disturbing regularity. Traditionally, examples such as these have forced Americans into either an awkward public conversation or an even more awkward public silence on the matter.

Certainly, abortion has been an extremely divisive issue in the United States for decades. Strong opposition groups organizing to eliminate the procedure are met with other groups intent on identifying for many that abortion is seen as a necessary part of women's overall reproductive health care.[9] Versions of these bills varied by states but were famously mandating what opponents called invasive medical procedures, requiring the woman to look at the fetus via ultrasound or, in the case of the Texas law, listen to the fetal heartbeat before they would be allowed to proceed.

Part of the controversy was exacerbated by the relatively new US Department of Justice definition of rape announced by Attorney General Eric Holder in January 2012, which expanded the term "rape" to include any penetration with an object against anyone's will.[10]

"Forcible rape" had been defined by the FBI's Uniform Crime Reporting (UCR) Summary Reporting System (SRS) as "the carnal knowledge of a female, forcibly and against her will." That definition, unchanged since 1927, was outdated and narrow. It included only forcible male penile penetration of a female vagina. The new definition is, "The penetration, no matter how slight, of the vagina or anus with any body part or object, or oral penetration by a sex organ of another person, without the consent of the victim."[11]

The past decade has seen vicious social and political arguments across social groups intending to set the agenda for what society will enact as its governing laws and policies. Before the US Supreme Court struck down all state bans on same-sex marriage in *Obergefell v. Hodges*, the issue was being litigated state by state, with Maryland and Washington state passing legislation allowing gay marriage, but opposition efforts are said to be mobilizing to send the issue to a referendum.[12] New Jersey also passed legislation in support of same-sex marriage, but the governor vetoed the measure.[13] The fight was brutal. Around that same timeframe a group of moms organized but failed to remove Ellen DeGeneres as the JCPenney spokesperson because she is gay,[14] and Dharun Ravi was convicted of a hate crime for spying on his gay roommate, Tyler Clementi, with a webcam. Clementi killed himself after the incident.[15]

Social attitudes affect educational objectives. In 2010 a county district attorney in the state of Wisconsin sent a letter to five school districts urging them to drop all sex education classes until the legislature could repeal a new law that had recently passed and signed by the governor.[16] In 2013 two high school students in Alabama began working with a team of state legislators to repeal a 1992 law that required educators to teach that being gay is a crime and "not a lifestyle acceptable to the general public."[17] Mississippi teachers, in 2014 were required by law to teach students that homosexual activity was illegal under the "unnatural intercourse" statute and that a "monogamous relationship in the context of marriage is the only appropriate setting for sexual intercourse."[18]

In 2015 Utah passed legislation to define abstinence only as the state's sex education program, legally mandating the elimination of instruction about sexual intercourse and contraceptive methods and disallowing both the mention of sex outside of marriage and any discussions about homosexuality and making sex education optional.[19] Kansas approved a teacher prosecution bill that would allow parents to prosecute teachers for teaching material they thought was "harmful to minors" and could result in a Class B misdemeanor, which could mean no more than six months in jail and a $1,000 fine.[20] The National Conference of State Legislatures (NCSL) has a collection of just how states are involved in providing sex education for public school children at http://www.ncsl.org/research/health/state-policies-on-sex-education-in-schools.aspx.

Whatever one's personal opinion might be about the effectiveness (or lack of effectiveness) in modern US sex education programs, serious questions are being raised about who needs sex education and how Americans understand basic aspects of sexual health. The United States ranks first among developed nations in both teenage pregnancy and sexually transmitted disease transmission.[21] Although teen pregnancy rates have declined considerably in past decades in the United States, the teen pregnancy rate is still highest in the United States at 57 per 1,000 15- to 19-year-olds.[22] Most people will have sex regularly throughout their lifetimes, with only 3 percent of people choosing never to have sex.[23] Young people are reported to be participating in oral and anal sex acts under the false belief that they can avoid sexually transmitted diseases or the idea they will still be considered a virgin on their wedding night.[24] On the other end of the age continuum, the Centers for Disease Control and Prevention (CDC) predicts that, within the next five years, 50 percent of people with HIV in the United States will be 50 years old or older. With the percentage of HIV increasing within this population by 16 percent between 2005 and 2008, researchers worried the numbers would continue to go up unless people in the advanced age group also spend more time thinking about sexual health and disease prevention. Numbers from 2016 suggested new diagnoses were declining; one in six HIV diagnoses in 2017 were in this group.[25]

People of various ages continue to demonstrate varying gaps in knowledge and understanding about the subject of sexual health. People young and old are raising questions about the parameters of what constitutes healthy sexual behavior. The previously mentioned Gallup poll illustrates how attitudes about sex and definitions of "appropriate" sexual behaviors vary over time and across demographics. The recent highly public political protests are reminding everyone just how controversial these questions remain in the United States. Different levels of exposure to accurate information, different levels of interest in what other people do and don't do, different attitudes about issues and definitions of morality are only a fraction of the many personal and socially chaotic conditions at play. Without question, these and other ongoing stories raise innumerable questions about the ability of the United States to establish parameters around a collective understanding of healthy sex and sexuality when people disagree about what that means. In fact, all of these conversations relate back to how citizens and communities across the United States choose to dialogue with each other on questions regarding sexual health and exactly what is meant by "health."

Profound divisions exist not only in the attitudes and opinions about sexual health but also across ranges of sexual behaviors whereby these decisions influence social attitudes about the classification of specific acts as deviant and criminal. It's a tricky business to outline "healthy" and "unhealthy" sexual behavior when people disagree about basic ideas. Sometimes, clarification between healthy and unhealthy behavior comes from watching how negative consequences are associated with a particular behavior. Social commentaries from countries outside the United States have famously suggested that US attitudes on sex reflect a fear-based, restrictive, sex-negative, or even "prudish" attitude toward sex.[26] But even when limiting the conversation to attitudes from within the United States and narrowing the conversation to a "simple" discussion about "healthy" sex and "normal" sexual development, controversy rages. The immediate question presented for consideration here is, what is healthy sex? The longer-term question for consideration is, what connections can be made between the conversation about healthy sexuality and sexual harm?

This chapter offers a variety of ideas and insights into ongoing conversations and controversies in the United States focused on what it means to be sexually healthy. Clearly, creating and advocating definitions and characterizations about what constitutes healthy sex and healthy sexuality is closely connected to the need to find a way to educate people in the United States once a curriculum can be identified and agreed upon. But what if opposing groups cannot reach a common understanding? What if people cannot ever agree about what constitutes sexual health? Any conversation about healthy sexuality requires making reference to multiple disciplines of study across the social and biological sciences, including psychology, sociology, and biology, as examples. Cross-discipline comparisons are always complicated because of unique definitional distinctions and disciplinary differences. While acknowledging the fact that more precise definitions might exist within different disciplines, content selected for inclusion in this conversation about healthy sexuality is intended to provide a backdrop for the forthcoming discussion about modern (primarily US) conceptualizations of sexual crimes and sex offenders and *is by no means intended to be seen as comprehensive coverage of the subject of sexual health.*

Information selected for inclusion in the chapter is intended to provide a review of some of the more fundamental ideas about the controversial parameters of healthy sexuality. While more comprehensive information about sex crimes, sex offenders, and the related social responses to sex crime controversies is covered in the chapters to follow, the discussion about healthy sexuality begins by asking "What is healthy sex?" and "When should informal and more formalized conversations about sex begin?" Attention is given to a plethora of terms and ideas and controversies around sexual identity development, sex education, and age-appropriate frameworks for describing the physical, biological, and emotional aspects of sex, including controversial conversations about sexually transmitted infections, masturbation, and gender and gay liberation. Emphasis is centered on consent, including distinctions between compliance and coercion. The conversation begs a final question: "Are groups of people, living in community, ever finished talking about the boundaries of healthy sex?"

WHAT IS "HEALTHY SEX"? TEN DEFINITIONS AND TWO MODELS

Consider the following definitions of sexual health:

1. **World Health Organization (WHO):** Sexual health is "the integration of the somatic, emotional, intellectual and social aspects of sexual being in ways that are positively enriching and that enhance personality, communication and love."[27]

2. **National Commission on Adolescent Sexual Health:**[28] Sexual health includes the ability to

   (a) develop and maintain meaningful interpersonal relationships;
   (b) appreciate one's own body;
   (c) interact with both genders in respectful and appropriate ways; and
   (d) express affection, love, and intimacy in ways consistent with one's values.

   Achieving sexual health requires the integration of psychological, physical, societal, cultural, educational, economic, and spiritual factors.

   Released as a consensus statement on adolescent sexual health, the statement was endorsed by 50 national organizations and over 35 professional organizations, including the American Psychological Association, Society for the Scientific Study of Sex, and Society for Adolescent

Medicine.[29] In contrast to most approaches to sexual health, which are narrowly focused on avoiding unwanted pregnancy and disease, the commission's statement articulated one of the most comprehensive approaches to adolescent sexual health to date by identifying the interplay between developmental processes of adolescence and sexual health and construing sexual health as a normative aspect of adolescent development.[30]

3. **US Surgeon General, David Satcher:** "Sexual health is inextricably bound to both physical and mental health. Just as physical and mental health problems can contribute to sexual dysfunction and diseases, those dysfunctions and diseases can contribute to physical and mental health problems. Sexual health is not limited to the absence of disease or dysfunction, nor is its importance confined to just the reproductive years. It includes the ability to understand and weigh the risks, responsibilities, outcomes and impacts of sexual actions and to practice abstinence when appropriate. It includes freedom from sexual abuse and discrimination and the ability of individuals to integrate their sexuality into their lives, derive pleasure from it, and to reproduce if they so choose."[31]

4. **Robinson and Colleagues Academic Research Articles:** "Sexual health is an approach to sexuality founded in accurate knowledge, personal awareness and self-acceptance, such that one's behavior, values and emotions are congruent and integrated within a person's wider personality structure and self-definition. Sexual health involves an ability to be intimate with a partner, to communicate explicitly about sexual needs and desires, to be sexually functional (to have desire, become aroused, and obtain sexual fulfillment), to act intentionally and responsibly and to set appropriate sexual boundaries. Sexual health has a communal aspect, reflecting not only self-acceptance and respect, but also respect and appreciation for individual difference and diversity, as well as a feeling of belonging to and involvement in one's sexual culture(s). Sexual health includes a sense of self-esteem, personal attractiveness and competence, as well as freedom from sexual dysfunction, sexually transmitted diseases, and sexual assault and coercion. Sexual health affirms sexuality as a positive force, enhancing other dimensions of one's life."[32]

5. **Wendy Maltz:** "Healthy sex involves the conscious, positive expression of our sexual energy in ways that enhance self-esteem, physical health, and emotional relationship. It is mutually beneficial and harms no one."[33]

6. **Sexuality Information and Education Council of the United States (SEICUS):** Sexual & Reproductive Health: "All people have a right to health care services that promote, maintain, and if needed, restore sexual and reproductive health. Health care providers should assess sexual and reproductive health needs and concerns as integral parts of each individual's health and wellness care and make appropriate resources available." (Note: Within their definition of sexual health SIECUS also has statements about adolescent health, access to repro-

ductive health, abortion, HIV/AIDS, and healthcare practitioner training. The full statements on each of these subdivisions within their full definition are included in the endnote.[34]

7. **National Sexual Violence Resource Center:** "Healthy sexuality means having the knowledge and power to express sexuality in ways that enrich one's life. It includes approaching sexuality interactions and relationships from a perspective that is consensual, respectful and informed. Healthy sexuality is free from coercion and violence."[35]

8. **Unitarian Universalist Association (UUA) of Congregations:** The following areas "constitute the foundation of a sexually healthy and responsible religious denomination:

   - Policies, bylaws and procedures
   - Full inclusion of women in denomination leadership
   - Full inclusion of LGBTQI (lesbian, gay, bisexual, transgender), persons
   - Sexually healthy religious professionals, including a.) required competencies for ministerial candidates, b.) sexually healthy and responsible seminaries, and c.) continuing education and support
   - Sexually healthy congregation programs and policies
   - Sexuality education, including curricula, training, implementation, and supervision
   - Sexual abuse and harassment prevention policies and procedures
   - Prophetic witness for sexual justice in the public square"[36]

9. **Focus on the Family:** "Let's think about how we can define sexual integrity. . . . The single most important question for us to ask is, 'How does God define sexual integrity?' . . . [O]ur strategy toward our kids' sexual development needs to be comprehensive. With this goal in mind, here's a list of questions to help you process your thoughts and questions about sexuality, including choices and circumstances:

   - Is it biblical?
   - Is it Christ-affirming?
   - Is it timeless?
   - Is it separate from the 'world'?
   - Is it equally sensitive to both males and females?
   - Is it service oriented?
   - Is it grounded in authentic intimacy?
   - Is it purposeful?
   - Is it connected to one's faith and spirituality?
   - Is it inspired by direction?
   - Is it visionary for future generations?
   - Finally, and most importantly, does the sexual choice or behavior reflect the spousal analogy found throughout Scripture, which teaches Jesus is the bridegroom of the Church?"[37]

10. **Advocates for Youth:** All young people have the right to reproductive and sexual health information, confidential, safe services and a secure stake in the future. Advocates envisions a world in which societies view adolescent sexual development as normal and healthy, treat youth as partners in promoting sexual health and value young people's relationships with each other and with adults. The core values of *Rights. Respect. Responsibility.*® (3Rs) animate this vision.

At a societal level, Advocates believes:

Rights. Youth have the right to accurate and complete sexual health information, confidential reproductive and sexual health services, and a secure stake in the future.

Respect. Youth deserve respect. Valuing young people means involving them in the design, implementation and evaluation of programs and policies that affect their health and well-being.

Responsibility. Society has the responsibility to provide young people with the tools they need to safeguard their sexual health, and young people have the responsibility to protect themselves from unwanted pregnancy and **sexually transmitted infections** (STIs), including HIV.

Further, Advocates believe *Rights. Respect. Responsibility.*® provides a framework for establishing healthy interpersonal relationships between young people and between youth and adults.

Rights. Young people have the right to be safe and healthy within their relationships—free from physical or emotional coercion. They have the right to make decisions based on their own personal values.

Respect. Young people demonstrate respect for each other within relationships by taking the needs of others into account. Parents and society as a whole should demonstrate respect for young peoples' relationships and help them to gain the emotional and communications skills key to establishing and sustaining healthy relationships.

Responsibility. Young people have the responsibility to protect their own emotional and physical health as well as that of their partners. Parents, families and society have the responsibility to nurture relationships with young people that are healthy, honest, and respectful.[38]

Without question, the idea of coming to an understanding or an agreement about what constitutes "healthy sexuality" is complicated by various social factors, including cultural and religious ideologies, family tradition, research from diverse academic disciplines, popular community groups, geography, and historical attitudes, to name just a few. Controversies are often exploited and expanded beyond comfortable limits in various media outlets, but what are the common themes? Given all of the current and historical controversy around this topic, is it possible to come to a collective understanding about what people in the United States identify as healthy sex and sexuality?

Table 1.1 WHO Definitions of Sexual Health

World Health Organization–Unofficial "Working Definitions"[1]

Sex—Sex refers to the biological characteristics that define humans as female or male. While these sets of biological characteristics are not mutually exclusive, as there are individuals who possess both, they tend to differentiate humans as males and females. In general use in many languages, the term sex is often used to mean "sexual activity", but for technical purposes in the context of sexuality and sexual health discussions, the above definition is preferred.

Sexuality—Sexuality is a central aspect of being human throughout life and encompasses sex, gender identities and roles, sexual orientation, eroticism, pleasure, intimacy and reproduction. Sexuality is experienced and expressed in thoughts, fantasies, desires, beliefs, attitudes, values, behaviors, practices, roles and relationships. While sexuality can include all of these dimensions, not all of them are always experienced or expressed. Sexuality is influenced by the interaction of biological, psychological, social, economic, political, cultural, ethical, legal, historical, religious and spiritual factors.

Sexual health—Sexual health is a state of physical, emotional, mental and social well-being in relation to sexuality; it is not merely the absence of disease, dysfunction or infirmity. Sexual health requires a positive and respectful approach to sexuality and sexual relationships, as well as the possibility of having pleasurable and safe sexual experiences, free of coercion, discrimination and violence. For sexual health to be attained and maintained, the sexual rights of all persons must be respected, protected and fulfilled.

Sexual rights—Sexual rights embrace human rights that are already recognized in national laws, international human rights documents and other consensus statements. They include the right of all persons, free of coercion, discrimination and violence, to:

- the highest attainable standard of sexual health, including access to sexual and reproductive health care services;
- seek, receive and impart information related to sexuality;
- sexuality education;
- respect for bodily integrity;
- choose their partner;
- decide to be sexually active or not;
- consensual sexual relations;
- consensual marriage;
- decide whether or not, and when, to have children; and
- pursue a satisfying, safe and pleasurable sexual life.

The responsible exercise of human rights requires that all persons respect the rights of others.

1 Ibid.

The fluidity of terms and concepts related to conversations about healthy sex and sexuality is illustrated in the first definition from the World Health Organization (WHO), which regularly brings together a group of international experts to update what it titled the "working definitions" of the terms "sex," "sexuality," "sexual health," and "sexual rights," acknowledging these terms as being subject to continuous change. See Table 1.1 for the full working definitions of these terms.[39] In fact, included with the WHO's "working definitions" was the following disclaimer: "These definitions do not represent an official WHO position, and should not be used or quoted as WHO definitions."[40]

The information presented throughout the chapter is a snapshot in time, a picture of efforts to understand sexual health in the United States today with the understanding that the sex-related definitions, social understandings, or conceptualizations should be considered "works in progress." In today's internet-driven society, the idea of a snapshot might be more appropriately replaced by the example of a video clip on YouTube, but the lack of firm definitions combines with the complexities of the subject matter to obscure the breadth and depth of the conversation about sexual health as a concept. As a result, the terms and ideas presented here are an educated starting point, offered for discussion and conversation rather than as a conclusive ending or final word on the subject.

THE CERTS MODEL AND MALTZ HIERARCHY[41]

The closing of the chapter offered 10 definitions of sexual health from a variety of organizations and institutions that have all identified an interest in helping people understand what sexual health might look like. Books, websites, blogs, faith communities, and educational research and resources reflect a need for education and discussion around healthy sexuality as a concept. In general the conceptualization of the terms "healthy sexuality" and "sexual health" is used here and throughout the text to reflect similar themes. **Healthy sexuality** refers to broad aspects of sexual health, including sexual and reproductive anatomy, biological sex, gender, gender identities, gender roles, sexual orientation, sex drive and sexual identity, and ways sexuality is experienced and expressed.[42] Two models of healthy sex have been selected for a more extended review here: Wendy Maltz's work at Healthysex.com and the Sexual Health Model from the Program in Human Sexuality at the University of Minnesota Medical School.

Wendy Maltz (2012) outlines the **CERTS model of healthy sex** at www.healthysex.com and argues healthy sexuality requires five conditions be met:

1. Consent
2. Equality
3. Respect
4. Trust
5. Safety

Consent means a person can freely and comfortably choose whether to engage in sexual activity (discussed more fully later in the chapter). All parties are conscious, informed, and able to stop the activity at any time during sexual contact. *Equality* means your sense of personal power is on an equal level with your partner's. Neither one of you dominates or intimidates the other. *Respect* refers to a positive regard for yourself and your partner. You also feel respected by your partner based on how your partner is treating you. *Trust* means you trust your partner on physical and emotional levels. You accept each other's needs and vulnerabilities and are able to respond to concerns with sensitivity. The fifth and final element of the CERTS model is *safety*, meaning you feel secure and safe within the sexual setting. You feel safe from the possibility of negative consequences, such as unwanted pregnancy, sexually transmitted infection, physical injury, and emotional harassment.

Several years ago, Maltz (1995) also outlined what she refers to as the **Maltz hierarchy of sexual interaction**.[43] Used as a therapeutic tool for survivors of sexual abuse, couples in relationship counseling, and general sex education, the Maltz hierarchy identifies **sexual energy** as a natural force that can be channeled along one of two routes: (1) the path to disintegration and disconnection or (2) the path to integration and connectedness. See Figures 1.1 and 1.2. Figure

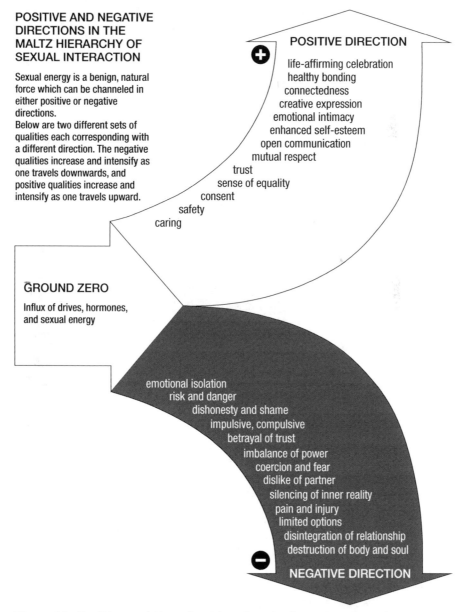

POSITIVE AND NEGATIVE DIRECTIONS IN THE MALTZ HIERARCHY OF SEXUAL INTERACTION

Sexual energy is a benign, natural force which can be channeled in either positive or negative directions.
Below are two different sets of qualities each corresponding with a different direction. The negative qualities increase and intensify as one travels downwards, and positive qualities increase and intensify as one travels upward.

⊕ POSITIVE DIRECTION

life-affirming celebration
healthy bonding
connectedness
creative expression
emotional intimacy
enhanced self-esteem
open communication
mutual respect
trust
sense of equality
consent
safety
caring

GROUND ZERO

Influx of drives, hormones, and sexual energy

emotional isolation
risk and danger
dishonesty and shame
impulsive, compulsive
betrayal of trust
imbalance of power
coercion and fear
dislike of partner
silencing of inner reality
pain and injury
limited options
disintegration of relationship
destruction of body and soul

⊖ NEGATIVE DIRECTION

Figure 1.1   Positive and Negative Directions in the Maltz Hierarchy of Sexual Interaction

Maltz, Wendy. "The Maltz Hierarchy of Sexual Interaction." Sexual Addiction & Compulsivity 2, no. 1 (1995): 5–18. https://doi.org/10.1080/10720169508400062.

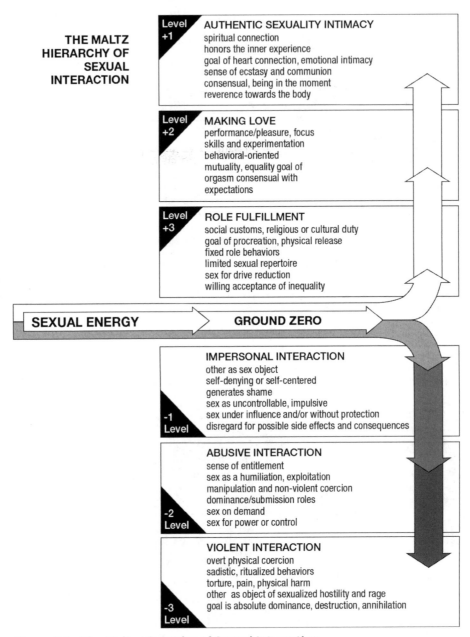

THE MALTZ HIERARCHY OF SEXUAL INTERACTION

Level +1
AUTHENTIC SEXUALITY INTIMACY
spiritual connection
honors the inner experience
goal of heart connection, emotional intimacy
sense of ecstasy and communion
consensual, being in the moment
reverence towards the body

Level +2
MAKING LOVE
performance/pleasure, focus
skills and experimentation
behavioral-oriented
mutuality, equality goal of
orgasm consensual with
expectations

Level +3
ROLE FULFILLMENT
social customs, religious or cultural duty
goal of procreation, physical release
fixed role behaviors
limited sexual repertoire
sex for drive reduction
willing acceptance of inequality

SEXUAL ENERGY **GROUND ZERO**

IMPERSONAL INTERACTION
other as sex object
self-denying or self-centered
generates shame
sex as uncontrollable, impulsive
sex under influence and/or without protection
disregard for possible side effects and consequences
-1 Level

ABUSIVE INTERACTION
sense of entitlement
sex as a humiliation, exploitation
manipulation and non-violent coercion
dominance/submission roles
sex on demand
sex for power or control
-2 Level

VIOLENT INTERACTION
overt physical coercion
sadistic, ritualized behaviors
torture, pain, physical harm
other as object of sexualized hostility and rage
goal is absolute dominance, destruction, annihilation
-3 Level

Figure 1.2   The Maltz Hierarchy of Sexual Interaction
Maltz, Wendy. "The Maltz Hierarchy of Sexual Interaction." *Sexual Addiction & Compulsivity* 2, no. 1 (1995): 5-18. https://doi.org/10.1080/10720169508400062.

1.1 explores the positive and negative aspects of sexual energy more fully by describing three levels of positive sexual encounters and three levels of sexual encounters of a more destructive nature. The positive sexual encounters begin with +1 Role Fulfillment, +2 Making Love, and +3 Authentic Sexual Intimacy. The negative numbers refer to –1 Impersonal Interaction, –2 Abusive Interaction, and –3 Violent Interaction.

THE SEXUAL HEALTH MODEL

While the CERTS model is useful as a tool for the parties involved in the sexual encounter, the focus is on the individuals in the act and their own personal motivations for the encounter. The **sexual health model**, on the other hand, integrates a significant amount of social and cultural commentary that includes sexual health for all people, including people with HIV/AIDS and other sexual concerns. Developed after years of observation and research, Robinson and her colleagues outlined this model as a resource to be used to target specific subcultural groups to enhance education and awareness about sexual health to address public health concerns, such as, in this case, the spread of HIV.[44] The 10 themes are outlined more fully in Table 1.2. The first theme seems simple enough: talking about sex. The organizers of this model suggest that it is important to be able to talk comfortably about sexuality, which they go on to describe as sexual values, sexual preferences, sexual attractions, sexual histories, and sexual behaviors.

Yet it seems important to ask, Are people in the United States comfortable talking about sexuality with other people? With friends? With family members? With sexual partners? How many people take the time to think about how their own individual attitudes compare to experiences of social convention and the personal attitudes of others regarding the different places where each one identified the acceptability of their individual limits? Perhaps certain conversations are acceptable among friends, whereas others are comfortable between partners. These are all good questions to begin thinking about when

Table 1.2   Ten Themes from the Sexual Health Model

1. *Talking about sex*—The ability to talk comfortably and explicitly about sexuality, especially one's own sexual values, preferences, attractions, histories, and behaviors.
2. *Culture and sexual identity*—Culture influences one's sexuality and sense of sexual self; individuals need to examine the impact of their cultural heritage on their sexual identities, attitudes, behaviors, and health because cultural meaning may influence unsafe or safer sex.
3. *Sexual anatomy functioning*—Sexual health assumes a basic knowledge, understanding, and acceptance of one's sexual anatomy, sexual response, sexual functioning, and freedom from sexual dysfunction and other sexual problems.
4. *Sexual health care and safer sex*—The practice of safer sex behaviors, knowing one's body, and obtaining regular exams for sexually transmitted diseases.
5. *Challenges*—Obstacles to sexual health include sexual abuse, substances abuse, compulsive sexual behavior, sex work, harassment, and discrimination.
6. *Body image*—The ability to expand narrow notions of beauty and encourage self-acceptance.
7. *Masturbation and fantasy*—Exploring the topic of masturbation and fantasy outside of the historical myths associated with sin, illness, and immaturity to normalize masturbation.
8. *Positive sexuality*—Shifting the view of sexual exploration from risk and disease to a positive, self-affirming perspective that leads to setting appropriate sexual boundaries and safer sex.
9. *Intimacy and relationships*—The ability to secure intimacy in relationships.
10. *Spirituality*—Congruence between one's ethical, spiritual, and moral beliefs and one's sexual behaviors and values.

exploring sex, sexuality, and sexual health and the boundaries between talk and action. Consider the issue of "talking about sex" in more detail.

The Sexual Health Model Theme #1: Talking about Sex

Conversations about sex in US culture can often result in controversy or conflict. In some ways, this culture is surrounded by sex—sexualized music, movies, and cartoons. Even kids' programming and video games are highly gendered and have sexualized themes. To be highly **gendered** means the media programs or games show overtly masculine or feminine social norms and ideologies often seen to be **socially constructed** or learned about through social interactions.[45] So, while young people are exposed to sex all around them in ads, TV, and music videos, as examples, in some places, talking about sex is often still seen as taboo. As Foucault[46] stated, if society talks about how "the secrets" of sex are not to be talked about, people are still talking about it. Said differently, people talk about sex all the time; they just don't talk about the "right" elements of sex.[47] However

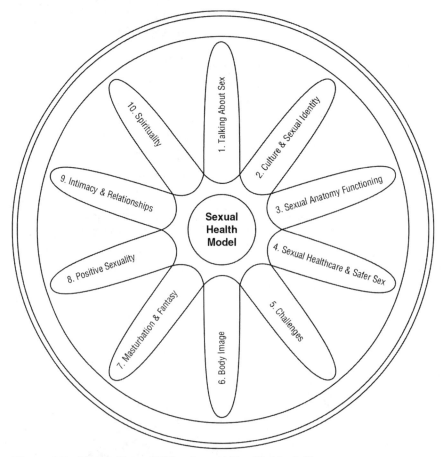

Figure 1.3   Illustration of "The Sexual Health Model"

Robinson, Bockting Rosser, Miner and Coleman. 2002. "The Sexual Health Model: Application of a sexological approach to HIV prevention." *Health Education and Research: Theory and Practice*, vol. 17, no. 1, pp. 43-57.

people in the United States choose to talk about sex, what is the role of sex education in this process? When is it appropriate to start talking about sex? Which aspects of sex do we talk about and at what age? At least three themes emerge as important for taking this conversation further: religion, gender identity, and the idea of gender bias.

Religious Communities and Sexual Health

Religious communities are often at the center of conflict when the conversation is related to sex. For example, the website for Focus on the Family, a Christian-based religious group, is very clear that sex should not happen outside of marriage, whether before marriage or after a marriage breaks down. Being strong advocates for making marriages work, Focus on the Family expresses concern about whether exposing children to the sexual behavior of parents who divorce and are dating might sexualize the child prematurely. For example, it suggests that "children can become sexualized as they witness their parents in sexually provocative situations or simply situations for mature adults. This sexualization, a type of covert sexual abuse, can alter or misdirect sexual development in the lives of our children."[48]

Children who have thoughts or questions about gender identity (discussed in more detail below) are encouraged to find their way back to heterosexuality through counseling and/or prayer.[49] The guidelines governing healthy sexuality are directly connected to a person's spiritual life and linked to the organization's interpretation of biblical teachings. While controversial in many groups, Focus on the Family continues to provide a loud and influential voice on matters of Christian sexual health in the United States.

Biblical representations of God's perspective on sexual health differ widely and reflect the strong role religion plays in the ongoing controversies regarding contemporary conversations about sexual health. Another Christian denomination reflects a dramatically different approach to the study of sexuality, and through many talks about sex has created perhaps the most comprehensive conversation about healthy sexuality in the United States, referred to as the Our Whole Lives (OWL) sex education curricula.[50] A joint project of the Unitarian Universalist Association and the United Church of Christ, the OWL series is intended to help participants make informed and responsible decisions about healthy sexual behavior with programs for grades K–1, 4–6, 7–9, 10–12, young adults (ages 18–35), and adults and is structured to provide facts about anatomy and human development as well as giving time to the spiritual, emotional, and social aspects of sexuality.[51]

Such a comprehensive presentation of information on sex, it would seem, might help to resolve many questions about how to talk about sex as a community, but, in fact, the conclusions about what is sexually appropriate were so dramatically different from each other that those who disagree will still find little if any common ground. The OWL program was based in part on the *Guidelines for Comprehensive Sexuality Education*, produced by professionals assembled by **SIECUS (Sexuality Information and Education Council of the United States)**[52]

and integrating research from a Kaiser Family Foundation report on sex education in America.[53] SIECUS is a nonprofit organization founded in 1964 by **Dr.
Mary Calderone**, who acted as the medical director for Planned Parenthood of
America and expressed concern about the lack of accurate information about
sexuality for both young people and adults.[54] SIECUS and other groups have
been associated with the idea of **comprehensive sexuality education**, defined by
SIECUS to refer to medically accurate, age-appropriate education that includes
information about abstinence and contraception.[55] It does not take long to find
other religious groups that strongly oppose various elements of the SIECUS curriculum.[56] The modest coverage of different religious attitudes in this section
does not even begin to reflect the expansive conversation about the relationship
between religion and sexuality.

GENDER IDENTITY AND SEXUAL HEALTH

Particular conflict in the discussion about healthy sexuality is linked to controversy in some social and political sectors around whether homosexuality, bisex-
uality, and transsexuality are "normal" or "healthy." This controversy introduces
a challenge to the humanity of some individuals who identify in these ways
by their detractors. This too is an idea steeped in religious ideology; however,
the controversy extends to medicine, biology, psychology, and beyond. In short,
sexual identity development happens in all people and refers to the process of
coming to understanding one's self as a sexual being. Even if one chooses not to
have sex, this decision is part of one's sexual identity. The academic and social
conversations (including the varied and diverse social, political, cultural, psychological, and religious aspects of these conversations) about categories and
classifications and ranges and variations of identity development, or even about
how sexual identity development happens, reflect disagreement about whether
these identities fall within "healthy" or "deviant" expressions of human sexuality and, in fact, human behavior. These controversies continue and are still
reflected in the way laws against homosexuality or engaging in homosexual sex
acts is enforced in the courts. Two gay men from the United States were arrested
in Dominica after they were spotted having sex on the balcony by someone on
the dock. Because sodomy is illegal in the port where the ship was docking, the
men were confined in jail until their court hearing. Although faced with a six-
month jail term, they pled guilty to the lesser charge of indecent exposure and
were fined $895 each and released.[57]

A number of scholars have written about the relationship between identity
development particularly as it relates to group membership and social strati-
fication along the lines of race, gender, social class, and sexual orientation.[58]
Also, the integrative biopsychosocial influences (e.g., biological aspects of development and maturation, gender norms, gender role socialization, culture and
religion, systemic homonegativity, and sexual prejudice and privilege) are often
overlooked, and some argue that *individual* identity development processes are
overemphasized when compared to the consequences of *social* identity development processes.[59] For academics, researchers, and scholars studying in this area,

talking about sex is a full-time job keeping up with all the new, interesting, and emerging elements of human sexuality that are being explored all the time.

Like so many of the issues relating to healthy sexuality, the collective discourse requires much more exploration and analysis than can be done here. The "genderbread" graphic presented in Figure 1.4 is intended to offer assistance in exploring the gender-related terms to enhance the general understanding of these issues. In short, **sexual minority** (similar to the idea of "ethnic minorities") is a term used to refer to people whose **sexual expression** (i.e., identity, orientation, practice, and sexual characteristics) differs from the majority, typically identified as heterosexual, or people attracted to others of the opposite sex/gender.[60] When people ask about **sexual orientation**, they are often referring to whether a person identifies as having feelings for someone of the same sex, the opposite sex, or both sexes. A **homosexual** is traditionally defined as a person who is attracted to and/or has sex with a person of the same gender. **Gender identity** refers to one's internally perceived **gender**,[61] which in various disciplines—particularly, in feminist critiques of traditional theories of behavior and development and the subsequent feminist theories and writings—is the term used to distinguish between biological sex and the social construction of gender, particularly exploring the range of characteristics used to distinguish maleness from femaleness, men from women, males from females, or girls from boys. While **gay** is the term most commonly used to describe males who are attracted to males, the term **lesbian** is used to describe women who are attracted to women. A **transgender** person identifies with or expresses gender identity that differs from the person's sex at birth. **Gender dysphoria** refers to a clinical term referencing discontentment or disconnection between a person's biological sex and their gender identity.

In some cases a young person may not identify as exclusively heterosexual.[62] Whatever one's individual, social, or cultural attitude about gender identity and sexual minorities, research suggests that, throughout the process of sexual identity development, many young people express questions about **heteronormativity**—the idea that heterosexuality is the only type of acceptable sexual identity. The social stigma attached to questions associated with sexual orientation and identity can be quite confusing for teens, particularly teens who do not receive support. Further, for decades studies have focused on why young people with a same-sex orientation are twice as likely to report suicide attempts and suicidal ideation and to abuse alcohol and feel hopeless, depressed, and victimized.[63] More about this is presented for consideration in chapter 3. Although many definitions are provided here, more comprehensive definitions may vary throughout the academic literature, particularly between community groups, social science research, and psychological and medical or clinical discussions of the terms. The history of homosexuality in the United States is discussed in chapter 5.

COMMODITY VERSUS PERFORMANCE MODEL: ILLUSTRATING GENDER BIAS?

Another critical aspect central to reflecting on how people in the United States are talking about sex pertains to the idea of **gender bias**, also known as **gender**

discrimination or **sexism**. This idea has been explored in greater detail within the sociological and psychological literature and, more specifically, around the gendered way sexual identity is characterized in society.[64] As with every rule, there are always exceptions; such is the case when discussing in generalities how men and women, as a group, present themselves. When talking about things "in general" or "as a rule," it is important to be careful to make note of the tendency to overgeneralize or attempt to represent ideas too broadly. With this in mind, consider the following: As a rule, mainstream values in the United States have reflected different attitudes about the sexual practices of men and women. As a rule, men were expected to seek out sex, and women were expected to resist having sex or to wait to have sex.[65] Popular cultural language talked about "the kind of women who have sex before marriage" as if having sex made them less valuable than woman who didn't have sex, or they were discussed as having been "used up." This language was presented in such a way as to trivialize, if not demonize, women who were sexually active. As a rule, men were expected to pursue sex, and women were expected to resist being pursued. As a rule, men were expected to "sow their wild oats" before marriage, and women were expected to be "chaste and pure" for their future husbands. As a rule, men were expected to be aggressive, and women were expected to be passive around the subject and/or activity of sex. Do these sexual "rules" sound like a thing of the past, or do they remain a gendered part of social realities today?

Many of the gendered messages about appropriate sexual boundaries were confounded in the movement(s) to secure women's rights as equal rights. Seminars and training sessions on identifying and ending gender inequality in the

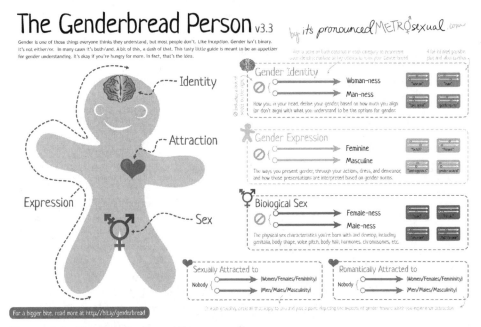

Figure 1.4   The Genderbread Person
Hues. "Genderbread Person v3.3 " The Genderbread Person." The Genderbread Person. Accessed November 6, 2019. https://www.genderbread.org/resource/genderbread-person-v3-3.

workplace, sexual harassment, domestic violence, and marital rape, for example, became popular in the 1980s and 1990s. In the mainstream, women were supposed to make themselves attractive to men while also being invited to see themselves as more than just their looks, and men were told women expected them to keep their sexual thoughts, and hands, to themselves. A considerable amount can be said about the use of sexually charged language to illustrate gender bias, "feminized" terms as put-downs, and sexually charged terms as the ultimate in name-calling. Examples among college women include those who are targets of such language if they rebuff a sexual advance or they are seen to relegate someone to the "friend zone."[66] Research suggests that young women and girls don't need to wait until college to be referred to as "bitches," "sluts," "whores," or even the c-word, something that used to be considered extremely offensive socially and culturally. However, the word was used repeatedly in the 2016 presidential election by opponents to describe Hillary Clinton, when she ran for president.[67] Words such as "man whore" and "player" seem to have less of a social sting for men than they do for women. Other terms are gendered in the sense that a "real man" would never be called such things or, if he were, would be expected to defend his "manhood" with violence.

Some have argued that sexual content, in some cases extremely *gendered* sexual content,[68] has been **normalized**, or seen as typical, in movies, music videos, TV, magazines, and advertising. Serious challenges have been leveled against the exploitation of sexuality for popular consumption as entertainment.[69] Although more is presented in chapter 6 about the commodification or consumption of sex through prostitution and pornography, here, it is important to know that men are targeted as the primary consumers of sex and women are the object to be consumed. Early feminist scholar Catharine MacKinnon famously explored the objectification of women in a sexual context when she said, "Man fucks woman; subject verb object."[70]

In 2008 Thomas Macaulay Millar outlined what he called the **performance model of sex**,[71] presented in sharp contrast to what he describes as the **commodity model of sex**, where the expression of sex is a commodity to be bought and sold.

> We live in a culture where sex is not so much an act as a thing: a substance that can be given, bought, sold, or stolen, that has a value and a supply-and-demand curve. In this "commodity model," sex is like a ticket; women have it and men try to get it. Women may give it away or may trade it for something valuable, but either way it's a transaction. This puts women in the position of seller, but also guardian or gatekeeper. . . . Women are guardians of the tickets, men apply for access to them. This model pervades casual conversation about sex: Women "give it up." Men "get some."[72]

Millar's explanation of the commodity model of sex can also be observed in the gendered nature of video game play, which sets up situations to suggest women who get "stuff" from the gamer will eventually agree to have virtual sex or get married in return.[73] Instead of being a trade-off between the "absence of no" and the "presence of yes," the performance model of sex suggests that sex should be seen as a collaboration, a consensual merging of two equal participants, like two musicians playing music together,[74] or, more specifically, playing music with no strings attached.

In the sexual health model, talking about sex seems to indicate everyone has a role to play in their own discovery of what sex means to them. They have a place to discover, explore, and understand the various aspects of their body, sexual feelings, and desires to be loved and to love and chart a course for how these things can be searched, studied, and investigated within a framework of self-awareness and confidence and with a healthy self-esteem.

THE SEXUAL HEALTH MODEL: #2 THROUGH #10

Notice that, so far, the entire discussion of the sexual health model has been sparked by simply using the *first* of 10 themes described by Robinson and her colleagues (2015)[75] and outlined in Table 1.2: talking about sex as a starting point for a conversation about healthy sexuality. Any number of conversations could have gone any number of different directions. At this stage, at least two things are noteworthy for purposes here: (1) seemingly infinitely more could be said about how people in the United States are "talking about sex," and (2) each of the 10 items identified in the sexual health model could also be discussed in great length. If it were not apparent at first review, anyone's attempt to understand sex more completely could easily and quickly become quite expansive and potentially complex.

The second theme introduced in the sexual health model is *culture and sexual identity*, the idea that culture influences one's sexuality and offers a sense of one's sexual self, suggesting cultural meaning may influence one's definition of **safe** or **unsafe sex**.[76] The third theme, *sexual anatomy functioning*, emphasizes the need to have a basic knowledge about sex, one's sexual anatomy, response, and functioning with freedom from sexual dysfunction and other sexual problems. The fourth element is *sexual health care and safer sex* and the ability to practice **safe sex** and check regularly for **sexually transmitted diseases**. The fifth element, *challenges*, highlights the need to be free from obstacles to sexual health, including sexual abuse, substance abuse, compulsive sexual behavior, sex work, or harassment and discrimination. The sixth theme is *body image*, seventh is *masturbation and fantasy*, eighth is *positive sexuality*, ninth is *intimacy and relationships*, and tenth is *spirituality*.

Certainly, every one of these areas of sexual health could be discussed at length, and, for some, controversies might erupt. So many questions remain, and research simply does not have answers for solving social conflict when social controversies are steeped in tradition and social customs. When is sexual behavior seen as compulsive, or how is sexual anatomy functioning differently in people who have suffered as victims of domestic violence or child sexual abuse? Each of the areas outlined in the sexual health model inspires a relatively clear understanding of sexual health, only to have that understanding explode wide open when the topics are researched in more detail. Feel free to explore each of these ideas more fully in classroom groups or independently. The themes reflect very individualized and personal attitudes and beliefs linked to family, religion, society and culture, individual experiences with sexuality, and sexual health. Remember too that an individual's attitudes and behaviors about sex often change over time, with age and life experiences.

When Is It OK to Start Talking about Sex?

In her award-winning video, *Raising Sexually Healthy Children*, psychotherapist and social worker Susan Adler suggests that, if a child is old enough to be sexually assaulted, they are old enough to learn age-appropriate information about sexual health.[77] Not everyone will agree with this idea, but, like so many other aspects of sexuality, the idea about when to begin discussions about sex with young people is extremely controversial. Whether young people are confronted with sex on TV shows or in the movies, or in the news of a local child abduction attempt, or as a scandal about teachers having sex with elementary students, or in the form of systemwide abuse from within various faith communities, or as alleged at Penn State in 2011, it seems kids are constantly exposed to messages about sex, some healthy and some unhealthy. Attention is given here to a series of themes contained in a collection of healthy sex programs, including abstinence only but expanding into comprehensive sexuality education beginning with the idea of consent, age, biology (physical), and psychology (emotional).

Consent, Compliance, and Coercion

The issue of **consent** will be presented multiple times throughout the text, adding nuance and broader context. Following the themes introduced earlier, attention is given here to three complementary terms: consent, compliance, and coercion. The national antisexual assault organization RAINN (Rape, Abuse, and Incest National Network) outlines three main considerations for determining whether a sexual act is consensual: (1) both people are old enough to consent, (2) both people have the capacity to consent, and (3) both people agree to the sexual contact.[78] Consent is often contrasted with **coercion**, or sexual encounters forced on a person. This might involve the use of a weapon, physical abuse, or other forms of pressure, but clearly sex is not agreed to freely. Like consent, coercion takes many forms and can include threats to one's job security, threats of violence, or the use of a weapon, as examples, but coercion can also be repeated pressure from a partner who will not take no for an answer and who just keeps asking until the other party says yes.

Comprehensive Sexuality Education

Although controversial in some circles, the SIECUS *Guidelines for Comprehensive Sexuality Education*, mentioned above, has been endorsed by the National Education Association (NEA) and the American School Health Association (ASHA) as a resource for developing appropriate school-based curricula.[79] Sex education programs in the United States have traditionally included information about the basics of reproduction and HIV/AIDS and other sexually transmitted diseases and infections alongside messages about abstinence. More recently, research is suggesting that parents strongly support expanding sex education in schools to include more controversial issues such as abortion, contraception beyond abstinence only, virginity pledges, and sexual orientation.[80] These research findings suggest sex education often reflects regional views, particularly when communities have **LGBTQI** (lesbian, gay, bisexual, transgender, queer, and intersexed) families, when young people are dealing with questions about sexual orientation or gender identity or are experiencing bullying in general or sexual-oriented bullying, or when the community might have reasons for ensuring sex and sexuality education is age appropriate for children.

Comprehensive sexuality education has four goals:

1. To provide accurate *information* about human sexuality.
2. To provide an opportunity for young people to develop and understand their *values*, *attitudes*, and *beliefs* about sexuality.
3. To help young people develop *relationship* and *interpersonal skills*.
4. To help young people exercise *responsibility* regarding sexual relationships, including addressing abstinence, pressures to become prematurely involved in sexual intercourse, and the use of contraception and other sexual health measures.[81]

Six key areas are considered to be essential for any comprehensive sexuality education program:

1. Human development
2. Sexual behavior
3. Relationships
4. Sexual health
5. Personal skills
6. Society and culture[82]

Some of the critical distinctions between sex education of the past and contemporary information about sex suggests that traditional sex education has focused on physical and biological information without emphasizing the importance of healthy relationships and a reliance on basic fundamentals, such as giving attention to the role of self-esteem and self-confidence in the decision to have sex. Although each of these issues could be focused on decisions about age appropriateness, the physical, biological, psychological, and emotional issues are discussed in greater detail below.

At What Age Is Sexual Education Appropriate?

In discussions about healthy sex, part of the challenge of educating children and young people lies in determining what constitutes the "age-appropriate" part of sex education. In the United States, this has proven particularly controversial because, historically, even adult behavior has been tightly regulated through legislation. This is especially true when people hear about sex education designed to begin with children as young as kindergarten. Various sex education programs outline the specific content in a sex education program differently; however, it is clear the content presented to a 5-year-old student in kindergarten is quite different from information about physical and biological aspects of a changing body in healthy discussions about puberty organized for students in middle school. These middle school discussions are also likely to differ from high school conversations, which might include information about pregnancy prevention, sexually transmitted diseases, and healthy relationships.

The Physical and Biological Aspects of Sex

The physical and biological aspects of sex are often the characteristics that get the most attention because they have to do with notable physical changes the body goes through in the aging process and in preparation for sexual activity. Most healthy sexuality programs do cover the physical changes the bodies will go through as they grow into puberty and then into adulthood. Understanding the menstrual cycle for women and the deepening of voices in men are often part of a healthy sexuality program. Questions about how to have sex fall within the common discussion about healthy sexuality because sex itself is about certain body parts and how babies are made.

The messages from society about how sex, gender, and sexual health are socially and culturally constructed are often excluded. One message to young people is that they are victims of their changing bodies. Adolescence is often treated as synonymous with "raging hormones" for young men, particularly emphasizing sex as a need or a goal to be reached that, once achieved, indicates having arrived at adulthood. The amount of work young people put into creating socially appropriate "feminine" or "masculine" bodies and identities is staggering. Regardless of efforts to identify an outward appearance for internal identities, something true of all youth whether straight or gay, young people spend a considerable amount of time focused on their "look" and how they are perceived by others. The social pressure for young men to present as **heteromasculine** and young women to present as **heterofeminine** is immense, as is clearly reflected in incidents of gay bashing and sexual bullying in the schools.[83]

To maintain a sexually healthy lifestyle, it is important to understand a decision to have sex comes with consequences. One of those consequences, of course, is an unplanned pregnancy. Another serious consequence of sexual activity is the possibility of contracting **sexually transmitted diseases (STDs)** or **sexually transmitted infections (STIs)**, including HIV/AIDS. Several types of **contraception** technologies are available to protect against pregnancy, but not all contraception protects against STDs/STIs. To prevent pregnancy and protect against STDs, abstaining from sex is taught in sex education programs as clearly the most effective option. Whether it is appropriate to discuss aspects of sex, such as referring to "making love" or addressing sexual issues within the broader context of a healthy relationship, it is the case that some sex education programs fall short in addressing the full range of issues related to sexual health.

Psychological and Emotional Aspects of Sex

In a highly gendered culture like that of the United States, it is not uncommon to see differences between how youth develop their attitudes about themselves and how they feel about sex. As children move into and through the teenage years, they all move at their own pace, which almost always seems like it is shockingly different from the experiences of their friends and peers—physical attractions, new relationships, romantic ideas of love, physical urges for sex, and lots of feelings. Feeling attractive, desirable, noteworthy, or lovable is part of the typical adolescent development process. The need to feel mature, or "act like a grown-up," or to feel accepted by another person is a powerful, natural, and sometimes awkward process that is not always managed well by adults. Many young people come from families that may not have an adequate understanding of healthy relationships; as a result, healthy sexuality is more difficult, if not impossible, for them. If the wants and needs of each party in a sexual encounter is discussed before finalizing a decision about participating in a sexual act, how many more sexual encounters would be healthy?

Communication: Language, Coercion, and Sexual Bullying

One study researching happiness suggested that 90 percent of a person's future happiness was based on who they marry.[84] The idea of building healthy relationships is a much more significant aspect of a healthy adult life; however, as young people in the US culture grow into adulthood, it is possible for them to see sex and relationships as the same thing. It is essential to remember that every person will have many relationships with no sexual component at all. Individuals need to learn how to have healthy disagreements and differences of opinions and when and how a relationship needs and can benefit from deliberate attention. Often, the case is that, even if someone is physically attracted to someone else, they will decide not to act on their feelings, whether they be physical or emotional, for a variety of reasons. Perhaps a person is married and they honor the institution of marriage. Perhaps a person is pursuing a rich and fulfilling career, and they do not want to be involved in a relationship at the time. The fact that most child abuse, child abductions, and violence in families happens between people in relationships is an indicator of how important it is to learn to communicate well with the people in our communities, at our workplaces, and in our households.

CONCLUSION: ARE WE EVER FINISHED TALKING ABOUT THE ESSENTIAL PARAMETERS OF HEALTHY SEXUALITY?

The chaos surrounding popular and public conversations intent on putting parameters around sexual health, as reviewed in the chapter introduction, suggests that the social and political discussions about healthy sex will be long-standing. The numerous definitions, models, and themes offered throughout the chapter highlight the multiple and varied attempts to define or clarify sexual health and introduced the dramatically different tone and context

Text Box 1.1.   Media Messages about Healthy Sexuality: Myths and Reclamations

In 2006 Dr. Mary-Lou Galician founded the Realistic Romance© Institute for Research and Education. In her work, she has focused on questions about how media have influenced unrealistic portrayals of sex, love, and romance. She identifies her work as "The Thinking Person's Relationship Remedy," and she has become known for her *7-Step Reality Check-Up©*. But she is perhaps more famous for her *Dr. FUN's Mass Media Love Quiz©*, all of which can be found on her website: http://www.realisticromance.com.

   Dr. Galician's 7-Step Reality Check-Up© was designed to assess how much mass media have created unrealistic expectations that may sabotage real-life romantic relationships. The following is quoted from her website:

   "With this process of critical thinking, you explode mass media myths and stereotypes that manipulate you and ruin your chances for a REAL-life happily-after-ever. (It's no wonder we're easily influenced—because we're surrounded 24/7 by these seductive but destructive media messages and images!)" (http://realisticromance.com/checkup.html)

   "The Purpose of REALISTIC ROMANCE® is to empower individuals and couples (and young people) . . .

- to recognize unhealthy and dangerous media myths and stereotypes of sex, love, and romance;
- to understand the harmful influence of these portrayals;
- to use the critical thinking skills of media literacy to "***dis-***illusion" media-created unrealistic expectations that sabotage real-life sex, love, and romance;
- to avoid using media myths and stereotypes as models for real-life behavior;
- to adopt healthy research-based relational strategies to achieve real-life romantic relationships that are more rewarding and fulfilling than media fantasies." (http://realisticromance.com/about.html)

REALISTIC ROMANCE®

Created by Dr. Mary-Lou Galician

www.realisticromance.com

12 Major Mass Media Myths & Stereotypes of Sex, Love, & Romance and Corresponding Prescriptions© for Healthy Coupleship

PARTNER IS PREDESTINED . . .

1. **Your perfect partner is cosmically predestined, so nothing/nobody can ultimately separate you.**

   Rx: CONSIDER COUNTLESS CANDIDATES.
   RIGHT AWAY, YOU KNOW . . .

2. **There's such a thing as "love at first sight."**

   Rx: CONSULT your CALENDAR and COUNT CAREFULLY.
   EXPRESSION NOT NECESSARY . . .

3. **Your true soul mate should KNOW what you're thinking or feeling (without your having to tell).**

Rx: COMMUNICATE COURAGEOUSLY.
SEXUAL PERFECTION . . .

4. **If your partner is truly meant for you, sex is easy and wonderful.**

Rx: CONCENTRATE on COMMITMENT and CONSTANCY.
CENTERFOLDS PREFERRED . . .

5. **To attract and keep a man, a woman should look like a model or a centerfold.**

Rx: CHERISH COMPLETENESS in COMPANIONS (not just the COVER).
ROLE OF GENDER (OR "REAL MEN") . . .

6. **The man should NOT be shorter, weaker, younger, poorer, or less successful than the woman.**

Rx: CREATE COEQUALITY; COOPERATE.
INTO A PRINCE (FROM BEAST) . . .

7. **The love of a good and faithful true woman can change a man from a "beast" into a "prince."**

Rx: CEASE CORRECTING and CONTROLLING; you CAN'T CHANGE others (only yourself!).
PUGILISM = PASSION . . .

8. **Bickering and fighting a lot mean that a man and a woman really love each other passionately.**

Rx: COURTESY COUNTS; CONSTANT CONFLICTS CREATE CHAOS.
TOTALLY OPPOSITE VALUES . . .

9. **All you really need is love, so it doesn't matter if you and your lover have very different values.**

Rx: CRAVE COMMON CORE-VALUES.
INCOMPLETE WITHOUT MATE . . .

10. **The right mate "completes you" — filling your needs and making your dreams come true.**

Rx: CULTIVATE your own COMPLETENESS.
OFTEN, ACTORS = ROLES . . .

11. **In real life, actors and actresses are often very much like the romantic characters they portray.**

Rx: (DE)CONSTRUCT CELEBRITIES.
NOT REAL/NO EFFECT . . .

12. **Since mass media portrayals of romance aren't "real," they don't really affect you.**

Rx: CALCULATE the very real CONSEQUENCES of unreal media.
(http://www.realisticromance.com/PDFs/QuizRxWeb.pdf)

Dr. FUN's Mass Media Love Quiz © 1995, 2000 by Dr. Mary-Lou Galician. All Rights Reserved.
Dr. Galician's Prescriptions© *for Getting Real About Romance* © 2000, 2001 by Dr. Mary-Lou Galician. All Rights Reserved.

expressed about the various aspects of sex within and across diverse cultures and communities across the United States. The CERTS model and the sexual health model provided the foundation for a discussion about several aspects of sex and sexuality, which represent a dramatically diverse, conflict-ridden history in the United States. In spite of increased efforts to mandate education, the controversy surrounding when and what to teach young people about sex in all its physical and emotional aspects remains.

In fact, the lack of agreement about various elements of the healthy sexuality discourse sets the stage for an even further complicated conversation about deviant sexuality in chapter 2. As the boundaries around healthy sexuality blur into the conversation about deviant sexuality, the various aspects of sexuality become even more complex and, as a result, even more controversial, making the chances for a common resolution to all the questions raised about sex unlikely if not impossible. Consequently, the controversies and the conversations continue.

KEY TERMS

CERTS model of healthy sex
coercion
commodity model of sex
comprehensive sexuality education
consent
contraception
Dr. Mary Calderone
gay
gender
gender bias
gender discrimination
gender dysphoria
gender identity
gendered
healthy sexuality
heterofeminine
heteromasculine
heteronormativity
homosexual
lesbian

LGBTQI
Maltz hierarchy of sexual interaction
normalized
performance model of sex
safe sex
sexism
sexual energy
sexual expression
sexual health model
sexual identity development
sexual minority
sexual orientation
sexually transmitted diseases (STDs)
sexually transmitted infections (STIs)
SIECUS (Sexuality Information and Education Council of the United States)
socially constructed
transgender

REVIEW QUESTIONS

1. What are the five elements of the CERTS model?

2. Why do you think the authors emphasized the difficulty of "talking about sex" as the first theme in the sexual health model?

3. What is the difference between the commodity model of sex and the performance model of sex as presented by Millar?

4. According to the information presented, what is the age of consent in your state?

5. What does the age of consent have to do with healthy sexuality?

DISCUSSION QUESTIONS

1. The conversation about gender identity brings to the forefront the topic of homosexuality and sexual minority populations. Is there any way to apply the CERTS model and the sexual health model to sexual minorities?

2. Feminist writers and scholars have done a significant amount of research about and challenged traditional sexuality. How does the conversation about the commodity model of sex reflect traditional sexual values that feminist writers and scholars are focused on changing?

3. Which of the definitions of sexual health makes the most sense to you? Can you find another definition you like even better? What aspects about that definition capture your interest and why?

4. Consider the information about ages of vulnerability to sexual violence and the question about whether comprehensive sexual education is appropriate for school-age children. What role does education play in sexual violence prevention?

5. Are we ever finished talking about sex?

NOTES

1. Leslie Feinberg, "We Are All Works in Progress," in *Women's Lives: Multicultural Perspectives*, 5th ed., ed. Gwyn Kirk and Margo Okazawa-Rey (New York: McGraw-Hill, 2009), 193.

2. "An Overview on Healthy Sexuality and Sexual Violence Prevention," National Sexual Violence Resource Center, 2012, accessed June 29, 2015, http://www.nsvrc.org/sites/default/files/SAAM_2012_An-overview-on-healthy-sexuality-and-sexual-violence.txt.

3. Jeffrey M. Jones, "Americans Hold Record Liberal Views on Most Moral Issues," Gallup, May 11, 2017, accessed August 19, 2019, http://news.gallup.com/poll/210542/americans-hold-record-liberal-views-moral-issues.aspx; Lydia Saad, "Doctor-Assisted Suicide Is Moral Issue Dividing Americans Most," Gallup, May 31, 2011, accessed June 24, 2015, http://www.gallup.com/poll/147842/doctor-assisted-suicide-moral-issue-dividing-americans.aspx.

4. Jeffrey M. Jones, "Americans Hold Record Liberal Views on Most Moral Issues," Gallup, May 11, 2017, accessed August 19, 2019, http://news.gallup.com/poll/210542/americans-hold-record-liberal-views-moral-issues.aspx; "Moral Issues," Gallup, accessed August 19, 2019, https://news.gallup.com/poll/1681/moral-issues.aspx.

5. Jones, "Americans Hold Record Liberal Views on Most Moral Issues."

6. Joy Wilke and Lydia Saad, "Older Americans' Moral Attitudes Changing: Moral Acceptance of Teenage Sex among the Biggest Generational Divides," June 3, 2013, accessed June 24, 2015, http://www.gallup.com/poll/162881/older-americans-moral-attitudes-changing.aspx.

7. Steve Karnowski and Amy Forliti, "Minnesota Archdiocese to Pay Clergy Abuse Victims the Catholic Church's Second-Largest Payout Ever," *Time*, May 31, 2018, https://www.yahoo.com/news/minnesota-archdiocese-pay-clergy-abuse-003007527.html

8. Suzanne Goldenberg, "LA Archdiocese Agrees $660M Payout for Sex Abuse Victims," July 16, 2007, accessed August 19, 2019, https://www.theguardian.com/world/2007/jul/16/religion.usa.

9. Sexuality Information and Education Council of the United States (SEICUS), "Position Statements: Definition of Sexual Health," SIECUS, accessed October 20, 2019. https://siecus.org/wp-content/uploads/2018/07/Position-Statements-2018-2.pdf; R. Kimball and M. Wissner, "Religion, Poverty, and Politics: Their Impact on Women's Reproductive Health Outcomes," *Public Health Nursing* 32, no. 6 (2015): 598–612, https://doi.org/10.1111/phn.12196.

10. Office of Public Affairs, "Attorney General Eric Holder Announces Revisions to the Uniform Crime Report's Definition of Rape," Department of Justice, January 6, 2012, accessed June 24, 2015, http://www.justice.gov/opa/pr/2012/January/12-ag-018.html.

11. US Department of Justice, "An Updated Definition of Rape," January 6, 2012, accessed August 19, 2019, https://www.justice.gov/archives/opa/blog/updated-definition-rape.

12. David Crary, "Bruising Gay-Marriage Showdowns Likely in 5 States," Associated Press, March 8, 2012, accessed October 20, 2019, https://bangordailynews.com/2012/03/08/news/nation/bruising-gay-marriage-showdowns-likely-in-5-states/.

13. "N.J. Gov. Christie Vetoes Gay Marriage Bill," *CBS News*, February 17, 2012, accessed June 24, 2015, http://www.cbsnews.com/8301-501365_162-57380574/n.j-gov-christie-vetoes-gay-marriage-bill/.

14. Lucas Grindley, "Ellen Wins: One Million Moms Group Concedes JCPenny Fight," *Advocate*, March 8, 2012, accessed June 24, 2015, http://www.advocate.com/News/Daily_News/2012/03/08/Ellen_Wins_One_Million_Moms_Backs_Down_in_JCPenney_Fight/.

15. Jonathan Allen and Aman Ali, "Student Guilty of Hate Crimes for Spying on Gay Roommate," *Reuters*, March 16, 2012, accessed June 24, 2015, http://www.reuters.com/article/2012/03/16/us-crime-rutgers-idUSBRE82F0VP20120316.

16. Mary Spicuzza, "Prosecutor Warns Teachers about New Sex Education Curriculum," *Wisconsin State Journal*, April 6, 2010, accessed June 24, 2015, http://host.madison.com/news/local/govt_and_politics/prosecutor-warns-teachers-about-new-sex-education-curriculum/article_0e1496a2-41e1-11df-aeea-001cc4c03286.html.

17. Katie McDonough, "Alabama Sex Education Law Requires Teachers to Say That Being Gay Is Illegal," *Salon*, March 21, 2013, accessed June 24, 2015, http://www.salon.com/2013/03/21/alabama_sex_education_law_requires_teachers_to_say_that_being_gay_is_illegal/.

18. Shadee Ashtari, "Mississippi Sex-Ed Law Permits Teachers to Instruct Students That Homosexuality Is Illegal," *Huffington Post*, April 8, 2014, accessed June 24, 2015, http://www.huffingtonpost.com/2014/04/08/mississippi-sex-ed_n_5110538.html.

19. Douglas Stanglin, "Utah Lawmakers Pass Abstinence-Only Sex Education Curriculum," *USA Today*, March 7, 2012, accessed June 24, 2015, http://content.usatoday.com/communities/ondeadline/post/2012/03/utah-oks-abstinence-only-sex-education-curriculum/1#.T1kzPoH4JMR; and Lisa Schencker, "Utah House Passes Bill to Allow Schools to Skip Sex Ed," *Salt Lake Tribune*, February 23, 2012, accessed June 24, 2015, http://www.sltrib.com/sltrib/utes/53570545-90/abstinence-allow-bill-education.html.csp.

20. Chris Arnold, "Teacher Prosecution Bill Approved by Kansas Senate," *KSN*, February 25, 2015, accessed October 20, 2019, https://www.ksn.com/news/teacher-prosecution-bill-approved-by-kansas-senate/.

21. Kathrin F. Stanger-Hall and David W. Hall, "Abstinence-Only Education and Teen Pregnancy Rates: Why We Need Comprehensive Sex Education in the U.S.," *PLOS ONE* 6, no. 10 (2011): e24658.

22. "Teen Pregnancy Rates Declined in Many Countries between the Mid-1990s and 2011: United States Lags Behind Many Other Developed Nations," Guttmacher Institute, January 23, 2015, accessed August 19, 2019, https://www.guttmacher.org/news-release/2015/teen

-pregnancy-rates-declined-many-countries-between-mid-1990s-and-2011. Note: The statistics are reported from developed nations for which complete statistics are collectable.

23. "Survey Reveals Surprising Sex Attitudes," *ABC News*, October 20, 2004, accessed June 24, 2015, http://abcnews.go.com/Primetime/News/story?id=174461&page=1#.T1k6QYH 4JMQ.

24. Avril Melissa Houston, Junyong Fang, Constance Husman, and Ligia Peralta, "More than Just Vaginal Intercourse: Anal Intercourse and Condom Use Patterns in the Context of 'Main' and 'Casual' Sexual Relationships among Urban Minority Adolescent Females," *Journal of Pediatric Adolescent Gynecology* 20 (2007): 299–304; "Sex Education and Other Programs That Work to Prevent Teen Pregnancy, HIV and Sexually Transmitted Infections," accessed October 20, 2019, https://www.advocatesforyouth.org/wp-content/uploads/storage// advfy/documents/sciencesuccess.pdf.

25. Ashley Milne-Tyte, "More Older People Contracting HIV/AIDS," Voice of America, November 30, 2010, accessed June 24, 2015, https://www.voanews.com/science-health/ more-older-people-contracting-hivaids; "HIV among People Aged 50 and Older," Centers for Disease Control and Prevention, updated September 18, 2018, accessed August 19, 2019, https://www.cdc.gov/hiv/group/age/olderamericans/index.html.

26. R. Walters, *Primers for Prudery: Sexual Advice to Victorian America* (Baltimore, MD: Johns Hopkins University Press, 2000); Kaye Wellings et al., "Sexual Behavior in Context: A Global Perspective," *The Lancet* 368, no. 9548 (2006): 1706–28, accessed June 29, 2015, http:// www.thelancet.com/journals/lancet/article/PIIS0140-6736percent2806percent2969479-8/ fulltext; "European Sex Attitudes versus American Sex Attitudes," *TeenNow California*, November 16, 2010, accessed June 29, 2015, http://tnca.wordpress.com/2010/11/16/euro pean-sex-attitudes-versus-american-sex-attitudes/; and Lisa Belkin, "A Different Kind of Sex Talk with Teens," *New York Times*, November 5, 2010, accessed June 29, 2015, http://parent ing.blogs.nytimes.com/2010/11/05/a-different-kind-of-sex-talk-with-teens/.

27. World Health Organization, "Education and Treatment in Human Sexuality: The Training of Health Professionals," *WHO Technical Report Series*, no. 572 (1975): 5–33.

28. Debra W. Haffner, "Facing Facts: Sexual Health for America's Adolescents: The Report of the National Commission on Adolescent Sexual Health," *SIECUS Report* 23, no. 6 (1995): 2–8.

29. Debra W. Haffner, "Facing Facts: Sexual Health for America's Adolescents," *Journal of Adolescent Health* 22, no. 6 (1998): 453–59.

30. Deborah L. Tolman, Meg I. Striepe, and Tricia Harmon, "Gender Matters: Constructing a Model of Adolescent Sexual Health," *The Journal of Sex Research* 40, no. 1 (2003): 4–12.

31. "The Surgeon General's Call to Action to Promote Sexual Health and Responsible Sexual Behavior," US Department of Health and Human Services, Office of the Surgeon General, July 2001, accessed June 29, 2015, http://www.ncbi.nlm.nih.gov/books/NBK44216/.

32. Beatrice "Bean" E. Robinson, "Sexual Health Model," in *The International Encyclopedia of Human Sexuality*, ed. Patricia Whelehan and Anne Bolin (Wiley, 2015); Beatrice "Bean" Robinson, Walter O. Bockting, B. R. Simon Rosser, Michael Miner, and Eli Coleman, "The Sexual Health Model: Application of a Sexological Approach to HIV Prevention," *Health Education Research* 17, no. 1 (2002): 43–57, https://academic.oup.com/her/article/17/1/43/764423.

33. Wendy Maltz, "What Is Healthy Sex?," HealthySex.com, accessed June 29, 2015, https://healthysex.com/healthy-sexuality/part-one-understanding/what-is-healthy-sex/.

34. "Issues: Sexual & Reproductive Health," SIECUS, accessed August 19, 2019, https:// siecus.org/issues/; "SIECUS Position Statements,"

"Adolescent Sexual Health. SIECUS believes that becoming a sexually healthy adult is a key developmental task of adolescence. Professionals, including educators, healthcare providers, and social service providers, should promote adolescent sexual health by providing accurate information and education about sexuality, and by assuring access to sexual and reproductive health care. Society can enhance adolescent sexual health by providing access to comprehensive sexuality education and affordable, sensitive, and confidential reproductive healthcare services.

Access to Reproductive Health Services. SIECUS believes that all people, regardless of age or income, should have access to affordable, confidential sexual health services including, but not limited to, access to methods of contraception and disease prevention, testing for HIV and other sexually transmitted diseases, and prenatal care.

Abortion. SIECUS believes that every woman, regardless of age or income, should have the right to obtain an abortion under safe, legal, affordable, easily accessible, confidential, and dignified conditions. Every woman is entitled to have full knowledge of the options available to her, and to obtain complete and unbiased information and counseling. SIECUS believes that abortion counseling and services should be provided by professionals specially trained in this field. SIECUS believes that it is unethical for any organization to *use anti-abortion propaganda, misinformation, manipulation, or fear and shame tactics to dissuade women facing unintended pregnancy from exercising their right to choose.* SIECUS further believes that violence against abortion providers and harassment intended to impede women's access to these providers are unconscionable attempts to undermine women's reproductive rights and should be decisively prosecuted by the justice system.

HIV/AIDS. SIECUS believes that the global HIV/AIDS pandemic needs to remain a top priority for governments, non-governmental organizations, philanthropic entities, corporations, academic institutions, medical professionals, scientists, the media, and societies around the world. Individuals need access to accurate information about HIV/AIDS, as well as evidence-based prevention programs and methods. HIV testing, treatment, and care must be widely accessible and affordable, and only provided with informed consent. All HIV/AIDS testing, treatment, and care and any related reporting requirements should be done in a manner that ensures the privacy and confidentiality of the individual. Governments and private entities must work together to ensure progress in reducing the spread of HIV and improving care and treatment options for those individuals already impacted by the pandemic.

Healthcare Practitioners Training. SIECUS believes that all healthcare practitioners should be well trained in the areas of sexuality and sexual and reproductive health. Professional training for all healthcare practitioners, including continuing education programs, should address medical, ethical, legal, and cultural aspects of sexuality. Healthcare practitioners are expected to provide care that is unbiased and meets the medical and psychological needs of each patient."

35. "What Is Healthy Sexuality and Consent?," National Sexual Violence Resource Center, 2015, accessed August 19, 2019, https://www.nsvrc.org/sites/default/files/saam_2015_what-is-healthy-sexuality-and-consent.pdf; also used by "Healthy Sexuality: A Guide for Advocates, Counselors, and Prevention Educators," National Sexual Violence Resource Center, 2012, accessed October 20, 2019, https://www.nsvrc.org/sites/default/files/2012-03/SAAM_2012_Healthy-sexuality-a-guide-for-advocates-counselors-and-prevention-educators.pdf.

36. Rev. Debra W. Haffner, "Toward a Sexually Healthy and Responsible Unitarian Universalist Association," *Religious Institute*, August 2010, accessed June 29, 2015, http://www.uua.org/documents/haffnerdebra/sex_health_responsible.pdf.

37. Rob Jackson, "Healthy Childhood Sexual Development," Focus on the Family, January 1, 2004, accessed June 24, 2015, https://www.focusonthefamily.com/parenting/healthy-childhood-sexual-development/.

38. "The Vision: Rights. Respect. Responsibility," Advocates for Youth, 2019, accessed October 20, 2019, https://3rs.org/3rs-curriculum/.

39. "Gender and Human Rights: Sexual Health," World Health Organization, accessed June 29, 2015, http://www.who.int/reproductivehealth/topics/gender_rights/sexual_health/en/.

40. Ibid.

41. Maltz, Healthysex.com.

42. This is a compilation of concepts from the models presented here.

43. Wendy Maltz, "The Maltz Hierarchy of Sexual Interaction," *Sexual Addiction & Compulsivity: The Journal of Treatment & Prevention* 2, no. 1 (1995): 5–18.

44. Robinson, "Sexual Health Model," 1115–354.

45. Peter L. Berger and Thomas Luckmann, *The Social Construction of Reality: A Treatise in the Sociology of Knowledge* (New York: Anchor Books, 1967).

46. Michel Foucault, *The History of Sexuality*, vol. 1, *An Introduction* (New York: Pantheon Books, 1978).

47. See, for example, Leslie Kantor and Vincent Guilamo-Ramos, "New 'Let's Talk Month' Poll Reminds Us That Sex Ed Begins with Parents," *RH Reality Check*, October 10, 2011, accessed October 20, 2019, https://rewire.news/article/2011/10/10/new-lets-talk-month-poll-reminds-us-that-sex-ed-begins-with-parents/.

48. Jackson, "Healthy Childhood Sexual Development."

49. See, for example, "The Right to Counseling for Unwanted Same-Sex Attractions: The Right to Seek Change and Live in Alignment with Chosen Values: Our Position," Focus on the Family, 2008, accessed June 24, 2015, http://www.focusonthefamily.com/socialissues/social-issues/the-right-to-counseling-for-unwanted-same-sex-attractions/the-right-to-counseling-for-unwanted-same-sex-attractions-our-position.

50. "Our Whole Lives: Lifespan Sexuality Education," Unitarian Universalist Association, accessed June 24, 2015, http://www.uua.org/re/owl.

51. Ibid.

52. "Guidelines for Comprehensive Sexuality Education, 3rd ed.," SIECUS, accessed August 20, 2019, https://siecus.org/wp-content/uploads/2018/07/Guidelines-CSE.pdf.

53. "Sex Education in America: A View from Inside the Nation's Classrooms," Kaiser Family Foundation, September 1, 2000, http://www.kff.org/youthhivstds/3048-index.cfm.

54. "Our History," SIECUS, accessed October 20, 2019, https://siecus.org/about-siecus/our-history/.

55. "Guidelines for Comprehensive Sexuality Education," accessed October 20, 2019, https://siecus.org/wp-content/uploads/2018/07/Guidelines-CSE.pdf.

56. M. Grossman, "You're Teaching My Child What?: The Truth about Sex Education," The Heritage Foundation, August 9, 2010, https://www.heritage.org/education/report/youre-teaching-my-child-what-the-truth-about-sex-education.

57. Mark Johanson, "Dominica: Gay Men Arrested for 'Buggery' on Caribbean Cruise Plead Guilty to Indecent Exposure," *International Business Times*, March 22, 2012, accessed June 29, 2015, http://www.ibtimes.com/articles/318149/20120322/dominica-gay-men-buggery-caribbean-cruise.htm#0_undefined,0_; Carlisle Jno Baptiste, "2 U.S. Men Arrested on Gay Cruise in Caribbean," March 22, 2012, accessed October 20, 2019, http://www.nbcnews.com/id/46821004/ns/travel-news/t/us-men-arrested-gay-cruise-caribbean/; Jonathan Lloyd, "Dominica Anti-Sodomy Law Lands Gay Cruise Ship Passengers in Custody: A Man on a Dock Told Authorities He Saw the Two California Men Having Sex Aboard a Passing Cruise Ship," *NBC Los Angeles*, March 22, 2012, accessed June 29, 2015, http://www.nbclosangeles.com/news/local/Gay-Cruise-Ship-Dominica-Buggery-Sodomy-Charges-143819716.html.

58. See, for example, N. A. Fouad and M. T. Brown. (2000). "Role of Race and Social Class in Development: Implications for Counseling Psychology," in *Handbook of Counseling Psychology*, edited by S. D. Brown and R. W. Lent, 379–408 (Hoboken, NJ: John Wiley & Sons Inc.); Roger L. Worthington, Holly Bielstein Savoy, and Elizabeth R. Vernaglia, "Heterosexual Identity Development: A Multidimensional Model of Individual and Social Identity," *The Counseling Psychologist* 30, no. 4 (2002): 496–531, doi:10.1177/00100002030004002; S. R. McCarn and R. E. Fassinger, "Revisioning Sexual Minority Identity Formation: A New Model of Lesbian Identity and Its Implications," *The Counseling Psychologist* 24, no. 3 (1996): 508–34, http://dx.doi.org/10.1177/0011000096243011.

59. Roger L. Worthington, Holly Bielstein Savoy, Frank R. Dillon, and Elizabeth R. Vernaglia, "Heterosexual Identity Development: A Multidimensional Model of Individual and Social Identity," *The Counseling Psychologist* 30, no. 4 (2002): 496–531.

60. Lars Ullerstam, *The Erotic Minorities: A Swedish View* (London: Calder & Boyars, 1967).

61. Cynthia J. Telingator and Kelly T. Woyewodzic, "Sexual Minority Identity Development: A Review of Process and Effects," *Psychiatric Times*, December 16, 2011, accessed June 24, 2015, http://www.psychiatrictimes.com/child-adolescent-psychiatry/sexual-minority-identity-development?pageNumber=2.

62. Ibid.

63. Telingator and Woyewodzic, "Sexual Minority Identity Development"; Ronald F. C. Kourany, "Suicide among Homosexual Adolescents," *Journal of Homosexuality* 13, no. 4 (1987): 111–17; Rob Cover, *Queer Youth Suicide, Culture and Identity: Unliveable Lives?* (London: Routledge, 2010).

64. One excellent history of gender bias and/or discrimination is provided by Tito Boeri, E. Patacchini, and G. Peri, eds., *Unexplored Dimensions of Discrimination* (Oxford University Press, 2015). See also a new index for measuring discrimination by Selin Dilli, Sarah G. Carmichael, and Auke Rijpma, "Introducing the Historical Gender Equality Index," *Feminist Economics* 25, no. 1(2019): 31–57, doi:10.1080/13545701.2018.1442582.

65. Tiffany Sharples, "Young Love," *Time*, January 17, 2008, accessed June 24, 2015, http://content.time.com/time/magazine/article/0,9171,1704687,00.html.

66. L. LaDue, personal communication with the author, March 6, 2012.

67. Amber Phillips, "A Donald Trump Adviser Just Called Clinton the C-Word in a Tweet," *Washington Post*, November 1, 2016, https://www.washingtonpost.com/news/the-fix/wp/2016/11/01/a-texas-state-official-just-called-clinton-the-c-word-in-a-tweet/?utm_term=.e9e2db14d446.

68. See, for example, the documentary media series by Jean Kilbourne, *Killing Us Softly*, https://shop.mediaed.org/killing-us-softly-4-p47.aspx.

69. See, for example, Pamela Paul, *Pornified: How Pornography Is Damaging Our Lives, Our Relationships, and Our Families* (New York: Times Books, 2005); Gayle Dines, *Pornland: How Porn Has Hijacked Our Sexuality* (Boston: Beacon Press, 2011); and Wendy Maltz and Larry Maltz, *The Porn Trap: The Essential Guide to Overcoming Problems Caused by Pornography* (New York: HarperCollins, 2010).

70. Catharine MacKinnon, "Feminism, Marxism, Method, and the State: An Agenda for Theory," *Signs: Journal of Women in Culture and Society* 7, no. 3 (1982): 541.

71. Thomas Macaulay Millar, "Toward a Performance Model of Sex," in *Yes Means Yes!: Visions of Female Sexual Power and a World without Rape*, ed. Jaclyn Friedman and Jessica Valenti (Berkeley, CA: Seal Press, 2008), 29–42.

72. Ibid., 36.

73. Alex Raymond, "Women Aren't Vending Machines: How Video Games Perpetuate the Commodity Model of Sex," Gamecritics.com, August 26, 2009, accessed October 20, 2019, http://www.gamecritics.com/alex-raymond/women-arent-vending-machines-how-video-games-perpetuate-the-commodity-model-of-sex.

74. Millar, "Toward a Performance Model of Sex," xx.

75. Robinson, "Sexual Health Model"; Robinson et al., "The Sexual Health Model."

76. Ibid.

77. Susan Adler with Louise Welsh Schrank, "Raising Sexually Healthy Children: Sexual Development, Sexual Abuse Prevention & Self Esteem for Children Under Seven," Learning Seed Video, 1998.

78. "Legal Role of Consent," RAINN, accessed August 20, 2019, https://www.rainn.org/articles/legal-role-consent.

79. "In Good Company: Who Supports Comprehensive Sexuality Education?," SIECUS Public Policy Office, updated October 2007, accessed August 20, 2019, https://www.get realeducation.org/sites/default/files/In_Good_Company.pdf.

80. "National Study on Sex Education Reveals Gaps between What Parents Want and Teachers Teach: Parents Think Schools Should Cover More: From Abstinence to Homosexuality," Henry J. Kaiser Family Foundation, September 26, 2000, accessed June 29, 2015, https://www.kff.org/wp-content/uploads/2000/09/3048-nr-sex-education-in-america-a-view -from-inside-the-nations-classrooms.pdf; "What Do Parents Think about Sex Ed?," University of Minnesota, The Division of Adolescent Health and Medicine, Department of Pediatrics, http://www.moappp.org/Documents/Parents_sexedF1.pdf.

81. Debra W. Haffner and Eva S. Goldfarb, "But Does It Work?: Improving Evaluations of Sexuality Education," August–September 1997, accessed August 21, 2019, https://siecus.org/ wp-content/uploads/2015/07/ButDoesItWork.pdf, 2.

82. Ibid., 5.

83. See, for example, Harold S. Koplewicz, "LGBT Teens, Bullying, and Suicide: What Are the Causes and How Can We Help?," Child Mind Institute, accessed August 21, 2019, https://childmind.org/article/lgbt-teens-bullying-and-suicide/; Jens Erik Gould, "The Lawrence King Case: In Court, Has the Bullied Become the Bully?" *Time*, August 25, 2011, http:// content.time.com/time/nation/article/0,8599,2090287,00.html; R. Perrone and L. Kalsnes, "Anoka-Hennepin School District Sued for Discriminating against LGBTQ Student," February 25, 2019, https://www.aclu-mn.org/en/press-releases/anoka-hennepin-school-district -sued-discriminating-against-lgbtq-student.

84. "Healthy Relationships," California State University, Fullerton, Women's Center and Human Services Department, accessed June 24, 2015, http://www.fullerton.edu/university blues/healthy_relationships/building_healthy_relationships.htm.

2

Defining Deviance, Dysfunctions, and Disorders

◆ ◆ ◆

Every society develops standards, rules, and norms for the sexual behavior of its members. These norms may differ a great deal from one society and one historical period to another, but in any case they result in dividing people into two groups: those who conform to the norms, i.e., the "normal" persons, and those who deviate from the norms, i.e., the "abnormal" persons or "deviants."

—E. J. Jaeberle, *The Sex Atlas*[1]

Politically, the major types of feminism have confronted the gendered social order in three different ways: *reform, resistance,* and *rebellion.*

—Judith Lorber, *Gender Inequality: Feminist Theories and Politics*[2]

Finally, you'll come to understand why our best hope of solving some of the most troubling problems of our age hinges entirely on the *amoral* study of sex.

—Jesse Bering, *Perv: The Sexual Deviant in All of Us*[3]

IF AMERICANS AS A COLLECTIVE are conflicted or confused about what constitutes "healthy" sexuality, as discussed in chapter 1, the conflict and potential confusion elevate exponentially when attempting to define and outline deviant sexual behavior, which is the next topic for deliberate reflection and exploration to be examined here. A quick review of the internet offers demonstrations both visually and verbally of just about any kind of sex act imaginable. The forms and shapes sex takes on the internet reveal something about the levels and degrees of difference in the general public's appetite for sex-related images and stories. Perhaps they don't mind the full-on exposure themselves, but they don't want their children exposed to such things, at least until a certain age. For whatever reasons, people will choose to either explore these unfamiliar themes or not; they will then either choose to go further in their explorations or not.

A search for answers to why people do what they do drives society on many levels. When it comes to talking about sex, religious authorities have outlined appropriate boundaries, and such boundaries are seldom questioned. Yet, if 10 images or stories were isolated from a given internet source for consideration, would people who reviewed those images agree about whether the stories or images were associated with a "healthy" or "unhealthy" sexual expression? Consider the continuums presented here. At one end are the kinds of sex acts society sees as healthy (Figure 2.1), and at the other end are behaviors everyone agrees no one would see as healthy (Figure 2.2).

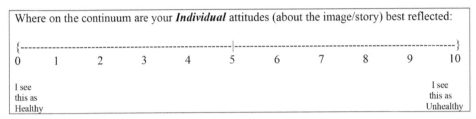

Figure 2.1 Individual Attitudes: Healthy to Unhealthy

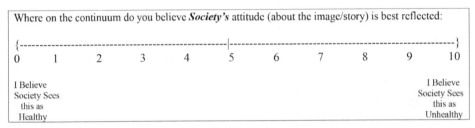

Figure 2.2 Individual Assesments of Social Attitudes about Healthy to Unhealthy

By taking the example of a sexual act or practice found on the internet, it is possible then to find a point on the continuum that represents either the evaluator's ideas or their perception of society's attitude in general on the subject. If one end of this continuum is "healthy" and the other end is "unhealthy," does the area in the middle represent some kind of deviance? If one continuum represents a person's individual attitude or opinion and another represents how someone thinks the larger society would respond, do the differences between what an individual believes and what they think society believes give insight into an individual's perceptions of their own level of "deviance" if they differ from the attitudes they attribute to the society around them? Would additional assessment of attitudes about sexual deviance create a convergence around what should be sanctioned and punished, or would these 10 sample issues demonstrate expanding differences within the range identified on the continuum? And what about whether the acts/images/stories should be legal or illegal?

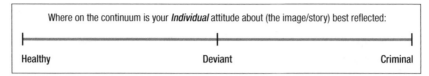

Figure 2.3 Individual Attitudes about Sex Topics from Healthy to Deviant

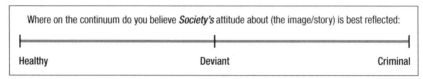

Figure 2.4 Individual Assesments on Social Attitudes on Sex Topics from Healthy to Deviant

Consider the continuums in Figures 2.3 and 2.4, which have been modified to include assessments about deviant and criminal acts. Maybe a person thinks watching **pornography** (porn for short) is immoral. Pornography refers to the use of images and films about sex as a form of sexual stimulation (see chapter 6). Because an individual thinks porn is immoral, they don't watch it, but they also don't think it is necessarily unhealthy, just a little higher on the scale toward deviant. Or perhaps they assess it as being unhealthy and believe that it should be banned or criminalized. Is it possible one person could place pornography on the more "deviant" end of the continuum, suggesting that it is criminal, and someone else might not consider it to be criminal and even place it toward the healthy end of the continuum?

Because one person finds a particular act, in this case, the use or creation of pornography, in the middle or more toward the healthy side of the continuum, what does that mean for assessing the larger social attitude? How many areas of the kinds of sexual behaviors one sees on the internet would people agree about? How many areas would reflect a dramatic difference between groups or even over time? What if every sex act known to humans was placed on the continuum? Do individual attitudes or larger social attitudes drive the next steps for addressing the issue of sexual appropriateness as a society? How do attitudes compare with research data? At this point, as unclear as people are about coming up with a definition of "healthy sexuality," it seems like it might be easier to agree about what is healthy than it would be about what is assessed as unhealthy or deviant and should be regulated. So what should we do?

The imprecise and controversial classifications of sexual deviance provide the central theme for consideration in this chapter. Much like the lack of clear separation between healthy sex and deviant sex, discrepancies in ideologies are also evident in the disagreement between classifications of deviant sex acts and sex crimes. These social ambiguities and the hidden aspects of their practice affect the ability to identify and respond to assertions of sexual harm. Beginning with an introductory discussion of deviance in general, the chapter summarizes how scholars and researchers have developed descriptions, models, and definitions of deviance. The contributions from traditional works and feminist ideology are highlighted, paying particular attention to the critique of objectivity and, more explicitly, offering a brief overview of the feminist concerns about gender bias in defining and outlining social control efforts regarding sex. After exploring the general conceptualization of deviance, consideration shifts to the conceptualizations of sexually deviant behavior. Various parameters of sexual deviance are reviewed to explore the parameters of the definition further.

DEFINING DEVIANCE

"Deviance" as a concept is contrasted with other similar terms, more commonly used in the vernacular of the street, as in "a delinquent"; in a therapeutic environment, as someone who is "behaving in an atypical way"; in the classroom, as someone described as "disruptive"; or in a conversational social setting where the actions are transferred to the actor who is identified or comes to be known as "a deviant." The hidden or secret aspects of sexual deviance, linking what in 1963 **Howard Becker** notably discussed as secret deviants and persons who are falsely accused of deviance, discussed in more detail below, are explored as an introduction to several examples of questionable or controversial social responses to behaviors that the larger society labels as deviant.

Efforts to definitively define deviance are ongoing. Several primary social science studies on the subject of deviance are overviewed here. Works of sociologists Emile Durkheim, Howard Becker, and Kai Erickson begin the dialogue by outlining several basic themes in the emergence of the study of deviance. Three different constructions of deviance research from Adler and Adler[4]; DeKeseredy, Ellis, and Alvi[5]; and Heckert and Heckert[6] follow. Their works reflect the use of different organizational categories within the larger study of deviance and an expansion beyond a **dichotomous**, or dualistic—two-sided model of deviant classifications in which behavior is seen as either deviant or normal. A third primary area of importance within the discourse on deviance is the shift in ideology and perspective coming from within the feminist critique of traditional crime and deviance theory. After a brief introduction to the general understanding of deviance, a more comprehensive review of various aspects of the study of sexual deviance is presented for consideration.

THE DEVIANCE DISCOURSE[7]

One of the earliest academic pieces about deviance came from Emile Durkheim (1895) in *Rules of the Sociological Method*, in which he asserted crime is normal.[8] His observations that all societies report some measure of crime led him to conclude that crime must serve a social function. In fact, the idea that crime serves a social function has been identified by some sociologists as the foundation for a group of criminological theories known as **functionalism**. Kai Erikson suggested that deviance can be defined as "conduct which is generally thought to require the attention of social control agencies—that is, conduct about which 'something should be done.'"⁹ Albert Cohen's *Deviance and Control* defined deviance as "behavior that violates normative rules."¹⁰ **Normative rules** are social rules based on **norms**. Norms are behavioral codes or prescriptions that guide people into conformance and social acceptability.¹¹ Much of the discourse in the emerging field of deviance studies in the 1960s asked fundamental questions about who actually sets the standards for determining, deciding, and enforcing society's normative rules. These fundamental questions, particularly around sexuality, persist.

In *The Wayward Puritan: A Study in the Sociology of Deviance*, Kai Erikson used Durkheim's assessments of the functionality of crime and wrote about how behaviors were used to test or reinforce the limits of a group's ideals and values. Among his observations, he noted that the boundaries of acceptability are always shifting, the sanctions for deviance are often not easily relayed through language, and the deviant forms of conduct often seem to be sustained by the very control agencies charged with their elimination.¹² In other words, to preserve social order, it is important to know when the boundaries of acceptable behavior get crossed. Having people cross those boundaries of unacceptability and then having other people reacting to those people who cross those boundaries provides the necessary pushback from other members of society who seek to secure compliance from those committing questionable or deviant behaviors and offers the exchange as a tool or a resource for the rest of society for determining the limits of socially acceptable and unacceptable behaviors.¹³

Another famous work on defining deviance came in 1963 in *Outsiders: Studies in the Sociology of Deviance* by Howard Becker.¹⁴ Becker reacted against what he argued were the two prevailing models of deviance at the time, the **statistical model** and the **medical model**. The *statistical model of deviance* used simple mathematics. Assessments of "normal" were achieved by simple tabulations of the largest numbers. Most people do not get As on a test; they get Cs. Scores on an exam are an easy way to see how, statistically speaking, most people's behaviors (grade performance) fall within the standard distributions of "normal" found on a bell-shaped curve, as illustrated in Figure 2.5.

The *medical model*, also known as the disease model, considered deviant behavior as an indication of illness or a disease. If someone was deviant, their

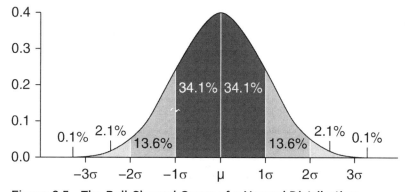

Figure 2.5   The Bell-Shaped Curve of a Normal Distribution

actions indicated the need for treatment from a member of the medical establishment to receive the help they needed to heal—to return to normal. To rid the person of their difficulty was seen as needing to rid them of the disease afflicting them. To cure them of the disease was to offer healing to restore the person to health. The medical model made a lot of sense until people raised questions about what actually falls within the range deemed healthy. This issue was central for Becker, who wrote:

> The simplest view of deviance is essentially statistical, defining as deviant anything that varies too widely from the average. . . . Similarly, one can describe anything that differs from what is common as a deviation.[15]
>
> A less simple but much more common view of deviance identifies it as something essentially pathological, revealing the presence of a "disease." This view rests, obviously, on a medical analogy. The human organism, when it is working efficiently and experiencing no discomfort, is said to be "healthy." When it does not work efficiently, a disease is present.[16] . . . The medical metaphor limits what we can see much as the statistical view does. It accepts the lay judgment of something as deviant and, by use of analogy, locates its source within the individual, *thus preventing us from seeing the judgment itself as a crucial part of the phenomenon.*[17]

The medical establishment's ability to determine the definition of normal was being challenged from various social sectors, and Becker described the limitations he saw within these prevailing models used to describe deviance. Who decided the limits of acceptable, particularly when people disagreed about the characterization of a specific act or behavior? Becker proposed what at the time must have seemed like a fairly radical idea, that the designation of an act as deviant was not solely locked in the act of deviance itself but, instead, the attachment of the *label* of deviant emerged from within the social response that followed the act. Specifically, in introducing what came to be called the **labeling theory**, Becker suggested a deviant label is not applied unless the group observing the behavior produces a reaction to the phenomenon being observed. Becker said that

> *social groups create deviance by making the rules whose infraction constitutes deviance* [italics in original], and by applying the rules to particular people and labeling them outsiders.[18]
>
> Insofar as a scientist uses "deviant" to refer to any rule-breaking behavior, and takes as their subject of study only those who have been labeled deviant, (they) will be hampered by the disparities between the two categories.[19]
>
> If we take as the object of our attention behavior which comes to be labeled as deviant, we must recognize that we cannot know whether a given act will be categorized as deviant until the response of others has occurred. Deviance is not a quality that lies in a behavior itself, but in the interactions between the person who commits an act and those who respond to it.[20]

With this work, Becker forever added to the landscape of deviance studies by introducing what has been discussed as the **social reaction, or labeling, the-**

ory and **symbolic interaction process**. People are thought to relate to each other through meanings attached to symbols, such as nice cars, where they live, what school they go to, or what they do for a living. All of this information known about or associated with a person becomes symbols of how that person wants to be or will be perceived by others. Humans make meaning in the world through this dynamic process of actions and reactions (social interaction). People also make assessments about the "other" or label others based on what they see. Imagine what Becker might have said had he been working when social media were part of the social conversation. Certainly, the idea of **relativism**—the philosophical idea that knowledge, truth, and morality are not absolute—as it is applied in the field of sociology has tentacles extending back to the time of Plato and before and reaching out to academic fields of future study.[21]

Becker's work, among so many others' work to follow,[22] was also considered to be a verification of the idea that there is no fixed social reality. Deviance is not an idea that is either present or absent and the same across time. Deviance was argued to be dependent on social context, an idea that has been referred to as **social relativism**. The fact that people have studied life in similar ways—from the same historical, social, cultural, or religious perspective—but perceived the meaning of things quite differently hints at the idea of social relativism. Understandings of the idea of God is one example. Many people are born into religious families who share religious traditions. Some will continue to live within those religious traditions and structures, whereas others will go in search of meaning in the form of other religious or spiritual traditions. Although people accept to varying degrees the idea that an individual religion is the right or only religion, the question about whether there is one Truth or varied ways of knowing truth is a deeply debated philosophical issue.

True to form, social scientists do not agree about social relativism, suggesting that some social values do, in fact, remain constant and unchanging. Challenges to the idea of relativism come from researchers such as Barbara Costello, who suggests that the use of "harm caused" is a fixed way to assess which acts are considered deviant.[23] Efforts to expand the conceptualization of deviance have produced typologies, or categories, for defining deviance beyond a dualistic, or deviant/nondeviant, classification, as illustrated by Heckert and Heckert, who outline definitions for four types of deviance with a focus on shifting the idea that deviance is only seen to be underconforming and negatively conceived.[24]

Building on Becker's social relativism, Richard Quinney, in *The Social Reality of Crime*, suggested crime was fostered by social conflict, with one group establishing and attempting to maintain control over another. Laws reflect the interests of the dominant class, according to Quinney, and the creation and enforcement of laws is characterized by conflict and struggle between groups with conflicting interests.[25] Those groups with the most power have the capacity to define and enforce social rules and ideas. He outlined six principles to demonstrate his idea:

1. Official definition of crime: Created by the dominant class in an apolitically organized society.

2. Formulating definitions of crime: Definitions of crime are composed of behaviors that conflict with the dominant class.
3. Applying definitions of crime: Definitions of crime are applied by the class that has the power to shape the administration and enforcement of laws.
4. How behavior patterns develop in relation to the definitions of crime: Behavior patterns are structured in relation to definitions of crime so that people engage in behaviors likely to be treated as criminal.
5. Constructing the ideology of crime: An ideology of crime is constructed and diffused by the ruling class to secure its hegemony.
6. Constructing the social reality of crime: The social reality of crime is constructed by the formulation and application of definitions of crime, the development of behavior patterns in relation to these definitions, and the construction of an ideology of crime.[26]

Certainly, many sociologists and criminologists have worked to define aspects of deviance, which warrant closer consideration; however, **William J. Chambliss** is one of the final deviance scholars presented for consideration here. Chambliss is known for a breadth of sociological research that includes gang studies, studies of corruption in the military and in government, and vagrancy laws. One of his most famous research studies is *The Saints and the Roughnecks*, for which he observed for two years two groups of adolescent boys.[27] The group known as the "Saints" comprised eight young white men from "good" upper middle-class families. The group identified as the "Roughnecks" included six boys from working-class families. Chambliss presented many interesting questions from his work, primary among them was why the Saints were identified as good, upstanding young men when they were in fact more delinquent than the Roughnecks. Further, community members, including teachers and police officers, knew about the delinquent behavior of the Saints but would explain it away by saying they were "sowing wild oats" or "just boys being boys," whereas they saw the behavior of the Roughnecks as problematic.

Chambliss identified the reasons for the difference in treatment between the groups as being visibility and demeanor. The Roughnecks were more visible and aggressive when confronted, whereas the Saints remained more hidden and, when addressed by police, were apologetic and penitent. Perhaps the most important assessment about the difference in treatment was Chambliss's assertion that the delinquencies of middle-class youth seemed less serious than the delinquencies of lower-class youth because of the difference in enforcement "by the way the law enforcement system is organized and who has the power to affect it."[28] Chambliss identified at least two important questions in his study: "How many poor, young men—black, brown, and white—incarcerated for minor offenses, would be in college today instead of prison had they been treated by the police and the community the way the Saints were treated? How many Saints would be in prison instead of going on to college had they been treated as the Roughnecks?"[29] In this study and throughout his career, Chambliss demonstrated an interest in understanding the role class and social power play in labeling certain behaviors as deviant or criminal.[30]

Consider the following social situation. A person goes to a local bar and starts getting flirty with people, sidling up to those who look like they have had too much to drink and chatting with them. While drinking is not likely to be supported in a work situation or at a job interview, most people go to a bar to relax, so finding people who have had too much to drink at a bar might not be much of a surprise. But take this scenario further. The idea that a person can commit an act, such as excessive drinking, in one social setting and raise little or no social reaction is made more interesting when they commit that same behavior in a different social setting and are viewed as inappropriate or deviant.

This scenario shifts and changes depending on the people at the bar, in other words, the *social interactions* in these exchanges. What would be said about a young male who had learned the best way to "hook up" with women was to go to a bar and identify who had had the most to drink. Maybe among a certain group of friends, this would be common practice: go to the bar, find women who are drunk, chat them up, and take them home and have sex. Is this deviant behavior or just the way things are done? In most states, if a woman has been drinking in excess, it is impossible for her to give consent.[31] Consequently, the dynamics of that encounter change to a possible criminal event. Yet, in college towns across the country, this type of behavior is not uncommon. In fact, it is so common that any type of social reaction is unlikely and the behavior is almost expected.

One student described this scenario as the "hunt," in which men are the hunters and women the hunted. In fact, a documentary film, titled *The Hunting Ground*, was released in 2015, which highlighted rape crimes on college campuses.[32] Another student, female, described the practice established within her group of friends: they would go to the bar together in a group, and, if any of the friends in the group had too much to drink, the designated driver was responsible for "cock-blocking," a term they used for steering their friends away from guys who were pushing hard for a hookup at the end of the night. Where do these kinds of scenarios fit into the discussion on healthy sexuality in chapter 1? Where might they be placed on the continuum of healthy, unhealthy, deviant, or criminal behavior? How similar or different will people's assessment of this situation as being either healthy or deviant be? How might the dynamic of this social situation change if a person looked up from their drink and saw one of their parents having a drink at the bar?

The collective bodies of work offered by Becker, Quinney, and Chambliss as an introduction to the study of deviance open various doors to important questions about the assessment of individual behavior but also about the role of social power in defining deviant behavior. Certainly, the field of deviance studies continues to find various ways to study the formal and informal responses to questionable human social behavior. Important questions are raised about the role of society in identifying and labeling behaviors as deviant. From that deviant classification, questions are raised about whether to move the social response to something more formal, to a law with related enforcement provisions. Of course, the idea that police and other enforcement agencies might use their power in unbalanced ways also proves to be another important area of study for sociologists, criminologists, and criminal justice practitioners. More about police and the justice system is presented in section III.

PRIMARY THEMES: THREE CATEGORIES IN THE STUDY OF DEFINING DEVIANCE

In the world of deviance, Adler and Adler are somewhat famous, if not extremely well known, for the fact that their book *Constructions of Deviance: Power, Context, and Interaction* is in its sixth edition. Their ongoing efforts to represent the parameters for studying and defining deviance outline three perspectives: (1) the **absolutist perspective**, (2) the **relativist perspective**, and (3) the **social power perspective**.[33] The *absolutist perspective* suggests that defining deviance is a simple task and assumes that most people agree about what constitutes deviant behavior; it identifies behavior and legal guidelines or laws as objective facts.[34]

> Deviance, then, is not viewed as something determined by social norms, customs, or rules, but something that is intrinsic to the human condition, standing apart from and existing before the creation of the socially created codes. According to absolutists, deviant attitudes, behavior or conditions by any name would be recognized and judged similarly. People have backed up this belief system by pointing to the existence of universal taboos surrounding such acts as murder, incest and lying.[35]

Imagine an example where the parents of two teenagers find out they are having sex. For purposes of illustration, this behavior is identified as a violation of the norms of the family or church and is thus identified as unacceptable behavior. Perhaps the parents say, "Having sex at your age is inappropriate, unacceptable, and irresponsible. You are grounded until further notice and forbidden from ever seeing that person again." Perhaps they send the teen home or call the other parents to outline what happened. This is an example of an absolutist perspective of defining deviance. Without question, the infraction is seen as wrong, and the parents believe anyone in their situation would do the same thing by responding to the inappropriate, or deviant, action.

The Becker tradition of social interactionism, as discussed earlier, might best reflect a *relativist perspective*. This means that definitions and classifications of deviant acts are likely to be seen differently, depending on the people and events involved. In this way, the idea of defining deviance is simple: if you have no social reaction, then there is no deviance because a social reaction implies deviance and no social reaction implies acceptance. For Becker, and other relativists, to identify a specific act as deviant is to expect groups to hold different values and, as such, they respond differently.

In the example of the young people having sex, perhaps everyone goes happily along in the world until the parents discover their teenagers are having sex. The teens have been having sex for months, but the parents never knew. No one is viewed differently because the parents are not aware of what is happening; there has been no opportunity for the reaction. The point of discovery, according to the relativist perspective, will be an important moment. Imagine some possible responses. The parents sit down with the young people and say, "If you are going to have sex, be safe." Imagine they have a long conversation, with both young people involved, and then the parents end the conversation by asking "Do you have any questions?" No negative reaction suggests no deviance label will be applied and no social control agent—within the family or in the form of law enforcement—is utilized.

The act of having sex before being married is the same in each scenario. Social reaction theorists, or those who subscribe to the relativist perspective, are much more interested in the *reaction* the parents had to the premarital sex for determining whether the act of premarital sex is deviant. According to social reaction theorists, the reaction the parents offer when they discover the young people are sexually active is the point at which a deviance classification is invoked or ignored. Whether the young people are seen as deviant in large part is determined by how the parents respond after learning about the behavior. Are there other ways that scenario might have gone?

The third category of deviance defining is the **social power perspective**.[36] Also referred to as the **critical approach**,[37] the focus is on the political nature of crime and how power is used to establish not only what is defined as socially acceptable but also how laws and social rules are enforced. Instead of focusing exclusively on individual actions and actors, the emphasis for critical criminologists is placed on the system and the inherent inequality of a social system that at its core was built on (and remains functioning because of) an inherent oppression of larger social groups. Most traditional discourse about these oppressed groups is linked to race, class, and gender. In fact, several subdivisions of criminological thought are reviewing the ways laws get used by people and powerful social groups to promote and protect their interests. The ability to establish certain acts as crime and to assess whether something is deviant or acceptable are characterizations of social power that disproportionately fall to those in privileged economic, social, and political positions.[38]

In the scenario with the two young people, the social power perspective might play out differently not only because of who the other "offending" party was but because of who their family is or how power is distributed between the people comprising the couple. Perhaps the girl was 15 and her partner was 17. Concern might be expressed about who had the power in that exchange and how the young woman might have been pressured by an older boy, or how an older woman might have unduly influenced a younger man. Perhaps the parents knew the young person or knew the young person's parents to be well-established doctors in the community. How would the power dynamics of that relationship change if the young woman were 17 and the young man were 15 or one person were from a poor family and one from a fairly affluent family?

The *social power perspective* of deviance defining shares characteristics of social relativism and the conflict perspective, emphasizing the influence that powerful groups and classes have in the definition and application of laws.

Consider if one of the two young people in that couple had been of a different race or one of the young people involved was from the "wrong side of the tracks." How would the scenario differ if the young people were of the same sex? How is the enforcement of the potential infraction likely to differ depending on whether the parents are the parents of the young woman or the young man? Would the response or possibility of classifying this as a deviant act differ if there were an unwanted pregnancy? Would the parents' reaction be different if other people, such as a church group, found out about the behavior of the young people? What if the parents were political figures and news of the relationship was made public?

Without question, differences exist in how scholars and researchers have approached the study of deviance and deviance defining. Whether centering deviance within the actor, as in the *absolutist perspective,* or linking the definition of deviance to the social reaction process that follows the act and the actors, as in the *relativist perspective,* or focusing the concern on who has the power to do the defining and either enforce the rules or look the other way and allow inappropriate, deviant, or even illegal activities to go unpunished, as in the *social power perspective,* an understanding of all of these ideas is essential to have a nuanced discussion of deviance and deviance defining. And like many other themes throughout the chapter, an interested, enterprising student who elects to explore further will find a veritable candy store of ideas.

FALSELY ACCUSED AND SECRET DEVIANT

Part of Howard Becker's classic work *Outsiders* included a classification system of deviant types (see Table 2.1): (1) falsely accused, (2) secret deviant, (3) pure deviant, and (4) conforming.[39] For the purposes of discussion around the topic of deviance, it is important to understand the typologies, particularly the **secret deviant**, or the person who commits deviant behavior but who is never caught. As a result, this person goes about their activities without ever being labeled or judged for their "deviant" behavior. People who are **falsely accused** are those who are in fact conforming to the standards of normal behavior but are identified and wrongly labeled as a "deviant." Consider a young girl whom kids are bullying in high school. They start a rumor that she had sex with several guys who are in on the prank and swear the story is true. Or consider a kid who is relentlessly teased for being gay but is not actually gay. These young people are what Becker describes as "falsely accused." They are perceived as deviant but in fact are actually conforming to the "acceptable" rules of social behavior. What must it be like to see yourself as "pure deviant" or "secret deviant" as defined by society, your faith communities, your family, and your friends?

Table 2.1 Howard Becker's Sequential Model of Deviant Behavior

	Obedient Behavior	Rule-Breaking Behavior
Perceived as Deviant	Falsely Accused	Pure Deviant
Not Perceived as Deviant	Conforming	Secret Deviant

Throughout his career, Becker is said to have expressed the most interest in the categories of the secret deviant and the falsely accused. The secret deviants might be those young kids who are having sex in private but are telling people they believe in the values of waiting until marriage. No one has assessed the situation, so no judgments are reflected back identifying these young people as deviant. Yet they know they are in conflict with their own stated beliefs and the beliefs of the people around them (parents and friends). How much are these attitudes and ideas different today as opposed to the 1990s, or 1960s, or before?

The Feminist Critique: Objectivity and the Communal Process of Defining Deviance

The contributions of feminist perspectives to sociology and criminology are immense. Some might argue both disciplines will never be the same because people, mostly women under the banner of feminism, asked other people, mostly men under the banner of scientific inquiry, to expand the way in which they asked their questions. Particularly, this meant focusing on the differences between men and women, rather than assuming the experiences of men and women were similar enough to combine or that men spoke in a unified voice with and for women. In addition to asking for and expecting the opportunity to frame questions of the day using their own voice, the idea of the feminist perspective being addressed as a critique is connected to the idea that feminists were also challenging the methods used in traditional scientific methods, most specifically in the study of the social sciences. Relying on a long history of scientific inquiry linked to the notion of **objectivity**, or the idea that "truth" rests outside of perceptions about the world as an idea of object that can be measured and studied. Scientific objectivity suggests that any bias about the subject a researcher brings to the experiment or research project can be set aside and will not be a factor in the execution of the analysis.

To ensure subject testability and reliability over time (the **validity** of the research), the subjectivity of the researcher must be separated from the objectivity of the process. The feminist critique suggests objectivity is not possible.[40] For social science researchers, the challenge of social relativism, reflected in the conversations about defining deviance discussed above and the feminist critique, suggests the social science observers too often come with a particular agenda. To outline and measure the idea of healthy sex and deviant sex is not an objective assessment, as traditional research methods might have people believe. The idea that assessing certain aspects of sex as healthy and other aspects of sex as deviance in a feminist perspective suggests there might be questions about who is defining the terms and setting the agenda for making these distinctions.

A Gendered Analysis?

Individuals learn about the world based on their experiences in the world. It is not surprising victims of abuse are more likely to expect to be abused.[41] In their social reality, this has been their experience, so this is what they come to expect. Men behave one way. Women behave another way. Young girls behave one way and young boys another. Several groups of parents have made headlines over the past several years because they deliberately and intentionally did not tell people the gender of their child when they were born, instead intending their child to be free from gendered stereotypes as long as possible. In one case, the parents referred to the child as "the infant," tossed out pink and blue for yellow, and allowed boy clothes or girl clothes, girl toys or boy toys, it mattered not.[42] Another set of parents with a similar ideal have been cautioned through media stories covering their decision, which has raised significant public interest. Some child development experts express strong concern suggesting the path these parents have chosen for their child could be "potentially disastrous" and yet others disagree saying many people who do not fit extremely hyperfeminized and hypermasculinized versions of maleness and femaleness would be relieved of a different brand of psychological harm if they were accepted for who they are as they are outside of society's gender constructions.[43]

Interesting too is the fact that people are sometimes born **intersex**, a term used for a variety of conditions in which a person is born with a reproductive or sexual anatomy that doesn't seem to fit the typical definitions of female or male. People may not realize they are intersex until puberty, or they might live their whole lives and not know. Although these classifications are controversial, research suggests that between 1 in 1,500 to 1 in 2,000 births meet this classification.[44] The controversies in this area are central to whether people who are born with both male and female characteristics as they are born are identified as deviant. The idea of being different could just be that, different. However, the shame often associated with these medical conditions seems to reflect fear of a strongly critical social response. Social outrage can be leveled against the families seeking social change by challenging how gender definitions restrict their family member's freedom to express themselves in any of many ways.

Society has long tried to tell us what to see as important or what to challenge as unacceptable. In 1984 sociologist **Edwin Schur** combined material from women's studies and deviance sociology in the study *Labeling Women Deviant: Gender, Stigma, and Social Control*, looking specifically at what he called "female deviance." Schur talked about the specific characteristics associated with women who were seen as deviant by the larger society and linked this to men's "devaluation of femaleness in general."[45] In short, women are subjected to labeling processes by men, and women's behavior is then labeled as deviant. Now, at about that same time, social scientists, mainly women, were beginning to ask questions about why women committed such low rates of deviance and crime as a group when compared to men.[46] Schur's work was used by other women to explore how "women's lower status relative to men makes them more vulnerable to the 'deviant' label, and how this threat of being labeled reinforces women's social subordination"[47] in the workplace, and how stigmatization can have dramatic influence on choices women make in their everyday lives.[48]

In 2018, just before driving his van through a crowded sidewalk in Toronto, Canada, a young man posted about an "incel rebellion" and brought more focused attention to what is being called the Incel Movement. Short for "involuntary celibate," men who identify as "incel" congregate on a few online forums and are united by the fact that women, who they say are shallow or obsessive and superficial, refuse to have sex with them.[49] After further investigation, police discovered the young man made reference to members of an online community who are often misogynistic, calling for rape or other forms of extreme violence.[50]

In 2006 a school shooting in Nickel Mines, Pennsylvania, was front-page news for weeks. Many of the headlines captured the horror as an unexpected and brutally violent act took the form of a school shooting in this quiet Amish community. In an op-ed piece for the *New York Times*, Bob Herbert focused coverage on a different element of the story.[51] Before the shooting, the killers separated the girls from the boys, telling the boys to leave. Ten girls were shot, five were killed, and several were molested. Herbert was struck by two things: (1) the fact that only girls were targeted and (2) the fact that the media coverage of this event didn't seem to notice that only girls were targeted. He asked why this fact was hidden behind the neutralized phrase "school children," and he asked readers to think about how society covers up gendered violence, with a series of fundamental questions about what this says about US society, about the ease with which this society uses women's bodies, and their sexuality in ads and for product sales while at the same time violence done to them as a specific social group is dismissed. Does violence against women get overlooked? How often is violence unnamed?

Women's groups and feminist studies have asked critical questions about the traditional role gender plays in individual and social development from within a culture that expresses strong opinions about the forms and shapes of masculinity and femininity. Questions about the undercurrents, or the "discourse" as Foucault (from the introduction) frames the conversation, invite further fundamental questions about the role gender plays in how each person sees themselves. These academic studies and social conversations are ongoing and have produced some fascinating studies in masculinity along the way.[52]

A Critique of Objectivity

In addition to asking questions about how culture is framed in traditionally male ways, inviting the US culture to think about the effect of gendered differences between men and women on people and in society, the feminist critique of traditional crime theory carried in with it a series of challenges to ways of measuring and studying crime with what feminists argued were male aspects and ideologies within mainstream crime theory. Referred to critically as "the malestream," the idea among feminist thinkers and writers was to establish the importance for separating the collective US cultural narrative in meaningful ways from the issues and ideals prioritized by males in the larger society but reflected in the attitudes and theories studied by male criminologists (and other scholars). Perhaps it is not surprising the research interests established by men were not exclusively identified as important by women scholars.

This aspect of research method and data collection is discussed more directly in section II; however, it is important here to speak briefly about the challenges brought to traditional ways of understanding society and, more specifically for the purposes here, the idea of crime and deviance. Deviance studies and challenges to traditional models of social research offered a fundamental critique about whether social science researchers could truly separate their ideas on crime from their larger world view. In the hard sciences, the goal was an objective pursuit of "truth." In the social sciences, feminists were asking whether objectivity was possible.

The voices associated with the feminist critique have splintered, and related research is in fact currently host to a diverse array of social commentaries and critiques.[53] Collectively, however, the focus on critical assessments of how power is distributed and displaced through various groups and the role of objectivity in the world and in social science inquiry are two important themes. These important themes connected directly to works in other social sciences studies, including antiracism work, queer studies, and a return to Native studies on peacekeeping as examples. All are engaged with questions of how power is used within the system by some groups and some people to diminish the experiences and expressions of other groups.

Sexual Deviance

Due in large part to the contributions of feminist writers, a significant amount of attention has been given to the ways sexual exploitation and violence merged. Interestingly, not all people who participate in a sex crime, even the most egregious kinds of sex crimes, such as rape, or incest, or manipulating the affections of a child with the intent to molest that child, are referred to openly as deviants, even sexual deviants. For years, leaders in the Catholic Church knew about priests who were abusing children, and they would relocate them, rather than arrest them and seek justice for the victim. Fathers who molest their children are often identified as abusers, but charges are seldom filed. In fact, significant disagreements exist about how to apply specific labels such as "criminal" and "deviant" to people who commit sex offenses. In fact, significant concerns have been expressed by victim advocates about the fact that

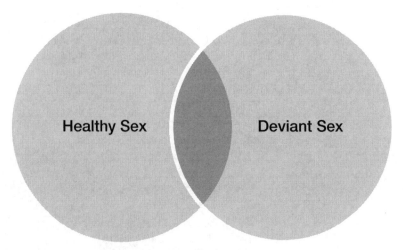

Figure 2.6   The Line Between Sexual Health and Sexual Deviance Is Not Clearly Defined

victims of sexual crimes are also ostracized to a degree and therefore seen as deviant as a result of their victimization.[54]

Efforts to get clear about the differences between healthy and deviant sexual expression requires additional consideration. For discussion purposes, Figure 2.6 is used to illustrate what it might look like if a circle could be drawn around every healthy sex act and another circle around everything collectively identified as sexually deviant. Generally speaking, deviant sex or deviant expressions of sexuality refer to sexual acts or expressions not offensive enough to warrant formal legal sanctions but that may elicit informal social concerns about their practice, such as disapproving glances or a stern conversation from a concerned individual.

Without question, defining the parameters of sexual deviance is no easier than trying to secure agreement about what actually constitutes sexual health. The ambiguity between where the ideological limits of healthy and deviant sex start and stop is reflected in the overlapping area of the Venn diagram in Figure 2.7. The shaded area suggests that there are some things people will disagree about in their assessments of healthy versus deviant sex. One person might think it is deviant to have sex before marriage, and another person might think making a life partner choice is so important that the sexual relationship has to be explored before making a marriage commitment and not doing so would be unhealthy.

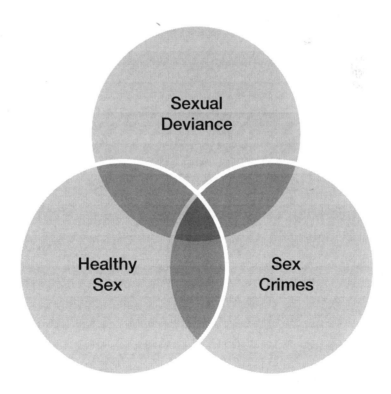

Figure 2.7   Multiple Overlaps Between Sexual Health, Deviance, and Sex Crimes

The goal here is not to assess one position as right or wrong but to offer various ways the range of divergent perspectives on the subject have been outlined or illustrated. Clearly, the areas of disagreement about the parameters between healthy and deviant sex are not so neatly and easily identified.

Defining Sexual Deviance

Think about what knowledge and information might be important for someone to intelligently consider the concept of "sexual deviance." To begin, it might be important to pay attention to aspects of popular culture and review what is presented as healthy or unhealthy. This could include looking at what people in the world normally see every day, but perhaps stepping back, using a critical eye, and really looking—both at what you are used to seeing and what you don't typically look at, if that seems possible. When considering social phenomena, which classification of deviance seems to fit best? When an act or activity is identified as deviant, more specifically *sexually* deviant, is it possible to say whether the act is attributed to an individual (the absolutist perspective), or society's response (the relativistic perspective), or to a power differential (the social power perspective) between the people involved? If walking down the street, an observer noted a homosexual couple holding hands, the response might be varied. For example, (1) "This is probably not a safe place for a same-sex couple to display public affection; I should warn them"; (2) "This kind of thing is wrong, wrong, wrong, and, as mayor of this town, I will make sure a law is passed to make sure no one else behaves in this way in our town"; or (3) "What a happy looking couple." As these observations about sexual deviance are made, consider not only the actions being observed but also the social responses. Consider the media, TV, commercials, movies, music, music videos, news stories, how stories are covered and written, in what geographic locations certain stories are covered, or what big events happen but are not discussed or are casually dismissed as unimportant.

What about research? As examples, consider academic research, agency reports, government reports, think tanks and social advocacy programs, historical records, hospital admissions, and definitions of related terms like sexual abuse. What do experts say about healthy/unhealthy sexual behaviors? This might include medical doctors, counselors, therapists, researchers, and leaders from faith communities. Is that everything? Consider police reports, court dockets, legal practices, status offenses (behaviors that are illegal only for minors) legislation, crime statutes, definitions of sex crimes, sex offender treatment policies and practices, psychological therapy, medical research, community correctional practices, and community reactions to sex offender releases in communities. Do all of these areas offer important information necessary for understanding the parameters of healthy and unhealthy sexuality? Does talking about law enforcement agencies imply a discussion of crime, not deviance?

Let's say Ron and Samantha are completing a class research project and have studied the many and varied ways people talk about sex in their local community. They have consulted research reports, talked to experts, and reflected on popular cultural expressions. Ron is interested in finding a way to quantify the

Table 2.2   A List of Sexual Attitudes and Behaviors

Hooking up/one-night stands/flings	Flirting	Telling sexual jokes	Pornography:
Friends with benefits	Flirting while dating another	Cross-dressing (aka transvestites)	• Hardcore porn
Masturbation	Dressing to be sexy	Cross-dressing (M/F)	• Racist porn
Premarital sex	Dress sexy while dating other	Cross-dressing (F/M)	• Ageist porn (older people)
Oral sex	Dating multiple people at the same time	Androgynous dress	• Simulated children or young people
Anal sex		BDSM	
Multiple partner sex		Spanking/hitting	• Anime porn
Orgies	Dating multiple people at the same time without telling the people you are dating	Handcuffs/tying down	• Toon porn
Swinging		Bestiality	
Watching others		Sex before the age of 18	
Stripping		Sex before the age of 16	
Performing lap dances	Open marriage	Sex before the age of 14	
Receiving lap dances	Polyamory		
Sexual activity after the ages of 70, 75, 80	Polygamy		
	Homosexuality		
Sexual activity over 80	Divorce		
	Extramarital affairs (aka adultery/cheating)		

terms to establish clear parameters around which acts, terms, or ideas reflect sexual deviance. Consider Table 2.2: A List of Sexual Attitudes and Behaviors.

Looking at Table 2.2, where would "hooking up" go? Is this acceptable or deviant sexual behavior? Samantha says it is easier to discuss the idea of hooking up on the continuum. Is hooking up just getting together, or does hooking up refer to having casual sex? Does it matter how casual, or what is meant by casual sex? Just to add some clarification, Ron decides hooking up will refer to a one-night stand or a fling. Is this healthy or unhealthy? Is there a gendered dynamic in this assessment? Is there a power dynamic present? As they think about whether to put hooking up in the healthy or unhealthy sex category, other questions get raised about whether hooking up after a party is the same as a spontaneous phone call between friends who have an established friends with benefits understanding.

Look at the list again. Where on the continuum would hooking up or friends with benefits be placed? Where would fornication or premarital sex go, more toward the healthy end or more toward the middle? Could the sexual behaviors outlined in Table 2.2 easily be placed on the continuum between sexual health and sexual harm? Somewhere in the middle are the acts considered to be sexually deviant. Is the boundary outlining sexually deviant acts clearly reflected? How would the boundary Ron and Samantha identified change if they decided to ask more people to help them resolve any of the disagreements they had in the classification process? Do you think soliciting opinions from more people will help clarify the parameters or make the task of defining parameters even more difficult?

Ron and Samantha cannot agree. Also important to note is the fact that deviant behavior is not always harmful behavior, although people do tend to see healthy, deviant, and harmful moving along from one end of that linear continuum to the other. But like assessments of deviance, assessments of harm are also complex. Some might argue assessments of harm are socially relative, like assessments of deviance, and are dependent on who is outlining the assessment of health and harm. It is possible Samantha and Ron might assess harm and deviance differently and their assessment of one term might affect the definition of the other.

When those limits of enjoyment, acceptability, or repulsion related to certain sexual acts or sexually charged behaviors are identified differently, this emphasizes our earlier categories: (1) the absolutist perspective: some people are wrong about what is healthy and unhealthy, (2) the relativity perspective: people do different things in different places, and (3) the social power perspective: the idea that assessing certain behaviors as acceptable or unacceptable is linked to political and social power over other groups when they disagree about these issues. Each of these subjects, sexual health, sexual deviance, and sexual harm, can be discussed in this way.

The idea that any one person who assessed these characteristics as healthy or harmful might change their mind with time and experience must be noted. To get two people to agree about how they want to behave sexually might not be that difficult. Disagreements might happen, but consent requires collaboration and creative resolutions that are agreeable to both parties. But is it possible for families, or faith communities, or cities and local communities, or state governments to agree about how these ambiguous boundaries are reflected in the law? Like many other themes, the more one looks for clarification, the more complicated the idea becomes.

The more Samantha and Ron studied this list, the more they disagreed about which classifications should be considered healthy and which ones were deviant

Table 2.3 Reflecting on Ranges of Behaviors: Deviant and Sex Crime Classifications

1. No one talks about it; it's impossible to know what people do.
2. Few people talk about it, but what people say doesn't match what they actually do.
3. These acts are outside acceptable boundaries for young people; adults do participate in these acts, but they don't talk about them or tell kids how bad it is to do them. But kids know adults are doing them and are left wondering "what's up with that?"
4. These acts are illegal in some places and repealed in other places, and, although people disagree, few are ever charged or prosecuted for doing them.
5. Everyone does these things, but you still don't talk about them except with close friends.
6. Not everyone in society approves of these things, but some folks do them, while others are curious about doing them.
7. These acts are universally considered deviant, but people do them in secret and they are usually undetected.
8. These acts are clearly deviant and potentially harmful but not illegal, and people do them anyway, mostly in secret.
9. These acts in some forms are illegal, but some people do them anyway in secret.
10. These acts are without question illegal; only disturbed people would do them.

or criminal. When they added more people, they added more controversy and a wider range of justification and explanations. When it came time for their report, they concluded by saying it is more important to make sure the couple is practicing consensual sex than it is to worry about which sex acts they were performing, leaving the definition of deviance up to each couple. When addressing questions, one of their classmates asked, "If you leave the definition of sexual deviance up to each couple, what role does the state play in outlining standards of sexual harm when consent is not present?" Ron and Samantha decided that was an excellent question but was outside the scope of their research project.

A GENDERED ANALYSIS OF DEVIANCE

The fact that all people would see the world differently may or may not be a surprise. When discussing the classifications of deviance, however, researchers, especially early criminologists, focused the bulk of their intellectual interests and research dollars on studies of young men and delinquent boys. Delinquent labels were traditionally applied only to young women for sex-related activities. Researchers noted the presence of women in gang research[55] or in research on delinquency,[56] for example, but the focus was on the boys. Their presence was explained as necessary for gang members to have access to sex.

For a young woman, having sex was enough to bring down the full force of a criminal justice system response, even if no other crime had been committed.[57] Over the past several generations, having sex before being married was a deviant, if not socially, devastating act—for women. Shotgun weddings or being shipped away to relatives if a pregnancy were discovered were social responses intended to protect the woman and her family from social disgrace. In 2012, citizens in Morocco erupted in protests after a 16-year-old girl killed herself by eating rat poison after being forced to marry her rapist.[58] A Canadian court found family members guilty of killing three teenage sisters and a family companion amidst allegations the girls had dishonored their family by defying family norms related to discipline, dress, dating, socializing, and using the internet.[59] In the United States, Orange County, California, made headlines when social workers, over a two-year period, were reported to have persuaded fifteen pregnant teenage girls (the youngest was 13) to marry the baby's father (the oldest was 30) to escape the legal consequences of their sexual activity; the marriages were authorized by a juvenile court judge.[60] Age of consent laws for sex are fairly well known and understood, but many states that set limitations for sex also have lower ages or no age limits for getting married when the child has the parent's permission.[61] They were too young to be deemed mature enough to make decisions about sex but not about marriage.

In Texas a 22-year-old avoided prosecution for having sex with a 14-year-old when the family court judge declared their relationship a common law marriage.[62] Sentiment is linked to questions about patriarchy and the gendered language associated with men controlling the lives of women and having the state facilitate that exploitation by the creating or interpreting of laws in ways that protect a rapist from prosecution and coerce or force a woman to marry the person who abused and/or impregnated her when she was legally defined a "child." The idea of marriage as a socially sanctioned option to protect the family from shame and humiliation or whether it will save local governments welfare money[63] invites all kinds of social criticism about the role of gender (and race and class) in both formal and informal social sanctions regarding sex and behaviors identified as sexualized, whether directly related to sex or to behavior seen as sexual.

Age of consent violations are more likely to see charges filed when the partners are of the same sex.[64] When the age gap is wider, engaging in same-sex sexual activity may result in a much harsher criminal penalty than heterosexual sex.[65] Parents, some of whom may be unhappy to find out their child is having gay sex, will often support state declarations of juvenile **status offense** classifications, actions only illegal for people under 18, and suggest they are "in need of supervision." The result is these kids are sometimes placed in foster care, group homes, or juvenile detention facilities.[66]

For some people, the telling of an offensive joke or a scene in a movie or music video that emphasizes women for their sexuality is described as harmful. The reality TV shows *Toddlers and Tiaras* or *Teen Mom* have been repeatedly challenged by people who think these kinds of social situations are harmful or potentially harmful for the young people involved. Again, looking at the linear continuum, are these activities healthy, deviant, or criminal? They are not illegal, so to what degree does the controversy surrounding the show make them deviant, or are they just controversial, and what would be the difference? What are the parts boys play in these programs? How are boys lives gendered in similar but different ways?

SEXUAL DISORDERS AND DYSFUNCTIONS

Like Samantha and Ron, many researchers are studying aspects of sexual deviance to understand more about sexual health and sexual harm or crimes. Psychology plays an important role in these efforts, as does the medical profession; sociologists; and other disciplines, such as women's studies, communication studies, international studies, and more. Although theories of sex offending behavior and treatment practices are discussed in more detail in section III, attention is given here to several terms and concepts used rather casually in the study of sex offending behavior. Many of these terms are used overly broadly or in a pejorative way, but important distinctions should be made to ensure, at least throughout this text, how the terms are used and what they have come to mean in other areas of related study.

The term **sexual disorder** is an umbrella term that lumps together sexual concerns identified as problems in sexual functioning, desire, or performance. Frank Weber, the clinical director of a statewide sex offender treatment program in Minnesota and author on the subject of sex offender treatment protocols suggests that

> all sexual disorders have distressing and repetitive sexual fantasies, urges or behaviors in common. These fantasies, urges or behaviors must occur for a significant time and must interfere with either satisfactory sexual relations or

everyday functioning in order for a diagnosis to be made.... [T]hey typically recognize the symptoms as negatively impacting their life, but feel as if they are unable to control them.[67]

This can include issues of sexual or gender identity, sexual performance, and sexual addiction. **Sexual dysfunction** is commonly used to refer to an event during the act of sex that is or becomes problematic for one or both partners.[68] Restrictions in sexual function can be caused by stress, heart conditions, depression, or other medical conditions that affect desire, arousal, or orgasm. An example is erectile dysfunction, or impotence, a condition that prevents men from achieving or attaining an erection. **Sex addiction**, or sexual compulsivity, is a controversial topic because experts disagree about how to assess whether someone is having too much or not enough sex. If the drive or desire for sex interferes with a person's everyday functioning, professional help might be a necessary solution.

PARAPHILIA AND PARAPHILIC CLASSIFICATIONS

The American Psychological Association defines a **paraphilia** as a mental disorder characterized by "recurrent, intense, sexual urges and sexually arousing fantasies" lasting at least six months and involving (1) nonhuman objects, (2) the suffering or humiliation of one's self or one's partner (not merely simulated), or (3) children or other nonconsenting people.[69] See Table 2.4 for a list of several paraphilias. A much more extensive list of paraphilias is included at the end of the text in appendix B.

Another way to think about paraphilias is to consider them in the category of contact or **touch offenses** and noncontact, minimal contact, or **nontouch offenses**. Touch offenses involve physical contact with the victim by the offender and the nontouch offenses are illegal or inappropriate activities that

Table 2.4 A List of Paraphilia

Paraphilia	Description of Attraction
Urophilia	Urination, particularly on others and/or being urinated on
Somnophilia	Sleeping or dead people
Exhibitionism	Exposing one's self to others sexually without their consent
Stigmatophilia	Body piercings and tattoos
Asphyxiophilia	Strangulation, aka autoerotic asphyxiation
Zoophilia	Animals
Necrophilia	Corpses
Infantophilia	Pedophilia with attraction to children 5 years old or younger
Hebephilia	Early pubescent children
Pedophilia	Prepubescent children
Sadism	Inflicting pain on others without their consent
Partialism	Specific nongenital body parts
Masochism	Suffering, being beaten, bound, or otherwise humiliated
Klismaphilia	Enemas

Table 2.5   Contact and Noncontact Paraphilia

Eight Main Paraphilias from DSM-IV-TR	
Noncontact/Minimal Contact Paraphilia	**High Contact Paraphilia**
Exhibitionism	Sexual masochism
Frotteurism	Sexual sadism
Voyeurism	Pedophilia
Fetishism	
Transvestic fetishism	

do not involve direct contact with the victim, such as telephone scatologia or calling a victim (either unknown or known to the offender) in a way that is sexually arousing to the offender. A paraphilia list classified as touch/nontouch is provided in Table 2.5.

ASYLUMS AND ABUSE: "TREATMENT" AS "REEDUCATION"

Attention was given earlier in the chapter to the work of Howard Becker, who identified a typology of deviance, including the ideas of falsely accused and secret deviants. As the conversation moves away from healthy, considers the idea of deviant, and then moves toward looking at how society manages and handles sexual crimes, it is particularly important to pay attention to the role society plays in the assessment and administration of definitions of deviance alongside the idea about creating justice. Earlier consideration was given to the gendered dynamic of delinquency and the idea of labeling women, young girls, and homosexuals as deviants. The phrase **Madonna/Whore** was used in reference to traditional views of women as being either "saintly," like the Holy Mother (also referred to as the Madonna), or unpure, sexual, or a whore. There was little to no room in between. This kind of social attitude is changing; however, people of different genders are still treated differently and judged differently for openly sexual behaviors.

This section is intended to further discuss the social responses to sexual behavior. Chapters 4 and 5 deal with the history of sexual harm and violence in the United States. It is important to think about not only the individuals who are "tagged," or "labeled," and therefore challenged with a deviant label but to also reflect about how system definitions and laws and practices affect people unfairly. When women were identified as too feeble to work in the business world, they were falsely accused. Other women at that time were secretly deviant because they held jobs but didn't want anyone to know. The idea of women being deviant for working seems laughable today. However, attempts to catch sexual deviants can have harsh consequences in the lives of people in both directions when they are falsely accused or the law fits but is not applied and people remain secretly deviant as they perpetrate more sex crimes.

Attention is given here to the role the system plays in creating those secret deviants and falsely accused. Women, particularly young women, who are identified as acting out sexually have often been labeled "incorrigible" and sent to halfway houses or institutions. In many cases, the treatment was a "reeducation" program, which taught young women that it was not acceptable to challenge authority.[70] Numerous historical reports outline cases where young women like these were further exploited by the people who were hired as caretakers in those institutions where they were placed as punishment for being "deviant," more specifically, "sexually deviant."[71] The same thing can be said for homosexuals. The traditional response to homosexuality was institutionalization, either treatment, which was said to "correct" this "deviant" behavior, or in some cases prison. To this day, there are programs that propose to "treat" and "heal" people from what they identify as the "disease" of homosexuality, in spite of consistent scientific literature refuting these claims.[72]

Too many questions remain about the role government plays in the sexual lives of its citizens. At the same time, no one would disagree with the need to make laws to protect people, particularly children and young people, from sexual harm and abuse. As this segment winds down, and as the focus shifts to assessing differences between sexual deviance and sexual crimes, give specific attention to the use of formal and informal social controls as well as the spaces where individual behavior and social influences intersect.

DISTINGUISHING BETWEEN SEXUAL DEVIANCE AND SEXUAL OFFENDING

It might be easy to see some overlaps between healthy sex and deviant sex or deviant sex and criminal sex acts. But does it seem possible that people would be in such disagreement about a sexual act or attitudes about sexual behavior that some groups identify as a healthy act, while other groups identify that same act as deviant, and still others would say that same act should be outlawed and made illegal? Is it possible that a sex act could be found controversial enough for people to disagree so widely? Consider oral or anal sex. Before the Supreme Court decision in *Lawrence v. Sherman* (2003) changed the illegal status of sodomy laws, oral sex was still on the books as illegal in many states, even between husband and wife. A Florida legislator attempted to take the law against cohabitation off the books in Florida, saying it was outdated and unfair to prosecute and punish people under such a law when the state has recorded approximately 544,907 residents are in violation of the state's law[73] and subject to a $500 fine and 60 days in jail.[74] His efforts to remove the law failed, with legislators saying they still supported the spirit of the law.[75] Although not heard in the 2011 session, the repeal request was sent to committee to be heard in the 2012 session and eventually was signed into law in 2016.[76]

Also, consider the example of homosexuality. Sex acts between consenting same-sex adults were illegal in most US states until 2003 when the Supreme Court ruled (*Lawrence v. Texas*) state bans prohibiting same-sex relations amounted to an unconstitutional violation of the right to privacy. Despite the fact that sex acts between same-sex adults have been documented throughout history, the classification of homosexual behavior as healthy, deviant, or criminal has differed dramatically depending on the time in history, the society, or the community being considered. (A more comprehensive review of the legal challenges and activities in the LGBTQI community is included in chapter 4.) Social attitudes about homosexuality seem to depend a great deal on religious and moral convictions, which perhaps everyone can agree differ widely between social groups and geographic locations.

Roughly ten years after the 2003 *Lawrence v. Texas* Supreme Court decision, the modification in legal definition has not wholly transformed contemporary social attitudes. In fact, almost a decade after the Supreme Court ruling, the Montana legislature actively demonstrated its disregard for the higher court's decision by actively refusing to remove the relevant laws from its state statutes.[77] Evangelical leaders from the United States traveled to Africa in support of antigay practices and seemingly in support of countries that support the death penalty for people who are identified as gay.[78] Antigay rhetoric continues in the United States. Efforts to legalize marriage are still controversial. In Minnesota, after a series of teen suicides, the Anoka-Hennepin school district was embroiled in legal battles and community controversies about whether it is appropriate for teachers to use the word "gay" in public schools. In the face of harsh, divisive, and vocal opposition, however, gay rights advocates and their allies remain steadfast in their pursuit of equal rights, consistently rejecting the idea that intimate relationships between gay couples are any less healthy than heterosexual couples. How many people walk around as secret deviants or falsely accused because of the rigid social attitudes about appropriate or healthy sexual expression. Does making laws and "protecting" the freedom of some come at the expense of freedom of others? What if, as in *Lawrence*, the court undoes years, centuries, or decades of criminal prosecution in a single day? How do these kinds of decisions and changes influence future discussions of deviance defining and crime classifications and criminal prosecution?

Table 2.6 helps elucidate characterization and classification of sexually deviant acts. Some of those acts are illegal, but people do them all the time without sanction. Some of the acts characterized by older generations as offensive or "just plain wrong" are viewed differently by a younger person.

To complicate things further, attempts to clarify the parameters of sexual deviance invite a similar effort to differentiate between deviant sex acts and acts designated as illegal. Just as ideological differences are evident between definitions of sexual health and sexual deviance, controversy also exists between deviant and criminal classifications of sex practices. Again, using the Venn diagram illustration, if it were possible to draw a line around all things healthy and all things deviant, and now all things criminal, there is still obvious overlap. As indicated in Figure 2.7 an illegal act might also be considered a deviant act, but a clear delineation does not always follow. Some acts are believed to be healthy in one group but completely unacceptable in another, so much so that the group might move to make those actions illegal.

Table 2.6 A Model for Discussing Normative and Deviant Social Attitudes about Sex in the United States

Degrees of Deviance	The Act Is Legal	The Legal Status Varies	The Act Is Illegal
Close to 100% Deviant	BDSM Genital modification Online porn Gay bath houses Swinging/open Marriage Men's/women's clothes Going to sex toy shops Celibacy—nonreligious	PORN Abortion/process Bestiality Adultery, female Genital modification Anal sex/hetero Drunk sex Anal sex/homosexual Sex with a person younger than 16	Child porn Child sex tourism Commercial exploitation of children Sex trafficking Drugs for sex Drug people to get sex Polygamy Prostitution Revenge porn
Deviant Status Varies	Homosexuality Women's/men's clothes Strip clubs/stripping Sexting (adults) Fetishes/partialism Interracial marriage	PORN Adultery, male Hooking up Status offenses Sending naked pictures	Nontouch, e.g., telephone scat, exhibitionism, and voyeurism Sexting, children and young people Touch offenses, e.g., frotteurism
Close to 100% Socially Acceptable	Cohabitation Erotica Sex before marriage, aka hooking up and friends with benefits Delayed marriage Divorce Not having children Celibacy—religious Fantasies/fantasizing	Oral sex	

CHAPTER SUMMARY AND REVIEW

The range of social behaviors included in a conversation about deviant behavior is extensive. Even after reviewing existing definitions of deviance and narrowing the conversation to sexual deviance, much remains. Clarifying the gap between what constitutes popular notions of normal behavior and deviant behavior is essential for thinking forward about ways to focus that larger conversation on the kinds of behaviors to be regulated through social policy and punishment. After a brief review of the study of deviance, attention was given to the way society has studied deviance and to the transitions happening to the larger study of social sciences making way for feminist theories and an expansion of ways to think about researching social science, deviance, and sexual deviance specifically.

Text Box 2.1.   Media Messages about Sexual Deviance

Consider: This image is from research in 1986 by Malamuth and Briere[1] in which they suggest a model by which current forces, including the media, may affect individual behavior. Focused on what they identify as a series of mutually influencing factors, they suggest one's own attitude about the actions of others may change but that change in attitude does not necessarily change their individual behaviors. Review and discuss the themes presented.

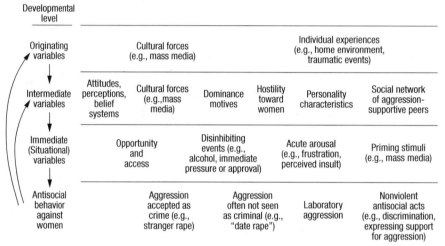

Figure TB 2.1   Hypothesized environmental influences on antisocial behavior against women
Malamuth, N. M. and J. Friere. 1986. Journal of Social Issues, vol 42, no. 3., p. 78

Consider: Media violence. In 2009, the Council on Communication Media published a policy on the effects of media violence that suggested that "exposure to violence in media, including television, movies, music, and video games represents a significant health risk to the health of children and adolescents."[2]

Consider: Cartoon violence. Consider the emerging genre of anime. Consider the cartoons that embed adult humor and adult content in the shows. Consider the cartoons that are absolutely intended to appeal to an adult market. Do the limits of art, humor, and media originally designed to appeal to children warrant closer attention? In what ways?

Consider: Disney and Nickelodeon have been criticized for focusing on adult themes. A December 2017 article in the *New York Post* announced to parents, "The Disney Channel is no longer safe for our kids."[3] When are kids ready to think about adult things, and when is it appropriate that those themes become about sex?

Consider: Slasher films. Horror movies have long since integrated sex and violence. An October 2017 review[4] asks questions about how this affects our understanding of human sexuality. What happens when we seek violence, but we don't see the sexuality?

Consider: Gaming violence. In 2014, *Grand Theft Auto V* was pulled from store shelves after concerns were raised about the elements of sexual violence and murder of women embedded in the game. Media critic Anita Sarkeesian published her review of several instances of violence against women in many popular video games that did not receive the "sexual violence" warning/rating.[5]

Consider: After being targeted as a problem, for hiding sexual violence throughout the gaming platforms, in late 2018, researchers at the University of New Hampshire designed two video games intending to educate students on what to do if they are witness to or the victim of asexual assault, sexual harassment, or stalking.[6]

Consider: In 2006, the United Kingdom started a public awareness campaign with the theme "Sex: It's worth talking about." In a related effort, focus was directed at addressing an increase in sexually transmitted infections (STIs) with the theme "Condoms: Essential Wear."

- Would such a program be seen as deviant in the United States?
- How do these efforts help or hinder efforts to expand conversations on healthy sexuality?
- What might be an approach that would be effective in the United States?
- How is the public awareness message reflected in movies and television?

Notes

1. Neil M. Malamuth and John Briere, "Sexual Violence in the Media: Indirect Effects on Aggression against Women," *Journal of Social Issues* 42, no. 3 (1986): 78.

2. Council on Communications and Media, "Media Violence," *Pediatrics* 124, no. 5 (2009): 1495–503. http://pediatrics.aappublications.org/content/124/5/1495.full.

3. Julie Gunlock, "The Disney Channel Is No Longer Safe for Our Kids," *New York Post*, December 8, 2017, accessed September 1, 2019, https://nypost.com/2017/12/08/the-disney-channel-is-no-longer-safe-for-our-kids/.

4. Kalyn Corrigan, "How Horror Movies Conjure Nightmares Out of Human Sexuality," *Collider*, October 24, 2017, accessed September 1, 2019, http://collider.com/sexuality-in-horror-movies/#final-girl.

5. Susan Cox, "Sexual Violence Is Present in More Games than 'Grand Theft Auto V,'" *Rewire.News*, December 11, 2014, accessed September 1, 2019, https://rewire.news/article/2014/12/11/sexual-violence-present-games-grand-theft-auto-v/.

6. Lindsay McKenzie, "Combating Sexual Violence with Video Games," *Inside Higher Ed*, August 22, 2018, accessed September 1, 2019, https://www.insidehighered.com/quicktakes/2018/08/22/combating-sexual-violence-video-games.

The chapter includes a review of various examples of early research on deviance and a discussion about what turns out to be a fairly arbitrary process of defining sexual deviance. Emphasis is placed on the way sexual deviance is defined differently for heteronormative boys and girls, and from young people who are ascribed to or active in the LGBTQI communities. The idea of clinical assessments of sexual disorders and dysfunctions is presented for review and consideration, taking the conversation beyond a socially assessed condition to a condition that is ascribed by a doctor or psychiatrist; however, it is evident that there is disagreement within professional communities about the classifications of physical and psychological disorders related to biological and psychological assessments of sexual behaviors. More discussions about the theoretical explanations and treatment responses are provided in chapters 9 and 13. The paraphilia classifications are introduced, giving attention to a series of more commonly discussed attractions and the related characterization, paying particular attention to the ideas of touch and nontouch offenses.

The idea of systemic abuses was introduced and overviewed, highlighting examples of past practices of institutionalizing people who were determined to have been behaving inappropriately. Ironically, or perhaps as a direct result of these issues being reviewed and raised, several studies and the related historical records from some of these same institutions are being released, which suggest that significant accounts of abuse happened in these very institutions created to protect or educate children.[79] A brief overview is offered, with a callout to the larger historical reflections being offered in section II, highlighting several systemic sexual abuses throughout US history that too often remain absent from the current conversations about sexual deviance, harm, and crime. A concluding conversation invites a place for considering the all-important distinction between sexual deviance and sexual offending. The bulk of the text moving forward is focused on the idea of identifying and defining sexual offending behaviors and looking more closely at the people who commit those offenses. Paralleling those conversations are related conversations about when a specific sexual act is determined to be a sexual offense and how the social system responds.

KEY TERMS

absolutist perspective	pornography
critical approach	relativism
dichotomous	relativist perspective
Edwin Schur	secret deviants
falsely accused	sex addiction
functionalism	sexual disorder
Howard Becker	sexual dysfunction
intersex	social power perspective
labeling theory	social reaction, or labeling, theory
Madonna/Whore	social relativism
medical model	statistical model
normative rules	symbolic interaction process
norms	touch offenses/nontouch offenses
objectivity	validity
paraphilia	William J. Chambliss

REVIEW QUESTIONS

1. What are the three characterizations of deviance outlined in the chapter?

2. What are the two primary themes from feminist discourse presented for consideration?

3. Becker highlighted two types of deviance as the most interesting, which the authors apply to sex crime and sexualized violence. What are they, and where in Becker's work can they be found?

4. According to the text, what are the differences between a sexual disorder and a sexual dysfunction? How do these ideas relate to sexual deviance?

5. How were mental institutions historically used to address questions of sexual deviance?

DISCUSSION QUESTIONS

1. In what ways has deviance been defined in both subtle and dramatic ways in your social experiences?

2. Have you seen the statistical, medical, or social reaction definitions of deviance often in social settings in your life?

3. Is it possible to be a victim to sexual aggression and not know you have been victimized?

4. How many people do you think fall into the category of secret sexual deviant, as this idea is presented in the chapter?

5. Is it possible to commit a sex act and not know you committed a sex act? Please explain.

NOTES

1. Erwin J. Haeberle, *The Sex Atlas: New Popular Reference Edition* (New York: Continuum International Publishing Group, 1983), Chapter 10, accessed October 20, 2019, https://www.literatur.hu-berlin.de/de/forschung/archive-forschungsstellen/forschungsstelle-kulturgeschichte-der-sexualitaet/archive-for-sex-research.

2. Judith Lorber, *Gender Inequality: Feminist Theories and Policies*, 5th ed. (New York: Oxford University Press, 2012), 9.

3. Jesse Bering, *Perv: The Sexual Deviant in All of Us* (New York: Scientific American/Farrar, Straus and Giroux, 2013), ix.

4. Patricia A. Adler and Peter Adler, *Constructions of Deviance: Power, Context, and Interaction*, 6th ed. (Belmont, CA: Wadsworth Publishing, 2009).

5. Walter S. DeKeseredy, Desmond Ellis, and Shahid Alvi, *Deviance and Crime: Theory, Research and Policy*, 3rd ed. (Cincinnati, OH: Anderson Publishing, 2005).

6. Alex Heckert and Druann Maria Heckert, "Using a New Typology of Deviance to Analyze Ten Common Norms of the United States Middle-Class," *The Sociological Quarterly* 45, no. 2 (2004): 209–28; Alex Heckert and Druann Maria Heckert, "Using an Integrated Typology of Deviance to Expand Merton's Anomie Theory," *Criminal Justice Studies: A Critical Journal of Crime, Law and Society* 17, no. 1 (2004): 75–90.

7. Adler and Adler's *Constructions of Deviance* (2009) is a collection of writings on deviance that represents a compilation of foundational themes in deviance scholarship; it was extremely helpful as I made decisions about how to narrow the material included here.

8. Emile Durkheim, *Rules of the Sociological Method* (New York: The Free Press, 1982).

9. Kai T. Erikson, "Notes on the Sociology of Deviance," paper presented at the 55th Annual Meeting of the American Sociological Association, New York, 1960, accessed August 21, 2019, https://www.soc.umn.edu/~uggen/Erikson_SP_63.pdf.

10. Albert K. Cohen, *Deviance and Control* (Englewood Cliffs, NJ: Prentice Hall, 1966), https://www.questia.com/library/66993/deviance-and-control.

11. William Graham Sumner, *Folkways: A Study of Mores, Manners, Customs, and Morals* (Boston: Ginn and Company, 1906); Adler and Adler, *Constructions of Deviance: Power, Context, and Interaction*, 6th ed. (Belmont, CA: Wadsworth Publishing, 2009), 44.

12. Kai T. Erikson, "On the Sociology of Deviance," in *Constructions of Deviance: Power, Context, and Interaction*, 6th ed., ed. Patricia A. Adler and Peter Adler (Belmont, CA: Wadsworth Publishing, 2009), 110.

13. Kai T. Erikson, *Wayward Puritans: A Study in the Sociology of Deviance, Classic Edition* (Upper Saddle River, NJ: Prentice Hall, 2004).

14. Howard S. Becker, *Outsiders: Studies in the Sociology of Deviance* (New York: The Free Press, 1963).

15. Ibid., 4.

16. Ibid., 5.

17. Ibid., 6.

18. Ibid., 9.

19. Ibid., 14. Italics in the original.

20. Ibid., 14.

21. Maria Baghramian, "A Brief History of Relativism," in *Relativism: A Contemporary Anthology*, ed. Michael Krausz (New York: Columbia University Press, 2010), 31–52.

22. Additional references regarding social relativism and the social construction of reality include Peter L. Berger and Thomas Luckmann, *The Social Construction of Reality: A Treatise in the Sociology of Knowledge* (New York: Anchor Books, 1967). Critical theories and feminist theories can be explored in I. Moyer, *Criminological Theories: Traditional and Nontraditional Voices and Themes* (Sage, 2001), Chapters 8 and 9.

23. Barbara Costello, "Against Relativism: A Harm-Based Conception of Deviance," in *Constructions of Deviance: Power, Context, and Interaction*, 6th ed., ed. Patricia A. Adler and Peter Adler (Belmont, CA: Wadsworth Publishing, 2009), 46–52.

24. Heckert and Heckert, "Using a New Typology of Deviance" and "Using an Integrated Typology of Deviance."

25. Richard Quinney, *The Social Reality of Crime* (Piscataway, NJ: Transaction Publishers, 1970).

26. Ibid., 167.

27. William J. Chambliss, "The Saints and the Roughnecks," *Society* 11, no. 1 (1973): 24–31.

28. Ibid., 28.

29. Ibid.

30. See, for example, William J. Chambliss, *On the Take: From Petty Crooks to Presidents* (Bloomington, IN: Indiana University Press, 1988).

31. J. Bjorhus, "Rape, Alcohol and Consent Are under Review by State Sexual Assault Task Force," *Star Tribune*, November 15, 2018, http://www.startribune.com/rape-alcohol-and-consent-are-under-review-by-state-sexual-assault-task-force/500437262/.

32. Kirby Dick, dir., *The Hunting Ground* (New York: RADiUS-TWC, 2015), film.

33. Adler and Adler, *Constructions of Deviance*, 27.

34. Ibid., 2.

35. Ibid., 3.

36. Ibid., 7.

37. DeKeseredy, Ellis, and Alvi, *Deviance and Crime*, 22.

38. Walter S. DeKeseredy and Martin D. Schwartz, *Contemporary Criminology* (Belmont, CA: Wadsworth Publishing, 1995).

39. Becker, *Outsiders*.

40. I. Moyer, *Criminological Theories: Traditional and Nontraditional Voices* (Thousand Oaks, CA: Sage, 2002).

41. B. Van der Kolk, "Developmental Trauma Disorder: Toward a Rational Diagnosis for Children with Complex Trauma Histories," *Psychiatric Annals* 35, no. 5 (2005): 401–408, https://doi.org/10.3928/00485713-20050501-06.

42. Yvonne Roberts, "Lucky Boy Raised without Gender Stereotypes," *The Guardian*, January 21, 2012, accessed June 24, 2015, http://www.theguardian.com/commentisfree/2012/jan/22/yvonne-roberts-gender-neutral-children.

43. Susan Donaldson James, "Baby Storm Raised Genderless Is Bad Experiment, Say Experts," *ABC News*, May 26, 2011, accessed June 24, 2015, http://abcnews.go.com/Health/baby-storm-raised-genderless-gender-dangerous-experiment-child/story?id=13693760; Anna North, "Mom Says Baby Storm Is Not 'Genderless' After All," *Jezebel*, May 30, 2011, accessed June 24, 2015, http://jezebel.com/5806733/mom-says-baby-storm-is-not-genderless-after-all; Natasha Dantzig, "Where Is He or She Now? An Update on the Great Genderless Baby Storm of 2011," December 31, 2011, accessed June 24, 2015, http://www.popsugar.com/moms/Update-Genderless-Baby-21090247.

44. "About," Intersex Society of North America, accessed June 25, 2015, http://www.isna.org.

45. Edwin M. Schur, *Labeling Women Deviant: Gender, Stigma, and Social Control* (New York: Random House, 1984).

46. Alice Rossi, *Gender and the Life Course* (Chicago: Aldine Transaction, 1985), 124.

47. Hannah Riley Bowles and Michele Gelfand, "Status and the Evaluation of Workplace Deviance," *Psychological Science* 21, no. 1 (2010): 49–54.

48. Andrew James McGrath, "The Subjective Impact of Contact with the Criminal Justice System: The Role of Gender Stigmatization," *Crime and Delinquency* 60, no. 6 (2010): 884–908.

49. Alex Hern, "Who Are the 'Incels' and How Do They Relate to Toronto Van Attack?," April 25, 2018, accessed August 31, 2019, https://www.theguardian.com/technology/2018/apr/25/what-is-incel-movement-toronto-van-attack-suspect.

50. Jason Wilson, "Toronto Van Attack: Facebook Post May Link Suspect to Misogynist 'Incel' Subculture," April 25, 2018, accessed August 31, 2019, https://www.theguardian.com/world/2018/apr/24/toronto-van-attack-facebook-post-may-link-suspect-with-incel-group; Hern, "Who Are the 'Incels'?"

51. Bob Herbert, "Why Are We Not Shocked?," *New York Times*, October 16, 2006, accessed June 24, 2015, http://www.nytimes.com/2006/10/16/opinion/16herbert.html.

52. Michael Kimmel, *Angry White Men* (New York: Nation Books, 2017); Nigel Edley, *Men and Masculinity: The Basics* (London: Routledge, 2017); Jackson Katz, *The Macho Paradox: Why Some Men Hurt Women and How All Men Can Help* (Sourcebooks, 2006).

53. One excellent review of feminist theories and the politics that shape them is offered in Judith Lorber, *Gender Inequality: Feminist Theories and Politics* (New York: Oxford University Press, 2012).

54. Mandi F. Deitz, Stacey L. Williams, Sean C. Rife, and Peggy Cantrell, "Examining Cultural, Social, and Self-Related Aspects of Stigma in Relation to Sexual Assault and Trauma Symptoms," *Violence Against Women* 21, no. 5 (2015): 598–615, doi.org/10.1177/1077801215573330.

55. Frederick Thrasher, "The Gang: A Study of 1,313 Gangs in Chicago," 1927, https://www.ncjrs.gov/App/Publications/abstract.aspx?ID=198646.

56. Cohen, *Deviance and Control*.

57. Meda Chesney-Lind and R. G. Shelden, *Girls, Delinquency and Juvenile Justice*, 4th ed. (Wiley Blackwell, 2014).

58. Nora Fakim, "Morocco Protest against Rape-Marriage Law," *BBC*, March 17, 2012, accessed June 24, 2015, http://www.bbc.co.uk/news/world-africa-17416426.

59. "'You Have No Place in Civilised Society': Muslim Family Jailed for Life after 'Despicable' Honour Killing of Three Teen Daughters Who Dared to Date Boys," *Daily Mail*, January 30, 2012, https://www.dailymail.co.uk/news/article-2093513/Afghan-family-guilty-honour-killing-Canada.html.

60. Kate Sutherland, "From Jailbird to Jailbait: Age of Consent Law and the Construction of Teenage Sexualities," *William and Mary Journal of Women and the Law* 9, no. 3/2 (2003): 324.

61. "State-by-State Marriage 'Age of Consent' Laws," FindLaw, accessed August 31, 2019, https://family.findlaw.com/marriage/state-by-state-marriage-age-of-consent-laws.html.

62. Nina Perales, "Cultural Stereotypes and the Legal Response to Pregnant Teens," in *Mother Troubles: Rethinking Contemporary Maternal Dilemmas*, ed. Julia E. Hanigsberg and Sara Ruddick (Boston: Beacon Press, 1999).

63. Vincent Schodolski, "Pregnant Teens Urged to Marry Adult Partners," *Toronto Star*, September 21, 1996, quoted in Kate Sutherland, "From Jailbird to Jailbait: Age of Consent Law and the Construction of Teenage Sexualities," *William & Mary Journal of Race, Gender, and Social Justice* 9, no. 3 (2003): 324, accessed June 29, 2015, http://scholarship.law .wm.edu/cgi/viewcontent.cgi?article=1167&context=wmjowl.

64. Donna Minkowitz, "On Trial: Gay? Straight? Boy? Girl? Sex? Rape?," *Out*, October 1995, 99, 145.

65. "'Romeo and Juliet Law' Gives Gay Teen 16 Years More in Prison Than Heterosexual Would Serve," *ACLU*, September 28, 2001, accessed June 29, 2015, https://www.aclu.org/ news/romeo-juliet-law-gives-gay-teen-16-years-more-prison-heterosexual-would-serve.

66. Colleen Sullivan, "Kids, Courts, and Queers: Lesbian and Gay Youth in the Juvenile Justice and Foster Care Systems," *Law and Sexuality* 6, no. 31 (1996): 32–34.

67. Frank Weber, Core Professional Services, personal communication with the author (from forthcoming book).

68. Rachel Yehuda, Amy Lehrner, and Talli Y. Rosenbaum, "PTSD and Sexual Dysfunction in Men and Women," *The Journal of Sexual Medicine* 12, no. 5 (2015): 1107–19, doi .org/10.1111/jsm.12856.

69. Eric Hickey, *Sex Crimes and Paraphilias* (Pearson, 2006). Specifically, J. Healy, Chapter 7.

70. Stephanie Coontz, *The Way We Never Were* (New York: Basic Books, 2016).

71. Ibid. See also S. Coontz, *The Social Origins of Private Life* (Verso, 1988).

72. E. Hooker, "The Adjustment of the Male Overt Homosexual," *Journal of Projective Techniques* 21 (1957): 18–31. See also J. S. Bohan, *Psychology and Sexual Orientation: Coming to Terms* (New York: Routledge, 1996).

73. "Florida Legislature Seeks to Repeal Obsolete Cohabitation Statute," *Fort Lauderdale Divorce Lawyer Blog*, September 15, 2011, accessed June 25, 2015, http://www.fortlauder daledivorcelawyerblog.com/2011/09/florida-legislature-seeks-to-r.html.

74. Jeff Cull, "ILLEGAL!? Some Florida Laws Forbid Things You Might Never Have Imagined," *Fort Myers Florida Weekly*, May 3, 2007, accessed June 24, 2015, http://fortmyers .floridaweekly.com/news/2007-05-03/top_news/001.html.

75. "Lawmaker Pushes to Repeal Florida Law That Makes Cohabitation a Crime," CNN, accessed September 1, 2011, http://www.cnn.com/2011/US/09/01/florida.cohabitation.law/ index.html.

76. Hilary Hanson, "Finally, Unwed Couples Can Legally Live Together in Florida," *Huffpost*, April 7, 2016, https://www.huffpost.com/entry/unwed-unmarried-couples-flor ida-law_n_57068015e4b0a506064e5bca?guccounter=1&guce_referrer=aHR0cHM6Ly 93d3cuZ29vZ2xlLmNvbS8&guce_referrer_sig=AQAAAGPooU8XlXwPB0n8Ic3Vd 51NpWnyJSjnqxC1rErb6OgXz30ngPSdmnbvYF3fCSN3nsaMm7rZi3CcahLeC8M 0FgG6HwQ9PmhEdnl0CtHezrzrq4qRG6gPxhezSDmVhncncEZHzZBCq1KnP 8gIxr1QuN_9Z58oqXIE-hdQLXw99pab.

77. "It's Still Illegal to Have Gay Sex in Montana, Years after Supreme Court Ruling," *LGBTQ Nation*, March 18, 2011, accessed June 25, 2015, http://www.lgbtqnation .com/2011/03/its-still-illegal-to-have-gay-sex-in-montana-years-after-supreme-court-rul ing/. Kansas similarly refuses to decriminalize gay sex; see Justin Kendall, "Gay Sex Is Still Illegal in Kansas, and Lawmakers Won't Do Anything about It," *The Pitch*, March 10, 2011, https://www.thepitchkc.com/gay-sex-is-still-illegal-in-kansas-and-lawmakers-wont -do-anything-about-it/.

78. Jessica Boutchie, "Globalizing Hatred," *Harvard Political Review*, March 15, 2019, https://harvardpolitics.com/covers/globalizing-hatred/.

79. Louise Hide and Joanna Bourke, "Cultures of Harm in Institutions of Care: Introduction," *The Social History of Medicine* 31, no. 4 (2018): 679–87.

3

So How Are the Children?

It is easier to build strong children than to repair broken men.

—Frederick Douglass[1]

Let us put our minds together and see what life we can make for our children.

—Sitting Bull[2]

THE MASAI, ONE OF THE OLDEST TRIBES in Africa, famously use a powerful greeting when they connect with others from various tribes. The question asked is, "Kasserian Ingera?" Translated, this means "How are the children?"[3] The welfare of the children is used to measure the welfare of the society as a whole. If the same greeting were offered in the United States, what would the likely response be? So, when we discuss sexual abuse and its related harms, how *are* the children?

Experts and policy makers describe child sexual abuse as both a "silent epidemic" and a public health emergency.[4] When considering the life of a child, it seems impossible to know how many are affected by sexual violence and to what degree. But when various social conditions and events are considered, perhaps it is not too much of a stretch to say all children and young people are affected by sexual harm in one way or another, often in events outside their control. Some of the more prominent examples are sexual bullying, unwanted touch, eroticized and sometimes violent subthemes of images in ads, the hypersexualized body, and issues related to negative body image. The dynamics of hurtful, harmful, or abusive behaviors in households are underscored by events within the family, in emerging dating relationships, or in headline-grabbing stories of colossal breaches of personal and public trust when community leaders, church officials, teachers, or coaches are found to be sexually abusing kids.

Events like these suggest that children and young people don't always have a choice about setting the stage and planning out the educational process of their choosing when it comes to learning lessons about appropriate and inappropriate sexual conduct. People will make meaning out of these events in a variety of ways, and, from what psychologists and sociologists report in related research, the consequences of victimization are quite varied. (More about the issue of sexual abuse and victimization is included in chapter 8.) Many, many questions have been structured but have not produced definitive answers. How affected are children and young people in the United States who have been directly or indirectly influenced by sexual harm and sexual violence? Before you proceed further, feel free to use the continuum in Figure 3.1 as one way to facilitate a discussion about popular social perceptions and assessments about sexualized harm or sexualized violence on the lives of young children. Ask yourselves and your classmates basic questions about how children are affected by the issues presented for discussion here.

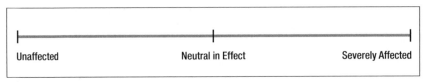

Figure 3.1 Individual Assesments of Perceived Impact

If young people are insecure about their bodies or get the message they are unattractive or unlovable, how do their feelings affect their ability to feel secure in the world and evolve into a healthy sexual relationship? If young people grow up to believe love equals sex, does this restrict or limit their experiences of love and sex in the world? At what point do cultural and media messages, name-calling, and bullying interrupt or negatively influence healthy sexual development? If you don't feel "strong enough" or "pretty enough" because social messages emphasize these qualities as gendered qualities and not human qualities, how do those ideas influence who a person becomes in the world? Abuse, particularly sexual abuse, has been equated to "soul murder."[5] Why does abuse seem to have less of a dramatic effect on some people? How are physical harms translated by a person into mental and/or emotional harms? At what point does incessant bullying become a life-altering harm?

With all of the socially conflicting messages about healthy sex and relationships, parents might try to selectively wrap up ideas about sex tied with a "they're too young to understand any of that stuff anyway" ribbon or a "we'll talk to them when they get older" bow. How do these social realities influence the dynamics of child victims and provide sexual offenders with unintended or unrestricted access to children and young people? How many kids do not get essential information about how to understand what is abusive and how to prevent abuse or what to do if abuse happens?

Whether or not it is possible to determine how many children grow up being negatively affected by direct or indirect exposure to sexualized violence, contradictory messages about sex abound. Sexualized images are on display virtually everywhere kids go, whereas, at the same time, kids often get the impression that the subject of sex is taboo. The wistfully romanticized "happily-ever-after" themes from G-rated Disney movies to R-rated romantic comedies break down a bit when guys get teased for getting "dragged" to these movies and girls become starry-eyed about what they think their future life should be. Kids hear "Sex is disgusting and nasty" as well as "Sex is a beautiful gift; save it for someone special." The truth is, of course, it can be both.

Examining the problem of sexual assaults and the effect of sexual violence and harms on the lives of the youngest American citizens requires a willingness to look at some unpleasant social realities. Although data isn't readily available for kids who do not identify as male or female, the CDC tells us that LGBTQI youth are victimized at an equal or higher rate than their straight peers. Consider the following statistics:

- One in three girls and one in seven boys will be sexually abused at some point in their childhood.[6]
- In as many as 93 percent of child sexual abuse cases, the child knows the abuser.[7]
- Children victims of other forms of crime, violence, and abuse are more at risk for sexual violence.[8]
- Most sexually abused children never come to the attention of authorities.[9] Estimates suggest that between 12 percent[10] and 30 percent[11] of abuse is reported.
- Of reported child sexual abuse approximately, 30 percent is successfully prosecuted.[12]
- One of the first books about child sexual abuse in the United States was written in 1981.[13]

Despite the disagreements and contradictions about when to share and how much to share with children and young people regarding healthy sex (chapter 1), the wide-ranging experimentation and questions about definitions of deviant sexuality (chapter 2), and all the efforts to get clarity around the relevant issues, an unknown number of young people will have their individual sexual "self" formed in undesirable ways at the hands of someone else, without adequate knowledge, awareness, resources, or any ability to understand or discuss what happened or what is happening to them. Gaining a realistic understanding about the dynamics of child sexual abuse and the consequences of that abuse on children and young people through adulthood is an important step in understanding the dynamics of sexual abuse.

This chapter presents current information about child sexual abuse and a review of how children, adolescents, teens, and young adults facing abuse differ in their needs and challenges. While the legal world recognizes childhood ending at the age of 18, more recent brain research suggests the brain continues to develop through the late 20s.[14] Much of the world, including the United States, did not historically recognize childhood as a unique or particularly interesting segment in time where chronological age, biological or physiological age, and social age interconnect in meaningful ways.[15] Consequently, certain statistics presented here reflect the biological focus, rather than the legal cutoff, with some data reflecting issues affecting young people into their 20s.

Research too often comes in the form of conflicting reports and competing definitions. For this reason, the chapter begins with a brief conversation about the difficulties associated with research on child sexual abuse and several important definitions. Attention is given to the vulnerable populations of young people, including runaways, physically abused, or young people facing questions or rejection as a result of sexual identity development. A brief introduction to social conditions and professions at high risk for attracting adults who abuse children, giving specific attention to the need to focus on *behavior*, rather than on physical features of the person and/or that individual's standing in the community. The chapter concludes with a brief overview reviewing the importance of education, awareness, and communication as key components to sexual violence prevention strategies for children and young people. (Additional information on victims/survivors is presented in chapter 14. Detailed research about sexual abuse experiences and statistics in adult populations and throughout the life span is included in chapter 7. Concentrated information about juveniles who commit sex offenses is presented in chapters 9 and 13.)

A NOTE ON SEXUAL ABUSE RESEARCH

Because each research project has a diverse goal or ideal, sometimes, studies on the same subject appear to reflect, and, in fact, *do* reflect, contradictory findings. In fact, some of the most central understandings of child abuse written by **Sigmund Freud** have been soundly challenged to mixed reviews. In the early 1900s, Freud traveled to the United States and introduced the country to the ideas of infantile sexuality, the drama of sexual conflict in the family, the case histories of female patients, and the idea that the sexual instincts permeated human life.[16] Early in his work, Freud put forward the seduction theory, the idea that child sexual abuse caused "hysteria," a Victorian term often used to reflect psychological harm in women. Freud later changed this view inexplicably, suggesting the reports of young girls being molested usually by their fathers were fantasies described in the more popular and well-received **Oedipus complex**.[17] Perhaps the harshest critique along this line is that Freud changed his assessments of his clients' stories to protect his social and political standing after hearing that one of his clients, the daughter of a friend in good social standing, alleged such abuse.[18]

> In 1896, with the publication of two works, *The Aetiology of Hysteria* and *Studies on Hysteria*, he announced that he had solved the mystery of the female neurosis. At the origin of every case of hysteria, Freud asserted, was a childhood sexual trauma. But Freud was never comfortable with this discovery, because of what it implied about the behavior of respectable family men. If his patients' reports were true, incest was not a rare abuse, confined to the poor and the mentally defective, but was endemic to the patriarchal family. Recognizing the implicit challenge to patriarchal values, Freud refused to

identify fathers publicly as sexual aggressors. Though in his private correspondence he cited "seduction by the father" as the "essential point" in hysteria, he was never able to bring himself to make this statement in public. Scrupulously honest and courageous in other respects, Freud falsified his incest cases. In *The Aetiology of Hysteria*, Freud implausibly identified governesses, nurses, maids, and children of both sexes as the offenders. In *Studies in Hysteria*, he managed to name an uncle as the seducer in two cases. Many years later, Freud acknowledged that the "uncles" who had molested Rosalia and Katharina were in fact their fathers. Though he had shown little reluctance to shock prudish sensibilities in other matters, Freud claimed that "discretion" had led him to suppress this essential information.[19]

Famous psychologists, including Carl Jung and Eric Erikson, reviewed the case studies in which Freud reported on his findings of his studies on hysteria, which were largely linked to the patient he referred to as "Dora."[20] Significant challenges to Freud's assertions would come during the 1960s through the 1980s, a period focused on women's and children's rights, also known as **second-wave feminism**. The researchers' ability to restrict themselves to an objective reading of the "facts" has been handily challenged, and there are many more examples. The American Psychological Association found itself embroiled in a controversy over the findings of the **Rind et al. study** in 1998, reporting (among other things) the effects of self-reported harm suggested that child sexual abuse was not always negative for the child.[21] Popular at the time, radio talk host Dr. Laura (Schlesinger) exploded the controversy wide open, and a first-ever condemnation of the research by both houses of Congress (July 1999)[22] was the result of the extensive social outcry. Although the central theme of their study was confirmed by other researchers,[23] the initial article was heavily critiqued for various methodological concerns and coupled with assertions that the authors were attaching themselves to groups known to be "pro-pedophilia."[24]

These are two among many of the more controversial psychological studies focused on efforts to better understand child sexual abuse, perpetrators, and the effects on victims. In spite of the professional disagreements regarding the research findings, the effect of these controversial findings on the existing and future research in the field is also of critical importance. The need to read diverse and varied studies as well as to understand research methods and related questions and critiques is evident. To ensure a broader understanding of the essential, relevant variables for future analysis related to the study of the human mind and social interactions, the need for caution and critical reflection remains.

Research Limitations and Liabilities

Historical attitudes and ideas infiltrate efforts to interpret data and, as discussed throughout various segments of the book, the issue of whether humans can truly be objective in how they view the world has been soundly challenged and continues to be routinely called into question. **Dr. Jim Hopper**'s website on child abuse is extremely thorough, but one of the more interesting aspects of the page is less about the fact that he is a clinical instructor at Harvard

Table 3.1   What Is Child Sexual Abuse?

At the extreme end of the spectrum, sexual abuse includes sexual intercourse or its deviations. Yet all offenses that involve sexually touching a child, including nontouching offenses and sexual exploitation, can be just as harmful and devastating to a child's well-being.

Touching sexual offenses include:	Nontouching sexual offenses include:	Sexual exploitation includes:
• Fondling • Making a child touch an adult's sexual organs • Penetrating a child's vagina or anus no matter how slight with a penis or any object that doesn't have a valid medical purpose	• Engaging in indecent exposure or exhibitionism • Exposing children to pornographic material • Deliberately exposing a child to the act of sexual intercourse • Masturbating in front of a child	• Engaging a child or soliciting a child for the purposes of prostitution • Using a child to film, photograph, or model pornography

These definitions are broad. In most states, the legal definition of child sexual abuse or exploitation is an act of a person—adult or child—who forces, coerces, or threatens a child to have any form of sexual conduct or simulation or rape or other forms of sexual exploitation with children.[1]

1 "Definitions of Child Abuse and Neglect," Child Welfare Information Gateway, accessed November 26, 2019, https://www.childwelfare.gov/pubPDFs/define.pdf.

Medical School and more about the fact that the entire conversation on child abuse begins with an easy-to-understand explanation of how research findings can be difficult to understand and interpret (see Table 3.1, and check out his website at www.jimhopper.com).

One of the most important things to understand about social science research is just exactly how humbling it is to work in the field of social research. Great researchers have been known to say, "I have been studying for years and I know so little." Few social science researchers are certain about their topic when they start, and while, it is possible to gain a sense of the field, it is often the case that acquiring a "full" understanding feels impossible because every research question addressed often invites more questions, rather than providing definitive answers.

Term Descriptions and Distinctions

Without question the condition of the human body changes at a remarkable pace between birth and puberty. As different as an infant is from a toddler, a "child" is different from a "tween," preteen, or adolescent, and a teen is different from an adult. Conversations about child sexual abuse collectively focus on the need to make sure children and young people are safe from harm. These same safety goals get convoluted when the term *child* is used to refer to a 3-year-old and a 15-year-old. The questions a 3-year-old would have about their body would be very different than questions a 15-year-old would have about their body, feelings, relationships, and the possibility of dating. Part of the controversy identified in defining "healthy sex" includes questions intent on better understanding the developmental needs of children as they transition through childhood and into the age of majority. Sexual abuse affects children in disproportionate ways, without provocation, and sometimes without a full awareness on the part of the child that they are being abused or exploited for another's purposes. Before moving on to the broader discussion of abuse, attention is given to the importance of clarifying the definitions of "child" and "sexual abuse."

Defining "Child"

The law defines a child as anyone under the age of 18. As discussed in chapter 2 with regard to the age of consent, the issue of age and sex is not so clearly delineated. Today, as was discussed, the age of consent in all US states is between 16 and 18. It was not long ago, however, that children married as early as 12 and 14 in the United States. While no longer customary, it is still legal in the United States for a child to marry before the age of 18 "with parental consent and/or under religious or customary law."[25] Kansas, which had no restrictions on marriage age with parental or judicial approval as recently as 2006, set a prohibition against marriage before the age of 15. Georgia also set the state's minimum marriage age to 16 that same year.[26] Although clear about the age selected for marriage, the first sentence in the article is "Kansas may have seen the last of its child brides." Although finding a place within the legal structure, researchers and mental health experts continue to study the effects of early sexual debut on people who meet a legal definition for marriage but who are still younger than the legal age of adulthood. (More on child brides in the United States and globally is discussed in chapter 6.)

Discussion specifically focused on "child prostitution" suggests that distinctions need to be made between the language of "child" and "youth," identifying the framing of child prostitution as counterproductive for young people who are constituted as subjects by an infantilizing discourse that positions them as prostitutes, not as victims of prostitution.[27] The use of the term "child prostitute" has also been recently challenged because it is a crime to have sex with a child. Therefore, the term "sexually trafficked child" has been adopted by frontline professionals as a more realistic term for describing what is occurring because a child is not able to be compliant in their own victimization.[28] Research is also focused on better understanding the effect of child sexual abuse on children of different ages. For example, a toddler will likely not have the capacity to understand or the vocabulary to explain what abuse is and how to talk about it, but, even if they are too young to understand being abused, physical and/or psychological implications from the abuse may result. (More on victimization is in chapter 14.)

For years, juvenile courts and child welfare agencies have used the well-known "best interest of the child" standard for assessing appropriate system response to the needs of young people. Based in the idea of *parens patriae*, the court and appointed agents are to engage the child as a kindly parent. Juvenile courts and other service providers for young people seem to be reflecting a new trend, referred to as "the adulteration of youth crime," and, in court processes, young people are treated as adults.[29] In sex-related cases, young people are increasingly being treated and sanctioned as adults. In perhaps one of the most famous, if not extreme, cases, in 1944 George Stinney, a 14-year-old black boy, was accused of murdering two white girls, ages 11 and 8. In what was believed to have been a coerced confession, he was said to have admitted to wanting to have sex with the older girl. Pronounced innocent seventy years after his execution in December of

2014, a judge reviewing the case announced that he was not guilty, pointing to various violations of due process and determining he had been unfairly convicted by the all-male, all-white jury.[30] How young is too young for a person to consent to having sex? How young is too young for an offender to be prosecuted? Questions about the age appropriateness of sexually active young people are a large part of this dynamic, regarding efforts to regulate the actions of teens and older people who hurt children. (Chapter 10 has more on laws and policies.)

Defining "Sexual Abuse"

Definitions of sexual abuse vary, socially and legally. A relatively common definition is "any sexual activity involving a child where the consent is not or cannot be given."[31] The American Psychological Association defines sexual abuse as any "unwanted sexual activity, with perpetrators using force, making threats or taking advantage of victims not able to give consent."[32] "Older children," distinguished as age 12 and up, were identified to be at greater risk than younger children.[33] Issues associated with the sociopolitical and legal definitions of child sexual abuse are not new; in fact, in 1986 the focus on terms was described as having an effect on the way research was collected and tabulated, which affected findings and incidents reported.[34] Sexual abuse can happen between adults and children, an older teen and a younger child, or minors who agree to have sex but are younger than the age of consent. Distinctions about how age plays a part in definitions of abuse are critical for reflecting on the research and policy intended to regulate and respond to victims as well as individuals accused of sexual offenses. See Table 3.2 for more on child sexual abuse.

Table 3.2   Inappropriate Sexual Behavior Scale

1	2	3	4	5
Sexualized Expression	Cooperative Sexualized Expression	Emotional Abuse of Sexualized Nature	Emotionally Coercive Sexual Abuse	Physically Coercive Sexual Abuse
Sex writing Sex drawing "Dirty" talk Masturbation Childish sex calls	Mutually consenting sex games Curious exploration	Exhibitionism Voyeurism Obscene calls Frottage	Premeditated genital contact with Narcissism Manipulation Thinking errors	Forcible demeaning and/or brutal sexual contact

© David Ziegler

YOUTH AT RISK: CONTEMPORARY CHILD AND ADOLESCENT SEXUAL VICTIMIZATION

An accurate estimate of sexual harm and other child abuse and neglect statistics is difficult to determine because complex data collection and reporting systems come from various agencies and organizations throughout society. Reports come from medical professionals, psychologists, academics, government agencies, and community groups, to name just a few. Narrowing the focus of accessible research sources, as is the case here, does not eliminate the breadth and depth of concern and questions raised on how child abuse, particularly child sexual abuse, is framed and analyzed. Data collected is never as easily replicated and translated to real-life policy responses as individuals and researchers might like. As a result, sexual abuse statistics, like sex offender statistics, are often convoluted and difficult to compare across researcher focus and subject nuance.

Without doubt, children are a vulnerable population. While some children who suffer harm are able to have other positive and nurturing relationships, a lack of resources can make children and young people vulnerable in ways that increase the likelihood of their exploitation. Further, various laws and policies are being designed in an effort to address the growing and evolving needs of children.

PHYSICAL VIOLENCE, ABUSE, AND NEGLECT

Violent crime in general suggests juveniles ages 12 to 17 experience victimization in nonfatal violence at a rate two and a half times greater than adults do.[35] Youth experiencing physical abuse, sexual abuse, or neglect at home or within the community are affected by another set of risk factors related to making the choice to run away. A total of 26 percent of homeless males and females reported being the victim of sexual abuse in at least one incident.[36] In the same study, researchers found that the vast majority of runaway youth, 82 percent, had experienced physical abuse at least once and many runaway youth had experienced numerous kinds of physical abuse. In a different sample of runaway youth respondents, 60 percent had allegedly experienced physical abuse, 42 percent had experienced emotional abuse, 48 percent had been neglected, and 21 percent disclosed surviving sexual abuse.[37] Street youth ages 12 to 19 were interviewed in three major cities. The rates of abuse were high in this study as well. Seventy percent of the females reported being sexually abused, and 35 percent reported being physically abused. Among males, the rates of sexual abuse were at 24 percent, and 35 percent reported having been physically abused.[38] The relationships between physical violence, sexual abuse, and exploitation require further exploration.

CHILD SEXUAL ABUSE

Conservative estimates on sexual assault suggest that 20 percent of US women and between 5 and 10 percent of US men report being sexually abused in their childhood.[39] The National Study of Missing, Abducted, Runaway and Throwaway Children (NISMART-3) research, conducted in 2013, showed significantly lower rates of missing children than did the 1999 results of the same study.[40] These results indicate a rate of 4.6 children per 1,000 were directly affected by a sexual offense in that one calendar year in the 1999 study.[41] Depending on the population studied and definitions used, 2 to 62 percent of woman and 3 to 16 percent of men will be identified as victims of child sexual abuse.[42] In fact, among females, almost 30 percent of all forcible rapes occur before the age of 11 years, and another 32 percent occur between the ages of 11 and 17.[43]

Roughly one-third of offenses were reported to law enforcement. (See more about police response in chapter 11.) Though all genders are affected, boys are less likely to report sexual abuse than girls, so the numbers in reference to male survivors could be higher than reported.[44] With the low reporting percentages illustrated here, it is easy to see why the reported numbers vary depending on the report and the definition of terms used by the researcher. The US Department of Health and Human Services compiled a list of the possible consequences of child sexual abuse on the victims. Children who are sexually abused may come to believe the world is not safe and adults cannot be trusted, but, depending on resiliency factors and support from nonoffending caregivers, children are not all affected in the same way. See the main points presented in Text Box 3.1.

Text Box 3.1. Factors Affecting the Impact of Sexual Abuse

Some factors that can affect the impact of child sexual abuse include:

- The relationship of the abuser to the child and how much of the abuse caused a betrayal of trust
- The abuser's use of friendliness or seduction
- The abuser's use of threats of harm or violence, including threats to pets, siblings, or parents
- The abuser's use of secrecy
- How long the abuse occurred
- Gender of the abuser being the same as or different from the child
- The age (developmental level) of the child at the time of the abuse (younger children are more vulnerable)
- The child's emotional development at the time of the abuse
- The child's ability to cope with their emotional and physical responses to the abuse (for example, fear and arousal)
- How much responsibility the child feels for the abuse

Note: The family's immediate response to learning about the sexual abuse and ongoing acceptance of what the child reveals play a critical role in the child's ability to recover and return to a healthy life.[1]

Note

1. "Parenting a Child or Youth Who Has Been Sexually Abused: A Guide for Foster and Adoptive Parents," US Department of Health and Human Services, December 2018, accessed September 3, 2019, https://www.childwelfare.gov/pubPDFs/f_abused.pdf.

Extrafamilial and Intrafamilial Sexual Abuse (Incest)

Sexual contact between people of the same family is commonly understood and defined to be **incest**. The definition has been expanded, however, to include people who act sexually toward someone for whom they are designated as caretaker.[45] Incest is identified as one of the most damaging types of sexual abuse due to the breach of trust that happens because the abuse is perpetrated by individuals on whom the victim trusts and depends. In addition, support can also be lacking and pressure to keep silent powerful because fear of the family breaking up can be overwhelming to the victim of abuse as well as other family members.[46] Adults who were incestuously victimized as a child by adults often suffer from low self-esteem, difficulties in interpersonal relationships, and sexual dysfunction. They are at an extremely high risk of many mental health disorders, including depression, anxiety, phobic avoidance reactions, substance abuse, borderline personality disorder, and posttraumatic stress disorder.[47] Father–daughter and stepfather–daughter incest is most commonly reported, with most of the remaining reports consisting of mother–daughter, stepmother–daughter, mother–son, or stepmother–son incest. Prevalence of parental child sexual abuse is difficult to assess due to secrecy and privacy; some estimates show 20 million Americans have been victimized as children by parental incest.[48]

A long-standing history of blaming the victim is a hallmark of sexual abuse, and sexual abuse within families is no different. Certainly, aspects of blaming the victim have been associated with Freud's work, discussed earlier, in which he denied sexual abuse and asserted instead that such stories expressed sexual fantasies about older father figures. Thankfully, the cultural tide is shifting as professionals, parents, and children are taught that the responsibility for the abuse lies with the abuser and not with the person being harmed.

Incest abuse can lead to **traumatic bonding**, which is "a form of relatedness in which one person mistreats the other with abuse, threats, intimidation, beatings, humiliations and harassment but also provides attention, some form of affection, and connectedness."[49] In other words, coming forward to tell is complicated by the fact that there are parts of the relationship the child may feel like they need and want to keep. Losing the attention and affection that appear to be separate from the abuse can feel like a threat or a potential void not worth the risk. There is also the very real concern the report may not be acted on due to, for example, denial, family shame, or fear of how it will change the family's living situation.

The responsibility to advocate for safety from a relative is a large burden to place on a child's or teenager's shoulders. In cases of abuse, only about 30 percent of survivors reveal their abusive situations; the other cases are either spotted by an eyewitness or inferred from vague comments.[50] A child living in a home where incest is the norm may never hear personal safety messages like "you are special and deserve to be safe" and "keep telling until someone believes you." Sadly, 51.9 percent of those who reported mistreatment to a parent were still being abused a year after the disclosure.[51] Incest occurs under a veil of secrecy and shame. Even after the veil is lifted, the abuse continues more than half of the time. The attention and affection trap can be very confusing and traumatic when positive attention is inextricably tied to the harm of sexual abuse and the person who is charged with keeping the child safe is the one perpetrating or ignoring the harm.

Sex Trafficking, Kidnapping, and Commercial Exploitation

Youth who have already been victimized may turn to **survival sex**, which means selling sex to meet basic needs, such as shelter, money, food, or drugs, as one way of survival. In one survey, it was determined that approximately 28 percent of street youths and 10 percent of shelter youths reported having engaged in survival sex.[52] This same study points out the dangers inherent in survival sex that "[m]ake it among the most damaging repercussions of homelessness among youths." In one study of homeless youth it was reported:

> The sample had a high prevalence of several mental disorders, including conduct disorder with aggression, major depression, and alcohol and drug abuse. Almost half had attempted suicide. Nearly all the adolescents were sexually active; about a third had more than ten partners in the previous year. About a third reported trading sex for money, food, or drugs. Although most had basic knowledge of HIV transmission and used some form of birth control, little more than half had used a condom in the most recent sexual encounter, and 18 percent reported sex with intravenous drug users.[53]

Suicide attempts are also present among the populations of runaway and homeless youth.

According to Molnar's survey of runaway and homeless youth:

> Forty-eight percent of the females and twenty-seven percent of the males had attempted suicide. The mean number of suicide attempts was 6.2 ($SD = 12.9$) for females and 5.1 for males ($SD = 7.6$). Sexual and physical abuse before leaving home were independent predictors of suicide attempts for females and males.[54]

The sexual and mental health of young people on the run is a serious concern. Some of these children are sexually exploited commercially because sex acts are bought and sold like a product. Because children cannot legally consent to sexual activity, the term **commercially sexually exploited child** more accurately represents what is happening to children through pimps, organized crime, and gang-initiated sexual assault for financial gain. Laws are beginning to reflect this change in attitude. In 2008, New York was among the first states to pass **safe harbor laws**, which protect children who are forced into illegal activities by treating them as victims, rather than as criminals. Connecticut, Illinois, Minnesota, and Washington followed in 2010. In June 2010, the Texas Supreme Court prohibited prosecuting prostituted minors. Since then, Vermont, Massachusetts, Florida, New Jersey, Tennessee, and Nebraska have passed legislation that makes children immune from prosecution.[55]

Children are brought into these conditions at a young age. The Paul and Lisa Program is a nonprofit agency working with children who are being commercially sexually exploited in New York City. Two of the employees reported the average age of a child being exploited commercially has decreased from 14 to 13 or even 12 in recent years.[56] The age at which children are first exploited can vary greatly, with different kinds of sex crimes occurring at different ages as reflected in this detailed risk-assessment report of commercially exploited youth.

> In general, organized crime units tend not to be involved with children younger than 9 years of age—not out of a sense of morality but because such young children are "too difficult" or "too hot" to handle. The exception to this pattern is the use of very young children as subjects of pornography—particularly if the children are foreign born. Our informants have denied using children under the age of 10 years as prostitutes, albeit some cases involving very young children have been identified by the public media.[57]

Children and youth living on the streets as runaways or being commercially exploited rarely have someone to advocate for their basic needs. Commercial exploitation of children has been compared to modern-day slavery because children are bought, sold, and traded for the highest price.

RUNNING AWAY AND OTHER MARKERS
OF VULNERABLE YOUNG PEOPLE

A **status offense** is a charge for conduct that is not a crime if it is committed by an adult.[58] Examples include running away, truancy, ungovernability or incorrigibility, violating curfew, and underage drinking, but sex can also be a factor. In a 2007 report, the American Bar Association identified over 400,000 youth arrested or held in limited custody by police because of a status offense.[59] Risk factors common to youth can affect their sexual health. One primary example is being a runaway. The national estimates of runaway and homeless youth run between 500,000 and 2.8 million.[60] Six percent of America's youth have self-reported as having run away within the past twelve months.[61] Runaway youth are a high-risk population that faces serious challenges, including a likelihood of sexual victimization. In gaining an understanding for the risks of the runaway youth population, the work to prevent the behavior is framed in the facts, which provide an accurate picture of the population at risk for crime and health concerns.

Runaway youth are often defined as adolescents who have left home for at least twenty-four hours without permission from a parent or guardian.[62] Most youth who run away are not gone for a long period of time. In fact, over 90 percent of runaways come home within a month, and more than 99 percent return within a year.[63] Not all youth, however, return home quickly. In a study done in the Hollywood area of Los Angeles, homeless teens were interviewed to determine the length of time this population had lived on the street. In this sample, the mean length of time for an adolescent youth to be homeless was 440 days, and the median response was 201 days.[64] More youths than adults end up in a situation where they are living on the streets. "The prevalence of youth home-lessness for a one-year period (measured as a percent of youth who experienced at least one night of homelessness in the last twelve months) is higher than the prevalence of adult homelessness for a five-year period."[65]

Nationally, females are more likely than males to run away.[66] The age group most at risk to run are youths ages 15 to 16 years old.[67] The National Runaway Safeline call statistics support the previously mentioned studies. Call data from the NRS showed that 74 percent of crisis callers under the age of 18 were female, whereas 26 percent were male. This same data reflects that the age of the youths most often calling in crisis are 15 to 17 years old at a rate of 59 percent.[68] Additional figures corroborate these findings that the majority of runaway youths were female between the ages of 15 and 16.[69]

Sexual Orientation

As stated previously, being rejected by family because of sexual identity issues can be one reason young people run away from home. In fact, in some states, young people who are below the age of consent and caught engaging in sexual activity with a same-sex partner are treated differently than heterosexual couples, with the penalties of jail time looming larger because some state Romeo and Juliet provisions are written to apply only to heterosexual couples.[70] More about the LGBTQI community is presented in chapter 5, but it is critical to note here that school climate surveys indicate that as many as nine out of ten LGBTQI students are harassed regularly in their routine at school.[71] One of the well-known and respected groups working to address the cultural discrimination and harassment of gay youths is the Trevor Project (www.trevorproject.org), a nonprofit organization that was originally formed to help prevent suicides among gay youths, which are estimated to be between two to seven times more likely than for straight youths.[72]

Statutory Rape

Statutory rape was introduced in chapter 2, but it is important to understand statutory rape from the perspective of both the offender and the victim. A divided Supreme Judicial Court ruled on a Massachusetts case where a 14-year-old boy was charged with statutory rape, but the three girls involved (two 12-year-olds and one 11-year-old) were not arrested under the same charge. The attorney in the case, Janice Bassil, said the law is clearly intending to protect all children under the age of 16. "You can't be the perpetrator and the victim, too." The dissenting opinion of the court focused on claims that the boy was a football player in high school, whereas the girls were still in elementary school. The boy was older, and there were claims that he sometimes pressured the girls into having sex. Meanwhile, the boy was expelled from school as a result of the charges.[73]

Sexting

Technology changes provide new challenges in promoting what is healthy. As young people adapt to new tools, they can make concerning and, sometimes, even harmful choices. The use of cell phones among young people continues to climb. Seventy-three percent of teens have access to a smartphone.[74] Fifty percent of teens feel they are addicted to their mobile devices, and 78 percent of teenagers check their phones once an hour.[75] Although most teens report more positive than negative experiences online,[76] the temptation to use technology for misplaced attention or affection can be a strong pull.

In addition to texting messages, teens can also text photos. **Sexting** is a term invented by the media that is believed to have first appeared in a British newspaper called *Sunday Telegraph Magazine* in 2005[77] and is now commonly used to refer to the sending or receiving of sexually explicit images electronically, usually via cell phones. How many teenagers are engaging in sending and receiving sexual images? One survey from 2012 had 18-year-olds self-report sexting behavior. Thirty percent of subjects stated that, yes, they had sent nude pictures at some point during the four years of high school and 45 percent said that they had received such pictures on their cell phones.[78] Even more telling, the most important motivation for sexting revealed in this study was pressure or coercion. In a different study from 2014, undergraduate students recruited from a large northeastern university completed an anonymous online survey concerning their engagement in sexting as minors.[79] These college students self-reported that 28 percent of them had sent photographic sexts while a minor. Interestingly, the majority of students (61 percent) were not aware that sending texts could be considered child pornography. In this same study, 59 percent of respondents reported that knowledge of legal consequences "would have" or "probably would have" deterred them from sexting.

Young people receive pressure from partners, crushes, and our culture to respond to attraction using cell phones as tools. "Teenagers' tendency toward exhibitionism and narcissism, their desire for intimacy in relationships, their desire and preoccupation with sexual exploration, and the hope of creating their identities as individuals who are attractive and desired may make them more vulnerable to the allure of sexting."[80]

A Legal Response

Although sexting is a relatively recent phenomenon, it has risen to a prominent place in social consciousness in large part because of the criminal justice system response. Sexting provides a legal challenge for courts and lawmakers struggling to determine what kind of punishment fits the crime.

Clearly, sending out sexual images of children is illegal. Federal law (18 U.S.C. § 2256) defines child pornography as "any visual depiction, including any photograph, film, video, picture, or computer or, other means, of sexually explicit conduct, where

- the production of the visual depiction involves the use of a minor engaging in sexually explicit conduct; or
- the visual depiction is a digital image, computer image, or computer-generated image that is, or is indistinguishable from, that of a minor engaging in sexually explicit conduct; or
- the visual depiction has been created, adapted, or modified to appear that an identifiable minor is engaging in sexually explicit conduct."

Text Box 3.2.   When Do Prosecutors File Charges in Sexting Cases?[1]

In a survey of 236 prosecutors handling sexting cases:

- Fifty-nine percent said that all (37 percent) or nearly all (22 percent) of their cases ended with *no* charges.
- Twenty-one percent said that most (7 percent) or all (14 percent) of their cases ended with charges filed. Four main themes prosecutors would file charges:

  1. Malicious intent/bullying/coercion or harassment (36 percent)
  2. Distribution (25 percent)
  3. Large age difference involved (22 percent)
  4. Graphic nature of the images (9 percent)

Note

1. Wendy Walsh, Janis Wolak, and David Finkelhor, "Sexting: When Are State Prosecutors Deciding to Prosecute?" The Third National Juvenile Online Victimization Study (NJOV-3), January 2013, http://www.unh.edu/ccrc/pdf/CV294_Walsh_Sexting%20&%20prosecution_2-6-13.pdf.

If a minor engages in sexually explicit conduct on their own cellular device and forwards the image on to their peers, that image can very well be deemed child pornography. Even though different states have different sexual consent ages, under 18 U.S.C. § 2256, the federal law considers individuals under the age of 18 to be children. If the youth in the image is under 18, the sexually explicit image is illegal. This social reality connects the practice of sexting with a possible prosecution for child pornography. A 2011 survey of law enforcement found that 18 percent of cases involving youth-created pornographic images (with no aggravating circumstances) progressed to the point of an arrest.[81] Child pornography laws, indecent exposure laws, and other child protection laws were designed to protect children and teens. It is not surprising then when the public is confused about how those same laws are also used to prosecute children and teens.

Community Response—Prevention

Because these sexting cases are happening around the country with no strong sense of consistency in the charges, trying to understand the laws has parents confused and frustrated. The National Center for Missing and Exploited Children (NCMEC) responded with an online "Policy Statement on Sexting."[82] According to its policy, the NCMEC "does not believe that a blanket policy charging all youth with juvenile or criminal violations will remedy the problem of sexting." NCMEC promotes education about consequences and the use of prosecutorial discretion to help navigate these situations. "A permanent record, juvenile or criminal, for any sex-related charge can have serious lifetime consequences for both the child/youth and parent, so considerable thought should be given before any filing of juvenile or criminal charges."[83] With coercion being a trend in the

---

Text Box 3.3.   Sexting: Education and Prevention

"If indeed young people are feeling pressure to be involved in sexting, the answer is not in education about the seriousness of legal implications. Rather opportunities should be created for young people to engage in discussions that challenge power dynamics in intimate partner relationships, by learning about sex and relationships from within a sexual ethics framework. The use of video and online educative resources that have received criticism for reinforcing gender stereotypes by shaming the initial producer of the image (usually a girl), could be a useful tool for debating these issues with young people. Furthermore, this study has implications for promotion of the 'bystander approach,' which involves teaching young men to recognize themselves as bystanders to violence against women. Stories shared of boys expressing their concern for the girl in the sexted image highlight the potential benefits of such approaches that involve young men in challenging the attitudes and behaviors of other young men."[1]

Note

1. Shelley Walker, Lena Sanci, and Meredith Temple-Smith, "Sexting: Young Women's and Men's Views on Its Nature and Origins," *Journal of Adolescent Health* 52, no. 6 (2013): 697–701.

---

asking, we would be better served with prevention messages that do not just focus on refusal skills and legal implications but also address the problems with asking someone to do something with sexual intent that is beyond their comfort zone. In other words, instead of focusing on just teaching the "Say No" message, the discussion should address gender dynamics, relationship expectations, consent, and the importance of respecting others enough to not continue to ask.

From a 2017 study that analyzed 462 stories of girls navigating sexting requests, seventy-six young women (31 percent) refused requests for photographs to varying degrees of success; 78.9 percent of the young women who attempted to refuse requests for photographs (N = 60) faced consequences for saying no: young men would reportedly persist in asking for pictures, get angry, or end the relationship. Because of these consequences, six of these young women did end up sending pictures.[84]

In defining sexting and presenting the dangers this behavior poses, it is apparent how much work remains to be done in the area of prevention, especially in discussions around coercion and consent. Additional academic research, focus groups with teenagers, legislative uniformity, and tools for parents and schools will be additional steps society must take to better educate and protect youth.

WHEN ADULTS HARM CHILDREN: FOCUS ON BEHAVIOR

People who harm children comprise a diverse group or population, making it difficult, if not impossible, to identify characteristics or create a type of the offender who might harm a child. This is a critical feature when considering how to prevent abuse and protect a child who reports abuse from further harm.

Assuming a person who is familiar to the child or a parent, someone often seen at the child's school or at the local community center where children go to swim, does not "look like" a child abuser or is not "the kind of person" who would harm a child in fact leaves children and young people vulnerable. (More information about people who perpetrate sexual abuse is offered in section III.) This segment gives specific attention to what is known about adults who harm children. Understanding this information is critical for adults to heighten their own awareness and practice intervention techniques that support kids and young people while also helping children and teens prepare prevention strategies when they find themselves in uncomfortable sexual situations.

Focus on Behavior, Not Relationship

Children have an image of what a dangerous person looks like and may not translate rules about safety to the polite, kind-looking individual who is known to their family. In the Denver Children's Hospital study, it was determined that, of the children seen in one year for sexual abuse, in 82 percent of the cases, the alleged offender was a heterosexual partner of a close relative to the child.[85] Family members are also a population of concern: 27 percent of sex offenses against children were family members with almost half of the offenders abusing children under 6 years of age and 42 percent abusing children ages 6 to 11 years.[86] A recent study indicates that a sex offender works to build trust with children in their circle by saying, "Children have comparatively little choice over whom they associate with, less choice perhaps than any population other than prisoners."[87] One of the main reasons that the nation's leading missing child agency, the NCMEC, no longer subscribes to teaching any kind of "stranger danger" curriculum is because most of the people who harm children sexually are family members or otherwise known to the child.[88] Although catchy, this particular phrase does not protect children from the greatest threat, especially when child molesters work hard to gain the trust of parents and children by putting themselves in the role of a family friend. Similar concerns have been raised about the ability of children to make necessary distinctions, as taught in the Good Touch/Bad Touch campaign, which is argued to give children confusing messages about unhealthy touches that might feel good or be considered "gentle molestation" but that children do not see as inappropriate.[89] Children may not disclose a touch they have been taught as "bad" because they believe that they, too, are bad. Instead of labeling touches, encouraging conversation about all touches, such as "in our family, we talk about touches," would better serve children than their trying to determine on their own what needs intervention.

Education, Awareness, Communication, and Resources

Although humans seem to have a natural aversion to talking about topics related to child sexual abuse, it is important to remove the cloud of secrecy offenders rely on to perpetrate their crimes. It should not be on the shoulders of a child to carry the responsibility for their body safety. A 30-year-old adult working to slowly violate a child's boundaries is nowhere close to a fair fight for a 4-year-old who has just begun to understand that their private parts are private. Adults must be the primary protectors of children. Education and awareness campaigns are important ways to enhance prevention efforts with opportunities for parents and caregivers to receive quality and accurate prevention information.

Similar to the continuums discussed in chapter 2, another continuum designed to help get clear about the kinds of behaviors that begin to cause concern and behaviors adults may want to watch for is worth considering.[90] Not all of the behaviors discussed in the first two categories are explored as inappropriate, but they could be issues of concern in a specific setting.[91]

Research suggests that people who are attracted to children represent a diverse population, also referred to as a **heterogeneous** population, with a variety of motivations and behaviors. (More about the types and behaviors of sex offenders is presented in chapter 7.) The range of abuses details the various kinds of abuse, from noncontact offenses, such as obscene phone calls, to contact offenses, such as fondling. It is important to say, once again, that different types of abuse affect victims differently. An offense that might seem minimal to an outside observer can have a dramatic effect on the victim/survivor. Having said that, different sex crimes are often delineated based on a varied assessment of harm, with, for example, harm involving a weapon being seen as more severe than harm without a weapon. (More on the legal issues regarding sex crimes is discussed in chapter 11.)

Consider the possibility of still another continuum to help explore the range of types of sexual harms, similar to the themes presented in the conversation about assessing deviance, as discussed in chapter 2, or with the continuum of sexual behaviors introduced in the introduction but focused on specific kinds of sexual acts that are identified as criminal within contemporary society. Remember, the effects of child abuse and sexual harms depend on many outside factors, as suggested above, including the duration of the abuse and the relationship of the victim/survivor to the offender. Be prepared to talk about the challenges for the system and the victim/survivor if sexual harm is ranked as being more or less severe.

CHAPTER SUMMARY: SO HOW *ARE* THE CHILDREN?

It is an intriguing question, the idea of thinking about the ways children could be or actually *are* held in the highest of regard in the hearts and minds of a community and then using that as an indicator of the overall health of that community. No matter how much one learns about the patterns of sexual offending behavior, it is impossible to know who might choose to commit an offense against a child. As parents, teachers, church leaders, and concerned community members, the knowledge that children are being targeted or bought and sold for someone else's sexual gratification is a frightening thought. More frightening, perhaps, is the fact that children are more likely to suffer sexual violence from parents; teachers; faith community leaders; and "concerned" community members, such as teachers, family friends, and neighbors.

Without question, this is not the answer anyone hopes for when they ask "How are the children?" When people are used as sexual commodities, their humanity is set aside. Abuse of children and young people happens at all ages and often before they have had the opportunity to develop their own safe networks of support. Arguably the most vulnerable, theirs can be an isolated existence. Their vulnerability, any feelings of isolation and the human desire to belong, make them ideal targets for people who are watching children, looking for and noting absent parents or parents who are overloaded or kids who are estranged from their families and communities. In short, this includes kids from all kinds of families. The idea that an individual works their way into a community in the same way they work their way into the lives, homes, and hearts of a young child highlights the need for all people in the community to be aware of appropriate boundaries with children of all ages. The current modern social reality includes sex offenders of all ages in local schools, communities, and religious groups. Offenders will traditionally look for positions of power and authority with children. Children need to understand their own boundaries, and they need to establish and develop healthy and respectful limits with others, both children and adults. Even with those advantages, not all children will age through their childhood without being harmed physically or sexually. For the child abuse survivor reading this chapter, it is important to remember that healed people heal people. Some of the best advocates in the field of prevention are people who were abused as children and decide that they want to help lead the charge for healthier childhoods for the next generation.

Before you proceed further, go back to the continuum that was presented at the beginning of the chapter in Figure 3.1. The questions were, How impacted are children and young people in the United States who have been affected or influenced by sexual harm and sexual violence? Has your perspective changed at all with regard to the way children and young people are influenced, in this case negatively, by exposure to various aspects of sexualized violence and harm, either directly or indirectly? When you asked your classmates basic questions about how children were affected by the issues presented here, what did they say? What do you and they say now? Referencing the health of children is an essential marker for assessing the social health and policy practice in contemporary America. Another important aspect of the conversation extends its wide reach back into the history of the country and the past practices and attitudes associated with sexual abuse and sexual exploitation. After looking at Text Box 3.4, in section II, focus turns to a series of examples of sexual violence in historical context and up through the current global conversations about gender and sexualized violence and harms.

Text Box 3.4.   Media Messages about Child Sexual Abuse

When considering the issue of sexual crimes and the process of identifying and holding offenders accountable, consider the following questions:

- What is the role for parents?
- What is the role for grandparents?
- What is the role for young adults?
- What is the role for educators?
- What is the role for schools?
- What is the role for community groups?
- What is the role for policy makers?
- What is the role for churches?
- What is the role for experts?
- What is the role for victims?
- What is the role for offenders?

Once you have assessed the role of each person or group listed, consider who or what is missing from the list. Then, think about how media influences how each one comes to understand the topic of sexual expression and sexual harms.

MEDIA-ting the Middle Ground

The US Department of Health and Human Services has an online media toolkit for working with traditional media and social media when the focus is on child welfare. The following is a public service announcement created for National Child Abuse Prevention Month.

A Collection of Sample Public Service Announcements
[30-second public service announcement aimed at building community involvement, including 10-second tag for local organization identity]

Voiceover (20 seconds): By working together as a community, we all can play a part in promoting children's emotional well-being and strengthening families. April is National Child Abuse Prevention Month. During this month and throughout the year, [INSERT ORGANIZATION NAME] is dedicated to supporting families and reducing the risk of child abuse and neglect.

Find out how you can play a part in creating positive change in our community.

Tag (10 seconds): Contact [INSERT LOCAL INFORMATION HERE] today at [INSERT PHONE NUMBER] or go to [INSERT WEBSITE ADDRESS] for more information.

[30-second public service announcement aimed at building parent and caregiver awareness, including 10-second tag for local organization identity]

Voiceover (20 seconds): Being the best parent you can be involves taking steps to strengthen your family and finding support when you need it. Parenting isn't something you have to do alone. When you have the knowledge, skills, and resources you need, you can raise a happy, healthy child. Find out more about activities and programs in your community that support parents and promote healthy families.

Tag (10 seconds): Contact [INSERT LOCAL INFORMATION HERE] today at [INSERT PHONE NUMBER] or go to [INSERT WEBSITE ADDRESS] for more information.[1]

Follow-up:

- How effective are public service announcements in the effort to eliminate child abuse?
- If education is the goal, where else are resources for families available in your community?
- If abuse happens disproportionately within families, where can those being harmed elicit support outside of families?
- With confusing and contradictory messages about sexual health and sexual harm accessible in so many media formats, what are the important considerations that accompany the fact that technology is available to children well before preschool?

Deciding Which Messages We Carry Forward

The *media literacy movement* refers to a collection of educational practices and curriculum resources focused on media literacy. **Media literacy** has been defined as "the ability to access, analyze and evaluate and communicate messages in a wide variety of forms,"[2] and used by a large number of scholars and educators to refer to the process of critically analyzing and learning to create one's own messages in print, audio, video, and multimedia.[3]

At the 1993 Media Literacy National Leadership Conference, five concepts were identified by US educators to be important for analyzing media messages:

1. media messages are constructed
2. media messages are produced within economic, social, political, historical and aesthetic contexts
3. the interpretative meaning-making processes involved in message reception consist of an interaction between the reader, the text and the culture
4. media have unique "languages," characteristics which typify various forms, genres and symbol systems of communication
5. media representations play a role in people's understanding of social reality[4]

Active in the media literacy movement, author and Media Education Foundation Board member Jackson Katz[5] offers the following questions as a vehicle for discussing media more comprehensively:

- Who produces most of the images and stories in mainstream media?
- Whose interests do the producers of media images represent? Do they present a realistic or distorted portrait of people or events?
- What stories about manhood and womanhood do media convey?
- Sex and violence might attract audiences, but what kinds of sex? Whose violence?
- When do media representations merely reflect existing relations of power, and when do they subvert them?

MEDIA MESSAGES SECTION II: How Does History Continue to Shape Modern Understandings of Sexual Harms and Sexualized Violence?

Section overview: The United States has a long history of sexualized violence acted out in a wide variety of social groups and between specific groups of people based on race and social standing, which was often driven by religious ideologies. What do we know about the history of rape within slave communities or as a weapon between indigenous people and the military or settlers of the early United States? How are those stories still with us as we talk about sexual violence and the kinds of harm present in society today? Historical accounts and statistics about sexual violence as it is researched and documented in the contemporary United States close the section.

Myths and Reclamations

When crime theories focus on critiques of the criminal justice system, attention is given at least in part to a seemingly simple question: "Who benefits?" The question is at its most basic a political one: Who benefits from the misrepresentation of social reality or the advancement of a socially distorted if not blatantly inaccurate reflection of crime commission or perpetrators of violence, in this case, particularly, sexualized violence and harm. Consider a few selected themes from section II, and be prepared to discuss, address, or answer the question: "Who benefits?"

Notes

1. US Department of Health and Human Services. Child Welfare Information Gateway: Protecting Children Strengthening Families. Online Media Toolkit. Sample Press Release for National Child Abuse Prevention Month, accessed November 11, 2013, https://www.childwelfare.gov/pubPDFs/NCAPM2019_SamplePSA_English.pdf

2. Renee Hobbs, "The Seven Great Debates in the Media Literacy Movement," *Journal of Communication*, 48, no. 1 (1998): 16, Center for Media Literacy, accessed September 3, 2019, http://www.medialit.org/reading-room/seven-great-debates-media-literacy-movement-circa-2001.

3. Ibid.

4. Ibid., 17–18.

5. Katz, J. 2006. *The Macho Paradox: Why Some Men Hurt Women and How All Men Can Help*. (Sourcebooks, Naperville, IL) p. 251.

KEY TERMS

commercially sexually exploited child
Dr. Jim Hopper
heterogeneous
incest
media literacy
Oedipus complex
parens patriae
Rind et al. study

safe harbor laws
second-wave feminism
sexting
Sigmund Freud
status offense
survival sex
traumatic bonding

REVIEW QUESTIONS

1. Describe how the Masai measure the welfare of the society as a whole. Please outline your support and/or concerns regarding this assessment.

2. Consider the segment on the research. Do a Google search for the definition of "child sexual abuse," and see how many ways this term is defined. Select your top three definitions, and be prepared to discuss the limits and usefulness of these definitions for research.

3. According to Dr. Jim Hopper, in his presentation about the limits of research, what role do emotions and moral commitments play in the reasoning and judgment required to conduct research?

4. The legal implications for sexting can be severe. Identify the possible legal consequences of sexting discussed in the chapter.

5. The chapter talks about incest being one of the most difficult types of sexual harm on many fronts. Why is this, and what are the family dynamics that make it hard to come forward?

DISCUSSION QUESTIONS

1. Why do you think that parents keep going back to "stranger danger" messages even when we know that they do not work?

2. Were you well prepared to advocate for your own needs and boundaries before your first relationship or crush? What might have helped you feel more comfortable?

3. What do you wish you would have known about sex and your body before you were in high school?

4. Looking back, what would you offer a younger brother or sister as advice and counsel for protection against child sexual abuse?

5. When you look at the issue of perpetrators, why do you think it has been easier for people to assess the way a sex offender *looks* rather than the way they *act*? How does this one idea increase a person's power of discernment?

NOTES

1. Frederick Douglass, quoted in Polly Greenberg, "Some Thoughts about Phonics, Feelings, Don Quixote, Diversity, and Democracy: Teaching Young Children to Read, Write, and Spell Part 1," *Young Children* 53, no. 4 (1998), 75.

2. Sitting Bull, quoted in *Indian Affairs Newsletter*, Association on American Indian Affairs, 1994.

3. Michael Gurian, *The Wonder of Girls: Understanding the Hidden Nature of Our Daughters* (Atria/Simon and Schuster, 2002), 179.

4. See, for example, Robert Freeman Longo, *Sexual Abuse in America: The Epidemic of the 21st Century* (Safer Society, 1997), 82; JoAnn Stevelos, "Child Sexual Abuse Declared an Epidemic: World Health Organization Publishes CSA Guidelines," *Psychology Today*, November 29, 2017, https://www.psychologytoday.com/us/blog/children-the-table/201711/child-sexual-abuse-declared-epidemic.

5. "Soul Murder," *Urban Dictionary*, accessed June 27, 2015, http://www.urbandictionary.com/define.php?term=Soul%20Murder; see also Leonard Shengold, *Soul Murder: The Effects of Childhood Abuse and Deprivation* (New York: Random House, 1991).

6. Marije Stoltenborgh, Marian J. Bakermans-Kranenburg, Lenneke R. A. Alin, and Marinus H. van IJzendoorn, "The Prevalence of Child Maltreatment across the Globe," *Child Abuse Review* 24, no. 1 (2015): 37–50, https://doi.org/10.1002/car.2353; Jean Renvoize, *Innocence Destroyed: A Study of Child Sexual Abuse* (London: Routledge, 2017); David Finkelhor, Anne Shattuck, Heather A. Turner, and Sherry L. Hamby, "The Lifetime Prevalence of Child Sexual Abuse and Sexual Assault Assessed in Late Adolescence," *Journal of Adolescent Health* 55, no. 3 (2014): 329–33, https://doi.org/10.1016/j.jadohealth.2013.12.026; Jim Hopper, "Child Abuse: Statistics, Research, and Resources," Jimhopper.com, last modified January 22, 2015, accessed June 29, 2015, http://www.jimhopper.com/abstats/.

7. "Children and Teens: Statistics," RAINN, accessed September 1, 2019, https://www.rainn.org/statistics/children-and-teens.

8. Emily M. Douglas and David Finkelhor, "Childhood Sexual Abuse Fact Sheet," accessed September 1, 2019, http://unh.edu/ccrc/factsheet/pdf/CSA-FS20.pdf.

9. Hopper, "Child Abuse."

10. Rochelle F. Hanson et al., "Factors Related to the Reporting of Childhood Rape," *Child Abuse & Neglect* 23, no. 6 (1999): 559–69, https://doi.org/10.1016/S0145-2134(99)00028-9.

11. David Finkelhor, *Childhood Victimization: Violence, Crime, and Abuse in the Lives of Young People* (New York: Oxford University Press, 2008).

12. Ibid.

13. Judith Lewis Herman, *Father-Daughter Incest* (Cambridge, MA: Harvard University Press, 1981).

14. Much is out about this now. See, for example, Catherine Lebel and Christian Beaulieu, "Longitudinal Development of Human Brain Wiring Continues from Childhood into Adulthood," *Journal of Neuroscience* 31, no. 30 (2011): 10937–47.

15. Harry Hendricks, "Constructions and Reconstructions of British Childhood: An Interpretive Survey, 1800 to the Present," in *Constructing and Reconstructing Childhood: Contemporary Issues in the Sociological Study of Childhood*, 2nd ed., ed. Allison James and Alan Prout (London: Falmer Press, 1997), 33–60.

16. John D'Emilio and Estelle B. Freeman, *Intimate Matters: A History of Sexuality in America* (Chicago: University of Chicago Press, 1998).

17. Jeffrey Moussaieff Masson, *The Assault on Truth: Freud's Suppression of the Seduction Theory* (New York: Ballantine Books, 2003); Herman, *Father-Daughter Incest*; Florence Rush, *The Best Kept Secret: Sexual Abuse of Children* (Upper Saddle River, NJ: Prentice Hall, 1980).

18. For more on hysteria, see, for example, Elizabeth Lunbeck, "Hysteria: Revolt of the 'Good Girl,'" in *American Sexual Histories*, 2nd ed., ed. Elizabeth Reis (Malden, MA: Blackwell Publishing, 2001), 211–29. For more on the feminist critique of Freud, see, for

example, Juliet Mitchell, *Psychoanalysis and Feminism: A Radical Reassessment of Freudian Psychoanalysis* (London: Penguin Books, 2000); and Kate Millett, *Sexual Politics* (New York: Doubleday, 1970).

19. Herman, *Father-Daughter Incest*, 9–10.

20. See, for example, Charles Bernheimer and Claire Kahane, *In Dora's Case: Freud-Hysteria-Feminism* (New York: Columbia University Press, 1990).

21. Bruce Rind, Philip Tromovitch, and Robert Bauserman, "A Meta-Analytic Examination of Assumed Properties of Child Sexual Abuse Using College Samples," *Psychological Bulletin* 123, no. 1 (1998): 22–53.

22. H.Con.Res. 107, "Expressing the sense of Congress rejecting the conclusions of a recent article published by the American Psychological Association that suggests that sexual relationships between adults and children might be positive for children," 106th Congress, July 12, 1999, Congress.gov, accessed September 1, 2019, https://www.congress.gov/bill/106th-congress/house-concurrent-resolution/107.

23. Heather M. Ulrich, Mickey Randolph, and Shawn Acheson, "Child Sexual Abuse: A Replication of the Meta-Analytic Examination of Child Sexual Abuse by Rind, Tromovitch, and Bauserman (1998)," *The Scientific Review of Mental Health Practice: Objective Investigations of Controversial and Unorthodox Claims in Clinical Psychology, Psychiatry, and Social Work* 4, no. 2 (2005–2006): 37–51.

24. Much has been written about this event, but see, for example, Anna Salter, *Predators: Pedophiles, Rapists, and Other Sex Offenders* (Cambridge, MA: Basic Books, 2003), 63–65.

25. Olga Khazan, "A Strange Map of the World's Child-Marriage Laws: When It Comes to Statutes Prohibiting Minors from Getting Married, the U.S. is More Like Latin America than Europe," *The Atlantic*, March 9, 2015, accessed June 27, 2015, http://www.theatlantic.com/international/archive/2015/03/child-marriage-map/387214/.

26. Associated Press, "Kansas Lawmakers Set Minimum Marriage Age to 15," *Fox News*, May 5, 2006, accessed June 29, 2015, https://www.foxnews.com/story/kansas-lawmakers-set-minimum-marriage-age-to-15. See also Daniel C. Vock, "Lawmakers Set New Ages for Marriage," *PEW*, June 1, 2006, accessed June 29, 2015, http://www.pewtrusts.org/en/research-and-analysis/blogs/stateline/2006/06/01/lawmakers-set-new-ages-for-marriage.

27. Lyvinia Rogers Elleschild, "Why Do 'Young People' Go Missing in 'Child Prostitution' Reform?," in *Sex As Crime?*, ed. Gayle Letherby, Kate Williams, Philip Birch, and Maureen E. Cain (New York: Routledge, 2011), 199–219.

28. Heather Montgomery, "Defining Child Trafficking and Child Prostitution: The Case of Thailand," *Seattle Journal for Social Justice* 9, no. 2 (2011): 775–811. See also Wendi J. Adelson, "Child Prostitute or Victim of Trafficking?," *University of St. Thomas Law Journal* 6, no. 1 (2008): 96–128.

29. John Muncie, "Adulteration," in *Dictionary of Youth Justice*, ed. Barry Goldson (Cullompton, Devon: Willan Publishing, 2008), 21.

Theoretical Criminologist John Muncie defines adulteration: "The unraveling of those processes of youth justice that were based on the recognition that children and young people should be dealt with separately and differently from adult offenders, in recognition of age-related differences in levels of capacity, competence, responsibility, and maturity."

30. Bill Chappell, "S.C. Judge Says 1944 Execution of 14-Year-Old Boy Was Wrong," *NPR*, December 17, 2014, accessed June 30, 2015, http://www.npr.org/sections/thetwo-way/2014/12/17/371534533/s-c-judge-says-boy-14-shouldn-t-have-been-executed.

31. Renee Z. Dominguez, Connie F. Nelke, and Bruce D. Perry, "Child Sexual Abuse," in *Encyclopedia of Crime and Punishment*, ed. David Levinson (Thousand Oaks, CA: Sage Publications, 2002), 202–207, accessed June 27, 2015, http://www.geocities.ws/ouclasses/ChildSexualAbuse.doc.

32. Alan E. Kazdin, *Encyclopedia of Psychology* (Washington, DC: American Psychological Association, 2000), 132.

33. "Understanding Child Sexual Abuse," American Psychological Association, December 2011, accessed June 27, 2015, http://www.apa.org/pi/about/newsletter/2011/12/sexual-abuse .aspx.

34. Gail Elizabeth Wyatt and Stefanie Doyle Peters, "Issues in the Definition of Child Sexual Abuse in Prevalence Research," *Child Abuse & Neglect* 10, no. 2 (1986): 231–40.

35. Katrina Baum, "National Crime Victimization Survey: Juvenile Victimization and Offending, 1993–2003," *Department of Justice*, August 2005, 1, accessed June 27, 2015, http://www.bjs.gov/content/pub/pdf/jvo03.pdf.

36. Kimberly Tyler et al., "Risk Factors for Sexual Victimization among Male and Female Homeless and Runaway Youth," *Journal of Interpersonal Violence* 19, no. 5 (2004): 503–20.

37. Jane Powers, John Eckenrode, and Barbara Jaklitsch, "Maltreatment among Runaway and Homeless Youth," *Child Abuse & Neglect* 14, no. 1 (1990): 87–98.

38. Beth Molnar et al., "Suicidal Behavior and Sexual/Physical Abuse among Street Youth," *Child Abuse & Neglect* 22, no. 3 (1998) 213–22.

39. D. Finkelhor, "Current Information on the Scope and Nature of Child Sexual Abuse," *The Future of Children*, Summer/Fall 1994: 31, http://www.unh.edu/ccrc/pdf/VS75.pdf.

40. Andrea J. Sedlak, David Finkelhor, and J. Michael Brick, "National Estimates of Missing Children: Updated Findings from a Survey of Parents and Other Primary Caretakers," June 2017, accessed September 2, 2019, https://www.ojjdp.gov/pubs/250089.pdf.

41. David Finkelhor, Heather Hammer, and Andrea J. Sedlak, "Sexually Assaulted Children: National Estimates and Characteristics," Department of Justice, August 2008, 2, accessed June 27, 2015, https://www.ncjrs.gov/pdffiles1/ojjdp/214383.pdf.

42. Charles Felzen Johnson, "Child Sexual Abuse," *The Lancet* 364, no. 9432 (2004): 462–70.

43. Dominguez, Nelke, and Perry, "Child Sexual Abuse."

44. Rochelle F. Hanson et al., "Correlates of Adolescent Reports of Sexual Assault: Findings from the National Survey of Adolescents," *Child Maltreatment* 8, no. 4 (2003): 266.

45. E. Sue Blume, *Secret Survivors: Uncovering Incest and Its Aftereffects in Women* (New York: Ballantine Books, 1998), 2.

46. Ibid.

47. Christine A. Courtois, *Healing the Incest Wound: Adult Survivors in Therapy* (New York: W.W. Norton & Company, 1988).

48. Jeffrey S. Turner, *Encyclopedia of Relationships across the Lifespan* (Westport, CT: Greenwood Publishing, 1996), 276.

49. Richard P. Kluft, "Ramifications of Incest," *Psychiatric Times* 27, no. 12 (2011), Modern Medicine Network, accessed September 3, 2019, https://www.psychiatrictimes.com/sexual-offenses/ramifications-incest.

50. Steven J. Collings, Sacha Griffiths, and Mandisa Kumalo, "Patterns of Disclosure in Child Sexual Abuse," *South African Journal of Psychology* 35, no. 2 (2005): 270–85.

51. Thomas A. Roesler and Tiffany Weissmann Wind, "Telling the Secret: Adult Women Describe Their Disclosures of Incest," *Journal of Interpersonal Violence* 9, no. 3 (1994): 327–38.

52. Jody M. Greene, Susan T. Ennett, and Christopher L. Ringwalt, "Prevalence and Correlates of Survival Sex among Runaway and Homeless Youth," *American Journal of Public Health* 89, no. 9 (1999): 1406–409.

53. M. Greenblatt, "The Prevalence of Psychotic Symptoms in Homeless Adolescents," *Journal of American Academy of Child and Adolescent Psychiatry* 29, no. 5 (1990): 724–31.

54. Molnar et al., "Suicidal Behavior and Sexual/Physical Abuse among Street Youth," *Child Abuse & Neglect* 22, no. 3 (1998): 213–22.

55. See, for example, Elizabeth S. Barnert et al., "Identifying Best Practices for 'Safe Harbor' Legislation to Protect Child Sex Trafficking Victims: Decriminalization Alone Is Not Sufficient," *Child Abuse & Neglect* 51 (January 2016): 249–62, https://doi.org/10.1016/j

.chiabu.2015.10.002; Polaris: Human Trafficking Issue Brief: Safe Harbor, Fall 2015, accessed September 3, 2019, https://polarisproject.org/sites/default/files/2015%20Safe%20Harbor%20Issue%20Brief.pdf.

56. Mia Spangenberg, "Prostituted Youth in New York City: An Overview," ECPAT-USA, March 2001, accessed June 29, 2015, https://d1qkyo3pi1c9bx.cloudfront.net/00028B1B-B0DB-4FCD-A991-219527535DAB/7922f23e-a266-44f4-aae4-0f525f3dbe7d.pdf.

57. Richard J. Estes and Neil Alan Weiner, "The Commercial Sexual Exploitation of Children in the U.S., Canada and Mexico," revised February 20, 2002, 18, accessed September 3, 2019, https://maggiemcneill.files.wordpress.com/2011/04/estes-weiner-2001.pdf.

58. Jessica R. Kendall and Catherine Hawke, "Juvenile Status Offenses: Treatment and Early Intervention," *Technical Assistance Bulletin*, no. 29 (Chicago, IL: American Bar Association, 2007).

59. Ibid.

60. Edith Fairman Cooper, "The Runaway and Homeless Youth Program: Administration, Funding, and Legislative Actions," *Congressional Research Service Report for Congress*, March 23, 2006, accessed June 29, 2015, https://digital.library.unt.edu/ark%3A/67531/metacrs9986/.

61. Rebecca Polley Sanchez, "Who Runs? A Demographic Profile of Runaway Youth in the United States," *Journal of Adolescent Health* 39, no. 5 (2006): 778–81.

62. Natasha Slesnick, *Our Runaway and Homeless Youth: A Guide to Understanding* (Greenwood Publishing Group, 2004), 11.

63. Heather Hammer, David Finkelhor, and Andrea J. Sedlak, "Runaway/Thrownaway Children: National Estimates and Characteristics," US Department of Justice, October 2002, accessed June 29, 2015, http://www.unh.edu/ccrc/pdf/MC18.pdf.

64. Milton Greenblatt and Marjorie J. Robinson, "Life-Styles, Adaptive Strategies, and Sexual Behaviors of Homeless Adolescents," *Hospital and Community Psychiatry* 44, no. 12 (1993): 1177–80.

65. B. G. Link et al., "Lifetime and Five-Year Prevalence of Homelessness in the United States," *American Journal of Public Health* 84, no. 12 (1994): 1907–12.

66. Sanchez, "Who Runs?"

67. Hammer, Finkelhor, and Sedlak, "Runaway/Thrownaway Children."

68. "National Trends on Youth in Crisis in the United States," National Runaway Safeline, 2017, https://www.1800runaway.org/trendreport2017/.

69. Powers, Eckenrode, and Jaklitsch, "Maltreatment Among Runaway and Homeless Youth."

70. Michael J. Higdon, "Queer Teens and Legislative Bullies: The Cruel and Invidious Discrimination behind Heterosexist Statutory Rape Laws," *U.C. Davis Law Review* 42, no. 195 (2008–2009), accessed June 29, 2015, http://heinonline.org/HOL/LandingPage?collection=journals&handle=hein.journals/davlr42&div=7&id=&page=.

71. Daryl Presgraves and Tom Chiodo, "GLSEN Study Finds Nearly 9 out of 10 LGBT Students Experience Harassment," Cision PRWeb, October 8, 2008, accessed September 3, 2019, https://www.prweb.com/releases/glsen/harassment-report/prweb1445714.htm. Download for the full report: http://www.glsen.org/download/file/NDIyMg==.

72. "Suicide Risk and Prevention for Lesbian, Gay, Bisexual, and Transgender Youth," Suicide Prevention Resource Center, US Department of Health and Human Services, 2008, accessed June 29, 2015, http://www.sprc.org/sites/sprc.org/files/library/SPRC_LGBT_Youth.pdf.

73. John R. Ellement and Andrew Ryan, "SJC Sees Possible Bias in Rape Case: Why Charge Only the Boy? Judges Bitterly Divided on Issue," *Boston.com*, February 7, 2009, accessed June 27, 2015, http://www.boston.com/news/local/massachusetts/articles/2009/02/07/sjc_sees_possible_bias_in_rape_case/; "Court Questions Whether Plymouth County Prosecutors Should Have Charged Preteen Girls in Rape Case: Teen Boy Claims Discrimination," *The Enterprise*, February 6, 2009, accessed June 27, 2015, http://www.enterprisenews.com/news/x439281556/Court-questions-whether-Plymouth-County-prosecutors-should-have-charged-preteen-girls-in-rape-case.

74. Pew Research Center, "Teens, Social Media & Technology Overview: Smartphones Facilitate Shifts in Communication Landscape for Teens," April 9, 2015, accessed September 3, 2019, http://www.pewinternet.org/2015/04/09/methods-teens-tech/.

75. "Dealing with Devices: The Parent–Teen Dynamic: Are We Addicted?" Common Sense Media, accessed September 3, 2019, https://www.commonsensemedia.org/technology-addiction-concern-controversy-and-finding-balance-infographic.

76. "Teens, Kindness and Cruelty on Social Network Sites," Pew Research Center: Internet & Technology, November 9, 2011, accessed September 3, 2019, https://www.pewinternet.org/2011/11/09/teens-kindness-and-cruelty-on-social-network-sites-2/.

77. Yvonne Roberts, "The One and Only," *Sunday Telegraph Magazine*, July 31, 2005: "Following a string of extramarital affairs and several lurid 'sexting' episodes, Warne has found himself home alone, with Simone Warne taking their three children and flying the conjugal coop" (22), quote from Wikipedia, accessed September 3, 2019, https://en.wikipedia.org/wiki/Sexting#cite_ref-SunTele_4-0.

78. Dr. Elizabeth Englander, "Low Risk Associated with Most Teenage Sexting: A Study of 617 18-Year-Olds," Bridgewater State University, 2012, accessed September 3, 2019, http://vc.bridgew.edu/cgi/viewcontent.cgi?article=1003&context=marc_reports.

79. Heidi Strohmaier, Megan Murphy, and David DeMatteo, "Youth Sexting: Prevalence Rates, Driving Motivations, and the Deterrent Effect of Legal Consequences," *Sexuality Research and Social Policy* 11, no. 3 (September 2014): 245–55.

80. Julie M. Sadhu, "Sexting: The Impact of a Cultural Phenomenon on Psychiatric Practice," *Academic Psychiatry* 36, no. 1 (January–February 2012): 77.

81. Janis Wolak, David Finkelhor, and Kimberly J. Mitchell, "How Often Are Teens Arrested for Sexting? Data from a National Sample of Police Cases," *Pediatrics* 129, no. 1 (2012): 4–12, accessed September 3, 2019, https://pediatrics.aappublications.org/content/pediatrics/129/1/4.full.pdf.

82. "Policy Statement on Sexting," NCMEC, September 21, 2009, https://www.mensen-handelweb.nl/system/files/documents/04%20mei%202015/National%20Center%20for%20Missing%20and%20Exploited%20children%20policystatementonsexting.pdf.

83. Ibid.

84. Sara E. Thomas, "'What Should I Do?' Young Women's Reported Dilemmas with Nude Photographs," *Sexuality Research and Social Policy* 15, no. 2 (2018): 192–207.

85. Carole Jenny, Thomas A. Roesler, and Kimberly L. Poyer, "Are Children at Risk for Sexual Abuse by Homosexuals?," *Pediatrics* 94, no. 1 (1994): 41.

86. Howard N. Snyder, "Sexual Assault of Young Children as Reported to Law Enforcement: Victim, Incident, and Offender Characteristics," Department of Justice, July 2000, 13, accessed June 27, 2015, http://www.bjs.gov/content/pub/pdf/saycrle.pdf.

87. David Finkelhor and Patricia Y. Hashima, "The Victimization of Children and Youth: A Comprehensive Overview," in *Handbook of Youth and Justice*, ed. Susan O. White (New York: Plenum Publishers, 2001), 59.

88. Karen Lewis Taylor, "Keeping Kids Safe in an Unpredictable World," WRAL.com, October 22, 2009, accessed September 3, 2019, https://www.wral.com/lifestyles/family/story/6260782/; "Keeping Your Children Safe Online: Why 'Stranger Danger' Doesn't Work," Wired, February 29, 2012, accessed September 3, 2019, https://www.wired.com/2012/02/keeping-your-children-safe-online-why-stranger-danger-doesnt-work.

89. Mary DeYoung, "The Good Touch/Bad Touch Dilemma," *Child Welfare: Journal of Policy, Practice, and Program* 67, no. 1 (1988): 60–68.
See also as an example: Natalie A. Cherrix, "'Good Touch, Bad Touch' May Send Confusing Message to Children About Sexual Abuse," Holly's House, accessed June 27, 2015, http://www.hollyshouse.org/uploads/3/2/0/9/32090669/notgoodbadtouch.pdf.

90. Dave Ziegler, "Inappropriate Sexual Behavior Scale," *Jasper Mountain*, 1987, accessed June 27, 2015, http://www.jaspermountain.org/inappropriate_sexual_behavior_scale.pdf.

91. Ibid.; see the report for full exploration, particularly page 4.

4

Historical Landmarks and Reflections on Sexual Deviance and Harm

◆ ◆ ◆

The relation between physical contact and emotional intimacy, notions of the sexed body, same sex and male-female bonds, pornography and sexual imagery, sexuality, concepts of marriage, love, friendship and family: these all have distinctive histories with their own meaning and significance.

—Kathy Peiss[1]

I believe studying history ought to make one uncomfortable. It should force a person to question his or her assumptions and beliefs. Ultimately, it should lead to the unsettling realization that present-day attitudes and ideas may someday be considered strange and illogical.

—David Allyn[2]

J. Marion Sims, a leading 19th-century physician and former president of the American Medical Association, developed many of his gynecological treatments through experiments on slave women who were not granted the comfort of anesthesia. Sims's legacy is Janus-faced; he was pitiless with non-consenting research subjects, yet he was among the first doctors of the modern era to emphasize women's health.

—Harriet Washington[3]

THE PRACTICAL APPLICATION OF early science, particularly the fields of psychology, sociology, and medicine, has proven to be significantly influential in the study of sex, known as **sexology**, for outlining the social and physiological parameters of sexual practices. Reflecting on how humanity managed the limits of human understanding at any given period in history, however, does not always illustrate the best characteristics associated with human nature. After a review of the European history, further reflection on the collective historical record offers up important aspects about US history often overlooked in the mainstream as communities throughout the United States continued to display tensions between law, religion, and science. The chapter begins with a brief review describing the contributions from Western civilization, particularly early Europe, as these attitudes and ideas influenced life in the US colonies.

Much like a family might have historically felt the need to hide an unwed mother[4] or a rape victim might be forced to marry her attacker in an attempt to "preserve the young woman's or the family's honor,"[5] cultural restraints in the form of religious ideology have played a significant role in defining the boundaries imposed on sexual practice and the punishment of sex crimes.[6] Through recent academic works on race, class, and gender in the United States,[7] the breadth of perspectives deliberating on the standard presentation of US history as historical fact shows an America well known for disregarding or intentionally dismissing various historical realities from the more widely held or "socially acceptable" historical narrative about sexual deviance and sexual harm. More recent feminist and social justice works focusing on the history of how sex was used to punish, silence, or ostracize smaller groups from the larger society offer some interesting insights into the attempts to give voice to marginalized groups silenced by the more popular historical record.

One person's abusing another has been attributed to individual action and, more recently, has raised questions about social dynamics of power and its expression. Sexual abuse is argued by some to be connected to a dynamic of social power that rests within both the individual and the individual's social position. Men are said to have power over women, whites over people of color, adults over children, and the rich over the poor. Patterns of abuse follow those same dynamics. For this reason, after the presentation of the more prominent historical narrative, attention is given to a review of the history of Native American culture and the role of sexuality during the European settlement of what is now the United States. Attention is also given to the important learnings about sexual violence and oppression in the United States regarding treatment of slaves and the documented history of African American families and sexual practices that emerged from within the institution of slavery. The chapter closes with a reflection on how deviance and crime have historically been defined. Further, how are challenges met or enhanced for criminal justice professionals when definitions of deviance and crime and the related enforcement of criminal acts are based on the actor, not the act, and, as such, punishment is mitigated for the socially influential?

AN AMERICAN NARRATIVE: OUTLINING THE AUTHORITY OF RELIGION, LAW, AND SCIENCE

Both the criminal justice system and religious institutions have been (and continue to be) the social institutions that were most influential in shaping sexual attitudes and behaviors in early America. In reality, much like today, laws were not always enforced, and religious worldviews did not always successfully produce a desired social practice. As a result, efforts by those in positions to outline legal and religious dictates throughout history did not necessarily reflect com-

Text Box 4.1. Brief Historical Timeline

1500s–1700s Commercial Revolution and expanded trade
Scientific Revolution: modern science, physics, astronomy, biology, medicine, and chemistry
Puritans to Colonial America
Enlightenment (18th-Century Europe)
1700s–1900 Industrial Revolution
1837–1901 Victorian era
First wave of feminism (1st WF)
1850 Second Industrial Revolution in United States and Germany: chemicals, petroleum refining, distribution, electrical industries, automobile
1860–1890 500,000 patents issued in United States
1864 Contagious Disease Act
1st WF continues
1869 Opening of first transcontinental railroad in United States
Grant's Peace Policy
1870s–1890s Gilded Age: United States assumed world leadership
1873 Comstock Act
1880s–1890s Freud, Krafft-Ebing, and Ellis researching sexual deviance
1886 Beginning of first wave of sexual predators
1890s–1920s Progressive Era: serious sexual offenders, including homosexuals and prostitutes, were labeled pathological
1st WF
Positivism: criminology focused on treatment/incapacitation
1893 *A System of Legal Medicine* published chapters on sexual crimes and indecent assault of children
1910–1915 First panic over sex killers
1914–1918 WWI considered end of Industrial Revolution
1920s Increasing concern regarding sexual dangers to children
1935 Increasing fears regarding sex offenders
1936 Beginning of second wave of sexual psychopaths
1939–1945 WWII Japanese comfort women
Holocaust, founding of United Nations
1948 Kinsey's *Sexual Behavior in the Human Male*
1949 Simone de Beauvoir's *The Second Sex* marks beginning of second wave of feminism (2nd WF)
1950s Rise of sexual psychopath legislation
1953 Kinsey's *Sexual Behavior in the Human Female*
1960s 2nd WF begins to take shape
1960s–1970s Liberal era "free love"
Dissipation of punitive reaction to sexual psychopaths
1969 Stonewall uprising
1973 *Roe v. Wade* US Supreme Court decision legalizing abortion and leaving regulation of abortion up to states
1976 Present Beginning of third wave of sexually violent predator
1990s Emergence of 3rd WF, multiracial and multiethnic feminism, feminist studies of men, constructionism, postmodernism, and queer studies
3rd WF
1990s Reemergence of sexually violent predator as result of child abductions
1991 Soviet Union collapsed
1994 Violence Against Women Act (VAWA) passed by US federal government
2003 *Lawrence v. Texas* US Supreme Court decision said sodomy laws were a violation of right to privacy
2004 VAWA reauthorized
2012 "War on women's reproductive freedom" claims presented through media and sweeping state efforts to restrict and/or remove abortion rights
2015 VAWA; Campus SaVE Act

mon social practice. The broader history of sex has arguably been more about religious definitions of morality than scientific assessments and biological analyses. Interactions between religious doctrine, secular law, and scientific explorations combined to shape the shifting and changing definitions and parameters of social and sexual practice in the United States, with the customs of the community leadership emulating a strong European influence.

A European Cultural Legacy: Law and Religion . . . and Politics

Society's laws and religious beliefs historically competed to stand above each other as having the more direct influence on regulating sexual behavior. In fact, the ancient **Code of Hammurabi**, drafted by the King of Babylon (1795–1750 BC) and considered to be the oldest document outlining laws and their corresponding punishments, is said to begin and end with prayers and other addresses to the gods.[8] The Code of Hammurabi was created in an attempt to regulate what is believed to be the oldest metropolis in the world (located in what is today an area in Iraq just south of modern-day Bagdad) and featured 228 laws intending to regulate social behavior. One section in the law was dedicated to sexual crimes and accusations. The husband had exclusive rights to his wife's sexuality and was also granted legal permission to participate in sexual relations outside of marriage. Wives who committed adultery were to be thrown in the river with their lover, although, if one party was pardoned, the other half had to be pardoned as well.[9]

Strengthening the idea that religious ideology was a driving force in early attitudes about sex, famous contemporary sex historians **Vern and Bonnie Bullough** linked the classification of many sexual acts as "against nature" or as crimes "not fit to be named" to a tradition engrained in Christianity through the well-known Pauline Epistle to the Romans.[10] Linking the observable elements of sexual practices found in nature to humans offered a distinct, if not arbitrary, line between what sexual acts were identified and practiced as "natural," with all others being considered "against nature."

Religion has historically had a tremendous influence on social behavior and how the law governing sexual behavior has developed and been applied in the United States. In the **Puritan** north, a religious message was said to leap out from every page of the criminal codes. Masturbation, fornication, adultery, sodomy, buggery, and every other sexual practice that inched off the line of traditional sex as approved by the Bible was outlawed, and the punishments for sexual crimes could be severe. Captain Kemble, who famously kissed his wife in public after returning home on a Sunday from three years at sea was made to stand for several hours in the stocks as a consequence.[11] At some points in time, attitudes about sex were so restrictive that men were encouraged to seek sex with "unclean women" (prostitutes) and leave the purity of their wives intact, except for the procreation of children.[12]

Aspects of sex and sexual attitudes defined as "healthy" were confined within **patriarchy**, a rigid, traditional social ideology where the male is identified as the primary authority figure throughout society. The idea of a wife's obligation to "obey" her husband and that a husband cannot rape his wife in marriage because she agreed (before God) in the marriage vows to grant her husband open-ended sexual access remained present in the United States until the feminist movement in the 1960s.[13]

The **colonial history** of the United States began with the European settlement of British colonies until the time of their Declaration of Independence in 1776, operating within four distinct regions: (1) New England, (2) the Middle Colonies, (3) the Chesapeake Bay Colonies, and (4) the Lower South. While the events of the colonies differed dramatically, some events stand out as common examples, such as the 1670 fornication trial of Anne Chase.[14] For unmarried women who conceived, regardless of their social standing or reputation for proper comportment, there was no chance of a rape trial. Sexual behavior was closely followed not to squelch it but to ensure it followed the appropriate setting and purpose: as a duty and joy within marriage and for the purpose of procreation.[15] Research in colonial Pennsylvania suggested that rape was prosecuted in proportion to the rank, character, and situation of the victim.[16] Because the women who were most likely to be raped were lower class, it was often the case that their offenders would be found not guilty in court. As a result, like in Pennsylvania, a significant number of rape events in most English colonies were not reported at all. Silence was indeed described as a standard of the day for both victims and victimizers.[17]

Another prominent event in the eighteenth century scandalized Europe when images and artifacts of sex acts and sex symbols were uncovered in 1749 near Naples, Italy. The volcanic eruption of Mount Vesuvius in 79 AD locked the city of Pompeii under four to six meters of ash. Almost 1,700 years later, an accidental discovery resulted in the creation of what has become known as the **Secret Museum**.[18] When Pompeii was being excavated, drawings and images of a sexual nature were uncovered. The artifacts from the ancient Roman culture were deemed by leaders of the day to be obscene, and women, children, and the poor were restricted from viewing the artifacts and drawings,[19] which were locked away under tightly controlled review by only educated, wealthy gentlemen and scholars.[20] The concept of pornography is believed to have its origin in the decision to annex these images, separating people who were granted access to sexualized images from people who did not have access. In modern times, the viewing of these images is monitored still, and access to the collection requires special permission.

Although the findings in Pompeii raise questions about contemporary understanding of erotic art and imaging, in the United States, as has been illustrated in various other places around the world, social standards identified as the correct standards of practice were also linked with religion through Christian missionaries. The wide range of diverse local customs in early America emphasizes the breadth of mixed-race households and, in many places, the acceptance of difference.[21] So much about the history of sex in the United States has been linked to assessments of European interpretations and the Christian religious tradition (or other religions closely affiliated with Christianity, such as Quakerism); the result is a gaping absence of any interest in reflections on non-Christian religious interpretations, such as Judaism, of sexual practices in the United States.[22] White male soldiers and settlers assumed the topless dress of some indigenous women indicated immodesty or promiscuity. The Christian ethics of the Puritan and Victorian eras continued to emphasize sex as a means for procreation only, highlighting the need to exploit women of color as sexually accessible and ignore white women, who were said to require religious purity.[23] Whether through physical violence or regional and national efforts to obliterate "uncivilized" sexual practices, as more people migrated west, the influence of European and Anglo norms was more prominent, and battle lines between original nations and peoples and the European soldiers were often used to justify violence and sexual assault of indigenous women.[24]

Some US historians suggest that the dominant meaning of sexuality changed from a primary association with reproduction within families in the Colonial era to the association with emotional intimacy and physical pleasure more recently.[25] Beginning in the nineteenth century, with an extremely socially conservative period, referred to as the **Victorian era** (1837–1901), named for Queen Victoria of England, the shift in these ideas was argued to be connected to efforts to terminate the use of contraceptives. The emerging idea of **marital rape** was connected to the strict social practices of the day, yet the idea was being advanced that a woman should be able to sexually consent within marriage.[26] Activists in support of women's sexual autonomy were decried as advocates of irresponsible promiscuity, but their goals have been identified as the "theoretical and practical recognition of a woman's absolute right to self-ownership,"[27] a goal, some might argue, that continues into the present day.

Religious beliefs are deeply steeped in religious doctrine, historical interpretations, and religious tradition. In spite of the US constitutional ideal requiring the separation of church and state, Christian religious values have had a significant effect on the social and political climate of American life for centuries. This includes a steady influence in the conversations and definitions of healthy sex and sexual deviance. Where sex is concerned, sometimes, public attitudes do not match private behaviors. In contemporary America, the religious influence on sexual matters has been significantly tarnished by the series of child sexual abuse cases that emerged in the mid-1980s from within the US Catholic Church but rose to significant national prominence in 2002 when the *Boston Globe* covered the high-profile criminal prosecutions of five Roman Catholic priests.[28] The scandal expanded to include countries in Africa, Asia, Europe, Australia, and North and South America.

The world was shocked as stories of sexual abuse were discovered to have spanned thirty years in some cases. A secondary layer of the scandal unfolded when it was discovered that offending priests accused of abuse were knowingly relocated to unsuspecting parishes in an attempt to keep the Church blameless.[29] In one Alaskan community, individuals sued the Catholic Church amidst reports that 80 percent of the children in their community had been abused by Church officials.[30] Silence on events and incidents distorts the history of sexual violence and harm, masks the need for healing, and makes prevention efforts that accompany sexual harm a higher priority. And active litigation involving sexual abuse in the Catholic Church is still happening almost thirty years later. In February 2012, the Archdiocese of Milwaukee (Wisconsin) revealed "more than 8,000 previously unreported incidents of alleged sexual abuse against children." The charges are said to span sixty years and involve approximately one hundred offenders.[31] The Catholic Church isn't the only organized religion with ties to sexual abuse scandals, but the systematic response by some to cover up the abuse, the degree of the abuse, and the breadth of the scandal has made it a huge international public story.

Science and Academics . . . and Politics

The **Enlightenment** (eighteenth-century Europe) is perhaps the most well-known intellectual movement linked to the beginning of scientific advancements in seventeenth-century Europe (1600s) and dedicated to the promotion of science as a means to advance social conditions and, ultimately, connected to the Industrial Revolution. One of the first efforts to discuss the treatment of sex afflictions is documented in the work of **Dr. James Graham** (1745–1794), who was best known for his "Grand State Celestial Bed," which was designed to aid couples with sexual difficulties. Reports suggest that he charged by the night and made a considerable amount of money from his invention while his sex clinic in London, the Temple of Health, scandalized eighteenth-century English society. Argued to be a quack by doubters and a medical entrepreneur by supporters, he produced various writings to aid couples with sexual difficulties.[32] While his methods were seen as unconventional and ridiculous by today's standards, he is said to have had a great interest in sex research and assisting his patients with their reproductive concerns. Also, in 1837 Europe, **Alexandre Jean Baptiste Parent-Duchatelet**, authored *Prostitution in the City of Paris*, which was identified as the first work of modern sex research in his study of over 3,500 registered prostitutes in Paris.[33]

In the United States, on March 3, 1873, a federal law was passed making it illegal to send "obscene, lewd and/or lascivious" materials through the mail, championed by **Anthony Comstock**. This legislation famously included a ban on contraceptives, making it a federal offense to disseminate birth control through the mail or across state lines.[34] Twenty-four states followed the **Comstock Act**, formally restricting contraception at the state level. Although law enforcement agents were said to look the other way when it came to enforcing anti–birth control laws, in Connecticut, married couples using birth control in the privacy of their own home could be arrested and subjected to a one-year prison sentence under what was identified as the most restrictive anti–birth control state law in the country.[35]

With his 1886 work, *Sexual Psychopathy: A Clinical-Forensic Study*, **Richard von Krafft-Ebing**,[36] an Austro-German psychiatrist, established sexology as a scientific field of study. In 1897, **Havelock Ellis's** *Sexual Inversion*[37] was published, a work that did not describe homosexuality as a disease. Ellis is argued to have been one of the most influential scholars opposed to the Victorian sexual morality and emphasizing sexual restraint and a rigid code of personal conduct.[38] Also in 1897, German physician **Magnus Hirschfeld**, an outspoken advocate for sexual minorities, including homosexuals and transsexuals, founded the Scientific-Humanitarian Committee. The committee's motto was "Justice through science." It had established repealing the section of the German penal code that criminalized homosexuality in 1871 as a top priority for the group. After securing signatures from prominent Germans, political support was moving in the direction of repeal when the Nazi Party rose to power in 1920. Nazi opposition to homosexuality made the idea of repeal impossible.[39]

Sigmund Freud famously established his theories on psychoanalysis at the turn of the nineteenth century, also known as the **Progressive Era** in American history. Freud's research focused on sexual abuse as a cause of psychological harm, until he later retracted that idea and advocated the more common idea known today, which suggests that young girls who claim to have been sexually abused are actually recalling fantasies about having sex with these older male figures.[40]

Also at this time, serious sex offenders were labeled pathological or insane and sent to mental hospitals or asylums.[41] In 1888, multiple notoriously brutal attacks on mostly prostitutes in London were later attributed to a single serial killer, dubbed "Jack the Ripper."

In 1916, women's rights activist **Margaret Sanger** was arrested in violation of the Comstock Act when she opened the first birth control clinic in the United States. The result was the first modification to the Comstock Act, with a second modification to come in 1936, also prompted by Sanger, who publicly declared her goal to overturn the Comstock Act. The second modification to the Comstock Act made it possible for doctors to distribute contraceptives across state lines.[42]

Throughout the 1920s and 1930s in the United States, traditional sexual morality was at variance with people's actual behavior as exemplified by heterosexual relations outside of marriage becoming more common, even while popular commentary reflected concern that the traditional family was in trouble.[43] A young cultural anthropologist, **Margaret Mead**, published her classic work on the study of adolescent girls, *Coming of Age in Samoa* (1928), which upset many in the United States with its suggestion that women elected to have casual sex until they married.[44]

Alfred Kinsey (1894–1956) famously founded the Institute for Sex Research at Indiana University in 1947 and, after securing funding from the Rockefeller Foundation and conducting extensive research with his team, published *Sexual Behavior and the Human Male* (1948) and, in 1953, followed with the female version, titled *Sexual Behavior and the Human Female*. Kinsey himself was embroiled in legal controversy when US Customs intercepted images of sex Kinsey was importing as part of his collection but were identified as pornographic and seized in 1956. Kinsey died before this legal matter was resolved.

Kinsey's work has been challenged scientifically and has acquired many social critics.[45] Trained as a zoologist, his original research included studies on the gall wasp. Fascinated by the unique variations he found, when he turned his attention to human sexuality, biographers have suggested that Kinsey expected to see the same kinds of variations in human sexuality that he found in his studies of nature. Credited as the catalyst for the sexual liberation efforts of both women and the LGBTQI community,[46] Kinsey's work was one of the few scientific studies on sex that was intent on exploring the biology and physiology of sex conducted in the United States, until the publication of **Masters and Johnson**'s studies, *Human Sexual Response* (1966) and *Human Sexual Inadequacy* (1970). With research findings in sharp contrast to popular social attitudes of the day, perhaps it is not surprising that both Kinsey and Mead were heavily critiqued about their assessments on sexuality. Their assessments of sexual freedoms as a possible sexual practice produced significant challenges to the objectivity of their analysis, with critics suggesting that their work was more a statement about their own individual beliefs and attitudes about sexuality than the outcome of a scientifically valid process.[47]

The Medical Model . . . and Politics

While the scientific study of sex might seem to form the periphery of a conversation on sexual deviance and sexual crime, the backstory of sex in the United States is also a story of social myth meeting biological and, in some cases, medical ignorance at best and medical distortion at worst. Two primary examples include the medical and scientific research on masturbation and abortion. In the case of masturbation, medical science has made nearly a complete shift in popular social attitudes since the 1800s. Pregnancy prevention methods and abortion are believed to have an even longer reach back into history, as reflected in various cultures' use of traditional herbal remedies and treatments to prevent pregnancy. Unlike masturbation, which seems to be less of an issue today, the US controversy around abortion has more recently been heating up with questions about access to the birth control pill at the center of the nationwide controversy. Although legal today, restrictions are expanding, and these questions raise concerns about whether the United States as a country is ready to go back to a time when women who have abortions or use birth control illegally will be subject to prosecution and imprisonment. What might the punishment be for such a crime, and would there be any process for distinguishing between a natural miscarriage and an allegation of an induced abortion?

Masturbation
In the eighteenth and nineteenth centuries, prominent physicians, scientists, and religious leaders believed insanity, blindness, hearing loss, epilepsy, and mental retardation were caused by self-stimulation of the genitals. Sixty percent of medical and mental illnesses were blamed on masturbation.[48] In the nineteenth and early twentieth centuries, young boys were fitted with devices intended to disrupt an interest in masturbation or prevent "self-abuse."

In more contemporary times, researchers have documented the suffering and damage caused by religious and medical distortions applied to the topic of masturbation.[49] As recently as 1994, then Surgeon General Joycelyn Elders was fired by President Bill Clinton after she made public statements in support of teaching schoolchildren to masturbate as a way of avoiding the spread of the AIDS virus.[50] Still a topic of contemporary controversy, the Catholic Church considers masturbation a "venal and mortal sin."[51] In 2007, an additional sixty days in jail was added on to an inmate's sentence in Florida after he was charged with "indecent exposure" for masturbating in his cell.[52]

Efforts to reduce carnal urges that might take on the form of "self-abuse" were presented in a variety of ways, some of the most extreme being institutionalization. In 1829, **Reverend Sylvester Graham** took a new approach to reducing the likelihood of masturbation by creating health food and a healthy diet.[53] Linking bland foods to the idea of reducing one's sexual appetite, it is impossible to know how well the product worked for those purposes; however, the product is still marketed today as graham crackers. Another product, made by **Dr. John Harvey Kellogg**, who held a similar belief, is also still sold today: cornflakes cereal.

The degree to which masturbation is seen as a sin against God, an unhealthy practice, an act of deviance, or a doorway to other sex-related criminal charges is open to debate. The brief review about public and private conversations on the topic of masturbation is only one example of how cultural attitudes, religious ideology, medical professionals, and scientific studies merge in an attempt to direct a social agenda. The example of contraception and abortion offers a second, even more socially volatile, example.

Contraception and Abortion

Consider the topic of birth control and contraception, specifically abortion. This topic has been extremely divisive in the United States and is centered within a clash of social, legal, and religious ideologies and practices. Abortion was legal in the United States and not identified as a criminal behavior during the eighteenth and early nineteenth centuries under common law.[54] In an effort to protect women from being unsuspectingly poisoned by shady entrepreneurs whose products included harmful or fatal chemicals, states started to regulate the open sale of **abortifacient drugs**, chemicals intended to prevent pregnancy by inducing a miscarriage.[55]

Efforts in the medical community to make abortion illegal and restrict abortions began in the mid-1800s; however, class anxieties[56] and efforts to keep women at home raising children rather than in professional positions[57] were argued to be pushing the criminalization of abortion. Between 1860 and 1880, states passed laws across the United States that were framed after the Comstock Laws at the federal level, making abortion and birth control illegal under federal anti-obscenity legislation.[58] Abortion would be illegal for over one hundred years in the United States, until the 1973 Supreme Court decision *Roe v. Wade* decided abortion would again be legal and constitutionally protected up until fetal viability. Specific guidelines and conditions for abortion were left up to individual state governments. The US abortion controversy by no means ended with the 1973 Supreme Court decision. Almost fifty years later, efforts to amend or modify the effects of the ruling continue.

In a collective effort more than twenty states have moved to or introduced legislation to "amend the constitutional definition of a 'person' to include 'all members of the species Homo sapiens at any stage of development, including the state of fertilization or conception."[59] Referred to as "personhood amendments," part of the controversy is that these new definitions of a person would also make the use of birth control illegal.[60] In Oklahoma, consideration of the personhood bill resulted in Senator Constance Johnson, in an openly hostile reaction to what she identified as government intrusion into the arena of women's reproductive health, submitted an amendment to Senate Bill 1433, which read "any action in which a man ejaculates or otherwise deposits semen anywhere but in a woman's vagina shall be interpreted and construed as an action against an unborn child."[61] The degree to which government is involved in defining sexual health and reproductive practices after years of debate is still a volatile social issue across the United States.

When criminologists suggest that crime is "created" by society, the example of abortion serves as a useful illustration. When abortion is not defined by society as illegal, women who choose abortion are not identified as criminals. If, on the other hand, the act of abortion is made illegal, women who terminate an unplanned pregnancy will be violating the law and, therefore of course, will be classified as criminals. According to some versions of the personhood amendment, any woman and her doctor who intentionally terminate a pregnancy will be committing an act of murder and, if convicted, shall be sentenced to life in prison or the death penalty.[62] In that line of thinking, if birth control is made illegal, then women who use birth control will be committing a crime. Because 98 percent of all US women are reported to use hormonal birth control at some time in their lives,[63] the idea of outlawing contraception might seem like a shocking political position. In spite of the Catholic Church's opposition to birth control, even among Catholic women between the ages of 15 and 44 and amidst significant controversy, "Data shows that 98 percent of sexually experienced women of child-bearing age and who identify themselves as Catholic have used a method of contraception other than natural family planning at some point in their lives."[64]

The legal or illegal status of abortion has little, if any, influence on the many individuals who consider the act of abortion to be unacceptable on moral grounds. If someone is opposed to an abortion, they are not going to have an abortion. In this way, social action taken in the form of social policy and legislation has a significant part to play in the creation of boundaries around sexual practices or the unintended consequences of healthy sexual practices as illegal. Ironically, in contrast to the early effort to protect against maternal mortality by making abortion products illegal, in more contemporary America, one of the primary pushes to *legalize* abortion was to prevent maternal mortality.[65] Women reported being blindfolded and taken to hotel rooms or other makeshift operating rooms, rather than medical facilities, with procedures performed by people with little or no verification of medical knowledge. While abortion rates were said to account for 14 percent of maternal mortality at the end of the 1920s, research conducted in New York City reported maternal mortality rates rose steadily to 42 percent by the 1960s.[66] The illegality of abortion had produced a public-health disaster in communities across the country, especially for low-income and minority women who could not afford another child.[67]

The 1973 US Supreme Court decision gave individual states the right to determine the conditions under which abortions are made available.[68] As is the case with many legal changes, this court decision resulted from a social and political movement, including a series of ongoing legal challenges. Some of those ongoing challenges to abortion come from within religious communities,[69] including the Catholic Church, for example, which has been a long-standing opponent to abortion and birth control. Pro-choice supporters, those who support keeping access to abortion safe and legal, and agencies providing pregnancy prevention education, including birth control, also remain active globally. The lack of access to affordable birth control is argued to result in 49 million unintended pregnancies and 21 million abortions for 148 million women across sub-Saharan Africa and South-Central and Southeast Asia.[70] Clearly, abortion is a big issue worldwide, steeped in a convergence of social (including economic and political), legal, and religious conflict and controversy.

IN(DE)VISIBLE FROM THE MAINSTREAM

The traditional history of the United States is most often told as one story from one perspective, the perspective of the dominant group, the white middle to upper class. In this way, the idea of social relativism from high-profile deviance scholars and the collective feminist critique of traditional social science research outlined in section I fits right in once again. Looking closer, of course, history has many stories to tell. The collective histories as expressed by social and political minority groups are easily lost in a history presented as a mainstream representation of a singular collective experience or ideology.[71] In fact, anthropologists suggest it was very late indeed in human evolution before man's role in procreation was discovered because it is not immediately obvious. As recent as the 1960s, anthropological research suggests Christian missionaries were said to have informed tribal groups of the connection between sex and children who up to that point had their own creation stories about how babies happened, assuming sex was only for pleasure.[72]

People in the United States and throughout the world continue to demonstrate less than a comprehensive understanding of the finer points of the sex act and connections to sexual infection transmission as well as pregnancy. Popular but false stories suggested that, if a girl touched a boy, she could get pregnant or, if tongues were used during a kiss or pinky fingers touched, that was sex.[73] Erroneous assumptions, for example, that infections cannot be transmitted via oral sex, anal sex is "safe sex," and a woman cannot get pregnant when she is menstruating indicate ongoing social and biological ignorance about sex, sexual practice, and implications for sexual activity. If a young person turns to the internet to get their sex-related questions answered, they may intentionally or accidently encounter images, videos, and opinions that will generate even more questions for them. Yes, it is likely there still are young people with certain catalogs hidden under mattresses, but sexually provocative material may not always offer the most comprehensive, healthy, or age-appropriate information for children and young people and even adults.

In the presence of an enormous collection of anything, it makes sense to sort the different pieces into smaller, similarly themed groups in an effort to organize similarities and differences and present them in a meaningful way. For example, studies in the social sciences often do this when a smaller group is targeted to locate and isolate various aspects of the larger group deemed worthy of further consideration and ongoing study. Often, when those smaller pieces are put back together to tell the larger story, decisions have to be made about which aspects of history "make the cut" in the popular cultural narrative. As such, certain elements are highlighted, and others are omitted.

In human groups, sexual behavior is said to be socially regulated in some fashion or another because it involves the perpetuation of the species[74] and other such important factors as love, jealousy, social position, and pleasure.[75] Anthropologists and other social scientists who have studied the history of sex remind us of a time in America when nonliterate, specifically non-English–speaking, people are seen as "savages," at worst, or "uncivilized," at best, and therefore were automatically identified as sexually promiscuous, assuming no sexual values were present.

Many a nineteenth-century anthropologist had the typical bias of their time; when they discovered people who lived differently than they did, they immediately interpreted this difference to mean inferiority. For the nineteenth-century intellectual, in many cases, the logic was simply that, if the nonliterate were intelligent and moral, they would be living as Europeans did. Today, science makes no such extravagant claims regarding intellectual inferiority or primitive promiscuity, for we know there is no evidence to support such a position.[76]

Consider how gendered language from approximately fifty years ago feels awkward and exclusive. While this work highlights an awareness of inclusion in the area of cultural observations of "other," it also reflects a sense of gender exclusion common during that time period. Regardless of whether these omissions and exclusions are intended to separate and lessen the value or experiences of the "other," colonizing the land by European settlers was undoubtedly easier if "uncivilized heathens" were the ones being displaced. The shift necessary to see the land essential for US nation-building and expansion into what was identified as the "American West" required a story of "rugged individualism" or "cultural genocide." The consequences of interpretation affected the way these historical stories are remembered and carried forward in the collective social consciousness. The outcomes for the people in either of the more narrow versions of these stories are limited and incomplete.

Much has been written about the writing and rewriting of US history; the most obvious example is simple enough to illustrate this idea. For years, in elementary school classrooms across the country, a history of the United States was (and still is in some places) presented as the "discovery" of America, as if the land mass or the people living in the area did not exist before Columbus set sail. Clearly, the indigenous communities had lived within long-standing social and cultural traditions for thousands of years;[77] however, this historical reality has often been overlooked, simply not discussed, or deemed insignificant by historical accounts in the American mainstream.[78] This becomes an important connecting point because, in the historical reflection on sexual harm and sexual violence in America, the sexual experiences of a wide variety of cultural groups are central to the story but often omitted from the collective telling of that history.

Consider the US government policies that forced removal of Native American children from their families and placed them in boarding schools notorious for sexual abuse by Christian missionaries[79] or the use of African American women by slave owners for sexual gratification or "breeding" more slaves.[80] Again, it is important to consider how much of the knowledge about First Nations communities before European contact has been removed or set aside intentionally by a generic (some would say a "white-washed") presentation of the colonial history and "invaders from the East."[81] While scholars representing the original nations and peoples are among those working to preserve aspects of indigenous knowledge,[82] other social groups are indifferent or in support of past US policy makers who worked to deliberately culturally and physically exterminate the First Nations people to make room for "the land of the free and the home of the brave."[83]

Similar historical cautions can be offered regarding what is known about the legal and illegal treatment of slaves in the early history of the United States. When history looks backward, the deviant or criminal classifications of sexual abuses, whether against original nations and people or slaves by slave owners, have significantly different historical meanings and social consequences for the respective communities.[84] Yet these ideas represent only a few stories hidden, lost, or ignored by the larger society in more contemporary times, particularly around sexual harm and violence. Books have been written about the consequences of the misrepresentation of social history on the people and community groups affected, including white people and communities.[85] Attention is given here to the Native American communities and the African American slave communities as a central feature in the history of sexual deviance and crime in American history.

THE PRECOLONIAL NATIVE AMERICAN/FIRST NATIONS PEOPLE

The history of First Nations people in the United States has been preserved through a long oral tradition that predates contact with European settlers. As a result, the knowing of that history, especially for people outside First Nations communities, can be difficult. Given the dramatic difference between the cultures that collided when European settlers began exploring in what is now the Americas, efforts to understand just how those precolonial cultures ordered their daily, lived realities are often filtered through a Eurocentric lens. What is known about original nations and peoples' histories sometimes comes from accounts challenged as being gross distortions of the indigenous cultures by early European observers.[86] Some historians suggest that many original societies had drastically altered their behavior in response to the European presence long before any impressions of "traditional" life were ever formally documented.[87]

In the mainstream assessment, traditions among original nations and peoples are often discussed as one tradition and one cultural history, as *the* (singular) "Native American" community. To discuss precolonial communities as a singular unit of people working similarly and in solidarity with each other, however, is a misrepresentation of the long-standing First Nations history.[88] Populations of indigenous people are estimated to have been between 10 and 12 million strong in North America, with some estimates of as many as 100 million,[89] organized into more than 600 societies and speaking approximately 200 languages,[90] before being targeted for physical and cultural extinction by the US government. Efforts to fully understand the effects of the Native American genocide on indigenous people in the United States and Canada are sketchy, at best, from within the history documented by European settlers.

Researchers from within communities of original nations and peoples have argued sexual violence holds a central place in the combined histories of European/American settlers and First Nations people in the United States to the point that nothing short of sovereignty and reinstatement of treaty rights will begin the process of undoing those harms.[91] Because efforts to extinguish First Nations peoples, their customs and traditions, were so pervasive throughout the history of America, the effects of that desire to obliterate this culture and these people is argued to continue into the present day.[92] Because such a bold claim might be hard for non-Natives to imagine after so many years have passed since they were displaced and died or killed as a result of European expansion, evidence of the more contemporary attitude illustrating the acceptability of sexualized violence against indigenous women is offered in the form of a 1983 video game called "Custer's Revenge." Generated for the Atari gaming system by the video company Mystique, the goal of the game was for players to navigate Custer (the gamer) through rows of flying arrows to reach a Native woman tied to a pole and then rape her. With apologies to any indigenous people reading this, a potentially triggering description follows, outlining the degree of disregard some had/have for the indigenous experience generally and indigenous women in particular. When the gamer reached a specified point level, the image of the "squaw" woman shifts to a doggy-style posture. The marketing copy reads: "Whether his needs have been sated, or brought down by enemy fire, Custer will return again and again to get what he wants." The people who came together to create and pitch this idea, find funding for the prototype, produce this idea, and distribute the product banked on consumers' willingness to purchase this game and literally buy into this idea, over and over again, until Custer "gets what he wants."

While mainstream America was deciding whether the new Atari gaming system was worth the price of purchase for their children, it is interesting to think about the *century-long* forced separation of indigenous children from their families. They were legally taken by order of the US government, a process that was formalized in the United States under **Grant's Peace Policy** in 1869.[93] Historians agree that original communities were devastated by the degree of physical harms, including sexual abuse and deaths, indigenous children were subjected to at the hands of missionary workers, caretakers, and church officials.[94] And yet this is a story of sexualized harm and abuse that First Nations people have been trying to put in front of mainstream America for decades with little success. In 2003, a class action lawsuit was filed against the US government on behalf of anyone abused at Indian boarding schools operated under US government control and the Bureau of Indian Affairs from 1890 to the present (***Zepier v. United States***). The case was dismissed, and the group has taken their case directly to the Bureau of Indian Affairs.[95] Interesting comparisons might be made between the systematic abuse of children under US government control and the systematic abuse and cover-up that was edging its way into full public view in 2002 in the stories of child sexual abuse in the Catholic Church, discussed earlier in this chapter.

Many historical accounts about early contact between First Nations or indigenous people and settlers agree that Indians did not rape their captives.[96] In general, sex and violence were not equated as a measure of manhood or prestige among First Nations peoples; however, other reports suggest a captive woman had little protection if a man wanted to abuse her.[97] Stories about the stoic "savage" were idealized and played up in popular media. Power dynamics were quite different between US and original cultures, and the egalitarian placement of women within the kinship systems was noted, most often with derision, among American settlers documenting contact with the indigenous people.[98] The question of whether women were raped when taken captive in intertribal warfare has been difficult to assess by historical records because definitions of consent and rape are not clear.[99] Although various accounts of intertribal abduction do not reflect outward aggression toward tribal captors, other stories express how a woman might wait years to get revenge against those who captured her. The oral storytelling tradition of First Nations communities makes it difficult to provide authoritative assertions about the treatment of captives by First Nations communities, where options included becoming a slave, a concubine, or a wife.[100] In clashes between natives and white traders, violence did sometimes take the form of sexual violence, as documented in formal meetings between tribal leaders seeking redress from state officials for the aggressive harms done to indigenous women at the hands of soldiers and settlers.[101]

Historical records suggest that such ongoing harms resulted in increased tensions between original nations and peoples and settlers and marked setbacks in commercial trading and relations.[102] While research on the subject generally confirms little tolerance for interracial marriage by Europeans, accounts of casual sex between settlers and indigenous people are documented throughout the historical record. Letters from settlers describing offense and displeasure toward what was seen as sexual permissiveness within the First Nations communities regarding sexual experimentation before marriage are contrasted with accounts of trappers marrying indigenous women and being welcomed into the tribal community.[103]

One of the more prominently placed challenges for European culture to comprehend is what has been described as **two-spirit people**, the third gender (or third sex), or the third and fourth genders.[104] Alternative gender roles have been described as one of the most distinctive features shared between North American Native communities with over 155 tribal accounts reflecting the existence of a male **berdache**, a man who in keeping with social custom assumes a woman's role. About one-third of these groups documented similar types of a formal status for females who undertook a man's lifestyle.[105] The term "berdache" is said to have been first written in 1704 and documented in European anthropological publications in the late 1800s and early 1900s. The berdache presented itself differently (and by a different name in some tribes); however, several visible markers included cross-dressing and attributions of spiritual powers.[106] At present, the use of the term "berdache" has been called into question by some indigenous people who suggest that "two-spirit" better describes the tribal ideology and cultural history of alternative gender lifestyles in the community.[107] More recent scholarship highlights the hetero/ homo binary as a restrictive tool contributing to the vilification of any sexual standards not representative of the European cultural tradition.[108]

First Nations sexual culture was described by many accounts as uninhibited and permissive.[109] Young women were free to experiment sexually before marriage and did so with white as well as Native men, although accounts suggest that not all tribes shared the same attitudes and practices. In fact, marriage was not prescribed as an eternal bond,[110] with women being able to walk away from a relationship at their choosing.[111] Children were raised in the collective, which was another difficult idea for European cultural standards to comprehend. The use of natural abortive medicines was also noted in historical accounts,[112] and many of the stories about sexual relationships are presented as a natural and, in many ways, a humorous part of the human condition.[113]

For Natives, one of the few prohibitions where sex was concerned applied to a restriction of individual agency, or the use of force.[114] For Europeans, however, the list of sexual restrictions was much more extensive and included critiques of Native kinship systems, definitions of marriage and family, gender and power dynamics, and sex practices. English men and women who were sexually intimate with an Indian were liable to be stigmatized as "debased" or "defiled." Marriages and long-term Anglo-Indian sexual relations were seen as problematic in their cultural implications because Europeans had long identified themselves as being the social and cultural superior to the First Nations peoples.[115]

The history of settlement and occupation in the United States is well documented. The history of interactions with people who were here at the time the land was claimed for England is not so well documented. Scholars and historians are reflecting on written accounts of interactions between the two cultures, but many questions remain. Some of those questions relate to the numbers of children who were abused in boarding schools by missionaries or government employees, the treatment of indigenous women by white settles and traders, and the overarching attitude that European settlers were more "civilized" and more "human" than the original nations and peoples. The history of the systematic efforts by the US government to obliterate the First Nations traditions, customs, and religion are well-known and, in some areas, celebrated. The continued cultural divide is reflected in recent efforts to protect Native women on Native land from increased sexual violence. The Department of Justice studies indicate Native American and Alaska Native women are more than 2.5 times more likely to be raped or sexually assaulted than white women in the United States.[116] When interviewers talk to women directly, however, it is often the case that the official records do not reflect the full extent of sexual violence. An Amnesty

International report documented the groups of women interviewed "could not think of any indigenous women within their community who had not been subjected to sexual violence."[117] In the summer of 2010, the Obama administration passed the **Tribal Law and Order Act of 2010**, which was intended to address jurisdictional issues that left Native American and Alaska Native people, particularly women, vulnerable and without enforcement. The legislation is intended to assure women a police response, access to a rape kit, and the prosecution of the alleged offenders.[118] When looking back at the history of sexual violence in America, it is important to note the lack of access to judicial assistance and legal recourse afforded First Nations people, particularly around the issue of sexualized violence, throughout history and into the present day.[119]

THE AMERICAN SLAVE TRADE AND RACIALIZED RELATIONS

Like original nations and people in America, slave families experienced the forced separation of families and sexualized violence amidst a clash of cultural ideals while European settlers dictated the terms of those encounters as evidenced in the disparate application of the law based on race. This worked to perpetuate and reinforce racialized boundaries from the time of European contact in the United States and resulted in privileged and preferential treatment for the white community.[120] Unlike indigenous people, however, for US slaves, the forced separation of families was due in large part to the commodification of slave bodies by white slave owners. Children born to slaves were the property of the slave master, who had complete control over their domestic lives and relationships, and any member could be sold at any time at the master's discretion.[121] The sex lives of both male and female slaves were shaped by the world in which black slaves moved and interacted together and the other world in which blacks were constantly under the control and oversight of white authorities.[122]

In spite of hostile judgments from whites against interracial mixing and US **anti-miscegenation laws**, the criminalization of interracial marriage or sex between different races, various patterns of interracial sexual relations were described in the unsettled Western areas of the United States, specifically in the Southwest, which included the assimilation of whites into Indian or Mexican society.[123] As the Western area of the United States became more settled, the expectations of European Christianity became more rigidly enforced. In nineteenth-century America,

> sexuality continued to serve as a powerful means by which white Americans maintained dominance over people of other races. Both scientific and popular thought supported the view that whites were civilized and rational, while members of other races were savage, irrational, and sensual. . . . [S]tereotypes of immoral women of other races contributed to the belief in white superiority. . . . Patterns differed but in each region the belief that white sexual customs were more civilized, along with the assumption that Indian, Mexican, and black women were sexually available to white men, supported white supremacist attitudes and justified social control of other races.[124]

Under slavery, white masters assumed slaves to be sexually available to them. As a result, black women slaves were easily marked as sexually promiscuous by white standards.

Slave families were aware that their owners had final say about if and when they could marry and whom they could marry, if and when they could live or work together (even when married), and the fate of their children—or even if they were allowed to have children.[125] The slave community, in many ways, resembled examples of preindustrial and peasant societies. Although premarital sex might occur without stigma, most adults married and maintained stable unions, and sexuality was closely linked to reproduction.[126] Compared to social convention around such matters in the white community, the lack of rigid sexual practices within the slave community was used by some to support the mainstream notion that slave women were immoral and white sexual mores were more appropriate and civilized.

The complete lack of acknowledging rape of women in a legal sense, specifically when women of color and particularly slave women were involved, demonstrates how little white people were willing to acknowledge the existence of a system of racial and sexual exploitation and the role white people—particularly white men—played in establishing and maintaining that system.[127] This institutionalized rape of the female slave was often not noted as a crime. Male slaves who attempted to intervene against the sexual demands made by slave owners were often dealt with by physical violence or sold. In some cases, slave owners would claim they were having sex for breeding purposes, to increase their slave holdings. To this end, male slaves were also forced to have sex with female slaves selected by the slave owner, who would also determine the conditions of the sexual encounter.[128]

One well-known accounting about the sexual abuse, pursuit, and ongoing efforts by slaves to evade master–slave sexuality came from Harriet Jacobs, in 1861 Edenton, North Carolina, who published *Incidents in the Life of a Slave Girl*, which describes her being harassed by her master from the time she was 13 and living for seven years in her grandmother's tiny attic to escape.[129] In her book, Jacobs spends time talking about "The Jealous Mistress." These and other accounts highlight the effect the culture had on particularly white women, who were, in effect, being trained not to see what was in plain sight, the infidelity of their husbands with slave women. Researchers have uncovered accounts in diaries of white women suggesting that white men

> saw women—whether slave or free, wealthy or impoverished, cultured or untutored, black or white—as interchangeable. . . . [F]ree women circulated at a discount due to the ready availability of women who could be forced to obey. At the same time that jealous mistresses were angry over their husbands' adulterous conduct . . . slave women resented what they envisioned as their mistress' narcissistic self-pity, and returned their mistresses' anger in kind.[130]

As suggested here, the availability of black women as men's sexual partners has also raised questions about the harm done to relationships between white men and white women, with reports of white women refusing to relate at all with their husbands after discovering their infidelities.[131] In some cases, the extramarital sex was seen as a violation of God and an affront to their marriage, and in other cases it was seen as defiling the white race. Other historical records suggest that sexual standards among the poorer classes were less rigid, with more apparent opposition to the mainstream religious and cultural ideal of preserving white female purity.[132]

Historical records also suggest that white women pursued relationships with black men by their choosing.[133] In fact, one of the legacies of slavery was the "postbellum fiction" that such liaisons were largely circumstances of rape.[134] While many historical records reflect intolerance for a white woman's "indiscretion" and sex between mixed couples was illegal, some court cases do exist where a white man was not granted divorce from a wife who bore mixed children while married.[135] The legal standard used was whether the husband could prove the illicit relationship had caused more harm than would result from the ultimate dissolution of a white family. In fact, in 1892, approximately thirty years after the Emancipation Proclamation was issued by President Abraham Lincoln, **Ida B. Wells-Barnett** would be immortalized for her publication on the fallacy of black men rapists. An early leader in the civil rights movement and a fierce anti-lynching campaigner in the United States and Europe, Wells was subject to many death threats and notoriously carried a weapon. In one of her more famous articles, "Southern Horrors: Lynch Law in All Its Phases," she wrote:

> Nobody in this section of the country believes the old thread-bare lie that Negro men rape white women. If Southern white men are not careful, they will overreach themselves and public sentiment will have a reaction; a conclusion will then be reached which will be very damaging to the moral reputation of their women. . . . [T]here are many white women in the South who would marry colored men if such an act would not place them at once beyond the pale of society and within the clutches of the law. The miscegenation laws of the South only operate against the legitimate union of races; they leave the white man free to seduce all the colored girls he can, but it is death to the colored man who yields to the force and advances of a similar attraction in white women. . . .
>
> In Nashville, Tenn., there is a white man, Pat Hanifan, who outraged a little Afro-American girl, and, from the physical injuries received, she has been ruined for life. He was jailed for six months, discharged, and is now a detective in that city. In the same city, last May, a white man outraged an Afro-American girl in a drug store. He was arrested, and released on bail at the trial. It was rumored that five hundred Afro-Americans had organized to lynch him. Two hundred and fifty white citizens armed themselves with Winchesters and guarded him. A canon was placed in front of his home, and the Buchannan Rifles (State Militia) ordered to the scene for his protection. . . .
>
> The lesson this teaches and which every Afro-American should ponder well, is that a Winchester rifle should have a place of honor in every black home, and it should be used for that protection which the law refuses to give. When the white man who is always the aggressor knows he runs as great risk of biting the dust every time his Afro-American victim does, he will have greater respect for Afro-American life. The more the Afro-American yields and cringes and begs, the more he has to do so, the more he is insulted, outraged and lynched.[136]

In early America, accounts were offered that suggested that what actually went on in wealthy white households and what was carefully presented to the outside world were often two different things. Although often hidden beneath aristocratic aspirations and definitions of social and religious propriety, white households—presented as genteel and compassionate—often employed the same brands of violence used on slaves to secure compliance. The treatment of slaves was often visited on the white family, with little recourse from the courts, the church, or the community, and with all victimized parties in question seen to be responsible for the harm done to them. The human suffering as a result of the expression of control through violence is evidenced in the records of women and children of all races. (More information on the history of child sexual abuse and family violence as reflected in the mainstream community is presented in chapter 5.)

Only since the mid- to late twentieth century have theories about crime built on a critical review of the legal system as a mechanism for preserving rights and privileges for some while ensuring harsh penalties and sanctions for others. Critical theorists, feminist scholars, and peacemaking criminologists are working to better understand whether the existing legal system, a system these theorists argue is built by privilege to preserve privilege, can also serve to ensure basic legal protections, such as equal protection. The study of sex crimes is not only looking at certain kinds of sex offenders everyone wants to identify and prosecute. One particularly interesting aspect of studying sex crimes involves looking at the justice process and paying attention to which sexual acts are treated as criminal acts and under what circumstances. Again, reflecting on Becker's (1967) deviance classifications, introduced in chapter 2, the sexual violence demonstrated in both the First Nations communities and the institution of slavery raises questions about who defines whether an action is determined to be a deviant act or a criminal sexual assault. Becker suggested that, for an act to be defined as deviant, the larger group had to react to the harm done. Those acts of harm were not identified as either deviant or criminal in specific instances—instances when the offender was white and the victim was a person of color.

In other instances, particularly when the perpetrator was black and suspected of having committed a sexual crime against a white woman, the justice system seemed to work in the exact opposite way. These same people worked around the justice system, taking justice into their own hands as if there were an unspoken and accepted ideal that white people were entitled to apply the law when, where, and how they saw fit. The history of racism is part of the history of the United States that is often overlooked by mainstream. Sexual harm too has a legacy of people not seeing the harm or not acknowledging the act as being aggressive. When sexual harm happens and decisions are made outside the system about when, where, and how the law is to be applied, critical insights are offered about the conditions under which an arrest, a trial, or a conviction have a part to play in the US justice process, and this is particularly true as questions about justice are applied to incidents of sexual harm and violence in the United States throughout history and into the modern day.[137]

CHAPTER SUMMARY: A COLLECTIVE REFLECTION

This chapter includes a historical review of several socially prominent events with a particular focus on how various sex-related behaviors were identified as either deviant or criminal acts worthy of punishment or not even justifying a passing glance. A nontraditional (some will say "feminist," and others will say "critical") conceptualization of history produces a reflection on historical accounts of sexual matters as a collection of stories from different geographic locations, social positions, and periods over time and place. The history of sexual deviance and sex crimes in the United States is a compilation of religious ideology, legal guidelines, and scientific study. Mark Rifkin in his recent work, *When Did Indians Become Straight?*, references many Native writers who emphasize the fact that not all social systems have been organized around the idea of heterosexuality.[138] Although this is certainly not a credible idea in contemporary US culture, the ideas of alternative social structures are also the subject of branches of feminist and queer theories.

All of the current understandings of sexuality transpired amidst massive amounts of biological, social, religious, and cultural ignorance. A brief presentation of historical information provides a review of the study of sex alongside the controversies surrounding sexuality managed in a tug-of-war between religious ideology and sociolegal and political decisions with all of the limitations of science and (mis)information used to drive social and political agendas. Sexual violence has been prevalent throughout the history of the United States. Disparate versions of history suggest different brands of justice are meted out depending on the circumstances. Sometimes, these "circumstances" have to do with the race, class, or gender of the parties involved. Deliberate and intentional critical reflection on sexual harm and sexual violence is essential if a realistic picture of the social response to sexual harm is to help direct the social transformation necessary to remove sexual violence as a fact of social life. The past four decades of the twentieth century have been witness to massive amounts of social change in favor of addressing the needs of sexual assault victims and to address the prosecution of sexual crimes. Chapter 5 highlights three more contemporary experiences of institutionalized sexual harm for further consideration in the occurrence of child sexual abuse, marital rape and domestic violence, and social regulation of people in the LGBTQI community.

> **Text Box 4.2. Media Messages about History: Social Systems Structured That Sanction Sexual Violence**
>
> Who benefits and who is harmed when the collective social thinking maintains:
>
> - an active fear of the black male? Americans have been taught that young black men are perpetrators of crime in larger numbers than any other population. As a group, they are portrayed as rapists, gangsters, drug dealers, and murderers, whereas white people, usually men, have been portrayed as the "good guys," the police officers, the respected teachers, clergymen, coaches, or loving husbands and fathers.
> - the identification of First Nation people, particularly First Nation women, as "natives" or "savages" or "uncivilized heathens" or even as "animals" who are "less than human"?

KEY TERMS

abortifacient drugs
Alexandre Jean Baptiste Parent-
    Duchatelet
Alfred Kinsey
Anthony Comstock
anti-miscegenation laws
berdache
Code of Hammurabi
colonial history
Comstock Act
Dr. James Graham
Dr. John Harvey Kellogg
Enlightenment
Grant's Peace Policy
Havelock Ellis
Ida B. Wells-Barnett
Magnus Hirschfeld
Margaret Mead

Margaret Sanger
marital rape
Masters and Johnson
patriarchy
Progressive Era
Puritan
Reverend Sylvester Graham
Richard von Kraft Ebbing
Roe v. Wade
Secret Museum
sexology
Sigmund Freud
Tribal Law and Order Act of 2010
two-spirit people
Vern and Bonnie Bullough
Victorian era
Zepier v. United States

REVIEW QUESTIONS

1. Identify three contributions or ideas medicine and science made regarding the human understanding of sex that might be seen today as strange?

2. Consider the role of religion in the national conversation about the boundaries of appropriate sexual behavior. How is religion connected to the patriarchal social ideology present in the United States?

3. According to the chapter, Christian men were advised to seek sex outside of their primary relationship. Why?

4. Consider the section in the chapter on the Secret Museum. Who had access, and who was excluded from viewing the holdings? How is this connected to the contemporary conversation about pornography?

5. What piece of legislation was Margaret Sanger intent on repealing, which also resulted in her fleeing the country to avoid being arrested and ultimately serving time in jail? What was the result of her efforts?

DISCUSSION QUESTIONS

1. In what ways does history offer a history of white people, a history of black people, and a history of Native people instead of just a history of people? In what ways are historical stories seen as a collective history?

2. What role did religion play in the European history presented here? In the African American history? In the Native American history? In history today?

3. What aspects of history are not reflected here that are critical to thinking more fully about the history of sexual deviance and sex crimes?

4. What role did cultural differences between blacks and whites and whites and Natives play in the sexual conflicts represented throughout the periods of history discussed here?

5. Looking back, what characteristics of these cultures stand out to you today that you might not have noticed if you were living in that period of historical time?

NOTES

1. Kathy Peiss, *Major Problems in the History of American Sexuality: Documents and Essays* (Boston: Wadsworth Cengage Learning, 2002), xvi.

2. David Allyn, *Make Love, Not War: The Sexual Revolution: An Unfettered History* (New York: Routledge, 2001), xv.

3. Harriet A. Washington, *Medical Apartheid: The Dark History of Medical Experimentation on Black Americans from Colonial Times to the Present* (New York: Doubleday, 2007), x.

4. See, as examples, Elizabeth Pleck, *Domestic Tyranny: The Making of American Social Policy against Family Violence from Colonial Times to the Present* (Chicago: University of Illinois Press, 2004); Merril D. Smith, ed., *Sex without Consent: Rape and Sexual Coercion in America* (New York: New York University Press, 2001); John D. Wrathall, "Reading the Silences around Sexuality," in *Major Problems in the History of American Sexuality: Documents and Essays*, ed. Kathy Peiss (Boston: Wadsworth Cengage Learning, 2002), 16–23.

5. Pleck, *Domestic Tyranny*; Peiss, *Major Problems in the History of American Sexuality*.

6. Heather Whipps, "A Brief History of Human Sex," Live Science, July 27, 2006, accessed July 19, 2015, http://www.livescience.com/7088-history-human-sex.html.

7. K. Crenshaw, N. Gotanda, G. Peller, and K. Thomas, *Critical Race Theory: The Key Writings That Formed a Movement* (The New Press, 1996).

8. Charles F. Horne, "Introduction," Law Code of Hammurabi (1780 BC), 1915, accessed July 19, 2015, http://mcadams.posc.mu.edu/txt/ah/Assyria/Hammurabi.html#Introduction.

9. Horne, "Introduction."

10. Vern L. Bullough and Bonnie Bullough, *Sin, Sickness, and Sanity: A History of Sexual Attitudes* (New York: Garland Publishing, 1977), 25.

11. James A. Cox, "Bilboes, Brands, and Branks: Colonial Crimes and Punishments," *Colonial Williamsburg Journal*, Spring 03 (2003), accessed July 15, 2015, http://www.history.org/foundation/journal/spring03/branks.cfm.

12. Sharon Block, *Rape and Sexual Power in Early America* (Chapel Hill, NC: University of North Carolina Press, 2006), 14.

13. Stephanie Coontz, *The Way We Never Were* (New York: Basic Books, 2016), 88.

14. Else Hambleton, "'Playing the Rogue': Rape and Issues of Consent in Seventeenth-Century Massachusetts," in *Sex without Consent: Rape and Sexual Coercion in America*, ed. Merril D. Smith (New York: New York University Press, 2001), 27–45.

15. John D'Emilio and Estelle B. Freeman, *Intimate Matters: A History of Sexuality in America* (Chicago: University of Chicago Press, 1998), 16.

16. Jack Marrieta and G. S. Rowe, "Rape, Law, Courts, and Customs in Pennsylvania, 1682–1800," in *Sex without Consent: Rape and Sexual Coercion in America*, ed. Merril D. Smith (New York: New York University Press, 2001), 81–102.

17. Ibid.; Merril D. Smith, "Introduction: Studying Rape in American History," in *Sex without Consent: Rape and Sexual Coercion in America*, ed. Merril D. Smith (New York: New York University Press, 2001), 1–9.

18. "The History of Pornography (Ita)," Vimeo video, 19:17, posted by "Florence Video Productions," 2011, https://vimeo.com/19597578; see also Heather Whipps, "A Brief History

of Human Sex," Live Science, July 27, 2006, accessed September 4, 2019, https://www.live science.com/7088-history-human-sex.html.

19. Walter M. Kendrick, *The Secret Museum: Pornography in Modern Culture* (Berkeley, CA: University of California Press, 1996), 142.

20. "Pompeii—The Secret Museum," BBC Radio 4, September 21, 2002, accessed July 19, 2015, http://www.bbc.co.uk/radio4/history/pompeii.shtml.

21. J. Battalora, *Birth of a White Nation: The Invention of White People and Its Relevance Today* (Strategic Book Publishing, 2013), 27.

22. For more information about sexual practices outside of the Christian and European influences in the United States, see Reay Tannahill, *Sex in History* (London: Scarborough House Publishers, 1991); Bullough and Bullough, *Sin, Sickness, and Sanity*; Foucault, *The History of Sexuality*, vol. 1.

23. Tannahill, *Sex in History*, 133.

24. S. Deer, *The Beginning and End of Rape: Confronting Sexual Violence in Native America* (University of Minnesota Press, 2015), 74.

25. D'Emilio and Freeman, *Intimate Matters*, xv.

26. Jesse F. Battan, "In the Marriage Bed, Women's Sex Has Been Enslaved and Abused: Defining and Exposing Marital Rape in Late Nineteenth Century America," in *Sex without Consent: Rape and Sexual Coercion in America*, ed. Merril D. Smith (New York: New York University Press, 2001), 204–29.

27. Ibid., 209.

28. Matt Carroll, Sacha Pfeiffer, and Michael Rezendes, "Church Allowed Abuse by Priest for Years: Aware of Geoghan Record, Archdiocese Still Shuttled Him from Parish to Parish," *Boston Globe*, January 6, 2002, accessed July 20, 2015, http://www.boston.com/globe/spotlight/abuse/stories/010602_geoghan.htm.

29. M. Rezendes and the Globe Spotlight Team (M. Carroll, S. Pfeiffer, and M. Rezendes with editor W. Robinson), "Church Allowed Abuse by Priest for Years: Aware of Geoghan Record, Archdiocese Still Shuttled Him from Parish to Parish, *Boston Globe*, January 6, 2002. See also T. Doyle, A.W.R. Sipe, and P. Wall, *Sex, Priests, and Secret Codes: The Catholic Church's 2000 Year Paper Trail of Sexual Abuse* (Taylor Trade Publishing, 2006); and 40th Statewide Investigating Grand Jury Report 1, Interim—Redacted, August 14, 2018, https://assets.documentcloud.org/documents/4756976/READ-Pennsylvania-priest-abuse-grand-jury-report.pdf.

30. Tom Curran, dir., *Frontline: The Silence* (Boston, MA: PBS, 2011), television.

31. Annysa Johnson, "8,000 Instances of Abuse Alleged in Archdiocese Bankruptcy Hearing," *Milwaukee Journal Sentinel*, February 9, 2012, accessed July 19, 2015, http://www.jsonline.com/news/religion/archdiocese-bankruptcy-judge-allows-two-claims-to-stand-me44pue-139044534.html; Chuck Quirmbach, "Bankrupt Archdiocese Tries to Limit Abuse Claims," *NPR*, February 16, 2012, accessed July 19, 2015, http://www.npr.org/2012/02/16/146995458/bankrupt-wis-church-tries-to-limit-abuse-claims.

32. Lydia Syson, *Doctor of Love: James Graham and His Celestial Bed* (London: Alma Books Ltd., 2008).

33. Vern L. Bullough, *The Society for the Scientific Study of Sex: A Brief History* (Mount Vernon, IA: Foundation for the Scientific Study of Sexuality, 1989).

34. Chana Gazit, dir., *American Experience: The Pill* (New York: PBS, 2003), television.

35. Ibid.

36. Richard von Krafft-Ebing, *Psychopathia Sexualis: A Clinical-Forensic Study* (New York: Bloat Books, 1999).

37. Havelock Ellis, *Sexual Inversion* (Charleston, SC: Nabu Press, 2010).

38. Ibid.

39. J. D'Emilio, *Intimate Matters: A History of Sexuality in America*, 2nd ed. (University of Chicago Press, 1998), 133.

40. Jeffrey Moussaieff Masson, *The Assault on Truth: Freud's Suppression of the Seduction Theory* (New York: Pocket Books, 1988); Jeffrey Moussaieff Masson, *A Dark Science: Women, Sexuality, and Psychiatry in the Nineteenth Century* (New York: Farrar, Straus and Giroux, 1984).

41. Karen Terry, *Sexual Offenses and Offenders: Theory, Practice, and Policy* (Belmont, CA: Wadsworth Cengage Learning, 2006).

42. L. Reagan, *When Abortion Was a Crime: Women, Medicine, and Law in the United States, 1867–1973* (University of California Press, 1998).

43. Janice M. Irvine, *Disorders of Desire: Sexuality and Gender in Modern American Sexology* (Philadelphia: Temple University Press, 2005), 16.

44. Margaret Mead, *Coming of Age in Samoa: A Psychological Study of Primitive Youth for Western Civilisation* (New York: William Morrow Paperbacks, 2001).

45. See, for example, Judith Reisman's website, www.drjudithreisman.com; Sue Ellin Browder, "Kinsey's Secret: The Phony Science of the Sexual Revolution," *Crisis Magazine*, May 28, 2012, accessed July 20, 2015, http://www.crisismagazine.com/2012/kinseys-secret-the-phony-science-of-the-sexual-revolution.

46. Barak Goodman and John Maggio, dir., *American Experience: Kinsey* (Saint Paul, MN: PBS, 2005), television; Kinsey Institute, http://www.kinseyinstitute.org/.

47. "Kinsey Reports," The Rockefeller Foundation, https://rockfound.rockarch.org/kinsey-reports. See also, for example, J. Gathorne-Hardy, *Alfred C. Kinsey: Sex the Measure of All Things; A Biography* (Chatto and Windus, 1998).

48. David E. Greydanus, "Masturbation: Historic Perspective," *New York Journal of Medicine* 80, no. 12 (1980): 1892–96.

49. Michael S. Patton, "Twentieth-Century Attitudes toward Masturbation," *Journal of Religion and Health* 25, no. 4 (1986): 291–302.

50. Douglas Jehl, "Surgeon General Forced to Resign by White House," *New York Times*, December 10, 1994, accessed July 16, 2015, http://www.nytimes.com/1994/12/10/us/surgeon-general-forced-to-resign-by-white-house.html.

51. *Catechism of the Catholic Church* #2352: "Both the Magisterium of the Church, in the course of a constant tradition, and the moral sense of the faithful have been in no doubt and have firmly maintained that masturbation is an intrinsically and gravely disordered action," accessed July 20, 2015, http://www.vatican.va/archive/ccc_css/archive/catechism/p3s2c2a6.htm; see also "Straight Talk about the Catholic Teaching on Masturbation," beginningCatholic.com, 2006, accessed July 20, 2015, http://www.beginningcatholic.com/catholic-teaching-on-masturbation.html.

52. David Batty, "Prisoner Found Guilty of Masturbating in His Cell," *The Guardian*, July 26, 2007, accessed July 19, 2015, http://www.theguardian.com/world/2007/jul/26/usa.davidbatty6; see also Martha Neil, "8 Targets in Prison Masturbation Cases," *ABA Journal*, July 27, 2007, accessed July 19, 2015, http://www.abajournal.com/news/article/eight_inmates_in_prison_masturbation_case/.

53. Adee Braun, "Looking to Quell Sexual Urges? Consider the Graham Cracker," *The Atlantic*, January 15, 2014, accessed July 20, 2015, http://www.theatlantic.com/health/archive/2014/01/looking-to-quell-sexual-urges-consider-the-graham-cracker/282769/.

54. James C. Mohr, *Abortion in America: The Origins and Evolution of National Policy* (New York: Oxford University Press, 1979).

55. Leslie J. Reagan, *When Abortion Was a Crime: Women, Medicine, and Law in the United States 1867–1973* (Oakland, CA: University of California Press, 1998), 10.

56. Daniel Scott Smith, "Family Limitation, Sexual Control, and Domestic Feminism in Victorian America," *Feminist Studies* 1, no. 3/4 (1973): 40–57.

57. Bullough and Bullough, *Sin, Sickness, and Sanity*; see also Mary Roth Walsh, *Doctors Wanted: No Women Need Apply: Sexual Barriers in the Medical Profession, 1835–1975* (New Haven, CT: Yale University Press, 1977).

58. Linda Perlman Gordon, *Woman's Body, Woman's Right: Birth Control in America* (New York: Penguin Books, 1990); Janet Farrell Brodie, *Contraception and Abortion in Nineteenth Century America* (New York: Cornell University Press, 1997); Reagan, *When Abortion Was a Crime*, 13.

59. "State Policy Updates: Major Developments in Sexual & Reproductive Health," as of August 15, 2019, Guttmacher Institute, http://www.guttmacher.org/statecenter/updates/index.html.

60. "The Personhood Movement: Where It Came from and Where It Stands Today," ProPublica, https://www.propublica.org/article/the-personhood-movement-timeline.

61. Bill Clifford, personal communication with the author, February 12, 2012; C. Johnson, "About My 'Spilled Semen' Amendment to the Oklahoma Personhood Bill," *The Guardian*, February 9, 2012, https://www.theguardian.com/commentisfree/cifamerica/2012/feb/09/spilled-semen-amendment-oklahoma-personhood-bill.

62. Ari Armstrong and Diana Hsieh, "Why the 'Personhood' Amendment Is Anti-Life," Coalition for Secular Government, August 31, 2010, accessed July 19, 2015, http://www.seculargovernment.us/docs/a62.pdf.

63. Cathy Lynn Grossman, "New Surveys: Catholics Want Birth Control Coverage," *USA Today*, February 7, 2012, accessed July 16, 2015, http://content.usatoday.com/communities/Religion/post/2012/02/contraception-catholic-bishops-obama-hhs/1#.T3evtYH4JMQ.

64. Glenn Kessler, "The Claim That 98% of Catholic Women Use Contraception: A Media Foul," *Washington Post*, February 17, 2012, accessed July 16, 2015, http://www.washingtonpost.com/blogs/fact-checker/post/the-claim-that-98-percent-of-catholic-women-use-contraception-a-media-foul/2012/02/16/gIQAkPeqIR_blog.html.

65. Reagan, *When Abortion Was a Crime*, 39.

66. Ibid., 77.

67. Ibid., 214.

68. The Guttmacher Institute offers monthly information on legislation related to the abortion issue for each state: https://www.guttmacher.org/state-policy/explore/overview-abortion-laws.

69. *Abortion: What Does the Church Teach? The Orthodox Perspective on Abortion, As Presented to the United States Supreme Court in the Amicus Curae Brief* (Conciliar Press, 1995). See also L. W. Tentler, *Catholics and Contraception: An American History* (Cornell University Press, 2004).

70. Jessica Bowden, "Developing-World Women and the Need for Modern Contraceptives," *Imperfect Parent*, May 16, 2011, accessed July 19, 2015, http://www.imperfectparent.com/topics/2011/05/16/developing-world-women-and-the-need-for-modern-contraceptives/.

71. Barbara J. Bloemink and Lisa Gail Collins, *Re/Righting American History* (Katonah, NY: Katonah Museum of Art, 1999).

72. Tannahill, *Sex in History*, 41–42.

73. Goodman and Maggio, *American Experience: Kinsey*.

74. Adrian Forsyth, *A Natural History of Sex: The Ecology and Evolution of Mating Behavior* (Richmond Hill, ON: Firefly Books Ltd., 2001).

75. Ira L. Reisse, *Premarital Sexual Standards in America: A Sociological Investigation of the Relative Social and Cultural Integration of American Sexual Standards* (New York: The Free Press, 1960), accessed July 19, 2015, http://www.sexarchive.info/Reiss1/index.html; Reay Tannahill, *Sex in History*.

76. Reisse, *Premarital Sexual Standards*, Chapter 1, accessed July 19, 2015, http://www.sexarchive.info/Reiss1/html/chapter_1.html#a1.

77. Vine Deloria Jr., *God Is Red* (New York: Putnam, 2003).

78. Coontz, *The Way We Never Were*; James W. Loewen, *The Lies My Teacher Told Me: Everything Your American History Textbook Got Wrong* (New York: Touchstone, 2007).

79. See, for example, J. Fear-Segal and S. D. Rose, eds., *Carlisle Indian Industrial School: Indigenous Histories, Memories, and Reclamations* (University of Nebraska Press, 2018); W. Churchill, *Kill the Indian, Save the Man: The Genocidal Impact of American Indian Residential Schools* (City Lights Publisher, 2004).

80. Joy DeGruy Leary, *Post Traumatic Slave Syndrome: America's Legacy of Enduring Injury and Healing* (Portland, OR: Upton Press, 2005); H. Washington, *Medical Apartheid: The Dark History of Medical Experimentation on Black Americans from Colonial Times to the Present* (Anchor, 2008).

81. See, for example, the work of V. Deloria, *Red Earth, White Lies: Native Americans and the Myth of Scientific Fact* (Fulcrum Publishing, 1997).

82. See, for example, all of Vine Deloria Jr.'s work; Andrea Smith, *Conquest: Sexual Violence and American Indian Genocide* (Durham, NC, 2015); Paula Allen Gunn, *The Sacred Hoop: Recovering the Feminine in American Indian Traditions* (Beacon Press, 1992); S. Deer, *The Beginning and End of Rape* (University of Minnesota, 2015).

83. See, for example, D. W. Adams, *Educating for Extinction: American Indians and the Boarding School Experience, 1875–1928*, 3rd ed. (University Press of Kansas, 1995).

84. Joy DeGruy Leary, *Post Traumatic Slave Syndrome: America's Legacy of Enduring Injury and Healing* (Portland, OR: Uptone Press, 2005).

85. Loewen, *Lies My Teacher Told Me*; A. Wong, "History Class and the Fictions about Race in America," *The Atlantic*, October 21, 2015, https://www.theatlantic.com/education/archive/2015/10/the-history-class-dilemma/411601/; R. DiAngelo, *White Fragility: Why It's So Hard for White People to Talk about Racism* (Beacon Press, 2018).

86. Peiss, *Major Problems in the History of American Sexuality*.

87. Coontz, *The Way We Never Were*, 41.

88. D. St. Clair, Native American scholar, personal communication with author, June 26, 2011.

89. Ibid.

90. Coontz, *The Way We Never Were*, 42.

91. Andrea Smith, *Conquest: Sexual Violence and American Indian Genocide* (Durham, NC: Duke University Press, 2015).

92. Andrea Smith (Cherokee), Native studies scholar and cofounder of INCITE! Women of Color Against Violence, has placed sexual violence at the center of the harms committed against Native people and a cause of breakdown of the Native communities reflected in crime, domestic violence, drug abuse, and other social problems. In her award-winning book *Conquest: Sexual Violence and American Indian Genocide*, Smith argues US conquest of American Indian people continues to the present day. See also the #MMIW (Missing and Murdered Indigenous Woman) movement at the Coalition to Stop Violence Against Native Women: https://www.csvanw.org/mmiw/.

93. Smith, *Conquest*, 35.

94. Ibid., particularly Chapters 2, 5, and 6.

95. Ibid., 46.

96. Coontz, *The Way We Never Were*, 50. Smith, *Conquest*, particularly Chapters 1 and 7; Tannahill, *Sex in History*; Peiss, *Major Problems in the History of American Sexuality*; Smith, *Sex without Consent*, Chapter 1, 10–27; Drew Haden Taylor, "Indian Love Call," in *Me Sexy: An Exploration of Native Sex and Sexuality*, ed. Drew Haden Taylor (Vancouver, BC: Douglas & McIntyre, 2008), 20–32.

97. Alice Nash, "'None of the Women Were Abused': Indigenous Contexts for the Treatment of Women Captives in the Northeast," in *Sex without Consent: Rape and Sexual Coercion in America*, ed. Merril D. Smith (New York: New York University Press, 2001), Chapter 1, 10–26.

98. Wue-Ellen Jacobs, Wesley Thomas, and Sabine Land, eds., *Two-Spirit People: Native American Gender Identity, Sexuality, and Spirituality* (University of Illinois Press, 1997).

99. Nash, "'None of the Women Were Abused,'" 17.

100. Ibid., 22.

101. Richard Godbeer, "The Overflowing of Friendship," in *American Sexual Histories*, 2nd ed., ed. Elizabeth Reis (Malden, MA: Blackwell Publishing, 2001), 54.

102. Nash, "'None of the Women Were Abused,'" 23.

103. Godbeer, "The Overflowing of Friendship," 47.

104. See, for example, Will Roscoe, *Changing Ones: Third and Fourth Genders in Native North America* (New York: Palgrave Macmillan, 1998); Sue-Ellen Jacobs, Wesley Thomas, and Sabine Lang, *Two-Spirited People: Native American Gender Identity, Sexuality, and Spirituality* (Chicago: University of Illinois Press, 1997); Will Roscoe, *Living the Spirit: A Gay American Indian Anthology* (New York: St. Martin's Press, 1988).

105. Roscoe, *Changing Ones*, 7.

106. Ibid., 9.

107. Ibid., 17.

108. Mark Rifkin, *When Did Indians Become Straight? Kinship, the History of Sexuality, and Native Sovereignty* (New York: Oxford University Press, 2011); David Wallace Adams, *Education for Extinction: American Indians and the Boarding School Experience, 1875–1928* (Lawrence, KS: University of Kansas Press, 1995).

109. Kathleen M. Brown, *Good Wives, Nasty Wenches, and Anxious Patriarchs: Gender, Race, and Power in Colonial Virginia* (Chapel Hill, NC: University of North Carolina Press, 1996), 58–61.

110. Godbeer, "The Overflowing of Friendship," 52.

111. Coontz, *The Way We Never Were*, 155.

112. Godbeer, "The Overflowing of Friendship," 54.

113. Joseph Boyden, "Bush Country," in *Me Sexy: An Exploration of Native Sex and Sexuality*, ed. Drew Haden Taylor (Vancouver, BC: Douglas & McIntyre, 2008), 5–14.

114. See, for example, Mark Rifkin, *When Did Indians Become Straight? Kinship, the History of Sexuality, and Native Sovereignty* (New York: Oxford University Press, 2011); Haden Taylor, *Me Sexy: An Exploration of Native Sex and Sexuality*, 5–14; Jacobs et al., *Two-Spirited People*.

115. Godbeer, "The Overflowing of Friendship," 49.

116. Steven W. Perry, "American Indians and Crime: A BJS Statistical Profile, 1992–2002," *Bureau of Justice Statistics* (2004), accessed July 20, 2015, http://www.justice.gov/sites/default/files/otj/docs/american_indians_and_crime.pdf.

117. *Maze of Injustice: The Failure to Protect Indigenous Women from Sexual Violence in the USA*, Amnesty International, 2007, accessed October 20, 2019, https://www.amnestyusa.org/pdfs/mazeofinjustice.pdf.

118. Larry Cox, "President Obama Signs Tribal Law and Order Act," *Human Rights Now Blog*, August 2, 2010, accessed July 19, 2015, http://blog.amnestyusa.org/women/president-obama-signs-tribal-law-and-order-act/.

119. *Maze of Injustice.*

120. Bonnie Cermak, "Race, Honor, Citizenship: The Massie Rape/Murder Case," in *Sex without Consent: Rape and Sexual Coercion in America*, ed. Merril D. Smith (New York: New York University Press, 2001), 230–46; Lisa Lindquist Dorr, "'Another Negro-Did-It Crime': Black-on-White Rape and Protest in Virginia," in *Sex without Consent: Rape and Sexual Coercion in America*, ed. Merril D. Smith (New York: New York University Press, 2001), 247–64.

121. D'Emilio and Freeman, *Intimate Matters*, 85–108; Peiss, *Major Problems*, 142–86.

122. D'Emilio and Freeman, *Intimate Matters*, 86.

123. Ramon A. Gutierrez, *When Jesus Came the Corn Mothers Went Away: Marriage, Sexuality, and Power in New Mexico, 1500–1846* (Stanford, CA: Stanford University Press, 1991).

124. D'Emilio and Freeman, *Intimate Matters*, 86–87.

125. Brenda E. Stevenson, "Slave Marriage and Family Relations," in *Major Problems in the History of American Sexuality: Documents and Essays*, ed. Kathy Peiss (Boston: Wadsworth Cengage Learning, 2002), 159–72.

126. D'Emilio and Freeman, *Intimate Matters*, 97.

127. Ibid., 86.

128. Nell Irvin Painter, "Soul Murder and Slavery," in *Major Problems in the History of American Sexuality: Documents and Essays*, ed. Kathy Peiss (Boston: Wadsworth Cengage Learning, 2002), 173–85.

129. Ibid.

130. Ibid., 181.

131. D'Emilio and Freeman, *Intimate Matters*, 94.

132. Ibid., 96.

133. See, for example, Martha Hodes, "White Women, Black Men, and Adultery in the Antebellum South," in *American Sexual Histories*, 2nd ed., ed. Elizabeth Reis (Malden, MA: Blackwell Publishing, 2001), 147–60.

134. Clare A. Lyons, "Sex among the Rabble: 'The Histories of Some of the Penitents in the Magdalen-House, 1760,'" in *American Sexual Histories*, 2nd ed., edited by Elizabeth Reis (Malden, MA: Blackwell Publishing, 2001), 143.

135. M. Hodes, *White Women, Black Men: Illicit Sex in the Nineteenth-Century South* (Yale University Press, 1999), especially Chapter 4, 68–95.

136. Ida B. Wells-Barnett, "Southern Horrors: Lynch Law in All Its Phases," in *Major Problems in the History of American Sexuality: Documents and Essays*, ed. Kathy Peiss (Boston: Wadsworth Cengage Learning, 2002), 155, accessed July 16, 2015, http://www.gutenberg.org/files/14975/14975-h/14975-h.htm.

137. See, for example, D. Bell, *Faces at the Bottom of the Well: The Permanence of Racism* (Basic Books, 1993); I. Kendi, *Stamped from the Beginning: The Definitive History of Racist Ideas in America* (Bold Type Books, 2017).

138. Rifkin, *When Did Indians Become Straight?*

5

Shifting a Legacy of Institutionalized Sexual Violence and Harm

◆ ◆ ◆

The history of childhood is a nightmare from which we have only recently begun to awaken.

—Lloyd de Mause[1]

Domestic violence is not a problem of a few "diseased or dysfunctional" individuals, but rather is a problem rooted and nurtured in social relationships and structures. Because it is so embedded, stopping domestic violence requires a coordinated community response where health, justice, and social service systems join with educational, religious, and victim services to confront violence. No one institution can do it alone.

—Anne Ganley[2]

We are helpless to change the course of this violence unless, and until, we achieve a national consensus that it deserves our profound public outrage.

—Then Senator Joseph Biden[3]

Unfortunately, we've also seen a historic rise in the distribution of child pornography, in the number of images being shared online, and in the level of violence associated with child exploitation and sexual abuse crimes. Tragically, the only place we've seen a decrease is in the age of victims. This is—quite simply—unacceptable.

—Attorney General Eric Holder[4]

THE IDEA THAT THE WORLD TODAY is less violent and more peaceful than any previous period in human history was a provocative idea presented by Harvard psychologist Steven Pinker in 2011.[5] Offering evidence beginning from within the seventeenth- and eighteenth-century European Enlightenment (refer back to the timeline presented in Text Box 4.1 in chapter 4), the "humanitarian revolution" is argued to reflect the steady decline of forms of violence such as torture, slavery, despotism, duels, and extreme forms of punishment. In more contemporary society, particularly over the past 50 years, what Pinker refers to as the "rights revolutions" demonstrates extraordinary efforts to address human rights concerns, resulting in less violence against marginalized social groups, including ethnic minorities, women, children, members of the LGBTQI community, and animals.[6] A historical reduction in violence over time might indicate collective vision forward for reducing or eliminating the processes for inflicting harm and using violence and abuse to secure compliance. Reflecting on several modern social institutions and their influence on social attitudes about the use and acceptability of violence affords interesting insights into the specialized history of sexual violence.

Conversations about the possibility of declines in the social acceptability of violence are happening in spite of an excavation of what have been stories and illustrations of a sordid history of violence in the United States, in the wide open and in plain public view. Although slavery illustrates an example of what is now seen as a disreputable social practice, other harms were perpetrated behind closed doors and from within perhaps the most basic of social institutions: the family. In some cases aggressive acts between family members tolerated in the past as normal are now identified as abusive. As examples, such acts are referred to as **family violence, domestic violence, relationship violence,** and **dating violence**; expressions of this broader form of violence can be both physical and/or sexual in nature. Incest and marital rape, for example, are perpetrated between family members, and dating violence is perpetrated between people known to each other or relational partners. These abuses exist within a social framework where both formal and informal social sanctions for actions in the family and in intimate relationships were governed from within a church structure initially run exclusively by men, from within state governance primarily run by men, and from within past families whose historical practice and traditional authority designed to govern the family was assigned specifically to men as the heads of household. Because the abuses were handed out by men, usually against women and children, and most violence and sexual abuse are perpetrated at the hands of men, the gender and power dynamics warrant closer attention. (For more information about the dynamics of gender and power in sexual violence, see chapter 7's review of contemporary studies on sexual harm and the gendered analysis of deviance in chapter 2.)

This conceptualization of male superiority within social institutions, referred to as **patriarchy** (introduced in chapter 4), is used broadly to refer to social structures where fathers control families and families are organized as the units of social and economic power—an idea, some argue, which has more resonance historically than in contemporary family structures.[7] The formal historical sanctioning of the institution of marriage, by both church and state governments, as the center of family life where the male was determined to be the head of household is an important awareness to acknowledge. The family structure was (some would say *is*) also, and equally importantly, not only a system of male domination but also—for better or worse—a structure creating the expectation of parental domination over children. This traditional idea of domination, regulation, and control has been challenged. As a result, many reforms in the United States focused on disallowing violence and creating protections for women and children in tandem while also continuing to identify and define essential rights for these groups over the last century.[8]

The idea that family violence is socially and politically constructed suggests politics is used to define what is socially and politically accepted within a family as standard or accepted practice.[9] In his early studies on family violence, one of the early family violence researchers, Murray Straus, identified physical violence as the ultimate recourse for keeping subordinates in place.[10] Largely as a result of feminists, historiography researchers went back to look at a history more focused on family structures and, more specifically, on the occurrences of abuse.[11] Studying family systems in the 1600s to 1900s, historian Stephanie Coontz identified four family systems in the early years of the United States,[12] beginning with Native communities linked by *kinship systems*. European settlers in the colonies developed *household-family systems* primarily used for social reproduction or as a center for the production of consumer goods. The role of family in producing consumer goods challenged First Nation, or Native, social organizations, which did not lend themselves to the kind of Western expansion brought over from Europe.[13]

Family systems structured outside Western ideological design were dismissed as illegitimate or destroyed among Natives by advancing European settlement and deliberate US government actions to "civilize" Native children; African tribes were civilized through the institution of slavery and slave owners' regulation of slave marriage and reproduction.[14] In the 1820s, the *domestic family* emerged, with a clear division of labor between husbands and wives and a socialization of children into particular class values.[15] In the early 1900s, the family structure shifted again from parent–child to *couple-centered nuclear family units*. Each family system reflects a different set of ideals about individual relations to others in society.[16] In her follow-up work, studying family life from 1900 to 1990,[17] Coontz argues that the myths about family life, in many ways, live larger as idealized images rather than actually being based in historical reality[18]—a harsh historical reality where the home is said to be one of the most dangerous places for women and children.[19]

At its basic element, history offers a collection of individual stories describing people's lives, and every life is lived differently. Efforts are made to present various examples of the range of events in early America, which complicates the contemporary conversations about sexual harm and sexual violence prevention. Although legal protections for women were documented in Massachusetts as early as 1641,[20] the actual enforcements to prevent violent practices within households and between intimate partners has remained an intense subject of social controversy.[21] While monumental aspects of sexual harm in these historical realities persist in the present day, other forms of resistance to mainstream ideologies on gender and sexuality are being fought "out loud and proud."[22] Battle lines are currently drawn between the gay community's fight for equality and social conservatives who oppose gay marriage and what is often referred to as a "gay lifestyle."[23] While each individual involved will certainly have their own individual ideas on the subject, young gay people are commonly known to die by suicide at an alarmingly high rate, for example, when compared to straight youth.[24] Social conservatives tend to collectively identify homosexuality as being "against God" and argue marriage should be legally defined as between a man and a woman.[25]

Structured similarly to chapter 4, this chapter outlines another set of three targeted historical reflections. The focus is on the aspects of harm perpetrated in the family, particularly regarding gendered and/or sexualized violence. The history of the subordination of women and children represents the first two of three aspects of family life identified for closer review. The lack of social sanctions and preventions against harm from within the family, particularly sexual harm, represents an institutionalized form of violence currently demanding more popular social and political attention. The third and final segment of the chapter is focused on the role of the family in two directions: (1) in its history of rearing children who identify as LGBTQI[26] and (2) in the larger history of collective efforts to secure—and resist—legal equality for and an expanded definition of family to include sexual minorities. The dynamics of family have included violence, and a portion of that violence has been linked to gender dynamics and is sexualized, while another form of implicit bias is to be found in the ongoing social debate and rejection of certain families within communities and by law based on sexual orientation. To understand crime linked to sexual acts and sexual orientation is to understand, at least in part, the dynamics of sex and power within the institution of what is legally identified as a family.[27]

A HISTORY OF CHILD ABUSE

The maltreatment of children is documented throughout history. **Infanticide**, the killing of infants and young children, was documented in biblical times. In early Rome, the father was given complete power to kill, abandon, or even sell his child.[28] Children of the poor suffered extensively throughout history based on the ability of the family unit to meet their needs for food and shelter. Both in the home and in schools, corporal punishment was used to secure compliance. An 1854 law in Massachusetts recommended death to a child over 16 years of age who was found guilty of cursing their parent unless it could be proven the parent did not raise the child in a Christian way.[29] Parents would often use children for labor or place their children in **indenture programs** from very young ages, where they would work or learn a trade in exchange for room and board. As the industrial revolution advanced, children were brought into the labor market as a means to save money because children worked for less than adults. Child labor laws vary from country to country and are still of concern around the world today.[30]

Even up through the twentieth century, school systems, like family systems, used corporal punishment in an effort to secure a child's compliance. Traditionally, children were considered to be the property of the father. Daughters were used by families and heads of households as a means for securing social standing or to barter for land and money. The marriage of really young girls was not uncommon in the United States and still happens in places around the world today.[31] Since early times throughout the world, fathers paid dowries for the marriage of their daughters, and, if no money was available, the daughters would be sent to the convent. (More on marriage practices for young girls at very young ages is covered in chapter 6.) Sexual violence was also present in other social systems. Early documentation exists of monks and priests treating young nuns as wives and threatening them with excommunication from the Church if they were to tell of their sexual abuse.[32] In 1548, England passed the first legal protection for children at risk of sexual abuse, protecting boys from forced sodomy, followed soon by another law in 1576 that protected girls younger than age 10 from forcible rape.[33] Again, the passage of the laws did not always result in active social protections and enforcement.

Churches and community programs were often sources of support for children and families, although that support depended on the community and the historical era. One of the first attempts to work in defense of children is found in the **Elizabethan Poor Laws,** a collection of laws passed beginning in 1601 through parish communities to assist the parents of impoverished children. In 1838, Charles Dickens wrote *Oliver Twist*, which would become the first of several novels he would write about the abandoned, abused, and neglected youth of the day that brought the issue of child abuse and neglect out to the larger social awareness.[34]

CHILD ABUSE PREVENTION EFFORTS

Orphan children in the United States were famously put on display in local train stations in late the 1850s through the late 1920s, when as many as 250,000 children from Eastern cities were sent to Midwestern and Western states in a program sponsored by the Children's Aid Society. Called the **Orphan Train Movement** and sponsored by child savers and well-known reformer **Charles Loring Brace,** the controversial program took children from impoverished families in "depraved urban surroundings and placed them with upstanding Anglo-Protestant farming families . . . determined to salvage the civil potential of poor immigrant children."[35]

In 1866, **Henry Bergh** created the American Society for the Prevention of the Cruelty to Animals and helped New York state pass legislation making cruelty to animals illegal. His collective action was referred to as **Bergh's War,** based on his enthusiasm in this effort. In 1874, Henry Bergh intervened on behalf of an abused child, **Mary Ellen Wilson.** Although historical reports differ, the abuse case set in motion a national effort to prevent child abuse using the legislation to prevent animal abuse because there were no laws to prevent child abuse.[36] In 1875, the **Society for the Prevention of Cruelty to Children** (SPCC) was established under **Elbridge T. Gerry,** the lawyer who prosecuted Mary Ellen's case.

As the New York City SPCC was replicated in other large cities, protective services for children began to reflect a more family-centered approach to child protection; under pressure from various social groups, in 1909 the White House Conference on Dependent Children introduced the idea of a US Children's Bureau to oversee the welfare of children, which was enacted in 1912. Although World War I became a national priority, between 1914 and 1918, the Keating-Owen Child Labor Act was passed in 1916 but challenged nine months later and ruled unconstitutional by the US Supreme Court in *Hammer v. Dagenhart.*[37] The **Child Welfare League of America** (CWLA) was established in 1920 as a large coalition of private and public agencies and is now the nation's oldest and largest organization serving vulnerable children and families.[38] The Social Security Act established aid to dependent children in 1935, in the middle of the Great Depression, with the **Fair Labor Standards Act of 1938** outlawing child labor, with the exception of children working in agriculture.[39] World War II, 1940 through 1945, soon followed, and in 1942 Congress authorized state grants to provide daycare for children of women doing work to benefit the war effort, as reflected by Rosie the Riveter, who became a social and cultural icon representing women working on the home front while the men were away at war.[40]

In 1946, Columbia University radiology professor **John Caffey** presented medical findings to suggest unexplained X-ray injuries might indicate child abuse. Amidst expansive social service legislation under President John F. Kennedy, **Dr. C. Henry Kempe** in 1962, then at the Department of Pediatrics, University of Colorado School of Medicine, presented the famous article "The Battered Child Syndrome" in the *Journal of the American Medical Association* (*JAMA*).[41] Initially focused on children 3 years and younger, the recommendation for medical professionals to look more closely at discrepancies between the information provided by the family and the clinical findings collected as an indicator of possible abuse became standardized as a result. The age recommendations changed to include children over the age of 3; however, the medical practice to compare family stories with a medical determination of probable causes of injury continues today.

Between 1960 and 1965, the CWLA Standards for Child Protection Services resulted in **mandatory child abuse reporting laws** in most states amidst the introduction of the War on Poverty announced by President Lyndon B. Johnson in 1964.[42] In 1972, the National Center for the Prevention of Child Abuse and Neglect was established to offer training and research on child abuse issues with the **Child Abuse Prevention and Treatment Act** (CAPTA) passed in 1974, providing federal funding to states in support of an array of child protection services, definitions of child abuse and neglect, research, and a national clearinghouse of child abuse and neglect information. CAPTA was reauthorized in 1978, the same year as the **Indian Child Welfare Act**, seeking to keep Indian children with American Indian families in response to an alarming number of Indian children being forcibly removed from their homes by both public and private agencies.[43] The CAPTA has been regularly reauthorized, revised, and amended to include attention to children and families and keeping children safe.[44]

CHILD SEXUAL ABUSE

Child sexual abuse can be defined from both a clinical and a legal perspective. According to the Child Welfare Information Gateway, a division of the US Department of Health and Human Services, two types of statutes define sexual abuse: (1) child protection (civil) and (2) criminal.[45] Child protection statutes tend to apply only to situations where the offenders are the children's caretakers. Criminal statutes outline prohibitions against specific sexual acts and the penalties. Criminal statutes prohibit sex with a child, regardless of the adult's relationship to the child.[46] US federal laws also define efforts to eliminate and prosecute child pornography, also known as the **sexual exploitation of children**.

> Images of child pornography are not protected under First Amendment rights, and are illegal contraband under federal law. Section 2256 of Title 18, United States Code, defines child pornography as any visual depiction of sexually explicit conduct involving a minor (someone under 18 years of age).[47]

Child sexual abuse issues are typically handled solely within a single state jurisdiction, unless the child is abused on federal lands, for example.[48] The Child Welfare Information Gateway's State Statute Series outlines a definition of child sexual abuse and, then, by state.[49] Consider the definitions from Minnesota, California, Texas, and New York in Text Box 5.1.

The American Psychological Association suggests that there is no universal definition of child sexual abuse but identifies the dominant position of an adult to be a central characteristic.[50] Sexual abuse was not widely studied until **David Finkelhor** surveyed college students in the late 1970s to determine whether they had been sexually abused.[51] Highlighting the convergence of the child protection movement and the feminist movement,[52] Finkelhor was one of the first academics to study sexual harm. Diana Russell's 1983 research suggested that 38 percent of women surveyed reported at least one sexual abuse experience before the age of 18, with 28 percent reporting abuse before the age of 14.[53] Child abuse research has exploded with attention being given to the ways academics, practitioners, medical personnel, research agencies, government agencies, and service agencies conduct and understand the definitions of harm and tailor their work and publications accordingly. Several variations of related definitions and harms are discussed below.

Text Box 5.1.   Minnesota Statutes, 2014. 626.556 Reporting of Maltreatment of Minors.

Subdivision 2: Definitions.

(d) "Sexual abuse" means the subjection of a child by a person responsible for the child's care, by a person who has a significant relationship to the child, as defined in section 609.341, or by a person in a position of authority, as defined in section 609.341, subdivision 10, to any act which constitutes a violation of section 609.342 (criminal sexual conduct in the first degree), 609.343 (criminal sexual conduct in the second degree), 609.344 (criminal sexual conduct in the third degree), 609.345 (criminal sexual conduct in the fourth degree), or 609.3451 (criminal sexual conduct in the fifth degree). Sexual abuse also includes any act which involves a minor which constitutes a violation of prostitution offenses under sections 609.321 to 609.324 or 617.246. Sexual abuse includes threatened sexual abuse which includes the status of a parent or household member who has committed a violation which requires registration as an offender under section 243.166, subdivision 1b, paragraph (a) or (b), or required registration under section 243.166, subdivision 1b, paragraph (a) or (b). https://www.revisor.mn.gov/statutes/?id=626.556

California Statutes: 2014. Penal Code Section 11164-11174.3

11165. As used in this article "child" means a person under the age of 18 years.

11165.1. As used in this article, "sexual abuse" means sexual assault or sexual exploitation as defined by the following:

(a) "Sexual assault" means conduct in violation of one or more of the following sections: Section 261 (rape), subdivision (d) of

Section 261.5 (statutory rape), 264.1 (rape in concert), 285 (incest), 286 (sodomy), subdivision (a) or (b), or paragraph (1) of subdivision (c) of Section 288 (lewd or lascivious acts upon a child), 288a (oral copulation), 289 (sexual penetration), or 647.6 (child molestation).

(b) Conduct described as "sexual assault" includes, but is not limited to, all of the following:

(1) Penetration, however slight, of the vagina or anal opening of one person by the penis of another person, whether or not there is the emission of semen.

(2) Sexual contact between the genitals or anal opening of one person and the mouth or tongue of another person.

(3) Intrusion by one person into the genitals or anal opening of another person, including the use of an object for this purpose, except that, it does not include acts performed for a valid medical purpose.

(4) The intentional touching of the genitals or intimate parts, including the breasts, genital area, groin, inner thighs, and buttocks, or the clothing covering them, of a child, or of the perpetrator by a child, for purposes of sexual arousal or gratification, except that it does not include acts which may reasonably be construed to be normal caretaker responsibilities; interactions with, or demonstrations of affection for, the child; or acts performed for a valid medical purpose.

(5) The intentional masturbation of the perpetrator's genitals in the presence of a child.

(c) "Sexual exploitation" refers to any of the following:

(1) Conduct involving matter depicting a minor engaged in obscene acts in violation of Section 311.2 (preparing, selling, or distributing obscene matter) or subdivision (a) of Section 311.4 (employment of minor to perform obscene acts).

(2) A person who knowingly promotes, aids, or assists, employs, uses, persuades, induces, or coerces a child, or a person responsible for a child's welfare, who knowingly permits or encourages a child to engage in, or assist others to engage in, prostitution or a live performance involving obscene sexual conduct, or to either pose or model alone or with others for purposes of preparing a film, photograph, negative, slide, drawing, painting, or other pictorial depiction, involving obscene sexual conduct. For the purpose of this section, "person responsible for a child's welfare" means a parent, guardian, foster parent, or a licensed administrator or employee of a public or private residential home, residential school, or other residential institution.

(3) A person who depicts a child in, or who knowingly develops, duplicates, prints, downloads, streams, accesses through any electronic or digital media, or exchanges, a film, photograph, videotape, video recording, negative, or slide in which a child is engaged in an act of obscene sexual conduct, except for those activities by law enforcement and prosecution agencies and other persons described in subdivisions (c) and (e) of Section 311.3.

(d) "Commercial sexual exploitation" refers to either of the following:

(1) The sexual trafficking of a child, as described in subdivision (c) of Section 236.1.

(2) The provision of food, shelter, or payment to a child in exchange for the performance of any sexual act described in this section or subdivision (c) of Section 236.1.

(Amended by Stats. 2018, Ch. 423, Sec. 112. (SB 1494) Effective January 1, 2019.)

https://leginfo.legislature.ca.gov/faces/codes_displayText.xhtml?lawCode=PEN&division=&title=1.&part=4.&chapter=2.&article=2.5

Texas Penal Code Title 5. Offenses Against the Person Sexual Offending Sec. 21.01. DEFINITIONS. In this chapter:

(1) "Deviate sexual intercourse" means:

(A) any contact between any part of the genitals of one person and the mouth or anus of another person; or

(B) the penetration of the genitals or the anus of another person with an object.

(2) "Sexual contact" means, except as provided by Section 21.11, any touching of the anus, breast, or any part of the genitals of another person with intent to arouse or gratify the sexual desire of any person.

(3) "Sexual intercourse" means any penetration of the female sex organ by the male sex organ.

(4) "Spouse" means a person to whom a person is legally married under Subtitle A, Title 1, Family Code, or a comparable law of another jurisdiction.

Acts 1973, 63rd Leg., p. 883, ch. 399, Sec. 1, eff. Jan. 1, 1974. Amended by Acts 1979, 66th Leg., p. 373, ch. 168, Sec. 1, eff. Aug. 27, 1979; Acts 1981, 67th Leg., p. 203, ch. 96, Sec. 3, eff. Sept. 1, 1981; Acts 1993, 73rd Leg., ch. 900, Sec. 1.01, eff. Sept. 1, 1994; Acts 2001, 77th Leg., ch. 739, Sec. 1, eff. Sept. 1, 2001.

Amended by:

Acts 2005, 79th Leg., Ch. 268 (S.B. 6), Sec. 1.124, eff. September 1, 2005.

Sec. 21.02. CONTINUOUS SEXUAL ABUSE OF YOUNG CHILD OR CHILDREN. (a) In this section, "child" has the meaning assigned by Section 22.011(c).

(b) A person commits an offense if:

(1) during a period that is 30 or more days in duration, the person commits two or more acts of sexual abuse, regardless of whether the acts of sexual abuse are committed against one or more victims; and

(2) at the time of the commission of each of the acts of sexual abuse, the actor is 17 years of age or older and the victim is a child younger than 14 years of age.

(c) For purposes of this section, "act of sexual abuse" means any act that is a violation of one or more of the following penal laws:

(1) aggravated kidnapping under Section 20.04(a)(4), if the actor committed the offense with the intent to violate or abuse the victim sexually;

(2) indecency with a child under Section 21.11(a)(1), if the actor committed the offense in a manner other than by touching, including touching through clothing, the breast of a child;

(3) sexual assault under Section 22.011;

(4) aggravated sexual assault under Section 22.021;

(5) burglary under Section 30.02, if the offense is punishable under Subsection (d) of that section and the actor committed the offense with the intent to commit an offense listed in Subdivisions (1)-(4);

(6) sexual performance by a child under Section 43.25;

(7) trafficking of persons under Section 20A.02(a)(7) or (8); and

(8) compelling prostitution under Section 43.05(a)(2).

(d) If a jury is the trier of fact, members of the jury are not required to agree unanimously on which specific acts of sexual abuse were committed by the defendant or the exact date when those acts were committed. The jury must agree unanimously that the defendant, during a period that is 30 or more days in duration, committed two or more acts of sexual abuse.

(e) A defendant may not be convicted in the same criminal action of an offense listed under Subsection (c) the victim of which is the same victim as a victim of the offense alleged under Subsection (b) unless the offense listed in Subsection (c):

(1) is charged in the alternative;

(2) occurred outside the period in which the offense alleged under Subsection (b) was committed; or

(3) is considered by the trier of fact to be a lesser included offense of the offense alleged under Subsection (b).

(f) A defendant may not be charged with more than one count under Subsection (b) if all of the specific acts of sexual abuse that are alleged to have been committed are alleged to have been committed against a single victim.

(g) It is an affirmative defense to prosecution under this section that the actor:

(1) was not more than five years older than:

(A) the victim of the offense, if the offense is alleged to have been committed against only one victim; or

(B) the youngest victim of the offense, if the offense is alleged to have been committed against more than one victim;

(2) did not use duress, force, or a threat against a victim at the time of the commission of any of the acts of sexual abuse alleged as an element of the offense; and

(3) at the time of the commission of any of the acts of sexual abuse alleged as an element of the offense:

(A) was not required under Chapter 62, Code of Criminal Procedure, to register for life as a sex offender; or

(B) was not a person who under Chapter 62 had a reportable conviction or adjudication for an offense under this section or an act of sexual abuse as described by Subsection (c).

(h) An offense under this section is a felony of the first degree, punishable by imprisonment in the Texas Department of Criminal Justice for life, or for any term of not more than 99 years or less than 25 years.

Added by Acts 2007, 80th Leg., R.S., Ch. 593 (H.B. 8), Sec. 1.17, eff. September 1, 2007.

Amended by:

Acts 2011, 82nd Leg., R.S., Ch. 1 (S.B. 24), Sec. 6.04, eff. September 1, 2011.

Section 21.06 was declared unconstitutional by Lawrence v. Texas, 123 S.Ct. 2472.

Sec. 21.06. HOMOSEXUAL CONDUCT. (a) A person commits an offense if he engages in deviate sexual intercourse with another individual of the same sex.

(b) An offense under this section is a Class C misdemeanor.

Acts 1973, 63rd Leg., p. 883, ch. 399, Sec. 1, eff. Jan. 1, 1974. Amended by Acts 1993, 73rd Leg., ch. 900, Sec. 1.01, eff. Sept. 1, 1994.

Sec. 21.07. PUBLIC LEWDNESS. (a) A person commits an offense if he knowingly engages in any of the following acts in a public place or, if not in a public place, he is reckless about whether another is present who will be offended or alarmed by his:

(1) act of sexual intercourse;

(2) act of deviate sexual intercourse;

(3) act of sexual contact; or

(4) act involving contact between the person's mouth or genitals and the anus or genitals of an animal or fowl.

(b) An offense under this section is a Class A misdemeanor.

Acts 1973, 63rd Leg., p. 883, ch. 399, Sec. 1, eff. Jan. 1, 1974. Amended by Acts 1993, 73rd Leg., ch. 900, Sec. 1.01, eff. Sept. 1, 1994.

Sec. 21.08. INDECENT EXPOSURE. (a) A person commits an offense if he exposes his anus or any part of his genitals with intent to arouse or gratify the sexual desire of any person, and he is reckless about whether another is present who will be offended or alarmed by his act.

(b) An offense under this section is a Class B misdemeanor.

Acts 1973, 63rd Leg., p. 883, ch. 399, Sec. 1, eff. Jan. 1, 1974. Amended by Acts 1983, 68th Leg., p. 509, ch. 924, Sec. 1, eff. Sept. 1, 1983; Acts 1993, 73rd Leg., ch. 900, Sec. 1.01, eff. Sept. 1, 1994.

Sec. 21.11. INDECENCY WITH A CHILD. (a) A person commits an offense if, with a child younger than 17 years of age, whether the child is of the same or opposite sex, the person:

(1) engages in sexual contact with the child or causes the child to engage in sexual contact; or

(2) with intent to arouse or gratify the sexual desire of any person:

(A) exposes the person's anus or any part of the person's genitals, knowing the child is present; or

(B) causes the child to expose the child's anus or any part of the child's genitals.

(b) It is an affirmative defense to prosecution under this section that the actor:

(1) was not more than three years older than the victim and of the opposite sex;

(2) did not use duress, force, or a threat against the victim at the time of the offense; and

(3) at the time of the offense:

(A) was not required under Chapter 62, Code of Criminal Procedure, to register for life as a sex offender; or

(B) was not a person who under Chapter 62 had a reportable conviction or adjudication for an offense under this section.

(b-1) It is an affirmative defense to prosecution under this section that the actor was the spouse of the child at the time of the offense.

(c) In this section, "sexual contact" means the following acts, if committed with the intent to arouse or gratify the sexual desire of any person:

(1) any touching by a person, including touching through clothing, of the anus, breast, or any part of the genitals of a child; or

(2) any touching of any part of the body of a child, including touching through clothing, with the anus, breast, or any part of the genitals of a person.

(d) An offense under Subsection (a)(1) is a felony of the second degree and an offense under Subsection (a)(2) is a felony of the third degree.

Acts 1973, 63rd Leg., p. 883, ch. 399, Sec. 1, eff. Jan. 1, 1974. Amended by Acts 1981, 67th Leg., p. 472, ch. 202, Sec. 3, eff. Sept. 1, 1981; Acts 1987, 70th Leg., ch. 1028, Sec. 1, eff. Sept. 1, 1987; Acts 1993, 73rd Leg., ch. 900, Sec. 1.01, eff. Sept. 1, 1994; Acts 1999, 76th Leg., ch. 1415, Sec. 23, eff. Sept. 1, 1999; Acts 2001, 77th Leg., ch. 739, Sec. 2, eff. Sept. 1, 2001.

Amended by:

Acts 2009, 81st Leg., R.S., Ch. 260 (H.B. 549), Sec. 1, eff. September 1, 2009.

Sec. 21.12. IMPROPER RELATIONSHIP BETWEEN EDUCATOR AND STUDENT. (a) An employee of a public or private primary or secondary school commits an offense if the employee:

(1) engages in sexual contact, sexual intercourse, or deviate sexual intercourse with a person who is enrolled in a public or private primary or secondary school at which the employee works;

(2) holds a certificate or permit issued as provided by Subchapter B, Chapter 21, Education Code, or is a person who is required to be licensed by a state agency as provided by Section 21.003(b), Education Code, and engages in sexual contact, sexual intercourse, or deviate sexual intercourse with a person the employee knows is:

(A) enrolled in a public primary or secondary school in the same school district as the school at which the employee works; or

(B) a student participant in an educational activity that is sponsored by a school district or a public or private primary or secondary school, if:

(i) students enrolled in a public or private primary or secondary school are the primary participants in the activity; and

(ii) the employee provides education services to those participants; or

(3) engages in conduct described by Section 33.021, with a person described by Subdivision (1), or a person the employee knows is a person described by Subdivision (2)(A) or (B), regardless of the age of that person.

(b) An offense under this section is a felony of the second degree.

(b-1) It is an affirmative defense to prosecution under this section that:

(1) the actor was the spouse of the enrolled person at the time of the offense; or

(2) the actor was not more than three years older than the enrolled person and, at the time of the offense, the actor and the enrolled person were in a relationship that began before the actor's employment at a public or private primary or secondary school.

(c) If conduct constituting an offense under this section also constitutes an offense under another section of this code, the actor may be prosecuted under either section or both sections.

(d) The name of a person who is enrolled in a public or private primary or secondary school and involved in an improper relationship with an educator as provided by Subsection (a) may not be released to the public and is not public information under Chapter 552, Government Code.

Added by Acts 2003, 78th Leg., ch. 224, Sec. 1, eff. Sept. 1, 2003.

Amended by:

Acts 2007, 80th Leg., R.S., Ch. 610 (H.B. 401), Sec. 1, eff. September 1, 2007.

Acts 2007, 80th Leg., R.S., Ch. 772 (H.B. 3659), Sec. 1, eff. September 1, 2007.

Acts 2009, 81st Leg., R.S., Ch. 260 (H.B. 549), Sec. 2, eff. September 1, 2009.

Acts 2011, 82nd Leg., R.S., Ch. 761 (H.B. 1610), Sec. 3, eff. September 1, 2011.

Sec. 21.15. IMPROPER PHOTOGRAPHY OR VISUAL RECORDING. (a) In this section, "promote" has the meaning assigned by Section 43.21.

(b) A person commits an offense if the person:

(1) photographs or by videotape or other electronic means records, broadcasts, or transmits a visual image of another at a location that is not a bathroom or private dressing room:

(A) without the other person's consent; and

(B) with intent to arouse or gratify the sexual desire of any person;

(2) photographs or by videotape or other electronic means records, broadcasts, or transmits a visual image of another at a location that is a bathroom or private dressing room:

(A) without the other person's consent; and

(B) with intent to:

(i) invade the privacy of the other person; or

(ii) arouse or gratify the sexual desire of any person; or

(3) knowing the character and content of the photograph, recording, broadcast, or transmission, promotes a photograph, recording, broadcast, or transmission described by Subdivision (1) or (2).

(c) An offense under this section is a state jail felony.

(d) If conduct that constitutes an offense under this section also constitutes an offense under any other law, the actor may be prosecuted under this section or the other law.

(e) For purposes of Subsection (b)(2), a sign or signs posted indicating that the person is being photographed or that a visual image of the person is being recorded, broadcast, or transmitted is not sufficient to establish the person's consent under that subdivision.

Added by Acts 2001, 77th Leg., ch. 458, Sec. 1, eff. Sept. 1, 2001. Amended by Acts 2003, 78th Leg., ch. 500, Sec. 1, eff. Sept. 1, 2003.

Amended by:
Acts 2007, 80th Leg., R.S., Ch. 306 (H.B. 1804), Sec. 1, eff. September 1, 2007.

New York—Child Sexual Abuse, 2014.
Aggravated sexual abuse in the first degree is a class B felony.
§130.75 Course of sexual conduct against a child in the first degree.

1. A person is guilty of course of sexual conduct against a child in the first degree when, over a period of time not less than three months in duration:
    (a) he or she engages in two or more acts of sexual conduct, which includes at least one act of sexual intercourse, oral sexual conduct, anal sexual conduct or aggravated sexual contact, with a child less than eleven years old; or
    (b) he or she, being eighteen years old or more, engages in two or more acts of sexual conduct, which include at least one act of sexual intercourse, oral sexual conduct, anal sexual conduct or aggravated sexual contact, with a child less than thirteen years old. *(Eff. 11/1/03, Ch. 264, L. 2003)*
2. A person may not be subsequently prosecuted for any other sexual offense involving the same victim unless the other charged offense occurred outside the time period charged under this section.

Course of sexual conduct against a child in the first degree is a class B felony.
§130.80 Course of sexual conduct against a child in the second degree.

1. A person is guilty of course of sexual conduct against a child in the second degree when, over a period of time not less than three months in duration:
    (a) he or she engages in two or more acts of sexual conduct with a child less than eleven years old; or
    (b) he or she, being eighteen years old or more, engages in two or more acts of sexual conduct with a child less than thirteen years old.
2. A person may not be subsequently prosecuted for any other sexual offense involving the same victim unless the other charged offense occurred outside the time period charged under this section.

Course of sexual conduct against a child in the second degree is a class D felony.

TYPES OF SEXUAL ABUSE WITHIN FAMILIES: INCEST, MARITAL RAPE, AND FAMILY VIOLENCE

Taboos against incest, or inappropriate sexual behavior between children and adults within families, appear throughout the earliest recorded history and appear to be universal. In Europe, biblical accounts and the Catholic Church are said to have restricted early incest taboos even further, but, by the 1900s, punishment through penal servitude or other types of incarceration was favored, suggesting that the responsibility for the sanctions shifted from religious to civil or state sanctions.[54] Normal family life has been outlined in various publications,[55] but families who cannot keep their relations within appropriate sexual bounds are identified as incestuous.

Argued to be a combination of social and individual pathology, the father most commonly described in the literature overcompensates for his feelings of powerlessness by assuming an overly authoritarian position.[56] A second orientation is marked by his withdrawal into a childlike state; however, the degree of abdicating adult responsibilities is viewed differently in the research.[57] It is critical to understand that abusers' behavior in incestuous relationships can present dramatically different pictures. In addition, the dysfunctional family dynamic often implicates the role of the mother, even when the incest is limited between the father and daughter, although extensive research has been done to suggest the mother is often unjustly blamed for either causing the abuse or for not intervening.[58] Siblings often collude with the behavior in an attempt to assure their own safety, which results in feelings of guilt later in life over their choice not to protect their sibling.

Abuse by mothers against children has been historically suggested to be far less common, although research on this has been challenged, suggesting fathers are more likely to commit extreme harm; however, the dynamics of abuse are complex.[59] When involving daughters, abuse is believed to be linked with significant dysfunction in the mother's childhood to the point of mental illness.[60] Often, because the mother sees the daughter as an extension of herself, rather as an independent person, the daughter does not learn to see herself as capable of functioning separately and will often remain dependent in relationships.[61] Mother and son incest is rare, although research shows victimized sons feel extreme guilt, feelings of worthlessness, betrayal, rage, and fear.

Although Sigmund Freud famously brought the subject of sexual abuse into popular discussion, researchers believe he did more to distract from the serious study of the topic.[62] In fact, Freud first put forward the idea that childhood sexual trauma was at the root of adult psychological problems, but he later changed that in preference of the idea that the stories of sexual abuse were fantasies, not real experiences. The effect of his professional decision has been devastating in part for victims of sexual violence because his views have so heavily influenced the field of psychology. Freud's reversal has been argued to be because he could not accept its implications that his own peers and colleagues in Viennese society were responsible for his patients' difficulties.[63] Although his motives are unclear, Freud's assessments discounted patients' reports of childhood sexual victimization, and perhaps even more devastating to the cause of sexual violence prevention was his placement of the blame of the sexual violation on the child rather than the adult.

The history of violence in the family is long-standing. (Attention is given in chapter 6 to the issue of domestic and intimate partner violence.) In addition to incest, sex was integrated into the family structure by religious teachings and social structural guidelines for how the family connected back to the larger community. One deeper aspect of this subordination and superiority of gendered family structures is also found in the experiences and perpetration of the integrated sexual violence found in examples of marital rape. (More on this is presented in chapter 6.)

The subject of child abuse has been acknowledged as a social problem in the United States since the early twentieth century. A focus on child sexual abuse has come much later, however. Critical reflection and questions about the extent of child abuse and the sexual nature of that abuse are ongoing. (Additional information about contemporary research findings on child sexual abuse is offered in chapter 6.) Most experts agree that the overarching assessment about child sexual abuse points in the same direction: child sexual abuse happens by people known to the child or from within the family circle. The family has been hailed both as a place to heal wounds from past social and cultural sexual misunderstandings[64] and as a place where children are most vulnerable.[65] Basic questions about how best to protect children from sexual harm while educating children about healthy sexuality remain controversial, with the center of that controversy seated in the family.

Table 5.1   How a Parent Might Overlook Abuse

Why might a parent not perceive potential harm?

1. Parents know the offender.
2. Parents are not familiar with the idea of abuse so do not see the signs.
3. Parents need the services of the potential abuser.
4. Parents trust the potential abuser.

Why might parents not provide adequate supervision for their child?

1. Parents may feel that the child can care for themselves.
2. Parents may feel unable to provide adequate supervision.
3. Parents may be unaware of unsupervised periods.
4. Parents may be otherwise occupied.
5. The child may initiate the separation.

THE DOMESTIC VIOLENCE MOVEMENT AND PREVENTION EFFORTS

The history of violence within family settings is long-standing. Although Francis Cobb wrote about "Wife Torture in England" in 1878, it was almost a century later before the issue was taken up in the United States with any success. Family violence includes violence between adults, between adults and children, and between siblings. Although the histories of abuse prevention efforts for children and women are interconnected, efforts to address the abuse between parents appeared most clearly from within the **battered women's movement**, loosely identified in the United States from the early 1970s through the 1990s.[66] Yet, as far back as history stretches, the experience of domestic violence is present and persists to the present day.

In 1824, the US Supreme Court justified domestic violence in the case of *Bradley v. State*,[67] where the court ruled a husband was allowed to "use salutary restraints in every case of a wife's misbehavior, without being subjected to vexatious prosecutions resulting in mutual discredit and shame of all parties concerned (p. 156)."[68] Over 50 years later, Maryland became the first state to write legislation outlawing wife beating in 1882, criminalizing the offense with 40 lashes for the first offense and a year in jail for a repeat offense.[69] After another 50 years, the 1970s saw a collective community action in the United States toward preventing domestic abuse in the home, including national hotlines for battered women, shelters, and national newsletters. Also, Del Martin's 1979 work *Battered Wives*[70] was published, and Oregon enacted legislation mandating arrest in domestic violence cases.

Between 1978 and 1984, various bills were presented to Congress to address the issue of domestic violence, but nothing passed the smaller subcommittees. In the 1970s, Lenore Walker was developing a theory described as the "battered woman syndrome,"[71] which, linked with the idea of learned helplessness, explores the consequences of violence against women in their intimate partnerships.

The RAINN resource page presents several reasons a woman might stay with an abusive partner in a dangerous relationship that include the following:

- still being positively reinforced by the "honeymoon" phase of the battering cycle
- economic dependence upon the batterer
- belief that they can keep the peace
- fear of danger if she were to leave
- threats made by the batterer to hurt her or her children if she left
- loss of self-esteem
- depression or loss of psychological energy necessary to leave[72]

The syndrome is thought to have four general characteristics:

1. The woman believes that the violence was or is her fault.
2. The woman has an inability to place responsibility for the violence elsewhere.
3. The woman fears for her life and/or her children's lives.
4. The woman has an irrational belief that the abuser is omnipresent and omniscient.[73]

Walker's cycle of violence was identified in three stages: (1) tension building, (2) acute battering, and (3) the honeymoon phase. Initially, these theories, particularly the battered person syndrome, were used in courts to defend women who killed their abusive partners.[74] Much has been written about the concerns and exceptions to this idea; however, the idea has maintained popular and academic attention. More recently, intimate partner violence has also been associated with posttraumatic stress disorder.

A review of police protocol to assure stricter arrest procedures in cases of domestic violence was being studied, but the subject rose to national prominence with the case of Tracey Thurman in Torrington, Connecticut. In 1983, after extensive efforts to secure police protection from her estranged husband, Tracey Thurman was stabbed 13 times in the chest, the neck, and the face by her estranged husband; after police arrived, he continued to kick her in the presence of the responding police officer. When three additional officers responded, no attempt was made to restrain the estranged husband while he continued to threaten Tracey, who was lying on the ground as a result of her injuries. Thurman sued the city of Torrington and in 1985 was awarded $2.3 million.[75]

With the growing movement to assess the occurrence of and social response to domestic violence, the Thurman lawsuit is considered by many to have been a critical point in the shift of public attitude and continued pursuit of enhanced individual accountability (treatment of offenders) and collective social action (police and legislative response). In 1984, the Family Violence Prevention Services Act finally passed, authorizing the Secretary of Health and Human Services to make grants to states to assist in supporting programs to prevent family violence and provide shelter and related assistance for victims and their dependents; however, this initiative did not bring the issue of domestic violence fully to public attention, which would not happen for another decade.[76] Issues like the treatment of Anita Hill in the sexual harassment hearing over the Supreme Court nominee Clarence Thomas and the 1994 murder of Nicole Brown Simpson are two examples of prominent issues that brought gender violence to the national consciousness again.

In May 1993, after a three-year investigation into the issue by the Senate Judiciary Committee, then Senator Joe Biden introduced the Violence Against Women Act. Linking the larger social attitude to a recent example of a callous disrespect for a sexual crime and an unwillingness to hold offenders accountable, Biden introduced the bill.

The result was the 1994 passage of the **Violence Against Women Act** (VAWA) as an effort to provide federal direction and resource support to the many state-run efforts providing services to victims of violent crimes. The VAWA was reauthorized in 2000, 2005, and 2013; fell out of compliance in 2018; and was reauthorized by the House in April 2019 but not put forward in the Senate.[77] Created in 1995 the **Office of Violence Against Women** (OVW) is a division of the US Department of Justice charged with providing "federal leadership in developing the nation's capacity to reduce violence against women and administer justice for and strengthen services to victims of domestic violence, dating violence, sexual assault, and stalking" by offering financial and technical assistance to communities across the country.[78]

TYPES OF INTIMATE PARTNER VIOLENCE

The National Institute of Justice defines **intimate partner violence**, historically called "domestic violence," as physical, sexual, or psychological harm by a current or former intimate partner or spouse and outlines four types: physical violence, sexual violence, threats of physical or sexual violence, and psychological/emotional violence with stalking as a related crime category.[79]

- **Physical violence** is the intentional use of physical force (e.g., shoving, choking, shaking, slapping, punching, burning, or using a weapon, restraints, or one's size and strength against another person) with the potential for causing death, disability, injury, or physical harm.

- **Sexual violence** can be divided into three categories: (1) the use of physical force to compel a person to engage in a sexual act unwillingly, whether or not the act is completed; (2) an attempted or completed sexual act involving a person who, because of illness, disability, or the influence of alcohol or other drugs, or because of intimidation or pressure, is unable to understand the nature or condition of the act, decline participation, or communicate unwillingness to engage in the act; and (3) abusive sexual contact.
- **Threats of physical or sexual violence** communicate the intent to cause death, disability, injury, or physical harm through the use of words, gestures, or weapons.
- **Psychological/emotional violence** traumatizes the victim by acts, threats of acts, or coercive tactics (e.g., humiliating the victim, controlling what the victim can and cannot do, withholding information, isolating the victim from friends and family, and denying access to money or other basic resources). In most cases, emotional violence has been preceded by acts or threats of physical or sexual violence.
- **Stalking** is often included among types of intimate partner violence. Stalking generally refers to harassing or threatening behavior that an individual engages in repeatedly, such as sending the victim unwanted presents, following or lying in wait for the victim, damaging or threatening to damage the victim's property, appearing at a victim's home or place of business, defaming the victim's character or spreading rumors, or harassing the victim via the internet by posting personal information.

Dating violence (discussed in more detail in chapter 7) is also included in discussions about intimate partner violence simply because the statistics demonstrate that violence against a dating partner, sometimes known as **breakup violence**, is being referred to as a "disturbing trend" in the United States. In 2013, Calgary resident Lacey Jones-McKnight was killed after breaking up with her former fiancé, who admitted to killing her; however, he disputes the events leading up to the murder.[80] Research suggests that one in three girls in the United States is a victim of physical, emotional, or verbal abuse from a dating partner—a number far exceeding rates of other types of youth violence.[81] Girls and young women between the ages of 16 and 24 experience the highest rate of intimate partner violence, almost triple the national average with 94 percent ages 16 to 19 and 70 percent ages 20 to 24 being victimized by a current or former boyfriend or girlfriend.[82] In 2005 the importance of addressing teen dating abuse was highlighted in the reauthorization of the Violence Against Women Act. In 2006, the first week of February was dedicated to dating violence awareness and prevention, and, then, in 2010 the campaign was expanded to the entire month. Teen Dating Violence Awareness Month, sponsored by Break the Cycle at breakthecycle.org and Love Is Respect at loveisrespect.org.

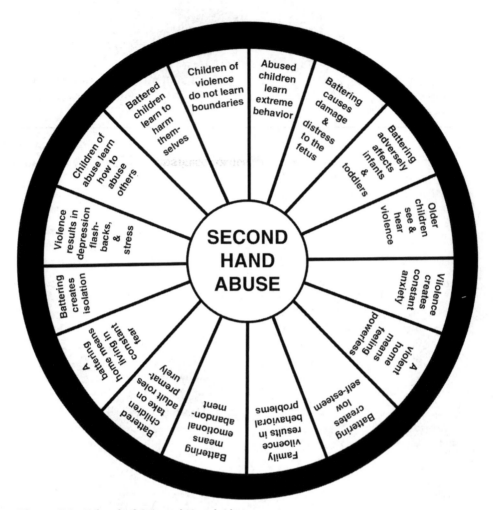

Figure 5.1 Wheel of Second Hand Abuse
© Ms. Kristina Korobov, Sr. Attorney for the National Center for the Prosecution of Violence Against Women.

THE LGBTQI MOVEMENT FOR EQUAL RIGHTS

One of the lengthiest and perhaps the most complex conversations about sexual attitudes in the United States and around the world is reflected in the history of organized resistance against the classification of homosexuality as a "deviant" lifestyle.[83] Controversy about the classification of physical and sexual interactions between people of the same gender as being sexually healthy, deviant, or criminal began with the Bible, if not before, and continues to this day. Cultural presentations of questions about sexuality, particularly the expression of sexual orientations, were undefined and ambiguous, and yet the hostile opposition to what is now defined as homosexuality was ever present in efforts to support the colonial American ideal.

> Though criminal records, church sermons, and other evidence reveal homo-erotic activity among the residents of the colonies, nothing indicates that men or women thought of themselves as "homosexual." . . . Colonists labeled what the twentieth century calls homosexual behavior as a sin and a crime, and aberrant act for which the perpetrator received punishment in this world and the next.[84]

The law stipulated harsh punishments for homosexual acts during colonial times, where the legal codes prescribed death for sodomy and instances can be found in the historical record of courts ordering the execution of men found guilty of this act.[85] Today, 93 nations in the world still punish homosexuality, and, in seven of those countries—Iran, Mauritania, Saudi Arabia, Sudan, United Arab Emirates, Yemen, and Nigeria—the punishment is death.[86] Most US states abolished the death penalty for sodomy. But, until 1950 in the United States, all but two states still classified sodomy a felony, and interactions between women and oral sex between men were defined within the sodomy and "crimes against nature" statutes.[87]

In the eighteenth century, the ideas about homosexuality in Europe reached well into the American mainstream. The practice of masturbation had been moved from the realm of religion to become a topic of study for medical practi-tioners and scientists. The writings and work of physician **Samuel A. D. Tissot**, who practiced in the Swiss city of Lausanne and advised the Vatican, had a profound influence in support of the idea that masturbation caused insanity.[88] Like some scientists of the day, much of Tissot's "science" reflected religious and cultural ideologies more than actual scientific method.[89] As evidence for such assertions, physicians offered their observations that large numbers of patients in mental institutions masturbated.[90] In the late 1880s through the end of the century, members of the medical profession were weighing in on the topic of homosexuality as a disease.[91]

Known throughout the world as one of the world's foremost authorities on sexual behavior and serving as a psychiatric consultant to the criminal courts of Germany,[92] **Richard Freiherr von Krafft-Ebing** published *Psychopathia Sexualis* in 1886. Argued to be one of the most influential books on the topic of sex, it was translated in many languages, was a best seller everywhere, and is still available today. **Sigmund Freud**'s *Three Essays on the Theory of Sexuality* went through many supplements and additions, with its first appearance in 1915 and the final edition presented in 1925. By the turn of the century, G. Stanley Hall, another noted psychologist, promoted the idea that early masturbation actually caused homosexuality.[93]

German attorney Karl Heinrich Ulrichs and Karl-Maria Kertbeny (who is credited with actually coining the term "homosexuality") were contemporaries opposed to the medicalization of homosexuality during the mid-nineteenth cen-tury. In spite of their efforts, homosexuality became known as a criminal form of insanity. French writer Paul Moreau's work attempted to bring the topic out of the courts and back into the medical profession for treatment, rather than punishment. To save "victims of such an illness from prison," it was preferred to bring them to the asylum.[94] Physician Benjamin Tarnowski attempted to distinguish between inherited and acquired sexual perversions based on studies of his own Russian patients.[95]

Inherited sexual perversions, like hysteria, epilepsy, alcoholism, anemia, and typhus, were a sign of a pathological condition, and such individuals were not to be punished. Acquired sexual perversion, though influenced by bad heredity, was developed by reading dirty books, keeping bad company, or living in too great luxury, and this kind of perversion should be punished.[96]

Magnus Hirschfeld campaigned for legal reform and was the first to attempt to organize a field of sexual studies. In 1908, he published the first *Journal for Sexology*. In 1913, he cofounded the first sexological organization, the medical Society for Sexology and Eugenics. In 1919, he opened the first Institute of Sexology and the first international sexological congress in 1921. In 1928, he cofounded the World League for Sexual Reform.[97] He cataloged what he referred to as sexual intermediary classifications ranging from masculine heterosexual male to feminine homosexual male; however, much of his data was destroyed by the Nazis in 1933.[98]

In 1948 in the United States, **Alfred Kinsey** (introduced in chapter 4) and a group of researchers published findings from a vast collection of interviews on the sexual behaviors of Americans: *Sexual Behavior in the Human Male* and *Sexual Behavior in the Human Female*. Both books went on to become best sellers; however, they were not without controversy. One of the driving forces within his research process was his own evolving interest in homosexuality[99] and his amazement at the number of people he found in prison for sex-related infractions, including homosexuality.[100]

A significant finding from his work was "The Kinsey Scale"—this heterosexual–homosexual rating scale was developed by Kinsey and colleagues to represent the data they had collected, which suggested that people did not fit neatly into exclusive categories of "homosexual" or "heterosexual."[101] Describing the world as a "continuum in each and every one of its aspects," Kinsey wrote:

> While emphasizing the continuity of the gradations between exclusively heterosexual and exclusively homosexual histories, it has seemed desirable to develop some sort of classification which could be based on the relative amounts of heterosexual and homosexual experience or response in each history. . . . An individual may be assigned a position on this scale, for each period in his life. . . . A seven-point scale comes nearer to showing the many gradations that actually exist.[102]

During this time, **Clellan Ford** and **Frank Beach**, also using a scientific approach, presented *Patterns of Sexual Behavior* in 1951, which found homosexuality across cultures and present in almost all nonhuman species. The American Psychiatric Association published its first official list of mental disorders in 1952 and included homosexuality under the classification of "sociopathic personality disturbance." In the mid-1950s, **Dr. Evelyn Hooker**, a psychologist, reported on her studies of gay men, suggesting that, other than their sexual orientation, her subjects in the study would be classified as "normal."

While the research findings of Kinsey, Hooker, and others resulted in more freedoms in the homosexual community in the United States, incidents of abuse and violence were present across the country. In Boise, Idaho, on November 2, 1955, after three men were accused of having sex with teenagers, a 15-month investigation of 1,400 people from area gay networks were questioned, dozens were arrested, and nine were imprisoned for as long as 15 years. That same year, on November 24, in the wake of the murder of a young boy, 29 Sioux City, Iowa, men suspected of being homosexual were committed to mental asylums as a preventive measure authorized by the state's "sexual psychopath" laws.[103]

On the heels of the civil rights and the feminist movements, leaders in the LGBTQI movement were organizing too. What was founded as the **Mattachine Society** in 1951 would grow into a national movement for homosexual liberation. The year 1969 brought about one of the biggest shifts toward equality when Dr. Evelyn Hooker advocated for the decriminalization of private sex acts between consenting adults and onlookers, watching a "typical" police raid of the Stonewall Inn, a small gay bar in Greenwich Village, NYC, erupted in violent opposition, known today as the **Stonewall uprising**, or the Stonewall riots. This date is used to mark the annual gay pride parade celebrated in June across the United States.[104] Issuing a statement in 1970 that homosexuality is a moral aberration, the Vatican reiterated the position of the Catholic Church.[105] Soon after, however, in 1973, the American Psychiatric Association removed homosexuality from its list of mental illnesses, with the American Psychological Association taking the same action in 1975.

As science increasingly presented homosexuality as another variant of "normal," the American mainstream was not of the same mind, nor were they willing to accept the scientific reports at face value. The idea that people who dated people of the same gender were acting within the range of normal human behavior was hard for some groups to accept. In 1980, Aaron Fricke had to sue his high school in a district court to be able to take his boyfriend, Paul Guilbert, to the senior prom.[106] Since then, openly gay relationships have been popularized in movies and TV and by celebrity weddings and adoptions, including Ricky Martin, Melissa Etheridge, Neil Patrick Harris, Wanda Sykes, Rosie O'Donnell, Ellen DeGeneres, Lady Gaga, and Chris Colfer.

In 1998, Matthew Shepard was murdered in Wyoming. The case garnered international attention in part because of the brutality of the killing and the focus on the fact that he was believed to have been killed because of his sexual orientation. Questions have been raised, however, about why his murder received so much attention when so many other gay and lesbians are also killed because they are gay.[107] Shepard was brutally beaten, tied to a fence post, and left for dead. Shepard's death happened around the same time the 1999 film *Boys Don't Cry* was released in the United States, based on the life and 1993 rape and murder of Brandon Teena, a transgendered man,[108] a story that received a second round of significant press after Hilary Swank won the best actress Oscar. The 2008 murder of 15-year-old Larry King by classmate Brandon McInerney was brought to the attention of national daytime viewers when a tearful Ellen DeGeneres profiled the story.[109] King was shot twice in the head in a computer lab at the junior high where he attended school. In September 2011, the judge declared a mistrial in the case when the jurors failed to reach a unanimous decision between the options of murder or manslaughter. The decision to try the shooter, who was 14 at the time, as an adult was also referenced as a point of contention among the jurors.[110] The decision was ultimately made by the California Attorney General to retry the case, and then McInerney pled guilty to second degree murder and voluntary manslaughter, rather than face the second trial, which could have produced a life sentence for the 17-year-old.[111]

As the second decade of the twenty-first century began, one of the most high-profile issues of controversy in the United States regarding homosexuality is focused on the right to marry. Support for legal recognition of same-sex marriage has shifted from a narrow majority opposed in 2009 to the recent Associated Press poll showing a narrow majority in support in 2011 but shifting into more favorable support in 2015.[112] In June 2011, the New York state legislature legalized gay marriage, making New York the sixth state (along with the District of Columbia) to legalize gay marriage, and the state of Virginia just passed legislation saying gay people could no longer adopt. In 2015, the US Supreme Court struck down all state bans on same-sex marriage, therefore legalizing same-sex marriage across the United States.[113]

The argument is made that people do not get involved in issues that don't affect them, so whether the issue is reparations, gay rights, or revisioning the "truth" about history, most people choose not to get involved. Schools in school districts across the country are trying to determine what policies and practices should be in place to prevent bullying and harassment of gay students amidst controversy and, in some cases, with deadly consequences. In an effort to combat this trend, well-known syndicated columnist Dan Savage has started a media campaign called "It Gets Better," organized in an effort to reduce the high incidents of suicide by gay youth.[114] While this goes on in the presence of mainstream media, with commercials on television and a large social media campaign, how people outside of the gay community respond to these efforts remains an open question.

CHAPTER SUMMARY: STATE-SANCTIONED RESTRICTIONS OVER PROTECTIONS

Social science research with an emphasis on families, particularly relating to topics like sex, has traditionally been seen more as "private" matters not to be discussed in public. Increasingly, attention to various aspects of family life is shedding light on a reality of family life that is, in some instances, a far cry from the "happily ever after" storybook romances. Relationships can be a significant source of discord, which can manifest itself in physical and emotional disruptions from within the family, with effects on everyone. Historically, derision and harassment were the standard treatment of LGBTQI families, and these external social pressures could increase difficulties within the household. Family violence in its many forms has been an unspoken burden to be managed, with negative and harmful effects on the couple and on the children. When people look back over the history of the United States, it is often through tainted reflections of socially determined assessments about what a "loving" family or a "loving" couple was supposed to look like. In those socially proscribed, idyllic, but unreal conditions, violence was seldom mentioned. Attention must be given to how families can learn to grow healthy children, have healthy relationships, and work to be a part of neighborhoods and communities where sexualized violence is not accepted.

Text Box 5.2. Media Messages about History: System-Supported Sanctions

Who benefits and who is harmed when the collective social thinking maintains

- the messages that young kids get, particularly young women, suggesting that using sex is the most effective way to get what they want in the world?
- the representation of romantic love and "happily ever after" fairy tales?
- the representation that to be "in charge" is a man's job and to "take charge" and to dominate others is true masculinity?

KEY TERMS

Alfred Kinsey
battered women's movement
Bergh's War
breakup violence
Charles Loring Brace
Child Abuse Prevention and Treatment Act
Child Welfare League of America
Clellan Ford
David Finkelhor
Dr. C. Henry Kempe
Dr. Evelyn Hooker
Elbridge T. Gerry
Elizabethan Poor Laws
Fair Labor Standards Act of 1938
Frank Beach
Henry Bergh
indenture programs
Indian Child Welfare Act

infanticide
intimate partner violence
John Caffey
Magnus Hirschfeld
mandatory child abuse reporting laws
Mary Ellen Wilson
Mattachine Society
Office of Violence Against Women
Orphan Train Movement
patriarchy
Richard Freiherr von Krafft-Ebing
Samuel A. D. Tissot
sexual exploitation of children
Sigmund Freud
Society for the Prevention of Cruelty to Children
Stonewall uprising
Violence Against Women Act

REVIEW QUESTIONS

1. What role does power have in the occurrence of sexual violence?

2. What organizations were the first to take action to protect children, and where did that happen?

3. What was Bergh's War?

4. Why was Dr. Alfred Kinsey such a controversial figure? What was his academic area of study?

5. Discuss the role John Caffey and Dr. Henry Kemp played in bringing the issues of child abuse into public discourse.

DISCUSSION QUESTIONS

1. What aspects of love, marriage, and family do you see reflected in this chapter? How are they similar to and/or different from the ideas of love, marriage, and family today?

2. The text talks about child abuse, family violence, and homosexuality as three examples of social issues that raised concerns but for which little was done and that these kinds of abuses were accepted or tolerated. Would you agree? Be prepared to justify your response and ideas.

3. How have elements of these social systems and structures changed since the time reflecting the information presented here? In the area of child abuse and prevention? In the area of family violence? In the area of homosexuality?

4. What, if anything, about these three basic issues remains controversial? In the area of child abuse and prevention? In the area of family violence? In the area of homosexuality?

5. What in the chapter did you find surprising or inspired you to dig deeper in an effort to secure a better understanding of the issues covered?

NOTES

1. Lloyd de Mause, "Our Forbearers Made Childhood a Nightmare," in *Traumatic Abuse and Neglect of Children at Home*, ed. Gertrude J. Williams and John Monday (Baltimore: Johns Hopkins University Press, 1980), 14–20.

2. A. Ganley cited in N. Nason-Clark, B. Risher-Townsend, and C. Holtman, *Religion and Intimate Partner Violence: Understanding the Challenges and Proposing Solutions* (Oxford University Press, 2018), 181.

3. Majority Staff of the Senate Judiciary Committee, *Violence Against Women: The Response to Rape: Detours on the Way to Justice*, United States Senate, 103rd Congress, accessed October 20, 2019, https://cyber.harvard.edu/archived_content/events/vaw/readings/DLRreadings.html.

4. Office of Public Affairs, "Attorney General Eric Holder Jr. Speaks at the National Strategy Conference on Combating Child Exploitation," Department of Justice, May 19,

2011, accessed July 18, 2015, http://www.justice.gov/opa/speech/attorney-general-eric-hold er-speaks-national-strategy-conference-combating-child.

5. Steven Pinker, *The Better Angels of Our Nature: Why Violence Has Declined* (New York: Penguin Books, 2012).

6. Ibid.

7. Linda Gordon, *Heroes of Their Own Lives: The Politics and History of Family Violence* (Chicago: University of Illinois Press, 1988), vi.

8. Ibid.; Stephanie Coontz, *The Social Origins of Private Life: A History of American Families* (New York: Verso, 1988).

9. Gordon, *Heroes of Their Own Lives*, 3.

10. Murray A. Straus, "Sexual Inequality, Cultural Norms, and Wife-Beating," in *Victims and Society*, ed. Emilio C. Viano (Washington, DC: Visage Press, 1976), 543–59.

11. See, for example, Ola W. Barnett and Cindy L. Miller-Perrin, *Family Violence across the Lifespan*, 3rd ed. (Thousand Oaks, CA: Sage Publications, 2011), 1–38, accessed July 17, 2015, http://www.sagepub.com/upm-data/38654_Chapter1.pdf; Angela Browne, *When Battered Women Kill* (New York: The Free Press, 1987); Lenore E. Walker, *The Battered Woman* (New York: Harper and Row, 1979).

12. Coontz, *The Social Origins of Private Life*, 7–40.

13. For Native colonization, see, for example, Robert Staples and Alfredo Mirande, "Racial and Cultural Variations among American Families: A Decennial Review of the Literature on Minority Families," *Journal of Marriage and the Family* 42, no. 4 (1980): 887–903; see also John A. Price, "North American Indian Families," in *Ethnic Families in America: Patterns and Variations*, ed. Charles H. Mindel and Robert W. Habenstein (New York: Elsevier, 1976), 248–70; Andrea Smith, *Conquest: Sexual Violence and Native American Genocide* (Durham, NC: Duke University Press, 2005); Tim Giago, *Children Left Behind: The Dark Legacy of Indian Mission Boarding Schools* (Santa Fe, NM: Clear Light Publications, 2006).

14. See, for example, David Wallace Adams, *Education for Extinction: American Indians and the Boarding School Experience, 1875–1928* (Lawrence, KS: University of Kansas Press, 1995); Ross Alexander Enochs, *The Jesuit Mission to the Lakota Sioux: Pastoral Theology and Ministry, 1886–1945* (Kansas City, MO: Sheed and Ward, 1996).

15. Steven Mintz and Susan Kellogg, *Domestic Revolutions: A Social History of American Family Life* (New York: Free Press, 1988); James Deetz and Patricia Scott Deetz, *The Times of Their Lives: Life, Love, and Death in Plymouth Colony* (New York: W. H. Freeman and Co., 2000); Richard Godbeer, *Sexual Revolution in Early America* (Baltimore: Johns Hopkins University Press, 2002); Kathleen M. Brown, *Good Wives, Nasty Wenches, and Anxious Patriarchs: Gender, Race, and Power in Colonial Virginia* (Chapel Hill, NC: University of North Carolina Press, 1996); Peter W. Bardaglio, *Reconstructing the Household: Families, Sex, and Law in the Nineteenth-Century South* (Chapel Hill, NC: University of North Carolina Press, 1995); Coontz, *The Social Origins of Private Life*.

16. Coontz, *The Social Origins of Private Life*, 35.

17. Stephanie Coontz, *The Way We Never Were: American Families and the Nostalgia Trap* (New York: Basic Books, 1992).

18. Ibid.

19. Antonia C. Novello et al., "A Medical Response to Domestic Violence," *Journal of the American Medical Association* 267, no. 23 (1992): 3132, accessed July 20, 2015, doi:10.1001/jama.1992.03480230024006; Teri Randall, "Domestic Violence Intervention Calls for More than Treating Injuries," *Journal of the American Medical Association* 264, no. 8 (1990): 939–40, accessed July 20, 2015, doi:10.1001/jama.1990.03450080021002.

20. "The Massachusetts Body of Liberties (1641)," Hanover Historical Texts Project, accessed July 20, 2015, https://history.hanover.edu/texts/masslib.html.

21. Margaret S. Groban, "The Federal Domestic Violence Laws and the Enforcement of These Laws," Minnesota Center Against Violence and Abuse, 2005.

22. Referencing the slogan often used as a symbol of gay pride.

23. See, for example, Matthew Vines, *God and the Gay Christian: The Biblical Case in Support of Same-Sex Relationships* (New York: Convergent Books, 2014); John D'Emilio, William B. Turner, and Urvashi Vaid, *Creating Change: Sexuality, Public Policy, and Civil Rights* (New York: St. Martin's Press, 2000); Bruce Bawer, *A Place at the Table: The Gay Individual in American Society* (New York: Simon & Schuster, 1994).

24. See, for example, Jay P. Paul et al., "Suicide Attempts among Gay and Bisexual Men: Lifetime Prevalence and Antecedents," *American Journal of Public Health* 92, no. 8 (2002): 1338–45; Michael King, "A Systematic Review of Mental Disorder, Suicide, and Deliberate Self-Harm in Lesbian, Gay, and Bisexual People," *BMC Psychiatry* 8, no. 70 (2008), accessed July 17, 2015, doi:10.1186/1471-244X-8-70.

25. See, for example, Justin Lee, *Torn: Rescuing the Gospel from the Gays-vs.-Christians Debate* (New York: Jericho Books, 2012); Justin R. Cannon, *The Bible, Christianity, and Homosexuality* (Charleston, SC: CreateSpace, 2008).

26. Note that various conversations with the literature about how to reference the LGBTQI community are ongoing. The references include LGBTQI for people who identify as lesbian, gay, bisexual, and transgender. With increasing regularity, reference is made to this community by adding Q, referring to "queer" or "questioning," and I, for intersex. The more traditional LGBTQI reference has been used here, with an open reference to the broad range of individuals included in that reference.

27. "LGBT-Inclusive Definitions of Family," Human Rights Campaign, accessed July 17, 2015, http://www.hrc.org/hei/lgbt-inclusive-definitions-of-family; see also Dominick Vetri, "The Gay Codes: Federal and State Laws Excluding Gay and Lesbian Families," *Willamette Law Review* 41 (2006): 881–84, accessed July 17, 2015, http://www.willamette.edu/wucl/pdf/review/41-5/vetri.pdf.

28. Mason P. Thomas Jr., "Child Abuse and Neglect, Part I: Historical Overview, Legal Material, and Social Perspectives," *North Carolina Law Review* 50 (1972): 293–349.

29. Cynthia Crosson-Tower, *Understanding Child Abuse and Neglect*, 3rd ed. (Boston: Allyn & Bacon, 1996).

30. Steven Otfinoski and Timothy J. Griffin, *The Child Labor Reform Movement: An Interactive History Adventure* (Minneapolis: Capstone Press, 2013); see also Russell Freedman, *Kids at Work: Lewis Hine and the Crusade against Child Labor* (Boston: HMH Books for Young Readers, 1998); Juliet H. Mufford, *Child Labor in America* (Hoboken, NJ: History Compass, 1970).

31. B. Blankley, "Analysis: Child Marriage Is Legal in 49 U.S. States." Watchdog, May 25, 2018, https://www.watchdog.org/national/analysis-child-marriage-is-legal-in-u-s-states/article_fbefbf04-5d0e-11e8-b6e6-cb9d5643bc13.html.

32. Crosson-Tower, *Understanding Child Abuse and Neglect*.

33. Jon R. Conte and David A. Shore, *Social Work and Child Sexual Abuse* (Binghamton, NY: The Haworth Press, 1982), 22.

34. Andrzej Diniejko, "Charles Dickens as Social Commentator and Critic," *The Victorian Web*, February 7, 2012, accessed July 20, 2015, http://www.victorianweb.org/authors/dickens/diniejko.html.

35. "Orphan Trains," The Adoption History Project, February 24, 2012, accessed July 20, 2015, http://pages.uoregon.edu/adoption/topics/orphan.html; see also Anthony M. Platt, *The Child Savers: The Invention of Delinquency* (New Brunswick, NJ: Rutgers University Press, 2009).

36. Eric A. Shelman and Stephan S. Lazoritz, *The Mary Ellen Wilson Child Abuse Case and the Beginning of Children's Rights in 19th Century America* (Jefferson, NC: McFarland & Company, 2005).

37. *Hammer v. Dagenhart*, 247 U.S. 251 (1918).

38. "Who We Are and What We Do," The Child Welfare League of America, accessed July 17, 2015, http://www.cwla.org/about-us/.

39. "Timeline of Major Child Welfare Legislation," The Child Welfare League of America, accessed July 17, 2015, http://www.cwla.org/wp-content/uploads/2014/05/TimelineOf MajorChildWelfareLegislation.pdf.

40. Emily Yellin, *Our Mother's War: American Women at Home and at the Front During WWII* (New York: Free Press, 2005); see also Doris Weatherford, *American Women and World War II* (Edison, NJ: Castle Books, 2009); Cheryl Mullenbach, *Double Victory: How African American Women Broke Race and Gender Barriers to Help Win World War II* (Chicago: Chicago Review Press, 2013).

41. C. Henry Kempe, "The Battered Child Syndrome," *Journal of the American Medical Association* 181, no. 1 (1962): 17–24.

42. "Timeline of Major Child Welfare Legislation."

43. "Indian Child Welfare Act of 1978," National Indian Child Welfare Association, 2015, accessed July 20, 2015, http://www.nicwa.org/indian_child_welfare_act/.

44. "About CAPTA: A Legislative History," US Department of Health and Human Services, July 2011, accessed July 20, 2015, https://www.childwelfare.gov/pubPDFs/about.pdf.

45. *Definitions of Child Abuse and Neglect: State Statutes Current through March 2019*, Child Welfare Information Gateway, accessed October 20, 2019, https://www.childwelfare .gov/pubPDFs/define.pdf.

46. Ibid., 4.

47. "Citizen's Guide to U.S. Federal Law on Child Pornography," Department of Justice, July 6, 2015, accessed July 20, 2015, http://www.justice.gov/criminal/ceos/citizensguide/citi zensguide_porn.html.

48. "Citizen's Guide to U.S. Federal Law on Child Sexual Abuse," Department of Justice, July 6, 2015, accessed July 20, 2015, http://www.justice.gov/criminal/ceos/citizensguide/citi zensguide_sexualabuse.html.

49. "State Statutes Search," US Department of Health and Human Services, accessed July 20, 2015, https://www.childwelfare.gov/topics/systemwide/laws-policies/state/?hasBeenRe-directed=1.

50. "Understanding Child Sexual Abuse," American Psychological Association, December 2011, accessed October 20, 2019, https://www.apa.org/pi/about/newsletter/2011/12/sexual -abuse.

51. Erna Olafson, David L. Corwin, and Roland C. Summit, "Modern History of Child Sexual Abuse Awareness: Cycles of Discovery and Suppression," *Child Abuse & Neglect* 17, no. 1 (1993): 7–24.

52. David Finkelhor, *Sexually Victimized Children* (New York: Free Press, 1981).

53. Diana E. H. Russell, "The Incidence and Prevalence of Intrafamilial and Extrafamilial Sexual Abuse of Female Children," *Child Abuse & Neglect* 7, no. 2 (1983): 133–46.

54. Crosson-Tower, *Understanding Child Abuse and Neglect*, 8.

55. Coontz, *The Social Origins of Private Life*; M. Rosenfeld, "Nontraditional Families and Childhood Progress through School," *Demography* 47, no. 3 (2010): 755–75. https:// www.ncbi.nlm.nih.gov/pmc/articles/PMC3000058/.

56. A. Nicholas Groth, "The Incest Offender," in *Handbook of Clinical Intervention in Child Sexual Abuse*, ed. Suzanne Sgroi (Lexington, MA: Lexington Books, 1982); Kathleen Coulborn Faller, *Understanding and Assessing Child Sexual Maltreatment* (Thousand Oaks, CA: Sage Publications, 1990).

57. Groth, "The Incest Offender"; Judith Lewis Herman and Lisa Hirschman, *Father-Daughter Incest* (Cambridge, MA: Harvard University Press, 1981).

58. Esther Deblinger et al., "Psychosocial Characteristics and Correlates of Symptom Distress in Nonoffending Mothers of Sexually Abused Children," *Journal of Interpersonal*

Violence 8, no. 2 (1993): 155–68; Faller, *Understanding and Assessing Child Sexual Maltreatment*; Ila J. Schonberg, "Distortion of the Role of Mother in Child Sexual Abuse," *Journal of Child Sexual Abuse* 1, no. 3 (1992): 47–61.

59. These are unsettled matters in the research; see, for example, D. Hosier, "Mothers More Likely to Be Abusive than Fathers, Study Suggests," Childhood Trauma Recovery, August 10, 2017, https://childhoodtraumarecovery.com/all-articles/mothers-likely-abusive-fa thers-study-suggests/; Christine Adams, "Mothers Who Fail to Protect Their Children from Sexual Abuse: Addressing the Problem of Denial," *Yale Law and Policy Review* 12, no. 2 (1994), https://digitalcommons.law.yale.edu/ylpr/vol12/iss2/7.

60. Crosson-Tower, *Understanding Child Abuse and Neglect*, 173.

61. Ibid., 175.

62. Finkelhor, *Sexually Victimized Children*, 8; see also Judith Lewis Herman and Lisa Hirschman, "Incest between Fathers and Daughters," *The Sciences* 17, no. 7 (1977): 4–7; Florence Rush, "The Freudian Cover-Up," *Chrysalis* 1 (1977): 31–45.

63. Rush, "The Freudian Cover-Up." See also F. Crews, *Freud: The Making of an Illusion* (Metropolitan Books, 2017).

64. Floyd M. Martinson, *Infant and Child Sexuality: A Sociological Perspective* (Saint Peter, MN: The Book Mark, 1973). See also J. Payne, *The Healing of Individuals, Families and Nations: Transgenerational Healing and Family Constellations*, Book 1 (Findhorn Press, 2005).

65. Finkelhor, *Sexually Victimized Children*.

66. See, for example, L. Walker, *The Battered Woman Syndrome*, 4th ed. (Springer Publishing, 2016); B. Russell, *Battered Woman Syndrome as a Legal Defense: History, Effectiveness and Implications* (McFarland, 2010).

67. *Bradley v. State*, 1 Miss 156 (1824).

68. Andrew Fulkerson and Shelly L. Patterson, "Victimless Prosecution in the Wake of *Crawford v. Washington*," *Forum on Public Policy* (2006), 2.

69. Ibid.

70. Del Martin, *Battered Wives* (Volcano, CA: Volcano Press, 1976).

71. Walker, *The Battered Woman*.

72. MNFirefly, "Ray Rice: Knowing When Say No to Domestic Violence and Abuse," September 9, 2014, http://www.chicagonow.com/active-suburbia/2014/09/ray-rice-knowing -when-say-no-to-domestic-violence-and-abuse/.

73. Walker, *The Battered Woman*, 95–97.

74. Browne, *When Battered Women Kill*.

75. "Domestic Violence—The Laws and the Courts: Landmark Legal Decisions," Library Index, accessed July 20, 2015, http://www.libraryindex.com/pages/2074/Domestic-Vio lence-Laws-Courts-LANDMARK-LEGAL-DECISIONS.html.

76. "Timeline of the Battered Women's Movement," National Center on Sexual and Domestic Violence, 2008, http://www.ncdsv.org/images/NYCHRADSS_TImelineBWM_2008.pdf.

77. Reauthorizing the Violence Against Women's Act has been uncertain in 2019. Although passed in the House of Representatives with modifications, it has been largely ignored in the Senate and has not been put forward for a vote.

78. "About the Office," Office on Violence Against Women, Department of Justice, accessed October 20, 2019, https://www.justice.gov/ovw/about-office.

79. "Overview of Intimate Partner Violence," National Institute of Justice, October 24, 2007, accessed July 20, 2015, http://www.nij.gov/topics/crime/intimate-partner-violence/ Pages/welcome.aspx.

80. "Calgary Police on Lookout for 'Breakup Violence' Trend: Disturbing Trend among Young People in the U.S. Is on the Rise," *CBC News*, November 1, 2013, accessed July 18, 2015, http://www.cbc.ca/news/canada/calgary/calgary-police-on-lookout-for-breakup-vio lence-trend-1.2326109; see also Meghan Grant, "Kristopher Guenther Tells Judge He Killed

Lacey Jones McKnight: Calgary Man on Trial for First-Degree Murder Didn't Show Any Emotion," *CBC News*, March 11, 2015, accessed July 18, 2015, http://www.cbc.ca/news/can ada/calgary/kristopher-guenther-tells-judge-he-killed-lacey-jones-mcknight-1.2990977.

81. Antoinette Davis, "Interpersonal and Physical Dating Violence among Teens," *The National Council on Crime and Delinquency Focus*, September 2008, accessed July 20, 2015, http://www.nccdglobal.org/sites/default/files/publication_pdf/focus-dating-violence.pdf.

82. See, for example, "Intimate Partner Violence in the United States, 1993–2004," Bureau of Justice Statistics, Department of Justice, December 20, 2006, accessed July 20, 2015, http://www.prisonpolicy.org/scans/bjs/ipvus.pdf; "Intimate Partner Violence and Age of Victim, 1993–99," Bureau of Justice Statistics, Department of Justice, November 28, 2001, accessed July 20, 2015, http://www.bjs.gov/content/pub/pdf/ipva99.pdf.

83. John D'Emilio, *Sexual Politics, Sexual Communities: The Making of a Homosexual Minority in the United States, 1940–1970* (Chicago: University of Chicago Press, 1983).

84. Ibid., 10.

85. Ibid., 14.

86. Lucas Ramón Mendos, *State-Sponsored Homophobia Report*, International Lesbian, Gay, Bisexual, Trans and Intersex Association, 2019, https://ilga.org/state-sponsored-homo phobia-report.

87. D'Emilio, *Sexual Politics, Sexual Communities*, 14.

88. Vern L. Bullough and Bonnie Bullough, *Sin, Sickness, and Sanity: A History of Sexual Attitudes* (New York: Garland Publishing, 1977); see especially chapter 5.

89. Ibid., 60.

90. Ibid., 60.

91. Vern L. Bullough, "Homosexuality and the Medical Model," *Journal of Homosexuality* 1, no. 1 (1974) 99–110; Jonathan Ned Katz, *Gay American History: Lesbians and Gay Men in the U.S.A.* (New York: Avon Books, 1978).

92. Bullough and Bullough, *Sin, Sickness, and Sanity*, 62.

93. Ibid., 206, note 17.

94. Ibid., 205.

95. See description of Tarnowski in Bullough and Bullough, *Sin, Sickness, and Sanity*, 206.

96. Bullough and Bullough, *Sin, Sickness, and Sanity*, 206, note 17.

97. "Magnus Hirschfeld (1868–1935)," Archive for Sexology, accessed October 20, 2019, https://www.ub.hu-berlin.de/en/literature-search/historical-collections/historical-and-special -collections-of-the-library/overview-of-the-historical-and-special-collections-of-the-library/ haeberle-hirschfeld-archive-of-sexology/haeberle-hirschfeld-archive-of-sexology.

98. Heike Bauer, *The Hirschfeld Archives: Violence, Death, and Modern Queer Culture* (Philadelphia, PA: Temple University Press, 2017).

99. Barak Goodman and John Maggio, dir., *American Experience: Kinsey* (Saint Paul, MN: PBS, 2005), television.

100. Ibid.

101. "The Kinsey Scale," Kinsey Institute, Indiana University, accessed July 18, 2015, https://kinseyinstitute.org/research/publications/kinsey-scale.php.

102. Ibid.

103. Michael Annetta, "November 24 in LGBTQ History," *The Lavender Effect*, November 24, 2013, accessed July 17, 2015, http://www.thelavendereffect.org/2013/11/24/novem ber-24-in-lgbtq-history-2/.

104. D'Emilio, *Sexual Politics, Sexual Communities*, 231–33.

105. Denise Carmody and John Carmody, "Homosexuality and Roman Catholicism," in *Homosexuality and World Religions*, ed. Arlene Swidler (Harrisburg, PA: Trinity Press International, 1993), 143–46.

106. "Who Are You Taking to the Prom This Year?," American Civil Liberties Union, accessed July 18, 2015, https://www.aclu.org/who-are-you-taking-prom-year.

107. M. Miller and S. Rich, "Hate Crimes Have Soared in D.C. Prosecutions Have Plummeted," *Washington Post*, August 21, 2019, https://www.washingtonpost.com/graphics/2019/local/dc-hate-prosecutions-drop/.

108. A. McCabe, "20 Years Later, 'Boys Don't Cry' Still Inspires Admiration and Debate," NPR, *All Things Considered*, October 21, 2019, https://www.npr.org/2019/10/21/771451650/20-years-later-boys-don-t-cry-still-inspires-admiration-and-debate.

109. "Ellen DeGeneres on 15-Year-Old Boy, Larry King, Killed for Being Gay," YouTube video, 2:38, posted by "Larry Goben," May 8, 2008, http://www.youtube.com/watch?v=PeM9w3L4H6I.

110. "Judge Declares Mistrial in Larry King Murder," *CBS News*, September 2, 2011, accessed July 18, 2015, http://www.cbsnews.com/news/judge-declares-mistrial-in-larry-king-murder-trial/; Sandy Banks, "Lessons from a Teen Student's Killing: Whatever Questions Remain after the Mistrial in the Killing of Gay Oxnard Student Larry King, This Much Is Clear: In Middle School, Kids Need Guidance," *Los Angeles Times*, September 5, 2011, accessed July 18, 2015, http://articles.latimes.com/2011/sep/05/local/la-me-0906-banks-20110906.

111. "California Teen Brandon McInerney Sentenced to 21 Years for Point-Blank Murder of Gay Classmate," *CBS News*, December 19, 2011, http://www.cbsnews.com/news/calif-teen-brandon-mcinerney-sentenced-to-21-years-for-point-blank-murder-of-gay-classmate/.

112. S. Clement and R. Barnes, "Poll: Gay-Marriage Support at Record High," *Washington Post*, April 23, 2015, https://www.washingtonpost.com/politics/courts_law/poll-gay-marriage-support-at-record-high/2015/04/22/f6548332-e92a-11e4-aae1-d642717d8afa_story.html.

113. *Obergefell v. Hodges*.

114. It Gets Better Project, http://www.itgetsbetter.org/.

6

Overexposed? A Picture of Contemporary Sexual Violence

Women can get killed by their prettiness.

—A fifth-grader[1]

"Why Aren't We Shocked?"

—Title of a *New York Times* article[2]

"No means yes; yes means anal."

—A chant repeated during a march through campus
by pledges to a Yale University fraternity[3]

LAYERS OF CONTROVERSY LINKED to ongoing efforts to describe, explain, and understand the boundaries of healthy, deviant, and criminal classifications of sexual practice remain relentlessly unresolved. Up to this point, several snapshots taken from within the larger US historical record have been offered for consideration in chapters 4 and 5 (and globally in chapter 6) to provide an illustration of the varying degrees socially sanctioned sexual violence and harm have existed throughout the world while at the same time remaining significantly absent in larger mainstream conversations. Continuing the metaphor, the information and history provided so far act somewhat like a still photograph—telling a story, serving as a reminder, but indicative of only a partial review of the larger and related events that made the picture possible. Placing the focus from within this broader social context is designed to serve as preparation for a more expansive contemporary conversation about various harmful expressions of sex, sexual deviance, and criminal sexual practices to be presented in the chapters to come.

Regardless of any noticeable historical shifts in these and related subject areas, the pernicious nature of such harmful actions can remain hidden in plain sight, depending on how the stories associated with those snapshots are compiled and the story is told. Research is an effort to take snapshots and put them together to tell a story. At least part of the tension existing at the heart of collective efforts to identify, define, and report information about topics related to sexual violence is directly connected to what are arguably flaws, and certainly disagreements, inherent within the system designed to study crime and justice more broadly.

In November 2011, the Centers for Disease Control and Prevention (CDC) put out the National Intimate Partner and Sexual Violence Survey (NISVS).[4] By January 2012, the report was at the center of a controversial national conversation about the perils of "**advocacy research**,"[5] or research argued by critics to be structurally skewed to prove the point under question, rather than to provide an objective assessment of the material being studied.[6] The "elastic" definitions of sexual violence used in the survey were criticized as "ambiguous" and said to be "letting the surveyors rather than the subjects, determine what counted as an assault."[7] Other concerns were raised about how the numbers presented in this form of research, an agenda focused on assessing victim experiences, differed so dramatically from the **Uniform Crime Report (UCR)** data, crime statistics tabulated and collected based on arrests made by local law enforcement and then reported to the Federal Bureau of Investigation (FBI) for compilation. One of the loudest critical assessments of the CDC report came to the national media from an author and resident scholar at a public policy research institute suggesting the following:

> The agency's figures are wildly at odds with official crime statistics. The FBI found that 84,767 rapes were reported to law enforcement authorities in 2010. The Bureau of Justice Statistics' National Crime Victimization Survey, the gold standard in crime research, reports 188,380 rapes and sexual assaults on females and males in 2010. Granted not all assaults are reported to authorities. But where did the CDC find 13.7 million victims of sexual crimes that the professional criminologists overlooked?[8]

The disparity in reported acts of sexual assaults is representative of the lack of a collective assessment about what actually constitutes acts of sexual violence and how those incidents and events are documented. The tenor of this report serves to open a big door where sexual assault advocates have been utilizing a window, if not a peephole. If the number of sexual assaults is not clearly known, how can communities and professionals respond?

Researchers, policy analysts, advocates, and prevention experts are among those suggesting the official statistics of sexual crimes significantly underestimate the sexual violence that happens in actual human experiences—for all genders and ages. If resource and policy decisions were shifted to reflect the findings presented in this CDC report, the implications would be dramatic. To add further debate to an already controversial subject, efforts by the federal government to collect statistics about sexual violence are undoubtedly going to change over time as a result of the 2012 change in the federal definition of rape, announced by Attorney General Eric Holder in January of that year. In the original definition, created in 1927, rape was defined as "the carnal knowledge of a female, forcibly and against her will."[9] In the new definition, rape is defined as "penetration, no matter how slight, of the vagina or anus with any body part or object, or oral penetration by a sex organ of another person, without the consent of the victim."[10]

In spite of the fact that various groups criticized the CDC's NISVS study, the University of Minnesota's Center for Leadership Education in Maternal and Child Public Health described the report on its web page as having been "designed to better describe and monitor the magnitude of sexual violence, stalking and intimate partner violence victimization in the United States."[11] After acknowledging the limitations of all research in the area of sexual violence studies, Karen Baker, director of the National Sexual Violence Resource Center (NSVRC), put out a public statement in support of the report. The NSVRC is an advocacy agency funded through a cooperative agreement by the CDC's Division of Violence Prevention, which identified the following reasons the NISVS research reports a higher prevalence of sexual violence than does the FBI's UCR and other reports. These include the following:

- NISVS asked about many types of "sexual violence" as an umbrella term. Rape is one type, but there are many other types of unwanted sexual behaviors that cause people to feel violated or unsafe. The FBI's UCR statistics measure only rape. Furthermore, until quite recently, the definition of rape used by the FBI was quite narrow and left out many instances that will be counted in the future.
- FBI statistics measure only reported rapes. Since 1929, crime data, such as reported rapes, has been submitted voluntarily by police departments. The data becomes a part of the UCR. Through the UCR, the FBI issues guidelines and definitions related to processing sexual assault cases, but not all police departments follow these guidelines.
- Rape is the most underreported crime in the United States for several reasons (knowing the offender, guilt, self-doubt, fear, shame, embarrassment, worries about being disbelieved or further traumatized, etc.). The majority of sexual assaults, an estimated 63 percent, are never reported to police.[12]
- NISVS asked not only about incidences that had occurred in the past year but also about victimization that occurred anytime in the participant's lifetime. This, of course, includes child sexual abuse, which is quite prevalent. About one in three girls and one in seven boys will be sexually abused before the age of 17.[13]

Interestingly, Baker said that the "behaviorally-specific questions" used in the data collection process, rather than being a weakness of the study, were actually one of the intentional design elements developed to make the study's findings more reliable.[14] Clearly, thoughtful and analytically minded people disagree. This research process described here is like many others—thoughtful people disagree about the methods used, the analysis of the data collected, and the best way to address and reduce the kind of behavior under study.

The systematic course of action designed by researchers to best gather information about any topic, in this case sexual violence, is also steeped in a long history of academic studies and related controversies regarding social science research methods. The nature of the process of research and data collection and analysis raised in both the collection of and reporting about crime statistics can be particularly controversial. In fact, the style of research methods presented by postmodern, feminist, and critical ideologies intentionally challenge traditional research in a variety of ways. The healthy debate around data collection methods and the interpretation of research findings in pursuit of a better understanding about the occurrence of sexual violence should be noted. The NSIVS study offers only one example of that dynamic, but the tension is important to note in a chapter, in a book, in an academic discipline, and in a body of research designed to present a collection of theories for review based largely on research studies created within this ongoing controversy.

As the attention here shifts from a historical reflection on hidden or ignored sexual violence to the documentation of contemporary events and acts of reported and recorded sexual violence, it is also important to note that the collective understanding of sexual violence has changed over time, as have the ways social science researchers work to study the phenomena. Research on sexual violence and related subjects certainly replicates the variety of ways different people and groups in society reflect on or talk about this particular social issue. Keep in mind that the difficulty of getting consistent, if not accurate, information about the subtle, covert, and even nonverbal aspects of coercion, compliance, and consent (central elements that most folks on all sides of the issue would agree comprise the core of the definition of rape, for example) will be reflected in the ways in which researchers and agencies organize the research agenda in play and the ideology driving that research. Note that, although discussed in more detail below and elsewhere throughout the text, traditional research has suggested good research and competent researchers do *not* allow individual attitudes and bias to affect the subject under study. Again, other researchers disagree and suggest that research happens from within individual perspectives, which will, in most cases, if not always, influence the subject being studied.

The NISVS report and the more recent FBI definition of rape provide examples of the degree to which social attitudes and cultural shifts might influence how sexual violence is documented, studied, and reported, yet even the conceptualizations of what is sex or what it means to sexualize something can produce deeply divisive conversations. In 2008, a reporter from *City Journal* took on what she considered the "campus rape myth," attributing flawed statistics and reasoning to several articles and studies with varied definitions of rape, reportedly attempting to better understand the parameters of rape on college campuses, where rapes and, more specifically, unreported rapes are argued to be high.[15] That same year, a researcher published a report in the journal *Contemporary Issues in Education Research*, suggesting that rape myths perpetuate rape in two ways: (1) rape is defined more narrowly than legal definitions, meaning someone who believes a rape myth might not report a potential rape event that actually does meet the legal definition of rape, and (2) rape myths blame victims for rape, which shames the victim into silence and results in unacknowledged rape.[16] In the summer of 2007, an article from the *Journal of Social and Personal Relationships* introduced the idea of **nonagentic sexual interactions**, referring to sexual experiences that occur against a person's will as being the result of a range of behaviors, including verbal pressure up through physical force.[17]

The idea that sexual touching can constitute coercion is a controversial idea to some, but at least some research seems to consistently find gender differences with regard to the influence of sexual coercion, suggesting that more women than men experience sexual coercion and more men than women use sexual coercion.[18] If such differences exist, how prevention education and policy or legal proscriptions are written will need to also differ. While certainly everyone will be likely to agree that a rape has occurred when there is a home invasion, a weapon is used, and sex is forced upon a person under those conditions. People are also likely to agree that a rape occurs when coercion, deceit, or trickery is present. Less agreement exists, however, about what constitutes coercion (discussed in detail in chapter 2), and, therefore, one of the critical elements argued to be a necessary element for defining rape has traditionally been unclear or means different things to different people. Addressing this lack of clarity becomes critical both for successfully educating people about sexual boundaries and for responding to harm caused when sexual boundaries are violated. What might be less obvious, though particularly relevant for the discussion here about the social reach of research, is the role the construction of those definitions (and individual perceptions of those definitions) plays in defining and directing popular as well as professional discernments on rape and other forms of sexual assault.

Again, examples can be helpful. In the wake of the public media release of court paperwork seeming to support multiple allegations of rape against entertainer Bill Cosby,[19] revealing his own statements regarding the use of drugs and sex with women, then President Barak Obama was asked at a press conference to comment on the crimes. While he refused to comment on the Cosby case, he made a very direct public statement, saying "If you give a woman—or a man, for that matter—without his or her knowledge a drug and then have sex with that person without consent, that's rape."[20] These public statements from a political figure were news in and of themselves after a number of politicians in the 2012 and 2014 election cycles made national headlines after using terms such as "real rape"[21] or "legitimate rape"[22] during interviews, suggesting not all rape is real or that there is a way to determine legitimate kinds of rape from other rapes (however those are identified and defined) not seen (by whom?) as legitimate. Although controversial among media pundits and politicians, and perhaps even throughout the mainstream US population, rape prevention educators and advocates are increasingly committed to clarifying and refuting aspects of rape used to perpetuate ideas seen as myths and social misunderstandings about sexual assault and rape and replacing them with more accurate, research-based information.

Efforts throughout the chapter are focused on including a wide range of information about various types of sexual violence, not necessarily to bring final resolution to the issue being referenced and, certainly, not to present any final sort of declarative statement of truth about what has been an unresolved, long-standing social and political dispute. The examples discussed above help create a platform from which to consider various ways people think about different aspects of the topics under study: the definition of sexual violence; what constitutes an act of sexual violence; and how sexual violence is identified, documented, and studied, to name just a few. All of these responses are influenced by social convention and are subject to change as a result of social events and shifts in personal attitudes (through education and life experiences, for example), including intentional collective action to create social change. And all of *this* is offered to lay some groundwork in preparation for upcoming discussions regarding the development of prevention efforts and to review laws, policy responses, enforcement, treatment, and punishment strategies.

A great deal of this chapter is focused on research limitations but also on the ways in which public and private assessments about sexual violence and harm seem to limit or restrict a more general ability to reach an understanding of the individual and/or the collective social will on responding to sexual violence as an individual and/or larger social harm. The structure of the categories of sexual harm presented for consideration in chapters 4 and 5 is supplemented and revisited here, giving attention to the contemporary documentation of incidents of sexual violence as described by race, gender, social class, and social convention. The contemporary review of types of sexual violence statistics from various sources also includes systemic elements of sexual violence often overlooked in the historical analysis of sexual assault, such as male rape and prison rape. The chapter closes with a presentation of and discussion about rape myths and some increasingly popular ways long-standing social controversies around sexual assault are being reframed in social media, inviting people to think differently about some of these longer-standing social attitudes.

CONTEMPORARY RESEARCH AND DATA COLLECTION ON SEX CRIMES

Before attempting to present research findings on sexual violence, consider two questions: (1) what are the most important things to learn about the current state of sexual violence, and (2) why is it so difficult to get good information about these kinds of controversial social issues? Whether an individual subscribes to the idea that the answers to these complex social questions are intentionally orchestrated by powerful groups within society or sees the answers to these questions as a consequence of innate individual behaviors, choices, and actions, popular mainstream attitudes about sex are vulnerable to flashes of information, particularly heinous information, which can then be used to influence individual attitudes or move social policy decisions in a specific direction.[23]

To best answer these questions more fully, it is important to focus on both the individual and the social structure of the society in which that individual operates. One way researchers attempt to address this is to give attention to a large collection of information that reflects issues over a longer period of time, rather than relying exclusively on the information presented from one study or a series of a few studies. Most people in the world do not spend the bulk of their time, much less a good portion of their entire life, studying the history of sex and deviance, or the criminalization of sexual deviance, or the classifications of sex crimes, or the laws and policies governing the punishment of sex offenders. When government policies are argued by critics to be unduly influenced by religious ideology in supporting, for example, abstinence-only education (discussed in chapter 1), for example, and research repeatedly demonstrates that abstinence-only education is not effective in preventing teen pregnancy or delaying teen sexuality, people on both sides of the issue attempt to make sense of the research by using the ideologies driving the thinking initially, either in support of the research findings or in opposition. The argument for the existence of "objective" research is challenged in these debates when the information produced in the research findings is heralded as a reason to continue or cut funding for a particular program supported by a particular ideology, for example. When the research findings have no influence on ideology or, more specifically, on individual action, meaning people read the findings but are not influenced by them, this is also important because, by rejecting the research, this raises questions about whether they are unaware of the implications or, in effect, rejecting the ideological framework of the researchers who conducted the research.

All of this may seem convoluted and downright confusing upon first review. It is critically important, however, to get a sense of how each person learns to interpret or accept the **objective nature of research** (introduced in chapter 3). If research suggests that young people increasingly learn about sex by researching pornographic material online,[24] critics might immediately counter the findings of this research by challenging the research method, the interpretation of the findings, or the way the questions were framed or organized, and, in this process, the critics will likely come up with an alternative argument. What anyone decides to do with this research is another question. Perhaps policy making and the legislative process are the goal. Perhaps people in a community use the information to make decisions about the sex education programs structured for schools. Regarding people who believe it is better for young people to learn about sex and sex-related violence through a structured educational program, action may be taken in one direction. On the other hand, if people believe sex education has always happened through trial and error and that is just fine, no action may be taken at all.[25]

Certainly, indicators of various levels of disagreement between different social groups are evidenced in society at large. The fact that these levels of disagreement carry themselves into the research community might not be a surprise. Many traditional researchers maintain the idea that research is not influenced by individual biases, although this idea has been resoundingly challenged in broader ideological and disciplinary circles, particularly criminal justice studies.[26] In the case of sexual assault and violence, the effects on the individual are diverse and can be profound (see more in chapter 14).

While research professes to educate in the collective, individual experience has been argued to be the greatest teacher of all. When a personal friend or family member or we ourselves have been affected by sexual assault, such an event can motivate people to get involved in efforts to reduce sexual violence. As individuals, what someone comes to know about sexual harm or sexual crimes might reflect the events of a specific personal experience or be the result of a lack of access to quality resources and information. Perspective is a powerful thing. Sometimes, perspectives and facts are easily confused. For example, the United States has earned a global reputation for its expansive resources, advanced educational systems, and cutting-edge technological innovation. Undoubtedly, aspects of this are true, yet the United States also has an international reputation for its endemic rates of violence, including gun violence,[27] serial killers,[28] and mass murders,[29] for example. Sadly, sexual violence too is an important part of this violent national legacy. Ironically, some argue the violence has become so commonplace that it has been rendered invisible. This has been argued very effectively when it comes to the idea of sexualized violence, as has been discussed throughout the book leading up to this point.

One way to review a great deal of information in a shorter project, as is the case here, is to identify some specific themes for consideration. A brief but deliberate review of four themes is presented for consideration. First, attention is given to the idea of researching research, doing the best to separate viable fact from superficial fiction and determine the degree to which truth can be found in the gray areas. Second, attention is given to the effects of the dark figure of crime as a difficulty within efforts to maintain ongoing reporting. A subtheme refers to the attention given to the myth-making tendency so prevalent throughout history and to the present day. Reflections on the way an idea is framed, followed by a brief conversation regarding the difference to be found when considering whether focus of an analysis should be on the individual, a microanalysis, or on the social-influencing factors of social systems and structures, a macroanalysis, or both is important to assure a common understanding about how these issues are being discussed in the larger context. Politicians are used to illustrate what is said in public about what society should do and is not necessarily what people actually do in private. Attention is given to a reality reflected in the breadth and depth of ways to make social meaning about sexual deviance and the problem of conflation, disciplinary separation, and interdisciplinary studies. Third, a presentation of statistics from a collection of popular research studies is offered for reflection and discussion. Fourth and finally, attention is given to a subject likely to be obvious to some but invisible to others, a review of some of the complexities associated with efforts to study sexual violence. In closing, as a supplement, the section looks at both formal and informal definitions of harm as reflected in various popular myths about rape and sexual violence.

Researching Research Resources

Data about sex crimes comes from a variety of sources, including the primary groupings of data from government sources, advocacy organizations, treatment practitioners, and academic communities (including legal and medical research). While researching the book, several individuals who are practitioners in the field of sexual violence prevention and in the correctional management sector suggested that 80 percent of sex offenders never get caught. This idea was supported later at a workshop when the presenter said "the best estimates suggest only 20 percent of sex offenders are ever caught and put in prison for their crimes."[30] Now, thinking about this number, can be tricky. Consider three things:

- A research project was designed to study how men understand "rape." This study was undertaken after findings suggested that, when men were asked whether they had ever raped someone, they would say no, but when they were asked whether they had ever held someone down or coerced them to have sex, a greater number would say they had.[31]

  Consider: Often, research on sex offenders comes from people under correctional supervision or students in college. Would this data point be assessed differently if the information were collected from individuals convicted of a sexual offense as compared to young men in a college setting?

- Eighty percent of victims never report their rape.[32]

  Consider: Research on sex offenders who have been caught suggests that they often will have significant numbers of victims before they get caught. So, if one person perpetrates a significant number of assaults against different people, to review this statistic with the idea that there are 80 sex offenders out there for every 20 arrested and convicted is misleading.

- Most sex crimes that result in a prison sentence are committed by people who have never before been convicted of a violent offense.[33]

  Consider: If this research were verified on a larger scale, what would it mean for the collective understanding about repeat offenders, offenders with multiple victims, or education and awareness programs?

Some of the larger issues around how sex crime statistics are discussed and interpreted are highlighted here. The importance of digging deeper when looking for the relevance and application of a research outcome cannot be over-emphasized. A generic representation of information does not tell the reader where the data was collected, and this always matters when someone is trying to understand the bigger picture. Keep this in mind as findings from several research projects are presented later in the chapter. Be sure to make note of the full citations and references for the information provided and review the full reports for more information.

Finding the 80/20, or Is It 90/10? Illustrating the Dark Figure of Crime
Over the past several years at conferences and in sessions or professional workshops, conversations with a collection of sex offender treatment practitioners, probation officers, researchers, and sexual violence prevention specialists have verified the idea that a great number of sex offenders are never caught. Research and sexual violence and child sexual abuse prevention advocates and activists, including prosecutors and defense attorneys, will confirm the **funnel effect**: if caught, fewer are convicted and, if convicted, even fewer do jail or prison time.

The idea reflected in the funnel effect (covered in more detail in chapter 10) has also been illustrated to the same effect with the image of an iceberg.

Although questions remain as to how many sex offenders are actively offending and remain undetected in communities, it is clear that common definitions and collaborative practices are most often informed by research and coupled with the history of related problems and experiences in a given community. As attention is given to the definitions of sexual violence, domestic violence, child sexual abuse, sexting, sex trafficking, and prostitution, it is critical to consider how research informs these processes. Each community is different, and the needs of each community will be reflected in those differences. Yet some common themes emerge.

It is important to understand that research is used to inform just about every stage in the criminal justice system where the responses to known sex crimes happen. All of these processes in the field rely on research: law enforcement decisions about the procedure for evidence collection, working with prosecutors to determine what charges are going to be filed, making referrals to medical professionals and advocates working to assure that the necessary information is provided if the case goes to court, and even assessing the event and how it is interpreted by professionals and practitioners. Understanding how these systems work together and having the ability to identify gaps in the system can produce more effective responses to victims and offenders or decrease the numbers of effective prosecutions of individuals convicted of committing a sex crime.

Even the offenders themselves, perpetrators of varying ages and offenses, have been confronted with their abusive behaviors; some acknowledge what they did was wrong, and others do not. Some offenders have mental health issues (more on the existing theories about why people offend in chapter 9), and some are uneducated or uninformed about the law. This was eerily indicated in the case of the rape of a high school girl in Steubenville, Ohio, which made national headlines. At one point, a student was taping the sexual assault.[34] When asked by prosecutors why he didn't stop the incident, he said, "It wasn't violent. I didn't know exactly what rape was. I thought it was forcing yourself on someone."[35] Another student said he didn't know what to do. Even the attorney in the case said "because she was silent doesn't mean she was objecting."[36]

How many rapes could be prevented if people were better informed about the parameters of a healthy sexual encounter? How likely is it a person would commit rape repeatedly if not caught, educated, treated and/or punished for their crimes? How many people who have committed sexual offenses but who have not been caught by the criminal justice system voluntarily go to treatment? While the research in this area is ongoing, research outcomes can be variable and even oppositional. So many questions remain. Even seasoned researchers must work continuously to keep up with the most up-to-date research, theories, and treatment responses that are designed to guide this work.

Federal and State Government Sources

Typically, government resources are usually considered to be relatively objective in the coverage of a multiplicity of issues of interest to those making public policy and drafting legislation at the federal, state, and local levels of government. Feel free to go to these websites and look around. Compare what the most current published research says about the information presented here to research offered from within your state or local community. How is what your state is doing similar to or different from the research and general attitudes of the researchers and practitioners at the federal level?

As has been stated elsewhere, every state will have a different structure within its state and local levels of governance to address the management and research about sexual violence prevention efforts, victim resources, and sex crime response. The amount of information generated on the subject is immense. Some of the publications generated years or even decades ago still have relevance, and yet some research can become outdated and is no longer useful, unless it is being considered in the social and historical context of the state or community for which it was developed. The process for securing information and using that information in the service of communities and agencies assisting anyone affected by sexual violence involves monumental state and local systems, working with researchers, practitioners, victims, and offenders. The goal, and the challenge, is to conduct research that produces accurate and useful information to advance the processes and practices already in place that are intended to reduce and/or respond to the topic of sexual violence.

Differentiating Facts from Fiction and Moral from Immoral: Constructing Acceptable Behavior

At least part of the controversy surrounding the study of sexual deviance and sexual crimes in the United States is centered in the study of sex itself. For example, the topic of sex education is convoluted even before any subject matter gets covered, in large part, because parents, caregivers, educators, lawmakers, and religious officials argue about where, as well as whether, when, and how, information about sex should be covered.[37] The long-standing myths about masturbation causing blindness or suggesting that young boys soak their testicles in ice water to cure tendencies toward "self-abuse" (an early reference to masturbation) are ready examples of what are now understood by the mainstream public as silly ideas presented as fear-based scare tactics or out of mythology, rather than steeped in scientific veracity. In this case, questions about sex education, adolescent development, and issues linked to eternal damnation are part of the bigger social, biological, and ideological question about whether masturbation is healthy, deviant, or sinful. In some instances, facts are presented as objective but have been hidden completely within a moral assessment proclaiming that a restriction of masturbation is connected in some way to a larger need to preserve social morality.[38]

In more contemporary times, sometimes, resources on sex continue to be presented in such a way as to make the facts and fictions indiscernible. Stories on the life of sex researcher Alfred Kinsey (discussed in chapter 2) suggest that much of the motivation for his shift in professional focus was linked to his personal frustration about finding information about sex coming from religious ideology and bad science or religious moralizing being presented as scientific dictums actually being more about sexual moralizing than acquiring a breadth of knowledge on the subject based in legitimate research and intentional scholarship.[39] **Sexology,** the deliberate and intentional focus on sex as an academically organized subject of study, didn't really begin in earnest in the United States until the 1960s[40] and is intended to place conversations about sex and society under the umbrella of one focused disciplinary analysis.

Books in popular culture outlining the parameters of healthy sex compete with books outlining sex with aliens;[41] sex and the supernatural, or paranormal sex;[42] and sex as art, which of course includes a range of images and pictures and degrees of violence as reflected in various popular books, magazines, music videos, and movies.[43] Adding another layer of information about sex are the books and workshops viewed from within the cultural complements of religion and spirituality,[44] politics,[45] science,[46] and history.[47] Still another layer of social reality happens when gender and sexuality are used in commercials, on billboards, and in various ads to sell products or services and the related effect media representations of sex and sexuality (both healthy and unhealthy) have on the viewing public.[48]

Research suggests that sexual violence prevention is linked to education and awareness about sexual violence and a well-informed education about sex is an essential part of that.[49] More recently, in the United States, research suggests that young people, especially young men, are more likely to learn what they know about sex from pornography, rather than in a forum focused on health and wellness.[50] Questions are raised about the effect of pornography on developing young people, particularly when research suggests that the average age young boys see porn is 11.[51] (More about the larger conversation on pornography is presented in chapter 6.) The possibility of learning any "facts" about sex in pornography is far outweighed by the "fictions" structured to entice a video sale. Studies on the history of sexual deviance and crime classifications illustrate how important it is to reach out to a wider review of information because the desire to restrict attention or emphasize one aspect of a social history reduces the scope of an idea or topic and, in some cases, prematurely results in the acceptance of that limited perspective as the truth, which makes it more easy to carry myths forward, rather than actual, factual information. As information is presented about the research being conducted to better understand this area, think about who might use this material, how it might be used, and how it might be limited in its scope or application.

As has been discussed in several places, the definition of what constitutes sexual aggression or sex crimes can vary from city to city and state to state. Certainly, individuals are influenced by the social events they see around them, and ideas about sex appeal are being pitched in various social arenas as an essential, potentially exchangeable commodity. Young people who might not otherwise be ready for sex feel pressured by peers and society to participate in activities they see on television and assume they are supposed to be doing too. In some cases, kids are so afraid to talk about sex that they do not feel comfortable seeking out even basic factual information, they secure information in secret, or they see sex as just another thing people do—no big deal. Most people would agree that it is important how kids come to know about sex. The consequences of how sex is portrayed in media is an influencing factor just like much about the ongoing conversation about the criminalization of sex is extremely controversial and divisive but also linked to "facts" and "fictions." Young people witness and develop perceptions about sex from within the society and social events they see all around them. All are matters of interest for researchers.

Public Words and Private Actions

Mainstream public conversations about all things related to sex often do not reflect the not-so-public sexual decisions individuals make in their own lives. Sometimes, these sexual experiences are initiated by individual choice, and, sometimes, those choices are imposed. People often present one attitude publicly and practice a different set of values privately. Consider past Democrat presidential candidate John Edwards, who cultivated a public persona as a "family man" but was later challenged when news of an affair and a baby was initially denied and then eventually acknowledged when the truth became public. In March 2008, Eliot Spitzer resigned as the governor of New York after the *New York Times* documented several meetings with highly placed prostituted women,[52] ironically, at the same time he took the lead in drafting what is argued to be one of the toughest anti–sex trade laws in the nation.[53] As the New York attorney general, a position he held before being elected governor, he was credited with aggressively pursuing the prosecution of a sex tourism and prostitution ring in New York City.

But also consider the fact that *how* different sex controversies are covered often varies, depending on who is involved. In June 2010, CNN announced Spitzer would join the agency as a political and economic commentator.[54] Not too long after, information was released about Arnold Schwarzenegger having an affair with his nanny, which produced a child, and Congressman Anthony Weiner's sexting scandal. The news organization CNN produced a brief retrospective about famous political sex scandals. When Spitzer's name was omitted, people took note.[55]

This sexual double standard, where a person might say one thing in public and do something else in private, complicates efforts to study ranges of sexual behavior as a lived human experience. In an effort to determine what can or should be classified as healthy, deviant, or criminal, concern arises about what the real effect of such a contradictory public presentation of sexual reality is when the private reality is very different. Questions arise about whether such silence about what people say and what people do contributes to acts of sexual harm and violence. This is particularly true when politicians make laws against the very things they are privately participating in.

In the United States, and elsewhere in the world, the LGBTQI (lesbian, gay, bisexual, transgender, queer, and intersexed) community has been forced to live a double standard or risk often life-threatening public censure or physical harm, even death, at the hands of those who see this behavior as threatening.[56]

When a sexual scandal erupts in America, it is not uncommon to see news reports out of some European countries that suggest the United States should review its "prudish" attitude about sex as a private matter between people, rather than a public statement about a person's character.[57] Problematic to a much more significant degree are those who take physical actions against people and use a sexual morality to justify abuse and harm. The spring of 2013 saw a series of violent attacks, including one deadly assault against gay men in New York City.[58] In fact, the National Coalition of Anti-Violence Programs (NCAVP) released its 2010 report suggesting that the data collected represented the second highest reported number of hate crimes against LGBTQI communities.[59] Statistics collected from within this community are presented below (more is offered in chapter 5).

Conversations about sexual expression, definitions of sexual deviance, and the definitions and criminalization of sexual harm have a long-standing place in American history. The lack of agreement and aggressive prosecution of certain segments of the population for legally codified, if not morally agreed upon, sexual activities is extensive. The story of history is impossible to tell without making decisions about what gets included and what gets excluded. In putting together information in preparation for a conversation about the state of sexual violence in the United States, it is important to think about who regulates what social priorities, what gets included in the retelling of historical events, and who benefits from the story as it gets told. While much has changed in modern-day America with its 24-hour news programs, streaming video, and instant Google searches, one thing that has not changed is the controversial nature of conversations about sex. Questions about what constitutes even a definition of the act of sex confound ongoing challenges with researching the differences between what people say about sex in public and what they actually do in private, which may in fact differ still from what they say others should be doing.

In June 2015, the US Supreme Court legalized same-sex marriage. In spite of national legal authority, multiple reports are documenting cases where marriage licenses have been denied and couples are being harassed. Regardless of the recent court ruling, same-sex relationships are defined as deviant by some groups in the population. Understanding what could be identified collectively as acceptable sexual practices would mean identifying concrete parameters within a range of healthy and deviant behaviors. As society's mainstream values shift and change, how is this possible? To take this idea further, identifying socially unacceptable sexual practices requires making distinctions between deviant and criminal sexual behaviors and then policing those behaviors. When people disagree about the parameters of a social reality as important as healthy sex and sexual harms, how are those decisions made, and who, by what authority, is entitled to make them?

Throughout the history of the United States, cases involving women who were battered were not straightforwardly defined as a harm or crime. Consider the following excerpt referring to gender violence, physical assaults, and ongoing abuse directed at women by men, often their husbands.

Such crimes were considered personal matters and not matters for the courts or for the police. There was no such thing as self-defense for battered women. . . . Western history is replete with laws authorizing men's use of violence against women in order to punish or control them. In ancient Rome, men were allowed to use physical force to discipline their wives. Coverture, a law that stated that a married woman's existence was incorporated into her husband's, was part of the Common Law of England and the United States throughout most of the 1800s. A wife had no existence of her own and no individual rights. She could not own property, vote, get an education, or even enter into a contract. If a wife were permitted to work, she was required to relinquish her wages to her husband. English rape laws considered rape a crime against the husband, father, or fiancé of the victim, but not a crime against the victim herself. Rape cases were settled when the injured male was compensated for the damage to his "property." And of course, there was no such thing as "marital rape," since wives could not legally refuse their husbands.[60]

Reflecting on the information about domestic violence presented in chapter 5, it is essential to think about how history shapes the current understanding of violence between dating couples or married couples, in families, in neighborhoods, and in faith communities across the country. Just as the more recent federal definition of rape offered a modified perspective about sexual assault and sexual violence to include men, it is essential to remember the fact that men can be victims of sexualized violence and this reality was not previously represented by the law. Further, men can be abused in relationships as well; increasingly, these social realities are being documented and warrant attention from researchers and policy makers. The dynamics of individual power and collective social power are at the center of the ongoing efforts to better understand how people use and abuse power as they work, live, and create intimate connections and relationships with other people. All of these areas require research to gain a better understanding.

Conflation, Separation, and Interdisciplinarity

Without question, efforts by researchers to describe, predict, and explain sexual expression, sexual aggression, and sexual abuse are ongoing and long-standing. Research studies about sex are cataloged across academic disciplines. In each of these disciplines of study, decisions about ways to make meaning of the world are structured around priorities set by the discipline. These priorities are often established in conjunction with research conducted in the field that is identified as interesting and innovative. Academic disciplines are organized in this way as a means for centralizing the subject of study in a collective area of expertise. The problem, of course, is that the gap that gets created between disciplines can become an unintended obstacle that prevents necessary exploration between related ideas and concepts that are separated by disciplinary boundaries.

While collaboration with other scholars interested in the same general concept can be an advantage, researchers and educators have more recently been criticized for creating "islands" of knowledge and unintentionally limiting the flow of information between disciplines in a way that more naturally reflects social reality.[61] For researchers, this narrowed scope may make their research efforts more manageable, but is it accurately reflecting the breadth and depth of the social conditions their research seeks to measure? That is harder to know, for sure.

The blending together of different ways to see a given topic often provides a new way to see the subject from a different perspective. In academic circles, this idea is captured in the term **interdisciplinary studies,** or the collaboration of topical studies between academic disciplines and expanding beyond one's home discipline. In the broader social and historical context, the postmodern term **master narrative,** or the primary story used to represent an idea,[62] reflects the idea of opening to the differences between reading history as a colossal yet static idea with a singular presentation, rather than as a collection of widely diverse individual narratives—plural—and whether (and/or how) those stories are constantly open to new interpretation as historical analysis or social interpretation continues to be analyzed.

When researchers and criminologists study aspects of sex crimes, including victims as well as offenders, decisions have to be made about how the story is going to be represented. Which snapshot will be taken? When questions are raised about victims, it might make more sense to study survivors of sexual assault, rather than all crime victims, with the understanding that there is a significant difference between being a victim of a financial crime, for example, and a sex crime. What is different about a person who commits a sex crime and a person who commits a financial crime? As a result, people studying human behavior are constantly trying to group people together to study them, based on common characteristics, and then they look for patterns and study the group from a new perspective.

The caution, of course, is found in the reviewing, or retelling, of a given series of events where those ideas uncovered about the group under study can easily be **conflated,** or collapsed and blended together, for the sake of brevity or to emphasize specific aspects of the story a researcher wants to highlight. The result can shift the facts of a given story into a different perspective or circumstance entirely, making history more a singular reflection of the attitudes of those relaying the story than including a perhaps more accurate representation of the variety of interpretations of these events as they happened and how they were viewed by and how they affected singular people and groups differently.

The study of sexual deviance and sex crimes offers countless examples of history being confronted with diverse interpretations of an event, and, in some cases, a moral judgment is used to describe the event that significantly influences how it is reflected to the community. This kind of blending together of ideas makes the telling of the story easier, but the story can also be used to direct social meaning in significant ways. When people casually refer to all sex offenders as pedophiles, for example, all illegal sexual behaviors are conflated in such a way as to obscure potentially weighty distinctions. Pedophilia, the persistent and predatory sexual attraction to prepubescent children, certainly does not describe all kinds of sex offenders. An 18-year-old convicted of a statutory offense for having sex with someone unable to give legal consent due to their age, may be a sex offender, but to assume he is a pedophile is not correct. To suggest that sex offender laws need to get tough on pedophiles is different from conflating those terms and saying the laws should be made tougher on sex offenders.

A more specific example of how certain social events sometimes conflate unrelated issues to produce long-term, unwarranted social consequences and stigmas is offered in a historical analysis of attitudes toward lesbian and gay people. In Memphis, Tennessee, in 1892, Alice Mitchell slashed the throat of her lover, Freda Ward, killing her. The subsequent murder trial of the "girl lovers" produced an international firestorm at that time. Assumptions and assessments about this murderous behavior were attributed unfairly and became even more stigmatizing and threatening to people who were thought to be or who self-identified as lesbian.[63]

In more contemporary times, an 18-year-old female high school student in Florida started dating a 14-year-old female high school student. Under Florida law, you must be 18 to consent to having sex, and, when the underaged girl's parents found out about the sexual activity, they pressed charges. As a result, the 18-year-old was arrested and charged with two counts of lewd and lascivious battery of a child.[64] She became an internet sensation when her parents tried to solicit support for her case online. She faced a 15-year prison sentence on each charge and would be required to register as a sex offender if she were found guilty. Cases that used to be very regional in nature now have the opportunity to go viral, for better or worse. Offered a plea deal early on, the 18-year-old insisted she had done nothing wrong and rejected the deal.[65] After violating the judge's orders not to see the 14-year-old, she was sent to prison and served four months in jail as part of a plea deal she ultimately did accept.[66]

Questions were raised about whether this kind of prosecution would have taken place if the relationship had been with a young man, rather than a young woman.[67] How many freshmen in high school date juniors or seniors? Consider this example and what is often referred to in the media as a dating "relationship." Because it is illegal in many states for a young person to have sex before a specific age (in most states, that age is 16, as discussed in chapter 2), an 18-year-old person who is involved sexually with someone age 15 is committing a crime. The idea about this being a relationship does not hold any weight in a court of law. Someone who is 14 cannot be in a sexual relationship, and someone who is 18, of legal age, is violating the law and at risk of being charged if they pursue a sexual relationship with someone who is unable to legally consent to sex. Yet these realities belie the lived experience of many young people growing up, and in fact some current efforts to change these kinds of laws are discussed in more detail in chapter 10.

Examples of highly publicized or sensationalized cases are not uncommon when the subject is sex. Sometimes, the cases come in the form of domestic violence murder cases, and, sometimes, cases fall on the other extreme, where both parties acknowledge sex was consensual but the law states otherwise. Efforts to understand how these kinds of public interest stories influence mainstream perceptions about the subject over time and how the laws or policies passed in the wake of such events are intended to regulate such activities or behaviors can be of great consequence for consideration by the justice system. In these cases, misperceptions about violence in gay and lesbian relationships can become a media focus, regardless of the fact that domestic violence happens between heterosexual couples with frightening regularity. Efforts to regulate sex offenders were less intended to regulate sex between young people and more likely to prevent predatory sex-offending behaviors. These are only a few research-related kinds of questions for those interested in studying sexual violence in its many forms.

Another powerful example that elicits similar kinds of complex questions and controversial attitudes is linked to the historic and contemporary attitudes about black males and how they are individually and collectively affected by the long-standing cultural focus in the United States on myths about the black male rapist. This myth was historically usually used by white men or a privileged white social structure as justification for lynching black men.[68] To best understand a controversial issue, it is important to research and develop an understanding of that issue from multiple perspectives.

Consider an example of another problem based on how incorrect information can be passed along, depending on how the issue is framed. When domestic violence is identified as a woman's issue, this excludes the effect on children growing up in violent homes and deemphasizes the need to target services and prevention strategies toward hyperaggressive batterers. It also creates an awareness gap for domestic violence happening in LGBTQI couples. Still other examples include the larger social translation of AIDS/HIV being discussed exclusively as a "homosexual disease" and the subsequent blaming of homosexuals, particularly the "deviant homosexual lifestyle,"[69] for the spread of the disease while leaving other people more vulnerable to exposure because of the lack of accurate social, political, and medical information on the subject. The incorrect idea of homosexuals "causing" AIDS or having sex with a virgin being a cure for AIDS requires the asking of similar questions about whether different sexually transmitted diseases, like syphilis, herpes, or the human papillomavirus (HPV), were attributed to a group of people rather than being discussed as a medical condition requiring prevention and treatment. All of these issues are subject to interpretation by people in communities around the country, and it is essential that efforts to better understand these social issues are directed by systematic research efforts.

Critical reflections of historical facts, historical interpretations, or any other research for that matter, requires mindful attention be given to the built-in limitations as well as obvious accidental and/or intended omissions or malicious misuses of the topic being studied. Because the social sciences are separated from the medical sciences, sometimes, the research, language, and subjects of study are not always merged together in such a way as to allow common understandings between the larger disciplines. This is equally true for the various related but isolated disciplines in the social sciences. Women's studies programs, ethnic studies programs, social work, sociology, nursing, public health, history, criminology and criminal justice, economics, and political science are all areas of study that might emphasize studies in sexuality. Each of these areas will have a disciplinary theme that is different from the disciplinary themes of other units. Issues are often framed and prioritized in different ways that influence the feedback and dialogue between and among disciplines. Throughout this chapter, although various aspects of US history are presented for review, it can be important to identify some guidelines for critical reflection, which will likely be different depending on the disciplinary focus.

A LASTING PORTRAIT OR A SINGLE SNAPSHOT? CONTEMPORARY RESEARCH ON SEXUAL VIOLENCE

A collection of information is presented below about the current state of various types of sexualized violence. The list is not exhaustive, nor are the categories rigid, meaning the categories for classifying and categorizing sexualized violence are represented differently in various places in the voluminous collection of related research. The goal here is to offer a collection of statistics and information from various organizations and government research groups that might offer a sense of the current state of sexual violence in the United States. Definitions are provided, but, as stated previously, it is important to note that certain terms mean different things to different people in different places and in different times. The goal is to offer a sense of the current state of sexual violence in the United States from multiple perspectives, rather than attempting to provide one definitive, or authoritative, statement or answer.

Conversations about what constitutes healthy sexuality are ongoing. Conversations about what constitutes sexual deviance are also evolving and shifting and have changed over time. Yet the social, cultural, and technological shifts that have taken place since Kinsey's work in the United States in the late 1940s to early 1950s seem to suggest a dramatic change in popular attitudes about how people explore and experience sex and sexuality. Acknowledging the vast quantity and sources of sexual violence information, we present a collection of statistics gathered from various research papers, government studies, and advocacy organizations for review throughout this section of the text. Each topic includes a brief introduction, followed by information from advocacy programs, government documents, and research studies.[70] The date of the report is included in the parenthetical reference after each bullet point, and the full reference for the report from which the data comes is included in the endnotes.

Touch/No Touch and Force/No Force

One way researchers, practitioners, and policy makers organize the sorting of sexual harms is to create a classification system of touch/no touch and force/no force. A good deal of conversation about sexual violence perpetration (as will be discussed in chapter 8's review of theories on sexual offending) is centered on issues related to child sexual assault and rape. When these actions are classified by law, they often include demarcations to assess harm done. This is done to determine whether the incident involved contact in the form of a touch or whether force was used, and then these acts are contrasted with no-touch offenses. Many questions remain, however, about the effects and consequences of coercion, compliance, and consent as applied to sex-related offenses historically, particularly where children and vulnerable populations are concerned. These terms will become more important when attention is given to the laws and public policy discussion in chapters 10 and 11.

Children and Sexual Violence

> If the adults who are sexual with children merely wanted sex, there are many lower-risk methods of obtaining it. In most cases it is not the touch itself that is harmful but the meaning behind the touch that hurts.
>
> —Mic Hunter, *Abused Boys*[71]

Much of the information presented in chapter 3 addressed several areas of child sexual abuse. The National Sexual Violence Resource Center includes a brief description about what child abuse is. It suggests that a person sexually abuses a child when "he or she exposes a child to sexual acts or behavior."[72] It is critical to realize that abuse is not always visible and many children do not report abuse because they love and/or trust the person who is abusing them or they do not realize that what is happening is abusive.[73] Forms of child sexual abuse include the following:

- Sex acts that involve penetration
- Touching the child's breast or genitals
- Making a child touch the perpetrator's breasts or genitals
- Voyeurism (when a perpetrator looks at a child's naked body)
- Exhibitionism (when a perpetrator shows a child his or her naked body)
- Showing a child pornography or using a child in the production of pornography
- Child sexual exploitation, such as sex trafficking
- Internet-based child sexual abuse, such as creating, depicting, and/or distributing sexual images of children online; stalking, grooming, and/or engaging in sexually explicit behaviors with children online

Attention here is given to some statistics provided from a collection of contemporary reports on child sexual abuse to supplement the information on child sexual abuse provided in chapter 3.

- Each year, 6.6 percent of American youth are exposed to a physical assault by one parent against the other (2009).[74]
- Over the course of their lifetimes, 25 percent of children are exposed to some sort of family violence (2009).[75]
- Nationally, 23 percent of sexual assault offenders were under the age of 18. About 4 percent were under the age of 12. Of the offenders who assaulted children under the age of six, 40 percent were themselves less than 18 (2000).[76]
- Of incest victims, 2 to 8 percent report sexual offenses (2003).[77]

- Studies suggest that up to 10 million children witness some form of domestic violence annually.[78]
- Men who as children witnessed domestic violence were two times more likely to abuse their own wives as were men who were born to nonviolent parents.[79]
- Children whose parents are going through divorce can become vulnerable and susceptible to victimization because they may feel alone and be seeking attention.[80]
- At the time of their first completed rape, 30 percent of women were between the ages of 11 and 17 (2011).[81]
- At the time of their first completed rape victimization, 12.3 percent of women were age 10 or younger; at the time of their first completed rape victimization, 27.8 percent of men were age 10 or younger (2011).[82]
- More than one-third of women who report being raped before the age of 18 report being raped as an adult (2011).[83]
- Of people who sexually abuse children, 96 percent are male, and 76.8 percent are adults (2011).[84]
- Only 12 percent of child sexual abuse is ever reported to authorities (1999).[85]
- The average age for girls to first become victims of commercial child sexual exploitation is 12 to 14 years old, and the average age at which boys first become victims of prostitution is 11 to 13 (2010).[86]
- In 2009, about one-third of arrests for internet sexual offenses in which the victim was identified involved child sexual abuse (2010).[87]
- Child sexual abuse is a significant risk factor for the development of mental health and behavioral problems in adulthood, especially depression and substance abuse (2003).[88]
- Children from lower-income families are more at risk than children from higher-income families (undated).[89]
- Children who are victims of other forms of crime, violence, and abuse are more at risk to be victimized in additional crimes as polyvictims (undated).[90]
- Child abuse and neglect cost the United States approximately $124 billion annually (2012).[91]

Rape and Sexual Assault

> Rape is rape.
>
> —President Barack Obama in response to questions raised
> by Rep. Todd Akin's use of the term "legitimate rape"[92]

> Rape is a criminal act whatever the circumstances. A woman riding the subway nude may be guilty of indecency, but she may not be raped. If she invites or even sells sex at 10:00 and refuses it at 10:45, the partner who disregards her refusal and forces sex is guilty of rape. If she is drunk, asleep, mentally defective, paralyzed or dead, she must not be raped. Why? Because sexual congress must be by consent.
>
> —Toni Morrison, author[93]

> Embedded, if unexamined, in all the talk is the rapidly shifting defini-
> tion of rape, the history of the derided but long-standing term "forc-
> ible rape," and the wildly varied databases on sexual assault. . . . Many
> experts now believe that rape is best understood as an act of unwanted
> bodily invasion that need not involve force.
>
> —Ethan Bronner, *New York Times* article[94]

The presentation of terms and categories about rape is problematic in attempting to understand what constitutes rape and the varying degrees of sexual assault
in efforts to research rape and sexual assault and in the formal documentation of
reports of rape and sexual assault from within the criminal justice system. Consider the following definitions presented from a collection of medical researchers
at the National Crime Victim Center (2011):

> Rape is a form of sexual assault that is defined as a felony crime in the USA
> and many other nations. The crime of rape has several major elements. First,
> rape involves some type of sexual penetration of the victim's vagina, mouth,
> or anus. Second, the sexual activity must be unwanted by the victim. Third, the
> tactics used by the perpetrator must involve (1) use of force or threat of force
> or other harm to the victim, (2) using alcohol or drugs to render a victim too
> incapacitated to control his or her behavior or protect themselves, or (3) taking
> advantage of a victim who is incapacitated or unconscious and who, therefore,
> is unable to protect themselves.
>
> *Forcible rape.* The tactic used by the perpetrator is force or threat of force
> or other harm to the victim or someone else (e.g., the perpetrator threatens to
> hurt the victim's children if the victim does not cooperate).
>
> *Drug- or alcohol-facilitated rape.* The tactic used by the perpetrator is
> to deliberately give the victim drugs or alcohol without her permission in an
> attempt to get her high or drunk and then to commit an unwanted sexual act.
>
> *Incapacitated rape.* The victim voluntarily uses alcohol or drugs and is
> passed out or awake but too drunk or high to consent or control her behavior.
>
> *Statutory rape.* The perpetrator has sexual penetration with someone who
> is defined by law as too young to be capable of giving consent.
>
> *Attempted rape.* This is a type of sexual assault that occurs when no sexual
> penetration as defined above occurs but an unsuccessful attempt by the perpe-
> trator to commit a rape as defined above has occurred.
>
> *Rape acknowledgement.* Not all women who have experienced an event
> that meets the legal definition of rape define what happened as rape, and there-
> fore they do not think of themselves as rape victims.
>
> *Unacknowledged rape.* An event that has the legal elements of rape but
> that is not perceived by the victim to have been a rape. Unacknowledged rape
> victims are victims of rape who do not acknowledge that what happened to
> them was a rape.[95]

Contrast these definitions with statutory structures. Every state's legal statutes around rape are different, so the statutory definitions used here will be illustrated by using Minnesota criminal sexual conduct provisions as an example.

609.342 CRIMINAL SEXUAL CONDUCT IN THE FIRST DEGREE[96]

Subdivision 1. **Crime defined.**

A person who engages in sexual penetration with another person, or in sexual contact with a person under 13 years of age as defined in section 609.341, subdivision 11, paragraph (c), is guilty of criminal sexual conduct in the first degree if any of the following circumstances exists:

(a) the complainant is under 13 years of age and the actor is more than 36 months older than the complainant. Neither mistake as to the complainant's age nor consent to the act by the complainant is a defense;

(b) the complainant is at least 13 years of age but less than 16 years of age and the actor is more than 48 months older than the complainant and in a position of authority over the complainant. Neither mistake as to the complainant's age nor consent to the act by the complainant is a defense;

(c) circumstances existing at the time of the act cause the complainant to have a reasonable fear of imminent great bodily harm to the complainant or another;

(d) the actor is armed with a dangerous weapon or any article used or fashioned in a manner to lead the complainant to reasonably believe it to be a dangerous weapon and uses or threatens to use the weapon or article to cause the complainant to submit;

(e) the actor causes personal injury to the complainant, and either of the following circumstances exists:

(i)   the actor uses force or coercion to accomplish sexual penetration; or

(ii) the actor knows or has reason to know that the complainant is mentally impaired, mentally incapacitated, or physically helpless;

(f) the actor is aided or abetted by one or more accomplices within the meaning of section 609.05, and either of the following circumstances exists:

(i)   an accomplice uses force or coercion to cause the complainant to submit; or

(ii) an accomplice is armed with a dangerous weapon or any article used or fashioned in a manner to lead the complainant reasonably to believe it to be a dangerous weapon and uses or threatens to use the weapon or article to cause the complainant to submit;

(g) the actor has a significant relationship to the complainant and the complainant was under 16 years of age at the time of the sexual penetration. Neither mistake as to the complainant's age nor consent to the act by the complainant is a defense; or

(h) the actor has a significant relationship to the complainant, the complainant was under 16 years of age at the time of the sexual penetration, and:

(i)   the actor or an accomplice used force or coercion to accomplish the penetration;

(ii) the complainant suffered personal injury; or

(iii) the sexual abuse involved multiple acts committed over an extended period of time.

Neither mistake as to the complainant's age nor consent to the act by the complainant is a defense.

* * *

It is important to note that this is the description of Criminal Sexual Conduct in the First Degree. There are First Degree, Second Degree, Third Degree, Fourth Degree, and Fifth Degree Criminal Sexual Conduct classifications in the state of Minnesota and statutory definitions of relevant terms, including scope, actor, force, consent, intimate parts, mentally impaired, mentally incapacitated, personal injury, physically helpless, position of authority, sexual contact, sexual penetration, complainant, coercion, significant relationship, patient, psychotherapist, psychotherapy, emotionally dependent, therapeutic deception, special transportation, predatory crime, and secure treatment facility.

The definitions of **sexual contact** and **sexual penetration** are included here:[97]

Subd. 11. Sexual contact.

(a) "Sexual contact," for the purposes of sections 609.343, subdivision 1, clauses (a) to (f), and 609.345, subdivision 1, clauses (a) to (e), and (h) to (o), includes any of the following acts committed without the complainant's consent, except in those cases where consent is not a defense, and committed with sexual or aggressive intent:

  (i) the intentional touching by the actor of the complainant's intimate parts, or

  (ii) the touching by the complainant of the actor's, the complainant's, or another's intimate parts effected by a person in a position of authority, or by coercion, or by inducement if the complainant is under 13 years of age or mentally impaired, or

  (iii) the touching by another of the complainant's intimate parts effected by coercion or by a person in a position of authority, or

  (iv) in any of the cases above, the touching of the clothing covering the immediate area of the intimate parts, or

  (v) the intentional touching with seminal fluid or sperm by the actor of the complainant's body or the clothing covering the complainant's body.

(b) "Sexual contact," for the purposes of sections 609.343, subdivision 1, clauses (g) and (h), and 609.345, subdivision 1, clauses (f) and (g), includes any of the following acts committed with sexual or aggressive intent:

  (i) the intentional touching by the actor of the complainant's intimate parts;

  (ii) the touching by the complainant of the actor's, the complainant's, or another's intimate parts;

  (iii) the touching by another of the complainant's intimate parts;

  (iv) in any of the cases listed above, touching of the clothing covering the immediate area of the intimate parts; or

  (v) the intentional touching with seminal fluid or sperm by the actor of the complainant's body or the clothing covering the complainant's body.

(c) "Sexual contact with a person under 13" means the intentional touching of the complainant's bare genitals or anal opening by the actor's bare genitals or anal opening with sexual or aggressive intent or the touching by the complainant's bare genitals or anal opening of the actor's or another's bare genitals or anal opening with sexual or aggressive intent.

Subd. 12. **Sexual penetration.**

"Sexual penetration" means any of the following acts committed without the complainant's consent, except in those cases where consent is not a defense, whether or not emission of semen occurs:

(1) sexual intercourse, cunnilingus, fellatio, or anal intercourse; or
(2) any intrusion however slight into the genital or anal openings:
   (i)   of the complainant's body by any part of the actor's body or any object used by the actor for this purpose;
   (ii) of the complainant's body by any part of the body of the complainant, by any part of the body of another person, or by any object used by the complainant or another person for this purpose, when effected by a person in a position of authority, or by coercion, or by inducement if the child is under 13 years of age or mentally impaired; or
   (iii) of the body of the actor or another person by any part of the body of the complainant or by any object used by the complainant for this purpose, when effected by a person in a position of authority, or by coercion, or by inducement if the child is under 13 years of age or mentally impaired.

*   *   *

The importance of these definitions cannot be understated because they influence how the actions are treated at each phase of the criminal justice process, by law enforcement, the legal system, the corrections officials, the department of health and human services, and the treatment practitioners. The need for clarifying the legal response may seem obvious upon first glance; however, the nuances of acts of sexualized violence require constant reassessments about which provisions cover the events under consideration. (More is presented on these questions in chapter 10.) Here, it must simply be made clear that the laws and statutes drafted to clarify the social response to sexual violence and harm is, at best, a guideline for moving forward. The better the laws are, the better the ability to provide services to victims to punish and/or offer treatment to offenders and then to address or redress harm in the community. Further, legally sanctioned definitions and terms also reflect how research on these crimes is conducted. When marital rape was not legally identified, for example, fewer formal research mechanisms were in place to study these incidents. Efforts to understand the incidents of violence in the family would be left to random reporting of incidents and stories, rather than conducting a systematic review of data and the social, legal, and political support for asking the necessary and relevant questions.

Selected basic information about victim responses and needs regarding the effects of rape and sexual assault is introduced in chapter 14. In addition to victims' needs, researchers who study those who are commonly victimized in society suggest that efforts to understand rape and sexual assault, as an example of harm, benefit from including information about a variety of aspects of both victims and offenders. The concept of **intersectionality** is important for understanding the role of **social location**, or a person's place in society, based on race, gender, and class, with significant influencing factors regarding the ways individual identity is seen to be socially constructed and subsequently affect, in this case, by sexualized violence. Intersectionality as a concept has been linked to the multiracial feminist movement, which has a long history of its own and produced research and writings that were not necessarily valued or prioritized by the initial mainstream feminist thinkers, who in large part assume all women speak from one social perspective.[98] Larger efforts to understand violence and oppression and even environmental harm stem from these initial efforts, which are primarily being acknowledged and expanded by feminist researchers.[99]

In short, a person might be gay, a Latino, an activist, a son of wealthy parents, and an immigrant to the United States. Although many people might see a gay man, or a Latino man, or a religious man, or simply a man, the idea of intersectionality and the importance of understanding social location invite a reflection about how people might reduce a person down to one thing, race, class, gender, the work they do, the car they drive, or their education, rather than see them as a composite or a fusion of these social experiences and exposures. The statistics presented below suggest that there is a significant difference between races and classes of people, still primarily women but increasingly including men, as victims. For those interested in understanding the social underpinnings of abuse, including information about the abusers as well as those groups most often harmed, these social variables are argued to hold some significantly important clues, which are easily overlooked when attention is given to traditional or mainstream constructions of how victims and offenders are viewed.

Frustratingly, though, when statistics are collected, it is often the case that much about the humanity of the people about whom these statistics are collected and reported is not captured. The focus here is on sexual violence, but the conversations about oppression and violence have broader application in US society. As a community of researchers and scholars, however, the idea of gender, ethnicity, and class often are treated as add-on issues, as if the people who fit these categories can be reduced to a narrow conceptualization of each category of male or female, black or white, rich or poor, as opposed to a fusion of all three. To see the extent of the limitations in efforts to understand the effects of harm, consider research on the long-term effects of nurses working with children and adults who have been harmed by sexualized violence. Researchers have suggested that the definition of "victim" be expanded to include those repeatedly exposed to of this kind of trauma.[100] But, because these people are "professionals" or are not "primary victims," assumptions are made about harm in the association.

A COLLECTION OF STATISTICS ON SEXUAL VIOLENCE

Efforts to understand social context are often limited by the use of statistics as an exclusive means of presenting social events. The significance of this expansive work from within the feminist tradition invites a reflection on how academics or other folks reading these statistics about sexualized violence actually see the people reflected in these statistics and offers a significant contribution to the way the individual stories reflected by those statistics are integrated into the hearts and minds of the people reading the statistics. The expressions of the humanity of people are always about so much more than one or two observable (or non-observable) characteristics. Having said all that, however, data collection methods are often structured in a more unidimensional way, and as a result the data presented below reflects those traditional categories.

Rape, Marital Rape, Domestic Assault, and Intimate Partner Violence

- Regarding female rape victims, 12 percent were assaulted when they were 10 or younger, but almost half of female victims said they had been raped before they turned 18, with about 80 percent of victims having been raped before they were 25.[101]
- Statistics from the US Department of Justice suggest that the percentage of rapes and sexual assaults committed by strangers remained consistent between 1993 and 2010 at approximately 24 percent (2012).[102]
- Using a controversial definition of rape (discussed earlier in the chapter), the NISVS reported that 1.3 million women may be victims of rape annually, which is significantly higher than the 188,380 Americans victimized 2010, with 84,767 assaults defined as forcible rapes in 2010 by the national FBI statistics from local law enforcement (2011).[103]
- There were 248,300 rapes/sexual assaults in the United States in 2007, more than 500 per day, up from 190,600 in 2005. Women were more likely than men to be victims; the rate for rape/sexual assault for persons age 12 or older in 2007 was 1.8 per 1,000 for females and 0.1 per 1,000 for males (2008).[104]
- More than half of women reported being raped by an intimate partner, and 40 percent raped by an acquaintance (2011).[105]
- Of all rapes, only 16 percent were reported to law enforcement.[106]
- Under at least one section of the sexual offense codes (usually those code sections regarding force), marital rape is a crime in all 50 states (2000).[107]
- Regarding married women, 14 percent report they were raped by their spouse. This percentage probably underestimates the true prevalence of marital rape (2011).[108]
- Of the women reporting, 23 percent reported rape and sexual assault as the only abuse in the marriage (2011).[109]
- Domestic violence has affected about 44 percent of women at some point during their adult lives, according to a recently published survey. Considerably fewer women, about 15 percent, reported domestic violence within the past five years from the date the survey was conducted, and that figure fell to about 8 percent for incidents in the past year (2006).[110]
- From 1994 to 2010, the overall rate of intimate partner violence in the United States declined by 64 percent, from 9.8 victimizations per 1,000 persons age 12 or older to 3.6 per 1,000 (2012).[111]
- Females ages 18 to 24 and 25 to 34 generally experienced the highest rates of intimate partner violence (2012).[112]
- Forty percent of family violence victims were injured during the incident. Of the 3.5 million victims of family violence between 1998 and 2002, less than 1 percent died as a result of the incident (2005).[113]

- Most family violence victims were white (74 percent), and the majority were between the ages of 25 and 54 (65.7 percent). Most family violence offenders were white (79 percent), and most were age 30 or older (62 percent) (2005).[114]
- Approximately 60 percent of family violence victimizations were reported to police between 1998 and 2002. The reporting rate among female victims was not significantly greater than the reporting rate among male victims. Among the 2.1 million incidents of family violence reported to police between 1998 and 2002, 36 percent resulted in an arrest (2005).[115]
- The CDC published data collected in 2005 that finds that women experience 2 million injuries from intimate partner violence each year (2008).[116]
- Total domestic violence victimizations, or crime committed by family members and intimates, increased slightly from 1.1 million in 2010 to 1.4 million in 2011.
- One in seven men reported having experienced severe violence at the hands of an intimate partner (2011).[117]
- Intimate partner violence made up 20 percent of all nonfatal violent crime experienced by women in 2001 (2003).[118]
- One in six women (16.2 percent) and 1 in 19 (5.2 percent) men in the United States reported stalking victimization at some point during their lifetime that had them worried about them or someone close to them being harmed or killed (2011).[119]
- Of the teens surveyed, 20 percent had posted nude or semi-nude pictures of themselves online (2008).[120]
- Nineteen percent of teens sent, received, or forwarded sexually suggestive nude or nearly nude photos through text message or email (2009).[121]
- Contradicting reports on sexting suggest numbers as low as 1 in 100 to 1 in 10 (2011).[122]
- The costs of intimate partner violence in the United States alone exceeded $5.8 billion per year: $4.1 billion are for direct medical and health care services, and productivity losses account for nearly $1.8 billion.[123]
- Women are much more likely than men to be victimized by a current or former intimate partner (2008).[124]
- Women are 84 percent of spouse abuse victims and 86 percent of victims of abuse at the hands of a boyfriend or girlfriend, and about three-fourths of the persons who commit family violence are male (2005).[125]
- After taking into account other risk factors for domestic violence, such as being abused or witnessing abuse between parents, carrying out frequent bullying as a child was linked to a fourfold increase in a man's risk for partner abuse.[126]

College Rape and Drug-Assisted Rape

- Findings indicate about 20 million women (out of 112 million women [18 percent]) in the United States have ever been raped during their lifetime. This includes an estimated 18 million women who have been forcibly raped, nearly 3 million women who have experienced drug-facilitated rape, and 3 million women who have experienced incapacitated rape.[127]

- Victims of drug-facilitated or incapacitated rape were less likely than victims of forcible rape to report to the authorities both in the general sample and in the sample of college assaults.[128]

- Of the nearly 6 million women currently attending US colleges, 673,000 (11.5 percent) have ever been raped. This includes an estimated half-million college women who have been forcibly raped; 160,000 who have experienced drug-facilitated rape; and over 200,000 who have experienced incapacitated rape (2000).[129]

- Between 1980 and 1990, 55 percent of gang rapes on college campuses were committed by fraternity members, 40 percent by sports teams, and 5 percent by others (1993).[130]

Stalking

- The US Justice Department's Bureau of Justice Statistics estimates that 3.4 million persons said they were victims of stalking during a 12-month period in 2005 and 2006. Women experience 20 stalking victimizations per 1,000 females age 18 and older, and men experience approximately seven stalking victimizations per 1,000 males age 18 and older (2009).[131]

- An estimated 3.3 million people age 18 or older were victims of stalking during a 12-month period (2006).[132]

- Seven out of 10 stalking victims know their offender in some capacity.[133]

- The percentage of persons stalked diminishes with age.[134]

Rape of Males

- Twenty-eight percent of male victims of rape reported that they were first assaulted when they were no older than 10 (2011).[135]

- More than half of the men who reported being raped said they were raped by an acquaintance (2011).[136]

- Approximately one in six boys are sexually abused before the age of 16 (2011).[137]

- The number of men who experience sexual abuse as children equals the number of men who develop prostate cancer, the most common cancer and second leading cause of death among men. Further, men with histories of childhood sexual abuse are more than four times the number of men with heart disease, the leading cause of death among men. (2012).[138]

- The US Department of Justice reports that 93 percent of victims under the age of 17 and 93 percent of victims age 18 and older were assaulted by someone they knew (2000).[139]

Focusing on First Nation Communities and Other Communities of Color

- Native women are assaulted more than twice as often as other women in the United States (2007).[140]

- Eighty-six percent of the rapes of Native women are by non–Native men. This compares to a 2004 report that found that 65.1 percent of rapes of white victims were white, and 89.8 rapes of African American victims were African American (2007).[141]
- One in three Native American women will be raped at some point in their lives (2007).[142]
- Indigenous women or women from racially and ethnically marginalized groups may fear state authority if the police have traditionally used coercive and violent means of criminal enforcement in their communities (2007).[143]
- Fifty percent of American Indian and Native Alaskan woman reported suffering physical injuries in addition to the rape; comparable figures for women in the United States are generally 30 percent (2004).[144]
- Native American women were victims in nearly 80 percent of the confirmed cases of rape and murder in Alaska over the past 15 years, when Native Americans make up only 16 percent of Alaska's total population (2007).[145]
- Native American women experience the highest rate of violence of any group in the United States, with an estimated 70 percent of sexual assaults never reported (2001).[146]
- One in 20 Latinas experienced intimate partner violence in the past 12 months (2005).[147]
- Latinas are only half as likely to report abuse to authorities as survivors from other ethnic and racial groups (2008).[148]
- Nearly half of Latinas did not report abuse to authorities (2008).[149]
- More acculturated Latinas are more likely to seek social services than low-acculturated Latinas (2006)[150]
- For every black woman who reports her rape, at least 15 black women do not report theirs (2003).[151]
- Approximately 40 percent of black women report coercive contact of a sexual nature by the age of 18 (2006).[152]
- The National Violence Against Women Survey (2006) found that 18.8 percent of black women reported rape in their lifetime.[153]
- Asian and Pacific Islander (API) women tend to report lower rates of rape and other forms of sexual assault (2004).[154]
- Like many other women of color, API women are subjected to derogatory and demeaning stereotypes about sexual availability.
- Sixty percent of black women are assaulted by the time they are 18.[155]

Focusing on LGBTQI Communities

- Of the 27 anti-LGBTQI murders in 2010, the second highest total recorded since 1996, 70 percent were people of color (2011).[156]
- Fifty percent of those who experienced hate violence did not contact the police for fear of further retaliation (2010).[157]
- In 2008, lesbians, gays, bisexuals, transgenders, or queer people (LGBTQI) reported 3,419 incidents of domestic violence to local antiviolence programs. Nine of these incidents resulted in murder.[158]

- In 2008, 51 percent of LGBTQI domestic violence victims were women, 42 percent were men, and 5 percent were transgender.[159]
- In cases where the age of the victim was known, 64 percent of LGBTQI domestic violence victims were age 30 and over, while 36 percent were under 30.[160]
- Stalking victims identified their stalker as a current or former intimate partner in 30.3 percent of cases.[161]
- When asked why they believed stalking behavior had begun, 16.8 percent of stalking victims said because the person had liked or had a crush on the victim and, 16.2 percent said it was to keep the victim in a relationship with the stalker.[162]

Institutional Abuses and Abuse of Vulnerable Populations

- *Ninety percent or more* (emphasis added) of people with developmental disabilities will be victims of sexual assault at some point in their lives.[163]
- Sexual abuse committed against a developmentally delayed person is most often committed by someone they know.[164]
- Difficulties in articulation may cause some disclosures to be misinterpreted or go unnoticed entirely.[165]
- There are offenders who look for people with disabilities because they know they will have difficulty disclosing the abuse and are more likely to be misunderstood or disbelieved.[166]
- There were 26,000 sexual assaults in the US military in 2012, more than 70 per day.[167]
- A study of navy personnel reported that 13 percent reported engaging in behavior that approximates legal definition of attempted or completed rape since the age of 14; among those men most (71 percent) reperpetrated.[168]
- Youth in adult prisons are five times more likely to be raped and more likely to commit suicide in an adult jail than in a juvenile facility.[169]
- A California study found that 59 percent of transgender inmates housed in men's prisons had been sexually abused while incarcerated, compared to 4 percent of nontransgender inmates.[170]

Additional information about various institutions implicated in higher percentages and averages of sexual abuses is presented in chapter 6.

COMPLEXITIES CHARACTERIZING SEXUAL DEVIANCE AND SEX CRIMES

Centering the idea of a sex crime on being defined as a sexual act that lacks **mutual consent** seems to suggest a notion of full agreement freely given. Another way to talk about mutual consent could be an easy standard to meet: no means no and yes means yes. But such an assessment has a clear disconnection from the lessons offered in a review of the practice of and social tolerance for aspects of sexual violence throughout history. The idea that "she didn't say no" has been taken as a yes is important. Based on the book *Yes Means Yes!*[171]

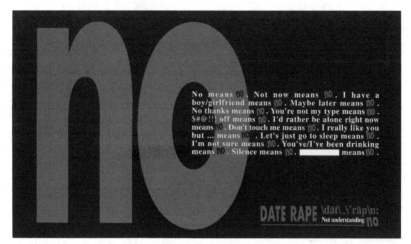

Figure 6.1   From the "No Means No" Campaign against Violence against Women and Gender-Based Violence.
© Canadian Federation of Students

and in part a response to the "No Means No" campaign against date rape (see Figure 6.1), the discussion of a sex-positive culture is emerging. The idea that only yes means yes, referred to as the **affirmative consent model**, includes a variety of conceptual shifts but is in part focused on acknowledging and respecting the role of both partners in the determination of the parameters of their own sexual pleasure without having any questions about what no might mean. If the answer is yes, everyone is clear. This idea of enthusiastic consent can trigger new discussions on how a sex-positive culture with clear communication can influence individual sexual choices.

It is estimated that between 64 and 96 percent of all rapes are never reported to criminal justice authorities and that only a small minority of reported cases, especially stranger–nonstranger assaults, are prosecuted.[172] (More on this is presented in chapter 10.) Recently, in the news, a woman in San Diego was fired from her teaching job, and her kids were asked to leave the same parochial school because of the escalating violence perpetrated by her husband. In cities across the country women—particularly poor women, which also means particularly women of color—have faced eviction from their homes after reporting a domestic dispute.[173]

In 1993, then Senator Joe Biden wrote the forward on a Senate Judiciary report, based on 1990 crime data from all 50 states, titled *Violence Against Women: The Response to Rape: Detours on the Road to Equal Justice*. In short, he summarized the report this way: "These findings reveal a justice system that fails by any standard to meet its goals—apprehending, convicting and incarcerating violent criminals: *98% of the victims of rape never see their attacker caught, tried, and imprisoned*" (italics in the original).[174]

When attention is given to sex crimes, the focus should rightfully be placed on whom—the offender or the victim? Traditionally, attention has been placed on the victim, with little or no public attention being given to conversation about the perpetrator of sexual harms beyond pitchfork-like mob mentalities that recommend "killing them," "cutting off their balls," or "doing unto others." The shift required in an effective focus on addressing and reducing the harm caused by sexual violence is missing the center point of much of the concern reflected here: most sexual offenses are committed by people known to the victim. Incidents of harm and sexual violence offer a typical scenario of an offender and a victim—someone perpetrating harm and someone being harmed—one aggressor and one target of that aggression. Ironically and historically, women are blamed for the behavior of the men in their lives who commit these acts of harm. While a great deal of attention is being given to the women as victims, less attention is given to the men who perpetrate these kinds of violent acts. Studies of the dynamics of oppression are powerful tools for reframing these events. Consider the following:

- Don't ask "Why does she stay?" Ask "Why does he hit?"
- Don't ask "Was she wearing a short skirt?" Ask "Why did he rape?"
- Don't ask "Was she drinking?" Ask "Why do some men rape?"

Yet, when you take the focus off of the victim and the offender and move to the larger systems and institutions in society, you find that many people argue that society too has a role to play in assessing and addressing the form and style of social rules outlined around individual relationship development. What social cues are directing these evolving parameters for young people and couples? What social institutions and systems also have a role to play in better understanding sexual violence and assault? What else can be done as a society to help empower survivors to report the offenses? When attention has been focused on sexual violence in the past, traditionally, the focus has stayed centered on the victim. (More on victim's issues is presented for discussion in chapter 14.) Even practitioners and advocates for sexual assault victims will say that, for too long, the victim has been at the center of the controversy of sex crimes, with people asking what she was doing or what she was wearing, rather than asking why a man would rape a woman. This is the same for domestic assault. People ask what she did or why she stays, rather than asking what kind of personal or social issues are at play that produce the conditions where a man will decide to hit his partner? What personal or social issues ever made violence against an intimate partner or family member socially acceptable?

A SNAPSHOT OF THE PORTRAIT OF SEXUAL VIOLENCE

This chapter opens by giving attention to the purposes and limits of social scientific research, particularly on crimes and activities seen to be of a private nature. Narrowing the scope to sex crime classifications, further consideration is given to the variability of terms and definitions as a result of individual state priorities and state-by-state implementation of varied local, state, and federal sex crime legislation (discussed in more detail in chapter 13). Data on sex crimes and sex offenses and sex offenders varies by year, by source, and by study. A snapshot of data and resources includes reviews to highlight the various ways research and media resources are used to describe the current state of sexual violence in the United States.

Also, as illustrated with the example of abortion in chapter 2, social assessments identifying behavior as either deviant or criminal are influenced by a variety of social realities. The nuanced perspective offered by studies on intersectionality provides what might be a more comprehensive way to look at these differences and see how they merge together in harmful social patterns. If the complete range of sexual behaviors is knowable and a reasonable discussion on that range of behaviors between various social groups is possible, would a consensus about acceptable or deviant and criminal classifications be achievable? Across the globe, sex as a topic of conversation and study has produced various social customs and practices with different taboos and restrictions in different social groups. The history of sex and sexual harm, like all historical analysis, is a dynamic process influenced by current attitudes combined with focused efforts to collect pieces from that past in the form of artifacts, letters, or stories. Historical interpretation is open to current interpretation. The information researchers think they know today about social realities of the past is always the subject of ongoing study and debate.

Statistics only capture snapshots, and researchers are left to make sense of what those still images might mean over time and which images might endure. In the United States, diverse interest groups compete to have their perspectives heard and acknowledged, making it is easier for larger groups or louder voices to overlook or set aside important social realities more evident in numerically smaller or socially marginalized social groups. The example of how First Nation or Native people in the United States have suffered a horrible history of sexual abuses at the hands of church officials, which was then compounded by US policy makers determined to see Native people destroyed both culturally and physically as the United States expanded west as well as individual actions taken by settlers interacting with Native people on a day-to-day basis and who benefited from the laws and policies—all of these elements are essential for both white people and people of color to understand fully whether they want to understand the true and full effect of their American heritage.[175] Female African American slaves were forced to have sex with slave owners at a time in history when those white, male, Christian slave owners, some of whom were married, acted in violation of both the legal system (anti-miscegenation laws) and religious ideologies (adultery/fornication) and yet were seldom prosecuted for these infractions.[176] For black or Native men, on the other hand, even an allegation of abuse was enough to create a lynch mob or a pervasive cultural myth that had little or no basis in historical fact.[177] The same act committed at a different time by a different person was punished very differently or not even noted at all. For this reason, in addition to studying the individual offender, criminologists and other social deviance researchers also study the social conditions and circumstances surrounding sanctions and prosecutions as well as social events that might warrant sanctions but were knowingly overlooked.

The parameters of marriage have also changed over time, for example, including the conditions under which divorce is permissible and whether marriage is possible at all, as in the case of gay marriage or marriage between people from different social classes or races. Collective social action intent on changing the laws identified as "bad" is often met head-on by supporters who intend to preserve the tone and content of those same laws that they describe as quite essential. How society responds to men who physically assault their wives or to the ways in which marriages and divorces could be granted are processed informally through the use of social sanctions, until, when deemed necessary or when political movements garner enough support, those actions are brought formally through the legal system. The use of formal and informal social processes is all a part of the sexual history in the United States. The lack of formal records and the use of informal processes make the efforts to collect sexual histories in the collective or in smaller social groups even that much more difficult.

In the United States, because the subject of sex in general has been and remains so controversial while efforts to punish sex offenders seem so energized, thoughtful critical reflection is timely. This social reality creates a strange blending of people who don't want to talk about sex but who are more than willing to offer up what they have to say about what should happen to perpetrators of sex crimes without really asking questions about what constitutes a sex crime or critically evaluating the effects of policy put in place to address sex crimes. Raising questions about what is right and wrong or what should be legal or illegal with regard to how the definition and design of the crime classification schemes are applied to perpetrators is linked in many ways to the research conducted and findings produced on these issues. Future research, laws, public policy, and prevention efforts are also linked to research findings.

Few would argue the need to find acceptable, even positive outcomes, for people who have been harmed or cause harm. Libraries are filled with books on related topics and themes, and, sadly, never a day passes without a sexual scandal or assault reported in the news in communities throughout the country. With each incident or media publication intent on illustrating the problems or ongoing issues related to sexual violence and harm, it seems people continue to identify sexual violence in a relatively fixed definition, where a line is crossed, rather than one that is actively under scrutiny and being modified over a continuum of acceptable and unacceptable behaviors. This shifting back and forth between acceptable and unacceptable behaviors can even be true in the eyes of both victims and offenders. Consider the example of a sexual assault where victims blame themselves when an offender was intentionally pushing personal and social boundaries. What role do social attitudes and social scripts have to do with this? How much influence does society have on each of us and our choices for individual actions? These are all great questions that have garnered a diversity of social science responses worthy of further and expansive exploration.

When attempting to offer a new view or clarify a more traditional view about appropriate or inappropriate sexual boundaries, how does society determine when a sexually explicit joke becomes offensive or when the use of sexually explicit language crosses the line and is seen as inappropriate or offensive? In spite of various dramatic changes in the way law enforcement agencies police sexual violence cases and attorneys prosecute these cases (see chapter 10), when does the larger society see sexual violence as a problem everyone has to confront in one way or another, rather than seeing it as solely a victim's issue, which mentally isolates the victim from themselves and the people they know and love? All of us, at one point or another, are confronted in our own lives and our own relationships with a situation for which we have to determine "No, that's too far, for me; not something I want to do," or "No, that's not something I want to see, even in a movie or on TV," or "That is so offensive, it should be made illegal." At some point, all of us must confront questions about how we, our kids, our families, or our communities make decisions about intimate relationships and sex.

Studies around sex, the statistics they produce, and the sexual attitudes and sexual behaviors represented in society require that a vast number of viewings, reflections, and visions be offered from many people throughout various social sectors to secure what might be referred to as a collective social "truth" about the state of events in the world. This is especially true for studies in sexual violence. Alfred Kinsey's research rose to national prominence in 1948 and 1953 after he wrote the twin volumes *Sexual Behavior in the American Male* and *Sexual Behavior in the American Female* and was supported in some circles, whereas the study's methodology, sampling method, findings, and data selected for inclusion in the study were heavily criticized by others.[178] Margaret Mead, an iconic figure in anthropology whose studies on adolescence and sexual practices were controversial at the time of their publication, has more recently come under new, although arguably discredited, scrutiny for her research methods and analysis.[179] Since language, cultural experience, and individual vantage points limit what is seen and experienced, it is not surprising when efforts to understand these complex issues are also restricted by time and place. The social and academic challenges offered in response to the scientific research of Kinsey and Mead exemplify some of the controversies associated with academic and scientific studies focused on the study of sex in general. Sensitivity to the limits of research is as important as the data presented in the more contemporary studies.

Ultimately, the information presented here is a snapshot of research data reflected in the 90-minute motion picture version of the longer book, which holds an even richer selection of the stories that come from one place and time in the life span of this subject of study. The historical study of all things offers an excellent example of how the dynamic story of past social realities is often reduced to specific stories and dates simply in the telling of the larger historical tale. The story of history itself is an interesting sociological query when one considers which stories are elevated and transferred as believable and which ones are reduced to insignificance or lost completely. As in the case of the sexual abuse of slave populations, sometimes, even the most common stories and controversies are not always captured and incorporated into a collective social understanding of the subject under study, in this case, sexual violence. Attitudes, opinions, and beliefs on many sides of the issue are presented within a sociopolitical, legal, or religious framework in an effort to garner support for directing guidelines governing the regulation or restriction of a wide range of sexual practices.

Research centers, think tanks, government and social service agencies, nonprofit organizations, and faith communities are only a smattering of outfits working to collect information about sexual harm, sex crimes, and sex offenders, all with an eye toward reducing and preventing sexual harm. Academic research focused on sex, gender, and family structure from American icons such as sex researcher Alfred Kinsey and cultural anthropologist Margaret Mead is easily suspect when academic arguments conflict with and are therefore thought to represent a challenge to social convention. Certainly, as is the case with both these researchers, their research continues to be critically challenged. Although structured to be a rigorous, objective assessment of social phenomena, academic research has limitations, and well-intentioned people have been shown to be driven more by ideology than objectivity, even in their use of the scientific method.[180] Even when the science is not challenged, popular interpretations might change, or additional research might be used to justify adjustments or compliance to past interpretations and social practice. Research once accepted as plausible is later challenged as limited, moralistic, ideological, flawed, and unscientific.[181] This dynamic, although sometimes unwieldy and messy, is arguably one of the best ways to introduce and review new ideas and present research findings for external review, or, in other words, to have the validity of the research be assessed by another researcher or research team in an effort to verify its credibility.

Another level of difficulty in researching sex crimes and sexual violence is reflected in the well-established social stigmas and taboos around sex and in the difficulty of studying crime in general. Social attitudes presented in popular culture as reflecting family values have been confronted by a stream of social activism in an attempt to change this traditional notion of what a family is and what is seen as acceptable sexual practices. This includes the challenges to gay marriage, nationally syndicated online blogs about sexual health and alternatives to traditional monogamous sex, and the related efforts to regulate, both formally and informally, these emerging social changes.

Without question, when reviewing data and information about sexual practices, sexual abuses, and the people who commit those sex offenses, critical reflection is required. As is becoming apparent, critical reflection is required when studying individual and collective understandings of sexual health, sexual deviance, social sexual past practice, and the social and legal definitions of sex crimes themselves. Yet, of all these areas, perhaps nowhere is that critical reflection more important and necessary than when reviewing the kinds of sexual violence humans perpetrate against other humans. The media coverage of acts of sexual violence offers an experience to educate ourselves about the sex crimes in our communities. The national coverage, however, of extreme kinds of sexualized violence can sometimes leave the impression that these extreme types of sexual violence are more prominent than they really are. This is important to know because, if efforts to protect against someone you do not know are promoted and believed to be accurate, it is possible to be even *more* vulnerable because the most common offenders are people known to you. As any student of crime prevention knows, it is not possible to protect yourself from everything, but, once the problem being confronted is clearly identified, efforts to address it are significantly enhanced. This is the case too with sexual violence prevention.

Cultural attitudes and traditions, religious principles, political processes, social ideology, economics, medical practices, technological advances, and legal guidelines all come together at different times and places throughout history to direct popular assessments of appropriate or inappropriate sexual expressions. In the United States, as if efforts to understand sexual harm and crimes from within a broader historical context are not complicated enough, research is suggesting that many of the preconceived notions surrounding sexual abuse appear to be largely based on misconceptions and misinformation rather than empirical evidence.[182] One of the most important realities for studying sexual violence is to have as clear a picture as possible about the scope of the problem. This means it is essential to do your research but also to understand the limitations of research. Having an understanding of the scope of the problem can help open ears and hearts and minds to the stories of those affected by sexual violence. Outlining the parameters of the problem is made more difficult when researchers, treatment practitioners, advocacy groups, and policy makers cannot agree on social and legal definitions, research protocols, and enforcement strategies. Ironically, in wrestling with these professional and disciplinary differences, further insights often emerge.

Text Box 6.1. Media Messages about Contemporary Sexual Violence

Who benefits and who is harmed when the collective social thinking maintains:

- a fear of strangers over a fear of people known to you?
- a culture where women are taught to seek attention using their bodies?
- a woman who has sex with multiple partners or is out at a bar drinking is likely to be up for sex and therefore is the kind of woman who is seen as "rapeable"?
- men are taught they are to be tough at all costs, aggressive to the point of using violence if necessary to secure compliance?
- the idea that someone loves "the wrong kind of person," or is a "freak of nature," or is likely to offer a less meaningful contribution in the world because of their gender expression or sexual identity?

After thinking about who benefits when cultural stories contrast lived reality, spend some time thinking about who loses and what they lose when these restricted social ideologies are offered as a sort of default way of thinking, that thing everyone just knows but no one really knows how they know it.

Consider how sex offenders benefit from the perpetuation of *false understandings* and common *media misrepresentations* of sexual offenders as people who look like an old man in a raincoat or a stranger hiding in the bushes. How is it that society continues to get the information about sex offending so wrong?

MEDIA-ting the Middle Ground

History
What differences might be discussed in the recording of history based on the race a person is born into? In other words, how might you remember

historical events or which historical events might you remember depending on the race of your family of origin?

How might attitudes be different if people come from a household where sexuality is respected and treated openly, without shame, compared to a family where various kinds of abuse, including verbal, emotional, physical, and sexual abuse were present?

How do the attitudes we see growing up affect our understanding of the world? What are our options if we learn later in life that what we learned about sex and relationships from within our home is not always true in the rest of the world and, in fact, what we learned in our home might have been harmful to us or to other family members?

What lessons do people get about how relationships work in the United States? What does it mean to be in a relationship with someone? What role does sex play in this dynamic?

Are there messages in today's popular culture that are as strange sounding today as some of the assumptions made throughout history, such as people should not be allowed to marry people from different racial categories or women should submit to sex with their husbands whenever their husbands demand sex?

Culture and Comedy

Comedian Dane Cook, who has been criticized about making sexist and racist jokes, had this to say about rape analogies:

> I think the word raped gets thrown around far too casually. You ever listen to a bunch of guys playing video games with each other online? It's like, "Ah man you shot me in the back dude. You raped me dude!" I'm pretty sure if I talked to a woman who's been through that horrific situation and I said, "What was it like, you know, being raped?" she's not gonna look at me and go, "Have you ever played Halo?"[1]

Here is an excerpt from an article about Cameron Esposito's comedy special "Rape Jokes" from 2018:

> In "Rape Jokes," her most recent comedy special, Esposito's ability to balance the hilarious with the poignant is on full display. Amid a light-hearted set that includes a story about a mortifying medical emergency and anecdotes about her upbringing, she shares her experience as a survivor of sexual assault.
>
> The story lands like a skillfully flown helicopter in an open field—unavoidable and with admirable grace.
>
> Her goal, she says, is to reframe assault as a lived experience instead of a topic for quips about perpetrators trying to reclaim their careers.[2]

Comedian Louis C.K. on dating:

> It takes courage to go on a date. Two very different kinds of courage; the male courage traditionally speaking is that he decided to ask. He went up to a random woman who he has no idea if she's going to like him or not, and he walks up to her, terrified. Everything in your whole body is saying go the f* home and jerk off. Don't do this. But he walked up and he says . . . sometimes if it works he says "do you want to go out sometime," and if it works, she says yes, and that's her courage. The courage it takes for a woman to say yes is beyond anything I can imagine. A woman saying yes to a date with a man is literally insane and ill advised. The whole . . . How do women still go

out with guys? Consider the fact that there is no greater threat to women, than men. We are the number one threat to women, globally and historically we are the number one cause of injury, and mayhem to women. We are the worst thing that ever happens to them. That's true. You know what our number one threat is? Heart disease. . . .

In November 2017, Louis C.K. admitted publicly that allegations of sexual misconduct made against him by five women were true.[3]

Amy Schumer on jokes about sexual assault:

"Any dude saying, 'I'm scared to be in a room with a woman now' or 'is it ok to say hello? I don't know the new rules,' STOP," she wrote. "What you are doing is belittling victims who have been wronged. . . . Stop making fun of the terror and indignity most of us have faced in our lives."

She continued, "If you're confused about the new rules. Just ask and don't make it a joke. Because that's harmful and we don't want to hear that kind of joke right now. Mmmmmkay?"[4]

In her stand-up acts, she has been heavily criticized for her storylines describing having sex with someone who will graduate from high school in three years, suggesting under the age of adulthood, if not under the age of consent, and also about initiating sex with someone who is really drunk. At least in part, the criticism has asked what the response would be if a male comedian used those storylines?[5]

Deciding Which Messages Move Forward

Consider the following statements from a collection of male and female writers on the topic of rape from the book *Yes Means Yes!: Visions of Female Sexual Power and a World without Rape*:[6]

"You should consider yourself lucky that some man finds a hideous troll like yourself rape-able" (p. 67).

"Rape is a complement, you stupid whore" (p. 67).

"As soon as I hook up with a girl I start to resent her . . . how can she be a high value female if she was that easy to get into bed?" (p. 33).

"Black strippers are lying whores" (p. 156).

"Why aren't we all socialized to expect and proactively ensure that every sexual interaction is marked by mutual enjoyment and respect?" (p. 199).

"Rapists are created; not born" (p. 198).

"My friends and I learned . . . that sexuality is tied to a boy's ability to play and win the 'get-some' game" (p. 200).

"Real sex education isn't porn education" (p. 311).

MEDIA MESSAGES SECTION III: What Do Experts Know about Sex Offenses, Sex Offenders, and the People They Harm?

Section overview: It is not uncommon to have individual researchers and social service providers focus on sex offenders exclusively in their work.

Nor is it uncommon for individuals who seek to focus on ways to assist people who have been harmed by sexualized violence to study on ways to support victims, exclusively. Section III reminds us of the interactive nature of sexual violence, again, leaning on what is known about the relationship dynamics of people who commit sexualized harms and the people who are harmed. Further, there are countries around the globe that also meet and must manage a vast array of sexualized harms. It seems each country has its own assessment and prioritization of these kinds of harms. While the reality may differ, is it possible to learn from the experiences other countries are addressing? The issues of pornography and prostitution, more commonly referred to as sex trafficking in many countries, and the dynamics of different laws and policies close the section.

Myths and Reclamations

Section III invites us to reflect on what we know about sex offenders, the people they harm, and the global context in which sexual violence in the United States is considered more fully. Conversations about sex offenders and the harm they perpetrate can contain a collection of social ideas reflecting more myths than facts. Strangely, research suggests the presentation of common myths even when refuted by facts is not an effective way to help people remember the facts because information is often used to support what a person already believes.[7] If a person learns something and then applies the information, making an assessment about the material can help reduce the likelihood of remembering the material incorrectly.

Notes

1. https://www.bing.com/videos/search?q=youtube+dane+cook+rape&view=detail&mid=29CCFA13FF3C5FAE103629CCFA13FF3C5FAE1036&FORM=VIRE.

2. Megan Thomas and Sandra Gonzalez, "Cameron Esposito Mixes Hilarious and Poignant with 'Rape Jokes,'" December 14, 2018, accessed September 9, 2019, https://www.cnn.com/2018/12/13/entertainment/cameron-esposito-comedy/index.html.

3. Joanna Walters and Molly Redden, "Louis CK Responds to Allegations of Sexual Misconduct: 'These Stories Are True.'" *The Guardian*, November 11, 2017, accessed September 9, 2019, https://www.theguardian.com/tv-and-radio/2017/nov/10/louis-ck-statement-sexual-misconduct-allegations-these-stories-are-true.

4. Sara M. Moniuszko, "Amy Schumer Slams Anyone Who Jokes about Sexual Assault: 'Stop Making Fun of the Terror,'" September 19, 2018, accessed September 9, 2019, https://www.usatoday.com/story/life/entertainthis/2018/09/19/amy-schumer-sexual-assault-jokes-stop-making-fun-terror/1356522002/.

5. "Mostly Sex Stuff—Class It Up," video, 2:26, posted by Comedy Central Stand-Up, August 14, 2012, accessed September 9, 2019, https://www.youtube.com/watch?v=XIKPA-4u4BU; "Wait a Second, Did Amy Schumer Rape a Guy?" Thought Catalog, May 6, 2014, September 9, 2019, https://thoughtcatalog.com/anonymous/2014/05/wait-a-second-did-amy-schumer-rape-a-guy/.

6. Jaclyn Friedman and Jessica Valenti, eds., *Yes Means Yes!: Visions of Female Sexual Power and a World without Rape* (Berkeley, CA: Seal Press, 2008).

7. Christina Peter and Thomas Koch, "When Debunking Scientific Myths Fails (and When It Does Not): The Backfire Effect in the Context of Journalistic Coverage and Immediate Judgments as Prevention Strategy," *Science Communication* 38, no. 1 (2016): 3–25, https://doi.org/10.1177/1075547015613523.

KEY TERMS

advocacy research
affirmative consent model
funnel effect
interdisciplinary studies
intersectionality
master narrative
mutual consent

nonagentic sexual interactions
objective nature of research
sexology
sexual contact
sexual penetration
social location
Uniform Crime Report (UCR)

REVIEW QUESTIONS

1. Define "nonagentic sexual interaction" and provide an example.

2. Identify three research challenges that confront anyone wishing to study sexual violence and related harms.

3. Consider the following statement: "Researchers cannot get completely accurate information on the number of sexual violence incidents, and, as a result, making policy with such limited information will be ineffectual." What might you suggest in response?

4. Identify two ways that the history of sexual violence and harm might affect the attitudes and social responses reflected in the data presented here.

5. The chapter discusses ways that society talks about sex (and other social subjects) using a "master narrative." How would you describe the primary story about sexual health and sexual harm or violence in your community? Does the research you see reflect that story?

6. In several places throughout the text, attention has been given to the ideas of consent, coercion, and compliance. Define each term and discuss how each one is related to the broader conversation about sexual violence and harm.

7. Discuss the importance of understanding sexual violence as it is related to children and young people and then as it is related to adults. What role does age play in how people talk about sexual violence and prevention?

8. Consider some of the data presented in the chapter on men as victims of sexual violence and harm. Describe three statistics that stood out to you, and consider how the information they provide affects the larger conversation of providing support to men who have been harmed by sexual violence.

9. Consider the information presented in the chapter and compare it to the information you see on social media or in movies and on TV. How are these themes similar and/or different?

10. The authors provide information suggesting that the material contained in this book is only one way to present and discuss sexualized violence and harm, that much more information exists in many different disciplines and interpretations will differ between communities, states, and geographic

regions. With so much variation, list three important themes or ideas to consider as you move beyond the statistics and into thinking about ways to enhance prevention efforts.

DISCUSSION QUESTIONS

1. Information in the chapter included a significant number of statistics about abuse that span a wide range of time. How does this information comport with your current understanding of sexual violence and harm?

2. A significant amount of information about sexualized violence and harm is not attainable because of a lack of reporting to official recording agencies or because the means to report is not available. What does the lack of reporting say about what communities know or do not know about sexual violence and harm and any given community's ability to address related concerns?

3. How is it possible to study sexual violence and work to create prevention objectives if the degree to which harm is happening is not discernable? Thinking about the community you are most familiar with, consider possible ways the subject can be addressed even without complete information about the degree of harm or the number of offenses committed. What areas of the community are working together to address concerns and meet needs?

4. Consider the subject of pornography. The disagreements about how society defines and policies related materials abound. What are some of the benefits and costs associated with banning materials deemed to be pornographic? What are some of the benefits and costs associated with legalizing materials deemed pornographic? Assume you are the mayor of your hometown, and citizens are asking for your leadership on this very issue. How would you approach the issue?

5. What thoughts are you left with as you consider the ways that information, data, and the classifications of sexual deviance and crimes happen?

NOTES

1. Emilie Buchwald, Pamela Fletcher, and Martha Roth, *Transforming a Rape Culture* (Minneapolis: Milkweeds Edition, 1995), 179.

2. Bob Herbert, "Why Aren't We Shocked?," *New York Times*, October 16, 2006, accessed August 24, 2015, http://www.nytimes.com/2006/10/16/opinion/16herbert.html.

3. Sandra Y. L. Korn, "When No Means Yes," *The Harvard Crimson*, November 12, 2010, accessed August 24, 2015, http://www.thecrimson.com/article/2010/11/12/yale-dke-harvard -womens/.

4. Michele C. Black et al., "The National Intimate Partner and Sexual Violence Survey (NISVS): 2010 Summary Report," National Center for Injury Prevention and Control, Centers for Disease Control and Prevention, November 2011, accessed August 24, 2015, http://www .cdc.gov/violenceprevention/pdf/nisvs_report2010-a.pdf.

5. Christina Hoff Sommers, "CDC Study on Sexual Violence in the U.S. Overstates the Problem," *Washington Post*, January 27, 2012, accessed August 24, 2015, https://www .washingtonpost.com/opinions/cdc-study-on-sexual-violence-in-the-us-overstates-the-prob

lem/2012/01/25/gIQAHRKPWQ_story.html; see also Bert H. Hoff, "The National Intimate Partner and Sexual Violence Survey and the Perils of Advocacy Research," *Menweb, Men's Voices Magazine*, April 16, 2012, accessed August 24, 2015, http://papers.ssrn.com/sol3/papers.cfm?abstract_id=2147574; Bert H. Hoff, "U.S. National Survey: More Men than Women Victims of Intimate Partner Violence," *Journal of Aggression, Conflict and Peace Research* 4, no. 3 (2012): 155–63.

6. See, for example, "Defining Sexual Violence in Impossibly Elastic Ways and Letting the Surveyors, Rather than Subjects, Determine What Counted as an Assault," No Pasaran blog, January 29, 2012, https://no-pasaran.blogspot.com/2012/01/defining-sexual-violence-in-impossibly.html.

7. Ibid.

8. Sommers, "CDC Study on Sexual Violence in the U.S. Overstates the Problem."

9. Susan B. Carbon, "An Updated Definition of Rape," Department of Justice, January 6, 2012, accessed August 24, 2015, http://www.justice.gov/opa/blog/updated-definition-rape.

10. Lynn Rosenthal, "Justice Department Announces Major Step Forward to Combat Rape," White House, January 6, 2012, accessed August 24, 2015, https://www.whitehouse.gov/blog/2012/01/06/justice-department-announces-major-step-forward-combat-rape.

11. Sharon G. Smith et al., "National Intimate Partner and Sexual Violence Survey: 2015 Data Brief," Centers for Disease Control and Prevention, accessed October 20, 2019, https://www.cdc.gov/violenceprevention/datasources/nisvs/2015NISVSdatabrief.html.

12. Callie Marie Rennison, "Rape and Sexual Assault: Reporting to Police and Medical Attention, 1992–2000," Department of Justice, August 2002, accessed August 25, 2015, http://www.bjs.gov/content/pub/pdf/rsarp00.pdf.

13. Karen L. Baker, "I Wish It Were True That Sexual Violence Is Being Overstated" (response to C. H. Sommers), National Sexual Violence Resource Center, February 21, 2012, accessed October 20, 2019, https://www.nsvrc.org/sites/default/files/Publications_NSVRC_Editorial_NISVS-Response.pdf.

14. Ibid.

15. Heather MacDonald, "The Campus Rape Myth," *City Journal*, Winter 2008, accessed August 24, 2015, http://www.city-journal.org/2008/18_1_campus_rape.html.

16. Rosemary Iconis, "Rape Myth Acceptance in College Students: A Literature Review," *Contemporary Issues in Education Research* 1, no. 2 (2008): 47–52.

17. Laurel Crown and Linda J. Roberts, "Against Their Will: Young Women's Nonagentic Sexual Experiences," *Journal of Social and Personal Relationships* 24, no. 3 (2007): 385–405.

18. E. Sandra Byers and Shannon A. Glenn, "Gender Differences in Cognitive and Affective Reponses to Sexual Coercion," *Journal of Interpersonal Violence* 27, no. 5 (2011): 827–45; see also Victoria L. Banyard et al., "Unwanted Sexual Contact on Campus: A Comparison of Women's and Men's Experiences," *Violence & Victims* 22, no. 1 (2007): 52–70; Cailey Hartwick, Serge Desmarais, and Karl Hennig, "Characteristics of Male and Female Victims of Sexual Coercion," *Canadian Journal of Human Sexuality* 16, no. 1/2 (2007): 31–44.

19. Daniel D'Addario, "Why Bill Cosby's Admission Should Put an End to the Era of Cosby Defenders," *Time*, July 6, 2015, accessed August 24, 2015, http://time.com/3947272/bill-cosby-drugged-women-quaalude-news/; Women in the World Staff, "35 Cosby Accusers Speak Out about Their Experiences," *New York Times*, July 27, 2015, accessed August 24, 2015, http://nytlive.nytimes.com/womenintheworld/2015/07/27/35-cosby-accusers-speak-out-about-their-experiences/.

20. Tom LoBianco, "Obama Defines Rape When Asked about Bill Cosby," *CNN*, July 16, 2015, accessed August 24, 2015, http://www.cnn.com/2015/07/15/politics/obama-cosby-rape-medal-freedom/.

21. Allison Yarrow, "Richard Mourdock's Comment Furthers Use of Rape to Win Election, Advocates Charge," July 14, 2017, accessed September 7, 2019, https://www.thedailybeast.com/richard-mourdocks-comment-furthers-use-of-rape-to-win-election-advocates-charge.

22. Lindsay Robertson, "Whoopi on Roman Polanski: It Wasn't 'Rape-Rape,'" *Jezebel*, September 28, 2009, accessed August 24, 2015, http://jezebel.com/5369395/whoopi-on-roman-polanski-it-wasnt-rape-rape; Charlotte Alter, "Todd Akin Still Doesn't Get What's Wrong with Saying 'Legitimate Rape,'" *Time*, July 17, 2014, accessed August 24, 2015, http://time.com/3001785/todd-akin-legitimate-rape-msnbc-child-of-rape/.

23. Karen Terry, *Sexual Offenses and Offenders: Theory, Practice, and Policy* (Belmont, CA: Wadsworth Cengage Learning, 2006).

24. Donna Bowater, "Pornography Is Replacing Sex Education," *The Telegraph*, December 16, 2011, accessed August 24, 2015, http://www.telegraph.co.uk/education/educationnews/8961010/Pornography-is-replacing-sex-education.html.

25. "Porn Literacy: A Key Ingredient in Sex Education for Today's Youth," *CNW*, March 5, 2013, accessed August 24, 2015, http://www.newswire.ca/news-releases/porn-literacy-a-key-ingredient-in-sex-education-for-todays-youth-512024401.html.

26. Moyer, *Criminological Theories: Traditional and Nontraditional Themes*.

27. "Break the Cycle," *The Guardian*, 2018, https://www.theguardian.com/us-news/series/break-the-cycle.

28. See, for example, J. Rosewood, *The Big Book of Serial Killers* (Create Space Independent Publishing Platform, 2017).

29. James Alan Fox and Jack Levin, "Multiple Homicide: Patterns of Serial and Mass Murder," *Crime and Justice* 23 (1998): 407–55. See also their book: *Extreme Killing: Understanding Serial and Mass Murder* (Sage, 2014).

30. This information was presented by colleagues from the Department of Corrections and the Department of Human Services, both in Minnesota. Because I could not confirm this information, I did not include a reference to the specific people making this claim.

31. S. Edwards, K. Bradshaw, and V. B. Hinsz, "Denying Rape but Endorsing Forceful Intercourse: Exploring Differences among Responders," *Violence and Gender* 1, no. 4 (2014), doi:10.1089/vio.2014.0022.

32. See, for example, K. Daly and B. Bouhours, "Rape and Attrition in the Legal Process: A Comparative Analysis of Five Countries," *Crime and Justice* 39, no. 1 (2010): 565–650, https://www.journals.uchicago.edu/doi/abs/10.1086/653101?journalCode=cj.

33. Lawrence A. Greenfeld, "Sex Offenses and Offenders: An Analysis of Data on Rape and Sexual Assault," Department of Justice, February 1997, accessed August 24, 2015, http://www.mincava.umn.edu/documents/sexoff/sexoff.pdf.

34. R. Goldman and S. Dooley, "Steubenville Rape Trial: Witness Testifies to Recording Alleged Assault," *ABC News*, March 15, 2013, accessed October 20, 2019, https://abcnews.go.com/US/steubenville-rape-trial-witness-testifies-recording-alleged-assault/story?id=18738378.

35. C. J. Carter and P. Harlow, "Alleged Victim in Steubenville Rape Case Says She Woke Up Naked," CNN, March 18, 2013, accessed October 20, 2019, https://www.cnn.com/2013/03/16/justice/ohio-steubenville-case/index.html. See, specifically, the coverage by Mark Law, "Teen Rape Case Moves Forward," *Herald Star*, October 13, 2012, accessed August 24, 2015, http://www.heraldstaronline.com/page/content.detail/id/578936/Teen-rape-case-moves-forward.html?nav=5010.

36. Law, "Teen Rape Case Moves Forward."

37. See, for example, M. Masland, "Carnal Knowledge: The Sex Ed Debate," *NBC News*, 2013, accessed October 20, 2019, http://www.nbcnews.com/id/3071001/ns/health-childrens_health/t/carnal-knowledge-sex-ed-debate/.

38. Information presented about famous sex researcher Alfred Kinsey has documented his frustration with morality being used as science as one of his primary motivators for working to study sex in a scientific way; however, that intention has been challenged by others who have suggested his own morality clouded his research. See, for example, D. Allyn, "Private Act/Public Policy: Alfred Kinsey, the American Law Institute and the Privatization

of American Sexual Morality," *Journal of Health Studies* 30, no. 3 (1996): 405–28, https://doi.org/10.1017/S0021875800024889; J. H. Jones, *Alfred C. Kinsey: A Life* (W.W. Norton and Company, 2004).

39. See, for example, Barak Goodman and John Maggio, dir., *American Experience: Kinsey* (Saint Paul, MN: PBS, 2005), television; "History of the Institute," The Kinsey Institute, accessed August 24, 2015, http://www.kinseyinstitute.org/about/history.html; "Alfred Kinsey," Biography.com, 2015, accessed August 24, 2015, http://www.biography.com/people/alfred-kinsey-9365493.

40. See, for example, J. Money, "History, Causality, and Sexology," *The Journal of Sex Research* 40, no. 3, (2003): 237–39, https://doi.org/10.1080/00224490309552187.

41. See, for example, H. Still, *Alien Sex: 19 Tales by the Masters of Science Fiction and Dark Fantasy* (Audio Studios on Brilliance Audio, 2015).

42. See, for example, Paul Deane and Paul Chambers, *Sex & the Paranormal: Human Sexual Encounters with the Supernatural* (London: Vega Books, 2003).

43. See, for example, D. Puccio and A. Havey, *Sex, Likes and Social Media: Talking to Our Teens in the Digital Age* (Ebury Digital, 2016); C. Smith, *The Routledge Companion to Media, Sex and Sexuality* (Routledge, 2017).

44. See, for example, D. Ray, *Sex and God: How Religion Distorts Sexuality* (Dogma Debate, 2013); C. Manning and P. Zuckerman, *Sex and Religion* (Cengage Learning, 2004); D. Hammack, *Rethinking Sex Ed: The Wisdom of Religion . . . without the Crazy* (Independent Publisher, 2018).

45. John D'Emilio, William B. Turner, and Urvashi Vaid, *Creating Change: Sexuality, Public Policy, and Civil Rights* (New York: St. Martin's Press, 2002); Kristin Luker, *When Sex Goes to School: Warring Views on Sex—and Sex Education—Since the Sixties* (New York: W.W. Norton & Company, 2007).

46. W. H. Masters and V. Johnson, *Human Sexual Response* (Ishi Press, 2010).

47. Reay Tannahill, *Sex in History* (London: Scarborough House Publishers, 1992); Michel Foucault, *The History of Sexuality*, vol. 1, *An Introduction* (New York: Pantheon Books, 1978); Vern L. Bullough and Bonnie Bullough, *Sin, Sickness, and Sanity: A History of Sexual Attitudes* (New York: Garland Publishing, 1977).

48. For economic issues, see M. Adshade, *Dollars and Sex: How Economics Influences Sex and Love* (Chronicle Books, 2013). Regarding media, see, for example, Mary-Lou Galician and Debra L. Merskin, *Critical Thinking about Sex, Love, and Romance in the Mass Media: Media Literacy Applications* (New York: Routledge, 2006).

49. See, for example, V. Banyard, E. Plante, and M. Moynihan, *Rape Prevention through Bystander Education: Bringing a Broader Community Perspective to Sexual Violence Prevention*, US Department of Justice, February 2005, https://www.mcrdpi.marines.mil/Portals/76/Docs/SAPR/SAPR_Bystander%20Research.pdf; V. M. Banyard, M. Moynihan, and E. Plante, "Sexual Violence Prevention through Bystander Education: An Experimental Evaluation," *Journal of Community Psychology* 35, no. 4 (2007): 463–81, https://doi.org/10.1002/jcop.20159; M. Flood, "Changing Men: Best Practice in Sexual Violence Education," *Women Against Violence* 18 (2005–2006): 26–36, https://eprints.qut.edu.au/103395/1/__qut.edu.au_Documents_StaffHome_StaffGroupR%24_rogersjm_Desktop_Flood%2C%20Changing%20men.pdf.

50. See, for example, J. Chirban, "Pornography: The New Sex Ed for Kids," *Psychology Today*, December 15, 2012, https://www.psychologytoday.com/us/blog/age-un-innocence/201212/pornographythe-new-sex-ed-kids; M. Jones, "What Teenagers Are Learning from Online Porn," *New York Times Magazine*, February 17, 2018, https://www.nytimes.com/2018/02/07/magazine/teenagers-learning-online-porn-literacy-sex-education.html.

51. Jennings Bryant and Dan Brown, "Uses of Pornography," in *Pornography: Research Advances and Policy Considerations*, ed. Dolf Zillmann and Jennings Bryant (New York: Psychology Press, 1989), 25–56.

52. Nina Bernstein, "Foes of Sex Trade Stung by the Fall of an Ally," *New York Times*, March 12, 2008, accessed August 24, 2015, http://www.nytimes.com/2008/03/12/nyregion/ 12prostitute.html; see also Alex Gibney, dir., *Client 9: The Rise and Fall of Eliot Spitzer* (New York: A&E IndieFilms, 2010), film; Peter Elkind, *Rough Justice: The Rise and Fall of Eliot Spitzer* (London: Portfolio, 2010).

53. N. Bernstein, "Foes of Sex Trade Are Stung by the Fall of an Ally," *New York Times*, March 12, 2008, https://www.nytimes.com/2008/03/12/nyregion/12prostitute.html.

54. "Spitzer, Parker to Host Primetime CNN Show," *CNN*, June 23, 2010, accessed August 24, 2015, http://politicalticker.blogs.cnn.com/2010/06/23/spitzer-parker-to-host-primetime -cnn-show/.

55. Jeff Poor, "Kurtz Rips Own Network for Omitting 2008 Eliot Spitzer Sex Scandal in Report," *Daily Caller*, May 22, 2011, accessed August 24, 2015, http://dailycaller .com/2011/05/22/kurtz-rips-own-network-for-omitting-2008-eliot-spitzer-sex-scandal-in -report/.

56. J. D'Emilio and William B. Turner, *Creating Change: Sexuality, Public Policy, and Civil Rights* (St. Martins, 2000); William B. Turner, *A Genealogy of Queer Theory* (Temple University Press, 2000).

57. Susan Milligan, "In Budapest, Sex Is No Scandal," *Washington Post*, February 1, 1998, accessed August 24, 2015, http://www.washingtonpost.com/wp-srv/politics/special/clinton/ stories/hungary020198.htm.

58. Cord Jefferson, "Vigils Continue for Mark Carson, Murdered in Anti-Gay NYC Shooting," *Gawker*, May 20, 2013, accessed August 24, 2015, http://gawker.com/vigils-continue -for-mark-carson-murdered-in-anti-gay-n-508908318; see also Taylor Berman, "Another Anti-Gay Attack Reported in New York City," *Gawker*, May 22, 2013, accessed August 24, 2015, http://gawker.com/another-anti-gay-attack-reported-in-new-york-city-509226262.

59. Maryse Mitchell-Brody and Andrea J. Ritchie, "Hate Violence against the Lesbian, Gay, Bisexual, Transgender and Queer Communities in the United States in 2009," *National Coalition of Anti-Violence Programs*, 2010, accessed August 24, 2015, http://www.calcasa.org/ wp-content/uploads/2010/07/NCAVP2009HateViolenceReportforWeb.pdf.

60. Sarena Straus, *Bronx D.A.: True Stories from the Sex Crimes and Domestic Violence Unit* (Fort Lee, NJ: Barricade Press, 2006).

61. M. Anft, "Breaking Professional Schools Out of Their Silos," *Chronicle of Higher Education*, April 30, 2017, https://www.chronicle.com/article/Breaking-Professional-Schools/239937; R. Craig, "College Silos Must Die for Students to Thrive," *Forbes*, April 14, 2017, https://www.forbes.com/sites/ryancraig/2017/04/14/college-silos-must-die-for-students-to-thrive/#539ff567222d.

62. Jean-François Lyotard, *The Postmodern Condition: A Report on Knowledge* (Minneapolis: University of Minnesota Press, 1984); Michael G. W. Bamberg and Molly Andrews, *Considering Counter Narratives: Narrating, Resisting, Making Sense* (Philadelphia: John Benjamins Publishing, 2004).

63. Lisa Duggan, *Sapphic Slashers: Sex, Violence, and American Modernity* (Durham, NC: Duke University Press, 2000).

64. Joseph Diaz, Jenner Smith, and Alexa Valiente, "Fla. Teen Jailed for Same-Sex Relationship with Underage Girlfriend Ready to 'Move On,'" *ABC News*, February 14, 2014, accessed August 24, 2015, http://abcnews.go.com/US/fla-teen-jailed-sex-relationship-underage-girl friend-ready/story?id=22504595.

65. Ashley Fantz, "Florida Teen Rejects Plea Deal in Controversial Same-Sex Case," *CNN*, May 26, 2013, accessed August 24, 2015, http://www.cnn.com/2013/05/24/justice/florida -teen-sex-case/.

66. Hunter Stuart, "Gay Florida Teen Kaitlyn Hunt Enters Plea Deal, Will Spend 4 Months in Jail," *Huffington Post*, October 3, 2013, accessed August 24, 2015, http://www.huffington post.com/2013/10/03/kaitlyn-hunt-plea-deal-jail-four-months_n_4036862.html.

67. Stephanie Slifer, "Kaitlyn Hunt Update: Fla. Teen Charged over Same-Sex Underage Relationship Rejects Plea Deal," *CBS News*, May 24, 2013, accessed August 24, 2015, http://www.cbsnews.com/news/kaitlyn-hunt-update-fla-teen-charged-over-same-sex-underage-relationship-rejects-plea-deal/.

68. Ida B. Wells-Barnett, "Southern Horrors: Lynch Law in All Its Phases," in *Major Problems in the History of American Sexuality: Documents and Essays*, ed. Kathy Peiss (Boston: Wadsworth Cengage Learning, 2002), 155, accessed July 16, 2015, http://www.gutenberg.org/files/14975/14975-h/14975-h.htm; see also Michael Fedo, *Lynchings in Duluth* (Saint Paul: Borealis Book, 2000).

69. Randy Shilts, *And the Band Played On: Politics, People, and the AIDS Epidemic* (New York: St. Martin's Press, 1987).

70. Please note that, in some cases, the information taken from advocacy websites and government websites includes data that have not been updated in over 10 years.

71. Mic Hunter, *Abused Boys: The Neglected Victims of Sexual Abuse* (New York: Ballantine Books, 1991).

72. "What Is Child Sexual Abuse? Info and Stats for Journalists," National Sexual Violence Resource Center, 2015, accessed August 24, 2015, http://nsvrc.org/sites/default/files/publications_nsvrc_media-packet_1.pdf.

73. David Finkelhor, Heather Hammer, and Andrea J. Sedlak, "Sexually Assaulted Children: National Estimates and Characteristics," Department of Justice, August 2008, 2, accessed August 21, 2015, https://www.ncjrs.gov/pdffiles1/ojjdp/214383.pdf.

74. Sherry Hamby et al., "Children's Exposure to Intimate Partner Violence and Other Family Violence," *Juvenile Justice Bulletin*, October 2011, accessed August 25, 2015, https://www.ncjrs.gov/pdffiles1/ojjdp/232272.pdf.

75. Ibid.

76. Howard Snyder, "Sexual Assault of Young Children as Reported to Law Enforcement: Victim, Incident, and Offender Characteristics," Department of Justice, July 2000, accessed August 25, 2015, http://www.bjs.gov/content/pub/pdf/saycrle.pdf.

77. John Ashcroft, Deborah J. Daniels, and Sarah V. Hart, "Youth Victimization: Prevalence and Implications," Department of Justice, April 2003, accessed August 25, 2015, https://www.ncjrs.gov/pdffiles1/nij/194972.pdf.

78. "Domestic Violence Statistics," DomesticViolenceStatistics.org, accessed August 25, 2015, http://domesticviolencestatistics.org/domestic-violence-statistics/.

79. Ibid.

80. Robin Sax, *It Happens Every Day: Inside the World of a Sex Crimes D.A.* (Amherst, NY: Prometheus Books, 2010), 77.

81. Black et al., "The National Intimate Partner and Sexual Violence Survey (NISVS): 2010 Summary Report."

82. Ibid.

83. Ibid.

84. "National Plan to Prevent the Sexual Abuse and Exploitation of Children," National Coalition to Prevent Child Sexual Abuse and Exploitation, 2012, accessed August 25, 2015, http://www.preventtogether.org/Resources/Documents/NationalPlan2012FINAL.pdf.

85. Rochelle F. Hanson et al., "Factors Related to the Reporting of Childhood Rape," *Child Abuse & Neglect* 23, no. 6 (1999): 559–69.

86. David Lisak et al., "False Allegations of Sexual Assault: An Analysis of Ten Years of Reported Cases," *Violence Against Women* 16, no. 12 (2010): 1318–34.

87. Ibid.

88. Frank W. Putnam, "Ten-Year Research Update Review: Child Sexual Abuse," *Journal of the American Academy of Child and Adolescent Psychiatry* 42, no. 3 (2003): 269–78.

89. Emily M. Douglas and David Finkelhor, "Childhood Sexual Abuse Fact Sheet," University of New Hampshire Crimes Against Children Research Center, May 2005, accessed June 27, 2015, http://www.unh.edu/ccrc/factsheet/pdf/CSA-FS20.pdf.

90. Ibid.

91. "Child Abuse and Neglect Cost the United States $124 Billion Annually," Centers for Disease Control and Prevention, February 1, 2012, accessed August 25, 2015, http://www.cdc.gov/media/releases/2012/p0201_child_abuse.html.

92. Dominique Mosbergen, "How Rape Is Defined around the World: Todd Akin's Comment, Julian Assange's Case Raise Questions over Definition," *World Post*, August 24, 2012, accessed August 25, 2015, http://www.huffingtonpost.com/2012/08/24/how-is-rape-defined-around-the-world_n_1823272.html.

93. Toni Morrison, *Birth of a Nation'hood: Gaze, Script, and Spectacle in the O.J. Simpson Case* (New York: Random House, 1997).

94. Ethan Bronner, "A Candidate's Stumble on a Distressing Crime," *New York Times*, August 23, 2012, accessed August 25, 2015, http://www.nytimes.com/2012/08/24/us/definition-of-rape-is-shifting-rapidly.html.

95. Heidi S. Resnick et al., "Rape and Other Sexual Assaults," in *Resilience and Mental Health: Challenges across the Lifespan*, ed. Steven M. Southwick et al. (Cambridge, MA: Cambridge University Press, 2011), 218–19.

96. Criminal Sexual Conduct in the First Degree, 609.342 Minnesota Statutes (2014), accessed August 25, 2015, https://www.revisor.mn.gov/statutes/?id=609.342.

97. Definitions, 609.341 Minnesota Statutes (2014), accessed August 25, 2015, https://www.revisor.mn.gov/statutes/?id=609.341.

98. See, for example, Patricia Hill Collins, *Black Feminist Thought: Knowledge, Consciousness, and the Politics of Empowerment* (New York: Routledge, 1991), 42; Patricia Hill Collins, "The Tie That Binds: Race, Gender and US Violence," *Ethnic and Racial Studies* 21, no. 5 (1998): 917–38.

99. Leslie McCall, "The Complexity of Intersectionality," *Signs: Journal of Women in Culture and Society* 30, no. 3 (2005): 1771–800.

100. Jennifer R. Wies and Kathleen Coy, "Measuring Violence: Vicarious Trauma among Sexual Assault Nurse Examiners," *Human Organization* 72, no. 1 (2013): 23–30.

101. Roni Caryn Rabin, "Nearly 1 in 5 Women in U.S. Survey Say They Have Been Sexually Assaulted," *New York Times*, December 14, 2011, accessed August 25, 2015, http://www.nytimes.com/2011/12/15/health/nearly-1-in-5-women-in-us-survey-report-sexual-assault.html.

102. Erika Harrell, "Violent Victimization Committed by Strangers, 1993–2010," Department of Justice, December 2012, 2, Table 1, accessed August 25, 2015, http://www.bjs.gov/content/pub/pdf/vvcs9310.pdf.

103. Rabin, "Nearly 1 in 5 Women."

104. Michael R. Rand, "National Crime Victimization Survey: Criminal Victimization, 2008," Department of Justice, September 2009, accessed August 25, 2015, http://www.bjs.gov/content/pub/pdf/cv08.pdf.

105. Ibid.

106. Dean G. Kilpatrick et al., "Drug-Facilitated, Incapacitated, and Forcible Rape: A National Study," Medical University of South Carolina: National Crime Victims Research & Treatment Center, February 1, 2007, 2, accessed August 25, 2015, https://www.ncjrs.gov/pdffiles1/nij/grants/219181.pdf.

107. "Marital Rape," Indiana Coalition Against Sexual Assault, RAINN, 2000, accessed August 25, 2015, https://rainn.org/pdf-files-and-other-documents/Public-Policy/Issues/Marital_Rape.pdf.

108. Jerrold S. Greenberg, Clint E. Bruess, and Sarah C. Conklin, *Exploring the Dimensions of Human Sexuality*, 4th ed. (Sudbury, MA: Jones and Bartlett Learning, 2011).

109. Ibid.

110. Robert S. Thompson et al., "Intimate Partner Violence: Prevalence, Types, and Chronicity in Adult Women," *American Journal of Preventative Medicine* 30, no. 6 (2006): 447–57.

111. Shannan Catalano, "Intimate Partner Violence, 1993–2010," Department of Justice, November 2012, accessed August 25, 2015, http://www.bjs.gov/content/pub/pdf/ipv9310.pdf.

112. Ibid.

113. Matthew R. Durose et al., "Family Violence Statistics: Including Statistics on Strangers and Acquaintances," Department of Justice, June 2005, accessed August 25, 2015, http://bjs.gov/content/pub/pdf/fvs02.pdf.

114. Ibid.

115. Ibid.

116. "The Facts on Children and Domestic Violence," Futures without Violence, August 2008, accessed August 25, 2015, http://www.futureswithoutviolence.org/userfiles/file/Children_and_Families/Children.pdf.

117. Black et al., "The National Intimate Partner and Sexual Violence Survey (NISVS): 2010 Summary Report."

118. Callie Marie Rennison, "Intimate Partner Violence, 1993–2001," Department of Justice, February 2003, 1, accessed August 25, 2015, http://www.bjs.gov/content/pub/pdf/ipv01.pdf.

119. Ibid., 2.

120. "Sex and Tech: Results from a Survey of Teens and Young Adults," Power to Decide (formerly the National Campaign to Prevent Teen and Unplanned Pregnancy), 2008, accessed October 20, 2019, https://powertodecide.org/what-we-do/information/resource-library/sex-and-tech-results-survey-teens-and-young-adults.

121. "Teen Online and Wireless Safety Survey: Cyberbullying, Sexting, and Parental Controls," Cox Communications, May 2009, accessed August 25, 2015, http://www.cox.com/wcm/en/aboutus/datasheet/takecharge/2009-teen-survey.pdf.

122. Ian Quillen, "Youth Sexting Not All That Common, Reports Find," *Education Week*, December 6, 2011, accessed August 25, 2015, http://blogs.edweek.org/edweek/DigitalEducation/2011/12/teen_sexting_not_all_that_comm.html.

123. "Domestic Violence Statistics."

124. Rand, "National Crime Victimization Survey: Criminal Victimization, 2008."

125. Durose et al., "Family Violence Statistics."

126. Kathryn L. Falb et al., "School Bullying Perpetration and Other Childhood Risk Factors as Predictors of Adult Intimate Partner Violence Perpetration," *Archives of Pediatrics and Adolescent Medicine* 165, no. 10 (2011): 890–94.

127. Kilpatrick et al., "Drug-Facilitated, Incapacitated, and Forcible Rape," 2.

128. Ibid.

129. Ibid.

130. C. Bohmer and A. Parrot, *Sexual Assault on Campus: The Problem and the Solution* (Lanham, MD: Lexington Books, 1993).

131. Katrina Baum et al., "National Crime Victimization Survey: Stalking Victimization in the United States," Department of Justice, January 2009, accessed August 25, 2015, https://www.victimsofcrime.org/docs/src/baum-k-catalano-s-rand-m-rose-k-2009.pdf?sfvrsn=0.

132. Shannan Catalano, "Stalking Victims in the United States—Revised," Department of Justice, September 2012, accessed August 25, 2015, http://www.bjs.gov/content/pub/pdf/svus_rev.pdf.

133. Ibid.

134. Ibid.

135. Ibid.

136. Ibid.

137. Ibid.

138. Ibid.

139. Snyder, "Sexual Assault of Young Children as Reported to Law Enforcement."

140. *Maze of Injustice: The Failure to Protect Indigenous Women from Sexual Violence in the USA*, Amnesty International, 2007, 2, accessed October 20, 2019, https://www.amnestyusa.org/wp-content/uploads/2017/05/mazeofinjustice.pdf.

141. Ibid., 4.

142. Ibid., 2.

143. Ibid., 4.

144. See, for example, Steven W. Perry, "American Indians and Crime: A BJS Statistical Profile, 1992–2002," Department of Justice, December 2004, accessed August 25, 2015, http://www.justice.gov/sites/default/files/otj/docs/american_indians_and_crime.pdf.

145. Jim Lobe, "One in Three Native American Women Suffers Sexual Assault," *FinalCall .com News*, May 14, 2007, accessed August 25, 2015, http://www.finalcall.com/artman/pub lish/printer_3482.shtml.

146. J. Collins, "The Status of Native American Women: A Study of the Lakota Sioux," https://www.drake.edu/media/departmentsoffices/dussj/2006-2003documents/StatusCollins .pdf.

147. Judith M. McFarlane et al., "Prevalence of Partner Violence against 7,443 African American, White, and Hispanic Women Receiving Care at Urban Public Primary Care Clinics," *Public Health Nursing* 22, no. 2 (2005): 98–107.

148. Maria J. Zarza and Rachel H. Adler, "Latina Immigrant Victims of Interpersonal Violence in New Jersey: A Needs Assessment Study," *Journal of Aggression, Maltreatment & Trauma* 16, no. 1 (2008): 22–39.

149. Ibid.

150. Sherry Lipsky et al., "The Role of Intimate Partner Violence, Race, and Ethnicity in Help-Seeking Behaviors," *Ethnicity and Health* 11, no. 1 (2006): 81–100.

151. Timothy C. Hart and Callie Rennison, "Reporting Crime to the Police, 1992–2000," Department of Justice, March 2003, accessed August 25, 2015, http://www.bjs.gov/content/pub/pdf/rcp00.pdf.

152. "Facts & Stats Collection: Sexual Violence in Communities of Color," Women of Color Network, June 2006, accessed August 25, 2015, http://www.doj.state.or.us/victims/pdf/women_of_color_network_facts_sexual_violence_2006.pdf; see also Black Women's Health Imperative, accessed August 25, 2015, http://www.bwhi.org.

153. Patricia Tjaden and Nancy Thoennes, "Extent, Nature, and Consequences of Intimate Partner Violence: Findings from the National Violence Against Women Survey," Department of Justice, July 2000, accessed August 25, 2015, https://www.ncjrs.gov/pdffiles1/nij/181867.pdf.

154. "Health Disparities Experienced by Racial/Ethnic Minority Populations," *MMWR* 53, no. 33 (2004): 755, accessed October 20, 2019, https://www.cdc.gov/mmwr/preview/mmwrhtml/mm5333a1.htm.

155. Brooke Axtell, "Black Women, Sexual Assault and the Art of Resistance," *Forbes*, April 25, 2012, accessed August 25, 2015, http://www.forbes.com/sites/shenegotiates/2012/04/25/black-women-sexual-assault-and-the-art-of-resistance/.

156. Michael Lavers, "70 Percent of Anti-LGBT Murder Victims Are People of Color," *Colorlines*, July 18, 2011, accessed August 25, 2015, http://www.colorlines.com/articles/70-per cent-anti-lgbt-murder-victims-are-people-color; see also "Hate Violence against Lesbian, Gay, Bisexual, Transgender, Queer, and HIV-Affected Communities in the United States in 2010," National Coalition of Anti-Violence Programs, 2011, accessed October 20, 2019, https://avp .org/wp-content/uploads/2017/04/2011_NCAVP_HV_Reports.pdf.

157. Ibid.

158. "Lesbian, Gay, Bisexual, Transgender, and Queer Domestic Violence in the United States in 2008," National Coalition of Anti-Violence Programs, 2009, 2, accessed August 25, 2015, http://www.cuav.org/wp-content/uploads/2012/08/5670_2008NCAVPDVReport.pdf.

159. Ibid., 20.

160. Ibid., 23.

161. Baum et al., "National Crime Victimization Survey: Stalking Victimization in the United States," 4.

162. Ibid., 5.

163. Dick Sobsey and Connie Varnhagen, "Sexual Abuse and Exploitation of People with Disabilities: Toward Prevention and Treatment," in *Special Education Across Canada: Issues and Concerns for the 90's*, ed. Marg Csapo and Leonard Gougen (Vancouver, BC: Vancouver Center for Human Development and Research, 1989), 199–218.

164. Sax, *It Happens Every Day*, 80.

165. Ibid.

166. Ibid.

167. J. Steinhauer, "Sexual Assaults in the Military Raise Alarm in Washington," *New York Times*, May 7, 2013, accessed October 20, 2019, https://www.nytimes.com/2013/05/08/us/politics/pentagon-study-sees-sharp-rise-in-sexual-assaults.html.

168. Stephanie K. McWhorter et al., "Reports of Rape Reperpetration by Newly Enlisted Male Navy Personnel," *Violence and Victims* 24, no. 2 (2009): 204–18.

169. Nancy Zang and R. Cole Bouck, "Overview of the 2003 Prison Rape Elimination Act (PREA): What It Means for the Michigan Department of Corrections (MDOC)," National Institute of Corrections, December 20, 2004, accessed August 25, 2015, http://bridgemi.com/wp-content/uploads/2015/04/PREA_SlideShow_MDOC_2004-12-20_112237_7.pdf; see also "Facing Prison Rape: How the Prison Rape Elimination Act Affects You," National Institute of Corrections, July 21, 2004, NIC Satellite Broadcast.

170. Valerie Jenness et al., "Violence in California Correctional Facilities: An Empirical Examination of Sexual Assault," Center for Evidence-Based Corrections, May 16, 2007, 3, accessed August 25, 2015, http://ucicorrections.seweb.uci.edu/files/2013/06/PREA_Presentation_PREA_Report_UCI_Jenness_et_al.pdf.

171. Jaclyn Friedman and Jessica Valenti, *Yes Means Yes!: Visions of Female Sexual Power and a World without Rape* (Berkeley, CA: Seal Press, 2008).

172. Bonnie S. Fisher, Francis T. Cullen, and Michael G. Turner, "The Sexual Victimization of College Women," Department of Justice, December 2000, accessed August 25, 2015, https://www.ncjrs.gov/pdffiles1/nij/182369.pdf; "Rape in America: A Report to the Nation," National Victim Center and Crime Victims Research and Treatment Center, April 23, 1992, accessed August 25, 2015, https://www.victimsofcrime.org/docs/Reports%20and%20Studies/rape-in-america.pdf?sfvrsn=0; Craig Perkins and Patsy Klaus, "National Crime Victimization Survey: Criminal Victimization 1994," Department of Justice, April 1996, accessed August 25, 2015, http://bjs.gov/content/pub/pdf/Cv94.pdf; Diana E. Russell, "The Prevalence and Incidence of Forcible Rape and Attempted Rape of Females," *Victimology* 7, no. 1-4 (1982): 81–93; David Lisak and Paul M. Miller, "Repeat Rape and Multiple Offending among Undetected Rapists," *Violence and Victims* 17, no. 1 (2002): 73–84.

173. Sandra Park, "Shut Up or Get Out: PA City Punishes Domestic Violence Victims Who Call the Police," ACLU, April 24, 2013, accessed August 25, 2015, https://www.aclu.org/blog/shut-or-get-out-pa-city-punishes-domestic-violence-victims-who-call-police; "How Domestic Violence Survivors Get Evicted from Their Homes after Calling the Police," *Rewire.News*, June 4, 2013, accessed October 20, 2019, https://rewire.news/article/2013/06/04/norristown-ordinance-and-impact-on-domestic-violence-victims-2/; Erik Eckholm, "A Sight All Too Familiar in Poor Neighborhoods," *New York Times*, February 18, 2010, accessed August 25, 2015, http://www.nytimes.com/2010/02/19/us/19evict.html?pagewanted=2&_r=0; Katie Miller and Sandra Park, "Calling the Police Can Get You Evicted," Shadowproof, March 17, 2011, accessed August 25, 2015, http://shadowproof.com/2011/03/17/calling-the-police-can-get-you-evicted/.

174. Alice Vachss, *Sex Crimes: Ten Years on the Front Lines Prosecuting Rapists and Confronting Their Collaborators* (New York: Holt Paperbacks, 1994), xi.

175. Andrea Smith, *Conquest: Sexual Violence and American Indian Genocide* (Durham, NC: Duke University Press, 2015).

176. See, for example, Stephanie Coontz, *The Way We Never Were: American Families and the Nostalgia Trap* (New York: Basic Books, 1992); Kathy Peiss, *Major Problems in the His-*

tory of American Sexuality: Documents and Essays (Boston: Wadsworth Cengage Learning, 2002); Smith, *Conquest.*

177. Angela Davis, *Women, Race, and Class* (New York: Vintage Books, 1983).

178. There are many excellent resources on Kinsey, including PBS biographies, books, and movies (see note 39). Perhaps the best resource for Kinsey remains the link to the Kinsey Institute for Research in Sex, Gender, and Reproduction at the University of Indiana, Bloomington: http://www.kinseyinstitute.org.

179. Reference is given here to the challenge Derek Freeman (*Margaret Mead and Samoa: The Making and Unmaking of an Anthropological Myth*, Harvard University Press, 1983) made to Margaret Mead's best-selling work *Coming of Age in Samoa* (1928), which suggests that Mead was "duped" by those she interviewed into presenting an incorrect understanding of their social lives. Dr. Martin Orans in *Not Even Wrong* (1996), titling the book after a phrase that refers to a critique of inquiry that cannot be proved or disproved, critiqued her application of the scientific process.

180. Physicist Wolfgang Pauli referred to science that was disconnected from testable hypotheses as "not even wrong."

181. This is an obvious assessment of social reality given the attitudinal changes in abortion, interracial marriage, cohabitation, and sex before marriage, as examples.

182. Timothy Fortney et al., "Myths and Facts about Sexual Offenders: Implications for Treatment and Public Policy," *Sexual Offender Treatment* 2, no. 1 (2007), accessed August 25, 2015, http://www.sexual-offender-treatment.org/55.html; see also "Myths and Facts about Sex Offenders," Department of Justice, August 2000, accessed August 25, 2015, http://www.csom.org/pubs/mythsfacts.html; Jill S. Levenson et al., "Public Perceptions about Sex Offenders and Community Protection Policies," *Analyses of Social Issues and Public Policy* 7, no. 1 (2007): 137–61; Jill S. Levenson and David D'Amora, "Social Policies Designed to Prevent Sexual Violence: The Emperor's New Clothes?," *Criminal Justice Policy Review* 18, no. 2 (2007): 168–99.

7

Focusing on People Who Commit Sexual Harms

A Sampling of Typologies, Theories, and Behaviors

Sexual aggression, in its many facets, represents institutionalized, normative behavior [and is] deeply ingrained and indelibly embedded in the social fabric.

—Prentky and Burgess, *Forensic Management of Sexual Offenders*[1]

According to the National Center for Missing and Exploited Children, there are 917,771 registered sex offenders in the United States and its surrounding territories. Breaking it down further, that's 279 registered sex offenders for every 100,000 people.

—Irma Wallace, "U.S. Cities Ranked by the Frequency of Registered Sex Offenders"[2]

As a survivor of sexual abuse, I am intimately acquainted with its horrors, yet I cannot believe convicted molesters are beyond redemption. . . . If society holds no hope for a molester's redemption, how can he learn to trust himself?

—Pamela Schultz, *Not Monsters: Analyzing the Stories of Child Molesters*[3]

EFFORTS THROUGHOUT THIS CHAPTER are primarily focused on reviewing the ways researchers and practitioners classify, describe, and explain characteristics of individuals who have committed sex-offending behaviors. This can include characteristics of the offenders themselves or focus on offender behavior. More traditional ways of studying sexualized violence include perhaps the most obvious: a focus on the individual who committed the offense. Starting in the mid-1950s, the study of crime in the main expanded its theoretical focus in some sectors to include the identification and exploration of various social and environmental characteristics and conditions. As crime theories continue to evolve as a discipline, this becomes evident in studies focusing on socially and culturally significant factors influencing the definition of sex crimes as well as their enforcement (discussed more in chapter 9). This also includes more recent studies on the role of social power. Here, attention is given to how researchers and practitioners evaluate the vast amounts of research and reports on criminal sexual behaviors, integrating the actual incidents and the people who commit crimes, including a sexual component. In addition to some basic terms, categories (referred to in the field as **typologies**) and theories attempting to explain current understandings of offense types are outlined and followed with a brief discussion of behavioral characteristics, as best they can be compiled in the aggregate. In closing, focused attention is given to several social systems where abuse has been prominent and persistent and that serve as ways to illustrate how researchers and practitioners are looking at society and social conditions using some of the newer structural theories in an effort to dialogue more completely about sexual harm and ultimately its prevention.

WHAT DOES RESEARCH ON SEX OFFENDERS REVEAL?

Throughout the text, attention has been given to both the individual and the social conditions in an effort to paint a bigger picture of what comes into view when focusing on sex offenses and offenders and the people they harm. A brief discussion about the broader research process will help bring this into sharper focus.

Researchers and practitioners develop and use theories in an attempt to explain sex offender behavior, to better understand why people offend in an effort to address the behavior, and to develop and then implement individual treatment plans for the offender and create laws and policies in an effort to protect communities. Society, more broadly, also uses similar kinds of information from research to develop support for victims and to inform prevention efforts. (These treatment designs and laws and policies are presented in greater detail in sections IV and V.) The overview presented here is focused on introducing information about how practitioners and researchers attempt to organize relevant information to better understand the **etiology**, or the root cause or set of causes, of sex-offending behavior.

Early efforts to define and understand sex offenders, and crime-committing behavior more generally, were focused on the individual offender. Collectively, theories focused on the offender are referred to as **micro theories**—think microscope and drilling down to a focus on the individual. Early practitioners and researchers might take a biological approach, for example, discussed in more detail below, inviting a medical review of the individual who committed the particular crime to see if they are ill.[4] As researchers continued their efforts, theoretical approaches began to focus beyond the individual offender to the broader social influencing factors. These theories, focused on better understanding how social factors influence an individual's behavior, are collectively referred to as **macro theories**. What role does family, or education, or religion, or geographic location, or government ideology, as examples, have on the choices people make—particularly those choices that lead to crime-committing behavior? And because the social sciences as a field of study is not static, or stationary, like a snapshot frozen in time, conditions under study are likely to change as soon as any given assessment is made.

To explore influences beyond the individual and include a broader exploratory focus on the social conditions as factors influencing an offender and offending behavior adds an additional layer to traditional, individual social inquiry. And, to follow, researchers began to think about the dynamic effects of individual characteristics and social characteristics. These groups of theories can be described as **interactionist** theories. The dynamics of both the research process and the subject of sex offenses, offenders, and the effect of sexual violence on society can be complicated. Seeking out the best way to understand the topic and share that understanding is an ongoing objective within related disciplines and in society more broadly.

The development of social science research processes extends well beyond the borders of the United States; social science inquiry takes place all over the world. This includes critical reflection on the processes of scientific inquiry itself. The collective history of social movements in the United States provides a unique insight into the popular social group challenges to the idea of accepting specific social conditions as a status quo. Social movements are designed to raise questions about how the design of social systems and social structures operates. These questions can be reflected in social science inquiry. As a result, researchers critically reflect on and analyze the effects of social structures, whereas others raise questions about the efficacy of social science inquiry. How are the decisions made regarding the groups researchers elect to study? Does social science inquiry seek out an assessment of "objective" truth, or does it serve a different purpose? These broader social structural critiques, particularly as they are used to discuss the study of crime, provide an additional level of analysis for researchers and practitioners, found at the level of social structures, and collectively are **critical criminology**, focused on the economics of power; **feminist criminology**, focused on the gender dynamics of power; and **peacemaking criminology**, focused on the role of violence and punishment in the quest for justice.[5]

Using these broader groups of theories, research is focused on learning what influence social structural factors might have on a person who goes on to commit a sex offense. The individual has historically and traditionally been centered in efforts to understand the specific crime or harm event. More recently, however, protracted efforts to better understand what might be described as a second layer of this sex-offending dynamic is being explored by asking what influence do society, social attitudes, social structures, and tradition have on the decision an individual makes to commit a sex crime or commit a sexual harm against another person? What social factors converge to create the conditions for which a crime is identified and enforced? Researchers interested in better understanding the effects of various social influencing factors on individual behaviors, particularly sexual deviance and harm, have increasingly explored various aspects of the social conditions that surround this original question—aspects that have been discussed traditionally but have not been called out and named for the purposes of more comprehensive research exploration.

A broader question, such as "What role do social conditions have in either supporting or decreasing the number of incidents of sexual violence in a given area over a given time?," invites a different focus and produces a different set of social and individual considerations from within the structure of the research and in the reported findings. When the issue of sexual abuse and offending includes questions about what is known about the individual offender as well as questions about the circumstances leading up to an offense and the social and cultural conditions in which these kinds of offenses occur, the pool of information researchers gather becomes more expansive.

In their 1998 work on sexual abuse in the United States, Robert Freeman-Longo and Geral T. Blanchard suggest studying the aspects of culture that continuously perpetuate the misuse of human sexuality and sexual behavior problems as being critical. This, they suggest, includes sexual crimes as well as sexually harmful behaviors.[6] Among the early **treatment practitioners**, those professionals working to assist or rehabilitate known offenders, were people working to encourage the viewing of sexual violence as a **public health issue**. Many implicated larger institutions and social systems as having a significant role to play in both reported and unreported rates of sexual abuse and violence.

We find it alarming that, on one hand, people are appalled by sexual abuse and sexual violence but, on the other hand, they spend billions of dollars on entertainment that is often abusive and distorts traditional values regarding human sexuality.[7]

Suggesting that the United States was suffering under what they referred to as a silent **epidemic**,[8] a significant upsurge in a particular event, the authors joined many voices asking questions about the way the issues of rape and child sexual abuse were being discussed in the larger societal context. Historically, relatively low numbers of sex crimes have been reported to police, but, in relatively recent years, reporting rates have increased (16 percent in 2011 and 23 percent in 2017[9]); however, the rates are still low compared to the number of individuals assaulted. RAINN reports that the self-reported rates of rape have fallen by more than half from 1993 to 2016.[10] These reported levels indicate significant swings, with some years higher and some lower. Yet communities of color and women on tribal lands report levels of assault that could be described as **endemic**, or something regularly found in a particular area among a particular group of people.[11] An endemic condition reflects a persistent prevalence of an event, in this case, sexualized violence, without an identifiable upsurge, peak, or reduction in the events under study.[12] With some minor fluctuations, sexual violence is argued to be a persistent area of concern across the US cultural experience, with particular sectors experiencing elevated levels of violence.[13] The core experience of sexual violence in the United States has become so common that pervasive questions are being raised about whether a decline in the numerical peak of these kinds of incidents can ever be expected.

To clearly understand the range of theoretical options used to explain sex offending, it is important to understand the full range of theoretical perspectives available for consideration. The expectation is that professionals in their respective fields of study may vehemently disagree about the best way to frame the subject of study. So here's a question: Who gets to decide which research findings better represent the "truth"? In areas of study that have been traditionally exclusive of women, the aspect of gender is glaringly obvious—more so when it is pointed out. All aspects of any question about whose word is given priority, whose studies are offered top billing, or whose research design is argued to best represent the needs of the discipline are important. Those asking questions about the traditional research and analytical model, a model some associate with the nearly exclusive masculine history of medical schools, higher education institutions, religious structures, and faith communities, are not only women.[14]

At the risk of oversimplification, it is possible to describe at least four ways to think about or group the theories being used to make sense of sex-offender behaviors. The first and more traditional way is at the individual, biological, or psychological level. The second is at a social or societal level with a focus on the role society plays—social rules, social traditions, and social customs—in the number of incidents of sexual harm or violence.[15] A third way, in this loosely ordered collection, raises questions about the connectivity between individual attitudes and social influences, an integration of influencing factors that come from the individual and society, collectively referred to as integrated theories. Finally, a fourth way to think about theory construction and development is to ask who has the power to define the questions being asked and who benefits from the definition of the social conditions as they are currently outlined? These theories are looking squarely at the role power plays in defining the social parameters and how those definitions are assigned or applied to others.

Confusion about the implications between research findings and a more complete understanding of the behaviors of sex offenders exists both among professionals and within the vast social networks, neighborhoods, and communities throughout the United States. A discussion about both social and psychological theories attempting to explain sex-offender behaviors would not be complete without also noting the social relativity of the processes and or the systems put in place to conduct these analyses. Remember that women who were identified as sexually promiscuous or people who were identified as homosexuals were identified historically by medical doctors and researchers as "insane" and, with socially determined provocation, they were in some cases institutionalized.[16] By contemporary medical standards, such a thing is unlikely to happen today; however, related social stigmas do remain in some social settings or come from specific social groups and are often too easily applied as a social sanction. If one thinks of how young people of high school age, particularly young girls, are talked about if they are thought to be having sex indiscriminately or with more than one person and then contrast this with how young men of the same age are responded to socially, this might prove to be a useful illustration of the variety of sexual deviant classifications, even today. With this in mind, efforts to reflect the most prominent typologies are presented below after a brief introduction to the *Diagnostic and Statistical Manual of Mental Disorders* (DSM) and the *International Classification of Diseases* (ICD).

THE *DSM* AND *ICD*: STANDARDIZED EFFORTS
TO CLASSIFY MENTAL DISORDERS

The *DSM* is a diagnostic tool and reference guide developed by the American Psychiatric Association (APA) and used by practitioners to classify mental disorders.[17] The latest edition of this text was 14 years in the making and officially introduced in May 2013. More commonly referred to as the *DSM-5*, indicating the updated fifth edition, the *DSM* is used in the United States and to varying degrees throughout the world.

In its evolving iterations over the years, the *DSM* has been referred to as the bible of modern psychiatry. This latest edition was released to much controversy and fanfare, after its publication date was delayed and the National Institute of Mental Health came out in opposition to some of the proposed changes.[18] Structured as a "living document," which can be changed piecemeal online as new evidence emerges,[19] some of these changes are actively being assessed and have been met with varied support and criticism.

The *DSM-IV-TR* (2000) identified a chapter on "Sexual and Gender Identity Disorders," which created three basic classes: (1) gender identity disorders, (2) sexual dysfunctions, and (3) paraphilias. **Paraphilia** is a term most often used in therapeutic settings and refers to a classification system set up by therapists and psychologists to collectively refer to mental disorders that consist of sexual urges, fantasies, and/or behaviors involving suffering or humiliations, nonhuman objects, children, and/or nonconsenting persons.[20] The *DSM-IV-TR* identifies eight primary paraphilias: voyeurism, exhibitionism, frotteurism, sexual masochism, sexual sadism, pedophilia, fetishism, and transvestic fetishism, with an additional classification of **paraphilias not otherwise specified** (NOS), which is a catch-all classification used for any of a variety of paraphilias not included in the manual but that are a source of distress.

While the eight primary paraphilia classifications were carried over into the *DSM-5*, there are some differences in chapter organization and terminology. The new *DSM-5* defines paraphilia as "any intense and persistent sexual interest other than sexual interest in genital stimulation or preparatory fondling with phenotypically normal, physically mature, consenting human partners."[21] Although the same eight topics are covered, the terms are now referenced as **paraphilic disorders:**

- Voyeuristic disorder—spying on others in private activities
- Exhibitionistic disorder—exposing the genitals
- Frotteuristic disorder—touching or rubbing against a nonconsenting individual
- Sexual masochism disorder—undergoing humiliation, bondage, or suffering
- Sexual sadism disorder—inflicting humiliation, bondage, or suffering
- Pedophilic disorder—sexual focus on children
- Fetishistic disorder—using nonliving objects or having a highly specific focus on nongenital body parts
- Transvestic disorder—engaging in sexually arousing cross-dressing

Similar to the *DSM-IV-TR*, the *DSM-5* acknowledges that dozens of distinct paraphilias have been identified and named; however, not all of them are included in the *DSM-5* but are classified as ***other specified paraphilic disorder*** and ***unspecified paraphilic disorder***. Although both additional categories can be applied to an individual who has symptoms characteristic of paraphilic disorders that "cause clinically significant distress or impairment in social, occupational, or other important areas of functioning predominate but do not meet the full criteria for any of the disorders used in the paraphilic disorders diagnostic class." The other specified paraphilic disorder is intended to be used in situations in which the clinician chooses to delineate reasons the criteria for the other paraphilias were not met; the use of unspecified paraphilic disorder is used when the clinician decides not to specify the reason the criteria are not met for a specific paraphilic disorder, including cases where a lack of information makes it impossible to finalize a diagnosis.[22]

The new *DSM-5* also incorporated a change in the diagnostic names used to reference and distinguish a paraphilia from a paraphilic disorder. A paraphilia that is currently causing distress or has resulted in personal harm or risk of harm to others is referred to as a paraphilic disorder. The diagnosis of a paraphilia, as explained in the revised version, highlights the reality that a paraphilia may be present, or even diagnosed, but may not require clinical intervention.[23] For example, **pedophilia** is a diagnosis in the *DSM-IV-TR*[24] with the following traits:

A. Over a period of at least six months, recurrent, intense sexually arousing fantasies, sexual urges, or behaviors involving sexual activity with a prepubescent child or children (generally age 13 years or younger).
B. The person has acted on these sexual urges, or the sexual urges or fantasies cause marked distress or interpersonal difficulty.
C. The person is at least age 16 years and at least 5 years older than the child or children in Criterion A.

Note: Do not include an individual in late adolescence involved in an ongoing sexual relationship with a 12- or 13-year-old.

A pedophile, then, is a person who has been diagnosed with pedophilia. It is important to note that *not all pedophiles act out sexually on their sexual urges*. This is the distinction being made in the new *DSM-5*. In fact, research is suggesting there is a conflict in the research community about the biology of a person attracted to children.[25] Some pedophiles are sexually satisfied by nonoffenses (discussed earlier in chapter 3), such as holding a child's hand or simply spending time with children, but they do not molest or rape children. Said in a different way, pedophilia describes the psychological *diagnosis* of a person and not the actual offending behavior.

Consider the example of kink. **Kink** refers to unconventional sexual preferences or behaviors and can include consensual practices of various paraphilias. As a result of the new *DSM-5*, a disorder is diagnosed only if the condition produces distress in the individual. For those who are interested in engaging in a paraphilia, if they are not distressed, then they would not meet the criteria to be diagnosed with a disorder. Simply put, the *DSM-5* will say that happy kinksters don't have a mental disorder but unhappy kinksters do.[26]

Various challenges have been raised about some of the new ways the *DSM-5* is proposing to discuss what constitutes a disorder. Arguments that were presented to remove paraphilias from the *DSM-5* completely have resulted in controversy because that would also remove pedophilia.[27] In support of the idea of removing paraphilias from the *DSM*, researchers suggest that people whose sexual practices are unusual or culturally forbidden should not necessarily be labeled as mentally ill.[28] And, in another ongoing controversy, the *DSM-5* organizers again chose not to include rape as a paraphilia. While the attitudes about identifying and diagnosing people who commit sex crimes against children have been long-standing, various task forces over the years have not been able to resolve questions about whether rape is a clinical disturbance, a criminal offense, or both. It is the inability to make a valid diagnosis with reliability that makes it impossible to define rape as a clinical disorder.[29] **Nicholas Groth,** a researcher who studied men and rape, raised questions about whether all nonconsensual sexual encounters are assaultive and suggested that mental health professionals have been slow to respond to rape as a possible sexual disorder.[30]

Questions remain about whether the *DSM* should generate a diagnosis for rapists, but the task force decision not to include a sexual violent or sexual predator classification was argued to be related to concern about a diagnosis using this language then being used by the criminal justice system to incarcerate more offenders under civil commitment provisions (discussed in more detail in chapter 12). Since at least the late 1980s, researchers have argued that some rapists report intense, repetitive urges to commit rape at an early age, which they argue suggests rape may meet the criteria in some cases for a paraphilia classification.[31]

While the controversy associated with professional efforts to identify and diagnose mental health issues is ongoing, it is important to be aware of a second evaluative tool, translated into 43 languages and reportedly used by more than 100 countries, the *International Classification of Diseases* (ICD).[32] According to the World Health Organization, about 70 percent of the world's health expenditures (USD 3.5 billion) are allocated using *ICD* for reimbursement and resource allocation.[33] The APA publishes the *DSM* for mental health professionals, and the rest of the health care industry uses the *ICD* for diagnostic codes.[34] Like the *DSM*, the *ICD* goes through periodic professional revisions. The *ICD-11* has been in the process of revision, over a decade in the making, with the anticipated approval in 2019, after adoption by member states, and implementation is scheduled for January 1, 2022.[35]

EARLY OFFENDER TYPOLOGIES AND CLASSIFICATIONS

Efforts to create typologies and subtypes of sex offenders are ongoing. Two of the most famous classifications were offered by Groth, Burgess, and Holmstrom in their construction of a rape typology[36] and then by Groth and Birnbaum in their construction of a typology for people who offended against children,[37] referred to them more commonly as **child molesters.** Groth, Hobson, and Gary and then Groth, Longo, and McFaden expanded the typology to include a sex-pressure event or a sex-force offense.[38] Offender typologies take several factors into consideration, including the offender, the offense, and the victim. The development and modification efforts illustrate clearly the fact that the efforts to explain the origin of sex-offending behavior are ongoing and ever evolving. Groth, in his comprehensive work *Men Who Rape: The Psychology of the Offender*, suggests that three patterns can be found in rape: (1) anger rape, (2) power rape, and (3) sadistic rape, with an assessment that rape is a psychological dysfunction either temporary and transient or chronic and repetitive.[39]

But, at the time, Groth stressed the reluctance to examine rape as a psychosexual disorder. Those are exacting words, for an assessment with supporters on both sides. His questions about whether mental health professionals have been slow to respond or were just plain wrong about not including rape as a type of paraphilia classification loom large and were raised again throughout the development of the *DSM-5*.[40] Clearly, the best way to classify characteristics and features of actions, behaviors, and harms is controversial even among professionals.

Initially, Groth and Birnbaum identified two groups of child sexual abusers: the fixated abuser and the regressed abuser (Table 7.1). Those who are classi-

Table 7.1 Fixated-Regressed Child Molesters

Typology	Motivation	Primary Victim Preference	Risk of Reoffending
Fixated Offender	• Having never developed an attraction to age-appropriate partners, the fixated offender has a persistent, continual, and compulsive attraction to children • Behavior emerges in adolescence • Offenses are premeditated in nature and do not stem from stressors • Most likely to be diagnosed with pedophilia/ephebophilia	• Extrafamilial • Female, prepubescent; male, prepubescent/adolescent • Typically recruits vulnerable children and engages in extensive grooming in order to ensure the continuation of the abuse	• Higher risk of recidivism • The risk of recidivism increases according to the number of victims
Regressed	• Offending stems from stressors in the individual's environment that undermine self-esteem and confidence • Behaviors emerge in adulthood • Offending is a departure from the offender's attraction to adults • Similar to rapists, the offender is not necessarily motived by sexual needs alone	• Intrafamilial, acquaintance • Gender varies, depending on who is accessible • Tend to victimize children to whom they have easy access	• Since they are not sexually fixated on children, they are at lower risk of reoffending if treated • Capable of feeling remorse for their actions

fied as a *fixated child sexual abusers* are described as individuals whose sexual desires and preferences revolve around children. Their attraction to children is thought to have developed during adolescence, and they are not likely to have healthy sexual contacts with age-appropriate adults as partners and are assessed as being emotionally immature.[41] **Grooming** behaviors, where the offender seeks to secure the trust of the child and/or family, are noted in this type of offender.[42] They are believed to offend against several children before being detected and are more likely to reoffend if they are not caught.[43] A *regressed child sexual abuser* is an individual who does not seem to be interested in children because they maintain relationships with adults; however, these child sexual abusers will resort to sexual contact with a child under duress or stress; their abuse is more likely situational, impulsive, and opportunistic.[44] Of these two classification categories, the fixated offender is more likely to reoffend.[45] They are thought to target male victims, whereas the regressed offender is likely to abuse young girls who are accessible, whether that means in the family or someone they know casually but someone who is available during their times of high stress.[46]

In the early rape typology, Groth, Burgess, and Holmstrom[47] outlined a **power rapist** and an **anger rapist**. Each category had two subcategories. The power rapist included the subcategories of the *power assertive rapist*, who regards the rape as an expression of his masculinity to control and dominate the victim, and the *power-reassurance rapist*, who will offend in an effort to counteract thoughts about sexual problems or feelings. The anger rapist includes an *anger-retaliatory rapist* and an *anger-excitement rapist*. The anger-retaliatory rapist commits rape to express anger, rage, and hostility toward their target, whereas the anger-excitement rapist derives erotic sexual pleasure in the humiliation or harm of another.[48] By 1979, Groth had added **sadistic rapist** to his categories, suggesting that both sexuality and aggression can become fused into a psychological experience known as *sadism* and the aggression itself becomes eroticized.[49] His findings suggested that 55 percent of the cases were power rapes, 40 percent were anger rapes, and about 5 percent were sadistic rapes, but he cautions about the final assessments because his sample was primarily convicted offenders.[50]

Efforts to be clear about the research being conducted follow along divergent lines as well. When studying sex offenders, getting clear about the use of terms is critical because sex offenders can be uniquely different in both motivation for committing the offense and response to treatment. The paraphilia and classification systems for the *DSM* are terms used to reflect a clinical diagnosis. Simkins conducted an exploratory study of sexually repressed and nonrepressed child sexual abusers to determine if or how they progressed differently in therapy by reviewing the offenders' **psychosexual histories**, a psychological assessment conducted of offenders prior to sentencing, usually to determine whether treatment might afford a viable option for the offender as the court weighs the possibility of a treatment and probation, rather than a jail or prison term.[51]

While efforts to get clear about how terms are used and the ways in which these concepts are structured for comparison, it is also critically important to note that, as people continue researching the subject and offer clarifications

Table 7.2   A Comprehensive Paraphilia Classification System[1]

Category I: Nonviolent Physical Paraphilia	Category II: Nonviolent Nonphysical Paraphilia
Examples: Swinging Exhibitionism Voyeurism Partialism Pedophilia/familial Transvestism	Examples: Telephone scatological Technophilia
Category III: Sadistic Paraphilia	**Category IV: Masochistic Paraphilia**
Examples: Sadism Pyromania	Examples: Masochism
Category V: Sadomasochistic Paraphilia	
Examples: Sadomasochism Apotemnophilia	

1 L. Shaffer and J. Penn. A comprehensive paraphilia classification system.

in the forms of typologies of offenders and offender characteristics, even the experts across disciplines may not be using a common language of terms as they are attempting to compare these emerging and evolving areas of research. For example, Baxter et al. studied **static information** about offenders, the information about the offenders that does not change, such as their age at first offenses, criminal history, family life, and education.[52] (More on both static measures and psychosexual evaluations is offered in chapter 12, on correctional management, and chapter 13, on treatment.) Table 7.2 overviews a multiplicity of treatment practitioners and researchers who have developed various classification systems, based largely on the motivation of the offender, in an effort to describe or explain what causes an offender to commit a sexually aggressive act.

Focused on the issue of paraphilia classification, Lisa Shaffer and Julie Penn (2006) published what they suggested might be a comprehensive paraphilia classification system, which is summarized in Table 7.2. It might be shocking to learn about the many more paraphilia classifications; however, most of these are not the central focus of treatment practitioners (as discussed in chapter 13).

PEDOPHILES, RAPISTS, AND A COLLECTION OF SEX-OFFENDER TYPOLOGIES

In spite of a lengthy list of paraphilias among practitioners in both the *DSM* and the *ICD* and in other publications, most studies on sex offenders and sex offending focus on the offenses of child molestation and rape, or they include both. As questions about the differences between individual involvement in paraphilia practices and the need for a paraphilic disorder diagnosis continue, research in real life suggests that the acts of sexual harm and aggression that police and

Table 7.3   Evolving Typologies for Describing Individuals Who Commit Sexual Harms

Cohen, Seghorn, and Calmas (1969)[1] identified four types of *rapists*:

1. The compensatory
2. The displaced aggressive
3. The sex-aggression diffusion
4. The impulse rapist

Groth, Burgess, and Holstrom (1977)[2]

The dynamics of power, anger, and sexuality are assessed to be present in every rape. This study looked to see which of these three dynamics were the primarily associated with each instance. Sexuality was found not to be the dominant issue in any of the behaviors studied.

Power rape
   Power-assertive rapist
   Power-reassurance rapist

Anger rapist
   Anger-retaliatory
   Anger-excitement

Groth (1978)[3] This study screened males who had been convicted of sexual crimes against children to determine if they were fixated on children as victims or had regressed from peer sexual relationships.

   Fixated
   Regressed

Groth (1979)[4]

Rape was described as having three main components: power, anger and sexuality, resulting in three types of offenders.

   Anger—Hostile.
   Power—Conquest.
   Sadistic—Anger and Power are eroticized.

Dr. Park Elliot Deitz (1983)[5] introduced the idea of the **situational sex offender**, someone who because of intoxication, social stressors, mood, and mental conditions engages in sex offenses due to situational factors.[6] Such offenders are "reasonably well adjusted and nonparaphilic men who committed their first offenses while drinking heavily, after being fired, during their wives' pregnancy, following a divorce, or during a depressive, manic or psychotic episode."[7] The **preferential sex offender** will have lifelong interest in specific illegal sexual acts, noting that many individual may have such preferences but never act on them.[8]

   Situational sex offender
   Preferential sex offender

Finkelhor (1984)[9]

Finkelhor continues to look at the division between fixated offenders, attracted to children from a young age and usually qualify for a pedophilia diagnosis, versus the preferential offender who is not solely attracted to children, but finds the child to be an easier target.

Knight and Prentky's (1990) Typology of Child Molestation[10] outlines four typologies:

   Opportunistic—impulse driven, subdivided into high and low social competence levels
   Pervasively angry—motivated by aggression, anger
   Vindictive—motivated by power and control, victim humiliation, subtyped into high and low social competence.
   Sexual rapists—either sadistic or non-sadistic with sadistic subdivided into overt or muted sadism, and non-sadistic subdivided into high or low social competence.

The Massachusetts Treatment Center: Child Molester Typology version 3 (MTC:CM3)[11]

Categories include degrees of fixation and amount of contact.

   Axis I fixation and level of social competence
   Axis II contact levels, interpersonal and narcissistic

Freund, 1990[12]

The courtship disorder hypothesis developed by Freund maintains that different paraphilias are all expressions of the same disorder (courtship disorder). This theory looks at the four stages of traditional courtship and asserts that when one of the steps is distorted, it becomes paraphilic.

Barbaree and Marshall (1991)[13] the role of sexual arousal in men during rape—6 models that describe men's sexual arousal to descriptions of rape are divided into two broad categories.

   The response control model—reduce the ability to suppress arousal in the presence of coercion or violence
   The stimulus control model—excited by deviant sexual cues

Lanning (1992)[14]—Not a why typology, but a how typology to be used by law enforcement to apprehend offenders.

   Situational—Offends against children not because of a preference for child victims, but because the situation.

   Regressed—Poor coping skills and low self-esteem. Acting out through Child Abuse due to external stressor.
   Morally indiscriminate—Child Sexual Abuse is an additional form of antisocial behavior in the offender who has a general pattern of causing abuse.
   Sexually indiscriminate—Willing to try anything sexual.
   Inadequate offender—Targets children because they seem to be non-threatening.

Preferential Child Molester—Sexual Preference for Children

   Seduction offender—courting children with attention, affection and gifts.
   Introverted offender—Has a preference for children, but lacks the skills to build a relationship with them.

Sadistic offender—Arousal tied to pain and suffering of victim.

Simon, Sales, Kaszniak, and Kahn (1992):[15] Continuous distribution of offenders rather than a dichotomous classification and suggested a continuum is more appropriate for using the fixated-regressed typology.

   fixated ——————————————————————————————————regressed

Simkins (1993)[16] this was an investigation to compare child abuse offenders on their progress in therapy and on other personality and research instruments. These offenders were put into three categories:

   Repressed
   Nonrepressed
   Exploitive

Barbaree et al. 1994[17]

Rapists were subtyped as either "nonsexual" (i.e., the opportunistic and vindictive subtypes) or "sexual" (i.e., the nonsadistic and sadistic subtypes). The nonsexual subtypes were more violent and resulted in greater victim damage.

Schwartz (1995):[18]

Outlined theoretical explanations for sexually deviant behavior including regressed are focused on external stressors. Other stressors listed included poor self-confidence, poor self-esteem, and a temporary departure from attraction to adults.

Berger 2000[19] Berger expanded on Groth's research from 1979.

   Power assurance
   Power assertive
   Anger retaliation
   Anger excitation

(continued)

Table 7.3 *Continued*

Dennis Stevens (2001):[20] Types of sex offenders were broken down into predatory and non predatory, but included aspects of six characteristics: hedonism, control, righteousness, situational, revenge, and visionary (responding to voices to fulfill divine directives).

Holmes and Holmes (2002)[21] described the following types of sex offenders:

Situational

Regressed
Morally indiscriminate
Naive/Inadequate

Preferential

Mysoped—Sadist, ritualized, no love for the victim, only interested in harm/death
Fixated

Holmes and Holmes (2009) included a different classification of *sex offenders*, from their 2002 work which outlining three types:[22]

1. **Sexual predator**, someone convicted of or pleaded guilty to committing a sexually oriented offense and who is likely in the future to commit additional sexually oriented offenses.
2. **Habitual sex offender**, someone who is determined by the sentencing court to have been previously convicted of or pleaded guilty to one or more sexually oriented offenses.
3. **Sexually oriented offende**r, a person who has been convicted of or pleaded guilty to committing sexually oriented offense.

1 Cohen, M., Seghorn, T., & Calmas, W. (1969). Sociometric study of the sex offender. *Journal of Abnormal Psychology*, 74(2), 249–255. doi: 10.1037/h0027185
2 Groth, AN, Burgess, W., & Holmstrom, LL. (1977). Rape: power, anger and sexuality. *Am J Psychiatry*, Nov;134(11):1239-43.
3 Groth, A. N., & Birnbaum, H. J. (1978). Adult sexual orientation and attraction to underage persons. *Archives of Sexual Behavior*, 7(3), 175–181. doi: 10.1007/bf01542377
4 Groth, AN. *Men Who Rape: The Psychology of the Offender* (New York: Plenum Press, 1979).
5 Dietz, PE. "Sex Offenses: Behavioral Aspects." In *Encyclopedia of Crime and Justice*. Ed. S.H. Kadish et al. New York: Free Press, 1983.
6 Lanning, K. 1986. *Situational and Preferential Sex Offenders, from Sexual Exploitation of the Child*, eds Frost, T. and M. J. Seng. (Loyola Univ) pp. 28-39.
7 Dietz, PE. "Sex Offenses: Behavioral Aspects." In *Encyclopedia of Crime and Justice*. Ed. S.H. Kadish et al. New York: Free Press, 1983, p. 1489.
8 Dietz, PE. "Sex Offenses: Behavioral Aspects." In *Encyclopedia of Crime and Justice*. Ed. S.H. Kadish et al. New York: Free Press, 1983, p. 1490.
9 Finkelhor, D. (1984). *Child Sexual Abuse: New Theory and Research*. New York: Free Press.
10 Knight, R.A., & Prentky, R.A. (1990). *Classifying sexual offenders: The development and corroboration of taxonomic models*. In W.L. Marshall, D.R. Laws, & H.B. Barbaree (Eds.), *Handbook of Sexual Assault: Issues, Theories, and Treatment of the Offender* (pp. 23–52). New York: Plenum.
11 Vandiver, D. and J. Braithwaite, M. Stafford. 2017. *Sex Crime and Sex Offenders*, Ch 4 Child Sexual Abuse, (Taylor and Francis) pp. 107-108.
12 Freund, K. (1990). "Courtship disorder." In W. L. Marshall, D. R. Laws, & H. E. Barbaree (Eds.), *Handbook of Sexual Assault: Issues, Theories, and Treatment of the Offender* (pp. 195–207). NY: Plenum.
13 Barbaree, H. E., & Marshall, W. L. (1991). *The role of male sexual arousal in rape: Six models. Journal of Consulting and Clinical Psychology*, 59(5), 621–630. doi: 10.1037//0022-006x.59.5.621
14 Lanning, K. V. (1992). *Child molesters: a behavioral analysis for law enforcement officers investigating cases of child sexual exploitation*. Washington, D.C.: National Center for Missing & Exploited Children.
15 Simon, L. M. J., Sales, B., Kaszniak, A., & Kahn, M. (1992). Characteristics of Child Molesters. *Journal of Interpersonal Violence*, 7(2), 211–225. doi: 10.1177/088626092007002007
16 Simkins, L. (1993). Characteristics of Sexually Repressed Child Molesters. *Journal of Interpersonal Violence*, 8(1), 3–17. doi: 10.1177/088626093008001001
17 Barbaree, H. E., Seto, M. C., Serin, R. C., Amos, N. L., & Preston, D. L. (1994). Comparisons Between Sexual and Nonsexual Rapist Subtypes. *Criminal Justice and Behavior*, 21(1), 95–114. doi: 10.1177/0093854894021001007
18 Schwartz, B.K., (1995). *Characteristics and Typologies of Sex Offenders*. In B. Schwartz (Eds). *The Sex Offender: Corrections, Treatment and Legal Practice*. New Jersey: Civic Research Institute, Inc.
19 Berger, R.D. (2000). *Successfully Investigating Acquaintance Sex Assault*. National Center for Women and Policing: OJP.
20 Dennis J. Stevens, *Inside the Mind of Sexual Offenders* (Lincoln, NE: Authors Choice Press, 2001), Chapter 13, especially, 207.
21 Holmes, R. M., & Holmes, S. T. (2002). Pedophilia and psychological profiling. In R. M. Holmes, & S. T. Holmes, *Profiling violent crimes: An investigative tool* (3rd ed.) (pp. 158-171). Thousand Oaks, CA: Sage
22 Stephen T. Holmes and Ronald M. Holmes, *Sex Crimes: Patterns and Behaviors*, 3rd ed. (Thousand Oaks, CA: Sage, 2009), 4.

courts deal with are not usually related to many of the paraphilia classifications outlined. Rather, those defined by the acts of sexual aggression in the criminal codes referred to, most commonly, a version of rape or sexual assault, child sexual abuse, and those acts related to child sex abuse, such as child pornography. Table 7.3 reviews a collection of the more commonly used sex-offender typologies, or groups sharing common features. The goal is to create a common language for researchers in an effort to assure comparisons between groups and research studies are similarly and consistently classified.

The chronological review of child sexual abuse, rapists, and sex offenders in the collective helps illustrate the various ways academics and other researchers and treatment practitioners attempt to describe and explain the themes that emerge in their individual and combined efforts to understand more about sex offenders as a larger group. These descriptive typologies provide a way for researchers and practitioners to create a common dialogue and to structure future research; however, they may change over time as more is learned.

Characteristics of Sexually Violent Perpetrators Involving Adult Males

Although specific attention has been given to pedophiles and the sexual acts against children, other areas of study attention have also been given to sexual assault of adult woman. (See the rape typologies outlined in Table 7.4.) People who commit rape comprise a heterogeneous population, and, although motivations for rape vary, the most common is power and control, and the most dangerous is the sadistic rapist. The following rape descriptions are common traits in men who rape women:

- Usually have negative views of women
- Endorse rape myths
- Condone violence
- Low self-esteem
- Sense of worthlessness
- Substance abuse problems
- Have problems managing or are unable to manage aggression
- Show signs of dysphoric mood states (specifically anger, fear, depression)
- Come from broken homes

Some of the characteristics for offenders who commit sexual assaults against children are the same or similar to the characteristics of the typologies used to explain sexual offenses against adults. Notably the *DSM* has no paraphilia classification for rape. Its absence reflects a controversy, and one side of the argument suggests that this represents a glaring omission of what is one of the largest categories for which sex offenders are arrested, convicted, and sentenced to treatment.[53] The other side of the argument suggests that the omission of sex offenders classifications focused on rape has to do with the fear by professionals that the courts would use this classification of mental illness as a means for committing convicted sex offenders to long-term mental health facilities. A long history of misuse of mental health facilities and the fairly recent deinsti-

Table 7.4 Summary of Rapist Typologies[1]

Typology	Primary Motivation	Characteristics
Compensatory	Sexual	• Only as much force as necessary • May have "courtship disorder" • Feelings of inadequacy • "Gentleman rapist"
Sadistic	Sexual	• Offender achieves gratification through pain and/or fear inflicted on victim • Often psychopathic • Offense may lead to sexual murder
Power/Control	Nonsexual	• An aggressive, pseudo-sexual act • Offender desires power and dominance over the victim • Motivation may be humiliation, degradation • Offender is often angry
Opportunistic	Nonsexual	• Recreational/situational offender who leads impulsive, adventure-seeking lifestyle • Assault often committed during another offense • Poor impulse control

1 From G. Robertiello and K. Terry, "Can We Profile Sex Offenders?: A Review of Sex Offender Typologies," *Aggression and Violent Behavior* 12, no. 5 (2007): 510.

tutionalization efforts of the 1970s and early 1980s is still fresh in the minds of treatment practitioners, researchers, and public health officials who remain concerned about assuring the reasons for institutionalization do not produce system-wide abuses.

Youth with Problematic Sexual Behavior

Juvenile sex offenders are different from the more commonly discussed adult sex offender population in their characteristics and motivations and the way they are treated and supervised.[54] Attention is focused on both male and female juvenile sex offenders, with recent statistics suggesting that as many as 50 percent of those who sexually abuse children are under the age of 18.[55] Juveniles are being charged for sexual crimes, from contact offenses to sexting.
　　Consider:

- Twenty to 50 percent of adolescents who have sexually abused children were themselves victims of physical abuse, and anywhere between 40 and 80 percent were victims of sexual abuse.[56]
- Children who express gender nonconforming behavior or presentation before age 11 (1 in 10 children) are more likely to be sexually abused. Gender nonconforming boys are especially at risk.[57]
- Forty-six percent of adolescent male sex offenders reported having experienced child sexual abuse (as compared to 16 percent of adolescent males who are not sex offenders reporting having experienced child sexual abuse).[58]
- It is of interest to note that, while arrests of adult women for sex offenses have decreased in recent years, the number of adolescent girls coming

to the attention of the juvenile courts for sex offenses has increased significantly. More specifically, between 1997 and 2002, juvenile cases involving female-perpetrated forcible rapes, other violent sex offenses, and nonviolent sex offenses rose by 6 percent, 62 percent, and 42 percent, respectively.[59]

- Researchers have noted a significant correlation between family dysfunction and sexually abusive behavior in juveniles.[60]
- Current research suggests that empathy deficits serve as an important etiological factor in juvenile sex offending.[61]

One of the biggest concerns about young people who commit sex offenses is the question about whether they can be effectively treated and subsequently rehabilitated. Research on characteristics and treatment specifically associated with female juvenile sex offenders is extremely limited.[62] The Center for Sex Offender Management (CSOM) invites caution when reviewing information about female offenders because the data on these offenders is so limited and might reflect more individual cases, rather than a collective. Experts agree that the lack of information about female offenders is extensive, and

[a]lthough females constitute a small proportion of the sex offender population, the percentage of sex offenders that is female increases as age decreases (Brown, Hull and Manesis, 1984; Fehrenbach and Monstersky, 1988; Moccio-Fonesca, 1998; Ray and English, 1995). Whereas females make up approximately 1 to 2 percent of the adult sex offender population, they make up approximately 10 percent of adolescent offenders (13–18 years of age) and nearly 20% of child offenders (12 years of age and under) (Ray and English, 1995). Overall, the age of onset for sexual offending in females is younger than the age of onset for males.[63]

Much of the victimization by adolescent females is the result of their exploring their sexuality in unacceptable ways.[64] The ability of the young person to develop empathy was seen to be as the result of a bond to the mother, which was shown to reduce the amount of sexual aggression in young men.[65] As has been discussed elsewhere throughout the text, it is important to understand issues like sexting will be significantly represented in this young age group. The use of phones, computers, and other technologies more common among and familiar to young people, which is likely to have a significant effect on the rates of sexual crimes attached to juveniles. (More will be discussed in chapters 10 and 11 with regard to the increase in opposition to sanctions in many of these cases.)

Perhaps of all sex-offender groupings, the least amount is known about female sex offenders. Like many other research samples in sex-offender research, the sample sizes are relatively small, making the generalizability of the findings nearly impossible. Experts agree, the lack of information about female offenders is significant, and efforts to understand this population of offenders are a significant area of need within criminal justice, juvenile, justice, and social service agencies.[66]

Because the reported offenses involving female perpetrators are extremely small, reliable information is difficult to obtain. Researchers at CSOM used arrest data, census and caseload data, and information from treatment programs and victimization reports to suggest the following:[67]

- Females account for less than 10 percent of the cases of all adults and juveniles that come to the attention of the authorities.[68]
- Female sex offenders, like male offenders, comprise a heterogeneous population.[69]
- Histories of childhood maltreatment, including sexual victimization
- Mental health symptoms, personality disorders, and substance abuse problems
- Difficulties in intimate relationships or an absence of intimate relationships
- A propensity to primarily victimize children and adolescents (rarely adults)
- A tendency to commit offenses against persons who are related or otherwise well known to them
- An increased likelihood of perpetrating sex offenses in concert with a male intimate partner

Although the numbers of female adult offenders and youthful female offenders is identified as small, between 1 and 3 percent, it is important to understand that the issues about reporting may be influenced by the social attitudes and

Table 7.5 Female Sex Offender Typologies[1] with Author

Author	Date	Classifications
Sarrel and Masters	1982	• Forced assault • Babysitter abuse • Incestuous abuse • Dominant woman abuse
McCarthy	1981, 1986	• Independent offenders of males (1986) • Independent offenders of females (1986) • Co-offenders and accomplices (1986) • Severely psychologically disturbed abuser (1981)
Mathews, Mathews, and Speltz	1989	• Teacher/lover • Predisposed • Male-coerced molester • *Exploration/exploitation • Psychologically disturbed
Mayer	1992	• Female rapist • Female sexual harassment • Mother molester • Triads • Homosexual molestations
Syed and Williams (building on Mathews et al., 1989)	1996	• Teacher/lover • Male-coerced • Angry-impulsive • Male-accompanied, familial • Male-accompanied, nonfamilial
Vandiver and Kercher	2004	• Heterosexual nurturers • Noncriminal homosexual offenders • Female sexual predators • Young adult child exploiters • Aggressive homosexual offenders

1 Typology layout adapted from Donna Vandiver, Jeremy Braithwaite, and Mark Stafford, *Sex Crimes and Sex Offenders: Research and Realities* (New York: Routledge, 2017), 190–91.

ideas linking men to sexual violence and thereby overlooking the possibility that women, too, can commit sex offenses at a higher rate than is reported.

Cybersex Offenders

Research on cybersex offenders, or sex offenders who use the internet in the furtherance of a sexual offense, is an emerging area of study. The numbers of cases, such as the Craigslist Killer,[70] dubbed so by the media after contact with the victims was made through ads placed on Craigslist, include a variety of high-profile instances where people meet someone in a chat room and then they meet in real life and are killed and murdered, such as victim 15-year-old Christina Long.[71] In addition to these extreme kinds of events facilitated by the internet, others have focused on the kinds of activities and information the internet, cell phones, and social media platforms have made available not only to the average person but also to sex offenders. These include:

- Sex education and information
- Commerce of sexually related goods
- Online sexual entertainment and masturbation
- Sex therapists
- Online dating to find both long-term partners and transitory sexual partners or swingers
- Online-only relationships
- Online personality or identity role creation
- Seeking digital images for sexual purposes
- Incel chat rooms
- Revenge porn[72]

Much has been written about the internet in "pathological" terms, including the idea that the multiplicity of ways to access sexual experience online are associated with the concept of "internet addiction," similar to online gambling addictions.[73] The concept of child pornography or child abuse imagery has been at the center of the concern about the internet and sex offending. In terms of convictions, child pornography has been the activity that constitutes internet-related sex crime focus at the present.[74] (More will be discussed about child pornography in chapter 9.) It is important to note that initial research about online offenders suggests that the cybersex offender is white, male, and younger than the general population of sex offenders[75] and more highly educated.[76]

If sex offenders are argued by some to be the most negatively revered criminal class, groups that advocate for the acceptability of child/adult sex are the noncriminal social class equivalent. The advent of the internet offers a variety of ways to advocate and educate people about the challenges being made to the social definitions of appropriate and inappropriate sexual interactions with children. Ultimately, their goal is to challenge the construction of abuse, suggesting that sexual interactions between children and adults do not necessarily prove harmful to the child. In fact, Amsterdam, the capital city of the Netherlands, perhaps best known for its red light district where prostitution and marijuana are legal, was confronted with the creation of a political party almost singly focused on creating a brief description of several international groups focused on reducing the social stigma, if not legalizing, sexual relations between young people, including children, and adults.[77]

Similar to ways researchers organize information for the purposes of study, focused in this case on sex offenses and offenders, one could discern at least three basic frames of reference in this discussion. One comes from treatment practitioners and the therapeutic community, focused on establishing effective treatment for offenders (discussed in more detail in chapter 13). A second voice is from law enforcement and public policy makers focused on establishing an appropriate public safety response to their goal of maintaining public safety (discussed in more detail in section IV). A third voice includes just about everyone else who has questions about sex-offending behaviors and sex offenders. This, to varying degrees, includes academics, policy makers, parents, people who have been harmed or know people who have been hurt, people who have perpetrated harm and their family and friends, and any other members of the public looking for a comprehensive way to discuss, address, and ultimately prevent this kind of harm.

SEX-OFFENDER THEORY CLASSIFICATIONS: A COLLECTION OF THEORETICAL FRAMEWORKS

Theories being developed to describe sex-offending behavior have been created in conjunction with work from various different, related, or overlapping disciplines of study. Consequently, researchers must take extra care to work across disciplines, among sexology, psychology, and criminology, as examples. Most researchers agree that assessments of sex-offending behavior are varied and often deferential to disciplinary emphasis and interests. Attention is given here to biological, psychological, sociological, and criminological explanations for sex-offending behaviors.

Biological

Theories that use a biological basis for their explanations begin with the assumption that some people are born with a predisposition to their particular sexual deviance or criminal behavior. Sexually deviant behavior, they argue, can be explained by biological or physiological abnormalities. In the case of a pedophile, for example, a biological theoretical explanation would suggest that an individual who committed sexually aggressive or harmful behaviors was born with a sexual predisposition toward being sexual with children. The idea that sexual deviance is connected to abnormalities in the body's biology or physiology has generated some interest in the world of sex-offender research. A sampling of biological focus includes structural explanations, focused primarily on abnormalities in the brain's structure, more specifically, temporal and frontal lobe abnormalities and cerebral blood flow.

Another area of study with regard to the biological explanations used as an explanation for sex-offending behaviors is found in the research on hormones, neurotransmitters, genetics, and sex chromosome abnormalities. Some researchers have argued that the aggressive sexual behavior is best explained by the role of androgens and androgen-releasing hormones in males.[78] The male body undergoes significant hormonal changes during puberty, the same time at which the sex drive increases. Biological theories are particularly interested in the role of testosterone in the male sex drive. With regard to rape, the questions are centered around whether this increase in testosterone or high levels of testosterone are connected in any way to increases in aggression. Marshall, Laws, and Barbaree[79] are among those who suggest that aggression and sex involve midbrain structures, such as the hypothalamus, septum, hippocampus, amygdala, and preoptic area, while the same endocrines activate sex and aggression.

The biological explanations for sex-offending behaviors have captured a smaller group of practitioners, in part, because a great deal of the research in this area has produced inconclusive or conflicting results.[80] Further, the research does not suggest that the biological factors alone are enough to prompt the kind of violence required for sexual offending. In fact, many researchers suggest that environmental and/or social learning factors must be present before events of sexual aggression are likely to happen.[81]

Cognitive Theories

Perhaps some of the earliest mainstream explanations for sexual offenders come from within the field of psychology. Early theories about possible sexual abuse were often linked to individual actions and behaviors. Psychological explanations for sexual deviance emerged in large part from the work of Austrian psychoanalyst Sigmund Freud (explored earlier in chapter 3). The review of sexual desires or perversions were argued to be the consequences of childhood deprivations.[82] According to Freud, there are four stages of psychosexual development: oral, anal, phallic, and genital. In his *Three Essays on the Theory of Sexuality*, written in 1905, Freud talked about sexual aberrations, infantile sexuality, and puberty. Unresolved childhood issues resulted in fixations on specific stages of development, which produced his famous sexually oriented anxieties and disorders: the Oedipus complex in men and the Electra complex in women, castration anxiety, and penis envy.[83]

Freud's theories have been heavily critiqued. However, when dealing with connections to the biological elements of how the body and mind work, how the physical elements of the body affect the mind, how perception is connected to the thoughts an individual has and the actions they then decide to take, psychologists are in the realm between the mind and the body. Cognitive theories and related research are linked to the study of how the brain works. Questions have been raised with regard to the role of mental retardation or other brain deficiencies and their relationship to sexual assault and victimization.

As part of the cognitive behavioral approach, treatment practitioners have been developing and exploring technologies and methods for grounding applied psychology and developing field approaches as a means to increasing the success of treatment or as part of the offender management process.[84] In short, several technologies and assessments in the evolution of these methods are included with a brief description in Table 7.6. (More contemporary processes

Table 7.6   Various Tests and Tools Used for Assessing Sex Offenders

---

Penile plethysmography, also known as phallometry, measures the level of a man's sexual arousal by placing a pressure-sensitive device around the man's penis and then presenting him with various sexually suggestive images. Increasingly controversial, legal challenges have been raised with regard to its use as a tool for monitoring individuals on supervised release.

The Abel Assessment for Sexual Interests was designed in 1995 to measure sexual interests and is used primarily to determine a tendency toward pedophilia and has undergone many revisions. Findings are questioned, and results are not admissible in some courts.

Self-report assessments are question inventories answered by individuals who have committed offenses, which might include personal history, education, employment, physical and psychological health, sexual development, family structure and dynamics, interpersonal relationships histories, prior abuse history (as victim and/or perpetrator), and attitudes toward treatment.

Cognitive modeling of sexual arousal and interest broadly refers to assessments of individual perceptions or thoughts that influence a person's emotional or behavioral response, exploring ways an offender needs help in identifying and responding to distorted or dysfunctional thinking, at times, leading up to or when an offense occurs.

The Implicit Association Test (IAT)[1] is a tool used in social psychology to determine the strength of a person's automatic association between concepts in an indirect way, applied to offenders to assess sexual interest in children or other associations with sexual violence.

---

1 Anthony G. Greenwald, Debbie E. McGhee, and Jordan L. K. Schwartz, "Measuring Individual Differences in Implicit Cognition: The Implicit Association Test," *Journal of Personality and Social Psychology* 74, no. 6 (1998), 1464–80.

are discussed in chapter 12.) The central idea underlying the different methods is that sexual interest will affect the cognitive processing of the observer, in this case, the offender.[85] Focused on assessing the treatment and management of sex offenders, at minimum, the goal is to identify the treatment needs and the response to treatment and reduce the overall risk of reoffense.[86]

Personality theories have also been introduced in an attempt to explain sex-offender personality types. Various personality traits have been associated with sexual-offending behaviors; however, not all of these characteristics are seen in all sex offenders. Antisocial and psychopathic personality disorders have been linked to behaviors and attitudes such as a lack of empathy, various narcissistic traits, sadistic traits, and disordered personality traits. This flows into the fact that sex offenders have been described as having trouble controlling their impulses, including expressions of hostility, anger, and aggression. Perhaps some of the most influential treatment protocols driving sex-offender treatment programs today are linked to what is referred to as **cognitive behavioral theories**. (The application of the theory as it is used in treatment protocols for sex offenders is discussed in more detail in chapter 13.) The research themes driving the study and theory development of cognitive behavioral theories include efforts to understand how the individual offender's thoughts affect their behavior. When the focus is placed on the way the offender's thoughts and behaviors work together, researchers and treatment practitioners pay close attention to the ways that their behavior, like the behavior of other humans, can be used to justify their actions,[87] referred to as **cognitive distortions**. Researchers have discovered a number of cognitive distortions common to sexual offenders, particularly those who are repeat offenders. Rather than focusing their thoughts on the harmful behavior, they deny the harm or focus on the behavior or actions of the victim, suggesting they caused the perpetrator to do what they did.

A common list of cognitive distortions might include:

- Children want and benefit from sexual contact with adults.
- Children can and do consent to sexual contact with adults.
- Children are under no pressure to have sex with an adult.
- Sexual contact between a child and an adult is not harmful.
- Children are sexually seductive.
- Adult men are entitled to satisfy their sexual needs, no matter what the cost to others.[88]

Additional psychological studies have been used to explore what has been referred to as **social information processing dysfunction**. The emphasis is given to the way an individual identifies social cues and interprets those ideas as they move a social situation forward into a social interaction.

Attachment theories offer another well-developed area of study with application to sex offenders. Again, the connections between the social world and the psychological development can be seen; however, early research observed rigid boundaries between the disciplines. Many sex offenders studied in treatment settings have been discovered to have significant difficulties in the creation and maintenance of intimate relationships. William Marshall, a researcher and clinical treatment service provider, has done interesting research on the role of what he describes as attachment, intimacy, loneliness, and the etiology and maintenance of sexual offending.[89]

As the theoretical explanations undergo more extensive academic review, it is clear that the boundaries of the psychological and the sociological do not remain so easily divided. Much of the work being done in the field of sex offender studies has developed an integrated model, including theories from psychology and theories from sociology. Attachment theories are certainly an example of a theory moving in that direction. It is helpful to note that, for those new to the field of study, **psychosocial theories** is another term used to reference theories that intentionally include the psychological with the sociological. Psychosocial theories about sexual offending would be centered around the idea that an active interconnection between psychology and sociology produces the characteristics (and, for researchers, the variables) that influence sexual behaviors and therefore inappropriate sexual behaviors. While academic disciplines love to create space between the fields of study, psychosocial theories remind us of the pesky, uncooperative areas of overlap.

Behavioral Theories

The use of classical and operant conditioning as it relates to sexual arousal and sexual offending is primarily connected with the process of reinforcements and punishments. Its application to the field of sexual deviance is attributed to researcher **Gene Abel** in the late 1970s.[90] In short, the focus is on individual behavior and the idea that there is not one identifiable disorder or problem that can explain deviant sexual behaviors. Rather, Abel and his colleagues identified sexually deviant behavior as an expression of other psychological disorders, which can be resolved through behavior therapy. In 1985, **S. C. Wolf** created a multifactor model for deviant sexuality, Cycle of Offending, which outlined a disturbed developmental history, such as physical or emotional abuse, with what he calls **disinhibitors,** which disrupt what would be the normal social controls against sexual deviance. Drugs or alcohol would be an example. Then, he argued that the offender has deviant sexual fantasies. These characteristics work together to generate and maintain an attraction to deviant sexual behaviors.[91] It isn't until something happens in the life of the offender that causes feelings of inadequacies or powerlessness that the offender may work to carry out the opportunity for an encounter and then seek to carry out the abuse. The offender will use distorted thinking to justify the actions.

INTEGRATIVE THEORIES AND MODELS OF SEX OFFENDING[92]

Reflecting a more integrated understanding of various disciplinary perspectives, references in discussions about sex crimes are increasingly referred to as integrated theories. In short, **integrative theories** attempt to expand the coverage of individual theories and offer connecting points between areas of diverse study. Most researchers and treatment practitioners will agree that sex offenders do not become sex offenders because of one specific incident. Increasingly, treatment practitioners attempt to use multifactor models. Several are presented briefly for review and consideration here.

David Finkelhor's Precondition Model (1984)

Commonly referred to as **Finkelhor's precondition theory**, this theory proposed a four-factor model, attempting to integrate various theories about why people initially commit abuse. In his model, he created a framework for thinking about preconditions to sexual abuse. To move into an occasion where one might sexually abuse, an individual must

1. have motivation to sexually abuse,
2. overcome any internal inhibitions against abuse,
3. overcome external factors that may act as inhibitors of abuse, and
4. overcome the child's resistance to the abuse.

Motivation to abuse may come from a variety of thoughts or situations and circumstances. Overcoming internal inhibitions means the offender must be able to rationalize or justify the events of offending to themselves by convincing themselves that what they did was not abusive or that the victim enjoyed the abuse. Overcoming external factors may be finding ways to get a child alone or begin building relationships with the family of the child in order to secure access to the child. Finally, the last step is to overcome the child's resistance to the abuse, which might include emotional manipulation, such as telling them how special they are or warning them not to tell anyone or they will get in trouble.

Marshall and Barbaree's Integrative Theory (1990)

The basic elements of this theory suggest that a connection exists between sex and aggression in males, referencing literature from neuropsychology that suggests that sex and aggression are mediated by similar networks and pathways throughout the body. The theory has been broken down into four basic features:

1. "Biologically endowed propensity for self-interest associated with a tendency to fuse sex and aggression"
2. Childhood experience
3. Sociocultural context
4. Transitory situational factors[93]

This theory suggests that, because men are biologically structured, neurologically wired, and hormonally prescribed to fuse sex and aggression, puberty is an important time to learn to regulate or inhibit this biological tendency, allowing them to interact in more socially acceptable ways and reduce the potentially harmful effects of these biological tendencies. Revisions to the original model, discussed here, were offered in 1999,[94] and in 2000[95] the earlier conceptualization was expanded.

Hall and Hirschman's Quadripartite Model (1991, 1992)

After reviewing the literature, Hall and Hirschman grouped sex-offending characteristics into four motivating factors they believe were significant to the etiology of sex offending:

1. Physiological sexual arousal
2. Cognitive appraisal
3. Affective dyscontrol
4. Personality problems or disorders

These researchers suggested that it is not the deviant sexual arousal alone that motivates deviant sexual behaviors but also how what they refer to as cognitive appraisals of arousal are important. The cognitive appraisal refers to the collective mental processes necessary for understanding emotions and behavior and the prediction of consequences for actions. Individual morality, belief in rape myths, or fear of being punished may be examples of thought processes that will affect the cognitive appraisal.[96] The authors propose that negative feelings of emotional pain, such as anxiety, guilt, and frustration, happen before an offense. These psychological states may act as a sort of push to offend, removing any previous barrier or inhibition to sexually offend. Finally, the issue of personality problems is more deeply steeped into the personality of the offender. A personality disorder is defined by the *DSM-IV* as a "pervasive pattern of 'inner experience and behavior' that is deviant from a person's cultural norms."[97] Once this is decided, then the specific personality disorder that applies must be determined.

Hall and Hirschman then focused on the role of motivation, by identifying four typologies and attempting to explain how they are connected to the four motivating factors outlined above. From a treatment perspective, Hall and Hirschman considered the last typology to be the most difficult to respond to treatment.[98]

Motivation: Sex Offender Typology[99]

1. Physiological sexual arousal characterized by excessive fantasy
2. Display sexual aggression only if it is arousing
3. Cognitive appraisal planning; less deviant arousal
4. Affective dyscontrol impulsive and predatory; unplanned violent and opportunistic
5. Personality problems or disorders; chronic developmental problems
6. Higher levels of general criminal and antisocial behaviors; violent acts

Malamuth's Confluence Model (1996, 1998)

The Malamuth confluence model is based on earlier work by Malamuth, Sockloskie, Koss, and Tanaka (1991); Malamuth, Heavey, and Linz (1993); and Malamuth, Linz, Heavey, Barnes, and Acker (1995)[100] to develop an integrated theory known as the confluence model of sexual aggression. The basic premise is that sexual aggression results from a synergistic confluence of several factors. Taken separately, sexual violence is unlikely, but sexual offending happens when elements within the environment merge. The three factors follow:

1. Promiscuous or impersonal sexual style: An immature or irresponsible approach to sexual activity with a corresponding lack of desire for sexual intimacy or the formation of long-term sexual relationships.
2. Hostile masculinity: A hostile and defensive orientation toward others, especially women, along with a hypersensitivity to perceived rejection and a gratification from achieving domination over women.
3. High-dominance, low-nurturance approach to interpersonal relationships: A personality style that suggests self-interested motives and goals, a lack of compassion or sensitivity, and little concern for harm toward others.

Although support has been offered for this theory since its development, questions have been raised about the reliance on evolutionary theories, its focus on relationships rather than potential individual factors, a concern that other important variables might have been left out, circular reasoning in some aspects of the theory, and a complete reliance on college students for the research studies.

Ward and Seigert's Pathways Model (2002)

The pathways model is focused on a particular type of sex offending: child sexual abuse by adults. Characteristics were integrated from Finkelhor (1984), Marshall and Barbaree (1990), and Hall and Hirschman (1991, 1992) to create four symptom clusters, which were then used to outline five different pathways intended to describe the development of deviant sexual behavior. Brief descriptions of the five pathways follow:

Pathway 1: Intimacy deficits—descriptive of an individual who offends if the preferred sexual partner is unavailable.

Pathway 2: Deviant sexual scripts—descriptive of individuals who have distorted thoughts about the way a sexual encounter might happen, misinterpreting affection or intimacy, even from children, as an interest in sexual activity.

Pathway 3: Emotional dysregulation—problems with emotional regulation create a condition in which an individual is faced with strong negative mood states that they are unable to relieve, so a sex offender might use sex with a child or a victim to restore emotional balance.

Pathway 4: Antisocial cognitions—descriptive of individuals who have attitudes and behaviors supportive of criminal behaviors, who embrace an antisocial lifestyle and have little regard for the emotional and psychological needs of others.

Pathway 5: Multiple dysfunctional mechanisms—descriptive of individuals who demonstrate aspects of the four clusters but with no particular type of problem as the most prominent.

Few studies have been done to fully test the pathways model, but criticism includes assessments of logical inconsistencies, a lack of complete description of the origins of the four clusters, narrow descriptions of the abuser types, incomplete explanations for how one moves from cognition to behavior, and little or no room for the pedophilia classification.

Ward and Beech's (2006) Integrated Theory of Sexual Offending (ITSO)

As efforts to reflect on the integrated theories and multifactor modeling used to expand the breadth and application of theories used to understand and treat sex offenders continue, it is clear that the overall field is in relatively early stages of development as a discipline.

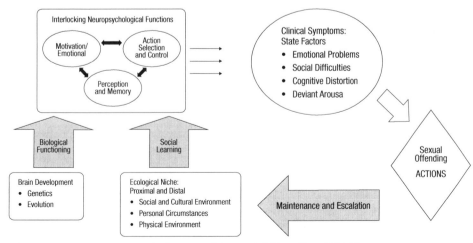

Figure 7.1 An Integrated Theory of Sexual Offending (ITSO)
Ward, T. and A. Beech. "An Integrated Theory of Sexual Offending," *Aggression and Violent Behavior* 11, no. 1, Jan-Feb 2006, 44–63. https://doi.org/10.1016/j.avb.2005.05.002.

Stinson, Sales, and Becker's (2008) Multimodal Self-Regulation Theory: A New Integration

A relatively new theory, outlined in graphic form in Figure 7.2, works to integrate developmental, psychological, and behavioral components in to explain the etiology of sex offending. Focused on what are described as self-regulation deficits emerging from childhood experiences, the authors propose these deficits shape the development of deviant sexual interest and arousal.[101] Integrating "a variety of psychosocial perspectives, drawing from child development theories, emotional and self-regulatory capacities, personality influences, and conditioning paradigms,"[102] the primary driving force is self-regulation.

Researchers and practitioners continue to investigate and examine new ideas for generating better understandings of people who commit sexual harms, looking for ways to enhance current treatment practices. The **Center for Sex Offender Management** serves as a national clearinghouse and technical assistance center to support state and local jurisdictions in the effective management of sex offenders. Although its primary focus is to develop and exchange information about sex-offender management it offers a variety of resources about sex offenders and victimization.

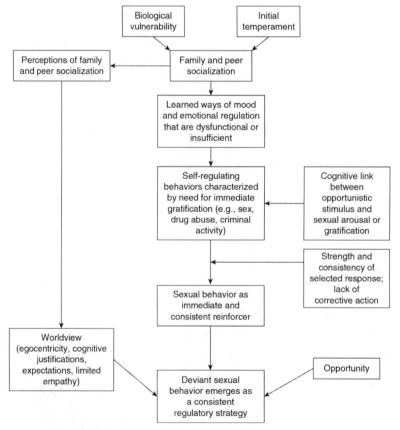

Figure 7.2   Multimodal Self-Regulation Theory

Stinson, Jill D., Judith V. Becker, and Bruce D. Sales. "Self-Regulation and the Etiology of Sexual Deviance: Evaluating Causal Theory." Violence and Victims 23, no. 1 (2008): 35–51. https://doi.org/10.1891/0886-6708.23.1.35.

SOCIOLOGICAL AND CRIMINOLOGICAL
EXPLANATIONS OF SEX-OFFENDING BEHAVIOR

As was the case with early efforts to study human behavior from within the field of psychology, sociologists and criminologists have separated from earlier schools of thought to focus on society and crime, respectively. Remember, efforts to better understand human sexuality, including deviant sexual activities, are evolving as an area of specialization within the medical field and include interdisciplinary approaches to the field of study. Other interdisciplinary studies focused on sex research include sexology. Although various subspecializations have emerged within more traditional disciplines, the focus here is on the theories commonly used to examine and attempt to explain sexual deviance and sex-offending behaviors.

SOCIOLOGICAL THEORIES AND TRADITIONAL CRIME THEORIES

Criminology is a subset of concentrated studies that emerged and later developed from within the larger body of sociological research. Using the sociological lens introduced above provides a window into ways to think about sexual offending. While sociologists as a discipline think more broadly about the institutions of society, criminologists think more specifically about the various aspects of society as they affect causes of and responses to crime. For those new to the study of these areas, this connection sometimes creates what might easily be seen as an overlap in these areas of study. Usually, criminologists study on the etiology of crime and theories to explain crime commission, the criminalization process, and the way the criminal justice system is structured to address issues of public safety as well as any critical reflections about the way the justice system executes these objectives.

In spite of academic evidence, the general population may retain other ideas about these associations. The goal of the social science research process is to help provide evidence for the connections between an idea and a well-supported theory. To take this further, the next level of challenges comes as social scientists work with practitioners to put theories into practice in the real world by creating programs and legislation to affect the kind of social change society supports. Several theories are selected for presentation here because they have been used by researchers in a specific effort to better understand sexual-offending behaviors.

Social learning theory. Perhaps one of the most prominent sociological theories, social learning theories is focused on the work of **Edwin Sutherland**'s work referenced as **differential associations**. Social learning theories suggest that all behavior is learned behavior. Whether one behaves in an extremely religious way or decides to hijack cars, these are learned behaviors. The application of social learning theory to the context of sexual behaviors and sexual offenses begins with the idea that, as humans, we learn to become sexual beings through our social interactions with others. As a result, it can also be argued from this theoretical perspective that sexually inappropriate behaviors are learned behaviors.[103]

Social control theories. Focused in part from the work of Travis Hirschi, instead of asking why people commit crime, social control theorists ask why people obey rules. Applied to sexual offending, theorists have suggested that society has constructed a continuum of sexual behaviors that are considered in society to be appropriate or inappropriate.[104] While the vast majority of people agree informally not to violate these socially proscribed values, Hirschi was curious to explain what role society had in maintaining an influence on people to the degree that they would secure compliance. These theories are dynamically reflective of the individual attitudes about society and the internal assessments of self-worth and connection to others in the community as solid influence on individual behavior. Coupled with this is a strong emphasis on classical theories, suggesting the importance of deterrence as a way to reduce future sex-offending behaviors.[105]

Social reaction theory (also referred to as labeling theory). The social reaction theory asks important questions about how people perceive others and how others see themselves as described by others in society. Once a social infraction is revealed and a person is labeled by others as deviant or even criminal, social reaction theorists argue that the individual is more likely to commit that deviant or criminal action because they have adopted or internalized the negative assessments others expect.

Table 7.7   Becker's Sequential Model of Deviant Behavior

	Obedient Behavior	Rule-Breaking Behavior
Perceived as Deviant	Falsely accused	Pure deviant
Not Perceived as Deviant	Conforming	Secret deviant

Another aspect of social learning theory was presented by Howard Becker (discussed earlier in chapter 2). When you consider, from a criminal justice system perspective, that some offenders are never caught for their sexual inappropriateness or sexual crimes, his conversation about falsely accused, secret deviants is interesting to think about further.[106] In short, people learn to behave in deviant and criminal ways in the same way people learn to comply, by exposure to friends and family and from things they see and hear about from within the larger society.

Rational choice theory. Linked to the early criminal justice theories that suggest that humans act out of free will, are hedonistic, and use reason and rationality as a means for assessing their individual actions, rational choice theory focuses on the idea that humans do not behave in a given way without thinking of the pros and cons and then actively making a choice for themselves. In fact, the criminal justice system is arguably built on the idea of holding people accountable for the decisions they make. The basic question for rational choice theorists is why are some people deterred by the current structure and proposed legal consequences and others are not. Applied generally, rational choice theory assumes that someone who takes a specific action has thought about that action and the consequences of that action and then chooses to do it anyway. Applied to sexual offending, an offender knows what they are doing is wrong; they assess the situation. They assess their likelihood of getting caught as being low, so they choose to commit a sexual assault because they make that deliberate choice.

Routine activities theory. Unlike most social theories, which focus on the individual, routine activities is focused more on the social environment in which an offender experiences the world. Linked with studies on crime prevention, the focus is centered on three things, referred to as the "crime triangle," which must be present at the same time in order for a crime to happen: a motivated offender, a suitable victim, and the absence of a likely intervening agent to prevent the event from happening. Offenders seek out places where their abusive patterns and practices might be easily conducted within opportunities, either accidental or actively solicited by the offender. Because so many events of child sexual abuse happen when offenders have unregulated access to children, places where children are become attractive occupational options for people who have a sexual interest in children. These also, as suggested by the crime prevention research, become places where options to intervene in the crime triangle are likely to provide reduction in abuse events.[107]

CRITICAL AND FEMINIST CRIMINOLOGY THEORIES: A CONTEMPORARY SHIFT IN FOCUS

Feminist criminological theories on sexual violence emerged in the United States in the 1960s, similarly asking questions about the role social systems and structures play on broader social understandings of sexualized harms. The feminist perspective is a critique of the mainstream, which some scholars refer to as the "male-stream," perspective[108] of the day, which is argued to be narrowly focused in a patriarchal worldview. The feminist perspective takes a structural perspective, with a great deal of the focus centered on the violence men perpetrate against women; initially, the focus was most particularly on rape. The focus was in demonstrating a cultural and historical oppression of women by men, using varying degrees of sexual violence based on gender. Susan Brownmiller's work *Against Our Will: Men, Women and Rape* (1975) suggests that the silence found around the topic of intrafamilial sexual abuse of children is rooted in sexual private property, which determined male attitudes toward rape, suggesting that women were private property and children were "a wholly owned subsidiary."[109]

For some who might oppose the feminist way of framing the conversation about sexual violence, the research seemed to be bearing out the idea first presented by the feminist critique of the traditional ways sexual and gender violence was assessed. And that basic shift in thinking is what is becoming increasingly evident in research and in real experiences of women's lives; the majority of violence doesn't come from a few "sexually violent" men but, rather, from a large number of men, mostly at the hands of people they know, including intimate partners, friends, and acquaintances.

Certainly women writers and scholars are not the only people asking questions about how the systems in the United States are discussing issues affecting women. Critical criminology is, like the feminist social critique, focused around an evaluation of the influence of larger social systems and the idea that long-standing social issues and concerns are steeped in cultural and social traditions about the larger aspects of society, including social systems and institutionalized violence and harm, and less about the individuals, highlighting the role culture serves as a significant influencing factor for shaping individual attitudes and beliefs.

DISTINGUISHING PERSONAL CHARACTERISTICS AND ROLES FROM BEHAVIORS

Because pedophiles and child molesters come from all walks of life, few common characteristics can be associated with people who sexually abuse children. As has been stated, the nature of sex offender behaviors is **heterogeneous**, very different between offenders, making it difficult (if not impossible) to create a generalized description of "a sex offender." Even though there is not one "type" of child molester, two common characteristics do stand out: child sexual abusers are predominately male and, most often, heterosexual. Current studies report that 95 percent[110] or 96 percent[111] of adults who sexually abuse children are male. Most child sexual abusers identify as straight in their consensual sexual acts.[112] All of the medical charts of sexually abused children seen in a Denver children's hospital during one year (July 1, 1991–June 30, 1992) were reviewed to see if a connection exists between sexual identity of the offender and the abuse of a child. In Dr. Carole Jenny's work, 352 medical charts were reviewed, and it was reported that the molester was a gay or lesbian adult in only two of the 269 cases in which the adult molester was identified. This worked out to less than 1 percent of the total cases[113] and disputes a common myth about the sexual orientation of those who commit a sexual offense against a child.

Focusing on the behavior of an individual, rather than the role or reason a person is around children, becomes a critically important distinction. When it comes to protecting children, it is important to focus on the way a child's boundaries might be tested and broken. A group leader of a youth service organization might be known by many people in the community, but blending in becomes more difficult if people do not make assumptions about that leader's place in the community, instead making note of inappropriate interactions. Children also need to be educated about the differences between appropriate and inappropriate exchanges, but we must always remember that it is up to adults to keep children safe. The goal is to make sure that inappropriate behaviors stand out so the "blending in" necessary for hiding abuse becomes less possible.

If a well-meaning adult is violating a child's physical boundaries (holding them down and tickling them despite the child's asking them to stop) and someone intervenes in a nonshaming way, it is very easy for the well-meaning adult to change their behavior. If, on the other hand, the adult is tickling the child and ignoring the pleas to stop as a way of testing the child's physical boundaries and someone steps in, that adult will learn their behavior is being monitored in the community. In both examples, the same response, explaining to an adult how certain behavior is not acceptable, can be received differently depending on the intention of the person pushing the child's boundaries. But, in both cases, the intervention is important for several reasons. First, the ultimate goal to stop the behavior is met; second, the inappropriate adult will learn people are watching; and, third, the child will learn they can say no and be heard in addition to getting a better sense of whom they can trust to hear them and whom they might want to avoid.

OFFENDER BEHAVIORS AND CHARACTERISTICS

What is known about people who sexually abuse children? The fact that individuals are known to be heterogeneous, or diverse, means it is hard to create a list of factors that apply to every offender. Here is a combination of what is generally agreed upon: child sexual abusers comprise a heterogeneous population and are mostly men with the following characteristics:

- Poor social skills
- Low self-esteem
- Feelings of inadequacy
- Sense of worthlessness and vulnerability
- Experience hindrances to normal adult relationships or previous frustrations with adult relationships
- See themselves as physically unattractive
- Problems with potency
- Feelings of humiliation and loneliness

Nonviolent child molesters coax, trick, or pressure a child into sexual activities.[114] Violent child molesters or rapists overpower and threaten their victims. A child molester may be a significantly older individual who *engages* in any type of sexual activity with individuals legally defined as children.[115] Again, the primary differences between a child molester and a pedophile are their actions. A child molester has touched a child inappropriately. A pedophile is a person who prefers to have sex with children. A pedophile may never act on their fantasies and, as a result, may never have sexually harmed a child, but a pedophile may also be sexually involved with an adult or might even be married. The thing that makes them a pedophile is the diagnosis. Studies vary on the marital status of pedophiles. Some prefer sex with adults but have sex with children because they are more vulnerable, and some have sex with an adult (a single mom, as an example) as a means to getting closer to children.[116]

It is impossible to know how many people have sexual fantasies about children and would prefer to have sex with children but simply do not. These people could be classified or diagnosed as pedophiles, although they will likely never be detected, unless they commit an offense against a child and are caught. Some additional terms related to this area include a **pederast**, or someone who commits sodomy (anal penetration) on a boy, usually refers to an adult male who sexually assaults a young boy.[117]

Although using the correct terminology for a certain behavior or diagnosis may not seem to be a solid step toward prevention at first glance, educated language can help shape educated dialogue. The confusion around the topic of child molestation is reflected in the confusion around the terms used to talk about those who hurt children or are attracted to children. The term **pedophile** does not describe all individuals convicted of a sex crime against a child, although it is often overused in the media and by concerned community members as a term to refer to people who sexually abuse a child. This can be an incorrect usage of the term.

Not all pedophiles act on their urges, so it is possible to be diagnosed as a pedophile and to never have offended against a child. Conversely, **child molestation** is a *behavior* and not a psychological diagnosis. A person who sexually abuses a child is deemed a child molester because of the demonstrated behavior. If the abuse was not due to sexual attraction but rather came out of a need for power and control, for example, the offending individual will *not* be considered a pedophile. Pedophilia is said, in the Western presentations of history, to have existed since Ancient Greece. During the Renaissance, prostitution involving young children was considered common fare. In 1898, Richard von Krafft-Ebing coined the term **pedophilia erotica**, defining it as "a morbid disposition, a psychosexual perversion, in which a sexually needy person is drawn to children."[118] In short, pedophiles are people who have a sexual interest in children. **Pederasty** refers to males over the age of 18 who are sexually attracted to and involved with young boys between the ages of 12 and 16. A pedophile is attracted to prepubescent children, and a **hebephile** is attracted to children who are postpubescent, or have gone through puberty. Through the National Center for Missing and Exploited Children (NCMEC), **Kenneth Lanning** has been developing a typological means by which to present seven patterns of behavior (rather than using psychological classifications or mental health diagnoses) to describe a child molester.

As the work continued, Lanning suggested, through his revised typology (Figure 7.3), the need to represent choices from along the lines of a continuum because the motivation (between situational and preferential) usually lies along a range, not as a static choice between two categories.

SEX-OFFENDING PATTERNS

Convicted sex offenders will admit that they identify a person as a target and increasingly exploit tickling or other "accidental" touching as a means to gain the child's trust. They demonstrate planning and awareness of the potential trouble by telling their partner, for example, there was a misunderstanding with this girl who might have taken something the wrong way, so the wife will assume innocence and possibly offer cover for the offender if the child confronts the offender.[119] Perhaps they tell the child no one will believe them and use threats to intimidate the victim.[120] It might not seem unusual for a teacher to take a group of kids out on a field trip or for a scout leader to take a group of kids on an overnight camping trip. These kinds of relationships, teacher and student, priest and altar boy, or boy scout leader and cub scout, are normal, natural experiences and offer young people opportunities for healthy experiences and skill-building sets. What becomes worthy of note is if one child is singled out, invited to more events, asked to stay late or overnight, or is inappropriately offered alcohol.

One of the most important terms for those interested in learning more about sex offenders is the term *grooming*. Grooming, mentioned earlier, is the

Motivation Continuum	
Biological/Physiological Sexual Needs	Psychosexual/Deviant
|============|============|============|============|============|============|	
Power/Anger Nonsexual Needs	Sexual Needs
(Not one or the other, but a continuum)	
Situational Sex Offender: (>More Likely)	**Preferential Sex Offender**: (>More Likely)
Less Intelligent	More Intelligent
Lower Socioeconomic Status	Higher Socioeconomic Status
Personality Disorders Such As	Paraphilias Such As
■ Antisocial/Psychopathy	■ Pedophilia
■ Narcissistic	■ Voyeurism
■ Schizoid	■ Sadism
Varied Criminal Behavior	Focused Criminal Behavior
Violent Pornography	Theme Pornography
Impulsive	Compulsive
Considers Risk	Considers Need
Sloppy Mistakes	Needy Mistakes
Thought-Driven	Fantasy-Driven
Spontaneous or Planned	Scripted
■ Availability	■ Audition
■ Opportunity	■ Rehearsal
■ Tools	■ Props
■ Learning	■ Critique
Method of Operation (MO) Patterns of Behavior	Ritual Patterns of Behavior
■ Works	■ Need
■ Dynamic	■ Static

Figure 7.3 Lanning's Motivation Continuum

Lanning, Kenneth V. "Child Molesters: A Behavioral Analysis, 5th Edition." National Center for Missing & Exploited Children, 2010; printed with permission from the National Center for Missing & Exploited Children

process of connecting with a person in an effort to assess how vulnerable they are to being pressured into or forced into a sexual relationship. The target is often a child or a young person but might also involve an adult. Groomers don't just groom their target; they also groom the target's family and the greater community. Some sex offenders have been known to date women who are single moms so they can help with the children, gaining access to the children for sexual purposes. The entire process of dating the mom, meeting the children, setting up a relationship as an interested adult, and attempting to gain the trust of the child is all part of the grooming process the individual orchestrates to gain access to future victims.

Seduction is another term worth highlighting. Seduction is a term used to refer to actions taken with the intention of encouraging someone to participate in a sexual encounter. Some sex offenders, however, can be known to suffer from cognitive distortions, or distorted thought processes, and as a result will convince themselves the victim, even if a small child, is an active and willing participant in the movement toward a sexual encounter. As an example, a healthy grandfather would easily hoist up their grandchild on their knee and think nothing of the encounter, except that the child wanted to be close to the grandpa for a hug. A person who suffers from cognitive distortion may see the child coming to sit on their lap as an indication from the child that they want to have sex with the grandfather. (More about these kinds of cognitive distortions is discussed in chapter 13, on treatment.)

Interestingly, most people who think and talk openly and publicly about sex offenders are unrelated to the field of sex offender studies and can easily be swept up in the socially popular idea that a sex offender is a creepy old man in a raincoat, someone unknown to them, or someone who might be easily identified as a sex offender because of how they look. Advocates, practitioners, and researchers alike are almost universal in their condemnation of these false ideas and work to educate the larger society about some of the incorrect assessments in the general public about sex offenders. In truth, just about every aspect of this notion has been challenged as false. As was discussed in chapter 3, sex offenders are *not* usually strangers to the victim. Of course, this cannot be said with 100 percent accuracy because there are a small percentage of stranger abductions. Further, it is apparent to anyone who has taken the time to look at sex offender registries in their state or in states across the country that offenders range in age, gender, occupation, class, race, education levels, number of offenses, types of offenses committed, and types of victim preferences. Remember, too, that there is no really clear understanding of how the sex offenders who are caught, as reflected by those state department sex offender registries, differ from the sex offenders who remain unknown to the police and other agents of the justice system. As a consequence it is difficult to know how well the offenders profiled in the registries reflect the larger unknown population of people who have committed sex offenses but have not been caught and/or convicted of the offense.

A child molester, whether they have been diagnosed as a pedophile or they are focused on power and control, may believe a child is attempting to seduce the adult. They see actions taken by the child as an indicator that the child has a sexual interest in the child molester. These kinds of distorted thoughts can become a part of the grooming process. There may be touching, tickle fights, and general horseplay, but, as part of the grooming process, this play goes too far and becomes sexualized for the offender; then, the events are used to condition the child toward more and more overtly sexualized kinds of interactions. Offenders are notorious for using these kinds of tactics to see how the child responds and, more importantly, whether they, the child molester, can take their desires to the next level. If a child resists, shows a lack of interest, or has a strong understanding of body boundaries, an offender might go looking for another young person who does not raise objections.

The idea of **luring** is important because it is not uncommon for a child molester or other individual to offer enticements in an effort to gain favor with their intended victim. This can happen with children, as in the case where a child might be lured into a car with candy or invited to see a puppy. It can also happen with adults. In some cases, the lure is the potential relationship. A person may be invited to a bar under the pretense of getting to know each other better, but, then when they are not looking, their date puts a drug in their drink and they become the victim of a discretely planned sexual assault. The most common lure is attention and affection.

After giving attention to the kinds of techniques offenders use, it is important to understand that these actions are a planned series of "multideterminant decisions."[121] In combining thoughts, feelings, and behaviors, the **offense cycle** describes the outcomes of these interactions.[122] Offenders use cognitive distortions to neutralize feelings of accountability, guilt, or shame, and researchers suggest that an understanding of the cognitive processes underlying the initiation, maintenance, and justification of sexual offending is vital for understanding treatment efforts,[123] although the altered thought processes required to act on feelings can vary in type and intensity.

FOCUS ON THE BEHAVIORS, *NOT* ON THE SOCIAL RELATIONSHIP

The term **sex offender** is commonly used to describe a person who has been convicted of committing any sex crime, whether a consensual statutory offense or a child abduction, sexual assault, or murder. In this context, the sex offender term is used to refer to a wide range of sexual behaviors identified as crimes. These examples represent how different offenders are and some of the perils that come from lumping different sex offenders into such a large generic term. One effort to address the disparity in the use of this generic term is the increased use of the term **sexual predator**. Although statements about what is known about offenders can be misleading, popular culture meets social science research in various ways as increasing efforts are made to understand the issues associated with sexual violence in US culture. Consider the following from *The Guardian* online:

> We actually know quite a bit about why men rape, and especially about the kinds of rapes that the media often calls "date rape" or "acquaintance rape"— rapes where the perpetrator knew the victim, or at least ran in the same social circles. Academics, researchers and sociologists have done in-depth studies on sexual assault and found that it's actually a small number of men who commit large numbers of acquaintance rapes. Most of those men intentionally target intoxicated women. They socially isolate them, ply them with alcohol to incapacitate them and intentionally push their boundaries to make them vulnerable. These repeat rapists are more likely to have rigid views of gender roles and are more angry at women than the non-rapist men. They perpetrate their crimes intentionally, but use our social narratives about rape to avoid prosecution. "These are clearly not individuals who are simply in need of a little extra education about proper communication with the opposite sex," says David Lisak. "These are predators."[124]

Sexual predator is also a term used to describe a sex offender; this term is used in legal situations, for example, in chapter 6, under discussions of who is reported on the sex offender registry, those persons who commit a crime that meets the legal definition of a **sexually violent person** or **sexually dangerous person**. Unfortunately, as is the case with the term *pedophile*, this term is often used generically to describe a person who has committed a sex offense, rather than being used to more accurately reflect a sex offender who has committed a crime for which community notification rules apply, as in this example. Another term, **sexually violent predator,** is also used with the intent to implement a legal definition or offer a more accurate definition of a person who commits a violent sexual act for which community notification rules apply and civil commitment considerations might be implemented within the Department of Corrections prior to the scheduled release of a designated sex offender back into the community. (More information about civil commitment and correctional management of sex offenders is offered in chapter 12.) The different classifications and the differential use of terms between and among those studying sex offenders are points of importance because, when the term "sex offender" is used broadly to refer to a vast array of criminal offenders, the nuances of each type of offender get lost.

SYSTEMS, INSTITUTIONS, AND SEXUAL ABUSE

Clergy abuse, abuse in families, and the number of cases of abuse by teachers, coaches, and trusted adults increasingly invite more focused attention regarding the occurrence of sexual abuse.

> Abuse of minors is most common in families and institutions where adults form mentoring and nurturing relationships with adolescents, including schools, religious organizations, sports and social organizations. Sexual assaults are most common among acquaintances, within relationships, in situations where there is an unequal power relationship (for example, abuse by a psychologist or a professor), or in closed institutions such as the military or prisons.[125]

In large part, perhaps because of myths suggesting offenders are more likely to be strangers, systems often overlooked in the traditional quest for "sex offenders" include schools, childcare settings (including after-school care programs and mentor programs), athletic organizations, religious institutions, prisons, and the military. Other analysis could include families, the film industry, colleges and higher educational institutions, and elderly care facilities. All of these systems meet the characteristics described above.

These institutional settings offer unique sets of conditions for the astute social observer to make note of as they review people and processes in place in these social settings when abuse happens. How does sexual abuse happen in so many public places and in so many different places in any given community without people who see people involved in abuse regularly, perhaps even every day? The name Larry Nassar, a world-renowned sports physician, became famous outside the world of gymnastics when allegations were made, followed by a very public trial accusing him of sexual abuse by several women and being sentenced to 175 years in prison.

The state of Pennsylvania conducted a grand jury review of the files of approximately 400 priests who had been credibly accused of sexual abuse, which was hidden in secret files in the archdiocese throughout Pennsylvania.[126] The issue of sexual abuse in the military has been a long-standing concern, particularly for women, but the stories of sexual assault, although seldom reported, also involve men. The stories of sexual abuse of soldiers by fellow soldiers suggest that a woman is more likely to be raped in combat by one of her fellow soldiers than she is to be injured in the line of duty.

Further, because sex offenders are seen to be so vilified in the general public, attention is given to the "prison justice" often expected to be meted out at the hands of fellow inmates should they find out the reason the offender has been incarcerated. In the days prior to former Penn State football coach Jerry Sandusky's very public trial and sentencing, the internet was filled with stories about people actively wishing Sandusky would "get his" in prison.[127] But rape in prison is illegal, just as it is outside of a prison setting.

A closer look at the institutional settings where abuse has been reported with some repetition expands and extends the focus to environmental factors and processes. This work has taken research in a new direction and invites public education and awareness on a whole new level. The shocking realization that sexual abuse, particularly child sexual abuse, has happened in places such as churches and schools, which we thought would be safe, warrants a closer look. Although the information presented here is only a brief introduction, attention is given to abuses in the Catholic Church, prison settings, and the military and closes with a brief discussion of systems and structures where abuse happens in places closer to home.

SEXUAL ABUSE IN RELIGIOUS INSTITUTIONS

Some might argue that the issue of abuse in the Catholic Church in the United States and around the world ushered[128] in a new era of attention and awareness on the subject of child sexual abuse. Sadly, the interest was not for their efforts to protect child victims of abuse but for their efforts to ignore or cover up abuse by priests. While the conversation about religious abuse has centered on the Catholic Church, other denominations have also been implicated in systems where children are sexually abused by religious leaders.[129]

Referring back, again, to the issue of data collection and research methods and the incomplete information collected on studies in social life, it is important to understand that the lack of research on religions, such as Scientology and Islam, does not suggest there is no abuse; rather, it suggests that these religions have not been studied.[130] Researcher, scholar, and author Karen Terry,[131] who has conducted research on the Catholic Church,[132] was involved in two recent projects sponsored by the United States Conference of Catholic Bishops: "The Nature and Scope of the Problem of Sexual Abuse of Minors by Catholic Priests and Deacons in the United States" and "The Causes and Context of Sexual Abuse of Minors by Catholic Priests in the United States, 1950–2010."[133] See the findings of each briefly highlighted in Table 7.9.

Table 7.8   Infamous Religious Abuse Cases in the United States

Year	Person	Location	Known Victims	Case Outcome
1981	Donald Roemer	Los Angeles	Convicted for 1	No prison; state mental hospital
1983	Gilbert Gauthe	Lafayette, LA	Dozens of boys	Served less than 10 years
1993	James Porter	Boston Area	100+ boys and girls	Sentenced 18-20 years
2002	John Goeghan	Boston, MA	130+	Killed in prison (2003)
2006–2013	Donald McGuire	Chicago, IL	Convicted for 1	25 years in prison (2009)
			Civil suit 6 men	$19.6 million settlement (2013)
		Madison, WI	Convicted for 2	Sentenced to 7 years but free on cases from 1960s appeal (2006)

1 McGuire conviction upheld on appeal in 2009. $19.6 million settlement involving 6 victims from the Chicago Province for the Society of Jesus.

Table 7.9   The Scope of Sexual Abuse in the Roman Catholic Church[1]

The Nature and Scope Study: Summary of Findings

The results of the Nature and Scope study showed that the total number of priests with allegations from 1950 to 2002 was 4,392, which was equivalent to 4 percent of priests in the ministry during that time. The number of individuals who made allegations of sexual abuse was 10,667. Abuse incidents peaked in the 1970s and early 1980s. This distribution was consistent across all regions of the Catholic Church in the United States as well as in all sizes of dioceses.

The study's goal: To determine the extent of the sexual abuse of minors by Catholic priests nationally from 1950 to 2002.

Information was compiled from:

- Data pertaining to offenses
- Data pertaining to abusers
- Data pertaining to victims
- Financial impact of the abuse crisis

The Causes and Context Study: Summary of Findings

"The abuse crisis was caused by a complex interaction of psychological, developmental, organizational, cultural, and situational factors. There was no single identifiable cause of the crisis, and no specific 'high risk' characteristics to help identify potential abusers. As with nonclergy sex offenders, priests with allegations of abuse who sexually abused minors constitute a heterogeneous population and very few were 'specialists' who sought out a particular type of victim (in regard to age/gender)."[2]

The study's goal: To explain what factors were associated with the abuse crisis and why there was a surge in abuse incidents in the 1970s and early 1980s.

Data came from:

- Existing longitudinal data sets
- Seminary documents
- Surveys of various groups within the Catholic Church
- Primary data
- Clinical data

1 Karen J. Terry, "Stained Glass: The Nature and Scope of Child Sexual Abuse in the Catholic Church," *Criminal Justice and Behavior* 35, no. 5 (2008): 549–69; see also Karen J. Terry, *Sexual Offenses and Offenders: Theory, Practice and Policy*, 2nd ed. (Belmont, CA: Wadsworth Cengage Learning, 2013).
2 Terry, *Sexual Offenses and Offenders*, 176.

SEXUAL ABUSE IN PRISON

Like other forms of sexual abuse, sexual abuse in prison can have serious physical, emotional, psychological, and behavioral consequences for the victim. As is the case with other forms of sexual assault, most of the information known about sexual assaults in prison comes from self-reported information. It is believed that both consensual and nonconsensual sex happen in prison, although it is not known how many sexual acts go unreported, at least in part, because sex is not legal in most prison settings.[134] The decision to report sexual acts is left up to the discretion of the prison guards; however, many agree that most reports come in for what is believed to be nonconsensual sex and, in fact, some of the allegations are against the guards and prison personnel.[135] Unfortunately, research on this area of sexual assault and violence is not very well known, and, after research has been done, often the conclusions are contradictory. For example, the book *The Myth of Prison Rape* suggests that the actual occurrence of sexual abuse was highlighted, reported, and elevated by advocacy groups, creating a sort of moral panic,[136] and other studies suggest that sexual assault rates in prison are high and inmates can expect to be the victim of multiple attacks by a variety of assailants.[137] Focus on the individual perpetrators and victims has produced prison research.

Further, the systemic analysis also offers interesting possibilities for exploring the relationship between historical social and sexualized abuses and sexualized violence in prison, suggesting, for example, that prison rape can be seen as a legacy of slavery and the lynch mob.[138]

SEXUAL ABUSE IN THE MILITARY

The award-winning documentary *Invisible War* outlines the dramatic amount of sexual assault in the military, attempting to expose a system-wide tolerance for the rape and sexual assault of female recruits and service members. As many as 500,000 women are believed to have been assaulted while actively in military service. The film highlights the lack of support and resources for these women, and men, and overviews a system in which women are often blamed for the assault and denied medical care and, sometimes, punished and demoted in rank if they file a claim. One theme that was presented repeatedly was the fact that single women were charged with adultery when they were raped by men who were married. Charges were filed against women who reported rape, but no charges were filed against the perpetrators. Discussion also centered around the incidents of male sexual assault. Because of the significantly higher numbers of men in the military, the numbers of sexual assault of men is likely to be even greater than the number of women, although these victimizations are seldom reported. Estimates suggest that 1 percent of males had been victims of sexual assault, which equals about 20,000 annually.[139]

Of the several critical issues raised in the film, experts describe the way the closed system of the military and the centralized command structure produce "a target rich environment for a predator"[140] and one that protects command. Further attention was given to the fact that the military attracts physically

---

Text Box 7.1.   Sexual Abuse in the Military: A Survey of Several Scandals

1991	Tailhook Scandal—Navy
1996	Aberdeen Proving Ground—Army
2003	Airforce Academy
2003–2004	Abu Ghraib Prison
2012	Marine Barracks, Washington, DC
2018	Inspector General Report: VA mishandled approximately 1,300 sexual trauma claims of the 12,000 sexual trauma benefits filed each year.

---

violent and aggressive men. In fact, a navy study found that 15 percent of incoming recruits had attempted or committed rape before entering the military, which represents a number twice the equivalent of the civilian population.[141]

In August 2013, after an increase in the number of assaults and a series of high-profile sexual allegations, Secretary of Defense Chuck Hagel ordered the military to screen employees for proper credentials, resulting in five dismissals and 55 suspensions.[142] In June, figures for 2012 estimated 26,000 service members were sexually assaulted, up from 19,000 in 2011.[143] Victims reported 3,374 incidents in 2012, and there were 238 convictions of those cases.[144] Broader research shows ranges from approximately 10 to 43 percent of women serving in the military report experiencing an attempted or a completed rape.[145] After these service officers leave the military, they can carry the consequences of their abuse with them into their civilian life.[146] Further, and of greater concern for sexual violence prevention efforts, is the fact that the people who perpetrate rape in military organizations, when discharged, are back in civilian communities. In review of the Department of Defense's Fiscal Year 2012 report, Senator Barbara Boxer of California famously suggested that such a large disparity between the estimated assaults, the assaults reported, and the numbers of convictions "means there are thousands of felons walking around—free and dangerous—in the military today."[147] Further questions remain about the degrees to which any predatory sexual behaviors continue when soldiers return to civilian communities and whether the military as a system, which promulgates images and narratives of sexual exploitation, violent sexuality, and female subordination, has in fact "helped to sustain a legal culture that reifies the connection between sexual violence and authentic soldiering."[148]

SEXUAL ABUSE IN SYSTEMS CLOSER TO HOME

The statistics showing how many people who are harmed by sexual violence actually know their perpetrator should give everyone pause. People might forget, but the family is a social institution. Schools, healthcare systems, athletics, after-school programs, and faith communities are foundational social systems many of us belong to and participate in regularly. How could abuse persist across all of these systems, and what can be done about it? Most people do not want to believe sexual abuse can be committed by someone they know or who knows their children, particularly by someone they trust to care for them. Abuse within family systems was discussed in chapters 3 and 6 and documents a stark reality. The horrible stories of incidents and/or long-standing abuses have been discovered in schools at all levels, from elementary schools through higher education, and, when these incidents occur, it seems they always take people by surprise. Outrage erupts. People are shocked.

Researchers are increasingly looking at social systems to assess how abuse might be better understood and how those systems might better structure themselves to protect against abuse events. Consider also at least two studies that have found domestic violence to be two to four times as prevalent in police officer families as it is in the general population.[149] When this is contrasted to the general population, the findings suggest that 40 percent of police officer families experience domestic violence, compared with 10 percent of families in the general population.[150] Given the role of police in the process of sexual assault prosecution, the relationship is important to explore more fully. Domestic violence, as in the case of discussing incest abusers, is often discussed differently and sometimes separately from other classes or types of sex offenses. As conversations about sex offenders continue, it is important to reflect on the system's procedural decisions to treat perpetrators of family violence differently from perpetrators of stranger sexual violence.

When considerations are given to the social systems and structures where abuse is commonly found, it is important to remember that most people do not commit sexual harm. Most teachers, for example, are highly qualified professionals who do great work and take good care of children. The persistence of these types of sexual offending behaviors is what has research on sex-offender theories expanding out into various systems and structures.

CHAPTER CONCLUSION

Much has been written throughout this text, and in society more broadly, about the shock and surprise that comes with allegations of sexual abuse and harm. Attention was given here to the early typologies created by researchers interested in better understanding what makes a person act against another person in a sexual way. Brief attention was provided to young offenders and female offenders after discussing the largest group of offenders, adult men. A description of theories, from criminal justice as well as professionals studying sex offenders specifically, was presented for review. The chapter closed with a review of social systems that are increasingly being referred to as places where sexual violence happens and is either ignored or denied, leaving those who study sex offenses and offenders wondering what can be done to prevent these harms if the option of studying them fully and where they happen is disabled by a lack of understanding. When these events happen, people are harmed whether or not a criminal justice response is initiated. Therefore, a review of circumstances and conditions surrounding incidents where abuse has been reported is discussed briefly in these theoretical applications.

Text Box 7.2.   Media Messages about Offenders: What Information about Sex Offenders Needs to Be Reclaimed or Reconsidered?

Fact: Generally, whether child sexual abuse or violence between adults, the offender is more often than not known to the victim. Stranger abductions do happen, but, as has been emphasized throughout the text, they are very rare.

Application: Knowing that a person is more likely to be injured by someone known to them and placing the blame for any possible offense on the perpetrator of that harm, not the victim, how might a group of college students use that information to elevate the safety of the people in their group if they were to go to a party on campus?

Fact: Researchers know perpetrators of sexual violence come from all sections of social groups, economic classes, and age categories.

Application: What is the best way to demonstrate an awareness of this reality in everyday life?

Fact: A content analysis of 323 *LA Times* articles published between 1990 and 2015 examined how stories in that paper represented victims and offenders of sexual violence. Findings suggested that terms and descriptions of the violence were used to justify retribution or harsh legal punishments, while adult victims, mostly women, were framed as responsible for their own victimization while also minimizing their importance as compared to child victims.[1]

Application: What recommendations would you make to people covering issues of sexual violence so that the coverage of those incidents reflects more of a reality of the offenses and offenders and victimization patterns, rather than playing into a narrow narrative about perpetrators and victims that leaves everyone less informed about the realities of sexual violence and harm?

What ideas and/or information do you bring to this conversation about sex offenders and people who have harmed other people in a sexualized way?

After considering the material presented in chapter 7 on offenders, what information from the media do you see requiring additional and particular focus for calling out inaccuracies?

What other facts that you are learning require adjustments to what you believed in the past about people who have committed sexual offenses?

Note

1. Rebecca A. DiBennardo, "Ideal Victims and Monstrous Offenders: How the News Media Represent Sexual Predators," *Socius: Sociological Research for a Dynamic World* 4 (October 5, 2018), https://doi.org/10.1177/2378023118802512.

The ongoing need to actively identify and assess the relationship between sexualized violence that happens in intimate relationships, in families, and in communities and at the hand of a stranger requires the collective ability of social scientists and practitioners to study the harm and create possible responsive alternatives that could prevent future harm. This is the primary focus of the theoretical work. How do researchers and practitioners better understand sexual-offending behaviors and their patterns, both as individuals and within society, and how can that collection of information be put together in a way that helps protect people from future harms? These questions are the heart of the chapter focus.

KEY TERMS

anger rapist
attachment theories
Center for Sex Offender Management
child molestation
child molesters
cognitive behavioral theories
cognitive distortions
critical criminology
Diagnostic and Statistical Manual of Mental Disorders (DSM)
differential associations
disinhibitors
Edwin Sutherland
endemic
epidemic
etiology
feminist criminology
Finkelhor's precondition theory
fixated child sexual abusers
Gene Abel
grooming
hebephile
heterogenous
integrative theories
interactionist
International Classification of Diseases (ICD)
Kenneth Lanning
kink
luring
macro theories
micro theories
Nicholas Groth
offense cycle

other specified paraphilic disorder
paraphilia
paraphilias not otherwise specified (NOS)
paraphilic disorders
peacemaking criminology
pederast
pederasty
pedophile
pedophilia
pedophilia erotica
personality theories
power rapist
psychosexual histories
psychosocial theories
public health issue
regressed child sexual abuser
S. C. Wolf
sadistic rapist
seduction
sex offender
sexual predator
sexually dangerous person
sexually violent person
sexually violent predator
situational sex offender
social control theories
social information processing dysfunction
social learning theory
static information
treatment practitioners
typologies
unspecified paraphilic disorder

REVIEW QUESTIONS

1. Clarify the distinctions between focusing on micro and macro perspectives.

2. Clearly delineate the difference between a clinical diagnosis and a legal definition.

3. List the effect of the fact that early studies, laws, and assault classifications were focused explicitly on male offenders and female victims.

4. What are the internal categories of the power and anger rapist, according to Goth et al.?

5. List at least three examples of integrative theories of sex-offending behaviors. Be prepared to discuss of their differences.

DISCUSSION QUESTIONS

1. Giving consideration to the theories used to describe people who commit sexual offenses requires thinking about the frames each individual carries and whether a researcher sees the elements of social theory from a more traditional analytical understanding or what is being referred to more collectively as a feminist analytical research design. Give this some attention. What have you and your friends come to think you know or understand about sex offenders or victims of sexual assault up to this point? It is not at all unusual to have a variety of frames of reference for a given subject, all of which are professing a particular "truth" and various challenges to the "truth" as it is presented by other frames, fields, and disciplines. Attempts have been made to offer several frames throughout this book, various ways to think about healthy sex, deviance, attention to victims, (chapter 14), and prevention (chapter 15), as examples. Consider the following: "Anyone who wears something like that out to the bar has to know she's asking for trouble" or "What was she expecting, after she was drinking like that?"

    Both of these ideas can be framed differently by asking "Why would anyone think that what a woman wears is at all related to the actions taken by another person, including the possibility of a sexual assault?" Or, in the second example, consider asking a person "Doesn't everyone know to avoid a sexual situation with a person who cannot give consent?" It is not uncommon to hear people ask "Why do women stay in a relationship after being hit or beaten by an intimate partner?" But the same question could be reframed to ask "Why do men hit women whom they claim to love?" In either case, the frame of reference a person carries with them into this conversation will likely dictate how these questions or related issues come up in the person's mind as they reflect on these questions. As the exploration of theory and sex offender etiology begins, it is essential to understand the frame each of us carries into the conversation. The goal is not to attempt to change any given individual's frame of reference but rather to help us understand what perspective we bring to the review of the material.

2. Consider the vast array of offender typologies offered here. How does one best make sense of these typologies, and how does understanding the typology help you understand the individual offender and the larger collective classification of "sex offenders." Why did the authors suggest that calling people "sex offenders" can be confusing? What benefit comes from referring to a person who committed a crime as a more specific action?

3. What are the implications for considering the theories focused on the individual offender and the theories that are focused on larger social and cultural attitudes and conditions?

4. Why do the authors suggest that it is important for individuals to focus on the behavior of sex offenders? How is this focus different from theories and typologies?

5. Consider the systems presented at the end where abuse patterns have been discovered, only to have uncovered the fact that abuse went on undetected for years. Some critics suggest that studying social patterns is not an appropriate or viable approach to the study of sex-offending behaviors, suggesting perhaps a focus on the individual is more appropriate. What do you say about social studies, individual studies, or both?

NOTES

1. Robert Alan Prentky and Ann Wolbert Burgess, *Forensic Management of Sexual Offenders* (New York: Plenum, 2000), 245.

2. Irma Wallace, "U.S. Cities Ranked by the Frequency of Registered Sex Offenders," Infographic Journal, March 14, 2019, accessed October 20, 2019, https://infographicjournal.com/u-s-cities-ranked-by-the-frequency-of-registered-sex-offenders/. See also "United States Marshals Service FY 2020 Performance Budget, Salaries and Expenses Appropriation," March 2019, https://www.justice.gov/jmd/page/file/1143886/download.

3. Pamela D. Schultz, *Not Monsters: Analyzing the Stories of Child Molesters* (Lanham, MD: Rowman & Littlefield, 2005), xvi.

4. See micro research on a specific offender. For example, there are several books that explore the life and crimes of Ted Bundy, including H. Aynesworth, *Ted Bundy: Conversations with a Killer* (Authorlink Press, 2000); A. Rule, *The Stranger Beside Me: The Shocking Inside Story of Serial Killer Ted Bundy* (Gallery Books, 1980).

5. See, for example, I. Moyer, *Criminological Theories: Traditional and Non-Traditional Voices and Themes* (Sage, 2001), for a thorough discussion of these collections of theories.

6. Robert Freeman-Longo and Geral T. Blanchard, *Sexual Abuse in America: Epidemic of the 21st Century* (Brandon, VT: Safer Society Press, 1998), 20.

7. Ibid., 21.

8. Ibid., 18.

9. Kathryn Casteel, Julia Wolfe, and Mai Nguyen, "What We Know about Victims of Sexual Assault in America," FiveThirtyEight, September 21, 2018, assessed September 9, 2019, https://projects.fivethirtyeight.com/sexual-assault-victims/.

10. "Sexual Violence Has Fallen by More than Half Since 1993," RAINN, accessed September 9, 2019, https://www.rainn.org/statistics/scope-problem.

11. See, for example, Amnesty International, *Maze of Injustice* (Amnesty International Publications, 2007); K. Fossett, "How Does a Country Develop a 60 Percent Rape Rate?,"

Foreign Policy, September 11, 2013, https://foreignpolicy.com/2013/09/11/how-does-a-coun try-develop-a-60-percent-rape-rate/; M. Finoh and J. Sankofa, "The Legal System Has Failed Black Girls, Women, and Non-Binary Survivors of Violence," January 28, 2019, American Civil Liberties Union, https://www.aclu.org/blog/racial-justice/race-and-criminal-justice/legal -system-has-failed-black-girls-women-and-non.

12. A. Feigh, personal communication March 2012, with Professor Roberta Gibbons, Min-neapolis Community and Technical College, and formerly of the Aurora Center.

13. Leah Fessler, "The Poorest Americans Are 12 Times as Likely to Be Sexually Assaulted as the Wealthiest," Quartz, January 3, 2018, accessed September 9, 2019, https:// qz.com/1170426/the-poorest-americans-are-12-times-as-likely-to-be-sexually-assaulted/.

14. See, for example, Robert Freeman-Longo and Geral T. Blanchard, *Sexual Abuse in America: Epidemic of the 21st Century* (Brandon, VT: Safer Society Press, 1998); J. Katz, *The Macho Paradox: Why Some Men Hurt Women and How All Men Can Help* (Sourcebooks, 2006); R. Jensen, *Getting Off: Pornography and the End of Masculinity* (South End Press, 2007); J. Friedman, *Yes Means Yes! Visions of Female Sexual Power and a World without Rape* (Seal Press, 2008); D. Savage, *American Savage: Insights, Slights, and Fights on Faith, Sex, Love, and Politics* (Penguin Group, 2013).

15. Support for this idea is offered in many works included throughout, particularly Free-man-Longo and Blanchard, *Sexual Abuse in America*; Moyer, *Criminological Theories*; Janus, *Failure to Protect*.

16. P. Adler and P. Adler, *Constructions of Deviance: Social Power, Context, and Interac-tion*, 7th ed. (Cengage Learning, 2011).

17. American Psychiatric Association, *Diagnostic and Statistical Manual of Mental Disor-ders, DSM-5* (American Psychiatric Publishing, 2013).

18. N. Rubinstein, "National Institute of Mental Health Will Not Support DSM-V," May 9, 2013, https://www.goodtherapy.org/blog/national-institute-of-mental-health-will-not-sup port-dsm-v-0509137.

19. Jerome C. Wakefield, "*DSM-5*: An Overview of Changes and Controversies," *Clinical Social Work Journal* 41, no. 2 (2013): 139–54, doi:10.1007/s10615-013-0445-2.

20. American Psychiatric Association, *DSM-5* (2013).

21. Ibid., 685.

22. Ibid., 705.

23. Ibid.

24. American Psychiatric Association, *DSM-IV-TR* (2000), 572.

25. Cord Jefferson, "Born This Way: Sympathy and Science for Those Who Want to Have Sex with Children," Gawker, September 7, 2012, accessed September 9, 2019, http:// gawker.com/5941037/born-this-way-sympathy-and-science-for-those-who—want-to-have -sex-with-children.

26. Jillian Keenan, "We're Kinky, Not Crazy," Slate, March 8, 2013, accessed September 9, 2019, http://www.slate.com/articles/health_and_science/medical_examiner/2013/03/sex ual_kinks_in_the_dsm_v_paraphilic_disorders_describe_unhappy_kinksters.html.

27. Charles Moser and Peggy J. Kleinplatz, "*DSM-IV-TR* and the Paraphilias: An Argu-ment for Removal," *Journal of Psychology & Human Sexuality* 17, no. 3-4 (2006): 91–109.

28. Ibid.

29. R. Flora, *How to Work with Sex Offenders: A Handbook for Criminal Justice, Human Service, and Mental Health Professionals* (New York: Hayworth Press, 2001), 95.

30. A. N. Groth, *Men Who Rape: The Psychology of the Offender* (New York: Plenum Press, 1990).

31. G. Abel, "Paraphilias," in *Comprehensive Textbook of Psychiatry*, ed. H. I. Kaplan and B. J. Sadock (Baltimore, MD: Williams and Wilkins, 1989), 1069–85.

32. World Health Organization, "International Classification of Diseases," http://www .who.int/classifications/icd/en/.

33. World Health Organization, "International Classification of Diseases (ICD) Information Sheet," http://www.who.int/classifications/icd/factsheet/en/index.html.

34. D. Foley, "DSM-5 vs. ICD-10-CM," *Journal of AHIMA*, August 10, 2016, accessed October 20, 2019, https://journal.ahima.org/2016/08/10/dsm-5-vs-icd-10-cm/.

35. World Health Organization, "WHO Releases New International Classification of Diseases (ICD-11)," June 18, 2018, accessed September 9, 2019, https://www.who.int/news-room/detail/18-06-2018-who-releases-new-international-classification-of-diseases-(icd-11).

36. N. Groth, A. Burgess, and L. Holmstrom, "Rape: Power, Anger and Sexuality," *American Journal of Psychiatry* 134, no. 11 (1977): 1239–43, doi:10.1176/ajp.134.11.1239.

37. N. Groth and H. Birnbaum, "Adult Sexual Orientation and Attraction to Underage Persons," *Archives of Sexual Behavior* 7, no. 3 (1978): 175–81, doi:10.1007/bf01542377.

38. N. Groth, W. F. Hobson, and S. Gary, "The Child Molester: Clinical Observations," *Journal of Social Work and Human Sexuality* 1, no. 1-2 (1982); A. N. Groth, R. E. Longo, and J. B. McFadin, "Undetected Recidivism among Rapists and Child Molesters," *Crime & Delinquency* 28, no. 3 (1982): 450–58, http://dx.doi.org/10.1177/001112878202800305.

39. Groth, N., *Men Who Rape: The Psychology of the Offender* (Basic Books,1979), l.

40. See, for example, A. Frances, "DSM 5 Confirms That Rape Is Crime, Not a Mental Disorder," *Psychology Today*, February 22, 2013, accessed October 20, 2019, https://www.psychologytoday.com/us/blog/dsm5-in-distress/201302/dsm-5-confirms-rape-is-crime-not-mental-disorder.

41. Groth and Birnbaum, "Adult Sexual Orientation and Attraction to Underage Persons."

42. William Edwards and Christopher Hensley, "Contextualizing Sex Offender Management Legislation and Policy: Evaluating the Problem of Latent Consequences in Community Notification Laws," *International Journal of Offender Therapy and Comparative Criminology* 45, no. 1 (2001): 83–101.

43. R. Przybylski, "Chapter 5: Adult Sex Offender Recidivism," Sex Offender Management Assessment and Planning Initiative, accessed October 20, 2019, https://www.smart.gov/SOMAPI/sec1/ch5_recidivism.html.

44. Michael Davis, "Differentiating Child Sexual Abusers," *InPsych* 35, no. 5 (2013), accessed September 9, 2019, https://www.psychology.org.au/inpsych/2013/october/davis.

45. Terry and Tallon, "Child Sexual Abuse"; R. Karl Hanson and Kelly E. Morton-Bourgon, "The Characteristics of Persistent Sexual Offenders: A Meta-Analysis of Recidivism Studies," *Journal of Consulting and Clinical Psychology* 73, no. 6 (2005): 1154–63; R. Mann, R. K. Hanson, and D. Thornton, "Assessing Risk for Sexual Recidivism: Some Proposals on the Nature of Psychologically Meaningful Risk Factors," *Sexual Abuse: A Journal for Research and Treatment* 22, no. 2 (2010): 191–217.

46. Hanson and Morton-Bourgon, "The Characteristics of Persistent Sexual Offenders"; Mann et al., "Assessing Risk for Sexual Recidivism."

47. Groth, Burgess, and Holmstrom, "Rape: Power, Anger and Sexuality."

48. Groth, *Men Who Rape*.

49. Ibid.

50. Ibid., 58.

51. L. Simkins, "Characteristics of Sexually Repressed Child Molesters," *Journal of Interpersonal Violence* 8, no. 1 (1993): 3–17, https://doi.org/10.1177/088626093008001001.

52. D. Baxter, W. Marshall, H. Barbaree, P. Davidson, and P. Malcolm, "Deviant Sexual Behavior: Differentiating Sex Offenders by Criminal and Personal History, Psychometric Measures, and Sexual Response," *Criminal Justice and Behavior* 11, no. 4 (1984): 477–501, http://dx.doi.org/10.1177/0093854884011004007.

53. See Flora, *How to Work with Sex Offenders*.

54. Karen Terry, *Sexual Offenses and Offenders: Theory, Practice, and Policy* (New York: Wadsworth Cengage Learning, 2013).

55. John A. Hunter et al., "Juvenile Sex Offenders: Toward the Development of a Typology," *Sexual Abuse* 15, no. 1 (2003): 27–48.

56. J. Hunter and J. Becker, "Motivators of Adolescent Sex Offenders and Treatment Perspectives," in *Sexual Aggression*, ed. J. Shaw (Washington, DC: American Psychiatric Press, 1998).

57. Andrea L. Roberts et al., "Childhood Gender Nonconformity: A Risk Indicator for Childhood Abuse and Posttraumatic Stress in Youth," *Pediatrics* 129, no. 3 (2012): 410–17, doi:10.1542/peds.2011-1804.

58. M. Seto and M. Lalumiere, "What Is So Special about Male Adolescent Sexual Offending?: A Review and Test of Explanations through Meta-Analysis," *Psychological Bulletin* 135, no. 4 (2010): 526–75.

59. Howard N. Snyder and Melissa Sickmund, "Juvenile Offenders and Victims: 2006 National Report," National Center for Juvenile Justice, March 2006, accessed September 9, 2019, https://files.eric.ed.gov/fulltext/ED495786.pdf.

60. Terry, *Sexual Offenses and Offenders*, 127.

61. N. Calley and S. Gerber, "Empathy-Promoting Counseling Strategies for Juvenile Sex Offenders: A Developmental Approach," *Journal of Addictions and Offender Counseling* 28, no. 2 (2008): 68–85; C. Farr, J. Brown, and R. Beckett, "Ability to Empathize and Masculinity Levels: Comparing Male Adolescent Sex Offenders with a Normative Sample of Non-Offending Adolescents," *Psychology, Crime and Law* 10, no. 2 (2004): 155–67, https://doi.org/10.1080/10683160310001597153.

62. Jennifer Vick, Ruth McRoy, and Bobbie M. Matthews, "Young Female Sex Offenders: Assessment and Treatment Issues," *Journal of Child Sexual Abuse* 11, no. 2 (2002): 1–23.

63. Terry, *Sexual Offenses and Offenders*, 123.

64. Donna M. Vandiver and Raymond Teske, Jr., "Juvenile Female and Male Sex Offenders: A Comparison of Offender, Victim, and Judicial Processing Characteristics," *International Journal of Offender Therapy and Comparative Criminology* 50, no. 2 (2006): 148–65.

65. J. Kobayashi, B. D. Sales, J. V. Becker, et al., "Perceived Parental Deviance, Parent-Child Bonding, Child Abuse, and Child Sexual Aggression," *Sex Abuse: A Journal of Research and Treatment* 7 (1995): 25, https://doi.org/10.1007/BF02254872.

66. "Female Sex Offenders: A Project of the Office of Justice Programs," Center for Sex Offender Management, US Department of Justice, March 2007, Washington, DC, accessed September 9, 2019, https://www.csom.org/pubs/female_sex_offenders_brief.pdf.

67. Unless otherwise designated, the information about female sex offenders comes from "Female Sex Offenders: A Project of the Office of Justice Programs."

68. Center for Sex Offender Management, "Female Sex Offenders," March 2007, A Project of the Office of Justice Programs, US Department of Justice, accessed October 20, 2019, p. 1, https://www.csom.org/pubs/female_sex_offenders_brief.pdf.

69. See, for example, G. Robertiello and K. Terry, "Can We Profile Sex Offenders? A Review of Sex Offender Typologies," *Aggression and Violent Behavior* 12, no. 5 (2007): 508–18, https://doi.org/10.1016/j.avb.2007.02.010.

70. Michelle McPhee, Dean Schabner, and Nikki Battiste, "'Craigslist Killer' Philip Markoff Commits Suicide," *ABC News*, August 15, 2010, accessed September 9, 2019, http://abcnews.go.com/US/craigslist-killer-phillip-markoff-commits-suicide/story?id=11405484.

71. Christopher Barry-Dee and Steven Morris, *Online Killers: Portraits of Murderers, Cannibals and Sex Predators Who Stalked the Web for Their Victims* (Berkeley, CA: Ulysses Press, 2010).

72. The last three items are modified from M. Griffiths, "Internet Addiction—Time to Be Taken Seriously?," *Addiction Research and Theory* 8, no. 5 (2000): 413–18. https://doi.org/10.3109/16066350009005587.

73. K. Sheldon and D. Howitt, *Sex Offenders and the Internet* (West Sussex, England: Wiley and Sons, Ltd., 2007).

74. Ibid., 7.

75. Kelly M. Babchishin, R. Karl Hanson, and Chantal A. Hermann, "The Characteristics of Online Sex Offenders: A Meta-Analysis," *Sexual Abuse* 23, no. 1 (2011): 92–123, doi:10.1177/1079063210370708.

76. Janis Wolak, David Finkelhor, and Kimberly Mitchell, "Child Pornography Possessors: Trends in Offender and Case Characteristics," *Sexual Abuse* 23, no. 1 (2011): 22–42, https://doi.org/10.1177/1079063210372143.

77. Cíntia Taylor, "Dutch Court Says Pedophilia Advocacy Group Martijn Can Continue," Daily Beast, July 11, 2017, September 10, 2019, https://www.thedailybeast.com/dutch-court-says-pedophilia-advocacy-group-martijn-can-continue.

78. Terry, *Sexual Offenses and Offenders*, 55.

79. W. L. Marshall, D. R. Laws, and H. E. Barbaree, eds., *Applied Clinical Psychology: Handbook of Sexual Assault: Issues, Theories, and Treatment of the Offender* (New York: Plenum Press, 1990).

80. See, for example, S. J. Hucker and J. Bain, "Androgenic Hormones and Sexual Assault," in *Applied Clinical Psychology: Handbook of Sexual Assault: Issues, Theories, and Treatment of the Offender*, ed. W. L. Marshall, D. R. Laws, and H. E. Barbaree, 93–102 (New York: Plenum Press, 1990).

81. See, for example, Leo Kreuz and Robert M. Rose, "Assessment of Aggressive Behavior and Plasma Testosterone in a Young Criminal Population," *Psychosomatic Medicine* 34, no. 4 (1972): 321–32; Hucker and Bain, "Androgenic Hormones and Sexual Assault."

82. P. Gay, *Freud: A Life for Our Time* (W.W. Norton, 1988).

83. Ibid., 37.

84. David Thornton and D. Richard Laws, *Cognitive Approaches to the Assessment of Sexual Interest in Sexual Offenders* (West Sussex, England: John Wiley and Sons, 2009).

85. Ibid., p. 225.

86. Ibid.

87. Gene G. Abel, Judith V. Becker, and Jerry Cunningham-Rathner, "Complications, Consent, and Cognitions in Sex between Children and Adults," *International Journal of Law and Psychiatry* 7, no. 1 (1984): 89–103.

88. S. Brown, *Treating Sex Offenders: An Introduction to Sex Offender Treatment Programmes* (Wilhan Publishing, 2005), 122.

89. See, for example, W. L. Marshall, "Intimacy, Loneliness, and Sexual Offenders," *Behaviour, Research, and Therapy* 27, no. 5 (1089): 491–504, https://doi.org/10.1016/0005-7967(89)90083-1; W. L. Marshall, "The Treatment of Sex Offenders: What Does the Outcome Data Tell Us?," *Journal of Interpersonal Violence* 8, no. 4 (1993): 524–30, https://doi.org/10.1177/088626093008004007.

90. Gene G. Abel, Judith V. Becker, Edward B. Blanchard, and A. Djenderedjian, "Differentiating Sexual Aggressives with Penile Measures," *Criminal Justice and Behavior* 5, no. 4 (1978): 315–32, https://doi.org/10.1177/009385487800500404.

91. S. C. Wolf, "A Multi-Factor Model of Deviant Sexuality," *Victimology* 10 (1985): 359–74.

92. The selection of integrated theories presented here were adapted from Jill D. Stinson, Bruce D. Sales, and Judith V. Becker, *Sex Offending: Causal Theories to Inform Research, Prevention, and Treatment* (Washington, DC: American Psychological Association, 2008).

93. Ibid., 142–43.

94. William L. Marshall, Dana Anderson, and Yolanda Fernandez, *Cognitive Behavioural Treatment of Sexual Offenders* (West Sussex, England: John Wiley & Sons, Ltd., 1999).

95. William L. Marshall and Liam E. Marshall, "The Origins of Sexual Offending," *Trauma, Violence, & Abuse* 1, no. 3 (2000): 250–63.

96. For additional information about Hall and Hirschman's integrated theory, see Stinson, Sales, and Becker, *Sex Offending*.

97. Jared DeFife, "DSM-V Offers New Criteria for Personality Disorders," *Psychology Today*, February 10, 2010, accessed September 10, 2019, http://www.psychologytoday.com/blog/the-shrink-tank/201002/dsm-v-offers-new-criteria-personality-disorders.

98. Stinson, Sales, and Becker, *Sex Offending*.

99. This review of Hall and Hirschman comes from Stinson, Sales, and Becker, *Sex Offending*, 149, and was put in tabular form by the author for ease of review.

100. Neil M. Malamuth et al., "Characteristics of Aggressors against Women: Testing a Model Using a National Sample of College Students," *Journal of Consulting and Clinical Psychology* 59, no. 5 (1991): 670–81.

101. Stinson, Sales, and Becker, *Sex Offending*.

102. Ibid., 167.

103. For more exploration of the theoretical applications to sex offending from a criminological perspective, see L. Zilney and L. Zilney, *Reconsidering Sex Crimes and Offenders* (Praeger, 2009).

104. Ibid., 13–15.

105. Ibid., 14, 33–39.

106. T. Ward, D. Polaschek, and A. Beech, *Theories of Sexual Offending* (John Wiley and Sons, 2006); Stinson, Sales, and Becker, *Sex Offending*.

107. For a more detailed discussion of how the routine activities theory can be applied to the larger discussion on sex-offending behavior, see Terry, *Sexual Offenses and Offenders*; Karen J. Terry and Alissa Ackerman, "Child Sexual Abuse in the Catholic Church: How Situational Crime Prevention Strategies Can Help Create Safe Environments," *Criminal Justice and Behavior* 35, no. 5 (2008): 643–57.

108. I. Moyer, *Theories of Crime and Justice* (Sage, 2001), chapter 11.

109. Susan Brownmiller, *Against Our Will: Men, Women and Rape* (New York: Fawcett Books, 1975).

110. David Finkelhor, Heather Hammer, Andrea J. Sedlak, "Sexually Assaulted Children: National Estimates and Characteristics," Office of Justice Programs, US Department of Justice, August 2008, 2, accessed September 10, 2019, https://www.ncjrs.gov/pdffiles1/ojjdp/214383.pdf.

111. Howard N. Snyder, "Sexual Assault of Young Children as Reported to Law Enforcement: Victim, Incident, and Offender Characteristics," Office of Justice Programs, US Department of Justice, July 2000, 11, accessed September 10, 2019, https://www.bjs.gov/content/pub/pdf/saycrle.pdf.

112. Groth, Hobson, and Gary, "The Child Molester."

113. Carole Jenny, Thomas A. Roesler, and Kimberly L. Poyer, "Are Children at Risk for Sexual Abuse by Homosexuals?" *Pediatrics* 94, no. 1 (1994): 41.

114. Carla van Dam, *The Socially Skilled Child Molester: Differentiating the Guilty from the Falsely Accused* (Binghamton, NY: Haworth Press, 2006), 19.

115. Ibid.

116. See J. Cavanaugh, "Some Aspects of the Diagnosis and Treatment of Pedophilia," in *Sexual Exploitation of the Child: Law Enforcement, Prosecution and Treatment Perspectives*, ed. Thomas M. Frost and Magnus J. Seng (Chicago: Loyola University of Chicago, 1986), 40–49; Lisa J. Cohen et al., "Impulsive Personality Traits in Male Pedophiles versus Healthy Controls: Is Pedophilia an Impulsive-Aggressive Disorder?," *Comprehensive Psychiatry* 43, no. 2 (2002): 127–34.

117. van Dam, *The Socially Skilled Child Molester*, 23.

118. Mary Edna Helfer, Ruth S. Kempe, and Richard D. Krugman, eds., *The Battered Child*, 5th ed. (Chicago: University of Chicago Press, 1997), 14.

119. See, for example, Alexandra Dickson and Vanessa Rother, dirs., *Close to Home*, 2001, Direct Cinema Limited.

120. A. Salter, *Predators: Pedophiles, Rapists, and Other Sex Offenders: Who They Are, How They Operate, and How We Can Protect Ourselves and Our Children* (Basic Books, 2003).

121. Terry, *Sexual Offenses and Offenders*, 71.

122. Ibid.

123. Tony Ward et al., "Cognitive Distortions in Sex Offenders: An Integrative Review," *Clinical Psychology Review* 17, no. 5 (1997): 479–507.

124. J. Filipovic, "Why the 'Nice Guys Commit Rape Too' Conversation Is Not Helpful," *The Guardian*, December 18, 2012, https://www.theguardian.com/commentisfree/2012/dec/18/nice-guys-commit-rape-conversation-unhelpful.

125. Terry, *Sexual Offenses and Offenders*, 161–85.

126. Report I of the 40th Statewide Investigating Grand Jury, Office of Attorney General, Commonwealth of Pennsylvania, July 27, 2018, https://www.attorneygeneral.gov/report/.

127. For example, D. Warner, "Sex Offender Sandusky Limited in Prison Due to Safety Concerns," *Reuters*, December 9, 2012, https://www.reuters.com/article/us-usa-penn-state-sandusky/sex-offender-sandusky-limited-in-prison-due-to-safety-concerns-idUSBRE8B70DO20121209.

128. Karen J. Terry, Margaret Leland Smith, Katarina Schuth, James R. Kelly, Brenda Vollman, and Christina Massey, *The Nature and Scope of the Problem of Sexual Abuse of Minors by Priests and Deacons*, prepared by the John Jay College of Criminal Justice for the US Conference of Catholic Bishops (Washington, DC: United States Conference of Catholic Bishops, 2011).

129. "Speaking Out: Faith Communities and Sexual Assault," *Connections*, Spring 2004, The Washington Coalition of Sexual Assault Programs, https://www.wcsap.org/sites/default/files/uploads/resources_publications/connections/FaithCommunities2004.pdf.

130. Terry, *Sexual Offenses and Offenders*, 168.

131. Ibid., 168, 172–77.

132. Terry et al., *The Nature and Scope of the Problem of Sexual Abuse of Minors by Priests and Deacons*.

133. Terry, *Sexual Offenses and Offenders*, 173–77.

134. M. Singer, *Prison Rape: An American Institution* (Praeger, 2013).

135. R. Walton, "National Prison Rape Elimination Commission Report," July 2009, https://www.ncjrs.gov/pdffiles1/226680.pdf. See also J. Kunselman et al., "Nonconsensual Sexual Behavior," in *Prison Sex: Practice and Policy*, ed. Christopher Hensley (Boulder, CO: Lynne Rienner Publishers, 2002), 45–61.

136. Mark S. Fleisher, and Jessie L. Krienert, *The Myth of Prison Rape: Sexual Culture in American Prisons* (Lanham, MD: Rowman & Littlefield, 2004).

137. J. S. Mair, S. Frattaroli, and S. Teret, "New Hope for Victims of Prison Sexual Assault," *The Journal of Law, Medicine & Ethics* 31, no. 4 (2003): 602–6, doi:10.1111/j.1748-720X.2003.tb00127.x.

138. Ian O'Donnell, "Prison Rape in Context," *The British Journal of Criminology* 44, no. 2 (2004): 241–55.

139. Kirby Dick, dir., *The Invisible War* (2012; Los Angeles: Cinedigm), 59:10.

140. Ibid., 1:05:35.

141. Ibid.

142. "60 Removed from U.S. Military Jobs in Sex Assault Review," *World Bulletin*, August 3, 2013, accessed October 20, 2019, https://www.worldbulletin.net/america-canada/60-removed-from-us-military-jobs-in-sexual-assault-review-h114480.html.

143. Ibid.

144. "Department of Defense Annual Report on Sexual Assault in the Military: Fiscal Year 2012," Department of Defense, May 7, 2013, accessed September 10, 2019, http://www.ncdsv.org/images/DOD_Annual-report-on-sexual-assault-in-the-military-FY2012_Exec Summ_5-7-2013.pdf.

145. Jessica A. Turchik and Susan M. Wilson, "Sexual Assault in the U.S. Military: A Review of the Literature and Recommendations for the Future," *Aggression and Violent Behavior* 15, no. 4 (2010): 267–77.

146. For more information, see D. Bostock and J. Daley, "Lifetime and Current Sexual Assault and Harassment Victimization Rates of Active-Duty United States Air Force Women," *Violence Against Women* 13, no. 9 (2007): 927–44, https://doi.org/10.1177/1077801207305232; M. Murdoch, J. Pryor, M. Polusny, M. Wall, D. Ripley, and G. Gackstetter, "The Association between Military Sexual Stress and Psychiatric Symptoms after Controlling for Other Stressors," *Journal of Psychiatric Research* 44, no. (2010); 1129–36, https://doi.org/10.1016/j.jpsychires.2010.09.009.

147. D. Cray, "Assault Issue Has Its Roots in the Culture," *Arizona Republic*, June 3, 2013, https://www.pressreader.com/usa/the-arizona-republic/20130603/281646777684211.

148. Elizabeth L. Hillman, "Front and Center: Sexual Violence in U.S. Military Law," *Politics and Society* 37, no. 1 (2009): 101–29.

149. See US Congress, House of Representatives, Select Committee on Children, Youth and Families, *On the Front Lines: Police Stress and Family Well-Being: Hearings before the Select Committee on Children, Youth and Families*, 102nd Cong., 1st sess. 1991, 32–48; see also Peter H. Neidig, Harold E. Russell, and Albert F. Seng, "Interspousal Aggression in Law Enforcement Families: A Preliminary Investigation," *Police Studies* 15, no. 1 (1992): 30–38; M. H. Culp, "Officer-Involved Orders for Protection: A Management Challenge," *The Police Chief* (March 2000): 10.

150. "Police Family Violence Fact Sheet," National Center for Women & Policing, accessed September 10, 2019, http://womenandpolicing.com/violenceFS.asp.

8

A Focus on People Harmed by Sexualized Violence

This is a tough issue. Many people have been hurt by sexual abuse. And many of these people have also been further traumatized by how people have responded to it—from family members doubting their stories to a criminal justice system that challenges their facts, their truth about what happened. We as authors acknowledge this. We tread into these waters with caution and utmost respect for those who have survived sexual abuse.

—Judah Oudshoorn with Michelle Jakett and Lorraine Stutzman Amstutz, *The Little Book of Restorative Justice for Sexual Abuse*[1]

[Ninety-five percent] of child molestation is done by a family member or close friend. No one wants to feel responsible for sending "Grandpa" to jail. No one wants to feel they broke up or exposed their family! And to children, that is the END of the world. Some adults scare children by threats not to tell.

—Aleesha Barlow, Tell Somebody Movement[2]

IN 1973, THE US SUPREME COURT ruled in **Linda R.S. v. Richard D.**, 410 U.S. 614 (1972), that the person seeking redress, the victim in the case, did not have the legal standing, or legal authority, to seek the legal outcome she had requested. In short, at the time, the legal belief was that a crime victim could not force a criminal prosecution because "a private citizen lacks a judicially cognizable interest in the prosecution or nonprosecution of another."[3] In the current legal structure, the state brings the legal charges, and, as such, if the prosecutors decided not to bring a case, the victim could not compel the prosecutor to do so. The Supreme Court did provide, however, a possible solution for addressing the situation by suggesting that Congress could "enact statutes creating legal rights, the invasion of which creates standing, even though no injury would exist without the statute."[4] In other words, the legal language would have to be in place to direct the courts if an expanded role for people who had been harmed was the desired objective.

Just under 10 years later, in 1981, then President Ronald Reagan proposed a National Crime Victim Rights Week, and several important events followed relatively quickly. In 1982, Reagan appointed a Task Force on Victims of Crime, and in 1983 the **Office for Victims of Crime** (OVC) was established in by the US Department of Justice within the Office of Justice Programs to implement the recommendations from the President's Task Force on Victims of Crime. The year 1984 produced a series of landmark initiatives, including the passage of the **Victims of Crime Act (VOCA),** which established the Crime Victims Fund to support state victim assistance programs. Also in 1984, the **Justice Assistance Act,** which funded state and local victim assistance programs was passed, and the **National Center for Missing and Exploited Children** was established as the national resource agency for missing children.

Also, during that time, the Task Force on Family Violence presented its recommendations, and Congress passed the **Family Violence Prevention and Services Act** (1984) to assist programs responding to people harmed by domestic violence. The **Concerns of Police Survivors** (COPS) was organized by relatives of officers killed in the line of duty. The Federal Bureau of Investigation (FBI) organized a victim/witness notification system, and the US Department of Justice organized victim/witness coordinator positions within its US Attorney's offices. The Office for Victims of Crime established the National Victim Resource Center, now named the **Office for Victims of Crime Resource Center** (OVCRC), to serve as a clearinghouse for OVC publications and other resources for victims. Without question, 1984 was a landmark year for movement toward establishing a more prominent role for and response to victims of crime in the US criminal justice system.

After a brief discussion about the use of the term "victim," attention is given to the history of victimology as an academic focus of study, followed by a review of legislation and federal government action to create legal protections for victims' rights. It must be mentioned that victim advocates were active in the community well before academic studies were well under way. A brief history of the study of victims is offered, with a focus on the **Victim Rights Movement.** Attention is then given to the consequences of sexualized harm and violence to those who are affected by the violence. After outlining victim impacts of harm, attention is shifted to the levels of harm caused by victimization in the families and communities where sexualized harms happen. A brief review of what to expect in the criminal justice system is introduced. (For more detail see chapter 11.)

The current understandings of the effects of harm on people are best reflected in the study of victims as a subdiscipline of psychology, social psychology, or criminology, or other social science fields. Another option, reflected from within the emerging field of **victimology,** the focused study on victims, is to focus on the victim from within an interdisciplinary area of study. This is the focus here. Although the field of victimization is deep and wide, this section is organized to explore victimization as it is in relationship to sexual offenses and the related dynamics from the individuals who have been harmed and within the dynamics of the larger society. Various aspects are discussed related to the social actions developed as emerging responses to these victimizing events and the individual and social processes being established for healing and prevention.

Text Box 8.1.   An Introductory List of Victimology Legislation Passed in the 1980s

---

1981: The first National Crime Victim Rights Week was established by then President Ronald Reagan.

1982: Victim and Witness Protection Act was passed to provide services in support of victims and witnesses who participate in the criminal justice system process.

1983:

- The Office for Victims of Crime (OVC) was established to implement the recommendations from the President's Task Force on Victims of Crime.

International Association of Chiefs of Police adopts Crime Victims' Bill of Rights.

1984:

- Victims of Crime Act (VOCA) established the Crime Victims Fund to support state victim assistance programs.
- Justice Assistance Act funded state and local victim assistance programs.
- National Center for Missing and Exploited Children was established as a national resource agency for missing children.
- The Task Force on Family Violence presented its recommendations to the president.
- The Family Violence Prevention and Services Act was passed to assist programs responding to people harmed by domestic violence.
- First National Symposium on Sexual Assault was held, cosponsored by OVC and FBI.
- Concerns of Police Survivors (COPS) was organized by relatives of officers killed in the line of duty.
- The Office for Victims of Crime Resource Center (OVCRC), initially named the Office of Victims of Crime, established the National Victim Resource Center to serve as a clearinghouse for OVC publications and other resources for victims.

1985: The Violent Criminal Apprehension Program (VICAP) is an FBI program responsible for the analysis of serial violence and sexual crimes, situated within the Critical Incident Response Group's (CIRG) National Center for the Analysis of Violent Crime.

A BRIEF COMMENT ON "VICTIM" TERMINOLOGY

The term *victim* is used to refer to a person who has been harmed by any given set of circumstances. The situation could be a natural disaster, such as forest fire or a hurricane, identity theft, or a scam by computer fraudsters. Victimology is centered on individuals who have had a crime perpetrated against them. Although victimology as a discipline is focused on the impacts of all kinds of crimes, this chapter is focused specifically on providing an overview of information about people who have been affected or harmed by sexual assaults and other kinds of sexualized violence. The use of the term "victim" is quite common in the news, in general social conversations, and throughout the historical development of research and disciplines working to better understand what can be learned about the impact of crime, the people harmed, and the circumstances and conditions where harm happened.

The more that has been learned about being a victim of crime and about the victimization process more generally, the use of the term "victim" has been called into question for a variety of reasons. There has been pushback from people who have lived through sexual violence that reject the label of victim because it can imply weakness or minimization. The term "survivor" has been claimed as a different way of defining their role in the experience of surviving a crime. This event happened, you were harmed by it, and in surviving the experience you can reclaim your voice. Modifications to this list have included advice from bloggers and other survivors who have added terms like "thriver" (step 3); server, someone who is determined to make good of the situation (step 4); and empowered server (step 5), which reflects confidence and a healthy recovery.[5]

The idea that there is one "victim" and one "offender" in one moment in time might imply a set of circumstances that do not reflect larger social influences. The dynamics of victimization can sometimes be more complicated than that. For example, if a young person is being bullied and teased, they might eventually hit the person taunting them and then be identified as the "offender," while the person doing the taunting and teasing is identified as the "victim." Such an assessment might be an easy classification for the playground teacher, but it does not fully reflect the larger dynamics at play.

Further, traditional references to a victim have implied a level of weakness, with the perpetrator assuming an implied position of strength or power. This idea has been increasingly challenged as more is learned about the dynamics of victimization. Whether intentionally or not, the idea that a victim is fully human before they were harmed and that they remain fully human after the incident is the focus of this larger discussion. Research findings have reported victims feeling reduced in some way after a harmful event and feeling seen only as a victim.[6] Consequently, people who had experienced some form of harm started using the term "survivor," particularly when referencing sexual assault.

It is possible that some might read this and see little differentiation between the terms; however, the idea is that a person might experience a horrible thing and feel changed by it in a negative way or as if that event defines them or their larger life experience. These things can be seen as happening *to them*, or it can be seen as an event or situation a person experiences as they might experience a variety of other events in life. One person might not ever elect to identify themselves as a victim, while acknowledging the victimization by stating themselves to be a victim might be really important for someone else who experienced similar events. In 1990, Lew and Bass wrote *Victims No Longer: Men Recovering from Incest and Other Sexual Child Abuse*. In 2009, Marilyn Nissim-Sabat wrote *Neither Victim nor Survivor: Thinking toward a New Humanity*, suggesting and perhaps summarizing the thoughts of others how the terms associated with victim and survivor, even perpetrator, by their construction and application devalue human agency in ways that undermine the larger issues associated with resisting violence and oppression more broadly.[7] How someone who has been harmed is seen by others can be as important as how they see themselves after a potentially horrible, harmful, incident. How these terms are defined by self and others can be significant.

There is power in what we call ourselves. Research suggests it is important for people who have been harmed by sexual violence to be able to tell their stories and use terms that have the most meaning for them. These nuances of the experience of a traumatic event and how a person comes to understand a difficult event in the context of their own lived experience warrant further reflection both in life and as a discipline of study. The term "victim" will be used here; however, seeing the complete humanity of individuals and people discussed as victims throughout this conversation is a priority.

A BRIEF HISTORY OF VICTIMOLOGY: THE STUDY OF VICTIMIZATION

The history of victimization studies follows closely the history of crime theory development, some of which was covered in chapter 7. The exclusive study of victims, however, did not emerge as a strong, stand-alone topic for study until the mid-twentieth century development of **victim typologies**. Similar to the way any other field of study creates common categories after identifying common themes, this refers to the varied categories created and used to study different types, in this case, of crime victims. **Benjamin Mendelsohn** coined the term "victimology" in 1940, referring to the more exclusive study of victims.[8] Today, three sets of theories about victimology are widely endorsed and will be discussed in more detail here: victim-based theories; interactional theories; and societal-based theories, with specific emphasis on **ecological theory**.[9]

Interestingly, Mendelsohn's assessment of the research he collected offered significant support for the idea that victims participated, at least to some degree, in their own victimization. His theories reflect **victim-based theories**, or those that are focused on the victim of a crime event. It might also be interesting to note the subjects of Mendelsohn's interviews were victims of sexualized violence, specifically rape victims. In his work, Mendelsohn identified six victim types, which were theoretically challenged and subjected to resounding criticism in the decades to come, but are described here as they were originally conceptualized.[10]

1. **The victim who is completely innocent**, someone who does not share any responsibility with the perpetrator.
2. **The victim with minor guilt and responsibility**, due to their own ignorance, is someone who could have expected some danger if they had thought about it and avoided the harm to themselves, such as a person attacked while walking on a dark street.
3. **The victim who is as guilty as the offender** (voluntary victim) and shares equally in the responsibility of their victimization; they chose to be a part of the interaction and common sense could have predicted danger.
4. **The victim who is slightly guiltier than the offender** (provoker) includes someone who seeks the damaging contact, for example, someone is provoked into committing a crime and is then injured.

5. **The victim who is exclusively responsible for their victimization,** such as someone who initiates an attack that leads to their injury.
6. **The imaginary victim,** or the individual who has suffered nothing at all, but who falsely expresses themselves to be a victim.[11]

In 1994, Zur argued that these early constructions of victimization were "controversial, inconclusive and incomplete, particularly with regard to guilt and responsibility" because cultural, demographic, and personal variables are important attributes for assessing culpability.[12] Various other research projects have worked to compile a list of victims and their vulnerability to victimization. A glimpse of some of the eventual pushback on these early victim-centered themes in victimology comes from indigenous communities, the LGBTQI community, and advocacy groups and from within communities of color, with additional protests coming from within various waves of the feminist movement. The pushback puts the responsibility of the act or the harm solely on the person who made the choice to cause harm and hopefully frees the person harmed from judgment or blame.

The idea of **victim precipitation**, the notion that a victim is to a degree responsible, or at least has a part to play in their victimization, has been a standard feature in victimology studies since its beginning, as presented above. A second group of theories used to discuss the study of victim theories highlights the challenges faced by researchers who risk fueling the idea of **victim blaming**, or the traditional notion that a victim is responsible in varying degrees for the harm done to them. Antiviolence educator Jackson Katz outlines how easily contemporary society has historically moved to victim blaming when discussing the role of the victim in an act of sexualized violence. At the same time, he suggests that what this also does is make the role of the perpetrator insignificant, if not invisible, in the ensuing conversations.[13] Efforts to support the victim seemed to shift focus away from the perpetrator. When the emphasis on the perpetrator is minimized, questions about the process for assuring accountability followed.

The idea of holding offenders accountable has become an almost intentional response to themes identified as victim blaming, forcing the narrative back to offender accountability. Interestingly, efforts to explain why people seem to inexplicably go to placing blame on the victim is presented in the idea that people want to believe they live in a fair or just world. This theory, referred to as the **just world theory**,[14] is based on the idea that people convince themselves that people who are harmed deserve that harm in order to be able to retain the belief that the world is a relatively predictable and sane place, in other words, the world is a "just" world. This idea perpetuates the idea that, if you don't do anything wrong, or, better yet, if you do good things, you are not likely to have bad things happen to you. These ideas are also connected to the ideas presented in many religious teachings, which suggest that, if you live according to God, then God will protect you. For sexual violence prevention experts, who see many victims who have done nothing wrong but who have been sexually victimized, the idea that these victims blame themselves for the hurtful actions is difficult, but the idea that the offenders too sometimes blame the victims for *their own—the offenders—actions* is of larger concern[15] and equally of interest to researchers.

The Women's Movement of the 1960s and 1970s is associated almost directly with the idea of feminism and the desire for equality between the sexes. Many groups, however, marched during that time in search of redress for social oppression and minimization—if not exclusion—from the kinds of social experiences other people, people in relative positions of power, maintained. The American Indian Movement, Gay Pride, the Civil Rights Movement, and workers' rights, to name a few, were intending to produce significant impact on efforts to address inequality in contemporary US society. A central part of the formal women's campaign was an effort to directly address what was argued to be the myth that women who were forcibly raped were somehow "asking for it," or they had somehow provoked the assault. The goal of this effort in this context at that time was to remove the blame for such violence from the victims, usually women, and place the blame for sexual assault squarely on the shoulders of the perpetrator, usually men, who committed the assault.[16] The more contemporary women's marches (2017, 2018, and 2019) and indigenous marches (2019) to raise awareness about, among other things, **missing and murdered indigenous women** are indications that critics support more attention or specific change on these issues. These and related efforts have produced broad-based support for the idea of **victim advocacy**, or support, for victims of sexual violence. These efforts have been extended to many areas of sexual violence victim support, including domestic and intimate partner violence, LGBTQI populations, indigenous communities and other communities of color, and battered women's networking; however, responses and support have not been met and/or distributed in equal measure.[17]

The second group of victimology theories presented for consideration here are **interactional theories**, which refer to theories that highlight the dynamic between victims and offenders and their environment. One of the most common interaction theories is **lifestyle routine activities theories**.[18] In short, personal characteristics, such as age, gender, or employment status, and/or lifestyle activities can increase or decrease a person's risk of victimization. Victimization research suggests that young, male, unemployed, and unmarried individuals are at the greatest risk, with drug use, indiscriminate socializing, crime commission, and prior victimization likely to increase one's exposure to victimization.[19] The second set of theories on victimization is focused more on activities associated with becoming a victim as the key focal point, rather than on the victims themselves.

The third group of victimology theories presented for consideration here are **societal-based theories** of victimology. These theories look at the root of crime and victimization in social structures, taking opportunity theories and considering how people's lived experiences differ based on social, economic, and political factors. Critical criminology, feminist criminology, and peacemaking criminology are examples of this in the field of crime studies, emphasizing the effects of power as it is expressed through economic structures, such as capitalism, gender bias, and the overarching use of violence for problem solving as examples of how inequalities in wealth, power, and authority are represented by different people, communities, and governments.

Ecological theory is increasingly being used as an integrative framework for understanding victimization through the interactivity of environmental and individual factors. This means that many events and people around us throughout our lives may factor into a full understanding of victimization, whether prior to the victimization, during the process of being victimized, or during the healing process and aftermath of the victimization, in both the long and short term. Consider the detailed overview of the theory offered below:

> Ecological theory sees individuals as influenced by intersecting levels of ecological systems: the *individual* (or ontogenetic), which includes factors internal to the individual such as personal characteristics and formative history; the *micro-system*, which considers peers, and cultural affiliations; the *exosystem*, which is the environment in which the person resides, his or her neighborhood and community including their limitations and resources; and the *macro-system* which includes those factors which are economic, social, and political in nature [italics added].[20]

One factor of significance in this theory is the fact that each of the ecological subsystems is thought to influence the range of choices and options available

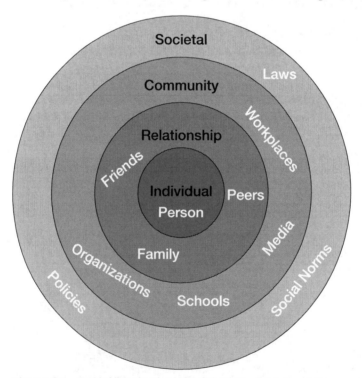

Figure 8.1   Social-Ecological Model of Social Influencing Factors

"3. What Is the Clinical-Community Relationships Measurement Framework?" AHRQ, U.S. HHS: Agency for Healthcare Research and Quality, 27 Mar. 2013, www.ahrq.gov/prevention/resources/chronic-care/clinical-community-relationships-measures-atlas/ccrm-atlas3.html.

to people both as individuals and as victims. Their range of perceived choices, decisions, and actions and behaviors will all be interactive from within a multiplicity of environmental influencing factors. As a result, how they see themselves before they were a victim, through the process of victimization, and in response to the victimizing event, the confluence, or coming together of these environmental conditions, or these various circumstances, will influence individual choices prior to and in response to a potential victimizing event.

Research on violence and victimization at the individual level (e.g., suicide), the interpersonal level (e.g., relations between people, in relationships or school bullying events or between married partners), and the group level (such as domestic or family violence, gangs, church abuses, and corporate crime), as well as critical assessments about the use of war and "for profit" prisons as a political or economic statement, all require an analysis of crime definitions and, as such, assessments of who is harmed.

THE VICTIM'S RIGHTS MOVEMENT

Since the 1940s, the examination of victims has expanded in many directions. Victim studies were generating a social response by the 1970s alongside the collection of social movements happening in the United States at the time. The early research and public education work around the issue of rape soon produced policy and advocacy organizations, such as **rape crisis centers** and **domestic violence shelters**. These were agencies where people who had been sexually assaulted could get resources, including counseling, financial assistance, housing, and legal assistance. Programming and advocacy that was also developed during this time period included programs for battered women and their children, as well as programming in hospitals (as will be discussed more fully in chapter 14).

Also important to remember is the fact that communities of color created programming within their communities in an effort to address the needs of the communities that were not being met by larger social and government programming. This is also apparent in efforts to identify the programs described as "forced dependency" used in meeting the treaty obligations between indigenous tribes and the federal government. Certain officials in the US government still identify the rights of members of the LGBTQI community to be undetermined or seek to overturn, rather than extend, rights to members of this social group. The responses to seek out government support to reduce victimization remain challenging.

Across the United States, work to directly and systematically address victim issues has enjoyed varying levels of support. The first crime victim compensation program is attributed to California legislation in 1965, following its leadership in victim rights with the first victim impact statement in 1976. The National Coalition Against Domestic Violence was formed in 1978, followed by Mothers Against Drunk Drivers (MADD) in 1980,[21] with the first Crime Victim's Bill of Rights passed in Wisconsin in 1980, followed in 1983 with the first Child Victim and Witness Bill of Rights.[22] Early sexual violence advocacy agencies were exclusively designed for women. Advocacy programs for male victims of sexual assault have yet to be realized at all in some areas, and where programs do exist, their relationship to programs for women and children is still being debated.[23]

The National Organization for Victim Assistance (NOVA) was created in 1975 as the first national victim assistance organization and is a larger nation-wide structure under which a broader collection of services to victims could be organized and made available.[24] In 1984, the Victim of Crime Act (VOCA) passed, which was discussed at the beginning of the chapter. It provided funds for victim assistance programs, victim compensation, and discretionary funding for research on victim needs.[25] Federal contributions to that funding source are made annually. In 1988, as an official agency of the US Department of Justice, the Office for Victims of Crime opened; its mission is to "enhance the Nation's capacity to assist crime victims and to provide leadership in changing attitudes, policies, and practices in ways that will promote justice and healing for all victims."[26] See Text Box 8.1, presented earlier in the chapter, for a list of major federal victim rights initiatives in the United States.

Marital rape was outlawed in all 50 states by 1993, and, when it was initially passed in 1994, the Violence Against Women Act (VAWA) was also passed as a landmark effort in victim rights, authorizing more than $1 billion in funding for programs to combat violence against women, with additional funding and prevention programming included. The road to sustaining the VAWA has been rocky.

In April 2004, the US Congress, after failing to pass a constitutional amendment, passed the Justice for All Act, a crime victims' rights act to strengthen the rights of victims of federal crimes. Critics disagree about whether the federal legislation should apply only to victims in federal crimes or be mandated at state levels of government, significantly impacting actions taken at the state level. At the current time, all states and the federal government have passed victim rights legislation, and 33 states have passed constitutional amendments to include victim rights.[27] The themes of victims' rights initiatives vary from state to state; however, major themes are included in Table 8.1.

In October 2016, the Survivors' Bill of Rights was passed; it

> identifies rights that must be afforded to sexual assault survivors in federal criminal cases, authorizes the Attorney General to administer grants to ensure that survivors receive certain notifications, and directs the Attorney General, in consultation with the Secretary of Health and Human Services, to establish a joint working group to *develop, coordinate, and disseminate best practices regarding the care and treatment of sexual assault survivors and the preservation of forensic evidence.*[28]

The working group identified six predominant themes:

1. Medical/forensic care
2. Trauma-informed approaches
3. Beyond DNA
4. Coordinated community response
5. Tracking evidence
6. Best practices and standards[29]

Table 8.1 Major Themes in Victim Rights Legislation (Varies from State to State)[1]

1. Right to Be Treated with Dignity, Respect, and Sensitivity
2. Right to Be Informed

   - the arrest and arraignment of the offender
   - bail proceedings
   - pretrial proceedings
   - dismissal of charges
   - plea negotiations
   - trial
   - sentencing
   - appeals
   - probation or parole hearings
   - release or escape of the offender

3. Right to Protection

   - police escorts
   - witness protection programs
   - relocation
   - restraining orders

4. Right to Apply for Compensation

   - medical and counseling expense
   - lost wages
   - funeral expenses

5. Right to Restitution from the Offender

   - lost wages
   - property loss
   - insurance deductibles

6. Right to Prompt Return of Personal Property
7. Right to a Speedy Trial
8. Right to Enforcement of Victims' Rights

1 "Get Help Bulletins for Crime Victims: Victims' Rights," National Center for Victims of Crime, accessed September 23, 2019, http://victimsofcrime.org/help-for-crime-victims/get-help-bulletins-for-crime-victims/victims'-rights.

Various resources for women and children have emerged around the globe, with several nations taking action to reduce or eliminate global sexual violence and exploitation. In 1985, the United Nations developed the **Declaration of the Basic Principles of Justice for Victims of Crime and Abuses of Power**.[30] Since that time and into the present, various countries, including Canada, the United States, and the United Kingdom,[31] have been working to establish a Victim's Bill of Rights, with the most recent effort in Canada said to have been reignited recently when a 17-year-old's suicide after an alleged rape and online harassment sparked public outrage.[32] (Chapter 9 reviews several international issues related to sexual exploitation.)

THE CONSEQUENCES OF SEXUAL VIOLENCE

Efforts to understand the full effect of sexual violence are ongoing. Data is being collected, reports are being written, specific groups are being studied and compared with other groups, all in an effort to best address questions and secure better levels of prevention. Attention is given to both more individual-ized impacts on sexual harm, followed by a review of levels of broader social impacts of sexualized violence. Although traditional reflection was given pri-mary to the scenario where a woman was the victim and the perpetrator was male, increasingly the full spectrum of gender and relationship types are being studied to better understand the similarities and differences in the groupings of people who have been harmed by sexualized violence. After a review of general responses victims have to sexual violence, attention is now being given addi-tionally to specific issues in relationships, in LGBTQI communities, for men and boys, and in communities of color.

VICTIMIZATION RESPONSES TO RAPE OR SEXUAL ASSAULT

Early studies on rape suggested that the coping strategies people who are raped used begin as the conditions for a sexual assault are being assessed.[33] Bodies can respond to danger in many ways, including fight, flight, or freeze. More recent research suggests a wide range of mitigating or coping skills are used by rape victims.[34] For example, the use of a weapon or a high level of aggression will likely be matched by the physical response of the victim.[35] Whether the victim was prepared in any way to meet a physical assault with a response will also determine the degree of response a victim offers under threat.[36] Consistently, research seems to indicate rape completion is less likely with almost any form of resistance[37] When bodies are in danger, it isn't usually the logical part of the mind that responds; it is often primal and somewhat automatic. This is another opportunity to make the point that the responsibility to prevent the crime should not lie on the shoulders of the victim but, instead, the person causing the harm.

Victims of sexual assault will have myriads of responses to the sexual assault. Some will happen immediately and some after an unspecified passage of time. Some of those responses will be physical and others more emotional. For exam-ple, one example is **tonic immobility**, or a form of profound moto inhibition usually associated with a situation of high fear, threat, and/or restraint.[38] Under threat, humans are known for a typical response of fight, flight, or freeze. This would be equal to the freeze response. Victims of a sexual assault might get angry or cry or yell, as other examples. As coping strategies emerge before an assault, so do coping strategies for surviving the attack, including threats, com-mands, or struggling. Some victims will focus on details or ways to remain calm or simply focus on something else.[39]

Victims will sometimes have other kinds of physiological responses that are more out of their control, such as choking, vomiting, or losing consciousness.[40] Victims who are assaulted with the facilitation of drugs or alcohol will have less recollection of the events and are unlikely to be able to resist their attacker.[41] A common drug used to incapacitate a victim is **rohypnol**, or GHB, and it can be ingested in a drink or food without the victim's knowledge.

As has been suggested in many places throughout this text, most sexual assault perpetrators are people known to the victim. Research suggests that, just like police response, the level of the relationship between the victim and the offender will influence how a victim responds to the assault.[42] (More about the police response is presented in chapter 11.) It is suggested by the DOJ's Office of Victims of Crime and the National Center for Victims of Crime that police investigations follow different investigative protocols for incidents where the perpetrators are known to the victims.[43]

Other responses to sexual violence can be longer term. In 1974, researchers Burgess and Holmstrom identified **rape trauma syndrome**, referring to the trauma experienced by a rape victim.[44] Initially, the focus was on the period immediately following the assault, the acute phase, typically weeks or days, and then a longer or protracted trauma, which could last for months or years. The phases of response were also discussed as real, regardless of whether the victim talked openly about them. Several people have created a variety of stages and phases attempting to describe with more clarity the process people go through after a sexual assault.[45]

Every person affected by sexual violence or sexual abuse responds differently. It is not uncommon for a person who experienced rape to have feelings of fear and anxiety and as a result need to take extra care to feel safe. This can include having people around them use a sympathetic tone and a nonjudgmental attitude.[46] Typical responses to rape and sexual assault can be emotional, including disbelief, fear, self-blame, anger, shame, and sadness. Responses vary with each person.[47] The need to communicate or express feelings will vary, but the immediate response to victims has been associated with the victim's **trauma response**, also referred to as **trauma-reaction symptoms**, which can affect a person's healing process. Sexual assault victimization (as either children or adults) can result in greater odds of drug abuse for lesbian, bisexual, and heterosexual women.[48] Research suggests that as many as 94 percent of women who are raped experience posttraumatic stress as a normal reaction to a shocking event.[49] Other mental health issues, such as depression, posttraumatic stress, guilt, and self-blame, may persist.

VICTIMIZATION RESPONSES TO CHILD SEXUAL ASSAULT

The process of helping children through sexual assault is evolving and has changed significantly. Past practices whereby children were encouraged to be silent or perhaps blamed for an assault are increasingly less likely. Resources for support are more prevalent. Parents or caregivers are encouraged to remind children that they are loved, the assault was not their fault, and the people around them will help them feel safe. Parents of children who have been assaulted are encouraged to seek support and may go through similar reactions: fear, shock, anger, anxiety, or depression.[50] This can make individual support and self-care essential for the child. Young children who are assaulted by a family member may have unexpected anger toward the nonoffending parent for removing the perpetrator from the house or may blame the nonoffending parent for not protecting them. They may want to talk about it a lot, or they may not want to discuss it at all. Increasingly, child advocacy centers (CACs) are being developed for children who have experienced sexual assault and abuse, where lawyers, social workers, police, medical professionals, and mental health professionals work together for the child and the family.[51] Professionals are continuing to change and adapt best practices as they continue to learn and respond to what is in the best interest of the child. Having experienced sexual assault as a child can influence a person's response to a later assault. Adults who were assaulted as children may experience more severe distress immediately after an assault and have a longer recovery time.[52]

VICTIMIZATION RESPONSES WITHIN INTIMATE PARTNERSHIPS

The effect of intimate partner violence within a relationship has been discussed in chapter 6 specifically. People are harmed and relationships may end as a result. But what about people whose family member or loved one is the victim of sexual violence? Attention is given here to supporting relationships and families where an individual has been assaulted by someone other than the partner or perhaps by someone known to the victim before they met their current partner but who is still affected by the trauma of the sexual assault. What can people who love and support victims of sexual violence do to help?

Research in this area is sparse but tends to reflect an awareness of and acceptance of rape myths as an important element. Several popular myths about rape and sexual assault are presented and discussed at the close of the chapter. Rape myths reflect this lack of education or understanding of the dynamic of sexual assault. More contemporary research suggests that attitudes about the degree to which a person blames the victim for an assault can be linked to whether people hold traditional understandings of male/female dynamics or more egalitarian attitudes.[53]

It is difficult, if not impossible, to set aside social attitudes about rape because the origin and effect of collective social beliefs is hard to identify or measure; however, for those who seek to support a loved one, the effect of a sexual assault of an intimate friend or partner can be similar to the experiences of the victim and can include anger, depression, a sense of despair, a sense of powerlessness, and outrage.[54] Fathers and brothers or boyfriends may have or express a desire for revenge[55] or fantasize about physically attacking the person.[56] Some partners will feel guilty or overprotective,[57] shame and humiliation, or helpless and therefore try to do too much or treat the victim like they are fragile and incapable of basic tasks as an overcompensation.[58] Also, specific consideration needs to be provided to any children in the household where a parent or sibling has suffered a sexual assault. Consistently, research suggests that children who were not directly affected should still be made aware of the event and be included in the healing process; however, they do not need to be made aware of the specific details of the event.[59]

VICTIMIZATION RESPONSES FROM MEN AND YOUNG BOYS

In the less typical cases where a woman is charged for assaulting a male, even if the person is a minor, court outcomes can sometimes reflect a rather dismissive cultural response, even negating the idea that any harm happened at all, rather than affording assistance for the young male victim.[60] Further, male-on-male sexual assault is a relatively new focus of mainstream study.[61] As was discussed in chapter 6, the federal definition of rape did not include the possibility of a sexual assault perpetrated against a man. Interestingly, the idea that a male would lose his masculinity if he were sexually assaulted, a common rape myth, parallels rape myths applied to women victims: that rape can and should be prevented by the person being assaulted, often leaving out or minimizing the role of the offender.

The response to sexual assault from men and boys reflects the effects of assaults on other survivors; however, men who were sexually abused as boys or teens may be affected differently than men who were assaulted as adults.[62] A common, although not complete, list of reactions from RAINN.org follows:

- Anxiety, depression, posttraumatic stress disorder flashbacks, eating disorders
- Avoiding people or places that remind you of the assault
- Concerns about sexual orientation
- Fear of "the worst" happening or a shortened future
- Feeling like "less of a man" or that you no longer have control over your body
- Feeling on edge, being unable to relax, and having difficulty sleeping
- Sense of blame or shame over not being able to stop the assault, especially if indications of arousal were present
- Increased sense of isolation
- Worrying about disclosing for fear of judgment

Newer research suggests that cultural attitudes and gendered expectations about sexual violence more broadly have historically overshadowed any perceived need for research in the area.[63] The information from the 2012 National Crime Victimization Survey findings, as discussed in more detail above, documented that 38 percent of incidents have been perpetrated against men, which sparked new research on the topic.[64] (Additional attention is given to outlining places for support for men and boys in chapter 14.)

VICTIMIZATION IN LGBTQI COMMUNITIES AND COMMUNITIES OF COLOR

Popular social attitudes undoubtedly default to a theme where the offender is male and the victim is female. Although smaller in number, according to current research, it is important to be attentive to the impacts of sexually abusive behaviors against members of the LGBTQI community. As with other subsets of sexual violence research groups, common themes emerge with regard to the impacts of violence. Gay and bisexual males are more likely than lesbians to experience sexual assault in relationships.[65] When placed side by side, gay, lesbian, and bisexual individuals reported higher rates of sexual violence within romantic relationships as compared to heterosexuals.[66] When compared to heterosexuals, higher rates of gay and bisexual males having experiences of sexual assault as children reported having substance use disorders. This dynamic was shared for females.[67] Further, gay and bisexual males who experienced sexual victimization within their relationships were more likely to abuse drugs and alcohol than gay and bisexual males who did not experience victimization in relationships.[68]

In addition to substance issues, other mental health issues were represented by people who had been victims of sexual offenses. Reports of high-risk sex behaviors were more likely in gay and bisexual male victims than nonvictims.[69] Women victimized by other women were seen to be more seriously affected by a loss of ability to trust perhaps because they saw their community as a place more likely to be free from violence.[70] Also, female victims of child sexual abuse or assault reported being younger in age when they questioned their sexual orientation, had consensual sex with another woman, or self-identified as lesbian when compared to women who were not victimized.[71]

Depression, substance use, and posttraumatic stress disorder and possible feelings of guilt, shame, and self-blame are just a few of the symptoms found in gay, lesbian, or bisexual victims of sexual abuse.[72] Attention is given to specialized responses to the LGBTQI community in chapter 14, as well as programming- and community-level responses raising awareness about victimization responses in communities of color.

LEVELS OF VICTIMIZATION IMPACT

In 1964, researchers Thorsten Sellin and Marvin Wolfgang identified three levels of victimization impact.[73] These three levels are primary, secondary, and tertiary victimization. **Primary victimization** refers to or affects the targeted victim. A second layering of victimization, discussed as **secondary victimization,** is more recently identified as people who were not directly victimized but are close friends or family members of the person assaulted and suffer from a result of the exposure to the victim or the scene of the victimization.[74] A final grouping of victim impact is discussed as **tertiary victimization**. In short, traumatic acts can create ripples and impact many lives. It is not uncommon for an entire community to feel the effects of a significant crime event. Tertiary victimization refers to the effect a crime has on the surrounding community. Research suggests that programmatic offerings at the secondary and tertiary levels have a positive impact on providing services to victims; additional research is needed to assess full viability.[75]

Consider the example of the rape that happened in Steubenville, Ohio, in August 2012. A female high school student was partying with friends and was later sexually assaulted by two different male high school students. Although she was reported to have awakened partially clothed, she didn't learn about the full extent of what had happened to her until pictures were posted to social media sites.[76] Clearly the young girl who was sexually assaulted was the primary victim in this case. The secondary victimization included the victim's parents, who were reportedly horrified by what had happened to their daughter. Perhaps friends of the young girl were reconsidering their own actions, when, in the days following the event, they might have felt bad that they had not intervened on her behalf. Perhaps they were negatively affected by their choice to not get involved, wondering if the outcome might have been different if they had offered to take her home or make sure she had folks looking out for her who could be trusted to ensure her safety. Teachers, investigators, or rape crisis counselors working with the case might also be identified as secondary victims. Finally, the larger community and perhaps people across the country who watched the story unfold could also have been negatively impacted. People in Steubenville, reportedly a tightly knit community, were shocked that something like this could happen in their community. The general sense of discomfort and fear of future such events or lingering effects of the incident could qualify as tertiary impacts of victimization.

Consider another example. A college town hears of the brutal beating and rape of a young woman near the college campus. The woman assaulted is the primary victim. The police and medical personnel who attend to her 911 call have never seen such a violent attack. As her friends and family learn of the event, they too will suffer secondary victimization impacts. They are not the person assaulted, but they are affected by the victimization event of their loved one or the event to which they responded. As the larger community hears about the event, perhaps friends watch each other more closely at the end of parties, or they remember having attended a class with the accused offender; they may take special care when they transport each other back to their campus housing or apartments after studying late. These might be examples of a tertiary level of victim impact.

Not surprising, the ecological model outlined earlier in the chapter is also an excellent graphical representation of the harm of sexualized violence at the community level, reflecting the initial impact, the larger impacts within families and friend circles, and then within the larger community. The impacts of trauma are likely to vary from case to case, city to city, and incident to incident. Increasingly, research is being conducted on the long-term effects of exposure by first responders or medical personnel to repeated trauma or a given significantly traumatic event, such as tornado or hurricane disasters, fatal automobile accidents, or child sexual abuse. When discussing victims, most often the primary victimization event is the focus of attention, and this makes sense given they are the most immediate person affected by an event. It is important to remember, too, the effects of the secondary and tertiary victim impacts.

IS THERE SUCH A THING AS A TYPICAL VICTIM RESPONSE? IN A WORD, NO

The United States has seen dramatic activism in the past 50 to 60 years around women's rights, violence prevention, sex crime victimization response, and prosecution, as well as sexual violence prevention efforts in the mainstream. Part of the research into this field of study has expanded because of efforts to understand the different levels of victim impact, as discussed above. Traditional research on victimization has typically focused on primary victimization. This section will overview what research offers regarding sexual violence victimization responses, including recommendations to people who are committed to offering love and support for those directly affected.

A PROCESS UNDER REVIEW: CRIMINAL JUSTICE SYSTEM IMPACTS ON VICTIMS

Much has been written about the important role police and hospital professionals play in the future health and wellness of a sexual assault victim/survivor. Research has shown those whom the victim comes in contact with first after an assault can set the tone for their healing and recovery. (Chapter 11 covers a significant amount of information on the criminal justice system and its process as it relates to identifying, arresting, processing, treating, and releasing individuals accused of committing sex offenses. Mention is made of the role of victims and advocates in that process.) Attention here is focused on research that highlights the effects of the current criminal justice system on the people who are victims as they are processed through this system.

In what is perhaps a poster case for potential system abuses of the victim is the case of accused rapist Luis Munuzuri-Harris, who acted as his own attorney and was therefore afforded by constitutional protection the opportunity to cross-exam the witness, the very person he was accused of having sexually assaulted. Although it is not typical, the case does demonstrate significant problems with the justice process where sexual assault is concerned. Early rape prevention advocates, researchers, and observers paid specific attention to the failings of the criminal justice system to protect women (at this time, almost all of the advocacy work was done by women for women), so much so that the process is referred to by many as the second assault. This highlights the fact that, in an adversarial justice process where the accused is innocent until proven guilty, a discredited witness would cast the much-needed shadow of a doubt necessary for the accused to be found not guilty. This justice system structure put the victim as the main target for discrediting the story of what happened, subjecting her to a second and very public round of abuse from this offender. This "assault," however, was legal and sanctioned by the justice system.

Steeped in a process of victim blaming, lawyers and other actors in the justice process would often reinforce the kinds of mentally and emotionally traumatizing experiences rape crisis centers were created to address. In addition to the treatment by the justice system itself were humiliating experiences in hospitals and police investigation processes. (See more about the development of the **sexual assault nurse examiner** [SANE] and sexual assault response team [SART] programs in chapter 11.)

While attention has been given to the social systems put in place to assist women and the ways in which the current justice system does not fully address some of these concerns, it must be noted that the evolution of these programs has resulted in a shift from early programs being run primarily by volunteers who were well meaning but not necessarily skilled, educated, or trained broadly about the issues they were confronting. Today, it is not uncommon for programs to have advocates who are highly trained social workers and counselors who understand the impact of trauma and have developed specialized knowledge about the process victims confront, personally first as a victim of sexualized violence and then in the system as a victim who reports the event to police and then throughout the entire justice process.

INFORMATION FOR PEOPLE WHO HAVE BEEN HARMED AND THE PEOPLE WHO LOVE THEM

As the result of a well-documented, lengthy history of sexual violence in the United States that has remained relatively accepted and unchallenged within mainstream culture for generations, part of the focus of early women's rights and sexual violence prevention advocates was to address and educate the masses about the popular and pervasive myths attached to sexual violence. Several of those early social attitudes may seem like ridiculous ideas no one would ever believe, but some are still being resoundingly challenged today.

Efforts to understand sexual violence as a cultural phenomenon, a "silent epidemic," or a "threat to public health" as discussed at the beginning of the chapter are argued by some to be directly linked to long-standing social attitudes and beliefs in rape myths, which offenders then use to justify sexualized violence against victims. Individual beliefs and attitudes about rape, fostered by attitudes reflected in the larger society, suggest to some perpetrators that sexually aggressive behavior, including rape, is justifiable.[77]

Consider the following:

2018: Greek males are more likely than non-Greek males to subscribe to traditional rape myths.[78]

2018: Students spontaneously articulated six types of rape myths in categories, including excusing perpetrators, trivializing sexual assault incidents, and blaming victims. The findings indicate that despite continued efforts on college campuses to eliminate or reduce students' rape myth endorsement, these beliefs continue to exist among undergraduate students. Additionally, often, students articulated rape myths that were subtler than rape myths measured with frequently used instruments, such as scale-based questionnaires.[79]

2017: Higher rape myths were associated with males, younger ages, lower GPAs, greater religiosity, greater alcohol consumption, and not knowing a victim of a sexual assault.[80]

2016: Comparing Japan, India, and the United States, researchers found college students in India, then Japan and then the United States were more likely to disbelieve a claim of rape.[81]

2006: It was found that men displayed significantly greater rape myth acceptance and greater negative attitudes toward rape victims. Additionally, participants with more traditional gender role beliefs, racist beliefs, and fundamentalist religious beliefs displayed more rape myth acceptance and more negative attitudes toward rape victims. Asian/Pacific Islander participants had more rape myth acceptance and more negative attitudes toward rape victims than did White participants.[82]

Because rape myth acceptance is an important determinant of sexual assault behaviors,[83] it can be impactful to call out false understandings. What research findings can be uncovered speaking to college attitudes and rape myths? A collection of more commonly referenced myths about rape are included at the close of the chapter.

Perhaps one of the most contentious focus areas of rape myths is directed toward the idea of **false reports**. A false report is a crime reported to a law enforcement agency that an investigation factually proves never occurred.[84] Research consistently finds the number of false reporting of sexual assault ranges from 2 to 10 percent. Again, report findings reflect different communities over different times, with different audiences. A 2010 study of 136 sexual assault cases in Boston from 1998–2007 found a 5.9 percent rate of false reports;[85] a 2009 multicommunity study, including 2,059 cases of sexual assault, found 7.1 percent false reports;[86] and a 2006 report of 812 reports of sexual assault from 2000–2003 found 2.1 percent false reports.[87] Research on false reports suggests the need for a careful consideration of findings because the definition of what constitutes a definition of a false report often falls outside of the definitions supported by most professionals in the field.[88] Research over time shows that the rates of 2 to 10 percent are likely inflated because of inconsistent definitions and protocols or a weak understanding of sexual assault.[89]

LEGACIES AND LEGISLATION: A BRIEF REVIEW

Chapter 10 provides a brief introduction to specific sexualized harms and the social policy that resulted from those crimes, some of which remain unsolved to this day. In few cases, the names of victims are held up as a remembrance of those people, often young people, who suffered unspeakable violence and death and who are dearly loved and sorely missed by friends and family left behind, trying to make sense out of what is surely a senseless action. The few names used in legislation, even legislation at the state level, do not come close to the number of people who have suffered varying degrees of sexualized harm at the hand of another person. The more people learn about sexual violence, the more they realize how prevalent it is and how likely it is for each of us to know someone whose life has been affected, either directly or indirectly by sexualized violence.

As efforts to look at the harm done come to a close and efforts shift to focusing on what next steps can be taken, it is important to spend a little time with some of the folks who have taken action in response to being a victim of sexual assault and lived to tell their story. Consider this chapter to be its own kind of vigil, a space to reflect upon the costs and consequences for individuals and societies affected by sexual violence. In this case, however, we have the luxury of gathering together to ask these questions and consider responses from each other in a quiet contemplative place, rather than in the aftermath of a specific horrific act.

The seemingly inexhaustible amounts of research covered in preparation for this text remind us without question that many people have been victims of sexual assault and have suffered in silence or gone on to seek assistance and led relatively normal lives after the assault. Even more have chosen to take their victimization and use their story to teach others about the effect of sexual violence and the need to expand sexual violence education and prevention efforts to better protect the communities throughout the United States. We honor the strength of those who have paved the way before us as researchers and writers and as we begin to think about actions we can take either as an individual or within a group to reduce sexual harm (the focus of chapter 15).

Sadly, news forums are replete with stories similar to these every day. The stories presented here were randomly collected from various news outlets and works on sexual violence; while any such collection of such stories is too long, creating an inclusive list is simply not possible. In so many ways, the lives of victims are changed by their victimization and changed in different ways again if they make that victimization known. They may be harassed or unfairly or inaccurately challenged, or their actions might be second-guessed by outsiders with little or no information about their experience. These individuals are mentioned here because it is so often the victims of abuse whose experiences provide education and information about the people and situations in which long-term sexual abuse or incidents of sexual assault occur, moving us one step closer to decreasing the number of sex crimes through sexual violence prevention efforts.

CHAPTER CONCLUSION

Attention throughout the chapter is focused on learning about the impact of sexual violence on the people who are harmed. Some victim responses to sexual harms will be similar; however, every person will move through the healing and recovery process in the aftermath of a sexual assault in uniquely their own way and in their own time. Attention was given to the history of victimology as an academic field of study and to the victims' rights movement in the United States. Some more pronounced victimization responses were discussed for rape victims, victims of child sexual assault, intimate partner violence, men and boys, the LGBTQI community, and communities of color. As the chapter closed, attention was given to the reality that sexual violence influences more than just the victim in that these events can be profoundly impactful on families, friends, and larger sectors of a community. A brief mention of the impact of the criminal justice system on victims and the ways families and loved ones seek to honor and support them and the person harmed by sexualized violence closed the chapter.

Text Box 8.2.   Media Messages about People Who Have Been Harmed by Sexual Violence

What information about people who have been harmed by sexual violence needs to be reclaimed or reconsidered?

Fact: Coverage in the chapter included a review of the idea of an "ideal" victim. Also, information has included several indications that the work of prevention programs and social service support does not reach all communities equally, with a significant number of indigenous women and African American women comprising a list of missing or victims of foul play at higher numbers. Further, women with more money receive more attention.

Application: What national or regional programming could be put in place to assure a more equal social response to people who have been sexually harmed or remain missing? What would be required to make that happen? To make that available in the locations where those resources are needed?

Fact: False reporting of sexual assault has consistently rested at between 2 and 10 percent. Researchers suggest confusion with the classification of false reports would very likely reduce that number if a consistent definition could be secured. On the high side, taking into account the number is likely overinflated, how does this influence your awareness around the common narrative that victims of sex crimes cannot be trusted to tell the truth, or they are in search of money, or they are seeking attention?

Application: When an incident of a false report is made known, attention can be given to the tragedy of that false claim. Being falsely accused is undoubtedly a horrible experience. What would be some ways to acknowledge the tragedy without elevating the false narrative of false reports?

What ideas and/or information do you bring to this conversation about people who have been harmed in a sexualized way?

After considering the material presented in chapter 8 on offenders, what information from the media do you see requiring additional and particular focus for calling out inaccuracies?

What other facts that you are learning require adjustments to what you believed in the past about people who have been harmed by sexualized violence?

KEY TERMS

Benjamin Mendelsohn
Concerns of Police Survivors
Declaration of the Basic Principles of Justice for Victims of Crime and Abuses of Power
domestic violence shelters
ecological theory
false reports

Family Violence Prevention and Services Act
interactional theories
just world theory
Justice Assistance Act
lifestyle routine activities theories
Linda R.S. v. Richard D.

missing and murdered indigenous
   women
National Center for Missing and
   Exploited Children
Office for Victims of Crime
Office for Victims of Crime Resource
   Center
primary victimization
rape crisis centers
rape trauma syndrome
rohypnol
secondary victimization
sexual assault nurse examiner
societal-based theories

tertiary victimization
tonic immobility
trauma response
trauma-reaction symptoms
victim
victim advocacy
victim blaming
victim precipitation
Victim Rights Movement
victim typologies
victim-based theories
victimology
Victims of Crime Act (VOCA)

REVIEW QUESTIONS

1. What was the decade with a wave of new action around victims' rights issues?

2. Outline the characteristics and the importance of the 1984 Victims of Crime Act.

3. Early crime theories placed a considerable amount of attention on the victim in their role in the crime itself. In what ways is this reflected in early research?

4. Explain fully the idea of the ecological theory and its visual representation.

5. Although it is important to remember everyone responds to rape or sexual assault differently, what are the most common responses people go through?

DISCUSSION QUESTIONS

1. Discuss the importance of considering the use of the terms "victim," "offender," "survivor," and "thriver." Consider this in the context of "neither victim nor survivor" and "victim no more."

2. How is disrupting myths around sexual violence related to supporting victims? What are some of the best ways to disrupt myths? Is the practice of myth busting more difficult than one might think at first glance?

3. Why do communities of color and indigenous communities warrant particular focus? Why does the history of violence in those communities get dropped from the main stories told about sexual violence and prevention efforts? What can be done to better address those concerns?

4. More will be coming regarding the role of the criminal justice system in responding to an incident of sexual harm in chapter 10. The impact of the system on victims is well known among professionals in the field. What can

be done about this to assure a fair trial for the accused and to protect the emotional and mental health of the person who has been harmed?

5. What pieces of working to assist a victim of sexual assault stand out? What might be more difficult for people who are friends and family members? What might be some ways to think about this that would be helpful should the information be needed? What are some local resources where information can be gathered?

NOTES

1. Judah Oudshoorn with Lorraine Stutzman Amstutz and Michelle Jacket, *The Little Book of Restorative Justice for Sexual Abuse: Hope through Trauma* (New York: Good Books, 2015), 3.

2. "From Hurt to Healer: The 'Tell Somebody' Movement." BlackDoctor.org, September 14, 2015, https://blackdoctor.org/465163/child-molestation-tell-somebody-movement/.

3. "History of Victims' Rights," National Crime Victim Law Institute, https://law.lclark.edu/centers/national_crime_victim_law_institute/about_ncvli/history_of_victims_rights/.

4. Ibid.

5. Licia Berry, "The 5 Stages of Healing from Trauma," Survivor Manual, 2013, accessed September 19, 2019, http://www.survivormanual.com/the-5-stages-of-healing-from-trauma/.

6. Much is written on this, but see, for example, Laurie A. Rudman and Kris Mescher, "Of Animals and Objects: Men's Implicit Dehumanization of Women and Likelihood of Sexual Aggression," *Personality and Social Psychology Bulletin* 38, no. 6 (2012): 734–46; W. L. Marshall, D. R. Laws, and H. E. Barbaree, eds., *Handbook of Sexual Assault* (New York: Springer Science+Business Media, 1990); Steve Loughnan et al., "Sexual Objectification Increases Rape Victim Blame and Decreases Perceived Suffering," *Psychology of Women Quarterly* 37, no. 4 (2013): 455–61.

7. Mike Lew and Ellen Bass, *Victims No Longer: Men Recovering from Incest and Other Sexual Child Abuse* (New York: HarperPerennial, 1990); Marilyn Nissim-Sabat, "*Neither Victim nor Survivor: Thinking toward a New Humanity. Theorizing Sexual Violence* (Lanham, MD: Lexington Books, 2009); Renée J. Heberle and Victoria Grace, eds., *Theorizing Sexual Violence* (New York and London: Routledge, 2009).

8. Benjamin Mendelsohn, *Rape in Criminology* (Giustizia Penale, 1940).

9. This distribution was presented by Albert R. Roberts, Cheryl Regehr, and Ann Wolbert Burgess, *Victimology* (Burlington, MA: Jones and Bartlett Learning, 2013), Chapter 3.

10. Mendelsohn, *Rape in Criminology*; Ofur Zur, "Rethinking 'Don't Blame the Victim': Psychology of Victimhood," *Journal of Couples Therapy* 4, no. 3/4 (1995): 15–36 as presented in Table 3.1 from Roberts, Burgess, and Regehr, *Victimology*, 77.

11. Roberts, Burgess, and Regehr, *Victimology*, 77.

12. Zur, "Rethinking 'Don't Blame the Victim,'" 17.

13. Jackson Katz, "Violence against Women—It's a Men's Issue," TedxFiDiWomen, November 2012, accessed October 20, 2019, https://www.ted.com/talks/jackson_katz_violence_against_women_it_s_a_men_s_issue.

14. Melvin Learner, *The Belief in a Just World: A Fundamental Delusion* (New York: Plenum, 1980).

15. See, for example, S. Blumenthal, G. Gudjonsson, and J. Burns, "Cognitive Distortions and Blame Attribution in Sex Offenders against Adults and Children," *Child Abuse & Neglect* 23, no. 2 (1999): 129–43, doi:10.1016/S0145-2134(98)00117-3; Ó. C. Ciardha, "A Theoretical Framework for Understanding Deviant Sexual Interest and Cognitive Distortions as

Overlapping Constructs Contributing to Sexual Offending against Children," *Aggression and Violent Behavior* 16 (2011): 493–502, doi:10.1016/j.avb.2011.05.001.

16. Roberts, Burgess, and Regehr, *Victimology*, 81.

17. Much has been written about the role poverty, race, and sexual identity play in increased experiences of sexualized violence and harm. See, for example, Leah Fessler, "The Poorest Americans Are 12 Times as Likely to Be Sexually Assaulted as the Wealthiest," Quartz, January 3, 2018, accessed September 19, 2019, https://qz.com/1170426/the-poorest-americans-are-12 -times-as-likely-to-be-sexually-assaulted/; Yasmin Jiwani and Mary Lynn Young, "Missing and Murdered Women: Reproducing Marginality in News Discourse," *Canadian Journal of Communication* 31, no. 4 (2006), https://doi.org/10.22230/cjc.2006v31n4a1825; and "*Maquiladora*'s Lost Women: The Killing Fields of Mexico—Are NAFTA and NAALC Providing the Needed Protection?" *Journal of Gender, Race & Justice*, 4, no. 137 (2000–2001), https://heinonline.org/HOL/LandingPage?handle=hein.journals/jgrj4&div=11&id=&page.

18. Lawrence E. Cohen and Marcus Felson, "Social Change and Crime Rate Trends: A Routine Activity Approach," *American Sociological Review* 44, no. 4 (1979): 588–608. http:// dx.doi.org/10.2307/2094589.

19. Bonnie S. Fisher et al., "Crime in the Ivory Tower: The Level and Sources of Student Victimization," *Criminology* 36, no. 3 (1998): 671–710, https://doi.org/10.1111/j.1745-9125.1998. tb01262.x; J. Lasley, "Drinking Routines/Lifestyles and Predatory Victimization: A Causal Analysis," *Justice Quarterly*, August 15, 2006: 529–42, accessed October 20, 2019, https:// doi.org/10.1080/07418828900090371; R. Morgan and J. Truman, "Criminal Victimization, 2017," December 2018, NCJ 252472, US Department of Justice, Bureau of Justice Statistics, accessed October 20, 2019, https://www.bjs.gov/content/pub/pdf/cv17.pdf.

20. Quote from Urie Bronfenbrenner, *The Ecology of Human Development* (Cambridge, MA: Harvard University Press, 1979), 10. On broader issues of development, see also Jay Belsky, "Child Maltreatment: An Ecological Integration," *American Psychologist* 35 (1980): 320–35, http://dx.doi.org/10.1037/0003-066X.35.4.320; Marion Bogo, *Social Work Practice* (New York: Columbia University Press, 2006); Carel B. Germain and Alex Gitterman, *The Life Model of Social Work Practice* (New York: Columbia University Press, 1996).

21. "The History of Crime Victims' Rights in America: An Historical Overview," Maryland Crime Victims Resource Center, 2014, accessed September 19, 2019, https://ovc.ncjrs.gov/ ncvrw2014/pdf/Landmarks.pdf.

22. J. Stein, "Wisconsin Senate Votes to Give Crime Victims New Constitutional Rights under Marsy's Law," *Milwaukee Journal Sentinel*, accessed October 20, 2019, https://www .jsonline.com/story/news/politics/2017/11/07/crime-victims-would-get-new-constitutional -safeguards-under-marsys-law-bill-before-wisconsin-senate/839822001/; The United States Department of Justice, "Rights of Child Victims," July 6, 2015, accessed October 20, 2019, https://www.justice.gov/criminal-ceos/rights-child-victims.

23. For example, L. Silverman, "More Domestic Violence Shelters for Men Opening," NPR, July 17, 2017, accessed October 20, 2019, https://www.npr.org/2017/07/15/537381161/ more-domestic-violence-shelters-for-men-opening.

24. See the history of the organization here: https://www.trynova.org/who-we-are/.

25. "Victims of Crime," National Institute of Justice, Office of Justice Programs, accessed September 23, 2019, http://www.nij.gov/topics/victims-victimization/rights.htm.

26. "OVC Fact Sheet: What Is the Office for Victims of Crime?" accessed September 23, 2019, https://www.ovc.gov/publications/factshts/what_is_OVC2010/intro.html.

27. "Get Help Bulletins for Crime Victims: Victims' Rights," National Center for Victims of Crime, accessed September 23, 2019, http://victimsofcrime.org/help-for-crime-victims/get -help-bulletins-for-crime-victims/victims'-rights.

28. "Survivors' Bill of Rights Act Working Group: Report to Congress October 2018," US Department of Justice and US Department of Health and Human Services, accessed September 19, 2019, page 4, https://www.justice.gov/ovw/page/file/1100476/download.

29. Ibid., 7.

30. United Nations, "Declaration of Basic Principles of Justice for Victims of Crime and Abuse of Power," 1985, accessed September 19, 2019, https://www.un.org/en/genocidepre vention/documents/atrocity-crimes/Doc.29_declaration%20victims%20crime%20and%20 abuse%20of%20power.pdf.

31. Deborah McGurran, "Calls for New Rights for Victims of Crime," BBC News, December 15, 2011, accessed September 19, 2019, www.bbc.co.uk/news/uk-england-16205713.

32. Canadian Press, "Victim's Rights Bill to Be Months in the Making: Nicholson," *i*Politics, April 23, 2013, accessed September 19, 2019, http://www.ipolitics.ca/2013/04/23/vic tims-rights-bill-to-be-months-in-the-making-nicholson/.

33. Anne Wolbert Burgess and Lynda Lytle Holmstrom, "Coping Behavior of the Rape Victim," *American Journal of Psychiatry* 133, no. 4 (1976): 413–18, https://doi.org/10.1176/ ajp.133.4.413.

34. Jessica Woodhams et al., "Behavior Displayed by Female Victims during Rapes Committed by Lone and Multiple Perpetrators," *Psychology, Public Policy, and Law* 18, no. 3 (2012): 415–52, http://dx.doi.org/10.1037/a0026134.

35. Jessica Woodhams and Claire Cooke, "Suspect Aggression and Victim Resistance in Multiple Perpetrator Rapes," *Archives of Sexual Behavior* 42, no. 8 (2013): 1509–16, http:// dx.doi.org/10.1007/s10508-013-0136-7.

36. Christine Gidycz, Amy Van Wynsberghe, and Katie M. Edwards, "Prediction of Women's Utilization of Resistance Strategies in a Sexual Assault Situation: A Prospective Study, *Journal of Interpersonal Violence* 23, no. 5 (2008): 571–88, https://doi.org/10.1177/0886260507313531.

37. Jongyeon Tark and Gary Kleck, "Resisting Crime: The Effects of Victim Action on the Outcomes of Crimes," *Criminology* 42, no. 4 (2004): 861–910, https://doi.org/10.1111/ j.1745-9125.2004.tb00539.x.

38. Grace Galliano et al., "Victim Reactions during Rape/Sexual Assault: A Preliminary Study of the Immobility Response and Its Correlates," *Journal of Interpersonal Violence* 8, no. 1 (1993): 109–14, https://doi.org/10.1177/088626093008001008.

39. Diane Daane, "Victim Response to Sexual Assault," in *Sexual Assault: The Victims, the Perpetrators, and the Criminal Justice System*, ed. Frances P. Reddington and Betsy Wright Kreisel (Durham, NC: Carolina Academic Press, 2017), 96. See also Burgess and Holmstrom, "Coping Behavior of the Rape Victim"; Woodhams et al., "Behavior Displayed by Female Victims during Rapes."

40. Daane, "Victim Response to Sexual Assault," 96.

41. Heather Littleton, Danny Axsom, and Amie Grills-Taquechel, "Sexual Assault Victims' Acknowledgment Status and Revictimization Risk," *Psychology of Women's Quarterly* 33, no. 1 (2009): 34–42, https://doi.org/10.1111/j.1471-6402.2008.01472.x; Nora Fitzgerald and K. Jack Riley, "Drug-Facilitated Rape: Looking for the Missing Pieces," *National Institute of Justice Journal*, April 2000, accessed September 23, 2019, https://www.ncjrs.gov/pdffiles1/ jr000243c.pdf.

42. Brian A. Feinstein et al., "Victim-Offender Relationship Status Moderates the Relationships of Peritraumatic Emotional Responses, Active Resistance, and Posttraumatic Stress Symptomology in Female Rape Survivors," *Psychological Trauma* 3, no. 2 (2011), 192–200, doi:10.1037/a0021652.

43. "Pocket Guide for Police Response to Sexual Assault," New York State Coalition Against Sexual Assault, 1998, accessed September 19, 2019, https://ovc.ncjrs.gov/sartkit/tools/lawen forcement/Pocket%20Guide%20for%20Police%20Response%20to%20Sexual%20Assault. pdf.pdf; "A Special Class of Victims," victimsofcrime.org, accessed September 19, 2019, https://victimsofcrime.org/docs/dna-protocol/baltimore_a-guide-for-developing-a-law-en forcement-protocol.pdf?sfvrsn=0.

44. Ann Wolbert Burgess and Lynda Lytle Holmstrom, "Rape Trauma Syndrome," *American Journal of Psychiatry* 131, no. 9 (1974): 981–86, doi:10.1176/ajp.131.9.981.

45. Aphrodite Matsakis, *The Rape Recovery Handbook* (Oakland, CA: New Harbinger Publications, 2003); Matt Atkinson, *Resurrection after Rape: A Guide to Transforming from Victim to Survivor* (Oklahoma City: RAR Publishing, 2004); and Wendy Maltz, *The Sexual Healing Journey* (New York: William Morrow, 2001).

46. T. Woods, "Responding to Victims of Crime, 2008, accessed October 20, 2019, https://ovc.ncjrs.gov/ovcproviderforum/asp/Transcript.asp?Topic_ID=101. See also as another example, The National Sheriff's Association, "First Response to Victims of Crime," Office for Victims of Crime, US Department of Justice, July 2010, accessed October 20, 2019, https://www.ovc.gov/publications/infores/pdftxt/2010FirstResponseGuidebook.pdf.

47. See, for example, "Sexual Assault Response Team (SART) Tool Kit," Office of Justice Programs, March 2011, accessed October 20, 2019, https://www.ncjrs.gov/ovc_archives/sartkit/.

48. See, for example, K. Lehavot, Y. Molina, and J. Simoni, "Childhood Trauma, Adult Sexual Assault, and Adult Gender Expressions among Lesbian and Bisexual Women," *Sex Roles* 67, no. 5-6 (2012): 272–84, doi:10.1007/s11199-012-0171-1.

49. Elyssa Barbash, "Overcoming Sexual Assault: Symptoms and Recovery," *Psychology Today*, April 18, 2017, https://www.psychologytoday.com/us/blog/trauma-and-hope/201704/overcoming-sexual-assault-symptoms-recovery.

50. See, for example, "Sexual Assault Response Team (SART) Tool Kit"; "Help Someone You Care About," RAINN, accessed October 20, 2019, https://www.rainn.org/articles/help-someone-you-care-about.

51. "How the CAC Model Works," National Children's Alliance, accessed September 19, 2019, https://www.nationalchildrensalliance.org/cac-model/.

52. Catalina M. Arata, "Coping with Rape: The Roles of Prior Sexual Abuse and Attributions of Blame," *Journal of Interpersonal Violence* 14, no. 1 (1999): 62–78, https://doi.org/10.1177/088626099014001004.

53. See, for example, Erin E. Ayala, Brandy Kotary, and Maria Hetz, "Blame Attributions of Victims and Perpetrators: Effects of Victim Gender, Perpetrator Gender, and Relationship," *Journal of Interpersonal Violence* 33, no. 1 (2015), accessed October 20, 2019, https://doi.org/10.1177/0886260515599160.

54. M. S. Cwik, "The Many Effects of Rape: The Victim, Her Family, and Suggestions for Family Therapy," *Family Therapy* 23 (1996): 95–116.

55. Ibid.

56. M. T. Notman and C. C. Nadelson, "The Rape Victim: Psychodynamic Considerations," *American Journal of Psychiatry* 133, no. 4 (1976): 408–13, https://doi.org/10.1176/ajp.133.4.408.

57. Silverman, D.C., "Sharing the Crisis of Rape: Counseling the Mates and Families of Victims." *American Journal of Orthopsychiatry* 48, (1978): 166–173.

58. Courtney E. Ahrens and Rebecca Campbell, "Assisting Rape Victims as They Recover from Rape: The Impact on Friends," *Journal of Interpersonal Violence* 15, no. 9 (2000), accessed October 20, 2019, https://doi.org/10.1177/088626000015009004.

59. "Helping Children Cope after a Traumatic Event," Child Mind Institute, accessed October 20, 2019, https://childmind.org/guide/helping-children-cope-traumatic-event/.

60. "Sexual Assault of Men and Boys," RAINN, accessed October 20, 2019, https://www.rainn.org/articles/sexual-assault-men-and-boys.

61. Richard Tewksbury, "Effects of Sexual Assaults on Men: Physical, Mental and Sexual Consequences," *International Journal of Men's Health* 6, no. 1 (2007): 22–35, https://riselearningnetwork.org/wp-content/uploads/2019/04/10.1.1.830.810.pdf.

62. "Sexual Assault of Men and Boys."

63. "High Prevalence of Sexual Victimization Detected among Men; Similar to Prevalence Found among Women in Many Cases," The Williams Institute, UCLA School of Law, April 30, 2014, https://williamsinstitute.law.ucla.edu/press/press-releases/high-prevalence

-of-sexual-victimization-detected-among-men-similar-to-prevalence-found-among-women
-in-many-cases/.

64. Lara Stemple and Ilan H. Meyer, "The Sexual Victimization of Men in America: New Data Challenge Old Assumptions," *American Journal of Public Health* 104, no. 6 (2014): e19–e26, doi:10.2105/AJPH.2014.301946.

65. M. Hester and C. Donovan, "Researching Same Sex Domestic Violence: Constructing a Survey Methodology," Sociological Research Online, December 11, 2017, accessed October 20, 2019, https://doi.org/10.5153/sro.1650.

66. M. L. Walters, J. Chen, and M. J. Breiding, "The National Intimate Partner and Sexual Violence Survey (NISVS): 2010 Findings on Victimization by Sexual Orientation," National Center for Injury Prevention and Control, Centers for Disease Control and Prevention, 2013, accessed October 20, 2019, https://www.cdc.gov/violenceprevention/pdf/nisvs_sofindings .pdf; S. C. Turell, "A Descriptive Analysis of Same-Sex Relationship Violence for a Diverse Sample," *Journal of Family Violence* 15 (2000): 281, accessed October 20, 2019, https://doi .org/10.1023/A:1007505619577.

67. T. Hughes, S. E. McCabe, S. C. Wilsnack, B. T. West, and C. J. Boyd, "Victimization and Substance Use Disorders in a National Sample of Heterosexual and Sexual Minority Women and Men," *Addiction* 105, no. 12 (2010): 2130–40, doi:10.1111/j.1360-0443.2010.03088.x.

68. Eric Houston and David J. McKirnan, "Intimate Partner Abuse among Gay and Bisexual Men: Risk Correlates and Health Outcomes," *Journal of Urban Health* 84, no. 5 (2007): 681–90.

69. S. Arreola, T. Neilands, and R. Díaz, "Childhood Sexual Abuse and the Sociocultural Context of Sexual Risk among Adult Latino Gay and Bisexual Men," *American Journal of Public Health* October 2009, accessed October 2019, https://ajph.aphapublications.org/doi/ full/10.2105/AJPH.2008.138925; D. Brennan, W. Hellerstedt, M. Ross, and S. Welles, "History of Childhood Sexual Abuse and HIV Risk Behaviors in Homosexual and Bisexual Men," *American Journal of Public Health*, June 2007, accessed October 20, 2019, https://ajph.apha publications.org/doi/full/10.2105/AJPH.2005.071423.

70. C. Kaukinen, "The Help-Seeking of Women Violent Crime Victims: Findings from the Canadian Violence Against Women Survey," *International Journal of Sociology and Social Policy*, August 2002, accessed October 20, 2019, https://www.emerald.com/insight/content/ doi/10.1108/01443330210790085/full/html.

71. J. Morris, G. Herek, and B. Levy, "Lesbian and Bisexual Women's Experiences of Victimization: Mental Health, Revictimization, and Sexual Identity Development," *Journal of Lesbian Studies* 2003, accessed October 20, 2019, doi:10.1300/J155v07n04_05.

72. Linda Garnets, Gregory M. Herek and Barrie Levy, "Violence and Victimization of Lesbians and Gay Men: Mental Health Consequences," *Journal of Interpersonal Violence* 5, no. 3 (1990): 366–83, https://doi.org/10.1177/088626090005003010; Jennifer M. Heidt, Brian P. Marx, and Sari D. Gold, "Sexual Revictimization among Sexual Minorities: A Preliminary Study, *Journal of Traumatic Stress* 18, no. 5 (2005): 533–40, https://doi.org/10.1002/ jts.20061; T. L. Hughes, T. Johnson, and S. C. Wilsnack, "Sexual Assault and Alcohol Abuse: A Comparison of Lesbians and Heterosexual Women," *Journal of Substance Abuse* 13, no. 4 (2001): 515–32, http://dx.doi.org/10.1016/S0899-3289(01)00095-5; M. Otis and W. Skinner, "The Prevalence of Victimization and Its Effect on Mental Well-Being among Lesbian and Gay People," *Journal of Homosexuality* 30, no. 3 (1996): 93–121, https://www.ncbi.nlm.nih .gov/pubmed/8743118.

73. Thorsten Sellin and Marvin E. Wolfgang, *The Measurement of Delinquency* (New York: Wiley, 1964).

74. See, for example, Charles R. Figley, *Compassion Fatigue: Coping with Secondary Traumatic Stress Disorder in Those Who Treat the Traumatized* (New York: Brunner/Mazel, 1995); B. Hudnall Stamm, ed., *Secondary Traumatic Stress: Self-Care Issues for Clinicians, Researchers and Educators* (Lutherville, MD: The Sidran Press, 1995).

75. Lucy Kirk et al., "Effectiveness of Secondary and Tertiary Prevention for Violence against Women in Low and Low-Middle Income Countries: A Systematic Review," *BMC Public Health* 17 (2017): 622, doi:10.1186/s12889-017-4502-6.

76. For more on the Steubenville rape case and the trial outcome see chapter 6.

77. R. Wegner, A. Abbey, J. Pierce, S. Pegram, and J. Woerner, "Sexual Assault Perpetrators' Justifications for Their Actions: Relationships to Rape Supportive Attitudes, Incident Characteristics, and Future Perpetration," *Violence Against Women* 21, no. 8 (2015): 1018–37, doi:10.1177/1077801215589380.

78. Taylor Martinez et al., "Good Guys Don't Rape": Greek and Non-Greek College Student Perpetrator Rape Myths," *Behavioral Sciences (Basel)* 8, no. 7 (2018): 60, doi:10.3390/bs8070060.

79. Julia O'Connor et al., "Students' Articulation of Subtle Rape Myths Surrounding Campus Sexual Assault," *Journal of College Student Development* 59, no. 4 (2018): 439–55, https://muse.jhu.edu/article/699391/pdf.

80. John C. Navarro and Richard Tewksbury, "Mythbusters: Examining Rape Myth Acceptance among U.S. University Students," *Journal of Student Affairs Research and Practice* 54, no. 4 (2017): 343–56.

81. Tamara Stephens et al., "Rape Myth Acceptance among College Students in the United States, Japan, and India, *Sage Open* 6, no. 4 (2016), https://doi.org/10.1177/2158244016675015.

82. B. L. Mulliken, "Rape Myth Acceptance in College Students: The Influence of Gender, Racial, and Religious Attitudes," Dissertation Abstracts International: Section B: The Sciences and Engineering, 66(11-B) (2006), 6285.

83. Stephens, "Rape Myth Acceptance among College Students in the United States, Japan, and India."

84. National Sexual Violence Resource Center, "False Reporting: Overview," Office on Violence Against Women, US Department of Justice, 2012, accessed October 20, 2019, https://www.nsvrc.org/sites/default/files/Publications_NSVRC_Overview_False-Reporting.pdf.

85. D. Lisak, L. Gardinier, and S. Nicksa, "False Allegations of Sexual Assault: An Analysis of Ten Years of Reported Cases," *Violence Against Women* 16, no. 12 (2010), https://doi.org/10.1177/1077801210387747.

86. K. Lonsway, J. Archambault, and D. Lisak, "False Reports: Moving the Issue to Successfully Investigate and Prosecute Non-Stranger Sexual Assault," *The Voice*, 3 (2009): 1, www.ndaa.org/ncpvaw_the_voice_newsletter.html.

87. M. Heenan and S. Murray, "Study of Reported Rapes in Victoria 2000–2003," Statewide Steering Committee to Reduce Sexual Assault, Australia, July 2006, accessed October 20, 2019, https://www.ncjrs.gov/app/abstractdb/AbstractDBDetails.aspx?id=243182.

88. Lisak et al., "False Allegations of Sexual Assault."

89. "False Reporting: Overview," National Sexual Violence Resource Center, accessed September 19, 2019, https://www.nsvrc.org/sites/default/files/Publications_NSVRC_Overview_False-Reporting.pdf.

9

Focusing on Global Issues of Sexual Violence and Harm

Can we bear to look? Can we afford not to?

—Robert Jensen, *Getting Off:*
Pornography and the End of Masculinity[1]

The rights (women) want:
   —we want to choose our husbands
   —we want to own land
   —we want to go to school
   —we don't want to be cut anymore (referring to female circumcision)
   —we want also to make decisions
   —we want respect in politics, to be leaders
   —we want to be equal.

   —Rebecca Lolosoli, from *Half the Sky* by Kristof and WuDunn[2]

As law enforcement and advocacy organizations across the nation have set forth a clear agenda for stopping the domestic trafficking of adolescents, the true challenge has been obtaining accurate scientific data that quantifies the scope of actual supply and demand.

   —Ernie Allen, President and CEO (2010) National
   Center for Missing and Exploited Children[3]

It is what we learn as girls. Our sexuality is dangerous. It causes men to do bad things to us. The idea is it's our fault. It took me years to undo all of these messages.

   —Interview with Candida Royalle in
   Working Sex by Marianne Macy[4]

MALALA YOUSAFZAI, a Pakistani schoolgirl, became an international symbol of gender violence when, at the age of 15, she was shot in the face by a member of an extremist group because of her active and vocal commitment to receiving an education—as a girl.[5] The fact that she did not die was hailed by many as a miracle. The youngest person ever to have been nominated for and to have received the Nobel Peace Prize, she has written a best-selling book and speaks all around the world about the 61 million children, both boys and girls, who do not have access to formal education.[6] Targeted for violence because she is a girl, she continues her work to secure educational access for all children.

Individual, localized incidents such as Malala's contrast sharply with global incidents that have a broad reach and involve international actors discovered in a 2013 international police operation titled **Project Spade** (Figure 9.1). After a three-year-long investigation, Canadian police disclosed to the world a sweeping international child exploitation investigation, which led to the rescue of 386 children around the world and produced the arrests of 348 people.[7] Aside from the horrible sexual abuse of children discovered, many seasoned investigators reported being shocked to find out how many arrested worked in jobs with children. Among those arrested included 40 schoolteachers or school administrators, 9 doctors and nurses, more than 30 people who volunteered with kids, 9 clergy, 6 police officers, and 3 foster parents.[8] Toronto-based owner of Azov Films, Brian Way instructed people around the world to create videos of children, mostly boys, ranging in age from 5 to 12 years. Many were from Eastern European countries.

The videos were then distributed to international customers in more than 50 countries. The company was said to have been running since 2005 and to have secured $4 million in revenue. In Canada, 108 people were arrested, 76 in the United States, and 164 in a collection of other countries.[9] After an initial sentence of 10 years, in 2017 Way was granted a six-month reduction in his sentence after alleging physical and verbal abuse in custody.[10]

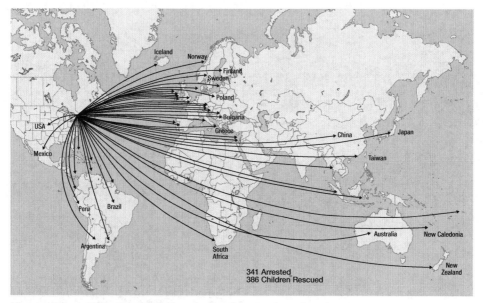

Figure 9.1 International Police Operation Project Spade
Used with permission from Toronto Police Service Child Exploitation Section.

Project Spade may have made headlines around the world, but trafficking stings have netted groups of people organizing sex for sale in states and cities around the world both before and since that police effort. In Chicago, Illinois, the National Day of Johns, a multijurisdictional operation, started in 2011, made its largest number of arrests (at 570) in 2015, resulting in the release of 68 victims, including 14 juveniles.[11] Although the United States is not often believed to be associated largely with sex trafficking, research shows the United States is actually driving the demand for trafficking. The past decade has seen actions across the country, producing varying numbers of arrests: 277 people arrested, including doctors and law enforcement officers, in a Florida police operation,[12] 75 arrested in Texas,[13] 23 in Oregon,[14] 7 in South Dakota,[15] and 58 in Minnesota,[16] as just a few examples.

Whether global in scope or an attack situated from within a small rural community half a world away, efforts to understand and prevent sexualized harms and abuse have generated what seem like an endless list of examples. Women throughout the world experience various kinds of gender-based violence or harms of a sexual nature. In fact, some of the acts are not defined as crimes by the government where the incident takes place, so it is not technically referred to or treated as a crime. Referred to collectively as **sexual and gender-based violence (SGBV)**, issues of violence against women including sexualized violence have produced efforts locally and globally to better understand SGBV and how to prevent this kind of harm or address the harm when acts of violence occur.

Pockets of efforts to give attention to violence against women around the world have likely always existed. In 1995, speaking before the United Nations Fourth World Conference on Women Plenary Session in Beijing, China, then First Lady Hillary Rodham Clinton made international news with her speech emphasizing women's rights as human rights, a strategic theme of the conference.[17] Argued at the time to have been a forceful presentation not only on human rights but also on the need for equal rights and legal protections for women internationally,[18] the speech included themes on SGBV protections. From that speech:

> Tragically, women are most often the ones whose human rights are violated. Even now, in the late 20th century, the rape of women continues to be used as an instrument of armed conflict. Women and children make up a large majority of the world's refugees. And when women are excluded from the political process, they become even more vulnerable to abuse. I believe that now, on the eve of a new millennium, it is time to break the silence. It is time for us to say here in Beijing, and for the world to hear, that it is no longer acceptable to discuss women's rights as separate from human rights.
>
> These abuses have continued because, for too long, the history of women has been a history of silence. Even today, there are those who are trying to silence our words. But the voices of this conference and of the women at Huairou must be heard loudly and clearly:
>
>> It is a violation of human rights when babies are denied food, or drowned, or suffocated, or their spines broken, simply because they are born girls.
>> It is a violation of human rights when women and girls are sold into the slavery of prostitution for human greed—and the kinds of reasons that are used to justify this practice should no longer be tolerated.

It is a violation of human rights when women are doused with gasoline, set on fire, and burned to death because their marriage dowries are deemed too small.

It is a violation of human rights when individual women are raped in their own communities and when thousands of women are subjected to rape as a tactic or prize of war.

It is a violation of human rights when a leading cause of death worldwide among women ages 14 to 44 is the violence they are subjected to in their own homes by their own relatives.

It is a violation of human rights when young girls are brutalized by the painful and degrading practice of genital mutilation.

It is a violation of human rights when women are denied the right to plan their own families, and that includes being forced to have abortions or being sterilized against their will.

If there is one message that echoes forth from this conference, let it be that human rights are women's rights and women's rights are human rights, once and for all. Let us not forget that among those rights are the right to speak freely—and the right to be heard.[19]

The issues Clinton emphasized so many years ago speak to ranges of harmful issues that can impact one person or entire communities or countries or exist internationally across many countries.

As described in chapters 4 and 5, definitions of terms used to explain, describe, and explore the range of acceptable sexual behaviors vary over time and location. Actions identified in the United States now such as rape, sexual assault, intimate partner violence, and marital rape were also viewed differently in different cultural, social, and historical contexts. Legal definitions and enforcement practices also vary dramatically between countries. It is important to consider what can be learned from other areas around the globe, while also understanding the information presented for inclusion here is intended to offer only a relatively cursory review. While it is certainly true different cultures have different traditions regarding marriage and dating, gender roles, and sexual practices, for example, the deeper social histories and traditions of each country are not the kinds of issues presented for in-depth consideration here.

When culture, language, and geographic differences are added into a discussion about an already complicated social issue, it is important to understand that even the process of social inquiry brings with it additional levels of complexities. In fact, the 2009 International Council on Human Rights Policy discussed some of the overlapping interests of sexual rights advocates and human rights advocates, suggesting "both continue to lack experience and language for thinking in a comprehensive and informed way about sex (in terms that are not moralized, naturalized or based on 'folk knowledge')."[20] Writer, scholar, and global advocate for children, Alice Miller, puts it this way:

In 2000, advocates and scholars (of whom the author was one) asked how coherent claims to sexual rights could emerge from distinct, often disjointed conversations about sexuality and rights that were taking place among people working on sexual violence against women, on sexual and reproductive health, on HIV/AIDS, on child abuse, and in Lesbian, Gay, Bisexual, Transgender, and Intersexed (LGBTQI) advocacy, to name a few of the relevant areas. By 2008, the unifying phrase 'sexual rights' was being used regularly in international and national fora; but the frequency of its use, particularly in academic and policy literature, is not yet always matched by clarity of legal content. Moreover, concerns about sexuality have evolved rapidly in the last decade in light of the HIV/ AIDS epidemic, as well as in response to recent migration and community displacement which has exacerbated anxiety about national borders. Notably, the recent globalisation of information systems, driven by the Internet and other new communicate on technologies (cell phones with video capacity, etc.) is driving new regulations on online content. With increasing frequency, attention to material with a sexual content is often coupled with claims around national security. Extremely powerful counter-attacks on sexual rights, reflecting the latter's impact, are linked to the emergence of an amalgam of political interests that draw together justifications based on religion, culture and nation to undermine human rights at the United Nations. In the context of these subversive, indeed repressive, elements, the silences between sexual rights movements and the policy gaps that exist are particularly troubling.[21]

The idea that sexual practices are regulated and punished, at least in some circles, seems to fly in the face of the objectives of those seeking human rights more broadly. To what degree can or should sexual practices be regulated, and/ or punished? This is an ongoing and hotly debated question.

The illustrations offered about the classification of human rights from within this global perspective on sexual rights and sexual violence parallel the primary theme offered by the structure and organization of this text but introduce connectivity between conversations in the United States on the subject with incidents and responses in many countries around the world. More specifically, if a person is not clear about what constitutes healthy sexuality and healthy sexual practices, actions to create or improve policy and regulate what is identified as inappropriate sexual behavior become impossible to clarify. As suggested in the quote above, religious, cultural, and national interests often collide in areas of importance, and for many who are harmed, preventing SGBV is essential. Efforts to bridge gaps in concepts, language, and definitions between countries regarding the larger questions and social responses to sexual behaviors and definitions of violence are ongoing and evolving, in some cases quite controversial, and require a significant investment in social and cultural understandings. Actions, behaviors, and interpretations of different cultural ideals around sex and sexuality can be framed from a perspective of information gathering and education sharing rather than moral judgments or indictments of cultural and community character. Such is the goal here. Although many of the acts will be SGBV, they may not be defined as a crime.

An overview of various types of sexual violence being documented around the globe follows. Beginning with a review of domestic and intimate partner violence, attention is given to several different forms that violence can take, including honor killings, acid attacks, female genital modification/mutilation, and finally child marriage and forced sterilization. The larger issue of sex trafficking begins with a focus on the commercial sexual exploitation of children and then addresses the often overlooked subject of abused men and boys. Further consideration is given to the role of the state in the process of making, by legal definition, the parameters outlining what events are determined to be harmful practice, offering examples from the LGBTQI communities, reproductive rights, and rape as a weapon of war.

Finally, the substantial and controversial issues of prostitution and pornography are introduced, along with a collection of issues being presented for consideration. Referred to commonly as the **commercial sex industry,** or as **sex work** more generally, aspects of the persistent controversy engendered between a contingent of sexual violence prevention advocates and people actively working in the commercial sex industry are reviewed. A segment on technology is offered as the chapter closes, highlighting how technology is being used in both media production and violence prevention efforts as technological advances make images easier to capture and distribute for financial compensation. A review of several high-profile efforts to create relevant laws and policies, often coming from international programs, agencies, or as the result of enforcement cooperatives, is included in chapter 11. International cooperation is particularly important to prevent international sex crimes and to define a legal structure to prosecute sexual offenses and offenders who target victims and commit sex crimes outside of the perpetrator's home country. Identifying a selection of types of sexual violence that have a global reach and an international response is the primary goal of this chapter.

SCANNING THE GLOBE: REVIEWING SEX PRACTICES, DEVIANCE, AND CRIMES AROUND THE WORLD

Award-winning journalist Lauren Wolfe, director of the Women Under Siege project, has been studying the reports of rape in Syria. She profiles people who share their stories of rape and sexual exploitation and has written the story of a family who was told to leave their daughter at an armed checkpoint or everyone in the car would be killed or the story of a mother, daughter, and sister in one family all of whom had been raped.[22] More than 20 percent of rape victims are reportedly killed after rape, some in an effort to destroy evidence of the crimes. These deaths also might be self-inflicted, or the victim might be killed by her family rather than be dishonored for the rest of her life by the assault.[23] Syria is an example of a community under significant duress, currently at war and heavily scrutinized from outside its borders.

As stories and themes are introduced from around the world, remember that the information is useful only as a beginning point for acquiring a deeper understanding of the country, the conditions, and the data collected. Keeping this in mind, perhaps some of the most active issues related to the international coverage of sexual violence in the last several years has come from India. India made headlines around the world for a series of rapes, including a brutal gang rape. In addition, however, a UN special report released in April 2013 suggested a more than 300 percent increase in child rape in the last decade—a number of cases that had been reported in juvenile justice homes run by the

Indian government.[24] A 2018 opinion piece in *The Guardian* identified sexual violence in India as "the new normal."[25]

In 1972, the rape of an impoverished tribal girl by two police officers at a rural police station produced a shocking series of events after the assault. First, when the victim decided to take her complaint to court and, second, when the accused were actually convicted, and finally, when the highest court in the land overturned the conviction and set the two police constables free.[26] Cultural attitudes and police practice were being called out amidst accounts of women being asked not to go out at night, or riddled with demeaning questions, or being disbelieved after assaults are reported. In another widely publicized case, police were reported to have pressured a victim to either marry one of her rapists or to reach a financial settlement with the man's family. Such stories are being elevated as unacceptable and presented for attention in the international media.[27]

The case sparked international outrage and produced public protests demanding action on rape prevention and legal accountability for the rapists, which produced reform throughout the country. In the nearly five decades since this event, pressure has been put on the Indian government to address the way sexual assaults are policed and investigated.[28] In 2012 and 2013, again, a series of high-profile rapes and protests were then followed by allegations of a mass rape by police in 2017. Long-standing efforts to generate change and reduce sexualized violence have been called into question as a result.[29]

Certainly, conversations such as these are not limited to India or Syria but, when taking a closer look, can be found in communities around the world. Questions remain about the degree to which sexual violence remains relatively hidden within a community or a country and how effective individual or community efforts are to define and affect the desired social change.

A BRIEF REVIEW OF SEVERAL INTERNATIONAL ISSUES

As information is collected and assessed, researchers and those concerned about preventing SGBV continue to seek ways to raise public and, in some cases, international awareness about the desire to reduce violence and harm generated against women. Increasingly, efforts to better understand violence against women also highlight the violence generated against the LGBTQI community and also against boys and men. Consider the following examples that bring international issues much closer to home.

Intimate Partner Violence (IPV) and Domestic Violence

> There is one Universal truth, applicable to all countries, cultures, and communities: violence against women is never acceptable, never excusable, never tolerable.
>
> —UN Secretary-General Ban Ki-Moon (2008)[30]

Within only the last 40 years has violence against women been acknowledged internationally as a global problem. The World Health Organization's (WHO)

2011 study, a survey at 15 sites in 10 countries, including Bangladesh, Brazil, Ethiopia, Japan, Namibia, Peru, Republic of Tanzania, Samoa, Serbia and Montenegro, and Thailand, suggests that, when either partner sees abuse as children, the likelihood of abuse is higher for those people in adulthood.[31] On the other side, when both the woman and her partner had completed secondary education, the rate of IPV was lower.

Various aspects of the subject of IPV in the United States were addressed in chapter 6; the issue of domestic violence and IPV has been argued to exist in every country in the world.[32] Some additional 2017 findings from the WHO[33] suggest:

- The younger the women were, the more at risk they were for IPV.
- About one in three women worldwide have experienced either physical and/or sexual IPV or nonpartner sexual violence in their lifetime.
- Globally, as many as 38 percent of murders of women are committed by a male intimate partner.
- Low education is among the factors in both perpetration and experiences of violence.

Domestic violence and IPV are argued to be the leading cause of homicide death in women globally[34] and are associated with increased levels of suicide and depression behaviors.[35] Data in 2010 from 141 studies in 81 countries showed that globally 30 percent of women aged 15 and over have experienced during their lifetime physical and/or sexual IPV.[36]

In 2013, the WHO, in collaboration with the London School of Hygiene and Tropical Medicine and the South African Medical Research Council, published its findings in support of the idea that violence against women is a significant public health issue across the globe. Its findings, focused on both IPV and sexual violence by someone other than a partner, suggested:

- Overall, 35 percent of women worldwide have experienced either physical and/or sexual intimate partner violence or nonpartner sexual violence. While there are many other forms of violence that women may be exposed to, this already represents a large proportion of the world's women.
- Most of this violence is IPV. Worldwide, almost one-third (30 percent) of all women who have been in a relationship have experienced physical and/or sexual violence by their intimate partner. In some regions, 38 percent of women have experienced IPV.
- Globally, as many as 38 percent of all murders of women are committed by intimate partners. Women who have been physically or sexually abused by their partners report higher rates of a number of important health problems. For example, they are 16 percent more likely to have a low-birth-weight baby. They are more than twice as likely to have an abortion, almost twice as likely to experience depression, and, in some regions, are 1.5 times more likely to acquire HIV, as compared to women who have not experienced partner violence.

- Globally, 7 percent of women have been sexually assaulted by someone other than a partner.

There are fewer data available on the health effects of nonpartner sexual violence. However, the evidence that does exist reveals that women who have experienced this form of violence are 2.3 times more likely to have alcohol use disorders and 2.6 times more likely to experience depression or anxiety.

The authors identified the "need to address the economic and sociocultural factors that foster a culture of violence against women," to be so massive globally as to require urgent international action.[37] Documented acts of violence between intimate or dating partners are present in the form of honor killings, acid attacks, female genital modification/mutilation, and child marriage and forced sterilization.

Honor Killings

> To combat the epidemic of honor killings requires understanding what makes these murders unique. They differ from plain and psychopathic homicides, serial killings, crimes of passion, revenge killings, and domestic violence. Their motivation is different and based on codes of morality and behavior that typify some cultures, often reinforced by fundamentalist religious dictates.
>
> —Phyllis Chesler, professor emerita and cofounder of the Association for Women in Psychology and the National Women's Health Network[38]

The **honor killings** are a cultural practice involving the killing or murder of women, usually daughters or wives, by family members, usually fathers or brothers. It is impossible to know precise numbers because the murders frequently go unreported, whether families claim the person went missing or killed themselves. Typically, honor killings occur in countries where family reputation predominates. The UN Commission on Human Rights has received reports from Bangladesh, Great Britain, Brazil, Ecuador, Egypt, India, Israel, Italy, Jordan, Pakistan, Morocco, Sweden, Turkey, and Uganda, with official governments condoning the practice in Afghanistan, Iraq, and Iran.[39] Affiliated in large part to the religious practice of Muslims, Hindu, and Sikh,[40] significant confusion exists because religious figures from within these faith communities are also actively speaking out against the practice and sometimes the consequences in the West include extending Islamophobia and silencing Muslim women who live in the United States.[41]

In the summer of 2013, CNN published a poll taken in Amman, Jordan's capital, with almost 50 percent of boys and one in five girls were reported to believe that killing a woman who has been dishonored or shamed her family is justifiable. One-third of the teens involved in the study advocated the practice.[42] Award-winning journalist Ayse Onal emphasized that the men who commit these crimes against their mothers, sisters, wives, and daughters often see the action as an inevitable outcome rather than a choice.[43] In spite of an increased punishment in the laws governing honor killings, between 5,000 and 20,000 women are believed to be killed in this way each year. The formal numbers in the United Nation's report are believed to be low, with experts suggesting many acts are documented as suicides or go unreported.[44]

Acid Attacks

Various incidents of women being attacked with acid have increasingly found their way to the international spotlight and onto the research agendas of those studying violence against women. The People's Republic of Bangladesh, a country in South Asia bordering India, is reported to have had approximately 300 such incidents annually with 78 percent of attacks happening against women. According to Acid Survivors Foundation (ASF) there have been 3,000 reported acid attack victims in the country since 1999. The most common reason given for the attacks is the refusal of marriage, denial of sex, or the rejection of romantic interest.[45] In late 2013, the Delhi High Court (India) upheld the life sentence of a man who killed his wife by throwing acid on her, referring to these kinds of attacks as one of the most "horrifying forms of gender-based violence."[46] Sometimes, acid from car batteries is used or toilet-cleaning products; the acid is used either internally or externally to cause harm to the woman.[47] Cases where the woman is held down and forced to drink the acid have been reported, while the more common cases are where the woman is approached, sometimes while sleeping, and doused with acid. The face is a popular target for attacks, with the intent of destroying the victim's physical appearance, but the result is often blindness. Acid Survivors Foundation (www.acidsurvivors.org) and Acid Survivors Trust International (www.acidviolence.org), both formed in 1999, are intent on addressing the needs of the victims, working to prosecute offenders who have historically gone unpunished by the legal system, and helping rebuild the lives of the survivors.[48] With increasing attention in India on issues of gender violence, the film *Saving Face* was the winner of the 2012 Academy Award for a documentary (short subject) (https://rocofilms.com/savf/) and profiles the stories of victims of acid attacks as a way to get the message out to educate and eradicate acid violence.[49] The role of **nongovernmental organizations** (NGOs) and nonprofit organizations, often international in scope that were created to address particular community needs, have bridged what some argue has been a failure of the state to ensure appropriate prevention, care, and prosecution of offenders who commit these kinds of crimes.[50]

Female Genital Modification/Mutilation

Since 2008, the UN Population Fund (UNFPA) and the UN International Children's Emergency Fund (UNICEF) have partnered on a global effort to end **female genital modification/mutilation** (FGM), also referred to as **cutting**, in one generation.[51] From the 2016 UNFPA/UNICEF report "Accelerating Change," the definition is offered as follows:

Female genital mutilation, also referred to as "female genital cutting," has been defined by the World Health Organization (WHO) as **"all procedures involving partial or total removal of the external female genitalia or other injury to the female genital organs for non-medical reasons"** (WHO 2008). Once characterized as "female circumcision," the word "mutilation" was adopted both to distinguish it from male circumcision and to stress the severity of the act (WHO, UNICEF, UNFPA 1997). A hybrid term—"female genital mutilation/cutting"— was coined by the UNFPA-UNICEF Joint Programme to underscore the importance of using non-judgmental terminology with practicing communities while emphasizing the fact the female genital mutilation/cutting constitutes a violation of the human rights of women and girls.[52]

Currently, the practice is believed to be concentrated in 30 countries, primarily located in Africa, with approximations of 125 to 200 million women and girls affected.[53] Statistics compiled in a comprehensive 2013 UNICEF report, in over half of the countries studied, the majority of the girls were cut from infancy and before the age of 5, with the rest of the countries reporting cutting between the ages of 5 and 14.[54] The damage done to the female genitalia is nonspecific, dependent on culture, tradition, and in some cases family history and local practice. Social acceptance is the most frequently cited reason for supporting the genital modification practice where in some cases the genitalia are sewn closed and, in other cases, all or part of the clitoris and/or the labia minora are excised.[55] Early work identified three types of female genital mutilation: (1) all or part of the clitoris is removed, (2) the clitoris and all or part of the labia minora are removed, and (3) removal of the clitoris, part or all of the labia minora with a bringing together of the flesh of the labia majora to cover the urethra and most of the vaginal opening.[56] In 1995, the WHO developed a typology of a fourth category, which includes everything not identified in types 1–3.

Historically, the term "female circumcision" was used to reference this practice of genital modification, which dates back to the fifth century BC.[57] Use of the term shifted in the 1970s, with increased international attention to the practice and concerns raised about the factual differences between FGM and male circumcision. Initially, concerns were centered on health risks, but as many as seven international conventions, dating between 1948 and 1996, have argued FGM is a human rights violation, the practice of which has no medical benefit.[58] These protestations have been met with broad support; however, cultural and geographic traditions run deep. Legislation at the national level to prevent or prohibit FGM varies from country to country.

Although most reports on and research about FGM come from Africa, Asia, and several Middle Eastern countries, FGM is increasingly being reported in the United States and Europe. Reports from Australia in early 2014 suggest that FGM is happening in numbers larger than the government is able to detect and record. Described as "hideous," "secretive," and happening under "very well-conspired arrangements," which are usually not detected because the crime is so secretive, officials typically find out about it only when there are complications from a procedure or in cases of marital breakdown.[59] Reports suggest that the effects of a procedure might not be detected right away. Negative effects are sometimes seen at various times in the life of the person on whom the procedure was administered, including six stages (1) immediate, (2) intermediate, (3) late, (4) at consummation of marriage, (5) at the delivery of the firstborn child, and (6) postnatal.[60] Many stories have been written about the experience of young women confronting ritual genital mutilation, including *Do They Hear You When You Cry?* (1999) and *Aman: The Story of a Somali Girl* (1995).[61] Migration and relocation have produced a need for medical staff and other care providers to be educated generally about the practice and its impacts.

Child and Forced Marriages and Forced Sterilizations

Various international organizations have created a space for publicly decrying the practice of child marriage. The 2016 Global Report by Human Rights Watch, a 2018 report by UNICEF, and a global partnership comprising more than 1,000 international organizations, called Girls Not Brides (founded in 2011),[62] are three high-profile examples. In 2014 Girls Not Brides published "A Theory of Change on Child Marriage," suggesting the need for long-term, sustained efforts to eliminate the practice with four primary strategies (1) empower girls, (2) mobilize families and communities, (3) provide services, and (4) establish and implement laws and policies around the world.[63]

While some people in communities are building global networks to assure women have the right to choose who or whether they want to marry, other countries are working to manage population by either promoting or outlawing unrestricted childbirth. In 2015, China ended a long-standing "one child" policy, which restricted families to one child. In 2018, it announced the possibility of removing restrictions on family size. Forced abortions or impossibly steep fines were used to secure compliance. The example of China's use of policies and practices in support of abortion and birth control contrast sharply to attitudes in the United States regarding abortion, for example, which is extremely controversial but linked to religious ideology, rather than government restrictions (although some might suggest the government's actions are linked to religious ideology).

The Chinese culture relies heavily on the patrilineal family line, so sons are expected to assist their parents in old age; however, girls are expected to care for their husband's family. As these public policy and cultural practices are presented for consideration here, technology has afforded the opportunity to determine the gender of the baby early, and, as in other places in the world, the decision to abort female fetuses or kill newborn babies, a practice known as infanticide, although much less common today, has been a centuries-old practice.[64] Ironically and interestingly, the numbers of men in some areas of China well outweigh the numbers of women as a natural consequence of the decline in female births. Although sex-selective abortion is illegal, the practice is believed to have been carried out widely.[65]

Issues related to the forced pregnancies or forced sterilization of women are certainly not limited to countries outside the United States. In September 2013, the state legislature of North Carolina agreed to spend $10 million to compensate people who were victims of forced and coerced sterilizations carried out under a North Carolina eugenics program. One hundred seventy-seven people have come forward. Ninety-nine percent of the victims were women, and 60 percent were black.[66] In the North Carolina eugenics program, anyone could request that someone be sterilized. The request was presented to a board, which would make the determination.[67] Thirty-three states in the United States had forced sterilization programs, with California's being the largest.[68] And the degree to which First Nation and indigenous women were routinely sterilized as a means for eliminating the indigenous populations is in dispute in the United States and around the world. In November 2018, sixty indigenous women in Canada filed a class action lawsuit against the government in Saskatchewan, claiming they were coerced to sign consent forms agreeing to have their fallopian tubes tied, some while in active labor, and others told they would not see their babies until they agreed.[69]

In other places around the world, the idea of forced sterilization is identified as a means to regulate and prevent the spread of HIV/AIDS. In spite of the ability of anti-AIDS drugs to prevent the spread of AIDS to the children of women with AIDS, sterilization procedures were performed. In Peru, as another example, national efforts to reduce population were connected with an estimated 2,000 women being sterilized without their knowledge.[70]

Clearly, the issue of sexual and reproductive rights has a long history of controversy, involving religious, political, and cultural conflicts. These issues are extremely divisive and powerfully disruptive of the social process and related conditions within countries, as well as in discussions across national lines. Attention will be given later in the chapter to considering the role of national government policies in regulating such controversies.

Human Sex Trafficking

Collective international efforts are under way to better understand the nature and scope of trafficking in persons, defined by the UN Office on Drugs and Crime as

> the recruitment, transportation, transfer, harbouring or receipt of persons, by means of the threat or use of force or other forms of coercion, of abduction, of fraud, of deception, of the abuse of power or of a position of vulnerability or of the giving or receiving of payments or benefits to achieve the consent of a person having control over another person, for the purpose of exploitation. Exploitation shall include, at a minimum, the exploitation of the prostitution of others or other forms of sexual exploitation, forced labour or services, slavery or practices similar to slavery, servitude or the removal of organs.[71]

At the same time researchers and practitioners seek to document more definitive answers for developing intervention and prevention strategies, movie makers have tagged sex trafficking themes as the stuff suspense thrillers are made of. One box office–busting example is the 2008 movie *Taken*, which centered the story line on two young women enjoying an international trip who were approached at the airport by a seemingly nice guy for the purposes— a pretense—of sharing a cab. After making note of where the women were staying, he later helps facilitate their abduction into the global sex trafficking underground. Liam Neeson portrays the avenging father and (minor spoiler alert) saves the day.[72] Followed by *Taken 2* (2012) and *Taken 3* (2014), the trilogy proved to be Hollywood gold, with a worldwide box office total of approximately $930 million.[73]

People clearly loved this story line as the plot for an action movie, yet, as news and stories of real-life sex trafficking were increasingly reflected in the news and on social media, people wanted to know more about whether and to what degree these and other films or TV programming content accurately reflected the trafficking experience. A more detailed review of commercial sex work is presented below, but a critical distinction is to be drawn between sex trafficking and prostitution. In 2000, the United States passed the **Trafficking Victims Protection Act (TVPA)**, and the United Nations adopted the "Protocol to Prevent, Suppress and Punish Trafficking in Persons, Especially Woman and Children." TVPA establishes human trafficking and offenses related to trafficking as a federal crime and outlines severe penalties for committing such actions.[74] The act established the Interagency Task Force to Monitor and Combat Trafficking, which is designed to assist in the implementation of the TVPA.

Since then, a search for distinctions between sex trafficking and prostitution has been under way with questions being raised about how the differences impact understandings of individual agency,[75] with the clear assessments of what constitutes coercion remaining in dispute.

The UN Trafficking Protocol prohibits the use of force or coercion for the "exploitation or prostitution of others or the use of underage children in prostitution." The NGO Exodus Road (www.exodusroad.com) provides a useful continuum for consideration, suggesting a range of force or coercion exists whenever sex is for sale. The "Spectrum of Sexual Exploitation" in Figure 9.2 may reflect a more nuanced understanding of what it means to be "forced" or "coerced" into a sexual exchange for money, but others might suggest this misrepresents the thoughts and choices of those who do in fact choose to be involved in sex work. The question about whether a healthy person would actually choose to sell sex for money is long-standing and ongoing and is discussed in more detail below. Policies and enforcement actions are being proposed to make sure no one is caught up in sex work against their will or being trafficked. For example, the state of Minnesota differentiates prostitution from sex trafficking by determining whether a third party is involved in the negotiation and/or transaction.

According to UN estimates, approximately 2.5 million people are being trafficked around the world at any given time, 80 percent of them women and chil-

| Adult who sells sex to pay for college tuition and rent | Runaway who sells sex to buy food and shelter | Keeps some of her profits but is threatened and abused by pimp | Promised job as a waitress; taken to a bar and sold for sex | Sold in masage parlor, passport taken, physically forced to stay | Minor kidnapped, taken across borders to brothel, sold day and night |

Spectrum of Sexual Exploitation

www.theexodusroad.com

Figure 9.2   Spectrum of Sexual Exploitation
The Exodus Road, theexodusroad.com

dren. Conservative estimates suggest that the sex industry generates some $32 billion annually. However, estimates of income generated from prostitution in one city, Las Vegas, are as high as $5 billion.[76]

In fact, many changes have been evidenced in the policies, policing, and prosecution of people who have traditionally been charged as prostitutes.[77] Chapter 10 talks more about some of those shifts in the laws and policies directing law enforcement responses; however, it is critical to highlight the fact that people involved in what has traditionally been referred to as prostitution are increasingly being treated as victims of exploitative practices, with language such as being "rescued from a trafficking situation" being used, followed by efforts to provide services and resources, rather than prosecuting those involved. More focused attention is given to prostitution and pornography below; however, specific attention is focused here on children, including men and boys—two topics that require a bit of focused attention before the larger conversation primarily because of the vulnerable status of children and the social stigma attached to sexual abuse of boys and men.

Commercial Sexual Exploitation of Children

The **commercial sexual exploitation of children (CSEC)** is the sexual abuse of a minor for economic gain.[78] The US Congress established the Exploited Child Unit within the **National Center for Missing and Exploited Children (NCMEC)** in 1996. National and international statistics on the sexual exploitation of children and young people vary widely because the practice is hidden and ranges from more isolated and individualized exploitation to a more persistent and systematized abuse (see Figure 9.3). As with various other definitional, practical, and ethical research considerations (discussed as methodological concerns resulting in incomplete data and/or varied and inconsistent research findings in chapters 3 and 6), it is difficult to generate any solid

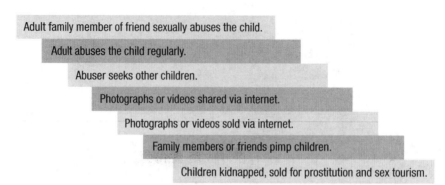

Figure 9.3   Continuum of Abuse and Commercial Exploitation
Originally published by the National Institute of Justice, US Department of Justice

estimates on this illegal activity.[79] Difficult to study, CSEC falls within the **dark figure of crime**, crimes that go undetected by professionals, including researchers and practitioners in the field.

The problems with collecting data and finding specific terms that encompass the various aspects of sex crimes and the commercial sexual exploitation of children were introduced in chapter 3. Historically, terms like "juvenile prostitution," "child sex rings," "child pornography," "child trafficking," "sex trafficking of children," and "child sex tourism" have been used to explain different ways to describe how children are exploited in the sex industry. Child sex rings and child sex tourism, terms still used in the media with some regularity,[80] have also been referred to as "**sex trafficking rings**"[81] or "child prostitution rings."[82] These and related terms generally refer to children and young people below the age of adulthood, usually 18, or in some cases the age of sexual consent, being kidnapped, coerced, or enticed into sexually abusive acts by a group of adult authority figures. Discussed in more detail at the end of this section, media messages have increasingly become the target for sexual violence prevention educators to raise awareness about how these terms are used in the news.

The number of young people, in these cases girls, victimized in this way was trending upward in late 2010 when at least three US states, New York, Michigan, and Minnesota, were identified as having double-digit increases in sex trafficking[83] (see Table 9.1).[84] Demands for state intervention when children being recruited who cannot consent but grow up in this way of living are also increasing.

The most popular outlets for CSEC include the internet and escort services. Women's Funding Network research findings suggested that "internet classifieds, without question, are the leading source for criminals to find girls for sex in these states." The 2009 report "Shattered Hearts: The Commercial Sexual Exploitation of American Indian Woman and Girls in Minnesota," produced results suggesting the trafficking of young native girls into prostitution remains a rarely discussed but significant and pervasive problem.[85]

Table 9.1   US Domestic Sex Trafficking via Internet and Escort Services

State	Six-Month Findings
New York—20% increase	**3,454 girls** were domestically sex trafficked in August, up from 2,880 in February (20% increase). **3,415 girls** were trafficked through ads posted on internet classifieds in August , up from 2,830 in February (21% increase). Monthly domestic sex trafficking in New York is more pervasive than annually reported incidents of teen suicide (54 instances), self-inflicted injuries (1,222 instances), or women of all ages killed by breast cancer (2,715 instances).
Michigan—36% increase	**159 girls** were domestically sex trafficked in August, up from 117 in February (36% increase). **142 girls** were trafficked through ads posted on internet classifieds in August, up from 102 in February (40% increase). **Only 20% of girls** advertised on internet classifieds in Michigan still appeared in ads two weeks later, which was the lowest "tenure" rate of domestically sex trafficked minors among the three states studied. Monthly domestic sex trafficking in Michigan is more pervasive than incidents of suicide among females under age 25 (31 incidents), infants who died from SIDS (46 incidents), or females under age 25 killed in car accidents (106 incidents).
Minnesota—55% increase	**124 girls** were domestically sex trafficked in August, up from 80 in February (55% increase). **112 girls** were trafficked through ads posted on internet classifieds in August, up from 68 in February (65% increase). Monthly domestic sex trafficking in Minnesota is more pervasive than incidents of teen girls who died by suicide, homicide, and car accidents (29 total); infants who died from SIDS (6 instances); or women of all ages murdered in one year (37 instances).

Text Box 9.1.   US Laws on Trafficking in Persons

The Victims of Trafficking and Violence Protection Act of 2000, as amended, provides the tools to combat trafficking in persons both worldwide and domestically. The act authorized the establishment of the State Department's Office to Monitor and Combat Trafficking in Persons and the President's Interagency Task Force to Monitor and Combat Trafficking in Persons to assist in the coordination of antitrafficking efforts.

05/28/15 Survivors of Human Trafficking Empowerment Act (Section 115 of the Justice for Victims of Trafficking Act of 2015)

03/07/13 Trafficking Victims Protection Reauthorization Act of 2013 (Title XII of the Violence Against Women Reauthorization Act of 2013)

01/01/08 William Wilberforce Trafficking Victims Protection Reauthorization Act of 2008

01/10/06 Trafficking Victims Protection Reauthorization Act of 2005

01/07/03 Prosecutorial Remedies and Other Tools to End the Exploitation of Children Today Act of 2003 (PROTECT Act)

01/07/03 Trafficking Victims Protection Reauthorization Act of 2003

01/07/03 US Leadership on HIV/AIDS, Tuberculosis, and Malaria Act of 2003

10/28/00 Victims of Trafficking and Violence Protection Act of 2000

An Intentional Note about the Sexual Exploitation of Boys and Men

There is much to be said about the development of masculine and feminine identities, and researchers more recently have argued that both masculinity and femininity are not binaries (comprising an either/or dichotomy) but rather grow and change with time.[86] In other words, the idea of nuances of gender expression as seen in the LGBTQI community or in the definitions of masculine and feminine identities are increasingly believed to be constructed differently for each individual and to change over time.[87] What social rules do men think they need to fit into and/or follow? Same with women: what aspects of femininity do women believe need to be followed to affirm their individual femininity? In the conversation about sexual violence, important questions are being asked about the ways men construct, establish, and reestablish their masculine identities, and the literature focused on describing men as individuals who purchase sex as **sex tourists** describes an imperial masculinity through which men live out their economic, racial, and geopolitical power.[88] The complexities of the economic, emotional, and embodied value of these sexual exchanges are being further studied,[89] as is the fact that women and same-sex clients also look for experiences in the sex tourism industry.[90] Studying men who are harmed by sexual violence is a relatively new area for researchers and service providers.

In Australia, www.oneinthree.com.au seeks to help the public understand the fact that statistics about family violence and abuse can be complex and often include the existence of male victims of violence.[91] Promundo, an international gender justice and violence prevention organization founded in Brazil in 1997, and the International Center for Research on Women (ICRW) have worked together since 2009 to research data on gender attitudes and has collected data from over 25 countries around the world as of 2017.[92] The 2012 International Men and Gender Equality Survey (IMAGES) data found

- 20 percent to 85 percent of men report having experienced psychological violence as children
- 26 to 67 percent of men report having experienced physical violence as children
- 16 to 44 percent of men report witnessing their mother being beaten by their father or another partner of hers
- 1 to 21 percent of men report having experienced sexual violence as children.[93]

It wasn't until the 1970s in the United States that state laws began to acknowledge that men could be victims of rape.[94] And as noted in chapter 6, it wasn't until 2012 that the FBI changed its definition of rape to acknowledged victims other than women. Also, statistics on how many men are assaulted are also reliable only to varying degrees. Increasingly, research is suggesting that men, like women, who are harmed by sexual violence also go through an individualized healing process. RAINN[95] suggests that men go through the following experiences in response to sexual assault (and be mindful, this process is not linear):

- Anxiety, depression posttraumatic stress disorder, flashbacks, and eating disorders
- Avoiding people or places that remind you of the assault or abuse
- Concerns or questions about sexual orientation
- Fear of the worst happening and having a sense of a shortened future

- Feeling like "less of a man" or that you no longer have control over your own body
- Feeling on edge, being unable to relax, and having difficulty sleeping
- Sense of blame or shame over not being able to stop the assault or abuse, especially if you experienced an erection or ejaculation
- Withdrawal from relationships or friendships and an increased sense of isolation
- Worrying about disclosing for fear of judgment or disbelief

As discussed in more detail in chapter 8, there are systems where the documentation of sexual offenses against men and boys are more common, such as the military and the Catholic Church. The lack of attention to men who have been sexually assaulted is increasingly being recognized; however, much more is to be learned.[96]

Increasingly, research efforts have attempted to understand the effects of exposure to violence on the mental health of men as adults. As mentioned in several places throughout the text, the now famous **Adverse Childhood Experiences (ACEs)** research has been focused on explaining and exploring the relationships between exposure to abuse as children and mental and physical ailments, including early death.[97] Research coming out of indigenous communities is also suggesting a need to reflect on the idea of **intergenerational transmission,** the idea that there is an association between being a victim of or witness to violence during childhood and then struggling with internal or external expressions of harmful behaviors as an adult. Socially, and culturally, it is clear that men in communities of color, including black and indigenous communities, suffer from social and political associations with violence, which is hard to locate with individual acts of harm but rather being increasingly associated with social attitudes and pervasive cultural myths.

As much as boys and men have been left out of discussions regarding those who have been harmed by a sexual assault, data that came out in the 2012 National Crime Victimization Survey took many researchers and advocates by surprise, indicating that 38 percent of the sexual assaults/rapes reported were against men.[98] Research on the subject has supported this idea, that at least in federal surveys, a high prevalence of sexual victimization is found among men, similar to the prevalence found among women.[99] For reasons emphasized throughout the text, these ideas emphasize why it is important to understand the research and reflections on social attitudes more broadly, in addition to looking squarely at the offenders and the incidents of harm.

Text Box 9.2.   Child Pornography: Tony Krone[1]

Child Sexual Abuse Images:

1. Images depicting nudity or erotic posing with no sexual activity
2. Sexual activity between children or solo masturbation by a child
3. Nonpenetrative sexual activity between a child(ren) and adult(s)
4. Penetrative sexual activity between children and adults
5. Sadism or bestiality

Note

1. Modified from Tony Krone's Sentencing Advisory Panel 2002. The panel's advice to the court of appeal on offences involving child pornography. London: Sentencing Advisory Panel

QUESTIONING THE ROLE OF THE STATE
IN DEFINING SEXUAL HARMS AND CRIMES

Perhaps some of the most volatile issues relating to the identification and prevention of sexual violence come in the form of social issues identified as moral issues for the purposes of determining what the legal standards are for defining and identifying what is policed as acts of sexual violence and treated as a crime. While the current state of laws and enforcement practices in the United States are characterized more specifically in chapters 10 and 11, various controversies exist around the world with regard to determining what constitutes sexual violence, and then what constitutes a relevant and appropriate government response. As suggested above, questions about how cultural and social attitudes might get in the way of studying and interpreting research or creating effective social policy offer important reflections.

Consider the following series of events that happened in rapid succession in the state of Texas in the United States. In May 2011, Texas Governor Rick Perry signed a bill that required a **transvaginal ultrasound**, where a piece of medical equipment in the form of a probe is inserted into the woman's vagina, as a part of the process legally required if a woman consults a physician seeking an abortion.[100] Supporters of abortion bans argued this to be essential to "safeguard women's health," and then additional restrictions on abortion were put in place in July 2013 after intense media coverage and massive protests in the state capitol.[101] Opponents to abortion restrictions raised questions about the act of literally forcing such an invasive procedure, with some suggesting this process was "mandating rape."[102] This added fuel to the limits and legalities of "reproductive health" or "abortion access" debates, which continue in the United States to date.

Soon after the legislative controversy, Texas correctional officials and law enforcement found themselves embroiled in controversy when a lawsuit reported the guards at Live Oak County Jail were running a "rape camp,"[103] and around the same time dash cameras of two different traffic stops recorded vaginal and anal probes of two women that were conducted on the side of the road by law enforcement officers during what appeared on camera to be a routine traffic stop.[104] Because rape and sexual assault are often discussed in the context of the use of power and misuse of authority, questions were raised about the degree to which state enforcement agency officials, agency practices, or cultural attitudes might be part of the problem. If the goal is to reduce sexual harm and violence, to provide justice for victims, the aftermath of these kinds of experiences have researchers and sexual violence prevention advocates looking to state efforts and state authority via laws, policies, and practices to identify, direct, and regulate the boundaries of legal and ethical behavior.

In 2013, Texas made international headlines again over a different battle, this time a legislative fight for what became universally known as House Bill 2. Then Governor Rick Perry signed legislation intended to make abortions more difficult and to close dozens of clinics in that state.[105] A federal judge overturned it in August 2014, but it was a victory against the new round of abortion restriction laws that had the effect of closing down over half of the clinics that were used to provide services as the case worked its way through the courts. In the years that followed, additional laws that would criminalize women who got abortions were adopted in several states across the United States. That specific Texas legal and regulatory issue went on to the US Supreme Court, which agreed with the lower court and struck down the provision in June 2016. Although the language of "abortion rights" or "reproductive rights" remains largely controversial, in spite of the court victories, many of the providers forced to close still have not reopened because of the expense. In April 2019, Texas introduced a bill criminalizing all abortions, with no exceptions for rape or incest, and paving the way for a charge of homicide for any woman having the procedure.[106] Because Texas allows capital punishment for homicide, this could make it a crime punishable by the death penalty for both the women and the service provider. Although there was little support for the bill, in an interview, Representative Tony Tinderholt, who introduced the bill, said the impact would require people to "consider the repercussions of the sexual relationship that they are going to have."[107] The legislation met with hostile reactions; however, Georgia and Kentucky were among other states proposing laws and policies related to addressing the issue of abortion, in spite of such actions being in violation of current federal laws.

This sampling of issues raised in the state of Texas provide an example of the importance of state and government actions for determining what gets treated as a crime and who gets treated as a criminal. Further concerns focus on who is harmed, who gets supported, and who gets punished by actions taken on behalf of the state, what should be the limits of state power, and what might be required as redress for those harmed by the powers of the state. The goal here is to present a collection of international issues that have produced similar questions about the role of the state in making decisions about the practices and protections imposed on individuals as they relate to sex-related matters and the definitions of crime. The issues included offer only a few examples: (1) gender identity and sexual orientation, where acts in some countries throughout the world are punishable by death; (2) reproductive rights, including forced marriages, child marriages, forced sterilization, and forced abortions; and (3) an exploration of state-sanctioned use of sexual assault and rape as a weapon of war.

International Sanctions Based on Sexual Orientation and Gender Identity

Late in 2013, the EU's high court in Luxembourg ruled refugees who face prosecution for committing homosexual acts in their home country have the right to asylum in the EU.[108] This is historically ironic, perhaps, because anti-gay laws, in Africa, for example, are arguably linked to the legacy of European colonial rule.[109] The EU Court's ruling was not seen as a distinct victory, however, because the ruling left the decisions about asylum to determinations about how rigidly the law was being enforced by the home country.[110] Stonewall, the lesbian, gay, and bisexual charity, published a 2010 report highlighting the fact that consensual acts between same-sex adults are criminalized in 80 member states of the United Nations and six of these countries list homosexuality as a justification for the death penalty.[111]

Persecution of lesbian, gay, and bisexual people around the world has included execution, torture, rape, and murder in countries that have passed laws in support of equal rights for everyone regardless of sexual orientation. The first openly homosexual person spoke at a UN human rights forum in 1992, noting the lack of representation of lesbian women and gay men.[112] In 1993, at the Vienna World Conference on Human Rights, three LGBTQI organizations were accredited to a UN meeting and participated.[113] Today, these asylum claims are coming from people in more than 100 countries who face punishments such as **corrective rape**, discussed in more detail in chapter 6, but referring to the forced sexual encounter of a gay person by a straight person who is said to believe such an encounter will "cure" the person of their homosexuality. Proscribed punishments include torture, jail, and even death.[114]

State-Regulated Reproduction: Are Reproductive Rights Human Rights?

The international human rights organization Amnesty International begins its 2012 report, "Realizing Sexual and Reproductive Rights: A Human Rights Framework," as follows:

> Women's equality, their ability to make their own decisions freely and without coercion, is central to any effective population and development policy. More than 18 years since the world's governments adopted a landmark Programme of Action on population and development, it is clearer than ever that the autonomy of women and girls—to decide, free of coercion and violence, whether, when and with whom to be sexually active; whether and when to become pregnant and have children; and whether or not to marry—is fundamental to any effective progress.[115]

Referencing the **Programme of Action,** adopted in Cairo in 1994, also known as the **Cairo Consensus,** these efforts reflected a forward-looking, 20-year vision for its focus on reproductive health rights, as well as women's empowerment and equality.[116] Yet the issue of **reproductive rights** gets captured internationally in conversations about abortion and individual rights, including bodily integrity and individual liberties for women.

The International Women's Health Coalition featured the stories of 17 women in El Salvador referred to as *Las 17* (the 17 women) who were young and poor when they went to a public hospital after having obstetric complications. El Salvador has a total ban on abortion since 1998. The women, all of whom were accused of having tried to abort their fetus, were arrested and sentenced to terms ranging from 12 to 40 years with significant questions remaining about the adequacy of their legal defense.[117] The number in the story of the 17 has grown to 25 women in jail for murder, who instead say they suffered miscarriages, stillbirths, or pregnancy complications.[118] This issue has attracted support globally and is being advanced by international human rights organizations.[119]

In December 2018, an 18-year-old who faced a 20-year prison term after being accused of attempted abortion was released from prison. She said she did not get prenatal care for the child, who is now almost two, because she didn't know she was pregnant. Her mother brought her to the hospital when she found her bleeding and in pain. At the hospital, the doctor suspected an abortion, so the police were called. The baby was found alive, but the young woman was charged with attempted abortion, denied bail, and sent to jail. Court documents suggest she had been abused repeatedly by her stepfather since the age of 11 or 12. Her release was hailed as a victory, but also drew international attention to the other women, many of whom have other children, who are still in prison on similar charges. In spite of the fact that these issues are controversial on an international stage, countries have the authority to make laws according to their collective social will and/or governing structure. Advocacy groups such as Amnesty International, however, include sexual and reproductive rights as an essential part of preventing and ending gender-based violence.[120] See the following text box for a review of what Amnesty International has created as a list of sexual and reproductive rights.

Allegations about efforts to terminate pregnancies are presented alongside stories of women who became ill as a result of or during the pregnancy and who were forced to carry the baby to term. In Romania, public health issues are raised in relation to the conversations about **pronatalist policies**, which incentivize populations to reproduce and often support the life of the fetus over the life of the mother. The result is the highest maternal mortality rate in Europe (approximately 150 per 100,000) and thousands of unwanted children in institutions.[121]

Text Box 9.3. Have You Ever Thought about Your Sexual and Reproductive Rights?[1]

Everybody has sexual and reproductive rights. States have an obligation to ensure that everyone can freely, without fear, coercion, or discrimination:

- Make decisions about her or his own health, body, sexual life, and identity.
- Ask for and receive information about sex, contraception, and related health services.
- Decide whether and when to have children.
- Choose whether or not to marry and what type of family to create.
- Have access to comprehensive and integrated sexual and reproductive health services. Nobody should be deprived of health care or information on the basis of who they are or what they can afford.
- Live free from rape and other violence, including forced pregnancy, abortion, sterilization, marriage, or female genital mutilation/cutting.

Note

1. "Realizing Sexual and Reproductive Rights: A Human Rights Framework," Amnesty International, 2012, accessed September 29, 2019, 2, http://www.amnesty usa.org/pdfs/RealizingSexualAndReproductiveRightsHumanRightsFramework.pdf.

Conversations about reproductive health also involve the parameters around which women are available to men for sex, as determined by culture, tradition, and government mandate.

Rape as a Weapon of War

> Besides soldier violence perpetrated against civilian populations, a significant role was also played by irregular forces, most notably, by partisan guerrillas and civilian vigilantes. Ethnic nationalist partisan forces perpetrated especially brutal sexual violence against women and girls of "enemy" nationalities. Likewise, after liberation civilian reprisals were fairly common throughout Europe against so-called "sexual collaborators," that is, against women excoriated for providing "sexual comfort" to the enemy during the German occupation.[122]
>
> During the civil war in El Salvador, state forces reportedly perpetrated sexual violence, male political detainees were frequently subjected to sexual torture, and women suffered sexual torture and rape in detention, as well as rape and other sexual violence in the context of military incursions. In sharp contrast, sexual violence by the rebel FMLN was quite rare. Civil war in Sierra Leone, by contrast, featured widespread rape and sexual violence by fighters from many armed groups, both rebel and government. Often, the violence took the form of gang rape, sexual slavery, or sexual torture. Conflict in the former Yugoslavia presents yet another example of variation. Here, it appears that rape by Bosnian Serb forces was both widespread and systematic, having been ordered or explicitly tolerated by key military figures and directed at particular ethnic groups. As the broad differences between these cases suggest, sexual violence during armed conflict is a complex phenomenon, yet it still is often understood through the lens of a few well-known episodes.
>
> —United States Institute of Peace, 2013, Special Report #323[123]

Today, as has been the case historically, rape and other forms of sexualized violence are all too often used as a weapon of war, a tool to break individual bodies, as well as the spirit of families and communities.[124] Anyone interested in history likely understands the use of the term "spoils of war" to include the use of rape by "victors" over the "conquered" people. President Abraham Lincoln is said to have famously issued General Order No. 100, known as the **Lieber Code of 1863**, which set clear codes of conduct for Union soldiers, as well as establishing legal recourse for rape if the code were violated—with penalties including death.[125] In spite of this specific directive, many women—particularly slave women—were vulnerable to rape during the American Civil War as indicated by court records, but in an unprecedented turn, as many as 450 cases of rape were prosecuted in the US Army, most of the perpetrators serving 10 years and a dishonorable discharge.[126] Many examples exist where competing sides have used sexual exploitation as a weapon against the people under siege in military battles as a form of torture, humiliation, and even genocide. Increasingly, researchers have been referencing a shift in current thinking about war and gender violence, as seen in the recognition that rape in wartime is not a by-product of war but rather an integrated, purposeful policy used by command.[127]

Many Americans were shocked to see images taken from Abu Ghraib prison in Iraq, where naked hostages were being led around by US soldiers on a dog collar and being tortured by attaching electrodes to their genitals, but further photos and information came out later that suggested various acts of rape, including sexual assaults with objects, happened at the hand of prison officials.[128] It is also clear that the use of rape is not only perpetrated by the enemy army. Kelly Dawn Askins, a human rights attorney, scholar, activist, and author of *War Crimes Against Women: Prosecution in International War Crimes Tribunals* (1997),[129] suggests that allies also perpetrate sexualized harm. Such was certainly the case with Josef Stalin's Red Army during the "liberation" of Germany in World War II. Although the exact extent of the sexual violence has been challenged, Red Army soldiers were reported to have raped as many as 2 million German women between the initial period of occupation and past the end of active military engagement, to include women being liberated from concentration camps.[130] A poem by Aleksandr Solzhenitsyn, a captain in the Red Army during WWII who spent years in prison for speaking out against wartime abuses and Stalin, includes reference to child rape and murder:

> A moaning, by the walls half muffled:
> The mother's wounded, still alive.
> The little daughter's on the mattress,
> Dead. How many have been on it?
> A platoon, a company perhaps?
> A girl's been turned into a woman,
> A woman turned into a corpse.[131]

Perhaps one of the most well-known examples of rape in wartime is the example of the **Comfort Women**, also during WWII. Japanese and South Korean women were recruited for work in factories or encouraged to help with the war effort. But, instead of work, the women were taken to secluded areas where they were expected to perform sex acts for Japanese soldiers.[132] The social and cultural humiliation of the affected women was profound; however, the humiliation handed to them by the Japanese government was suggested to have been even more brutal when, after creating a military-prostitution system of an estimated 200,000 women, the government denied that the acts of sexual servitude ever happened.[133]

The first **comfort station**, a small series of rooms where soldiers would line up for sex, was established in 1932. Accounts suggest initial women used in the comfort stations were prostituted women who volunteered to work for the military. Recruitment then shifted to the local population where women were tricked or kidnapped into sexual slavery. Reports vary; however, the number of women believed to have been held as comfort women ranged up to 400,000. Three-fourths of the women died, and many were left infertile because of the damage done to their body by the physical assaults and the ravages of disease.[134]

The history of the comfort women has been rife with controversy, from the Japanese government's denial of the event as recently as 2007[135] to public claims the women's stories are not credible or that all of the women who were involved in the comfort stations were not forced but had volunteered.[136]

During the more recent Bosnian war (1992–1995), the United Nations estimated between 20,000 and 50,000 women were raped as a result of that conflict, and, in Sierra Leone (1991–2002), the numbers of rape were estimated between 50,000 and 64,000. During the Rwandan genocide, an estimated 500,000 women were raped during 100 days of conflict.[137] In 2008, the Democratic Republic of the Congo reported rapes on both sides of the civil war in that country.[138] The examples of sexual degradation are horrific, including gang rapes; rapes committed in front of the entire community; male relatives forced to have sex with their daughters, mothers, or sisters; women used as sex slaves and forced to eat excrement or the flesh of murdered relatives; women murdered with bullets from guns forced into their vaginas; and men forced to simulate having sex in holes dug in the ground with razor blades stuck in the holes.[139] These acts were not random acts of violence but deliberate attempts to dehumanize and destroy entire communities.[140]

South Africa is reported to have one of the highest rates of sexual assault in the world. A country of 52 million people, South Africa has more cases of rape reported to the police each year than India, a country with a population of approximately 1 billion.[141] Five men were arrested and charged in October 2013, after the bodies of two toddlers, cousins, aged 2 and 3, were abducted in broad daylight and then found days later, raped and murdered, their bodies dumped in a public toilet.[142] Like the rape and murder of the young woman on a bus in India, this event produced global public outrage and protests, seeking more protections for women and more response from the justice systems both locally and globally.[143] Although not technically involved in an armed conflict, the estimates of one rape every 26 seconds prompted the Women's Media Center's Women Under Siege project, mentioned earlier, to publish a piece titled "Women in South Africa Are Living in a War Zone."[144] Many victims do not believe the justice system can offer necessary services or protect them, treat them with respect, support their claim through the system, or act as a deterrent to rapists.[145]

The complexities of addressing the global subject of multiculturalism, and the biases that can come as a result, cannot be understated. When approaching such an expansive issue from within the United States, where predominant cultural attitudes have either shifted from or have not supported practices such as forced marriage, honor killings, and female genital modification, it can be difficult to discuss the origins of these practices because of distance, a lack of contemporary and historical knowing, and the fact that smaller cultural groups are often discussed as monolithic, or as if they are one mindset, when in fact many people do not believe the same way or act in similar ways within a given country. As reflections are offered on these international issues, it is also important to remember these intercultural issues sometimes get entangled within international public policy, such as in the cases of immigration issues and economics, and the initial issue can get coopted or side tracked.[146] Further, the United States is not free from the controversies associated with socially and judicially controversial issues such as abortion, human trafficking, and sexual violence in war, as examples.

COMMERCIAL SEX WORK AND THE COMMERCIAL SEX INDUSTRY

The businesses of prostitution and pornography have a unique history in each country around the world. In the United States, just about every film described in the United States as "a western" profiles a story about the "wild west," which includes a town saloon with a brothel upstairs. In the presentation of many of these story lines, seemingly happy, vivacious, eager young women are ready to service equally eager male clients.[147] *The Best Little Whorehouse in Texas* was a popular Broadway musical in the late 1970s, and the film adaptation went on to become one of the highest-grossing movies of the 1980s. The 1990 movie *Pretty Woman*, also a film about prostitution, enjoyed dramatic box office success. The film was nominated for various awards and has been identified as the most popular and profitable films of all times.[148] Movies and story lines such as these provide a fertile ground for challenging and raising questions about how people come to learn about and understand what the lives of people who work in the sex industry are like in the real world every day, in both their personal and professional experiences.

Discussion as to whether *Pretty Woman* is a feminist classic speaking to women's empowerment and self-determination or "one of the most misogynist, patriarchal, classist, consumerist, and lookist movies ever to come out of Hollywood" is divisive and usually without common ground between factions.[149] This divide does not seem to be bridged by some of the more contemporary changes in laws and/or policies around how prostitution is treated by law enforcement, nor is social criticism smoothed by the increasing popularity of various genres of video pornography and expanding if not surprising (in some circles) successes in the mainstream of books and subsequent mainstream movies such as *50 Shades of Gray*, which centered on sexual acts of bondage and domination.[150]

To say that both the industries of prostitution and pornography have supporters and critics would be an understatement. Challenges are present it seems in just about every aspect of the industry. The use of violence, although variable, in both pornography and prostitution is a primary theme for concerns raised about the commercial sex industry, or the individuals and companies that exchange money or goods for sexual services more broadly.[151] The integration of violence, degrading and dehumanizing acts, and verbal harassment associated with prostitution and pornography is often at the center of the many controversial conversations surrounding the decisions to be made regarding regulating or legalizing aspects of sex work, more broadly.

As suggested in the section on sex trafficking above, one significant factor is whether there is a clear line between those who are involved by choice and those who are coerced in some way. Critics of acts identified as sex work raise various objections from a diversity of sectors, while a strong network of support is building in the international community for increased support for sex workers, primarily around disease prevention, personal safety, and the proposed benefits of **decriminalization**, removing legal restrictions.[152]

The controversy around prostitution, pornography, and other sex-related work is as long-standing as their social existence. But what is at the heart of the controversy? With thousands of years of social efforts to address these and related concerns, is the idea of realizing any sort of cooperative agreement ever going to be possible? What if, for the sake of discussion, the matter of commercial sex work could be reduced down to two central questions: *Are there people (primarily women, but not always) who actively and deliberately seek money in exchange for sex acts out of their own free will?* This question asks whether people work in the sex industry because they want to and they decide this for themselves from a healthy place, not because they have no other options, or because they think they will make good money, or because of manipulation—blatant or subtle (e.g., for the "love" of someone or because a coercive partner wants to sell their sexuality for some additional cash). Consider this question from the perspective of the individual and then with a focus on the possible influence of social conditions.

A second question could be, *Are a significant number of people (primarily men, but not always) going to be interested in seeking out sexual services regardless of the legal status of sex work?* Given history, the answer may seem obvious, but, if the answer is yes, other questions immediately follow: What is an appropriate social response? Is it important to know why people seek out sexual services? And, if sex work is common to countries around the globe, why do societies respond so differently?

Regardless of the answers to these basic questions, an element of either formal or informal social regulation is warranted. If, regarding the first question, no people report prostitution as a preferred livelihood, then society is left to regulate the broader forces of human trafficking. And if it is children who are being recruited when they cannot consent and then forced to grow up in this livelihood, will there ever be a "rescue"? If, however, there are people who choose this lifestyle, do laws, policies, and practices seek to regulate the individual choice, the industry, or both? As all of these and other more nuanced elements of the commercial sex industry take place in the world around us, the world of sex work is vastly different with the advent of the internet, and it is changing still.

Technological advances, discussed in greater detail in the segment below, have made access to commercial sex work open and available to anyone. The money to be made in the global marketplace is difficult to quantify because the characterization of prostitution and/or trafficking is different in different areas. A fundamental reason for the international trafficking in humans for sex is profits. The UN International Labor Organization (ILO) estimates $99 billion is generated by sex slavery.[153] That number does not include the mainstream sex toy stores or other sex industry stores that are legal. Industry market research reports suggest that the advancement of mainstream books like *50 Shades of Gray* and other cultural shifts in social acceptance of sex stores have created more market and sex-related products in mainstream stores like

Walmart and CVS.[154] How the larger conversations around these issues have been changing both internationally and in contemporary US markets is the central theme of this section. Attention is given to a common set of definitions, then to a collection of some of the most well-discussed, controversial themes within commercial sex work, including prostitution, pornography, and technical advances related to sexually oriented content. As the review of this area begins, one more fundamental question might emerge: Why is prostitution largely illegal if pornography is legal?

Definitions

Commercial sex work, the more generic term used for activities involving "the exchange of material goods such as money, food, drugs, transportation, housing, etc., for sexual services,"[155] is not the only way people talk about the **sex industry**, or the combination of industries and businesses that facilitate financial or other exchanges where sex is involved. Distinguishing **sexual commerce** from sex work includes people who work in the sex industry but do not trade in sexual services and include but is not limited to those who may work as managers, property owners, drivers, and telephone and camera operators. Sex work is generally understood to include but is not limited to street work, escort work, work in brothels, exotic dance clubs, paid domination, phone sex, web cam sex, and sexual massage.[156]

But commercial sex work is a relatively new umbrella term intended to reference the broader social issues associated with prostitution and pornography. **Prostitution** is the offering of something of value for sexual activity.[157] The US government defines **sex trafficking** as a form of human trafficking "in which a commercial sex act is induced by force, fraud, or coercion, or in which the person induced to perform such act has not attained 18 years of age."[158] Some sectors of have been accused of conflating what is historically known as prostitution with sex trafficking, suggesting prostitution is the more appropriate term when decisions about sex work are made by the parties involved, whereas sex trafficking refers to activities coerced in any way. It is not difficult to find a scenario where two people well versed in the subject of sex trafficking, sex work, and prostitution might disagree about whether a person is being exploited or acting of their own choice. In fact, some advocates believe strongly the idea of willingly being involved in sex work is not possible, suggesting instead that prostitution is always exploitive.

The term **pornography** is sometimes used to describe all sexually explicit books, magazines, movies, and websites, with a distinction made between **soft core** (nudity with limited sexual activity not including penetration) and **hard core** (graphic images of actual, not simulated, sexual activity including penetration). Pornography is also distinguished from **erotica** (material that depicts sexual behavior with mutuality and respect), leaving pornography as the term for material depicting sex with domination or degradation.[159]

Within the fields of related study, as well as in the broader society, the limits and parameters intended to outline what is to be done to define and address the legal status of many aspects of commercial sex work are controversial. Two primary groups opposing pornography and prostitution are religious organizations, which condemn sex work on moral grounds as a violation of religious values, and women's advocacy groups, on the grounds that individuals are objectified and exploited.

Efforts more recently have revolved around making sure that someone who is 18 or younger involved in sex work in any capacity will be treated as a victim of trafficking, thus criminalizing the adults. Because the state laws were not equally applied, some people younger than 18 were being charged and convicted of prostitution in spite of the fact that they were legally minors. As a result, safe harbor laws have been passed in the United States, and just over 30 states have provisions that treat the young person as a victim and provide services.[160]

Depictions of sex and displays of sexuality are present throughout history in various artistic forms and representations, but only certain images and terms used to describe those displays have been defined as pornographic through the application of specific legal meaning; however, the social definitions seem rather fluid. Incorporating **bondage, discipline, sadism, and masochism (BDSM)** within a sexual encounter, as an example, is a practice older generations might describe as way outside of the mainstream, perhaps even dangerous and in need of regulating, whereas younger people might see that as less than noteworthy. Whereas most adults have a general understanding of both prostitution and pornography, the reality of expanded access to a wide variety of commercial sex work provided via the internet, cell phones, and global streaming platforms also produces a broader, more comprehensive discussion about the level of coercion, either subtle or overt, and expanded efforts to assure the absence of exploitation and abuse. A brief review of some of the current issues as they relate to the argument for or classification of sex crimes is presented for reflection and consideration.

A NOTE ON SEX TRAFFICKING, COMMERCIAL SEX WORK, AND THE COMMERCIAL SEXUAL EXPLOITATION OF CHILDREN

Conversations about prostitution have sometimes been collapsed into conversations about sex trafficking. Prostitution is often historically and sometimes jokingly described as the world's oldest profession, yet, more recently, an increase in awareness about the trafficking of humans for sexual purposes, expressly for the profit of a third party or company, has been isolated as a subject for deeper scrutiny and analysis, as discussed above. The idea that a person who has sex for money is not making their own individual choices is being targeted and resoundingly challenged by communities and enforcement agencies.

These larger public conversations among academics, practitioners, communities, and sex workers themselves are contrasted with conversations about whether the exchanges for sex are directed from within a larger syndicated crime structure with money as a motive. Sometimes described as a corollary or supplement to drug trafficking syndicates, human trafficking is attractive because it can be more profitable. Drugs can only be sold once, whereas people can be sold for sex over and over and multiple times a day for years.[161]

References to child pornography or commercial child exploitation are excluded from the following conversations about adult involvement in commercial sex work. Further, human trafficking more broadly is distinguished from the larger conversation about the degree to which adults participate willingly in commercial sex work. The gray areas of where legal limits are, or should be, and the remaining open questions, dynamic tension, and ongoing discussions and debates about the legal limits of those adult themes are acknowledged, as is the need for more analysis and data collection and critical review than can be offered here.

Prostitution and Pornography

Las Vegas, Nevada, in the United States has earned its reputation around the world as a center for vice, including gambling and prostitution. It is, famously, but erroneously, identified as the one place in the United States where prostitution is legal. Some will say prostitution is and has always been a social taboo. Others will say that it is linked to a long history of patriarchal control of messages about sex, with men being the dominators, controlling the narratives about sex and women being the subordinated or submissive party, awaiting instruction from men. Even women's rights groups have struggled to come to a collective understanding about what is the most empowering or the least oppressive way forward.

Catharine A. MacKinnon became well known for her early presence in the **feminist movement** of the 1970s and her work to establish legal standards for women who were trying to use the legal system to address sexual harassment in the workplace, for example. Until that time, a woman could be fired for not sleeping with her boss, for example, but have no recourse until MacKinnon created a legal claim for sexual harassment as a form of sex discrimination. The organizing idea was fairly simple: the legal system did not provide the protections women needed to protect them from men who would abuse their power. Some say even with these changes, the legal system still doesn't go far enough. Then, in the early 1980s elements of social activism involving the LGBTQI community and communities of color, with attention being given to how dominance and individual agency and legal protections worked more broadly, generated a response to what was largely labeled "anti-porn feminists," with what was identified as **sex positive feminism**.[162] These ideas about whether the law was necessary for protecting women or whether using the law was seen as minimizing the ability of women to act on their own interests set the stage for a larger social and political conversation, referred to as the **feminist sex wars**.

While academics and legal scholars were battling it out very publicly, also in the 1970s Candida Royalle was making adult films and argued publicly that celebrating all kinds of female desire was central to women's liberation.[163] In the mid-1980s, she became a director of adult films geared toward creating better working conditions for the actors and targeting women and couples as her audience. Calling her work a departure from traditional porn, Royalle suggested feminist porn centered women and choice and assured dignity to the performers. "Feminist porn is probably the only aspect of porn that focuses on making humane improvement for the people watching as well as the actresses in the videos."[164] Her work remains controversial, with some suggesting the term "feminist porn" is an oxymoron and others embracing the expanded standards in the adult film industry.

Raising questions about women's choice and expanding a market toward "erotic films" were both happening as the issue of prostitution was expanding into a global conversation, when in June 1975 a group of sex workers occupied a church in Lyon, France. Expressing their anger and frustration about the exploitation and criminalization they faced, that group became one of the first groups to draw attention to and discuss the need for protections and rights for sex workers. Two decades later in the early 1990s, sex workers in India tapped into and tagged onto the HIV/AIDS discourse, suggesting that the risks of this disease for sex workers must be addressed and they must be protected.[165]

In spite of an ongoing social stigma surrounding sex work, increased attention is being given to the numbers of people who seek out sex workers. In the summer of 2011, *Newsweek*, through the *Daily Beast*, put out an article titled "The John Next Door," suggesting estimates of men who pay for sex range from 16 to 80 percent, presenting the shocking idea that 99 percent of the studies in this area have been done on the women involved in prostitution, not the johns who pay for sexual services.[166] Sixteen to 80 is a huge range within that reporting, but like other subjects related to sex, the statistics are difficult to assess with complete accuracy. An estimate in 2000 suggested the United States has approximately 70,000 female prostitutes and set the average acts of prostitution with male customers annually at 700 per person, totaling approximately 50 million acts of prostitution each year.[167]

Should Prostitution Be Treated as a Crime?

Various countries reflect different social attitudes toward prostitution with many countries banning prostitution outright, as in the case of the United States, with the exception of the state of Nevada. Looking back several decades, attitudes about the legal status of prostitution around the world has changed over time and location. Generally, catering with some exclusivity to wealthy white men,[168] the legal standing of brothels reflected a significant change at the turn of the twentieth century as the result of religious group influences and assessments of immorality resulting in a total ban by 1920.[169] This included media representations, movies, and news coverage. More recently, the risk of violence has been noted as a significant threat for women in the sex work industry. The idea that a prostitute cannot be raped or that giving consent to one sex act includes unrestricted sexual access of any kind is a common misperception, yet this is reinforced in decisions producing media stories and public attitudes and has been associated with decision-making processes about arrests and prosecutions.

In 1991, 55 prostituted women working in Portland were interviewed about their sexual assault history. In this study, 78 percent of them reported being raped an average of 16 times annually by their pimps and 33 times a year by johns. Of the total 49 rapes, 12 were reported within the criminal justice system, and

Table 9.2   Prostitution around the Globe from World Population Review

Nations where prostitution is **legal as of 2019**:

Legal:
Chile, Colombia, Costa Rica, Cuba, Cyprus, Czech Republic, Demark, Dominican Republic, Ecuador, el Salvador, Ethiopia, Estonia, Finland, Germany, Greece, Argentina, Guatemala, Honduras, Hungary, India, Indonesia, Israel, Italy, Austria, Kenya, Kyrgyzstan, Latvia, Luxembourg, Malta, Mexico, Bangladesh, Netherlands, New Zealand, Nicaragua, Belgium, Panama, Paraguay, Peru, Poland, Portugal, Bolivia, Senegal, Singapore, Slovakia, Slovenia, Spain, Switzerland, Brazil, Turkey, Belize, Uruguay, and Venezuaela.

Nations where local laws **regulate or prohibit prostitution**:

Illegal:
Cambodia, China, Croatia, Dominica, Angola, Antigua and Barbuda, Grenada, Guyana, Haiti, Iran, Iraq, Jamaica, Afghanistan, Jordan, North Korea, South Korea, Liberia, Bahamas, Lithuania, Barbados, Philippines, Romania, Rwanda, saint kitts and Nevis, Saint Lucia, Saint Vincent and the Grenadines, Saudi Arabia, South Africa, Suriname, Thailand, Trinidad and Tobago, United Arab Emirates, Albania, Uganda, and Egypt.

Limitedly Legal:
Canada, France, Iceland, Australia, Ireland, Japan, Malaysia, Armenia, Norway, Sweden, United Kingdom, United States.

Citation: Countries Where Prostitution is Legal. (2019-10-10). Retrieved 2020-02-18, from http://worldpopulationreview.com/countries/countries-where-prostitution-is-legal/

no pimp or john was ever convicted of the offense.[170] In 1995, it was estimated that between 80 and 95 percent of all prostitution was pimp controlled across the United States.[171] In 2001, 183 Vancouver prostitutes were interviewed, and 68 percent had reported being physically assaulted in the previous six months, 68 percent were raped in the previous six months, 72 percent were kidnapped or confined in the previous six months, and 60 percent reported being the victim of an attempted murder in the previous six months.[172]

In 1999, Sweden changed the ground rules of prostitution practice when it became the first country to adopt the **Nordic model** on prostitution, which criminalizes the purchase of sex. Focusing the enforcement on the purchasers of sex, not the people doing sex work, this model is being considered in places throughout the United States.[173] Sweden reported street prostitution was reduced by half due to the sudden drop in demand in the short term and a shift in social attitude over the long term, with the majority of the Swedish population supporting the ban.[174]

Another shift in legal definitions happened in August 2018, when a US court permitted a civil claim by Kadian Noble, a British actor, against film producer Harvey Weinstein using the US Trafficking Victims Protection Act (TVPA). Since legal recourse for work-related sexual harassment and abuse was limited if not nonexistent before the 1970s, this case suggested the forced sexual acts were related to her career, therefore, making them commercial in nature.[175] Catharine A. MacKinnon's work from the 1970s was highlighted and extended to the more contemporary events, when in 2017 she wrote "[i]t was the legal recognition that broke the rule of impunity that the more power a man has, the more sex he can exact from those with less power."[176] She went on to say:

A lot of women's work, like the rest of women's lives, is sexualized. Working for tips in a restaurant to make anything close to a living wage, for example, largely requires women in effect to sell themselves sexually. The entertainment industry commodifies the sexuality of the women in it. The fact that so many of the exposed harassers in the entertainment field subjected their victims to a pornographic spectator sexuality, masturbating over them in real life like consumers do over women in pornography, is no coincidence. Pervasively normalized, this is what an endemic abuse looks like.

In its fundamental dynamics, sexual harassment turns real work into a form of prostitution. The imperative to exchange sex for survival, or its possibility whether real or not, rules women's inequality, hence women's lives, worldwide. In prostitution, virtually all of women's and girls' options are precluded except for this one, making her consent to it, or choice of it, fraudulent and illusory.[177]

The law is being continuously clarified as efforts are ongoing to assert legal utility further in finding ways to hold an individual accountable for using sex in connection with offers of career advancements or threatening to eliminate future prospects for career opportunities. The discussion about the role of prostitution in society is ongoing, with people falling out strongly on either side of the argument and even others working to suggest a middle way.

Should Pornography Be Treated as a Crime?

The expanded acceptance of pornography, the use or sale of pictures or images of sexually explicit materials intended to or for the purposes of sexual arousal,[178] has been identified as one of the biggest cultural shifts in mainstream American culture over the last 25 years.[179] In a recent Gallup poll, two-thirds of Americans identified pornography as morally wrong.[180] But, in spite of any moral trepidation, the porn industry is one of the largest money-making industries in the world.

It is easy enough to describe roughly how the characteristics of the pornography market have changed in recent years, but greater problems arise when attempting to provide quantitative figures since it is almost impossible to find estimations that clearly state their methods and sources. Estimates suggest general pornography generates $57 billion globally in revenues and $2.5 billion for internet pornography;[181] more recent data put the global 2006 revenues from pornography to $97 billion. China ($27 billion), South Korea ($26 billion), Japan ($20 billion), and the United States ($13 billion, $3 billion of which is generated by internet pornography) generate the majority of pornography revenues. Some estimates place pornography revenue as greater than the combined revenues of all professional football, baseball, and basketball franchises.[182]

As difficult as it is to determine the actual amounts of money associated with pornography, technology has made pornography increasingly available. In the early 1970s, pornography became mainstream in the United States with the production of films like *Deep Throat* and *Behind the Green Door* on old-school VHS videos. The advent of internet technology has exploded the sales and access even further, with both free porn sites (e.g., www.youporn.com, www.pornotube .com, www.xtube.com) and pay porn sites, which use free clips to get people to visit their sites. MindGeek, an online porn provider, suggest they are "pioneering the future of online traffic"; it has over 100 million daily visitors and is one of the top three consumers of bandwidth, right along with Netflix and YouTube.[183]

Aside from a broad definition, pornography can be difficult to define socially. As with other areas related to the discussion of sexual attitudes and acceptable parameters of sexual images, the definitions change over time and geographic location. Often, how pornography is defined is based on the context in which it is being considered. For example:

> [T]he definitions of what pornography is fall mainly into six different types, namely: (i) those that define "pornography" as the sale of sex for profit, (ii) those that define it as a form of bad art, (iii) those that define it as portraying men or women as, as only, or only as sexual beings or sexual objects, (iv) those that define it as a form of obscenity, (v) those that define it as a form of (or contributor to) oppression, and (vi) those that define it as material that is intended to produce or has the effect of producing sexual arousal. Definitions in the latter three categories are by far the most prominent.[184]

As is suggested in the more nuanced definition of what pornography is, the legal history of pornography has been a battle for defining the "obscene." Made famous in *Jacobellis v. Ohio* in 1964 by US Supreme Court Justice Potter Stewart in a case attempting to determine whether a film fell under protected speech provisions of the First Amendment, he wrote:

> I shall not today attempt further to define the kinds of material I understand to be embraced within that shorthand description ["hard-core pornography"], and perhaps I could never succeed in intelligibly doing so. But I know it when I see it, and the motion picture involved in this case is not that.[185]

Highlighting the difficulty of placing an objective assessment on what is ultimately a subjective cultural and social determination, the Stewart assessment is reflective of larger issues. In short, the idea of regulating pornography is daunting. People are using their iPhones and creating websites where they can stream porn and accept money to their PayPal accounts. The number of professional actors, producers, or distributors of pornography finding a place in the market is hard to determine.[186] In 1973, the courts in *Miller v. California* developed a three-part standard for assessing whether speech or expression can be labeled obscene, in which case it would not be protected by the First Amendment to the US Constitution and could be prohibited. See Text Box 9.4.

The impacts of the pornography industry on societies across the globe are also difficult to objectively assess without taking a deep dive. There is a lot of information from various sources on the subject. In 2015, for example, a meta-analysis of 22 studies from seven countries found that internationally the consumption of pornography was significantly associated with increases in verbal and physical aggression, among males and females alike,[187] while other research findings raise questions about associating pornography with self-reports of increased sexual violence.[188] Other reports suggest sexual violence has been decreasing over the

Text Box 9.4.   The Miller Test (1973)

In 1964, Supreme Court Justice Potter Stewart famously wrote in *Jacobellis v. Ohio*: "I shall not today attempt further to define the kinds of material I understand to be embraced within that shorthand description ["hard-core pornography"], and perhaps I could never succeed in intelligibly doing so. But I know it when I see it, and the motion picture involved in this case is not that."[1]

In 1974, the US Supreme Court established the test that judges and juries use to determine whether matter is obscene in three major cases: *Miller v. California*, 413 U.S. 15, 24–25 (1973); *Smith v. United States*, 431 U.S. 291, 300–302, 309 (1977); and *Pope v. Illinois*, 481 U.S. 497, 500–501 (1987). The three-pronged *Miller* test is as follows:

1. Whether the average person, applying contemporary adult community standards, finds that the matter, taken as a whole, appeals to prurient interests (*i.e.*, an erotic, lascivious, abnormal, unhealthy, degrading, shameful, or morbid interest in nudity, sex, or excretion);
2. Whether the average person, applying contemporary adult community standards, finds that the matter depicts or describes sexual conduct in a patently offensive way (*i.e.*, ultimate sexual acts, normal or perverted, actual or simulated, masturbation, excretory functions, lewd exhibition of the genitals, or sado-masochistic sexual abuse); and
3. Whether a reasonable person finds that the matter, taken as a whole, lacks serious literary, artistic, political, or scientific value.

Any material that satisfies this three-pronged test may be found obscene.

Note

1. In *Jacobellis v. Ohio*, 378 U.S. at 197 (Stewart, J., concurring) (emphasis added).

last decade while pornography usage has been increasing, suggesting pornography provides little or no influence worthy of rigid and steep regulation.[189] The amount of research in this area is truly prodigious, with strong statements on both sides advocating uncensored access and abstinence or getting rid of pornography completely. Close attention should be paid in the state-by-state assessments of pornography usage data sources when reviewing information, as well as when comparing across international standards. It seems few people studying the subject have not taken a side. The sides seem to break down in terms of moral issues, related to a desire to protect public health potentially harmed by pornography and the effects of porn usage on one side, and without question or apology people on the other side arguing for the preservation of individual rights, including the right to make money, and advocating the idea that pornography can be used as part of a healthy lifestyle.

The history of pornography is lengthy and filled with controversy. A full review of its social and legal history is outside the scope of the larger objectives here. Evidence is mounting that suggests reason to pay close attention to research as it adds to what is currently known about the long- and short-term implications of pornography usage on individuals and on the larger social environment.[190] A review of several of the basic controversies around the broad access and distribution of pornography, the issue of child pornography, and the issue of pornography's impact on relationships between intimate partners and across genders is offered for a brief review.

Access and Distribution

In 1988, the *Freeman* decision by the California Supreme Court made it legal to make pornographic films because the performers were identified as actors, not prostitutes. The US Supreme Court let the state court's ruling stand, and other states have followed the California standard. This answers the common question about why pornography is legal and prostitution is illegal: pornography is a performance protected by the first amendment, and prostitution is a sex act directly exchanged for money. However, the courts are having a hard time keeping up.

Questions have been raised regarding whether drawings or cartoon images can legally be modified for sexual purposes and defined as pornography. The internet has created various cartoon images, including pages based on famous Disney characters, Hello Kitty, or other popular cartoon images. In 2008, an Iowa district court jailed a manga collector for six months for owning "one or more drawing or cartoons that depict a minor engaging in sexually explicit conduct." Manga are comics created in Japan or by creators in the Japanese language. In *United States v. Hadley*, the defendant faced 20 years in prison and a $250,000 fine, so he reached a plea agreement, which was prosecuted under the PROTECT Act, designed to penalize commercial exploitation of children, discussed in more detail in chapter 10. Airport security checkpoints are increasingly being challenged with assessing the legal status of specific genres of pornography. By far, the central focus around the policing of pornography is connected to child pornography.

Child Sexual Abuse Imagery

Large international police operations, such as illustrated through the Spade Project, discussed at the opening of the chapter, provide insight into the extensive global networks created for trafficking in video images of children. Evidence collected in the 2001 Wonderland Club case confiscated images of children as young as 2 months old being sexually assaulted and tortured. To join, each new member had to supply 10,000 images of child porn, and membership extended to 13 countries.[191] Because child pornography is a multijurisdictional problem, global efforts have been put in place to provide legal redress and include:

1. The Optional Protocol to the (UN) Convention on the Rights of the Child on the Sale of Children, Child Prostitution and Child Pornography;
2. The Council of Europe's Convention on Cybercrime; and
3. The Council of Europe's Convention on the Protection of Children against Sexual Exploitation and Sexual Abuse.[192]

And because the legal jurisdictions of every country make international enforcement more complicated, the challenges and seeming contradictions are many. In the United States, even though child pornography is socially unpopular and illegal, the definition of what constitutes child pornography is being challenged in the courts and websites that take young people over the legal age and place them as character roles to look younger are extremely popular.

In 2002, the Free Speech Coalition, founded in 1991 as a nonprofit trade association for the adult industry, secured its first big victory with *Ashcroft v. Free Speech Coalition*. In that case, the US Supreme Court ruled the 1996 Child Porn Prevention Act was unconstitutional because its definition of child pornography was overly broad. The law was narrowed to cover only those images including *actual persons* who were under the age of 18, leaving room for computer-generated images and sites that make women of a legal age look more childlike. As a result of the *Ashcroft* ruling, internet sites with this genre of pornography proliferate. This distinction is not made in other countries, using Canada and the United Kingdom as comparative examples, but NRP, or Not Real People, stimulus sets refer to computer-generated images (CGI) expected to get better as technology improves, and are sometimes referred to as PCP, or **pseudo child porn**, because the "girls" or "children" being represented in the videos are situated in sexual encounters with teachers, fathers, religious figures, coaches, or any number of possible adult figures, including child molesters.[193]

In 2011, the Oregon Supreme Court ruled that it is not a crime to look at child pornography while surfing the internet, comparing the experience to going to a museum. Looking at things does not mean you have possession of them and, therefore, if an image is on your machine but it was not purchased, the legal definition of "possession" has not been met and a child pornography charge is not supported.[194] Clearly the courts, both in the United States and internationally have not offered their last ruling on these important legal parameters.

Family and Community Impact

Although the questions of child protection and women's empowerment are an entrée into an extremely controversial and long-standing debate about whether women who participate in sex work are coerced economically or participate by choice, communities and groups have moved in ways to reflect their attitudes toward sex work more specifically. One example is Northampton, Massachusetts, at the website nopornnorthampton.org. According to its web page, it aims to:

> increase awareness about the impact of porn on people and communities. We support the reasonable regulation of sexually oriented businesses in Northampton, Massachusetts and elsewhere. We ask businesspeople to balance profits with compassion. We do not advocate increasing government censorship of porn. For our positive vision of sexuality visit GreenSexuality.com.[195]

Research suggesting men becoming desensitized to porn, impacting personal sexual activities, calls into question the longer-term impacts of pornography usage.[196] In 2007, the University of Alberta (Canada) published a report suggesting one in three boys were heavy porn users, with boys aged 13 and 14 living in rural areas being the most likely to access pornography.[197] Ninety percent of males and 70 percent of females reported viewing porn at least once, while 33 percent of boys and 8 percent of girls viewed porn "too many times to count."[198] The author, a former sex education teacher, expressed the motivation for her research being a concern that excessive early exposure to porn may change the expectations young people have for relationships, both sexual and interpersonal, and may normalize what are considered by many to be risky sexual practices.

Longer-term psychological studies are calling into question what happens when young people use pornography to learn about sex, emphasizing research suggesting extreme amounts of gendered violence, intimacy issues, and problems developing relationships in general can result.

Recent studies suggested the overall chance of divorce doubled for both men and women who started using porn after getting married,[199] with divorce rates higher among young people (at 50 percent) and lowest among those 50 years old and over, which did not have a significant impact on relationship status. s

The Price of Pleasure: Pornography, Sexuality and Relationships, a 2008 documentary film, focused on studying the rise of the pornography industry and the impact of pornography on relationships. Focused primarily but not exclusively on the users of pornography in the United States, at one point it profiled a man attempting to explain the rise in anal pornography, saying this type of porn is produced for every man who was mad at his wife and wanted to "F*** her in the ass." Such a statement integrates anger, sex, and aggression at a minimum and begs the kinds of questions one might have about what he or anyone else might think any given relationship might actually look like. But it also raises questions about why people watch pornography.

When attention is given to a statement such as that, what attitudes and beliefs exist behind that kind of remark? Certainly, everyone knows that people in relationships argue and disagree. Fight the New Drug, an online movement to educate "on pornography's harmful effects on individuals, relationships, and society," at FightTheNewDrug.org, suggests porn harms in these three ways and takes site visitors to peer-reviewed research that explains the effect porn has on the brain, how porn affects relationships, and how pornography affects society more broadly.[200] Learning how to argue and forgive and bond with others is essential for developing and pursuing relationships in a healthy way, and FightTheNewDrug.org is only one of many public service agencies highlighting research suggesting the impact of porn is harmful long term. The National Center on Sexual Exploitation has suggested the age at first exposure and the pervasive use of pornography is "ground zero for all those concerned for the sexual health and wellbeing of our loved ones, communities and society as a whole."[201] In short, their findings suggest:

- (Negative) impacts on sexual violence and exploitation
- (Negative) impacts on adolescents
- (Negative) impacts on females
- (Negative) impacts on males

- (Negative) impacts on mental health
- (Negative) impacts on brain/evidence of addiction
- (Negative) impacts on sexually transmitted infections
- (Negative) impacts on relationships and sexual behaviors[202]

As attention is given to the tone and the underlying assumptions that drive the creation and use of pornography, what does it tell us as a larger society about our underlying expectations and assumptions about each other and our relationships? This brief review is focused on the impact of individuals who are not considered to have committed a sex crime but rather are just typical individuals who use pornography. What is the impact of pornography on people who have committed sex crimes? What is the impact, for some, of porn used as a substitute and, for others, used as a how-to guide and a stimulus to the event?[203]

Technology and Cybersex

Consider the 2013 police action in Amsterdam, Netherlands. After posting a computer-generated child in a video chat room as a 10-year-old Filipina girl named "Sweetie," over 20,000 men contacted the website. Referred to as **webcam child sex tourism,** the authorities raised the alarm internationally with their reports. In less than two and a half months, adults from 71 countries solicited Sweetie, and more than 1,000 men were caught trying to pay for the child to perform sex acts online: 254 were from the United States, 110 were from the United Kingdom, and 103 were from India.[204]

Part of the report out on the story at the time was the need for new policing techniques and practices to combat what was emerging as a new threat, using a technology and imaging systems that were developing rapidly around the world.–Cooperation between private business and focusing on the ability to collect payment, in other words following the money, have produced positive outcomes.

Additional moral and legal questions are evolving in a shared public conversation about what technology might produce. Moving off the online platform and into a manufactured form of real life, artificial intelligence (AI) programs in dolls that mimic human appearance can be voice activated with motors embedded into parts of their robot body increasingly being more "life-like."[205] Robots in the United States are made in the adult size, with physical features reflecting video gaming images of women, and features can be selected or made to order. A model resembling a 5-year-old girl is produced in Japan.[206]

Various issues have been raised about the moral appropriateness of the development of such sex-related technologies, with researchers and social critics asking questions about the "rights" of machines and comparing sex robots to prostitution and slavery,[207] as well as whether such images and technologies are an appropriate treatment option for offenders.[208] What is clear, however, is the fact that the technological advancements are happening rapidly.

The internet has also played a part in how people in search of sex find ways to solicit sex. This includes prostitution. Instead of driving around in a specific area of town or working underground networks, increasingly there are "low end" and "high end" sex work operations available online with customer reviews[209] and crowdsourcing opportunities.[210] Whether these new innovations are seen as advances or setbacks remains debatable.

The **Internet Crimes Against Children (ICAC) Task Force Program** is a national network of 61 coordinated task forces representing over 4,500 federal, state, and local law enforcement and prosecutorial agencies in the United States continually engaged in monitoring child abuse and exploitation on the internet.[211] In a national survey by the National Center for Missing and Exploited Children, the Crimes Against Children Research Center, and the Office of Juvenile Justice and Delinquency Prevention, 1,500 young people, aged 10 to 17, who were asked about their internet experiences reported increases in solicitations for sexual pictures, unsolicited requests for sexual material that were sometimes distressing, a continued prevalence of sexual solicitations, kids are quiet about victimization, and sometimes risky online behavior happens in groups with other kids.[212] Decisions about how to monitor products made and sold or images made available on the internet will undoubtedly be an ongoing focus of the sex industry and those seeking steeper regulation.

"EXOTIC" PEOPLE AND REMOTE LOCALES: REFLECTING OR RE-CREATING A RACIST HISTORY?

And to this day, few people seem willing to name and challenge the colonialist exploitation at the heart of the globalized prostitution business. Exhibit A: the increasing number of American and European men who travel to impoverished Third World countries to have sex with dark skinned young women and girls and boys. When you add that degree of overt racism to the already rampant sexism of prostitution, the problem can seem overwhelming.

—Jackson Katz, *The Macho Paradox*

Many Anglos, particularly white feminists, insist that the men of our culture created machismo and they conveniently forget that the men of their race make the rules.

—Emma Perez, *Sexuality and Discourse: Notes from a Chicana Survivor*[213]

For as many misunderstandings and misconceptualizations one culture has for another, adding assumptions about sex can expand the miscommunication gap. In 1983, Liza Dalby presented the book *Geisha*. In the preface to the first edition she wrote:

What geisha do and what they represent are intelligible only within their cultural context. Thus it has been necessary to discuss Japanese customs, history, law, social interaction, psychology, business practice, male-female relations, religious beliefs, dress, food, music, aesthetics, and consciousness of cultural identity, among other things, in order to say anything revealing about geisha.[214]

Earlier in the chapter, attention was focused on the idea that sexual exploitation occurs with white men traveling to impoverished countries to have sex with dark-skinned young people and children. Professor of sociology and women's studies, **Gail Dines** has spent two decades studying pornography, and part of her research highlights the racialized overtones of pornography.

> When men (regardless of race) ejaculate on her face and body, they often make reference to her skin color, and her debased status as a woman is seamlessly melded with, and reinforced by her supposed debased status as a person of color. In the process, her race and gender become inseparable and her body carries the status of dual subordination.[215]

Also from Dines:

> It is no surprise that Asian women are the most popular women of color in porn, given the long-standing stereotypes of them as sexually servile geishas, lotus blossoms and China dolls. Depicted as perfect sex objects with well-honed sexual skills, Asian women come to porn with a baggage of stereotypes that makes them the idealized women of the porn world.[216]

In reviewing the racialization of porn, various racial and religious groups are highlighted, each within specific genres of porn. Black women are also often situated in scenes where the juxtaposition of gender and race is also merged with class, making explicit references to the ghetto or abject poverty and referencing what poor women are willing to do when they really need the money[217] or using other dehumanizing themes that suggest a black woman is "untamed" or "in need of socialization," which is implied to be offered through sexual domination.[218] Research has also shown how black girls are seen as more adult at a younger age and how this plays into victimization.[219]

This is a powerful way to deliver racist ideology because it not only makes visible the supposed sexual debauchery of the targeted group but also sexualizes the racism in ways that make the actual racism invisible in the minds of most consumers and nonconsumers alike.[220]

And women are not the only racialized group exploited by the porn industry in significantly racist ways. Leaning on a deep mythos and horrifyingly racist history of the male form, pornographers capitalize on false perceptions of Asian men as effeminate and black men as racialized and sexualized outside of any acknowledgment of their humanity.

> "The likely negative consequences of legalized prostitution on a country's inflows of human trafficking might be seen to support those who argue in favor of banning prostitution, thereby reducing the flows of trafficking," the researchers state. "However, such a line of argumentation overlooks potential benefits that the legalization of prostitution might have on those employed in the indus-

try. Working conditions could be substantially improved for prostitutes—at least those legally employed—if prostitution is legalized. Prohibiting prostitution also raises tricky 'freedom of choice' issues concerning both the potential suppliers and clients of prostitution services."[221]

The Durbar Mahila Samawayan Committee (DMSC) is one of the largest and most successful sex-worker rights movements in the world.

Without question, the law limits aspects of pornography and prostitution. In the United States, there is long-standing disagreement about how to solve the problems of women who are bartered and traded in an economic marketplace. Questions are raised about the idea of sex work as real work, suggesting no one who had the choice would ever want to be involved in such an occupation. Yet efforts are being marshaled throughout the world, by advocate groups and labor movements, around the idea that sex workers need protection and seek the opportunity to use their own voices in the national and international efforts to secure legalization and regulation of the sex work industry.

CHAPTER CONCLUSION

The chapter began with a brief introduction of controversies receiving international attention, including conflicts conceptualizing the scope of the problem of sexual and gender-based violence as it is presented around the globe. The definition of human rights and questions about women's rights served as a starting place. International incidents of gender and sexualized violence include many of the kinds of crimes also happening in the United States. This might seem obvious, but conversations about global sex trafficking, prostitution, pornography, internet sexual crimes, commercial child sexual exploitation, and rape in war can sometimes be discussed as if they happen in other countries outside of the United States; however, these issues are present in the United States as well. Those who follow the global politics of sexual violence, in fact, might be less interested in directives or condemnation from the United States about local efforts to respond to sexual harm and gendered-violence in other countries because the United States is no closer to solving the problem of sexual violence today than it was decades or even centuries ago.

As the concept of sexual violence becomes more and more clearly articulated in communities across the United States and around the world, as more and more people openly discuss the elements of sexual activities and sexual harms, attention is given to questions about which elements are going to be regulated by individual nations as cultural or legal norms and to what degree. Technological advances create conditions in which all of these technological changes are happening within a global purview. Should the viewing of pornography produce jail time, or treatment, or rest within a discernable freedom to choose and not be regulated at all?

In the beginning of her 1996 book, *Working Sex: An Exploration of the Sex Industry from the People Who Actually Do the Work*, Marianne Macy speaks plainly:

I wrote this book. It's about sex. You bought this book. You had a pretty good idea what it was about, judging from the title. We just had a transaction based on sex and money. Let's get that straight right from the beginning.[222]

Gail Dines, longtime antiporn activist and author of *Pornland: How Pornography Has Hijacked Our Sexuality* suggested:

As pop culture begins to look more and more pornographic, the actual porn industry has had to become more hard-core as a way to distinguish itself from those images found on MTV, in *Cosmopolitan*, and on billboards.[223]

The idea that nonintimate conversations about sex permeate the lives of people in the United States and around the world, in film, advertising, on the internet, and in casual conversation is not news. Questions about the content invite—or invoke, require, or even demand, depending on your perspective—conversations about healthy sexuality, about definitions of deviance, and about the edges and consequences of the criminalization process. All of these conversations affect decisions about age-appropriate exposure and ongoing conversations about healthy sexual development, and yet the United States is a country that restricts sex education and actively sexualizes commercial exchanges. And as countries around the world decide what aspects of sex are going to bring them into contact with either the criminal justice system or a sex addiction treatment program, the more and more demand there is going to be for people focused on healthy sex education, sex offender treatment, and who can help address issues of addiction before the criminal justice system becomes involved.

Again, as is the case with just about every subtopic included in the pages of this text, a discussion of the definition, the morality, or the appropriate legality of sex work could occupy an entire book on its own. In the 1970s, Betty Dodson shocked the world when she openly discussed women's sexuality and held workshops to teach women about their genitalia and more specifically how to masturbate. When she wrote *Liberating Masturbation*, now called *Sex for One: The Joy of Selfloving*, Dodson was ridiculed from multiple sectors. Margaret Sanger was repeatedly arrested for selling birth control. People who are gay are threatened with capital punishment.

Today, with more conversations about sexual violence, sexual violence prevention, and ways to regulate potentially harmful behaviors, people on all ends of the spectrum are trying to clarify the parameters of the state to create laws that regulate sexual or gender-based interactions. Some of the most hotly contested elements in that discussion are related to the creation and distribution of pornography and the commercial sale of individual labor for sex with a specific eye on practices that minimize or eliminate the options for an individual to freely choose those encounters. After discussing emerging elements associated with **cybersex** and online environments, attention is given to the impact of global networks on nations comprising nonwhite populations, raising questions about the degree to which a banning of such activities in the United States will produce markets in "exotic" locals where economic opportunities might be significantly limited.

Text Box 9.5.   Media Messages about Global Issues: What Information about People Who Have Been Harmed by Sexual Violence Needs to Be Reclaimed or Reconsidered?

Fact: Narratives about sex trafficking have traditionally seemed to suggest that sex trafficking happens outside of the United States. This is true, *and* it also happens in the United States and can involve children, tweens, and people younger than 18.

Application: Identify three problems that can result from incorrectly implying that this kind of sexual violence and harm is less likely to happen in the United States.

Fact: Computers make sexually explicit materials easily available to people who might not otherwise be interested in pursuing illegal sexual materials such as child pornography. Further, the children or young people exploited in sexual images are often from outside of the United States. Consider again the PROTECT Act. Consider again, the stories of international police agencies uncovering a wide range of professionals (many working with children) who are trafficking in illegal sexually exploitive materials involving children.

Application: Outline primary, secondary, and tertiary programs (either create them and outline how you see them working, or conduct some research and identify them as they exist already) to address this problem.

What ideas and/or information do you bring to this conversation about sexual violence and harm in other parts of the world?

After considering the material presented in chapter 9 on global issues of sexual violence, what information from the media do you see requiring additional and particular focus for calling out inaccuracies?

What other facts that you are learning require adjustments to what you believed in the past about how sexualized violence is different in the United States from other countries around the world?

MEDIA-ting the Middle Ground

Sex offenses are more likely to be perpetrated against someone known to the offender than be committed by a stranger. Having this as a basic understanding helps people in the community better understand the larger dynamics and impacts when addressing the accountability of the perpetrator and the future needs of the person they harmed. Consider the following scenarios:

Scenario 1: In Alabama, court records of juveniles are sealed. To illustrate an example, consider a young 14-year-old committed a sex offense against a girl younger than 12, and he was found guilty of "enticing a child for immoral purposes." As a part of that process, he was expelled from school for one year. Three years later, the young girl's older brother is heading to class for the first day, and he sees the young man who had been convicted for the sex offense against his sister; he had reenrolled in school. The victim's family was horrified. They had been given no notice as to the possibility they would run into this person again at school. In Alabama, school is mandatory, and, as of January 2018, there were 1,306 juvenile sex offenders on the sex offender registry. Although the school principal can be informed of the juvenile's history, the information is considered confidential and can be shared only with teachers and staff who have supervision over the student. Disclosing confidential information held by the court is a misdemeanor. While the family of the victim is upset they will risk running into the offender during school events, state juvenile justice officials are concerned that sending the student to alternative education or the registration process itself could be too harsh and result in long-term collateral consequences that could have lifelong impacts on the young man as he gets older. Some states do not register juvenile offenders at all, suggesting instead that registration hinders the offender's future prospects for gainful employment, housing, and military service, as examples. Proposed legislation suggests a widening of the people to be notified to include the superintendent and the school board when the offender is released, but critics say that is not enough. The law was referenced to determine how to address the rights of the offender, but questions remained about treatment of the victim and her family.[1]

Scenario 2: Within the last decade, a child of divorced parents came home with indications of sexual abuse. Those allegations were confirmed by a medical doctor and the Department of Children Services. The family court judge used a court-appointed custody advisor, a psychiatrist, who downplayed the medical reports and instead suggested the father had not been diagnosed as a pedophile or child molester and as such should be awarded custody of the child. Further, the mom was warned not to talk with her son about the alleged abuse and had to stop taking him to doctors to be examined for signs of abuse.[2]

Scenario 3: A college student commits an offense against another college student. College student A files a complaint against college student B. College student B has been in trouble before on another campus for committing sexual assault; however, the report was contained within the university. The student was expelled, but there is no way the new university could have known about college student B's background. The previous infraction did not rise to the level of a mandatory report to police; however, significant information suggested that the student acted against the university's code of conduct. What obligations do universities have to report? What policies support modifying current practice? What programs can you find that seek to make changes in this area?

Deciding Which Messages Move Forward

In what ways do some offenders manipulate the emotions of unsuspecting people, people who are completely unrelated to the assault and would then see the offender as "a good person," in an effort to provide cover for offenses they would commit against others? To interrogate the messages presented from the media requires an interrogation of the efforts taken to discredit or silence victims. What is it that the community should know about a person who has been harmed by sexual violence?

In what ways is information about sexual assaults received differently about people from different social classes or about people who are seen as having "other" problems, which somehow means their expectation of body safety has been compromised?

Those who are ideal victims include children, some women and the elderly. Young men, the homeless, those with drug problems, sex workers, etc., may find it much more difficult to achieve legitimate victim status. In this sense, there is the danger of creating a hierarchy of victimization. Race, social class and status also play a role, and whether or not it is done intentionally, it is perpetuated by the media. Whether we agree or disagree with how the media chooses to report crimes and the impact it has on victims, as victim service providers, we have a role to assist victims dealing with the media and a unique opportunity to educate the media and the public about crime, victims and the impacts of reporting.[3]

In what ways are young people taught to grow into their sexually developing bodies, and in what ways are young people sexualized by society? "Residents said she dressed older than her age, wearing makeup and fashions more appropriate to a woman in her 20s. She would hang out with teenage boys at a playground, some said." This story involved an 11-year-old.[4]

MEDIA MESSAGES SECTION IV: In What Ways Is the Justice System Addressing Sexual Harm?

Section overview: Some of the most difficult decisions confronting a person who has been harmed by sexualized violence is how they will or *if* they will involve the criminal justice system. Consideration is given to the role of police in the initial response and investigation and then in the court process should the case go in that direction. Much has been written about the failings of the criminal justice system in its response to sexualized violence. Further, questions are raised about the role of laws and policies in actually making individuals safer. Do the laws and policies in place work? What other laws might be warranted? How does the law assist identification and support for victims? For offenders? Finally, the majority of people convicted of sex crimes will get out of prison. How are the impacts of those difficult harms navigated as a person returns to the community, to the family, or to the society after having committed an offense? What are the implications for both the victim and the offender when the system is built to release or diminish charges when a conviction is not possible? Issues of support and accountability are introduced.

Notes

1. Marty Roney, "Alabama Schools Struggle with Juvenile Sex Offenders in the Classrooms," *Montgomery Advertiser*, February 22, 2018, accessed September 30, 2019, https://www.montgomeryadvertiser.com/story/news/2018/02/22/alabama-schools -struggle-juvenile-sex-offenders-classrooms/301089002/.

2. Laurie Udesky, "Custody in Crisis: How Family Courts Nationwide Put Children in Danger," December 1, 2016, accessed September 30, 2019, https://100r.org/2016/12/ custody-2/.

3. "Understanding How the Media Reports Crime," Canadian Resource Centre for Victims of Crime, accessed September 30, 2019, http://crcvc.ca/publications/media -guide/understanding/.

4. Pelisek, C. July 13, 2017. Texas Gang Rape: How a horrific Case is Dividing a Town. The Daily Beast. Accessed November 29, 2019, https://www.thedailybeast.com/texas -gang-rape-how-a-horrific-case-is-dividing-a-town.

KEY TERMS

Adverse Childhood Experiences
  (ACEs)
bondage, discipline, sadism, and
  masochism (BDSM)
Cairo Consensus
comfort station
Comfort Women
commercial sex industry
commercial sex work
commercial sexual exploitation
  of children (CSEC)
corrective rape
cutting
cybersex
dark figure of crime
decriminalization
erotica
female genital modification/
  mutilation (FGM)
feminist movement
feminist sex wars
Gail Dines
hard core
honor killings
intergenerational transmission
Internet Crimes Against Children Task
  Force Program (ICAC)

Lieber Code of 1863
National Center for Missing and
  Exploited Children (NCMEC)
nongovernmental organizations
  (NGOs)
Nordic model
pornography
Programme of Action
Project Spade
pronatalist policies
prostitution
pseudo child porn
reproductive rights
sex industry
sex positive feminism
sex tourists
sex trafficking
sex trafficking ring
sex work
sexual and gender-based violence
  (SGBV)
sexual commerce
soft core
Trafficking Victims Protection Act
  (TVPA)
transvaginal ultrasound
webcam child sex tourism

REVIEW QUESTIONS

1. Briefly describe the following acts of gender-based violence discussed in the chapter:

    Honor killings
    Acid attacks
    Female genital modification/mutilation
    Child marriage and forced marriages
    Forced sterilization

2. When referring to the fact that a government has the power to "create" a sex crime, what does that suggest?

3. Be clear about the difference between human sex trafficking, the commercial sex industry, and prostitution. What is the controversy surrounding the use of those terms?

4. Describe at least one of the most shocking findings reflected in the international police operation Project Spade.

5. How does the commercial exploitation of children, referred to more casually in some places as child sex tourism, differ from the larger conversation of the commercial sex industry?

DISCUSSION QUESTIONS

1. Discuss the significance of centering the idea of human rights for the larger, global conversation about sexual violence prevention. What elements of social life will impact this idea?

2. Discuss the phenomenon "rape as a weapon of war." What elements of accountability are available to civilians in nations at war to prevent such practices?

3. Consider the advancements of computer technologies and the role those advancements play in virtual sex. Are the courts right to suggest that artistic work, drawings, and cartoon images are protected under the First Amendment? How does this comport with your concerns about protecting children from abuse and the fact that child pornography has a steady following in spite of its illegal status and significant penalties.

4. Discuss the issues raised by the theories that reflect on structural issues in society suggesting that "rape culture" is representative of attitudes outside of any specific individual and in fact is more reflective of broader misogynistic attitudes in society at large. How does the conversation about sexual violence as a public health concern seem to work with these social structural theories?

5. Get a group of your friends together, and address this question: Is legalizing sex work a viable answer to the global concerns about sexual exploitation? What information are they missing, to better understand your point of view? What information are they offering to you, which you are not finding compelling?

NOTES

1. R. Jensen, *Getting Off: Pornography and the End of Masculinity* (South End Press, 2008).

2. N. Kristof and S. WuDunn, *Half the Sky: Turning Oppression into Opportunity for Women Worldwide* (First Vintage Books, 2009).

3. "Minnesota's Child Sex Trafficking Profile Rising," *Pioneer Press*, September 8, 2019, accessed October 20, 2019, https://www.twincities.com/2010/09/08/minnesotas-child-sex-trafficking-profile-rising/.

4. M. Macy, *Working Sex: An Odyssey into Our Cultural Underworld* (Carroll and Graf Publishing, 1996), 34.

5. M. Yousafzai, *I Am Malala: The Girl Who Stood Up for Education and Was Shot by the Taliban* (Back Bay Books, 2015).

6. See, for example, her selection by *Time* magazine for the cover photo of its double issue coverage on the 100 most influential people in the world. *Time* April 29/May 6, 2013, 138–40.

7. "76 Americans Busted in Massive Global Child Porn Ring Including Police Officers, Teachers and Doctors as Nearly 400 Children Are Rescued," *Daily Mail*, November 14, 2013, accessed October 20, 2019, http://www.dailymail.co.uk/news/article-2507459/Global-child-porn-ring-busted-leading-rescue-nearly-400-children.html.

8. https://www.dailymail.co.uk/news/article-2507459/Global-child-porn-ring-busted-leading-rescue-nearly-400-children.html; http://worldnews.nbcnews.com/_news/2013/11/14/21462256-nearly-400-children-rescued-and-348-adults-arrested-in-canadian-child-pornography-bust.

9. D. Silva, "Nearly 400 Children Rescued and 348 Adults Arrested in Canadian Child Pornography Bust," NBC, https://www.nbcnews.com/news/world/nearly-400-children-rescued-348-adults-arrested-canadian-child-pornography-flna2D11599561.

10. "Toronto Child-Porn Czar Has 10-Year Sentence Reduced after Reports of Jailhouse Abuse," CBC News, August 9, 2016, accessed September 19, 2019, https://www.cbc.ca/news/canada/toronto/toronto-child-porn-czar-has-10-year-sentence-reduced-after-reports-of-jailhouse-abuse-1.3713680.

11. Charlotte Alter, "Over 570 Arrested in Super Bowl Sex Traffic Sting," *Time*, February 2, 2015, accessed September 19, 2019, http://time.com/3692993/super-bowl-sex-traffic-sting/.

12. Michael King, "Doctors and Cops among 277 Arrested in Human Trafficking, Online Prostitution Sting in Florida," nbc4i.com, August 15, 2019, accessed September 19, 2019, https://www.nbc4i.com/news/u-s-world/doctors-and-cops-among-277-arrested-in-human-trafficking-online-prostitution-sting-in-florida/1096287648.

13. "75 Arrested in Undercover Prostitution Sting in Montgomery County (Texas)," abc13, November 5, 2018, accessed October 20, 2019, https://abc13.com/75-arrested-in-undercover-prostitution-sting-in-montgomery-co-/4625662/.

14. "Undercover Human Trafficking Sting in Portland, Hillsboro Leads to 23 People Facing Charges," FOX 12, November 9, 2018, https://www.kptv.com/news/undercover-human-trafficking-sting-in-portland-hillsboro-leads-to-people/article_ac608bf4-e462-11e8-a408-6fd9fd88dc20.html.

15. Trevor J. Mitchell, "Seventh Man Charged after Sex Trafficking Sting," *Argus Leader*, August 27, 2018, September 19, 2019, https://www.argusleader.com/story/news/crime/2018/08/27/seventh-man-charged-after-sex-trafficking-sting/1115131002/.

16. Sarah Chandler, "A Closer Look at Minnesota's Sex Trafficking Problem," May 24, 2018, accessed September 19, 2019, http://www.minnesotamonthly.com/Minnesota-Life/A-Closer-Look-at-Minnesotas-Sex-Trafficking-Problem/; B. O'Brien, "Minnesota Arrests 58 in Child Sex Sting during NCAA Final Four Weekend," *Reuters*, April 10, 2019, accessed October 20, 2019, https://www.kotatv.com/content/news/11-men-arrested-in-sex-sting-operation-at-79th-Sturgis-Motorcycle-Rally-543158281.html.

17. United Nations, "Report of the Fourth World Conference on Women," Beijing 4-15 Sept. 1995, https://www.unsystem.org/content/fourth-world-conference-women-1995-0.

18. See this excerpt: "Speaking more forcefully on human rights than any American dignitary has on Chinese soil, Hillary Rodham Clinton catalogued a devastating litany of abuse that has afflicted women around the world today and criticized China for seeking to limit free and open discussion of women's issues here." Patrick E. Tyler, "Hillary Clinton, in China, Details Abuse of Women," *New York Times*, September 6, 1995, section A, page 1, http://www.nytimes.com/1995/09/06/world/hillary-clinton-in-china-details-abuse-of-women.html.

19. First Lady Hillary Rodham Clinton Remarks for the United Nations Fourth World Conference on Women, The United Nations Development Programme (UNDP), September 5, 1995, in collaboration with the United Nations Fourth World Conference on Women, https://www.un.org/esa/gopher-data/conf/fwcw/conf/gov/950905175653.txt.

20. "Sexuality and Human Rights: Discussion Paper," International Council on Human Rights Policy, 2009, accessed September 19, 2019, http://www.ichrp.org/files/reports/47/137_web.pdf.

21. Ibid., 7.

22. Lauren Wolfe, "Rape Is Shredding Syria's Social Fabric," CNN online, December 5, 2012, accessed December 25, 2018, https://www.cnn.com/2012/12/05/opinion/wolfe-syria-rape/index.html; see also Lauren Wolfe, "What's Going on in Syria Is about a Lot More than Chemical Weapons," *The Guardian*, October 26, 2013, accessed December 25, 2018, http://www.theguardian.com/commentisfree/2013/oct/26/syria-peace-talks-women-raped.

23. Ibid.

24. Report of the Special Rapporteur on Extrajudicial, Summary or Arbitrary Executions, Christof Heyns, UN General Assembly, April 26, 2013, https://www.ohchr.org/Documents/HRBodies/HRCouncil/RegularSession/Session23/A.HRC.23.47.Add.1_EN.pdf

25. Mari Marcel Thekaekara, "Sexual Violence Is the New Normal In India—and Pornography Is to Blame," *The Guardian*, August 9, 2018, accessed October 20, 2019, https://www.theguardian.com/commentisfree/2018/aug/09/sexual-violence-india-rape-pornography.

26. Basu, M. "The Girl Whose Rape Changed a Country. CNN.com, 2013, accessed October 20, 2019, http://www.cnn.com/interactive/2013/11/world/india-rape/.

27. Max Fisher, "India's Rape Problem Is also a Police Problem," *Washington Post*, January 7, 2013, accessed September 19, 2019, http://www.washingtonpost.com/blogs/worldviews/wp/2013/01/07/indias-rape-problem-is-also-a-police-problem/.

28. "India under Fire Again as Child Rape Cases Reach 'Epidemic' Proportions," Women's Agenda, April 22, 2013, accessed September 19, 2019, http://www.womensagenda.com.au/talking-about/world-of-women/india-under-fire-again-as-child-rape-cases-reach-epidemic-proportions/201304222023.

29. "Indian Police Accused of Mass Rape during Operation," *Aljazeera*, January 8, 2017, accessed September 19, 2019, https://www.aljazeera.com/news/2017/01/indian-police-accused-mass-rape-operation-170108151834228.html; "The Rapes That India Forgot," BBC News, January 5, 2018, accessed September 19, 2019, https://www.bbc.com/news/world-asia-india-20907755.

30. "Secretary-General Says Violence against Women Never Acceptable, Never Excusable, Never Tolerable, as He Launches Global Campaign on Issue," [press release], February 25, 2008, accessed September 19, 2019, https://www.un.org/press/en/2008/sgsm11437.doc.htm.

31. Tanya Abramsky et al., "What Factors Are Associated with Recent Intimate Partner Violence?: Findings from the WHO Multi-Country Study on Women's Health And Domestic Violence," *BMC Public Health* 11, (2011), http://www.biomedcentral.com/1471-2458/11/109.

32. M. Moore, "The Lancet Series on Violence Against Women and Girls: Prevention of Violence Against Women and Girls: What Does the Evidence Say?," Gender Violence and Health Centre, London School of Hygiene and Tropical Medicine, London, November 26, 2014, accessed October 20, 2019, http://same.lshtm.ac.uk/2014/11/26/lancet-series-violence-women-girls/.

33. World Health Organization, "Violence Against Women: Key Facts," November 29, 2019, accessed October 20, 2019, https://www.who.int/news-room/fact-sheets/detail/violence-against-women.

34. "Global, Regional, and National Age-Sex Specific Mortality for 264 Causes of Death, 1980–2016: A Systematic Analysis for the Global Burden of Disease Study 2016," *The Lancet*, 390, 1151–210, accessed October 20, 2019, https://www.thelancet.com/pdfs/journals/lancet/PIIS0140-6736(17)32152-9.pdf.

35. K. M. Devries et al., "The Global Prevalence of Intimate Partner Violence against Women," *Science*, June 20, 2013, accessed October 20, 2019, doi:10.1126/science.1240937.

36. K. M. Devries et al., "The Global Prevalence of Intimate Partner Violence against Women," *Science*, June 20, 2013, accessed October 20, 2019, doi:10.1126/science.1240937.

37. Global and Regional Estimates of Violence against Women: Prevalence and Health Effects of Intimate Partner Violence and Non-Partner Sexual Violence," World Health Organization, 2013, accessed September 19, 2019, https://apps.who.int/iris/bit stream/handle/10665/85239/9789241564625_eng.pdf;jsessionid=45C5859DD14BD 4B03E7544E0688737E0?sequence=1.

38. Phyllis Chesler, "Worldwide Trends in Honor Killings," *Middle East Quarterly* (Spring 2010), accessed September 19, 2019, http://www.meforum.org/2646/worldwide-trends-in -honor-killings.

39. Hillary Mayell, "Thousands of Women Killed for Family 'Honor,'" *National Geographic News*, February 12, 2002, accessed September 19, 2019, http://www.unl.edu/rhames/ courses/212/readings/honor-kil-ng.pdf.

40. Phyllis Chesler, "Are Honor Killings Simply Domestic Violence?" *Middle East Quarterly* (Spring 2009): 61–69, accessed September 19, 2019, http://www.meforum.org/2067/ are-honor-killings-simply-domestic-violence#_ftn5.

41. Sonya Fernandez, "The Crusade over the Bodies of Women," *Patterns of Prejudice* 43, no. 3–4 (2009): 269–86, http://www.tandfonline.com/doi/abs/10.1080/00313220903109185# .UopSYknna70; Chesler, "Worldwide Trends in Honor Killings."

42. Laura Smith-Spark, "Third of Teens in Amman, Jordan, Condone Honor Killings, Study Says," CNN, June 20, 2013, accessed September 19, 2019, http://www.cnn.com/2013/06/20/ world/meast/jordan-honor-crimes-study/.

43. Ayse Onal, *Honour Killing: Stories of Men Who Killed* (London: Saqi Books, 2008).

44. Rana Husseini, *Murder in the Name of Honor: The True Story of One Woman's Heroic Fight against an Unbelievable Crime* (London: Oneworld Publications, 2011); Ahmed Maher, "Many Jordan Teenagers 'Support Honour Killings,'" BBC News, June 20, 2013, accessed December 23, 2013, https://www.bbc.com/news/world-middle-east-22992365.

45. "Combating Acid Violence in Bangladesh, India, and Cambodia: A Report by the Avon Global Center for Women and Justice at Cornell Law School," Committee on International Human Rights of the New York City Bar Association, the Cornell Law School International Human Rights Clinic, and the Virtue Foundation, 2011, p. 1, accessed October 20, 2019, https://www.ohchr.org/Documents/HRBodies/CEDAW/HarmfulPractices/AvonGlobal CenterforWomenandJustice.pdf.

46. "Acid Attacks Horrifying Forms of Gender-Based Violence: Delhi High Court," DNA, November 14, 2013, accessed September 19, 2019, http://www.dnaindia.com/india/report -acid-attacks-horrifying-forms-of-gender-based-violence-delhi-high-court-1919243.

47. Kamal Kumar, "Acid Attacks: A Scar on India," *Aljazeera*, January 24, 2014, accessed September 19, 2019, http://www.aljazeera.com/indepth/features/2013/09/acid-attacks-a-scar -india-2013927165429393354.html.

48. "Combating Acid Violence in Bangladesh, India, and Cambodia"; see also "Stop Acid Attacks," Stop Acid Attacks blog, February 18, 2019, accessed September 19, 2019, http:// www.stopacidattacks.org/.

49. A film by D. Junge and S. Obaid-Chinoy, *Saving Face*, produced by David Combe, International, 52 minutes, 2012; S. Jothianandan, "Oscar-Winning 'Saving Face' Directors' Battle to End Horror of Acid Attacks," *Daily Beast*, July 13, 2019, accessed October 20, 2019, https://www.thedailybeast.com/oscar-winning-saving-face-directors-battle-to-end-hor ror-of-acid-attacks.

50. Elora Halim Chowdhury, "Negotiating State and NGO Politics in Bangladesh: Women Mobilize against Acid Violence," *Violence Against Women* 13, no. 8 (2007): 857–73, http:// vaw.sagepub.com/content/13/8/857.short.

51. https://www.unicef.org/evaldatabase/index_FGMC.html.

52. UNFPA-UNICEF, "Accelerating Change by the Numbers, 2016 Annual Report of the UNFPA-UNICEF Joint Programme on Female Genital Mutilation/Cutting: Accelerat-

ing Change," 2016, accessed October 20, 2019, https://reliefweb.int/report/world/accelerating-change-numbers-2016-annual-report-unfpa-unicef-joint-programme-female.

53. "Female Genital Mutilation," World Health Organization, January 31, 2018, accessed October 20, 2019, https://www.who.int/news-room/fact-sheets/detail/female-genital-mutilation.

54. UNICEF, "Female Genital Mutilation/Cutting: A Statistical Overview and Exploration of the Dynamics of Change," July 2013, p. 3, accessed October 20, 2019, https://www.unicef.org/cbsc/files/UNICEF_FGM_report_July_2013_Hi_res.pdf.

55. Ibid., 22.

56. Andrea Parrot and Nina Cummings, *Forsaken Females: The Global Brutalization of Women* (Lanham, MD: Rowman & Littlefield, 2006).

57. Uriel Elchalal et al., "Ritualistic Female Genital Mutilation: Current Status and Future Outlook," *Obstetrical & Gynecological Survey* 52, no. 10 (1997): 643–51.

58. Rogaia Mustafa Abusharaf, ed., *Female Circumcision: Multicultural Perspectives* (Philadelphia: University of Pennsylvania Press, 2006).

59. "A Report on the National Female Genital Mutilation Summit by Dr. Comfort," Australian Department of Health, September 2013, accessed October 20, 2019, https://www1.health.gov.au/internet/main/publishing.nsf/Content/report-fgms.

60. Abusharaf, *Female Circumcision: Multicultural Perspectives*, 10.

61. V. Barner, *Aman: The Story of a Somali Girl* (Vintage, 1995); F. Kassindja, *Do They Hear You When You Cry?* (Delta Books, 1999).

62. "The Elders, Who Co-Founded Girls Not Brides, Celebrate Their 10th Birthday," Girls Not Brides, July 18, 2017, accessed September 19, 2019, https://www.girlsnotbrides.org/elders-co-founded-girls-not-brides-celebrate-10th-birthday/.

63. "Theory of Change on Child Marriage," July 2014, accessed September 19, 2019, https://www.girlsnotbrides.org/wp-content/uploads/2014/07/Girls-Not-Brides-Theory-of-Change-on-Child-Marriage.pdf.

64. Therese Hesketh, Li Lu, and Zhu Wei Xing, "The Effect of China's One-Child Family Policy after 25 Years," *New England Journal of Medicine* 353, no. 11 (2005): 1171–76, accessed September 19, 2019, http://discovery.ucl.ac.uk/8938/1/8938.pdf.

65. Ansley J. Coale and Judith Banister, "Five Decades of Missing Females in China," *Demography* 31, no. 3 (1994): 459–79; Petra Löfstedta, Luo Shusheng, and Annika Johansson, "Abortion Patterns and Reported Sex Ratios at Birth in Rural Yunnan, China," *Reproductive Health Matters* 12, no. 24 (2004): 86–95; Zhuochun Wu et al., "Perinatal Mortality in Rural China: Retrospective Cohort Study," *BMJ* 327, no. 7427 (2003): 1319, https://www.bmj.com/content/bmj/327/7427/1319.full.pdf; "Forced Abortion Is Not a Choice," Women's Rights without Frontiers, accessed September 19, 2019, http://www.womensrightswithoutfrontiers.org/index.php?nav=forced_sterilization.

66. Jessica Cussins, "Involuntary Sterilization Then and Now," *Psychology Today*, September 5, 2013, accessed September 19, 2019, http://www.psychologytoday.com/blog/genetic-crossroads/201309/involuntary-sterilization-then-and-now.

67. I. Carmon, "For Eugenic Sterilization Victims, Belated Justice," MSNBC, June 27, 2014, accessed October 20, 2019, http://www.msnbc.com/all/eugenic-sterilization-victims-belated-justice.

68. Elizabeth Cohen, "North Carolina Lawmakers OK Payments for Victims of Forced Sterilization," July 28, 2013, accessed September 19, 2019, http://www.cnn.com/2013/07/26/us/north-carolina-sterilization-payments/index.html.

69. Zachary Prong, "Canada's Shame: The Coerced Sterilization of Indigenous Women," *New Internationalist*, November 30, 2018, accessed September 19, 2019, https://newint.org/features/2018/11/29/canadas-shame-coerced-sterilization-indigenous-women.

70. Rafael Romo, "Peruvian Authorities Reopen Investigation into Forced Sterilizations," CNN, November 17, 2011, accessed September 19, 2019, http://www.cnn.com/2011/11/17/world/americas/peru-sterilizations/index.html.

71. UNODC, "Human Trafficking," accessed September 19, 2019, https://www.unodc.org/unodc/en/human-trafficking/what-is-human-trafficking.html#What_is_Human_Trafficking.

72. R. Ebert, "Review: *Taken*," January 28, 2009, accessed October 20, 2019, https://www.rogerebert.com/reviews/taken-2009.

73. "*Taken*," Box Office Mojo, accessed September 19, 2019, https://www.boxofficemojo.com/franchises/chart/?id=taken.htm.

74. "Human Trafficking: Current Federal Laws," accessed September 19, 2019, https://polarisproject.org/current-federal-laws; see also "Victims of Trafficking and Violence Protection Act of 2000," October 28, 2000, accessed September 19, 2019, https://www.state.gov/j/tip/laws/61124.htm.

75. Kate Butcher, "Confusion between Prostitution and Sex Trafficking," *The Lancet* 361, no. 9373 (2003): 1983; see also Carole S. Vance, "Innocence and Experience: Melodramatic Narratives of Sex Trafficking and Their Consequences for Law and Policy," *History of the Present* 2, no. 2 (Fall 2012): 200–28.

76. "Melissa Farley," Prostitution Research & Education, accessed September 19, 2019, http://prostitutionresearch.com/pub_author/melissa-farley/.

77. For example, see "Stopping Human Trafficking: FBI Works with Partners to Get Traffickers Off the Streets," *FBI News*, January 30, 2018, accessed October 20, 2019, https://www.fbi.gov/news/stories/human-trafficking-prevention-month-2018; S. Marcin, "Prostitution and Human Trafficking: A Paradigm Shift," *Law Enforcement Bulletin*, March 5, 2013, accessed October 20, 2019, https://leb.fbi.gov/articles/featured-articles/prostitution-and-human-trafficking-a-paradigm-shift.

78. "Commercial Sexual Exploitation of Children: What Do We Know and What Do We Do About It?" National Criminal Justice Reference Service, US Department of Justice, December 2007, accessed September 19, 2019, https://www.ncjrs.gov/pdffiles1/nij/215733.pdf.

79. See, for example, Margaret Melrose, "Labour Pains: Some Considerations on the Difficulties of Researching Juvenile Prostitution," *International Journal of Social Research Methodology* 5, no. 4 (2002): 333–51.

80. Charlotte Alter, "1400 Children Exploited in U.K. Child Sex Ring, According to New Report," *Time*, August 27, 2014, accessed September 19, 2019, http://time.com/3195725/1400-children-exploited-in-u-k-child-sex-ring-according-to-new-report/.

81. Michael McLaughlin, "Child Sex Trafficking and Drug Dealing Ring Arrests: Colorado Attorney General John Suthers Charges 14," *Huffington Post*, January 31, 2012, accessed September 19, 2019, http://www.huffingtonpost.com/2012/01/31/child-sex-trafficking-colorado_n_1243966.html.

82. See, for example, J. DeGarmo, "The Shocking Truth of Child Sex Trafficking," *HuffPost*, November 18, 2016, accessed October 20, 2019, https://www.huffpost.com/entry/the-shocking-truth-of-child-sex-trafficking_b_582de812e4b0eaa5f14d417d.

83. ; see also "Six Month Report: Domestically Sex-Trafficked Minors on the Rise in Key States," Women's Funding Network, September 15, 2010, accessed September 25, 2104, http://minnesota.publicradio.org/features/2010/09/documents/sex-ad-study.pdf.

84. Collins, Amy Fine. "Sex Trafficking of Americans: The Girls Next Door." *Vanity Fair* 24 May 2011. Accessed October 20, 2019, http://www.vanityfair.com/politics/features/2011/05/sex-trafficking-201105.

85. "Shattered Hearts: The Commercial Sexual Exploitation of American Indian Women and Girls in Minnesota," Minnesota Indian Women's Resource Center, 2009, accessed September 19, 2019, http://www.niwrc.org/sites/default/files/documents/Resources/Shattered-Hearts-Full.pdf.

86. R. W. Connell, *The Men and the Boys* (Berkeley, CA: University of California Press, 2000).

87. R. W. Connell, "Change Among the Gatekeepers: Men, Masculinities, and Gender Equality in the Global Arena," *Signs* 30, no. 3 (2005): 1801–25.

88. K. McCabe and S. Manian, *Sex Trafficking: A Global Perspective* (Lexington Books, 2010); J. O'Connell Davidson "'Child Sex Tourism': An Anomalous Form of Movement?," *Journal of Contemporary European Studies* 12, no. 1 (2004): 31–46; Megan Rivers-Moore, "Almighty Gringos: Masculinity and Value in Sex Tourism," *Sexualities* 15, no. 7 (2012): 850–79.

89. See, for example, "An Introduction to Human Trafficking: Vulnerability, Impact and Action," United Nations Office on Drugs and Crime (Vienna), (United Nations, 2008), accessed October 20, 2019, https://www.unodc.org/documents/human-trafficking/An_Introduction_to_Human_Trafficking_-_Background_Paper.pdf; E. Wheaton, E. Schauer, and T. Galli, "Economics of Human Trafficking," *International Migration* 48, no. 4, (2010), doi:10.1111/j.1468-2435.2009.00592.x.

90. See, for example, S. Louie, "Female Sex Tourism: What Are the Ethics of Exploiting Ethnic Minorities in Sex Tourism?," *Psychology Today*, September 20, 2019, accessed October 20, 2019, https://www.psychologytoday.com/us/blog/minority-report/201909/female-sex-tourism; C. Mendoza, "Beyond Sex Tourism: Gay Tourists and Male Sex Workers in Puerto Vallarta (Western Mexico)," *International Journal of Tourism Research* 15, no. 2 (2013), doi:10.1002/jtr.1865.

91. "Misinformation about Family Violence," 1in3, accessed September 19, 2019, http://www.oneinthree.com.au/misinformation/.

92. "International Men and Gender Equality Survey (IMAGES)," Promundo, accessed September 19, 2019, https://promundoglobal.org/programs/international-men-and-gender-equality-survey-images/.

93. Manuel Contreras et al., "Bridges to Adulthood: Understanding the Lifelong Influence of Men's Childhood Experiences of Violence: Analyzing Data from the International Men and Gender Equality Survey," April 2012, accessed September 19, 2019, https://promundoglobal.org/wp-content/uploads/2014/12/Bridges-to-Adulthood.pdf.

94. F. Reddington, "Male Victims of Sexual Assault," in *Sexual Assault: The Victims, the Perpetrators, and the Criminal Justice System*, 3rd ed., ed. F. Reddington and B. Kreisel, 185–90 (Carolina Academic Press, 2017).

95. "Sexual Assault of Men and Boys," RAINN, accessed September 19, 2019, https://www.rainn.org/articles/sexual-assault-men-and-boys.

96. Richard Tewksbury, "Effects of Sexual Assaults on Men: Physical, Mental and Sexual Consequences," *International Journal of Men's Health* 6, no. 1 (2007): 22–35. http://dx.doi.org/10.3149/jmh.0601.22.

97. Vincent J. Felitti et al., "Relationship of Childhood Abuse and Household Dysfunction to Many of the Leading Causes of Death in Adults: The Adverse Childhood Experiences (ACE) Study," *American Journal of Preventive Medicine* 56, no. 6 (2019): 774–86. https://doi.org/10.1016/j.amepre.2019.04.001.

98. Jennifer L. Truman, Lynn Langton, and Michael G. Planty, "Criminal Victimization, 2012," US Department of Justice, October 2013, accessed September 19, 2019, https://www.bjs.gov/content/pub/pdf/cv12.pdf.

99. Lara Stemple and Ilan H. Meyer, "The Sexual Victimization of Men in America: New Data Challenge Old Assumptions," *American Journal of Public Health* 104, no. 6 (2014): e19–e26, https://www.ncbi.nlm.nih.gov/pmc/articles/PMC4062022/.

100. Jessica Luther, "The Trans-Vaginal Ultrasounds You Didn't Hear About: Ignoring Anti-Choice Extremism in Texas," Global Comment, April 2, 2012, accessed September 19, 2019, http://globalcomment.com/ignoring-anti-choice-extremism-in-texas/; Jake Miller, "Texas Governor Rick Perry Signs Controversial Abortion Law," CBS News, July 18, 2013, accessed September 19, 2019, http://www.cbsnews.com/news/texas-governor-rick-perry-signs-controversial-abortion-law/.

101. Miller, "Texas Governor Rick Perry Signs."

102. Norma Gattsek, "Mandating Rape in Virginia," Feminist Majority Foundation, February 16, 2012, accessed September 19, 2019, https://feminist.org/blog/index.php/2012/02/16/mandating-rape-in-virginia/.

103. Cameron Langford, "2007–2000: 'Rape Camp' in Live Oak County Jail," Texas Jail Project, April 1, 2015, September 19, 2019, https://texasjailproject.org/2015/04/rape-camp-in-live-oak-county-jail/; Hunter Stuart, "Texas Sheriff's Jail Ran 'Rape Camp,' Where Female Inmates Were Repeatedly Violated Lawsuit Alleges," *Huffington Post*, December, 6, 2017, accessed September 19, 2019, https://www.huffingtonpost.com/2013/06/18/texas-rape-camp_n_3459920.html.

104. Candice Bernd, "State-Sanctioned Rape in Texas: Business as Usual," Truthout, April 8, 2013, accessed September 19, 2019, http://www.truth-out.org/news/item/18058-state-sanctioned-rape-in-texas-business-as-usual.

105. K. Brooks, "Texas Governor Signs Strict Abortion Law That Sparked Protests," *Reuters*, July 18, 2013, accessed October 20, 2019, https://www.reuters.com/article/us-usa-abortion-texas/texas-governor-signs-strict-abortion-law-that-sparked-protests-idUSBRE96H05920130718.

106. Anna North, "A Texas Bill Would Allow the Death Penalty for Patients Who Get Abortions," April 11, 2019, accessed September 19, 2019, *Vox*, https://www.vox.com/policy-and-politics/2019/4/11/18304825/abortion-texas-tony-tinderholt-death-penalty-bill.

107. Lyanne A. Guarecuco, "Lawmaker: Criminalizing Abortion Would Force Women to be 'More Personally Responsible,'" *Observer*, January 27, 2017, accessed September 19, 2019, https://www.texasobserver.org/texas-lawmaker-no-abortion-access-would-force-women-to-be-more-personally-responsible-with-sex/.

108. "Court Orders Asylum for Persecuted Gays," Spiegel Online, November 7, 2013, September 19, 2019, http://www.spiegel.de/international/europe/european-high-court-rules-persecuted-gays-must-be-offered-asylum-a-932423.html.

109. "The Fight Against Discrimination Must Go On," Spiegel Online, April 5, 2013, September 19, 2019, http://www.spiegel.de/international/world/spiegel-interview-with-dutch-gay-human-rights-activist-boris-ditrich-a-892800.html.

110. "Bigotry by Degrees," *The Economist*, November 16, 2013, accessed September 19, 2019, http://www.economist.com/news/europe/21589914-level-persecution-determines-when-gays-can-claim-asylum-europe-bigotry-degrees.

111. N. Miles, *No Going Back: Lesbian and Gay People and the Asylum System* (Stonewall, 2010).

112. Alya Z. Kayal, Penny L. Parker, and David Weissbrodt, "The Forty-Fourth Session of the UN Sub-Commission on Prevention of Discrimination and Protection of Minorities and the Special Session of the Commission on Human Rights on the Situation in the Former Yugoslavia," *Human Rights Quarterly* 15, no. 2 (1993): 410–58, http://www.jstor.org/stable/762545.

113. Douglas Sanders, "Getting Lesbian and Gay Issues on the International Human Rights Agenda," *Human Rights Quarterly* 18, no. 1 (1996): 67–106, http://muse.jhu.edu/journals/human_rights_quarterly/v018/18.1sanders.html#REF3.

114. "Bigotry by Degrees."

115. "Realizing Sexual and Reproductive Rights: A Human Rights Framework," Amnesty International, 2012, accessed September 19, 2019, http://www.amnestyusa.org/pdfs/RealizingSexualAndReproductiveRightsHumanRightsFramework.pdf.

116. United Nations, "Programme of Action of the International Conference on Population Development," 2014, accessed September 19, 2019, https://www.unfpa.org/sites/default/files/pub-pdf/programme_of_action_Web percent20ENGLISH.pdf.

117. Shena Cavallo, "In El Salvador, a Woman Who Miscarries Can Get a 50-Year Prison Sentence," International Women's Health Coalition, September 3, 2014, accessed September 19, 2019, http://iwhc.org/2014/09/el-salvador-woman-miscarries-can-get-50-year-prison-sentence/.

118. A. Moloney, "Salvadoran Woman Jailed for Abortion Crimes Hopes for Early Release—Rights Groups," *Reuters*, December 8, 2017, accessed October 20, 2019, https://www.reuters.com/article/us-el-salvador-abortion/salvadoran-woman-jailed-for-abortion-crimes-hopes-for-early-release-rights-groups-idUSKBN1E229D.

119. E. Malkin, "They Were Jailed for Miscarriages. Now, Campaign Aims to End Abortion Ban," *New York Times*, April 9, 2018, accessed October 20, 2019, https://www.nytimes.com/2018/04/09/world/americas/el-salvador-abortion.html.

120. "Amnesty International Women's Health, Sexual and Reproductive Rights," Amnestyusa.org, 2019, accessed October 20, 2019, https://www.amnestyusa.org/themes/womens-rights/womens-health-sexual-reproductive-rights/; Amnesty International, "Five Wins for Women's Rights," March 2019, accessed October 20, 2019, https://www.amnesty.org/en/latest/campaigns/2019/03/five-wins-for-womens-rights/.

121. P. Stephenson et al., "Commentary: The Public Health Consequences of Restricted Induced Abortion: Lessons from Romania," *American Journal of Public Health* 82 no. 10 (1992): 1328–31, doi:10.2105/AJPH.82.10.1328.

122. Jeffrey Burds, "Sexual Violence in Europe in World War II, 1939–1945," *Politics & Society* 37, no. 1 (2009): 35–73, https://doi.org/10.1177/1059601108329751.

123. Dara Kay Cohen, Amelia Hoover Green, and Elisabeth Jean Wood, "Wartime Sexual Violence Misconceptions, Implications, and Ways Forward," United States Institute of Peace, 2013, accessed September 19, 2019, http://www.usip.org/sites/default/files/resources/SR323.pdf.

124. Kevin Gerard Neill, "Duty, Honor, Rape: Sexual Assault against Women during War," *Journal of International Women's Studies* 2, no. 1 (2000): 43–51, https://vc.bridgew.edu/cgi/viewcontent.cgi?article=1642&context=jiws; see also Ishita Chowdhury and Mark M. Lanier, "Rape and HIV as Methods of Waging War: Epidemiological Criminology's Response," *Advances in Applied Sociology* 2, no. 1 (2012): 47–52, https://www.scirp.org/pdf/AASoci20120100005_45136691.pdf.

125. Crystal N. Feimster, *Southern Horrors: Women and the Politics of Rape and Lynching* (Cambridge, MA: Harvard University Press, 2011).

126. K. Murphy, *I Had Rather Die: Rape in the Civil War* (Coachlight Press, 2013).

127. Doris E. Buss, "Rethinking 'Rape as a Weapon of War,'" *Feminist Legal Studies* 17 (2009): 145–63. doi:10.1007/s10691-009-9118-5.

128. Duncan Gardham and Paul Cruickshank, "Abu Ghraib Abuse Photos 'Show Rape,'" *The Telegraph*, May 27, 2009, accessed November 17, 2013, http://www.telegraph.co.uk/news/worldnews/northamerica/usa/5395830/Abu-Ghraib-abuse-photos-show-rape.html.

129. K. Askin, *War Crimes Against Women: Prosecution in International War Crimes Tribunals* (Martinus Nijoff Publishers, 1997).

130. Norman M. Naimark, *The Russians in Germany: A History of the Soviet Zone of Occupation, 1945–1949* (Cambridge and London: Harvard University Press, 1995); see also Antony Beevor, *The Fall of Berlin 1945* (New York: Viking Penguin, 2002).

131. Alexander Solzhenitsyn, *Prussian Nights: A Poem*, trans. Robert Conquest (New York: Farrar, Straus and Giroux, 1977), 197; see also Glynn Young, "Poets and Poems: Aleksandr Solzhenitsyn and 'Prussian Nights,'" *Tweetspeak Blog*, accessed September 19, 2019, http://www.tweetspeakpoetry.com/2014/05/20/poets-poems-aleksandr-solzhenitsyn-prussian-nights/; Alfred M. de Zayas, *Prussian Nights–Alexander Solzhenitsyn: Prussian Nights: A Poem.* Trans. Robert Conquest. (New York: Farrar, Straus and Giroux, 1977. Pp. 113.) and Alexander Solzhenitsyn: Ostpreussische Nächte. trans. Nikolaus Ehlert. (Darmstadt: Luchterhand, 1976. Pp. 87. DM 20.), *The Review of Politics* 40, no. 1 (1978): 154–56, http://journals.cambridge.org/action/displayAbstract?fromPage=online&aid=5337684.

132. See, for example, Yoshimi Yoshiaki, *Comfort Women*, trans. Suzanne O'Brien (New York: Columbia University Press, 2002); Nora Okja Keller, *Comfort Woman* (New York: Penguin Books, 1998); George Hicks, *The Comfort Women: Japan's Brutal Regime of Enforced Prostitution in the Second World War* (New York: W.W. Norton and Co., 1997).

133. Cheah Wui Ling, "Walking the Long Road in Solidarity and Hope: A Case Study of the 'Comfort Women' Movement's Deployment of Human Rights Discourse," *Harvard Human Rights Journal* 22, no. 1 (2008): 63.

134. See, for example, Anne-Marie L.M. de Brouwer, *Supranational Criminal Prosecution of Sexual Violence* (Antwerp: Intersentia, 2005).

135. Dan Fastenberg, "Japanese Sex Slavery," *Time*, June 17, 2010, accessed November 17, 2013, http://content.time.com/time/specials/packages/article/0,28804,1997272_1997273_1997286,00.html.

136. Frankie Edozien, "'Comfort Women' Controversy Comes to New York," *New York Times*, May 10, 2012, accessed November 17, 2013, http://rendezvous.blogs.nytimes.com/2012/05/10/comfort-women-controversy-comes-to-new-york/?_r=0.

137. Lauren Wolfe, "Where Is the 'Red Line' on Rape in War?" CNN, September 17, 2013, accessed September 19, 2019, http://www.cnn.com/2013/09/17/opinion/wolfe-red-line-on-rape/.

138. "Atrocities beyond Words," *The Economist*, May 1, 2008, 57, accessed September 19, 2019, https://www.economist.com/middle-east-and-africa/2008/05/01/atrocities-beyond-words.

139. Ibid.

140. Ibid., 58.

141. "Diepsloot Toddlers: South African Rape and Murder Charges," *BBC*, October 18, 2013, accessed September 19, 2019, http://www.bbc.co.uk/news/world-africa-24581412.

142. "Overview of Human Trafficking and NIJ's Role," National Institute of Justice, February 25, 2019, accessed September 19, 2019, https://www.nij.gov/topics/crime/human-trafficking/pages/welcome.aspx.

143. "Residents Protest as Toddler Murder Accused Appear," News 24, October 24, 2013, accessed September 19, 2019, http://www.news24.com/SouthAfrica/News/Residents-protest-as-toddler-murder-accused-appear-20131024.

144. Shazdeh Omari, "Women in South Africa Are Living in a War Zone," Women's Media Center, October 29, 2013, accessed September 19, 2019, http://www.womensmediacenter.com/women-under-siege/women-in-south-africa-are-living-in-a-war-zone.

145. "Rape Survivors' Guide to the Criminal Justice System in South Africa," One in Nine Campaign, 2012, accessed October 20, 2019, https://www.ru.ac.za/media/rhodesuniversity/content/studentzone/documents/A_Rape_Survivors_Guide_to_the_Criminal_Justice_System_in_South_Africa.pdf. See their work online at oneinnine.org.za in Johannesburg, South Africa. Another example is Rape Crisis, an organization in Cape Town, South Africa, working to educate, create awareness, and inspire change at Rapecrisis.org.za.

146. Moira Dustin and Anne Phillips, "Whose Agenda Is It?: Abuses of Women and Abuses of 'Culture' in Britain," *Ethnicities* 8, no. 3 (2008): 405–24, https://doi.org/10.1177/1468796808092451.

147. Anne Seagraves, *Soiled Doves: Prostitution in the Early West* (Hayden, ID: Wesanne Publications, 1994).

148. "Top 10 Most Profitable Movies of All Time," The Wondrous, accessed September 19, 2019, http://thewondrous.com/top-10-most-profitable-movies-of-all-time/.

149. "Why 'Pretty Woman' Should Be Considered a Feminist Classic," Bitch Flicks, January 16, 2015, accessed September 19, 2019, http://www.btchflcks.com/2015/01/why-pretty-woman-should-be-considered-a-feminist-classic.html#.VMg6SMLnYeg.

150. Emanuella Grinberg, "Explaining 'Fifty Shades' Wild Success," CNN, February 7, 2017, accessed September 19, 2019, http://www.cnn.com/2012/07/13/living/fifty-shades-buzz-50-shades-success/.

151. A. Nichols, T. Edmond, and E. Heil, *Social Work Practice with Survivors of Sex Trafficking and Commercial Sexual Exploitation* (Columbia University Press, 2018); L. Gerassi

and A. Nichols, *Sex Trafficking and Commercial Sexual Exploitation: Prevention, Advocacy, and Trauma-Informed Practice* (Springer Publishing Company, 2017).

152. Richard S. Ehrlich, "U.N. Report Calls for Decriminalizing Prostitution," *Washington Times*, October 24, 2012, accessed September 19, 2019, http://www.washingtontimes.com/news/2012/oct/24/un-report-calls-decriminalizing-prostitution/?page=all.

153. "ILO Says Forced Labour Generates Annual Profits of US$ 150 Billion," ILO News, May 20, 2014, accessed September 20, 2019, https://www.ilo.org/global/about-the-ilo/news room/news/WCMS_243201/lang—en/index.htm.

154. "Adult Stores Industry in the US–Market Research Report," IBISWorld, May 2019, accessed September 20, 2019, https://www.ibisworld.com/industry-trends/specialized-mar ket-research-reports/consumer-goods-services/lifestyle-stores/adult-stores.html.

155. J. L. Postmus, ed., *Sexual Violence and Abuse: An Encyclopedia of Prevention, Impacts, and Recovery* (Santa Barbara, CA: ABC-CLIO, 2013), 561.

156. Ibid.

157. Ibid., 439.

158. "Overview of Human Trafficking and NIJ's Role."

159. Postmus, *Sexual Violence and Abuse*, 395.

160. "Human Trafficking Issue Brief: Safe Harbor," Polaris, fall 2015, accessed September 20, 2019, https://polarisproject.org/sites/default/files/2015percent20Safepercent20Harbor percent20Issuepercent20Brief.pdf.

161. See Carrie A. Bohnert, Aaron W. Calhoun, and Olivia F. Mittel, "Taking Up the Mantle of Human Trafficking Education: Who Should Be Responsible?" *AMA Journal of Ethics* 19, no. 1 (2017): 35–42. doi:10.1001/journalofethics.2016.19.1.ecas4-1701; see also Tim Talley, "Official: Trafficking More Profitable than Drugs," *Washington Times*, September 24, 2014, accessed September 4, 2018, http://www.washingtontimes.com/news/2014/sep/24/oklahoma -house-to-study-human-trafficking-crimes/.

162. See, for example, Jaclyn Friedman and Jessica Valenti, *Yes Means Yes!: Visions of Female Sexual Power and a World without Rape* (New York: Perseus Books, 2008); Janet Halley, *Split Decisions: How and Why to Take a Break from Feminism* (Princeton, NJ: Princeton University Press, 2006).

163. C. Royalle, *How to Tell a Naked Man What to Do: Sex Advice from a Woman Who Knows* (Touchstone, 2004).

164. "Feminist Porn," Candida Royalle, accessed September 20, 2019, http://candidaroy alle.com/feminist-porn/.

165. The SANGRAM/VAMP Team, "The VAMP/SANGRAM Sex Worker's Movement in India's Southwest," Association for Women's Rights in Development, 2011, accessed September 20, 2019, https://www.awid.org/sites/default/files/atoms/files/changing_their_world_2_-_ vamp_-sex_workers_movement_in_indias_southwest.pdf; Srilatha Batliwala, "Changing Their World: Concepts and Practices of Women's Movements," Association for Women's Rights in Development, 2011, accessed September 20, 2019, https://www.awid.org/sites/ default/files/atoms/files/changing_their_world_2ed_full_eng.pdf.

166. Leslie Bennetts, "The John Next Door," *Daily Beast*, April 24, 2017, accessed September 20, 2019, https://www.thedailybeast.com/the-john-next-door.

167. Devon D. Brewer, John J. Potterat, Sharon B. Garrett, Stephen Q. Muth, John M. Roberts Jr., Danuta Kasprzyk, Daniel E. Montano, and William W. Darrow, "Prostitution and the Sex Discrepancy in Reported Number of Sexual Partners," *PNAS* 97, no. 22 (2000): 12385–88, https://doi.org/10.1073/pnas.210392097. See these additional assessments: Devon D. Brewer, John M. Roberts Jr., Stephen Q. Muth, and John J. Potterat, "Prevalence of Male Clients of Street Prostitute Women in the United States," *Human Organization* 67, no. 3 (Fall 2008): 346–56, https://www.jstor.org/stable/44127359?seq=1#page_scan_tab_ contents; John M. Roberts Jr. and Devon D. Brewer, "Estimating the Prevalence of Male

Clients of Prostitute Women in Vancouver with a Simple Capture–Recapture Method," *Journal of the Royal Statistical Society*, April 2006, accessed October 20, 2019, https://doi.org/10.1111/j.1467-985X.2006.00416.x.

168. John D'Emilio and Estelle B. Freedman, *Intimate Matters: A History of Sexuality in America*, 3rd ed. (Chicago: University of Chicago Press, 2012), 297.

169. V. Bullough, *Sin, Sickness and Sanity* (Plume, 1977).

170. Emilio and Freedman, *Intimate Matters*, 297.

171. Kathleen Barry, *The Prostitution of Sexuality* (New York: New York University Press, 1995).

172. Leonard Cler-Cunningham and Christine Christenson, "Studying Violence to Stop It: Canadian Research on Violence against Women in Vancouver's Street Level Sex Trade," *Research for Sex Work* 4 (2001), https://www.nswp.org/sites/nswp.org/files/research-for-sex-work-4-english.pdf.

173. S. Kingston and T. Thomas, "No Model in Practice: A 'Nordic Model' to Respond to Prostitution?," *Crime, Law and Social Change* 71, no. 4: 423–39, May 2019, accessed October 20, 2019, https://link.springer.com/article/10.1007/s10611-018-9795-6.

174. "Nordic Model," Scandinavian Human Rights Lawyers, accessed September 20, 2019, http://humanrightslawyers.eu/human-trafficking/nordic-model/.

175. E. Durkin, "Harvey Weinstein: Judge Allows Sex Trafficking Case to Move to Trial," *The Guardian*, August 14, 2019, accessed October 20, 2019, https://www.theguardian.com/film/2018/aug/14/harvey-weinstein-trial-sex-trafficking-latest-news.

176. Catharine A. MacKinnon, "How Litigation Laid the Ground for Accountability after #MeToo," *The Guardian*, December 2017, accessed September 20, 2019, https://www.theguardian.com/commentisfree/2017/dec/23/how-litigation-laid-the-ground-for-accountability-after-metoo.

177. Ibid.

178. Michael C. Rea, "What Is Pornography?" *Noûs* 35, no. 1 (2001): 118–45, https://doi.org/10.1111/0029-4624.00290.

179. Rebecca Leung, "Porn in the USA," *60 Minutes*, November 21, 2003, accessed September 20, 2019, http://www.cbsnews.com/2100-18560_162-585049.html.

180. Lydia Saad, "Doctor-Assisted Suicide Is Moral Issue Dividing Americans Most," Gallup, May 31, 2011, accessed September 20, 2019, http://www.gallup.com/poll/147842/doctor-assisted-suicide-moral-issue-dividing-americans.aspx.

181. Fabio D'Orlando, "The Demand for Pornography," *Journal of Happiness Studies* 12, no. 1 (2011): 51–75, doi:10.1007/s10902-009-9175-0.

182. Williams, L. *Porn Studies* (Duke University Press, 2004).

183. David Auerbach, "Vampire Porn," *Slate*, October 23, 2014, accessed September 20, 2019, https://slate.com/technology/2014/10/mindgeek-porn-monopoly-its-dominance-is-a-cautionary-tale-for-other-industries.html.

184. Rea, "What Is Pornography?," 118–45.

185. *Jacobellis v. Ohio*, 378 U.S. at 197 (Stewart, J., concurring).

186. Lily Karlin, "Duke Porn Star Belle Knox on the 'SVU' Episode Based on Her Story," *Huffington Post*, October 24, 2014, accessed September 20, 2019, https://www.huffingtonpost.com/2014/10/24/duke-porn-star-svu_n_6041258.html?ec_carp=8825984435536173108.

187. Paul J. Wright, Robert S. Tokunaga, and Ashley Kraus, "A Meta-Analysis of Pornography Consumption and Actual Acts of Sexual Aggression in General Population Studies," *Journal of Communication* 66, no. 1 (February 2016): 183–205.

188. Silvia Bonino et al., "Use of Pornography and Self-Reported Engagement in Sexual Violence among Adolescents," *European Journal of Developmental Psychology* 3, no. 3 (2006): 265–88.

189. Conor Friedersdorf, "Is Porn Culture to Be Feared?" *The Atlantic*, April 11, 2016, accessed September 20, 2019, https://www.theatlantic.com/politics/archive/2016/04/porn-cul ture/477099/.

190. Grant Hilary Brenner, "4 Ways Porn Causes Problems," *Psychology Today*, March 5, 2018, accessed September 20, 2019, https://www.psychologytoday.com/us/blog/experimenta tions/201803/4-ways-porn-use-causes-problems.

191. Martin Bright and Tracy McVeigh, "This Club Had Its Own Chairman and Treasurer. Its Business Was Child Abuse," *The Guardian*, February 10, 2001, accessed September 20, 2019, https://www.theguardian.com/uk/2001/feb/11/tracymcveigh.martinbright.

192. "Child Pornography: Model Legislation & Global Review," 8th ed., 2016, International Centre for Missing & Exploited Children, accessed September 20, 2019, https://www.icmec.org/ wp-content/uploads/2016/02/Child-Pornography-Model-Law-8th-Ed-Final-linked.pdf.

193. See N. Malamuth and M. Huppin, "Drawing the Line on Virtual Child Pornography: Bringing the Law in Line with the Research Evidence," *New York University Review of Law and Social Change* 31 (2007): 773–827.

194. Aimee Green, "Oregon Supreme Court Rules That Simply Viewing Child Pornography on the Internet Isn't Illegal," *The Oregonian*, January 10, 2019, accessed September 20, 2019, https://www.oregonlive.com/pacific-northwest-news/index.ssf/2011/01/oregon_supreme_ court_rules_that_simply_viewing_child_pornography_on_the_internet_isnt_illegal.html.

195. See "About Us," NoPornNorthampton.org, accessed October 20, 2019, www.noporn northampton.org.

196. Pamela Paul, *Pornified: How Pornography Is Transforming Our Lives, Our Relation- ships, and Our Families* (New York: Times Books, 2005).

197. "1 in 3 Boys Heavy Porn Users, Study Shows," Phys.org, February 23, 2007, accessed September 20, 2019, http://www.physorg.com/news91457852.html.

198. Ibid.

199. Samuel L. Perry and Cyrus Schleifer, "Till Porn Do Us Part? A Longitudinal Exam- ination of Pornography Use and Divorce," *Journal of Sex Research* 55, no. 3 (2018): 284–96, accessed September 20, 2019, https://enough.org/objects/Till_Porn_Do_Us_Part_A_Longitu dinal_Exam_fnv.pdf.

200. See, for example, "Brain, Heart, World: A Documentary in Three Parts," accessed October 20, 2019, https://brainheartworld.org/.

201. "Pornography and Public Health: Research Summary," National Center on Sexual Exploitation, August 2, 2017, accessed September 20, 2019, http://endsexualexploitation .org/wp-content/uploads/NCOSE_Pornography-PublicHealth_ResearchSummary_8-2_17_ FINAL-with-logo.pdf.

202. Ibid.

203. Gail Dines, G. 2010. *Pornland: How Porn Has Hijacked Our Sexuality.* (Boston: Bea- con Press, 2010), 161, note 35.

204. Angus Crawford, "Computer-Generated 'Sweetie' Catches Online Predators," *BBC News*, November 5, 2013, accessed September 20, 2019, https://www.bbc.com/news/ uk-24818769; see also "Becoming Sweetie: A Novel Approach to Stopping the Global Rise of Webcam Child Sex Tourism," report by Terre des Hommes Netherlands, November 2013, accessed October 20, 2019, https://www.terredeshommes.org/webcam-child-sex-tourism.

205. Kathleen Richardson, "Sex Robot Matters," *IEEE Technology and Society Maga- zine*, June 2016, accessed September 20, 2019, http://prostitutionresearch.com/wp-content/ uploads/2017/08/Sex-Robot-Matters.pdf.

206. Samuel Osborne, "Japanese Company Manufactures Lifelike Child Sex Dolls for Paedophiles," *Independent*, January 13, 2016, accessed September 20, 2019, https:// www.independent.co.uk/news/world/asia/japanese-company-manufactures-lifelike -child-sex-dolls-for-paedophiles-a6811046.html.

207. Ibid.

208. Ethel Quayle and Max Taylor, "Child Pornography and Internet: Perpetuating a Cycle of Abuse," *Deviant Behavior* 23, no. 4 (2002): 331–61, https://doi.org/10.1080/01639620290086413; Roc Morin, "Can Child Dolls Keep Pedophiles from Offending?" *The Atlantic*, January 11, 2016, accessed September 20, 2019, https://www.theatlantic.com/health/archive/2016/01/can-child-dolls-keep-pedophiles-from-offending/423324/; Ryan C.W. Hall and Richard C.W. Hall, "A Profile of Pedophilia: Definition, Characteristic of Offenders, Recidivism, Treatment Outcomes and Forensic Issues," *Mayo Clinic Proceedings* 82, no. 4 (2007): 457–71, https://doi.org/10.4065/82.4.457.

209. Scott Cunningham and Todd D. Kendall, "Examining the Role of Client Reviews and Reputation within Online Prostitution," in *The Oxford Handbook of the Economics of Prostitution*, ed. Scott Cunningham and Manisha Shah (Oxford, UK: Oxford University Press, 2016), 9–32, http://scunning.com/reputation.pdf.

210. Allison Schrager, Christopher Groskopf, and Scott Cunningham, "How the Internet Changed the Market for Sex," Quartz, November 5, 2017, accessed September 20, 2019, https://qz.com/1065881/how-the-internet-changed-the-market-for-sex/.

211. Internet Crimes Against Children Task Force Program, https://www.icactaskforce.org/

212. Janis Wolak, Kimberly Mitchell, and David Finkelhor, "Online Victimization of Youth: Five Years Later," 2006, accessed September 20, 2019, http://www.unh.edu/ccrc/pdf/CV138.pdf.

213. Emma Perez, "Sexuality and Discourse: Notes from a Chicana Survivor," in *Chicana Lesbians: The Girls Our Mother Warned Us About*, ed. Carla Trujillo (Berkeley, CA: Third Woman, 1991), 163.

214. L. Dalby, *Geisha* (University of California Press, 1983).

215. Dines, *Pornland: How Porn Has Hijacked Our Sexuality*.

216. Ibid.

217. Ibid., 127.

218. Ibid.

219. Maya Finoh and Jasmine Sankofa, "The Legal System Has Failed Black Girls, Women, and Non-Binary Survivors of Violence," ACLU, January 28, 2019, accessed September 20, 2019, https://www.aclu.org/blog/racial-justice/race-and-criminal-justice/legal-system-has-failed-black-girls-women-and-non.

220. Dines, *Pornland: How Porn Has Hijacked Our Sexuality*, 140.

221. "Does Legalized Prostitution Increase Human Trafficking?," Harvard Law and International Development Society, June 12, 2014, https://orgs.law.harvard.edu/lids/2014/06/12/does-legalized-prostitution-increase-human-trafficking/.

222. Marianne Macy, *Working Sex: An Exploration of the Sex Industry from the People Who Actually Do the Work* (Carroll and Graf Publishing, 1996).

223. Dines, *Pornland: How Porn Has Hijacked Our Sexuality*, 140.

10

Laws, Public Policy, and Legislative Action

◆ ◆ ◆

[P]ublic policy in the United States regarding sexual offenders is based on misinformation and fear, and ignores what we know about sexual offenders and sexual crimes.

—Michael Miner[1]

Victim and community measures to manage sex offenders ordinarily only address convicted sex offenders. However, research shows that the vast majority of sex offenders are never reported, let alone tried and convicted. Contrary to the popular myth of "stranger danger," children and youth are far more at risk of sexual abuse from adults they know. The same holds true for adult victims of sexual assault. Research shows that the vast majority of sex offenders know their victims, yet measures are generally designed to address situations in which the sex offender is presumed to be a stranger to the victim.

Community members need to understand the limitations of current measures to manage convicted sex offenders, because without this critical knowledge, the enactment of measures can lead to a false sense of security, thereby putting children at even greater risk.

—National Alliance to End Sexual Violence[2]

WITHOUT QUESTION, having a better understanding of the dynamics of sexual violence and its history, legislative origins, and important definitions provides a solid foundation for anyone thinking about how individuals and communities can best respond to this kind of violence and work toward prevention. The primary legal intent behind the laws and policies focused on sex offenders put in place starting in the late 1990s was to increase public safety and decrease **sex-offender recidivism,** or the commission of a subsequent sexual offense by an individual who had previously been convicted of a sex crime.[3] The implications of those legislative efforts are still under review from various angles, and, beginning almost immediately after implementation, questions were raised as to whether the laws as they were drafted and are currently enforced have actually met the objectives lawmakers and community members had in mind when the legislation was designed.

Efforts to prevent sexualized violence stretch back into periods of time influenced by religious practices, social or cultural philosophies, community events or attitudes, and individual and family life, as well as by legislators and city governments.[4] Sex-offender laws and policies have evolved differently in each community, and the history and legislative response to localized needs will reflect those community differences. Increasingly, a vast array of researchers, scholars, and practitioners who work to better understand sex crimes and explore and/or create a related social response spend a notable amount of those conversations critically assessing the existing laws, policies, and public practices designed to hold an offender accountable. A short reflection is provided on the important role of state governments, and the diversity of responses put in place to address sexual violence and related harms follows. A timeline of federal legislation is offered as an introduction to a review of the complicated questions being raised regarding primary pieces of those national initiatives. A brief presentation of information about the legislation and its pathway into existence is provided, with an overview of critical social reflection about various controversial provisions of the legislation closing the chapter.

A BRIEF STATEMENT ABOUT STATE-LEVEL SEX-OFFENDER LEGISLATION

Each state in the United States has identified and advanced legislation in the past decade[5] working toward delineating what community members and legislators in that state define as an appropriate response to the problems raised by sexual offenses and related conduct. Part of that legislative effort is focused on designing a system to regulate people who commit sex offenses, and part of the state action is in response to localized concerns about maintaining public safety. In 1947, California passed a sex-offender registration law that required offenders who had been convicted of specific offenses to register with local police.[6] In 1990, the state of Washington, for example, crafted the first contemporary protocol to regulate sex offenders, titled the **Community Protection Act**.[7] The actions were directly related to two significant events involving repeat offenders, one who, while incarcerated, bragged about looking forward to killing again should he ever be released who would then go on to assault and murder three young boys. The second case involved a perpetrator who had over 20 years of history committing sexual violence and who, almost immediately after being released from prison, kidnapped a 7-year-old boy, sexually assaulted him, and then left him for dead. Both men had completed their sentences and, in spite of behaviors of concern, had served their time and were released.[8] Almost immediately, efforts were under way to address the collective community concern.

The Community Protection Act was designed to give the state more control over sex offenders perpetrating extreme behavior and included provisions on civil commitment, offender registration, community notification by police when any offender identified as a sexually violent predator was released, treatment options in prison, community supervision upon release, and expanded sentences for certain sexual offenses.[9] Many of these provisions are discussed in more detail below. Born out of tragic events in a short span of time in both Seattle and Tacoma, proponents of the legislation saw the purpose of the law to be a significant move toward crime prevention, as well as offering law enforcement tools to assist with management and oversight of offenders living in their jurisdiction. Many of the ideas were later replicated at the federal level and implemented widely in other states.

As has been discussed in other places throughout the text, several states gave specific attention to rape laws in the 1970s. The social and cultural attitudes of the time were questioning the use of capital crimes, or the death penalty, for the crime of rape, and advocates were challenging low conviction rates of rape in the court systems.[10] A Supreme Court challenge in 1977, *Coker v. Georgia*, ended the use of the death penalty for the crime of rape, resulting in a more varied state response to rape, with rape laws most commonly being drafted in the first, second, and third degree or classified as aggravated or simple assault, based on the degree of coercion and/or the use of a weapon, the degree of harm to the victim, and the age of the victim.[11]

Advocates watched while women who made allegations of rape were asked by the court to bring corroborating information, in fact, suggesting that the word of the woman alone was not enough to warrant further proceedings.[12] Juries were often instructed, or given a statement by the judge before deliberating the case, that accusations were easily made and immensely difficult to defend against. Advocates seeking reform argued these statements could easily create a prejudice against the victim, and, although it took considerable time, the practice is no longer common.

Two other issues were raised by reformers working to balance the legal scales for rape victims seeking justice: the marital exception provision and rape shield laws. The **marital exception** was linked back to English common law, which suggested that the wife was considered a man's property and as such was to be available for sex at his request. Eventually, all states created legislation making spousal rape illegal; however, the particular characteristics of the laws vary from state to state. The final issue for presentation regarding the efforts reformers undertook with regard to how rape was treated in the courtroom included what were called **rape shield laws**. Once a victim took the stand, there were no legal protections. As such, defense attorneys would bring in issues about her sexual behavior, personal habits, emotional stability, and various other elements of her life, related to the case or not. In short, the goal was to discredit the witness in an attempt to create doubts about the individual's character and, by default, the claims made in the case under review. Although the debate on this was vigorous, it is the case that exactly what can be asked of a victim during a court proceeding will differ from state to state and be based on past practice and judicial discretion.[13]

Many of these changes were fought using state legislative houses across the country as the battle ground. Various elements of these early state practices became modified and used at the federal level and will be discussed below in more detail. For example, one concern raised is that states generate specific legislation in response to a specific and extremely horrible incident, which can then prioritize and drive the demand for immediate action before any complicated or nuanced research findings can be done or well-considered options are fully explored and vetted. With that reflection, however, comes a critique of laws, suggesting they may not have the intended effect but instead have **collateral consequences,** or unintended, often negative consequences impacting the offenders after release. Concerns that the laws are too restrictive, making it harder to successfully reintegrate into society after a prison term, have raised questions about what a sex offender needs to be successful and, more importantly, having the resources and support needed to prevent future offending behaviors after release from prison.[14]

Many of the state processes reflect the federal policies, including **offender registration, community notification, residence restrictions,** and **civil commitment,** all discussed in more detail below. The reality is that states can vary widely in their development of sex-offender policy. Serious students of the subject will want to affirm local practices and networks in their area. Courts are affirming legal challenges,[15] and researchers and critics have questions about the effectiveness of the laws passed and whether other options might prove to be better suited for future prevention. Calls for reform seem ever present, so much so, in fact, that different state efforts to create socially acceptable social policy to regulate people who have committed sex offenses has been rather famously described as a "race to the bottom to see who can most thoroughly condemn this group of offenders," one of the most despised and ostracized population of convicted criminals.[16]

In 2018, the state of Missouri considered legislation to amend its existing requirements for sex offenders to register for a lifetime, with no exceptions. Extreme by any measure, even while some are raising questions, states are touting a need to get tougher. Although the measure did not pass, there can be implications. This is a much more stringent registration requirement than other states, and as a result many offenders choose to move out of state where registration requirements are not as severe, sometimes away from family and support.[17] With increased attention being given to assessing the efficacy of laws and policies designed for regulating sex offenders, expanded calls for assessments to determine whether the laws and policies actually have the desired effect may also require an expanded range of creative alternatives.

A BRIEF HISTORY OF FEDERAL SEX-OFFENDER LEGISLATION IN THE UNITED STATES

The early Americas relied heavily on English common law for the legal framework being implemented the United States, and as a reminder punishment for the crimes of rape and sodomy could include death. Although the punishments varied state by state,[18] at the turn of the nineteenth century, churches in communities held significant sway, and as such the community would also sometimes dole out informal justice for infractions through the Catholic Church.[19] As the twentieth century approached, science was increasingly a social and medical tool used in large part to replace punishment-oriented philosophies with treatment. Laws at this time generally reflected that social ideal, and offenders were seen to have uncontrollable sexual urges, which needed to be addressed medically.[20] While science was advancing in some sectors, factions in the US government were focused on regulating immoral activity. Working to address, define, regulate, and punish sexual activity was at the top of the list. As an example, the **Mann Act of 1910** made it a felony to transport any "woman or girl for the purpose of prostitution or debauchery, or for any other immoral purpose." Used primarily for arresting men who had sex with underaged girls, the legal language of "immoral purpose" created a wide application in the courts and came to include the legal classification of **miscegenation**, referring to interracial sexual relationships. Collectively, legislation in the period around the 1930s to as late as the 1950s commonly referred to sex crime laws as the "sexual psychopath laws," designed to remove individuals who had committed a sex offense from society until evidence could be offered that they had been rehabilitated.[21] Social science researchers in the 1950s started challenging the efficacy of these treatments and tested these legal proscriptions.[22] As a result of medical and academic challenges, the late 1950s to 1970s saw a significant number of treatment facilities shut down, referred to as **deinstitutionalization**, or the removal of people from institutions utilized for treatment. The 1960s and 1970s saw a significant amount of social turmoil, protests, and marches about racial and gender justice, and, during the 1970s, several decisions in the US Supreme Court demanded focused attention on the rights of the accused offenders, which resulted in the famous **Miranda rights** police officers read to anyone accused of a crime. Over time, questions regarding concerns about violations of offenders' constitutional protections, the efficacy of treatment, and a social and cultural shift to punishment over treatment saw those laws replaced.[23]

The 1980s brought in a "get tough" attitude toward crime. Another monumental US Supreme Court decision in 1982, *New York v. Ferber*, put the rights of children front and center when the Court ruled that making child pornography and its distribution was illegal, over the traditional practice of prioritizing individual rights to privacy. As examples, attention was given to incest, rapes perpetrated by someone known to the victim (at the time, called "acquaintance rape"), aspects of gender and sexual orientation, and domestic violence, which would become a national movement. Also, as indicated above and discussed more completely in chapter 11, legal standards were opening up to women, and research was expanding to shift some long-standing social attitudes, including a fundamental idea that continues to be misrepresented into the present: the idea that *rape is much more likely to be perpetrated by someone the victim knows.* This was a significant shift from the earlier misleading focus on stranger rape.

In the 1990s, a series of incidents of abductions, sexual assault, and murder involving children and young people produced a climate of outrage, and several federal laws resulted. The "get tough on crime" attitude continued into the next decade with the **Violent Crime Control and Law Enforcement Act** (1994), also referred to as the Clinton Crime Bill, an approach President Clinton himself would decades later come to criticize as significantly flawed and which critics say attributed to the contemporary problems of mass incarceration. A significant element of the crime bill was focused on initial efforts to track individuals convicted of sex offenses by requiring them to register with law enforcement. Certainly, the undercurrents prioritizing treatment or punishment as a response to serious crime seemed to swing back and forth like a pendulum, a dynamic theme that continues to this day. A collection of the most instructive federal laws focused on sex offenders and offenses is presented below, followed by an evaluation of their efficacy.

A TIMELINE OF PRIMARY CONTEMPORARY FEDERAL SEX-OFFENDER LAWS IN THE UNITED STATES

1990—**Jeanne Clery Disclosure of Campus Security Policy and Campus Crime Statistics Act** (originally known as the Crime Awareness and Campus Security Act) requiring all colleges and universities that participate in federal financial aid programs to document and publish information about crime on and near their campus. The law is named for Jeanne Clery, a 19-year-old freshman at Lehigh University who was raped and murdered in her campus residence hall by another student in 1986.

1994—**Jacob Wetterling Crimes Against Children and Sexually Violent Offender Registration Act** mandates that each state create a program to register sex offenders. This bill required states to implement public registries of individuals who commit crimes against children. The legislation was named after Jacob Wetterling, who was 11 years old in 1989 when he was abducted and whose whereabouts remained unknown for almost 30 years. In 2016, the perpetrator confessed to Jacob's abduction and revealed the location of the remains in rural Minnesota, approximately 30 miles from where Jacob was taken. Jacob's parents, Patty and Jerry Wetterling, rose to national prominence in their efforts to create legal protections and advocate for children's safety.

1994—**Violence Against Women Act** (VAWA) was introduced by then Senator Joe Biden and reauthorized under Bill Clinton in 2000 to include more programs and provisions for cyberstalking and dating violence and an increased emphasis on immigrant populations. In 2006 under G. W. Bush, the legislation was reauthorized and included additional provisions. A long legislative battle in 2013 ensued due to opposition to additional provisions to include services for immigrants, an extension of services to protect victims in same-sex partnerships, and questions about budget appropriations produced, but regardless the act was reauthorized in early 2013.

Similar partisan opposition to efforts to renew or add to the legislation was impacted by a government shutdown in 2018–2019 with reauthorization measures passed through the House but not addressed by the Senate as of early 2019.

1996—**Megan's Law**, created as an amendment to the Wetterling Act, required the release of relevant sex-offender information to the public for protection from sexually violent offenders. This has collectively become known as community notification, reflective of the 1990 Washington state legislation. Megan's Law is named for 7-year-old Megan Kanka, of New Jersey, who was abducted, sexually assaulted, and murdered by a neighbor who was a repeat violent sex offender.

1996—**Pam Lychner Sexual Offender Tracking and Identification Act of 1996** is another amendment to the 1994 Jacob Wetterling Act. This act allowed the FBI to establish a national database of the names and addresses of sex offenders to be held in a National Sex Offender Registry (NSOR). The provisions required state law enforcement officials to regulate information collected from registered offenders and allowed the dissemination of the information gathered by the FBI. The act is named for Pam Lychner, who became a victims' rights advocate after she narrowly escaped an attack by a repeat sex offender. Ms. Lychner and her two daughters were killed in the crash of TWA flight 800 off Long Island in 1996.

1996—**Child Porn Prevention Act (CPPA)** was an attempt to make simulated child pornography illegal, but, in 2002, the US Supreme Court (*Ashcroft v. Free Speech Coalition*) held that portions of the CPPA were unconstitutional because the descriptions were overly broad. The legislative response to the court ruling resulted in the PROTECT Act (2003), discussed in more detail below.

1997—**Departments of Commerce, Justice, and State, the Judiciary, and Related Agencies Appropriations Act of 1998** (also known as the Jacob Wetterling Improvement Act) included updates and amendments to portions of the Jacob Wetterling Act and the provisions outlined in its modifications. Among its requirements were mandates that states participate and set up a protocol for participation, with heightened registration requirements for sexually violent offenders, including members of the US Armed Forces who were convicted in any civilian or military court. Such offenders must register in their state of residence, as well as in the state where they work or go to school if those locations were in a different state. If they relocated, they had to register in the state of their new residence. Additionally, the Bureau of Prisons was to notify state officials when a sex offender was released. The act also included a motion from Congress that each state shall create laws prohibiting the stalking of juveniles.

2000—**Victims of Trafficking and Violence Protection Act** as amended combats trafficking in persons, especially into sex trade, slavery, and involuntary servitude. The statute authorizes the Office to Monitor and Combat Trafficking in Persons and the President's Interagency Task Force to Monitor and Combat Trafficking in Persons to coordinate antitrafficking efforts and was signed into law by President Clinton and then reauthorized by the Bush, Obama, and Trump administrations.

2003—**PROTECT (Prosecutorial Remedies and Other Tools to End the Exploitation of Children Today) Act** "comprehensively strengthens law enforcement's ability to prevent, investigate, intercept communications in an effort to prosecute and punish violent crimes committed against children."[24] One of the first tools was the establishment of a national **AMBER Alert** program, including the appointment of an AMBER Alert coordinator and state support for developing AMBER Alert communication systems. Attention was also given to establishing the means to prosecute US citizens who travel abroad or outside the United States for sex with children (sex tourism). States were required to develop websites that contained the information about the sex offenders, and the Department of Justice was required to host a website with links to every state. The sanctions for offenders were enhanced, moving child abduction to 20-year minimum and the production of child pornography to 15–30 years and provided lifetime imprisonment for offenders who were convicted of two serious sex offenses against children. Finally, anyone released from prison after committing an offense against a child would be required to be on supervised release for life.

2003—**Prison Rape Elimination Act (PREA)** is focused on the prevention, identification, prosecution, and internal response by correctional officials to allegations of sexual violence in prison. It was in large part a response to a 1994 Supreme Court case, *Farmer v. Brennan*, in which the court ruled the state has an obligation to keep people incarcerated free from sexual assault.

2006—**Dru Sjodin National Sex Offender Public Website,** which is included within the wide-ranging Adam Walsh Child Protection and Safety Act, establishes a nationwide online sex-offender database. The database allows the public to search for sex-offender information by zip code or geographic radius. The law is named for Dru Sjodin, who was abducted in North Dakota, sexually assaulted, and murdered by a repeat violent sex offender.

2006—**Adam Walsh Child Protection and Safety Act**, also known as the Sex Offender Registration and Notification Act (SORNA), replaced the requirements and updates of the Jacob Wetterling Act and its amendments and strengthened multiple areas of law relating to the protection of children in an effort to encourage a national standard. The act is named for Adam Walsh, of Florida, who was abducted and murdered in 1981 at the age of 6. His father, John Walsh, became a national TV personality recognized as an advocate for victims of violent crimes. As of 2014, 17 states, three territories, and 63 tribes had implemented SORNA requirements from the Adam Walsh Act.[25] Within the Adam Walsh Act is the **Office of Sex Offender Sentencing, Monitoring, Apprehension, Registering, and Tracking (SMART)**, which was authorized to implement and administer the standards of the Adam Walsh Act and assist professionals at the state level with anything they need to ensure public safety.[26]

2008—**Keeping the Internet Devoid of Sexual Predators (KIDS) Act** was passed to address the issues of online safety for kids by requiring the collection of internet identifiers as part of the offender registration process.

2010—**Katie's Law**, also known as the Katie Sepich Enhanced DNA Collection Act, provides funding to states to implement minimum and enhanced DNA collection processes for any felony arrest. The bill is named after Katie Sepich, who was raped and killed. Skin and blood samples found under her fingernails and the DNA profile believed to be her attacker's were sent to the **Combined DNA Index System (CODIS)**, where a match was found. After being confronted with the DNA evidence, the killer confessed.

2010—**Federal civil commitment upheld by the Supreme Court.** The US Supreme Court ruled in *Gundy v. United States* that the authority of Congress did in fact allow the continued civil commitment of sex offenders after they have completed their criminal sentence, by convincing a judge the individual still poses a danger. In other words, after a federal inmate comes close to completing their sentence, if the government deems them a sexually violent person and a judge agrees, the government can continue to hold the individual until they assess the individual as no longer a threat. See also *Kansas v. Hendricks* (1997) on civil commitment.

PUBLIC RESPONSE AND CRITICAL REFLECTION ON SEX-OFFENDER LEGISLATION IN THE UNITED STATES

In 2007, Human Rights Watch released "No Easy Answers: Sex Offender Laws in the US." On the cover was a grief-stricken mom, **Patty Wetterling**, holding a photo of her son Jacob, who at that time had been missing since 1989.[27] She had become known nationally for the work she was doing to help create better ways to supply resources for law enforcement, enhance public safety, and protect people from violence. Here, however, almost 20 years after her son's abduction, she was among an increasing number of people asking hard questions about the policies regulating sex offenders. From the report summary:

> Human Rights Watch appreciates the sense of concern and urgency that has prompted these laws. They reflect a deep public yearning for safety in a world that seems increasingly threatening. Every child has the right to live free from violence and sexual abuse. Promoting public safety by holding offenders accountable and by instituting effective crime prevention measures is a core government obligation.
>
> Unfortunately, our research reveals that sex-offender registration, community notification, and residency restriction laws are ill-considered, poorly crafted, and may cause more harm than good:
>
> - The registration laws are overbroad in scope and overlong in duration, requiring people to register who pose no safety risk;
> - Under community notification laws, anyone anywhere can access online sex-offender registries for purposes that may have nothing to do with public safety. Harassment of and violence against registrants have been the predictable result; and
> - In many cases residency restrictions have the effect of banishing registrants from entire urban areas and forcing them to live far from their homes and families.
>
> The evidence is overwhelming, as detailed in this report, that these laws cause great harm to the people subject to them. On the other hand, proponents of these laws are not able to point to convincing evidence of public safety gains from them. Even assuming some public safety benefits, however, the laws can be reformed to reduce their adverse effect without compromising that benefit. Registration laws should be narrowed in scope and duration. Publicly accessible online registries should be eliminated, and community notification should be accomplished solely by law enforcement officials. Blanket residency restrictions should be abolished.[28]

Reflecting on the decade of expansion on sex-offender laws and policies, related research, and legal challenges or court reviews, the idea that these laws would be challenged at all, much less by a mother whose child was still missing, might have been a surprise to some. Now, after the decade of legal action and, with over a decade of time and additional research supporting the challenges presented in the Human Rights Watch report, significant consideration is being given to what aspects of the current process work and what might need review and change. A summary of research related to the major legislation is presented below.

RESEARCH ON LEGISLATIVE IMPACTS

The last two decades have produced a significant number of critical reviews offered regarding several primary features of the sex-offender laws. With organizations in every state working to produce changes to the current state of sex-offender laws, related efforts could be described as a kind of collective learning and action.[29] While federal law requires states to register former offenders convicted of certain crimes, a state could elect to increase the number of offenses that require registration. Aspects of consequences of laws intended to be "tough on crime" can also have little or no influence,[30] or worse, produce the opposite effects.[31] Further, the idea that all states are enacting severe sanctions and penalties on individuals convicted of committing sex offenses is not accurate. Some states such as Texas, Florida, and Arizona have implemented more oversight, whereas other states have implemented only registry and notification laws.[32]

In addition, after all of the work required to get a law passed and implemented, those laws sometimes fall short. In 1998, a young woman went missing, but, at 19 years old, she was considered too old to be covered under the Missing Children's Act of 1982, which requires the reporting of anyone under 18 who goes missing to the National Crime Information Center (NCIC). Her parents helped to pass Suzanne's Law in 2003 (as a part of the National AMBER Alert bill), which requires police to immediately take reports of missing 18- to 21-year-olds and enter that information into NCIC. The act of naming a law after a loved one is referred to as a **legacy law**.[33] Friends and family are not alone in their work to change legislation and policy following a high-profile crime, hoping to make improvements to the current system. Many of the federal laws are named after loved ones. It is important to note that legislation named after crime victims may not always result in the outcome the families intend. Sometimes, the law does not pass or is not funded. And, sometimes, the impact of the law can reach well beyond the initial idea.

Researchers have also cautioned about the difficulty assessing the impact of any given law when several laws are put in place at the same time and utilized together.[34] Because different states utilize different protocols, it is potentially deceptive to attempt to make meaningful comparisons across states. Also, much of the legislative response has been to sex crimes that are unusual and rare,[35] such as stranger abduction. Consideration is given to the basic costs and benefits of three of the major pieces of federal sex-offender legislation—sex-offender registries, community notification, and residence restrictions—and a few practices more commonly utilized at the state level, including driver's civil commitment, community license notification, chemical castration, lifetime supervision, and electronic monitoring.

Sex-Offender Registration

The Wetterling Act was designed to establish guidelines for states to track sex offenders. Returning to a community after prison, past offenders would have to register their place of residence with local law enforcement and have their address confirmed once a year for 10 years.[36] For those committing more violent sex crimes, their address would be confirmed four times a year for the rest of their lives. In the case of the Wetterling abduction, police speculated the incident was committed by a sex offender, but they did not have a centralized database of people who had committed these kinds of crimes in the past to either eliminate suspects quickly or focus in on in the investigation.

The idea with the Wetterling Act was to help provide law enforcement with information about possible offenders, but the information was not to be shared unless public safety was deemed an issue. That provision changed with Megan's Law. Because Megan was taken by a sex offender who moved into her neighborhood, her parents argued that they should have been told about the release of the offender, speculating that they would not have let her play outside had they known. In response to their daughter's murder, they worked to pass legislation that would require public safety officials to notify the community when a sex offender moved into the neighborhood.

The Wetterling Act and Megan's Law were updated and integrated into the Adam Walsh Act (2006), also referred to as the Sex Offender Registration and Notification Act (SORNA). The information required of all sex offenders includes:

- Name
- Social security number
- Home, work, and school address
- License plate number
- Vehicle descriptions of any vehicles they own or drive
- Date of birth
- Email addresses
- Pseudonyms used for instant messaging programs
- Passport numbers
- Phone numbers
- DNA, fingerprints, palm prints, and information about the offense for which they were convicted

When an offender is scheduled to travel, they must report their plans to local law enforcement, which may notify officials in the destination city.

The degree of contact with law enforcement depends on the classification the offender receives coming out of prison. The SORNA provisions establish a **three-tiered system**, with each tier having its own specific registration guidelines.

Tier-three sex offenders are the individuals who are being released with a higher statistical probability of reoffending. These offenders are required to register for life and must renew their registration every three months. Tier-two sex offenders are predicted to be less likely to reoffend than tier-three offenders but more serious than tier-one offenders and must register for 25 years. Tier-one offenders must register for 15 years and are considered to be the least likely to reoffend. It is important to note that just because someone has a higher probability of reoffending does not mean that they will reoffend.

The goal of sex-offender registries is to provide information so parents and communities can better protect people in the community, particularly children.[37] Modifications and clarifications to the initial legislation have followed. For example, the **Campus Sex Crimes Prevention Act** (2000) required notification of either enrollment or employment at any institution of higher education. Of particular concern is how registries are impacting young people. Another modification, commonly referred to as **Romeo and Juliet provisions**, states that those who have engaged in consensual sex with a victim at least 13 years old and the offender is no more than four years older than the victim, the offender could be exempted from registration.

Interestingly, *Marie Claire*'s 2011 survey of states with juveniles on the sex-offender registry highlighted the issue of juveniles being placed on the registry for what are consensual sex acts under the age of 18[38] and dubbed in the media as "the accidental sex offender."[39] One example that has received national coverage is of Frank Rodriguez, who was a 19-year-old Texas teen when he had sex with his then 15-year-old girlfriend and was reported to police by her mother. Frank was arrested and, faced with the possibility of a long sentence, pled guilty to an offense that would not require jail time but seven years on probation and registration as a sex offender. The thing that makes this case unusual is that he later married his girlfriend and now they have four children.

A more recent report by Human Rights Watch profiles an 11-year-old boy who was put on the sex-offender registry in Texas, which emphasizes the impact of the sex-offender registry process when it is applied to young people without modification. Although most juvenile records are disclosed only to law enforcement, most states provide sex-offender registry information to the public to be in compliance with community notification laws (discussed below). Failure to adhere to registration and community notification can result in a felony conviction, adding additional challenges for families when young convicted offenders cannot live in a household with other children and particularly when research suggests putting young offenders on registries does not advance public safety.[40]

Research has shown that the information on the registry is often inaccurate or unknown.

Questions have been raised about the accuracy of the information included or whether it is appropriate for sex offenders who abuse children, but not adults.[41] Another study found no steady effect on the impact of registries on rape rates.[42] No research to date offers validity for the idea that the registration of sex offenders actually meets the objectives set out in the legislation, including assisting law enforcement, deterring offenders from reoffending, deterring other potential offenders from committing an initial offense, and providing information to community citizens that will help prevent future victimizations.[43]

Community Notification (Megan's Law)

Often linked together with the registration process, the community notification element of Megan's Law has had swift application. Implementation at the federal level was tied, with registration provisions, to federal funding allocations for state law enforcement. As a result, all states were in compliance rather quickly.[44] The influences of the legislation are mixed, with research suggesting no effect on the enhancement of public safety,[45] and at least preliminary findings in Minnesota suggested a reduction in sex-offender recidivism.[46]

Residence Restrictions

Many states have taken the action to enact additional regulatory laws in an effort to expand public safety, intending to protect local communities against sex offenders. Residence restrictions allow for communities to establish locations, set by specific distance parameters, where sex offenders can live or more specifically where they can and cannot go. Based on the idea that sex offending is a crime of opportunity and proximity to targets, laws have been designed to restrict access to parks, schools, daycares, sports arenas, libraries, churches, and other places where children congregate. Although the distance and specific restricted locations vary depending on the state or local jurisdiction, it is not unusual for the policy to suggest restrictions of 1,000 to 2,500 feet.

Without question, the state of Florida has a reputation for the extensive work it has done to implement residence restrictions for sex offenders. The Florida Department of Corrections reported that a total of 140 local ordinances had been enacted by 44 of the 67 counties in Florida and that 104 ordinances covering 22 percent of the total number of jurisdictions in the state made it illegal to live near bus stops.[47] As a result, the homeless population of offenders exploded. Between 2006 and 2010, the entire underside of the Julia Tuttle Causeway had become a relocation camp for approximately 1,000 sex offenders who could not find housing after they had been released from prison. One offender was issued a driver's license with his address listed as Julia Tuttle Causeway.[48] The city of Miami ended up suing the state of Florida in an effort to get some attention focused on relocating the offenders. The American Civil Liberties Union suggested the 2,500-foot restriction was too severe and housing options would expand for offenders if the restriction were lowered to 1,000 feet.

In March 2011, Lisa Ling aired an episode of *Our America* focused on sex offenders in Florida, highlighting the makeshift camps in the swampy unincorporated areas of the city that do not prohibit sex-offender housing.[49] Many offenders relocated to an area outside of Hialeah city limits, and reports suggest almost 300 people were living in tents and had the area listed as their legal residence, a requirement of probation. The group lives with no electricity and no running water or bathroom facilities and creates a difficult reality for the local stores where the residents go to use the bathroom facilities.[50] In spite of the fact that Florida has brought national attention to the issue of residence restrictions, other states also utilize the practice, although significant differences exist in the length of the boundary (from 500- to 2,500-foot restrictions) or the type of sex offender targeted (for example, the law may apply only to offenders who have victimized children).[51]

In spite of their popularity among the general public, research findings indicate little support for the idea that the behaviors of sex offenders are influenced by residence restriction or that they make the public more safe.[52] The multiple layers of restrictive ordinances (city, county, or state) make the study of impact of the practice difficult; however, more research is needed to assess the influence of community notification on public safety. Additional research themes have expanded to include focused attention on assessing the full impact of the unanticipated hardship, or collateral consequences, the policy is having on offenders working to move beyond their offense and reintegrate into the community. Further, court cases have overturned resident restrictions,[53] and cities are reconsidering policies in consultation with law enforcement officials who have a much more difficult time tracking offenders who have no home address and as studies suggesting homeless offenders are as much as four times more likely to commit a subsequent offense.[54] Perhaps, most importantly, the premise of the law was to prevent a child abduction or a sexual offense by a stranger, a fear that has been resoundingly challenged by researchers and public awareness educators who emphasize the fact that an estimated 93 percent of sexually driven crimes are committed by a family member or someone known to the victim. Therefore, any "stranger danger" directives used to inform these public policies and community practices are misplaced.[55]

Additional Options for Sex-Offender Management in the Community

State and local governments are allowed to implement more restrictive laws than the minimum guidelines established by the federal government, set out most recently by the Adam Walsh Act in 2006. States have also implemented programs or passed legislation directed at enhanced management of sex offenders. Five additional practices—civil commitment, lifetime supervision, driver's license notations, chemical castration, and electronic monitoring—are reviewed briefly.

Linked back to the 1990 state of Washington Community Protection Act, mentioned above, offenders who were thought to create a public threat were assessed at the end of their prison confinement, and a determination was made as to whether they remained a threat to the community and should be classified as a **sexually violent predator,** or similar term, and referred for civil commitment or an involuntary civil commitment or held indefinitely until their mental condition improved enough for them to be released into society. Although the characteristics of what constitutes a sexually violent predator vary from state to state, the state of Washington, for example, defines a *sexually violent person* to be any person:

- Who has been convicted of or charged with a crime of sexual violence; and
- Who suffers from a mental abnormality or personality disorder;

- Which makes the person likely to engage in predatory acts of sexual violence if not confined in a secure facility.[56]

The state of Minnesota uses the term *sexually dangerous person*, which has three elements to the definition:

- First, it must be demonstrated that the person has engaged in a course of "harmful sexual conduct" in the past. Sexual conduct is "harmful" if it creates a substantial likelihood of causing serious physical or emotional harm to another person. Certain crimes are presumed to cause such harm, unless proven otherwise in a particular case. For example, felony-level criminal sexual conduct crimes are presumed to qualify as "harmful sexual conduct." Additionally, a number of other violent crimes are presumed to be "harmful sexual conduct" when they are motivated by the person's sexual impulses or are part of a pattern of behavior that has criminal sexual conduct as its goal. These crimes include murder, manslaughter, felony-level assault, robbery, kidnapping, false imprisonment, incest, witness tampering, arson, first-degree burglary of a dwelling, terroristic threats, and felony-level harassment and stalking.
- Second, it must be shown that the person has manifested a sexual, personality, or other mental disorder or dysfunction.
- Third, it must be proven that, as a result of this mental disorder or dysfunction, the person is likely to engage in future acts of harmful sexual conduct.[57]

The civil commitment issue has been under serious legal review; however, the US Supreme Court has upheld the state's sexual predator laws as constitutional. See *Kansas v. Hendricks*, where an offender in Kansas was civilly committed after having served his prison sentence for assaulting a child. He challenged the commitment, and the Supreme Court upheld the Kansas sexual predator law as constitutional. The issue of civil commitment remains controversial with advocates on both sides, suggesting a range of legal and financial issues with the practice. In the state of Minnesota, a federal appeals court in January 2017 reversed the 2015 lower court ruling declaring the Minnesota Sex Offender (civil commitment) program unconstitutional because no one had been released from the program. The US Supreme Court refused to hear the case, leaving the Eighth Circuit's ruling to stand. The appellate court decision was then followed by the conclusions to a class action lawsuit on behalf of the program participants, initiated in 2011, and settled in fall of 2018 with the dismissal of the remaining petitioner's claims, requiring individuals to bring claims, rather than to bring them as a class.[58] The judge did speak out on several issues he argued were a shock to the court's conscience, emphasizing the continued confinement of the only woman in the program, the elderly, people with cognitive impairments, and those who had committed their offenses while they were juveniles. In 2019, the Minnesota Sex Offender program confined approximately 732 offenders who were determined to be a threat to the public and placed in the civil commitment at the end of their confinement.[59]

Additional processes were put in place to provide alternative sanctions for sex offenders, including **lifetime supervision,** to address repeat offending and require high-risk offenders to be monitored within the community for the rest of their lives.[60] Several states have required offenders to display a notation identifying their registration status on their driver's license in an effort to help improve compliance.[61] Some states have experimented with **chemical castration** (discussed in more detail in chapter 12), where eligible offenders can choose to be injected with a synthetic hormone in an effort to reduce sexual arousal. Finally, states are also incorporating electronic GPS monitoring devices in addition to the traditional community release protocols. The protocol also varies from state to state, with Florida requiring convicted child sexual abusers to wear a GPS device for the rest of their lives.[62]

The wide scope of the Adam Walsh Act revised the elements of registration and community notification introduced by the Wetterling Act (1994) and Megan's Law (1996) to outline expanded regulations for sex-offender oversight. Tensions exist; however, while questions are being raised about the efficacy of these practices, elements are being extended to other crimes, for example, drug crimes, expanding the application and use of the registration and notification processes. In total, the structure and content of efforts to legislate sex-offender behavior and community protections are difficult to evaluate, leaving the implications and the effectiveness of the legislation uncertain. The variation of laws and application in different states makes it difficult to pull out the full effects any given policy makes, and analysis is ongoing. Individuals in the community are not following the policy and research debates about how well programs are working and continue to focus on the stranger sex offender, rather than the social reality that most people will know their offender. This reality alone might significantly influence future laws seeking to address sex-offender behavior, victim support, and community criminal justice system responses.

CHAPTER CONCLUSION

Early efforts to provide a legal framework for preventing sexual violence and harms and redress when a harm happens started in approximately the mid-1990s and are more recently being challenged. Some of those challenges are coming to the larger conversation in different ways from different states. Other challenges are coming from larger conversations involving police, attorneys, or other law enforcement professionals raising specific questions about enforcement at either the early stages or after release from prison. Other legal challenges come directly from individuals affected. Treatment practitioners working with offenders in prison and after their sentence has been served are raising issues brought out by families and offenders frustrated with the number of obstacles offenders must face while working to comply with the laws that sometimes have unanticipated consequences or create circumstances that too easily register as a violation of their community release and put them back in prison.

Text Box 10.1.   Media Messages about Legislation

Research has suggested that many of the laws put in place to protect children and other victims of sexual violence are not having the positive intended effect policy makers were hoping for when those laws were designed and implemented. Consider the primary elements of the laws presented in chapter 10. One of the realities policy makers confront is the fear and panic related to sex offenders and the possibility of sex offenses happening to people they love and care about. When people are afraid and policy makers respond by making laws in a climate of fear, history has shown us that the intended outcomes are not fully achieved. In some cases, the effort completely fails. Consider the nature of formal laws and informal community "policing." Could you design a kind of public service announcement that might help your community better meet the objectives policy makers intended for the communities they represent? What community groups would you talk to with your message?

The heterogeneous nature of sexual offending is mentioned several times throughout the text. As laws are crafted, they are structured to treat all offenders the same or similarly. What other ideas might inform an effort to create a legal response that considers a small percentage of offenders are strangers? Does the stranger offender warrant different treatment under the law? A larger percentage of offenders are known to the victim. Does a known offender who is family warrant a different legal response than someone who is a neighbor, a teacher, or a babysitter? If the known offender is family, does the relationship of the offender, whether they are parent or partner, warrant a different legal response?

More broadly, the public attitude about sex offenders and the related classification as a sexually violent person is seen by many as extremely punitive, calling for locking all sex offenders up or placing them under lifetime supervision in the community. The subject is in an awkward transition between what is currently in place, what communities want to see changed, and what is a balanced approach to provide public safety and manage the related costs and larger implications of such a broad policy. Further, efforts to meet offenders' needs can fly in the face of the needs victims identify, which are argued by victim service providers and families of victims to easily get lost in the focus on a criminal response and focus on the offender. Although efforts to prevent harms are actively engaged, questions about how to connect with the larger number of offenders who are not reported or do not get prosecuted through the criminal justice system raise questions about the existing legal and social processes currently in place for responding to sexual violence and related harms.

KEY TERMS

AMBER Alert
Ashcroft v. Free Speech Coalition
Campus Sex Crimes Prevention Act

chemical castration
civil commitment
Coker v. Georgia

collateral consequences
Combined DNA Index System
  (CODIS)
community notification
Community Protection Act
deinstitutionalization
Gundy v. United States
Kansas v. Hendricks
legacy laws
lifetime supervision
Mann Act of 1910
marital exception
Megan's Law
Miranda rights
miscegenation

New York v. Ferber
offender registration
Office of Sex Offender Sentencing,
  Monitoring, Apprehension,
  Registering, and Tracking
  (SMART)
Patty Wetterling
rape shield laws
residence restrictions
Romeo and Juliet provisions
sex-offender recidivism
sexually violent predator
three-tiered system
Violent Crime Control and Law
  Enforcement Act

REVIEW QUESTIONS

1. The legislation presented for consideration here is largely applicable at the federal level. What aspects of these federal laws do you see in your community?

2. States are required to post information about former offenders in a registration process. Where are the local resources for the public information posted about sex offenders? What, if any, additional offenses trigger registration in your state?

3. The Violence Against Women Act (VAWA) was in limbo as this book was going to press. What is the current status of that legislation? If the legislation has been passed, what additions or concessions were made in the most recent iteration of that law?

4. Which law from the state of Washington created a process that would later be implemented in other states or at the federal level?

5. Which 2006 law updated the 1994 Jacob Wetterling Act and the 1996 Megan's Law?

DISCUSSION QUESTIONS

1. Critical questions have been raised about the efficacy of sex-offender legislation and its impact on offenders and in the community. Given that research is increasingly moving in that direction, what process makes the most sense for moving forward when there is not a consensus on what actions to take?

2. Be prepared to consider how federal initiatives and local attitudes might clash. What social practices might assist efforts to prevent violence or even make legal measures unnecessary with the exception of for those most violent incidents?

3. How would you best describe the attitudes about sex offenders, sex-offender release, and sex-offender reintegration as it is reflected in your home community?

4. Research suggests that most people do not access the vast information available to learn about the sex offenders living in their community. Does this support or discredit the efforts to collect information on sex offenders? What are the benefits for keeping the information up to date and available to the public? Downsides?

5. One of the issues raised with regard to the decision about age of the victim is also the age of the offender. Can a person be a victim and an offender? If a young person, aged 10 or 12, initiated sex with another person who is older, say 14, but is still below the legal age of consent, who would be the "victim" and who would be the "offender"? How does this example fall outside the scope of what sex-offender legislation was intended to do? Does the Romeo and Juliet exception provide an appropriate remedy? Why or why not?

NOTES

1. Michael H. Miner, "Editorial: Is This Any Way to Develop Policy?" *Sex Offender Treatment* 2, no. 1 (2007), http://www.sexual-offender-treatment.org/54.html.

2. "Community Management of Convicted Sex Offenders: Registration, Electronic Monitoring, Civil Commitment, Mandatory Minimums, and Residency Restrictions," accessed March 2, 2013, https://vawnet.org/sites/default/files/assets/files/2016-09/CommunityManagement.pdf.

3. G. Duwe and W. Donnay, "The Impact of Megan's Law on Sex Offender Recidivism: The Minnesota Experience," *Criminology* 46, no. 2 (2008): 411–46, https://doi.org/10.1111/j.1745-9125.2008.00114.x; L. Sample and T. Bray, "Are Sex Offenders Dangerous?," *Criminology and Public Policy* 3, no. 1 (2003): 59–82, doi:10.1111/j.1745-9133.2003.tb00024.x; R. Zevitz, "Sex Offender Community Notification: Its Role in Recidivism and Offender Reintegration," *Criminal Justice Studies* 19, no. 2 (2006): 193–208, https://doi.org/10.1080/14786010600764567.

4. T. Doyle, A. W. R. Sipe, and P. Wall, *Sex, Priests, and Secret Codes: The Catholic Church's 2000 Year Paper Trail of Sexual Abuse* (Taylor Trade Publishing, 2006); Deborah W. Denno, "Life before the Modern Sex Offender Statutes," *Northwestern University Law Review* 92, no. 4 (1998), http://heinonline.org/HOL/LandingPage?collection=journals&handle=hein.journals/illlr92&div=41&id=&page=.

5. See, for example, L. Sample and C. Kadleck, "Sex Offender Laws: Legislators' Accounts of the Need for Policy," *Criminal Justice Policy Review* 19, no. 1 (2008): 40–62, https://doi.org/10.1177/0887403407308292; M. Petrunik, "Managing Unacceptable Risk: Sex Offenders, Community Response, and Social Policy in the United States and Canada," *International Journal of Offender Therapy and Comparative Criminology* 46, no. 4 (2002): 483–511, https://doi.org/10.1177/0306624X02464009.

6. "California Sex Offender Registry," State of California Department of Justice, accessed September 20, 2019, https://oag.ca.gov/sex-offender-reg.

7. Donna D. Schram and Cheryl Darling Milloy, "Community Notification: A Study of Offender Characteristics," Washington State Institute for Public Policy, October 1995, 2, http://www.wsipp.wa.gov/ReportFile/1208/Wsipp_Community-Notification-A-Study-of-Offender-Characteristics-and-Recidivism_Full-Report.pdf; see also Norm Maleng, "The Community Protection Act and the Sexually Violent Predator Statute," *University of Puget Sound*

Law Review 15, no. 821 (1992): 821–26, https://digitalcommons.law.seattleu.edu/cgi/view content.cgi?article=1366&context=sulr.

8. Wesley Allan Dodd is the perpetrator in the first case, and Earl Shriner is the offender in the second case.

9. "A Summary of Recent Findings from the Community Protection Research Project," Washington State Institute for Public Policy, February 1994, accessed September 20, 2019, https://www.ncjrs.gov/pdffiles1/Digitization/156450NCJRS.pdf.

10. Julie A. Allison and Lawrence S. Wrightsman, *Rape: The Misunderstood Crime* (London: Sage Publications, 1993).

11. Ibid.; C. C. Spohn, "The Rape Reform Movement: The Traditional Common Law and Rape Law Reforms," *Jurimetrics* 39, no. 2 (1999): 119–30.

12. Mary Ann Largen, "Rape-Law Reform: An Analysis," in *Rape and Sexual Assault II*, ed. Ann Wolbert Burgess (New York: Garland Publishing, 1988), 272.

13. Allison and Wrightsman, *Rape: The Misunderstood Crime*.

14. Keri B. Burchfield, "Residence Restrictions," *Criminology & Public Policy* 10, no. 2 (2011): 411–19, https://doi.org/10.1111/j.1745-9133.2011.00716.x; J. S. Levenson and K. M. Zgoba, "Sex Offender Residence Restrictions: The Law of Unintended Consequences," in *Sex Offender Laws: Failed Policies, New Directions*, ed. R. G. Wright, 180–89 (New York: Springer Publishing Company, 2015).

15. SMART Office, "Sex Offender Registration and Notification in the United States: Current Case Law and Issues," Smart.gov, March 2019, accessed October 20, 2019, https://www.smart.gov/caselaw/6-Other-Constitutional-Issues.pdf; Karen J. Terry, "What Is Smart Sex Offender Policy?" *Criminology & Public Policy* 10, no. 2 (2011): 275–82, https://doi.org/10.1111/j.1745-9133.2011.00707.x; Lisa L. Sample and Colleen Kadleck, "Sex Offender Laws: Legislators' Accounts of the Need for Policy," 19, no. 1 (2008): 40–62, https://doi.org/10.1177/0887403407308292.

16. R. Shepard, "Does the Punishment Fit the Crime?: Applying Eighth Amendment Proportionality Analysis to Georgia's Sex Offender Registration Statute and Residency and Employment Restrictions for Juvenile Offenders," *Georgia State University Law Review* 28, no. 2 (2012), Art. 7, accessed October 20, 2019, https://readingroom.law.gsu.edu/.

17. "Report: Missouri's Tough Stance Sending Sex Offenders to Surrounding States," News Channel 3, May 14, 2018, accessed September 20, 2019, https://wreg.com/2018/05/14/report -missouris-tough-stance-sending-sex-offenders-to-surrounding-states/.

18. P. Jenkins, *Moral Panic: Changing Concepts of the Child Molester in Modern America* (Yale University Press, 1998); L. Zilney and L. Zilney, *Perverts and Predators: The Making of Sex Offender Laws* (Rowman & Littlefield, 2009); L. Zilney and L. Zilney, *Reconsidering Sex Crimes and Offenders: Prosecution or Persecution?* (ABC-CLIO, 2009); E. Janus, *Failure to Protect: America's Sexual Predator and the Rise of the Preventive State* (Cornell University Press, 2006).

19. Doyle, Sipe, and Wall, *Sex, Priests, and Secret Codes*.

20. C. Leon, *Sex Fiends, Perverts, and Pedophiles: Understanding Sex Crime Policy in America* (New York University Press, 2011); P. Jenkins, *Moral Panic: Changing Concepts of the Child Molester in Modern America* (Yale University Press, 1998).

21. Zilney and Zilney, *Perverts and Predators*; D. Denno, "Life before the Modern Sex Offender Statutes," *Northwest University Law Review* 92, no. 1317 (1998), accessed October 20, 2019, https://ir.lawnet.fordham.edu/faculty_scholarship/113/.

22. E. Durkheim, "The Sexual Psychopath Laws," *Journal of Criminal Law and Criminology* 40, no. 5 (1950): 543–54, https://scholarlycommons.law.northwestern.edu/cgi/viewcon tent.cgi?article=3714&context=jclc.

23. R. Wright, *Sex Offender Laws: Failed Policies, New Directions* (Springer Publishing Company, 2015); C. Ewing, *Justice Perverted: Sex Offense Law, Psychology and Public Policy* (Oxford University Press, 2011).

24. "Fact Sheet PROTECT Act," Department of Justice, April 30, 2003, accessed September 20, 2019, http://www.justice.gov/opa/pr/2003/April/03_ag_266.htm.

25. Barbara K. Schwartz, ed., "Handbook of Sex Offender Treatment," Civic Research Institute, 2011, accessed September 20, 2019, https://civicresearchinstitute.com/toc/HSOT TOC.pdf.

26. "About SMART," Office of Justice Programs, US Department of Justice, accessed September 20, 2019, http://www.ojp.usdoj.gov/smart/about.htm.

27. "No Easy Answers: Sex Offender Laws in the US," Human Rights Watch, 19, no. 4(G) (2007), accessed September 20, 2019, https://www.hrw.org/sites/default/files/reports/us 0907webwcover.pdf.

28. Ibid., 3.

29. See, for example, National Association for Rational Sexual Offense Laws, reformsex offenderlaws.org.

30. Christina Mancini, *Sex Crime, Offenders, and Society* (Durham, NC: Carolina Academic Press, 2014), 213.

31. Kristen M. Zgoba, "Spin Doctors and Moral Crusaders: The Moral Panic behind Child Safety Legislation," *Criminal Justice Studies* 17, no. 4 (2004): 385–404.

32. Mancini, *Sex Crime, Offenders, and Society*, 229.

33. See, for example, laws outlined in Human Rights Watch, "No Easy Answers: Sex Offender Laws in the US," September 11, 2007, accessed October 20, 2019, https://www.hrw .org/report/2007/09/11/no-easy-answers/sex-offender-laws-us.

34. Mancini, *Sex Crime, Offenders, and Society*, 214.

35. Karen J. Terry, "What Is Smart Sex Offender Policy?" *Criminology & Public Policy* 10, no. 2 (2011): 275–82.

36. "About SMART."

37. Jill S. Levenson, David A. D'Amora, and Andrea L. Hern, "Megan's Law and Its Impact on Community Re-Entry for Sex Offenders," *Behavioral Sciences & the Law* 25, no. 4 (2007): 587–602, https://doi.org/10.1002/bsl.770.

38. Lauren N. Williams, "Kids on the Sex-Offender Registry: A *Marie Claire* Survey," *Marie Claire*, August 26, 2011, accessed September 20, 2019, http://www.marieclaire.com/ world-reports/news/teens-on-sex-offender-registry.

39. See Abigail Pesta, "The Accidental Sex Offender," *Marie Claire*, July 28, 2011, accessed September 20, 2019, https://www.marieclaire.com/culture/news/a6294/teen-sex-offender/.

40. "Raised on the Registry: The Irreparable Harm of Placing Children on Sex Offender Registries in the US," Human Rights Watch, May 2013, accessed September 20, 2019, https:// www.hrw.org/sites/default/files/reports/us0513_ForUpload_1.pdf; "US: More Harm Than Good," Human Rights Watch, May 1, 2013, accessed September 20, 2019, https://www.hrw .org/news/2013/05/01/us-more-harm-good; A. Agan, "Sex Offender Registries: Fear without Function?," *Journal of Law & Economics* 54, no. 1 (2011): 207–39, https://www.jstor.org/ stable/10.1086/658483?seq=1#metadata_info_tab_contents; S. Rozek, "The Sex Offender Registry: It's Not What You Think," *Criminal Legal News*, May 2018, 12, accessed October 20, 2019, https://www.criminallegalnews.org/news/2018/apr/19/sex-offender-registry-its-not -what-you-think/.

41. D. Lind, "Why the Sex Offender Registry Isn't the Right Way to Punish Rapists," Vox. com, July 5, 2016, accessed October 20, 2019, https://www.vox.com/2016/7/5/11883784/ sex-offender-registry.

42. B. E. Vásquez, S. Maddan, and J. T. Walker, "The Influence of Sex Offender Registration and Notification Laws in the United States: A Time-Series Analysis," *Crime and Delinquency* 54 (2008): 179–92.

43. Scott Matson and Roxanne Lieb, "Sex Offender Registration: A Review of State Laws," Washington State Institute for Public Policy, July 1996, September 20, 2019, https://www

.wsipp.wa.gov/ReportFile/1227/Wsipp_Sex-Offender-Registration-A-Review-of-State-Laws_ Full-Report.pdf.

44. Mancini, *Sex Crime, Offenders, and Society*; Karen J. Terry, *Sexual Offenses and Offenders: Theory, Practice and Policy* (Belmont, CA: Wadsworth Cengage Learning, 2006).

45. Rachel Bandy, "Measuring the Impact of Sex Offender Notification on Community Adoption of Protective Behaviors," *Criminology & Public Policy* 10, no. 2 (2011): 237–63, http://www.atsa.com/sites/default/files/LibraryArticles/Impact%20of%20notification.pdf ?origin=publication_detail.

46. Grant Duwe and William Donnay, "The Impact of Megan's Law on Sex Offender Recidivism: The Minnesota Experience," *Criminology* 46, no. 2 (2008): 411–46, https://doi .org/10.1111/j.1745-9125.2008.00114.x.

47. Jill S. Levenson et al., "Transient Sex Offenders and Residence Restrictions in Florida," July 2013, accessed September 20, 2019, https://floridaactioncommittee.org/pdf/SORR%20 and%20Transients%20in%20Florida%202013.pdf.

48. Greg Allen, "Bridge Still Home for Miami Sex Offenders," NPR, July 21, 2009, accessed September 20, 2019, https://www.npr.org/templates/story/story.php?storyId=1066 89642&ft=1&f=1001.

49. "State of Sex Offenders," *Our America with Lisa Ling*, March 1, 2011, accessed September 20, 2019, https://www.tvguide.com/tvshows/our-america-with-lisa-ling/episode-3-sea son-1/state-of-sex-offenders/309462/.

50. Douglas Hanks, "Tent Camp of Homeless Sex Offenders Near Hialeah 'Has Got to Close,' County Says," *Miami Herald*, August 23, 2017, accessed September 20, 2019, https:// www.miamiherald.com/news/local/community/miami-dade/article168569977.html.

51. Mancini, *Sex Crime, Offenders, and Society*, 232.

52. Phyllis Blood and Paul Stageberg, "State Legislation Monitoring Report: FY2008," Iowa Department of Human Rights, Division of Criminal and Juvenile Justice Planning, February 2009, accessed September 20, 2019, https://humanrights.iowa.gov/sites/default/ files/media/Monitoring%20Report%20FY2008.pdf; Grant Duwe, William Donnay, and Richard Tewksbury, "Does Residential Proximity Matter?: A Geographic Analysis of Sex Offense Recidivism," *Criminal Justice and Behavior* 35, no. 4 (2008): 484–504, https:// doi.org/10.1177/0093854807313690; Jill S. Levenson et al., "Public Perceptions about Sex Offenders and Community Protection Policies," *Analyses of Social Issues and Public Policy* 7, no. 1 (2007): 1–25, https://www.innovations.harvard.edu/sites/default/files/105361.pdf.

53. Lorelei Laird, "Courts Are Reconsidering Residency Restrictions for Sex Offenders," *ABA Journal*, July 1, 2015, accessed September 20, 2019, http://www.abajournal.com/maga zine/article/courts_are_reconsidering_residency_restrictions_for_sex_offenders.

54. S. Yoder, "New Evidence Says US Sex-Offender Policies Are Actually Causing More Crime," Quartz, December 21, 2016, accessed October 20, 2019, https://qz.com/869499/ new-evidence-says-us-sex-offender-policies-dont-work-and-are-are-actually-causing-more -crime/; S. Lee, A. Restrepo, A. Satariano, and R. Karl Hanson, "The Predictive Validity of Static-99R for Sexual Offenders in California: 2016 Update," July 13, 2016, accessed Octo- ber 20, 2019, http://www.saratso.org/docs/ThePredictiveValidity_of_Static-99R_forSexual Offenders_inCalifornia-2016v1.pdf.

55. Howard N. Snyder, "Sexual Assault of Young Children as Reported to Law Enforce- ment: Victim, Incident, and Offender Characteristics," US Dept. of Justice, July 2000, accessed December 3, 2009, http://www.ojp.usdoj.gov/bjs/pub/pdf/saycrle.pdf; Kelly K. Bonnar-Kidd, "Sexual Offender Laws and Prevention of Sexual Violence or Recidivism," *American Journal of Public Health* 100, no. 3 (2010): 412–19, doi:10.2105/AJPH.2008.153254.

56. "Sexually Violent Predators: Protecting Children and Families from Sexually Violent Predators," Washington State, accessed September 20, 2019, https://www.atg.wa.gov/sexu ally-violent-predators.

57. Jeffrey Diebel, "Sex Offenders and Predatory Offenders: Minnesota Criminal and Civil Regulatory Laws," Research Department Minnesota House of Representatives, January 2012, accessed September 20, 2019, https://www.house.leg.state.mn.us/hrd/pubs/sexofdr.pdf.

58. "Protracted Minnesota Sex Offender Program Suit Comes to End," *MPR News*, August 23, 2018, accessed September 20, 2019, https://www.mprnews.org/story/2018/08/23/long -running-minnesota-sex-offender-case-comes-to-end.

59. "Minnesota Sex Offender Program Statistics," Minnesota Department of Human Services, accessed October 20, 2019, https://mn.gov/dhs/people-we-serve/adults/services/sex -offender-treatment/statistics.jsp.

60. Marcus Nieto, "Community Treatment and Supervision of Sex Offenders: How It's Done across the Country and in California," Sacramento, CA: California Research Bureau, 2004.

61. Bonnar-Kidd, "Sexual Offender Laws and Prevention of Sexual Violence or Recidivism."

62. Kathy G. Padgett, William D. Bales, and Thomas G. Blomberg, "Under Surveillance: An Empirical Test of the Effectiveness and Consequences of Electronic Monitoring," *Criminology & Public Policy* 5, no. 1 (2006): 61–91, https://doi.org/10.1111/j.1745-9133.2006.00102.x.

11

The Criminal Justice System Response

Policing and Prosecuting Sexual Harm

When crimes are not reported to the police, victims may not be able to obtain necessary services to cope with the victimization, offenders may go unpunished, and law enforcement and community resources may be misallocated due to a lack of accurate information about local crime problems.

—National Crime Victimization Survey, August 2012[1]

The police response to sexual assault has been an issue for as long as I've been in law enforcement, and that's been more than 40 years. This is an issue that police shouldn't try to handle on their own. We need to work with courts, victims' advocates, crime prevention groups, and others to ensure that we treat rape victims with compassion, and to ensure that our processes are transparent. These partnerships strengthen every part of the process, from reporting every case and doing thorough investigations to helping reduce the trauma of victims.

—Philadelphia Police Commissioner Charles Ramsey, 2011[2]

My first lesson about sex crime prosecution was that perpetrators were not the only enemy. There is a large, more or less hidden population of what I later came to call "collaborators" in the criminal justice system. Whether it comes from a police officer or a defense attorney, a judge or a court clerk or a prosecutor, there seems to be a residuum of empathy for rapists that cross all gender, class, and professional barriers. It gets expressed in different ways, from victim-bashing to jokes in poor taste, and too often it results in giving the rapist a break.

—Alice Vachss, author and former chief of the
Queens, New York Special Victims Unit[3]

AS THE UNITED STATES began the transition into a new millennium, several indicators focused attention on sexual assault, arguably one of the most unreported or underreported of crimes. More specifically, efforts began to extend into sexual violence prevention. Using 1990 crime data from each of the 50 states, in 1993 the Senate Judiciary, under the direction of then Senator Joe Biden, released *Violence Against Women: The Response to Rape: Detours on the Road to Equal Justice*. The introduction to the report stated what many had suspected for some time:

> These findings reveal a justice system that fails by any standard to meet its goals—apprehending, convicting, and incarcerating violent criminals: 98% of the victims of rape never see their attacker caught, tried, or imprisoned.[4]

In 1999, the National Center for Policy Analysis reported arrests made in only 50 percent of the sexual assault cases reported, with only 16.3 percent of those arrested going to prison.[5] In 2002, research estimated that "between 64% and 96% of all rapes are never reported to criminal justice authorities and only a small minority of reported cases, especially nonstranger assaults, ever result in the successful prosecution of the offender."[6] In 2004, the General Social Survey reported that only 37 percent of women and 17 percent of men chose to involve the police in sexual assault claims.[7] Considering the fact that as many as 80 to 97 percent of victims of sexual assault know their attacker, if the goal is to identify, treat, and/or punish people who commit sexual assault, our system is falling short of that goal.

In September 2010, the Senate Committee on the Judiciary held hearings in response to concerns raised by the Women's Law Project, a local advocacy group focused on police mishandling of sexual assault cases.[8] The Women's Law Project, after reading an investigative report in the *Philadelphia Inquirer*, realized that there was a long-standing police practice to reduce sex crime to noncriminal classifications, to intentionally significantly reduce, if not eliminate, the legal requirement to further investigate sexual assault cases.[9] In fact, the Women's Law Project brought the issue to Congress citing the "chronic failure to report and investigate rape cases." A brief clip of Director Susan B. Carbon's comments is presented in Text Box 11.1.

The story of the police practice came to light after a young woman, Shannon Schieber, was murdered in the same neighborhood where similar attacks had happened but whose cases had been reduced to the noncriminal classification. Consider the testimony of Women's Law Project Executive Director Carol E. Tracy in the Text Box 11.2.

After reviewing the events brought to the Women's Law Project by people in communities throughout the United States, and before moving on to address specific issues about the damage rape myths can have on police officer attitudes and the limitations of the police reporting system, Tracy continued her remarks:

> Initially I thought the reports of egregious police conduct were isolated incidents. However, viewing the totality of the news accounts, it is clear that we are seeing chronic and systemic patterns of police refusing to accept cases for investigation, misclassifying cases to non-criminal categories so that investigations do not occur, and "unfounding" complaints by determining that women are lying about being sexually assaulted. They also show a shocking disregard and callous

Text Box 11.1.   2010 Meeting of the Committee on the Judiciary

Director Susan B. Carbon

U.S. SENATE, SUBCOMMITTEE ON CRIME AND DRUGS,
COMMITTEE ON THE JUDICIARY, WASHINGTON, DC.

The Subcommittee met, pursuant to notice, at 2:25 p.m., in room SD–226, Dirksen Senate Office Building, Hon. Arlen Specter, Chairman of the Subcommittee, presiding.

Present: Senators Specter, Cardin, and Klobuchar. Also Present: Senator Franken.

Rape in the United States the chronic FAILURE TO REPORT AND INVESTIGATE RAPE CASES TUESDAY, SEPTEMBER 14, 2010

OPENING STATEMENT OF HON. ARLEN SPECTER, A U.S. SENATOR FROM THE STATE OF PENNSYLVANIA

Chairman SPECTER. Good afternoon, ladies and gentlemen. The Criminal Law Subcommittee will now proceed with the hearing on the subject of rape.

This hearing has been requested by the Women's Law Project following an extensive series of articles by newspapers in many leading United States cities commenting about the inaccuracies on reports of rape, raising serious questions as to whether there are adequate steps being taken by police departments to catalogue the complaints, to investigate them, and to make the determination when rape, in fact, occurred. The statistics are staggering. Over 20 million women, or 18 percent of all women in the United States, have been victims of rape, and each year approximately 1,100,000 more women are victims of rape. The statistics show that 28 percent of the forcible rapes have victims under the age of 12, and 27 percent of forcible rape victims are in the ages of 12 to 17. Reportedly, only 18 percent of forcible rapes are reported to the police. . . .

Director of the Department of Justice's Office on Violence Against Women. In this role, she serves as liaison between the Department and Federal and State governments on crimes of domestic violence, sexual assault, dating violence, and stalking.

Director Susan B. Carbon

. . .

In my testimony today, I hope to provide a broader context for the scope of sexual assault and our collective responses to it. First, it is difficult to quantify the crime. Studies use different definitions of rape and different data collection methods. Some include only forcible rape or only rape that is reported to law enforcement. Our terminology is confusing as well. Sometimes we talk about rape, sometimes sexual assault, other times sexual violence. That being said, researchers estimate that about 18 percent of women in the United States report having been raped at some point in their lives.

For some populations, rapes or sexual violence are even higher. Nearly one in three—and I repeat, nearly one in three—American Indian or Alaska Native women will be sexually assaulted in her lifetime.

Sexual assault is also one of the most underreported crimes in America. The Bureau of Justice Statistics reports that the majority of rapes and sexual assaults of women and girls between 1992 and 2000 were not reported to law enforcement. Reasons for not reporting included fear of not being believed, a lack of trust in the criminal justice system, fear of retaliation or embarrassment, being too traumatized to report, or self-blame and guilt. Second, there are dramatic differences in the way that police departments, prosecutors' offices, and even courts respond to this crime across the country. Some communities have highly trained, coordinated teams of primary and secondary responders from health, law enforcement, legal, and victims services sectors. However, as you are going to be hearing from subsequent panels this afternoon, in other places victims are subjected to humiliating interrogations and are treated with suspicion by law enforcement. Collected evidence may sit for months or even years without being analyzed. In some areas of the country, there simply are no services.

Text Box 11.2.   2010 Meeting of the Committee on the Judiciary

WLP Executive Director, Carol E. Tracy Testimony

Because of the role the Women's Law Project played in Philadelphia, I have been contacted by journalists from the *St. Louis Post Dispatch*, the *New Orleans Times Picayune*, the *Baltimore Sun*, and the *New York Times*, who have reported similar problems in their cities. I have also discussed this issue with reporters from the *Cleveland Plain Dealer*, the *Journal Sentinel in Milwaukee*, and the *Village Voice*, who have also reported on this problem. Questions are being raised across the United States about sex crime data reported to the FBI:

- *The Baltimore Sun* reported that, since 1992, the number of Baltimore rape cases reported to the FBI has declined by 80% and, since 1991, the percentage of unfounded rape cases has tripled. From 2003 through 2010, police wrote reports for only 4 in 10 rape calls, signifying that patrol officers were rejecting cases prior to investigation.
- *The St. Louis Post-Dispatch*, reported that many St. Louis rape complaints were written up in informal memos, not counted in crime statistics, and then filed away for 1-2 years before being shredded, often before the statute of limitations had run out. The city's official rape tally declined during the 20 year period that the "memo" system was in place.
- *The Times-Picayune* reported that more than half of the reports of rape in New Orleans are put in a noncriminal category, raising questions about the accuracy of the department's recent rape statistics showing a sharp decrease by 37%.
- *The New York Times* reported that the number of rapes in New York City declined by 35.7% between 2005 and 2009. Yet since 2005, the number of sex crimes classified as misdemeanors rose 6%, and there was a dramatic increase in the rate at which forcible rape complaints have been "unfounded."
- *The Baltimore Sun* and *The Times-Picayune*, reported more homicides than rapes in Baltimore and New Orleans in 2009.

The translation of this data to real life presents horrifying events:

- *The Cleveland Plain Dealer* reported that a Cleveland victim was found to be "not credible" after she filed a complaint that she had been sexually assaulted by Anthony Sowell, a man who had spent 15 years in prison for a 1989 rape and registered as a sex offender upon his release from prison. Her complaint was unfounded even though she was bleeding when she flagged down a police cruiser and provided the police with detailed information about the assailant and the location of the assault, and the police took her to a hospital where she received stitches and found blood and signs of a struggle at Sowell's home. Police eventually found the remains of 11 women at Sowell's home, six of whom were murdered after police failed to pursue the complaints of this and one other woman.

- **The Journal Sentinel in Milwaukee** reported that the apprehension of a serial rapist, Gregory Tyson Below, prompted Milwaukee police to look into previously received complaints by three women who had been victimized by him and claimed they were not assisted by police when they reported the assaults. One woman was kidnapped from a nightclub and sexually assaulted over a period of several hours; she said she went to three different Milwaukee police stations to report the attack but gave up because officials kept telling her to go to a different station. Police arrived in the middle of the assault against the second woman, who was naked from the waist down, bruised and screaming for help; one of the officers asked her if the incident was a "dope date," as he had discovered a drug charge against the woman and did not believe her. No arrest was made in either case. The serial rapist re-offended after these reports were ignored and was eventually apprehended only after raping more women.
- **The Baltimore Sun** reported that a woman who had been raped at gunpoint and treated at a hospital for vaginal bleeding retracted her statement because of the intimidating and accusatory questioning she was subjected to by the police: "Why had she waited two hours to call police? Why didn't she flag down a squad car? Where was she coming from before she was assaulted? Who was she with?"
- **The Village Voice** reported that a woman was pushed into the woods by an unknown assailant, physically overpowered and held down while the perpetrator told her he wanted to have sex with her and masturbated against her. She was told by police officers, who had consulted with the Special Victims Unit, that the crime was a misdemeanor, "forcible touching," while she protested it was a felony, attempted rape. She was ignored.

indifference to victims who are interrogated as though they are criminals, are presumptively disbelieved, are threatened with lie detector tests and/or arrest, and are blamed for the outrageous conduct of perpetrators.

We believe this is a national crisis and that the factors contributing to it can be addressed through federal action. There is no question that sexual stereotypes and bias are a root cause of police mishandling of sex crimes. Less visible but no less responsible is the manner in which the FBI's UCR system defines, analyzes, and publicizes the incidence of sex crimes. The combination of bias and an unrealistic definition result in highly unreliable data on the incidence of sex crime in America.[10]

Largely in response to the issues raised in these congressional hearings, national efforts have been put in place to study law enforcement agencies and help improve their handling of sexual assault cases. The combined efforts of the Office on Violence Against Women and the **Police Executive Research Forum (PERF)** are presented below in more detail. The numbers of serious violent crimes not reported to police suggest that rape and sexual assault have been among the highest, at 63 percent (in 2010).[11] Reports documented from 1993 through 2017 suggest the rate of violent victimization reported to police declined

73 percent.[12] The 2017 victim reports suggest an increase in reporting of rapes or sexual assaults to police from 23 percent in 2016 to 40 percent in 2017,[13] suggesting some positive changes have resulted.

In December 2018, however, a strikingly similar story began to emerge. The *Minneapolis Star Tribune* concluded a nine-part series, beginning in July of that year, titled *Denied Justice*, which focused on how Minnesota's criminal justice system often fails victims of rape and sexual assault. Centered on the investigation and prosecution of sexual assault cases in the state of Minnesota, the history is troubling. Then state Attorney General Lori Swanson convened a sexual assault task force to examine the "failings in Minnesota sex crime investigations."[14] The task force comprised law officers, public health officials, and victim advocates with the goal of recommending reforms to the legislature. The attorney general gave the group a broad mandate "from reworking sex crime statutes, to proposing more funding for officers and training, to issuing best practices for police investigations."[15] Is this an echo of past criminal justice system bad practice, either slow to change or reflective of little to no change, or is the Minnesota case an additional marker of broader police efforts to usher in necessary changes to advance police response to sexual assault?

For those impacted by sexual assaults or working within the system, some of the changes in processing sexual assaults presented below and the exploration of statistics reflecting some changes in reporting numbers could be seen as an indication that the tide is changing and some of the concerns expressed are having a positive impact on the experiences of victims throughout the criminal justice system. Yet combined with the national information presented as "a national crisis" to Congress less than 10 years ago, Minnesota could simply become one more state in a long line of state departments of public safety called on to make an accounting to sexual assault victims after an extensive media investigation invited sharp focus.

The need to revise existing systems so they work better for victims was identified as the broad goal for the task force in the state of Minnesota, as it was in a 2012 national collaboration with the emerging national initiatives focused on improving police processes. Yet decades of long-standing mistrust of the criminal justice system's response to people who have experienced sexual violence has been identified as pervasive and documented at all phases of the justice system and in local, state, and federal levels of policing and prosecution.[16] The term **second rape**, coined in a 1991 book by the same title, and also described as a **secondary victimization**, refers to the long series of interrogations required of rape victims who report their assault, a process that can exacerbate the victim's initial trauma and make the experience seem "not worth it."[17]

A brief review of the criminal justice system in its entirety is presented for reflection and consideration as a starting point. A more detailed assessment of both the role of police and prosecution efforts in the cases of sexually motivated or gender-bias crimes follows and begins with police. The themes of police procedures and court processes and the interactions between police and prosecutors in making decisions about whether to take the case before trial are discussed with decisions about how convictions and punishments will be decided. (Punishment and treatment options for those convicted will be discussed in more detail in chapters 12 and 13. The role of advocates in the entire process will be discussed in chapter 14.)

The decisions police and prosecutors are confronted with are linked not only to the way the laws are written but also to how those laws are interpreted, enforced, prosecuted, and punished in the criminal justice system. Police can only arrest, and prosecutors can only prosecute cases they believe can be proven in court because of limited resources. In the cases of legislated protocols in court proceedings, anyone has the right to bring a case to court, and the law allows individuals to act as their own attorney. These fundamental structures of the legal system process have produced some difficult cases for victims of sexual abuse, including a case where an offender sued the victim he was convicted of stalking after he was released from prison[18] and even an accused rapist interrogating in open court the victim he was accused of raping.[19] Certainly, extreme anecdotes cannot be used as a standard for suggesting there is a problem; these and similar kinds of stories about the ineffectiveness of the criminal justice system response to sexual assault suggest that they influence an individual's decisions about whether to report an abuse event and speak more broadly to the need for system reform.

As is the case with the other elements of research on sexual assaults, gaps exist in what is reported, how those reports are interpreted, and how those reports influence police procedure. If the decision to move a case forward is based on the evidence collected to assure conviction, the decision to file charges, make an arrest, and then hand the case over to prosecutors all hinge on the initial police response. Attention will be given to police officer attitudes about sexual assault past and present, followed by a review of the role of the prosecutor's office, the structure and design of sex crimes response units, courtroom strategies, and the role of plea bargaining. Although advocacy work is a comparatively new addition to the way victims are directed through the criminal justice system, it has become an integral part of the processing of sexual assault cases. (More information about the role of advocates and the work they do both in and out of the justice system process is in chapter 14.)

THE CRIMINAL JUSTICE SYSTEM—A BRIEF OVERVIEW

The criminal justice system has long been heavily criticized for its response to, or more specifically, for its lack of response to, sexual violence incidents, including child sexual abuse, intimate partner violence, and reports of sexual assault in general. The criminal justice system is based on a principle of "innocent until proven guilty," with the idea that it is better to let a guilty person go free than it is to convict an innocent person. In this structure, a "tie" goes to the accused. In other words, in a case where no conclusive evidence of guilt exists, the accused will not be convicted. In the case of sex crimes, the offenses usually happen without witnesses, and, contrary to popular belief, often happen without physical injuries being present on a victim, even an extremely young victim. When a lack of facts corroborating the alleged crime is combined with a tendency toward nonreporting, it may seem obvious that arrest and conviction rates are low for sexual violence. Discussed generally, the criminal justice system comprises at least 10 phases or stages.

1. Reporting and/or the investigation of a crime by police
2. Arrest
3. Prosecution
4. Indictment
5. Arraignment—entry of a plea
6. Pretrial detention/bail
7. Plea bargaining process
8. Trial
9. Sentencing
10. Legal appeals

Because the criminal justice system is designed to release perpetrators rather than risk a false conviction, the losses of suspected perpetrators through the various decision-making points in the criminal justice system are said to resemble a funnel (see Figure 11.1). This **funnel effect** is argued to be particularly pronounced for victims of sexual crimes. The process begins, police respond to a large number of alleged crimes and/or infractions, and decisions must be made about the veracity of these claims. The top of the funnel refers to the large number of people who police confront, and the narrowing of the funnel indicates the lessening of the numbers of people who are retained in the system as their cases are

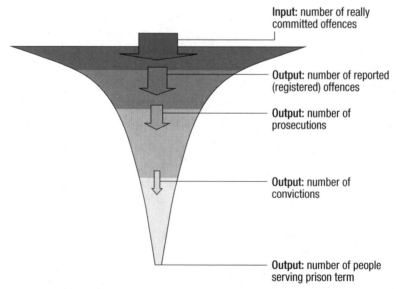

Figure 11.1   The Dark Figure of Sexual Assault Crimes and the Funnel Effect

Krajewski, Krzysztof. "Gaps in the Knowledge Base–Evidence in the Criminal Justice System and Its Implementation in Practice." European Monitoring Centre for Drugs and Drug Addiction. Identifying Europe's information needs for effective drug policy, Lisbon, Portugal.

processed through the system. At each stage of the criminal justice system process, the number of alleged offenders is reduced, and people who were initially identified as suspects are removed from the system. At the final stages of the process, where sentencing happens and punishments are offered, the fewest number of people are retained. In other words, the likelihood of receiving a legal sanction is reduced at each stage of the criminal justice system process, and, at least in theory, only those with significant evidence against them will be convicted.

The slope of this drop-off rate is particularly dramatic in the instances of sexual assault and prosecutions involving additional forms of gender violence. From the time of the assault to the time a victim makes a decision to report the event to police, a certain number of offenders avoid prosecution. From the time an event is brought to police and a decision is to be made about whether enough evidence exists to warrant an arrest, more alleged offenders are removed from the prosecution process. When police hand the cases over to prosecutors and, throughout the investigation process, police are often working closely with prosecutors, prosecuting attorneys must decide whether enough evidence exists to secure a conviction. Is the evidence they have enough to warrant bringing the case to trial? Does this case represent a likely conviction, or would the time, effort, and energy of the prosecutor's office be better spent on another case? If a decision to try the case is made, a conviction is not always an obvious outcome. A decision could be made to mediate the case, or the parties may reach a **plea bargain**, a negotiated deal usually for lesser time if the party admits guilt. If the case does go to trial, a conviction results, and, assuming the parties do not decide to appeal the decision, the process will continue to the sentencing phase to determine whether the person will go to prison or participate in a diversion or treatment program.

Research suggests the way law enforcement responds in sex crime cases will have a significant impact on both the adjudication of the case but also can direct the course of the impacts and treatment of the person who has been harmed.[20]

Interest in or information about people behind the sex-offender label is limited. Information about people who commit a sex offense but is never reported is simply unknown. In fact, few people go to a sex-offender treatment program without a state mandate in the form of a court order. As discussed in chapter 8 on victim responses to sexual assault, a significant number of people harmed by sexual violence do not report that harm. And because the numbers of successfully processed or prosecuted cases decrease at each level of involvement in the criminal justice system, *the accepted but unspecified reality is that most sex offenders never reach the point of being sent to treatment and/or prison.*[21] Criminal justice systems in communities across the country are left with a reality many people find unacceptable: A relatively small number of people who commit sexual assaults will get caught or serve time in prison. In fact, the low rate of reporting has led some to the conclusion that those incarcerated for sex offenses represent less than 10 percent of all sex offenders living in communities nationwide.[22]

Research indicates even the people who have committed sex offenses as defined by the law do not identify themselves as sex offenders or call what they did rape, even if they acknowledge perpetrating acts that meet the legal definition of rape.[23]

Asked "if they had penetrated against their (victim's) consent," said Dr. Mary Koss, researcher and professor of public health at the University of Arizona, the subject will say yes. Asked if he did "something like rape," the answer is almost always no. Studies of incarcerated rapists, even men who admit to keeping sex slaves in conflict zones, find a similar disconnect. It's not that they deny sexual assault happens; it's just that the crime is committed by the monster *over there*.[24]

Increasingly, this emerging and expanding range of research on sexual violence from perpetration through prevention lends support to the idea that working with convicted sex offenders is addressing only the tip of the iceberg. Acknowledging this is important for public education, research, treatment, and prevention efforts.

Without question, being convicted of a sexual crime increases the chance of being forced to go to treatment as a component of that conviction. Those identified by the system and prosecuted are assessed (as discussed in more detail in chapter 12) to determine the treatment needs before their final sentence is decided. This means state departments of corrections are often working hand in hand with treatment practitioners to establish the therapeutic planning, management, and oversight structure for convicted sex offenders.

Department responses to victims of sexual abuse vary widely; however, police in general have carried a reputation for clumsy if not inept handling of sexual assault incidents. Trainings are in place in some departments to advocate the department's ability to respond to rape victims with sensitivity and compassion, but whether officers actually are able to meet those training objectives is unclear.[25] The profession of policing itself has gone through dramatic cultural and attitudinal shifts around the issue. Current initiatives funded by the Department of Justice and led by the **International Association of Chiefs of Police (IACP)** are looking at ways to assist police departments in better responding to sexual violence by reviewing policies and procedures in an effort to better meet victim and community.[26] After a review of research on police attitudes about sexual violence and victims, attention is given to reporting trends and the basic processes of police investigation.

POLICE ATTITUDES ON SEXUAL ASSAULT: THEN AND NOW

Early research on police attitudes toward sexual assault compared attitudes of the police, offenders, and rape crisis counselors and found that police attitudes more closely reflected the attitudes of rapists than the attitudes of the victims or the sexual violence prevention advocates.[27] Further, like police, regular citizens' attitudes were also more similar to the rapists' attitudes when compared to the attitudes of rape crisis counselors.[28]

Rapists believed that rape prevention was the victim's responsibility, rape is motivated by sex, punishment should not be severe, victims encourage rape through their appearance and behavior, rapists are mentally disturbed, women should not resist during rape, a woman is less desirable after she has been raped, and rape is not motivated by power. Disturbingly, police officers' attitudes were found to be more similar to that of the rapists than the rape crisis counselors.

Citizens also displayed attitudes more similar to rapists than rape counselors. These findings are frightening. The individuals who are supposed to protect victims seem to identify more with the criminals than the victims. How are victims supposed to feel safe when police officers share similar attitudes with rapists?[29]

More contemporary research findings on police attitudes toward sexual assault victims reflect this difference by breaking down police officer attitudes into categories of male and female officers' attitudes as they reported out their findings.[30] Research has suggested police with more education (beyond high school or GED) were less likely to victim blame[31] and that increased levels of officer experience lead to decreased levels of rape myth acceptance by the officers.[32] Further, officers less inclined to believe rape myths often proved to be more skilled in interviewing victims.[33] While research has suggested the gender of the officer matters with regard to their view toward people who make rape allegations, research has also suggested female officers may be more likely than male officers to hold the victim partially responsible for the rape.[34] Again, as has been the case with other areas of study regarding sexualized violence, research offers inconclusive, if not contradictory, outcomes when the focus is sexual assault victimization.

Much more can be said about police attitudes regarding rape and gender violence, as well as about how the dynamics between different gendered perspectives on victimization and offending are expanding to include studies about the policing and punishing of rape and sexual assault of male victims. (The history of sexual violence and evolution of rape crisis centers across the United States is covered in more detail in chapter 6, and more focused attention is given to the role of social service agencies and individual efforts in assuring the treatment of and services for male sexual assault victims in chapter 13.) Attention here is focused on three areas of police response, child sexual abuse, rape, and domestic or intimate partner violence, in an effort to address several of the most important social issues in this area, while also attempting to reduce the area of this conversation down to a more manageable size.

REPORTING TO POLICE ABOUT SEXUAL VIOLENCE AND SEXUALIZED VICTIMIZATION

In January 2016, a former police officer in Oklahoma City was sentenced to 263 years in prison after being found guilty of sexually abusing several women while on duty.[35] Certainly an extreme case, yet interviews with police chiefs in 2008[36] suggested some do see sexual misconduct as a problem within their departments. While they report that serious or criminal forms of sexual misconduct (such as rape, sexual assault, sex with a minor) are rare, they also suggest less serious, noncriminal incidents, such as flirting on duty, consensual sex on duty, or pulling over a female driver to "get a better look," are more common.[37] The issue as to whether there can be "consensual sex" while a police officer is on duty was raised by the American Civil Liberties Union in 2018 in a New York case involving officers who were accused of rape by a woman in their custody. The DNA was matched in forensic evidence, and, after resigning from the department, ex-detectives faced rape and kidnapping charges.[38] Officers Richard Hall and Eddie Martins claimed in court proceedings that the sex was consensual, resulting in a media firestorm. In the spring of 2019, the initial charges were modified to official misconduct and bribery, but the outrage remained.[39]

Fundamentally, if rape is a crime of power and control, then police officers who were in the process of making an arrest should not be in a circumstance where sexual consent is even a consideration. A flurry of states, including Minnesota, Louisiana, Maryland, and Kansas, moved to pass legislation to close the "sexual consent" loophole, following New York's lead. In response to this and similar cases, however, approximately 30 states still allow the use of consent as a defense in allegations of sexual abuse when officers are on the job.[40]

Certain reports suggest law enforcement officers who commit this kind of sexual violence or abuse often target individuals who are criminalized, marginalized, or otherwise vulnerable to sexual abuse and/or exploitation in an effort to reduce the likelihood that their behavior will be reported.[41] If the people who were assaulted are also involved in sex work or the use of drugs, they fear they will be charged with a crime if they do not submit or they report their victimization.[42]

So what is an acceptable standard of behavior for law enforcement officers? Why do there seem to be so many questions around a subject area that many people would expect to be quite clear? What actions shift from acceptable behavior in general to acceptable police officer behavior? How do police officers' attitudes and behaviors affect their trustworthiness in the eyes of the public, particularly when police are argued to demonstrate misogynistic attitudes that reflect a gendered, sexually violent, racialized culture? More importantly, what kinds of training are warranted to assure a victim of a sexual crime is taken seriously by police and their perpetrator will be pursued?

Without question, law enforcement officers are painted with a broad brush when allegations of abuse rise to the level of public scrutiny and are presented in the media. Research suggests, like other sex offenders, the system or processes for when abuse happens seem to reflect similar themes to other sexual abusers and include the targeting of people in a vulnerable population, the use of systemic power and/or authority to gain trust or groom victims, and, in some cases, the use of fear to secure silence from the victims. While it might be clear that not all law enforcement officers are sexual offenders, or are even potential sexual offenders, it is also clear that when one officer is identified as abusing their power to secure sexual favors, all officers are suspect. This suspicion increases when the communities have endured long histories of sexual abuse and have been subjected to stories of a lack of adequate system response.

Certainly not all police departments warrant skepticism and suspicion. Police departments in communities everywhere are intended to provide vital support services to members of the community when they find themselves without the resources necessary for meeting any given set of unanticipated circumstances. It is also true that the examples offered in this chapter are only a small sampling of particular issues related to police response to sexualized violence and harm that have people asking questions about what they intend to do to address this persistent problem.

POLICE PROCEDURE IN CASES OF SEXUAL VIOLENCE AND HARM

Police departments vary in size and scope, with any given community's public safety priorities established by city or county administrations, based on budgets and public safety needs, often reflecting the cities and counties in which they operate. Efforts are included here to present a general sense of what a typical police department response would be to a report of sexual assault or abuse. These efforts in real time will be dependent on the circumstances, the officer, the victim, the department procedures, the district attorney, a sexual assault advocate (if an advocate agency is involved), and school or social service officials (if school or other child protective services are involved). Each case of sexual abuse is different, especially when children are involved. Research suggests a relatively standard, if not best practice, for police responding to reports of sexual violence. A few of those processes and related terms are presented for consideration.

POLICING CHILD SEXUAL ASSAULT, INTIMATE PARTNER VIOLENCE, AND ABUSE CLOSE TO HOME

Clearly, one of the most difficult areas of sexual abuse to identify, police, and prosecute is sexual abuse and sexual violence in the home. Early research, including Diana Russell's 1983 study, suggests that 2 percent of the cases of intrafamilial, within the family, and 6 percent of extrafamilial, outside of the family, child sexual abuse were reported to the police.[43] The idea that most children are sexually abused by someone they know, someone known to them or to their families, is a difficult social reality to absorb, especially when as a culture the more prominent notion, although *false* idea, is that children are in more danger from a stranger, or someone *not* known to them. In 1997, research out of the US Department of Justice suggested that domestic violence was the most common but least reported crime in America.[44] Domestic violence calls have a reputation for being some of the least favorite calls among police officers partly because of the potential volatility of the situation. How do police deal with the issue of sexual violence in places traditionally seen as private? Attention is given to the general process of police responding to sexual assault allegations, with a brief focus on specific issues within specific populations, including child sexual abuse, intimate partner violence, and in various potentially vulnerable communities such as LGBTQI or nursing care facilities, as examples. What aspects of the policing function are made more difficult or easier when working with families to address the issue of sexual violence in the home?

A GENERAL DESCRIPTION OF THE POLICE RESPONSE TO SEXUAL ASSAULT

So what happens if a woman has been at a party and wakes up in an unfamiliar area with no recollection of what happened but with a clear understanding or awareness that she has been involved in a sex act? If a woman goes to the police station with this story, what would be the likely police response? The truth is, the response would depend on the department and the particular officer who responded. When police respond to an allegation of sexual assault, the first decision is to assist the individual who has been harmed and to determine whether sufficient conditions warrant classifying the assault as a crime. A decision will be made as to whether there is enough evidence to make an arrest or whether the evidence collection will require additional time.

The Office of the Victims of Crime suggest three primary needs of victims after a traumatic event: (1) the need to establish a sense of safety, (2) the ability to express their emotional reactions to the incident, and (3) a clear set of expectations for what will be coming next.[45] (Additional information about the needs of victims during the initial response to allegations of sexual assault is provided in chapter 8.) The following text box provides a review of specific

---

Text Box 11.3.   Tips for Police Response to Sexual Assault Victims[1]

1. Be prepared for any kind of emotional response from the victims.
2. Avoid interpreting calmness as an indication that something serious did or did not happen; the victims could be in shock.
3. Approach victims calmly.
4. Ask victims whether they would like to contact a family member or a friend.
5. Offer to contact a sexual assault advocate. Ask whether they prefer a male or female.
6. Ask the victims whether they prefer a male or female police officer.
7. Do not appear patronizing or overprotective.
8. When collecting evidence and listening to the victims describe the events, remember that it is often difficult for victims to tell their story or aspects of the story that they do not want to remember. It is not uncommon for the details to change or be remembered out of order.
9. Encourage the victims to seek medical attention. Make sure the victims have transportation to the hospital and transportation to a final destination after the hospital.
10. Be mindful of the concerns victims of sexual assault will have, including telling a spouse or partner or family member, the possibility of becoming pregnant or getting a sexually transmitted infection, and worries that the incident could become public and/or that people including coworkers or neighbors might find out about the sexual assault.
11. Interview victims with extreme sensitivity.
12. Offer to answer any questions or provide resources to assure further assistance.
13. Encourage the victims to seek counseling.
14. Provide basic community resources that support people and families who have been impacted by sexual assault.

Note

1. Office for Victims of Crime. July 2010. *First Response to Victims of Crime: A Guidebook for Law Enforcement Officers*. National Sheriffs' Association. Preparation of this publication was supported by grant number 2005-VF-GX-4001, awarded by the Office for Victims of Crime, Office of Justice Programs, U.S. Department of Justice.

tips for police response when working with people impacted by sexual assault. Further, for reasons that might seem obvious, police response to accusations of sexual violence and harm will also vary, depending on the setting and the role of the officer as they respond to the scene. Attention is given briefly to several places where law enforcement officers assist with responses to allegations of sexual violence and/or harm.

POLICE RESPONSE TO ALLEGATIONS OF ABUSE OF A CHILD

Many schools today, whether elementary or high school, have a community service officer or police officer who works within the school during school hours. What would a police officer do if presented with a story by a school-aged child about allegations of sexual abuse? Because children are likely to be abused by someone they know, and this includes family, police undertake what is referred to as a **parallel investigation**, investigating the people closest to the child while at the same time focusing on other leads. Once the investigation has cleared the family of involvement, the investigation can focus fully on external leads. Although this can be difficult for people who are not involved, it is important for law enforcement to rule out family and other close relationships to assure no one is inadvertently overlooked. Referred to as "**inner circle assaults**," the truth of these statistics helps young people and their parents better understand the reality that being afraid of strangers is not likely to protect against sexual assault. When a parent refuses to believe someone known to them could commit a harmful act against their child, they provide a cover for the offender and perhaps make it possible for the abuse to continue or that another child will become the target of their abuse.

After a series of child abuse allegations at daycare centers hit the national news in the 1980s, focused attention was given to how law enforcement interview children and other vulnerable populations. It is essential that the people doing the interviews with the children are held to high standards in their training to ensure that the quality of the interview protocol is maintained.

POLICE RESPONSE TO ALLEGATIONS OF FAMILY OR INTIMATE PARTNER VIOLENCE

So what happens if a neighbor calls police and reports loud yelling and sounds of physical aggression at the house next door? Given that every situation is different, what would be a general guideline for a typical police response? (Chapter 6 highlights some of the current statistics about violence in the home.) An **order for protection**, also referred to as an OFP or a protective order, is a common tool used to support someone who has been threatened and can be issued by a judge to require one party to leave the other party alone, or to not contact them, or to stay outside a designated distance from where the holder of the OFP expects to be. Since the issue of family violence has historically been seen as a family secret or deemed a decision for the husband to make as the head of the household, law enforcement agencies were slow to assume any responsibilities for involvement in domestic situations.

The lack of police response was clearly illustrated in the 1984 case of *Thurman v. The City of Torrington*. In the 1980s, Tracey Thurman repeatedly reported abuse by her husband to police, secured a protection order, and consistently reported to police violations her husband made of the order. But police did not take action. On June 10, 1983, Tracey was stabbed 13 times by her husband 10 minutes after she called police. This case produced landmark legislation when in 1984 Tracy Thurman sued the Torrington, Connecticut, police department and 24 of its officers for failing to protect her from her violent, estranged husband.[46]

POLICE RESPONSE TO LGBTQI COMMUNITIES AND COMMUNITIES OF COLOR

For many of the reasons discussed above, various police departments across the United States have been forced to address questionable practices of police procedure and departmental attitudes toward the issues of gender bias and/or sexual violence. At the federal level, the US Marshals Service has been used to seek out, arrest, and return to prison offenders who have been convicted of a sex crime but who fail to register and "fall off the grid." (More about the management of sex offenders is offered in chapter 12.)

Reports by the organization INCITE! emphasize the "largely invisible" sexually exploitive experiences people experience at the hands of law enforcement, suggesting women of color and transgender people are especially vulnerable to a system of exploitation that does not keep statistics on allegations, complaints, or incidents of rape, sexual assault, sexual harassment, or coerced sexual conduct by police.[47] Two studies (Missouri and Florida) of law enforcement license revocations identified sexual misconduct on the job as the basis of revocation in almost 25 percent of the cases.[48] Further, the abuse is evidenced at local, state, and federal levels of police jurisdictions.

While individual crimes and incidents suggest a need for ongoing research and social reflection, when the field of consideration is expanded or narrowed, depending on the frame of reference, additional questions and concerns are evident. Native women have a complicated past with the broader reach of the criminal justice system. Because tribal governance typically includes local police for the tribe but also oversight from the federal government, the jurisdiction of oversight becomes complicated, and high numbers of sexual assaults on Native lands suggest perpetrators understand this legal loophole, putting tribal communities at increased risk for sexual violence. A 2008 report identified distrust of law enforcement as a significant reason Native women do not report sexual violence.[49]

SEXUAL ASSAULT PROSECUTION AND THE COURT PROCESS

Although a considerable amount of attention in the arena of sexual violence investigation and response has been given to policing systems, in the past several decades increased attention to the decisions made regarding whether to prosecute those cases has placed a spotlight on the prosecutor's office.[50] As is the case with many of the procedural elements of a sexual assault, from reporting the event to the punishment of the accused offender, much of the research is extrapolated from combining research from the information reported by victims, both those who do report and those who do not report, and from the offenders, those who are caught, and more recently by those who report potentially abusive and assaultive behaviors but do not see themselves as offenders, as discussed in chapter 7. As it stands, however, studies suggest that 82 to 86 percent of all rape cases were dropped by the criminal justice system, most during the investigative stage.

By now, it must be clear that most victims of sexual assault are known to the perpetrator. One issue about criminal law and criminal procedure important for better understanding the system response to sexual crimes is that past practice has been to lock on to the assumption that sex crimes are a one-time incident that happens between people who are strangers.[51] When the actual criminal behavior being confronted does not meet this typical assumption, as is the case in allegations of child sexual abuse and/or violence between partners, for example, the procedural rules can become an obstacle for successful prosecution.[52] The example offered is in the case of a child being sexually assaulted for years by a family member. If that child cannot provide specific dates for the abuse, the case could be thrown out by an untrained prosecutor, using the legal standard of "reasonableness"; however, critics of the system suggest that it is the court that is unreasonable.[53] This is only one example.

Courtroom procedures are directed by local statutory provisions, and, as a result, the nuances differ state by state and county by county. Typically, an alleged offender will make at least five or six court appearances: (1) when bail is set; (2) at the grand jury hearing, when a decision is made to determine whether there is enough probable cause or evidence to move forward with a trial; (3) at the arraignment, when a formal reading of the charges against the defendant happens and at which time they enter a plea of guilty or not guilty; (4) at any necessary court hearings, introducing motions or evidentiary rulings, for example, and possibly during any plea negotiations; (5) at trial; and (6) at sentencing. The crime victim usually appears only at the grand jury's presentation of evidence and at trial.

If each police response is unique, so is the case with each criminal prosecution. Each judge, jury, victim, prosecutor, and offender has a part to play in the way a given case is processed through the court. Sexual assault cases are hard to win if the victim is not perceived as relatively likeable and is not identifiable as a "**good victim**," someone the jury will easily connect with and find believable."[54] Characteristics of a good victim include the person having a job and a positive social status and being well educated, articulate, attractive (but not too attractive), demure (but not a pushover), and believable to a jury. In court, they should be upset to a point but not overly emotional and certainly not hysterical, or that could negatively impact the jurors' assessments. Convictions come more easily if the jury and the judge are presented with a good victim. But not all rape victims meet the good victim standard. Questions about these kinds of biases toward victims of sexual assault remain unsatisfactorily unaddressed under the current judicial system. Consider the following statement from a former prosecutor who specialized in sex crimes:

> Rapists tend to go to trial more than any other kind of criminal, believing in their souls that all men, including those on the jury would rape if only they had what it takes. They are supported too often in this belief by the fact that what the defense puts on trial is the victim.[55]

Experienced prosecutors have described the grand jury process, which is the process where the initial determination as to whether there is enough evidence to proceed to a trial, as a highly political process where a jury may choose to make a political statement rather than follow the law.[56] The concept of **victim blaming**, which is focusing attention on the victim of the crime rather than on the offender, has risen to national prominence in the United States in large part because of the efforts by sexual violence prevention advocates to shift the blame for sexual violence from the victim to the perpetrator. (This idea is discussed more fully in chapter 8 on victims.) Attitudes about sexual assault and victimization show up in the form of the various actors in the courtroom. Research supports the idea that a jury will look at an alleged rapist and say "but he looks like such a nice guy," while looking at a victim of a sexual assault and say "well she is not a virgin, and she was in a bad part of town, and she had been drinking," as if any of the actions on the part of the victim could be used to justify a violent sexual attack on one person by another.

It is at least part of the prosecutor's job to assess the mood and temperament of the judge, the jury, and the defense attorney while working to make the case on behalf of the victim. The prosecutor has the authority to assess the information from police and determine which relevant statutory violations have occurred and which ones can be proven in court. Although the judge is responsible for imposing a sentence on the defendant who is found guilty, the initial charges filed and any plea agreements are left up to the discretion of the prosecutors. The judge's sentencing power is different from a prosecutor's; once a person pleads guilty or is found guilty in a courtroom, the judge has the discretion to hand out a sentence anywhere within the statutory minimum or maximum.[57] A judicial decision to reduce the charges requires authorization from the prosecutor.

The initial charges are filed at the beginning of the process (and may be determined in conjunction with law enforcement), and plea bargaining arrangements are negotiated between defense counsel and the prosecutor, with the intention of reducing the load on the court and likely offering the defendant a lesser term than if they were found guilty in court. Unfortunately, research in police departments across the country supports the claims made by the Women's Law Project in Pennsylvania, discussed at the opening of the chapter, that some sex crimes are made invisible by overlooking the sexual violation when the charges are filed or the plea deal is reached. For example, charges of home invasion rape are reduced to robbery or burglary, and no reference is made to the sexual assault.[58] The case is closed, and the offender goes back out into the community with no record of sexual offending, no accountability to the victim, and perhaps most importantly, no information about resources and support for perpetrators of sexual harm and violence.

Although the use of plea bargaining serves a systemic function, not every-one—in some cases this might include the victim—agrees with the plea deal.

> The purpose of plea bargaining is manifold. For a defendant, it guarantees a specific punishment and avoids the gamble that a conviction could produce a greater punishment. . . . For a prosecutor, a plea bargain guarantees that a defendant will be assured punishment with the conviction noted on his rap sheet. Even with a seemingly strong case, there is no guarantee of a conviction at trial. . . . In child abuse and sex crime cases there are strong additional factors in favor of a plea bargain. In a sex crime, the victim is spared the ordeal of having to publicly recount an embarrassing and traumatic experience. It also spares her from having to face her attacker in court or having to deal with all of the accusations that come with cross-examination. In child abuse cases, there are similar factors along with the additional emotional trauma testifying can cause a minor. There is also the added difficulty of obtaining a conviction for sex crimes and crimes against children. It can be difficult for people to understand the lack of corroborative evidence in such cases. Also, conviction rates vary from county to county, and from state to state. . . . the low conviction rate often forces prosecutors to provide a low plea offer that is both unfair to the victim and unjust punishment for the crime, but better than nothing.[59]

The prosecutor is also responsible for making sure they have the evidence necessary for trial. Innovations in law and legal practice have made it possible under certain instances to use a recorded testimony or recorded forensic interview in cases where the victim was a child or where specific emotional harm might prevent the victim from testifying in front of the perpetrator, although many prosecutors will say they would rather have the testimony presented live in open court. In addition, the use of a **polygraph** test, also known as a lie detector test, is now permissible in courts, as well as the use of DNA evidence. The utilization of a **rape kit**, a process followed for the forensic collection of any physical material that could be used as evidence when tested to determine whether the material provides a DNA match to the offender. Since 2000, the process for assessing a DNA match has become more commonplace in court proceedings. With the implementation of the national **Combined DNA Index System (CODIS)** database, which is a searchable software program, laboratories maintain a forensic index of profiles from crime scene evidence. In many states, people convicted of sex offenses and who are required to register with local law enforcement (discussed in more detail in the chapter 12) are also required to submit a DNA sample, which is then included in CODIS.

Perhaps the most important part of a sex crime prosecution is the initial interview with the victim because two key questions are answered: (1) Was a crime committed (and what crime classification is appropriate), and (2) can the victim describe what occurred with enough credibility to withstand cross-examination?[60] This becomes a high burden for a person who has been assaulted and remains a contentious aspect of the court process for victims. Forensic interviewers follow protocol and training standards to get facts from the victim in such a way that they can be used in court.

If a person is arrested, they must be assessed as to whether they are fit to stand trial. If they are not deemed fit to stand trial, they will likely be placed in a mental health facility until such time when they might be determined by mental health professionals to stand trial. In *Jackson v. Indiana* (1972), the Supreme Court said the indefinite holding violated due process and that if the defendant could never become competent, they must be civilly committed or released.[61] If a person is "Jacksoned out," they are returned to civil commitment—an event seen as a particularly frightening possibility for seriously mentally ill individuals who could be released from a mental health facility back into the community with little or no oversight in the community.[62] If the accused is deemed capable of standing trial, another judicial process is required. The **McNaughton test** is used to determine the mental state of the individual and whether the defendant understood the nature and consequences of their actions *at the time the crime was committed*. While many in our society tend to lump all kinds of sexual assaults together, as has been emphasized throughout the text, *much variation exists between offenders who commit sexual crimes*. Consider the following excerpt from the work of the Los Angeles County District Attorney who specialized in prosecuting sex offenders:

> Adult sex crimes are less about *what* was done, and more about how the act was accomplished, primarily, whether there was consent. There are basically only seven ways to commit an adult sex crime: accomplishing a sex act by force, fear, violence, duress, undue influence, intoxication, and incapacity. Each of these has its own legal definition, yet all basically involve the appearance of consent while the circumstances show that actual consent was in fact not present (49).
>
> Children do not have the capacity to consent to a sex act as a matter of law . . . yet children have no understanding that it is sexual, or even what the offender wants to do to them. They simply do not understand sex. Another difference between adult sex crimes and child sexual assaults is that the age of the offender matters, as well as the age of the victim. . . . besides the victim's age, some victims take into account the difference between the age of the victim and the offender (51).
>
> Child sexual assault may involve a variety of different actions or behaviors. It includes the conduct most people think of first when they hear a term like "child sex crimes": rape, sodomy, oral copulation, finger penetration, digital penetration, and other physical contact aimed at sexual gratification (52).
>
> While rape is a serious crime . . . there are many other forms of child sexual abuse that can have equally damaging short- and long-term effects that have nothing to do with intercourse or penetration. . . . For example, [the] category of child sex crimes generally known as *sexual molestation* . . . includes photographing children, hiding a video camera in a dressing room, or sending sexually explicit letters or emails both about children and to children. Another category . . . *sexual exploitation* usually means some form of victimizing children for sexual gratification or financial profit (e.g., child pornography and child prostitution) (52). . . . [A] victim whose ability to articulate the abuse is weak due to a disability, the level of corroboration (for conviction) may need to be greater (80). Simply put, kids who will make poor witnesses (in court) are natural targets for sexual assault (89).[63]

Typically the alleged perpetrator's response to accusations of rape fall into three categories: (1) it never happened, (2) it was consensual, or (3) it wasn't me.[64] With DNA evidence acting as a powerful tool for the prosecution, the likely defenses are more easily reduced to two: (1) it wasn't me, or (2) sure it was me, but the sex was consensual.[65] Prosecutors must prepare to counter whichever defense is raised. Fortunately, with the right training and the collaborative efforts of a multidisciplinary team, prosecutors can use perceived weaknesses attributed to the victim as strengths and turn them into corroboration for why a child was targeted for abuse.[66]

When cases of sexual assault go to court, particularly in the case of young victims, it is the cross-examination that invites the most fear and trauma from the victims and the most outrage and systemic criticism from advocates and supporters. One child sex abuse prosecutor described this as the "blame the child to save one's own hide" defense.[67] Another tactic used by defense attorneys is to blame the people the child disclosed the abuse to and attack their credibility. This gets taken to extremes when the perpetrator invokes his right to represent himself at trial. Not only did he work hard to victimize the victim again in the process of cross-examination, but then after he lost the case, he appealed on the grounds that he had an inadequate defense.

To secure a conviction, the victim's story has to be corroborated by evidence, and the evidence must be compelling enough to convince a jury beyond a reasonable doubt. This corroboration can come in the form of evidence provided by the victim; evidence provided by the offender; or evidence provided by witnesses, the medical examination, or additional physical evidence, as examples.[68] The prosecution can seek a plea, and the defense can seek a reduction in charges all the way up until the time the jury returns a verdict. At that point, it becomes the judge's responsibility to sentence the accused, now the convicted offender. Often, a judge will reference a **presentencing report** before making a final decision about sentencing. Also referred to as a **presentencing investigation**, or PSI, the report includes a brief personal and arrest history generated for all felony convictions and is presented to the judge prior to sentencing. The report includes drug use history and can offer an opportunity for the defendant to make a statement about their guilt. After a conviction is handed down or a plea is reached, the victim is given an opportunity to make a statement to the judge, outlining how this crime has affected them and often requesting a certain sentence or statement to the offender upon sentencing. Known as the **victim impact statement**, these are sometimes offered to the judge or read before the court and into the official court record. (The use of probation as a treatment and/or management strategy is discussed further in chapters 12 and 13.)

CONTEMPORARY SYSTEM RESPONSES TO SEXUAL ASSAULT

In 2011, the Police Executive Research Forum (PERF) in preparation for a national conference and in response to local and national community concerns focused on "Improving the Police Response to Sexual Assaults." Organizers conducted a study on the ways police agencies respond to sexual assaults. While there was agreement that no single policy change can resolve all of the problems with sexual assault reporting and investigation, a great deal of those responding suggested police departments need to ensure that their officers develop a deeper understanding of sexual assault crimes.[69]

In general, police departments' organizational designs evolve to meet community needs, and their structural response to sexual assaults and sex crimes can be quite different. As many as 90 percent of police departments participate in **sexual assault response team (SART)** programs, although the structure of the programs vary.[70] SART programs include trained police, prosecutors, sexual assault advocates, and nurse examiners, among others as identified by the team and are credited with improved response to victims and increased likelihood that offenders will be arrested, charged, and convicted. Supporters of the program suggest that detectives who handle sexual assault cases form close relationships with the other SART team members to assure interpersonal and systemic issues are addressed to the positive outcome on any given case.

In fact most professionals in the field agree: Responding to child sexual assault and sexual violence requires a team.[71] The members of such a multidisciplinary team could include the victim advocate, folks from health services, social services, members of law enforcement, and legal services. Past Los Angeles District Attorney and child sex crime prosecutor Robin Sax suggests the following team members,[72] with each explained in brief below.

Advocates: Attend to the needs of the victim and make sure they understand the various elements of the criminal justice system as they are being required to participate in them as the charges and court proceedings progress.

Detective: Patrol police officers are usually the first to respond to a report of child sexual abuse for the preliminary investigation, so their role must not be minimized. It is important that first responders are aware of the need to protect evidence and secure the crime scene. Some departments recommend people who have experience with gathering forensic evidence specifically and exclusively for sexual crimes cases to be the police investigator, who is usually more experienced in addressing the nuances of sexual abuse investigation and fully understands the prosecutorial evidentiary needs to secure a conviction in court.

Doctor/Nurse Practitioner: Medical personnel can be professionally trained to respond to and manage sexual assault cases. Also referred to as SANE (sexual assault nurse examiner) programs, the idea is to use medical professionals who have specialized training, knowledge, and awareness about sex crimes to collect and gather any potentially key evidence that might later be used to corroborate the victim's story, as well as paying attention to cues and statements as they talk with the victim, to assist in securing information that might also be helpful to police in the investigation.[73]

Forensic Interviewer: In some places, this is the prosecuting attorney, the police investigator, or a specialist. There are also professionals who do this work as their main area of focus. A well-trained forensic interviewer can ask about the events in an effort to secure the necessary information to secure a conviction at trial, without further disturbing the victim.

Prosecutor: The legal representative who works for the city or county government agency, who will prosecute the alleged offender in court. The factors a prosecutor will consider are:

- Has a crime been committed?
- What crime was committed? Which penal code section is involved?
- Who committed the crime? What is the identity of the perpetrator?
- What connects the defendant to the crime? What kind of corroboration is there?
- What defenses are available? What will the defendant say?
- How strong is the victim's testimony? Is it believable and can it be corroborated?[74]

Social Worker: The social worker is responsible for assuring the children's needs are met, and the state's obligation to assure the child remains safe are met. Social workers are responsible for making sure the family stays together whenever possible. To this end, their job is to assure the child or the family receives the necessary counseling, education, oversight, and any other resources necessary.[75]

Assessments about sex crimes cases include strategies for educating the juries about the issues specific to sex crimes cases. If a judge did not believe rape between adults could happen if the victim and the offender knew each other, they could provide the jury instructions reflecting this prejudicial belief.[76] In cases involving children, juries sometimes have a hard time understanding that children often do not report abuse right away. Well-intended but ill-informed individuals might increase the number of dropped cases, or cases that are brought to the system through a criminal investigation but never referred to a prosecutor.[77] Special training for judges and prosecutors and police investigators is recommended so the process allows for the appropriate use of any evidence that can be used to prove or discredit a case. The IACP has developed a collection of best practices regarding sexual assault investigations in collaboration with local, state, and federal law enforcement, prosecutors, sexual assault advocates, medical professionals, and forensic experts.[78]

Recommendations to increase the number of prosecutions include submitting all children suspected of abuse a forensic interview and finding extra-legal services, including an advocate or social worker, to assure the children's safety concerns are addressed while decisions are made about whether to pursue a court case.[79] Remember, well-intended parents want to believe sexual abuse could not happen to their child. A larger percentage of children may have parents who are the perpetrators. This simple idea results in a significant system disruption in families when the primary presumptions revolve around the idea that parents will be responsible for protecting their child, not harming them.

Children don't tell, and it can be for the simplest reasons. They think they will get in trouble or the defendant has threatened to hurt them, or their parents or a sibling. And most often, children don't tell because they love the person who abuses them and they don't want to get the person in trouble.[80]

Whether it was a relationship based on love, fear, or bribery, it was the understanding of that relationship that helped the jury understand the victims and their behavior.[81]

Many batterers are charming in life, as they were when they first meet their victims. This is the case in various types of sexual assault cases, whether the couple is married, dating, or living together. In these cases, the manipulation of the victim is often a factor the prosecutor must deal with if the charges are to be successfully leveled. In the past, these cases would often be dropped or dismissed, and then the police and perhaps even the prosecutor's office would become very familiar with the cycle of violence in that household. For this reason, attention has also been given to what is referred to as evidence-based prosecution, or **victimless prosecution**. The prosecutor uses techniques and evidence collected by law enforcement allowing the case to proceed even without the cooperation of the alleged victim. Two more recent Supreme Court cases have impacted this option, limiting the application of hearsay exceptions (**Crawford v. Washington**, 2004) and the use of 911 call recordings (**Davis v. Washington**, 2006).

In cases where children are involved, the child is often attached to the offender, and although they are being victimized, the child is truly attached to or loves the perpetrator, whether they be the parent, a close friend of the family, or someone the child knows who has worked to secure the trust and affection of the child. In the case of violence perpetrated in the home, the victim might believe the offender will not hurt them again, or the family might seek counseling in hopes of restoring the family unit; in many cases, all parties want to seek the stabilization of the family unit, rather than see the family break up. In these cases, historically, if the abuse happened to a child under the age of majority, the state would take action on behalf of the child, and the offender would be processed through the system with the state taking on the role of the parent. However, if the child were unwilling to testify against the alleged offender or wouldn't engage during their forensic interview, the case might risk being tossed out. Often, in the case of intimate partner or family violence cases, unless the victim was willing to bring charges against the offender, police would not make an arrest and charges would not likely be filed. The use of victimless prosecution makes it possible for police and prosecutors to move forward with the case even without the consent or participation of the victim.[82]

Reasons for a victim, even as an adult, to choose not to prosecute a sexual crime are steeped in history, social convention, problematic policies in policing, and fears associated with future interactions with the offender, or the process of prosecution, to name a few. But just as is the case that not all victims fit the preferred classification of "good victim," not all battered women are justified in using the battered women's legal defense, or not all people accused of sexual violence are guilty and not all perpetrators are men. It is critical that each case be investigated and led by a presentation and collection of facts, rather than giving deference to the stereotypes and myths about what abuse and abusers "look like." With intimate partners, whether dating, married, separated, or divorced, it was sometimes the case that a complaint would be filed by one party, only to be followed by a retaliatory complaint from the other party. These cases are called **cross complaints** and refer to cases where both parties have filed complaints against each other. In many cases, this can become a vicious cycle for both parties where the court process is used as another weapon by one party to abuse the other.[83] Much has been written about the court process in marital dissolution and child custody, which is beyond the scope of the topic here. Few would disagree that the proceedings seldom produce the kind of clear resolution or outcome either party seeks.

CHAPTER CONCLUSION

Without question, police and prosecutors are on the front line of a justice system that is arguably often broken when it comes to addressing sex crimes. Author and advocate Alice Vachss, a former chief of the Special Victims Unit in the Queens district attorney's office in New York, called people "collaborators," when they would choose not to take action to stop sexual violence when they were confronted with the opportunity. Social attitudes about violence in the household and expectations about police response to that violence have changed. (More attention is given in chapter 15 to the broader social issues associated with a more collective community response to rape and sexual violence, said to influence the police response in the communities they serve.) Attention here is focused on police and the prosecutorial process. The legislative choices that outline procedural directives for both the prosecution and the police will differ based on city, county, and state regulations, as well as jurisdictional interpretation of national policy and federal legislation. (More about current laws and reflection on key legislation directed at addressing the issues related to the regulation and management of sex offenders is presented in chapter 10.)

Keeping in mind that entire disciplines, including social work, departments of human services, community programs, and national programs, have been developed to help address the issue of child harm and abuse makes it easier to see that paying attention to children's needs is everyone's job. This idea, however, flies in the face of cultural conditioning, which suggests that people's private lives are not to be interfered with, and this includes how people raise children. Policing issues of sexual harm and sexual violence are difficult for daycares, schools, and educational programs, as well as after-school programs and community programs, including Boy Scouts, Girl Scouts, and other programs developed for and centered on kids. Families, faith communities, and groups where relationships develop are places where abuse can happen. To put the entire task of policing sexual violence on police departments and agencies limits potential outreach. Young people report abuse to people they feel they can trust, and this in fact may be an adult in an after-school program or a friend's parent. In this way, everyone benefits if the local community resources are known and familiar.

Text Box 11.4. Media Messages about Police, Courts, and Corrections

Depending on the community, an individual might get different messages about whether the police are the best place to report a crime. Depending on where an individual lives, that person's questions about the effectiveness of the criminal justice system might extend to the entire system. Depending on the experiences a person has had or the experiences of friends and families or of a given community, their beliefs about whether they would be taken seriously in reporting a sexual assault may be impacted—one way or the other. What if the messaging around sexual violence and harm, in other words, victim blaming, not believing their stories, small prosecution and conviction rates, and lenient sentencing, could be understood by the public as the decriminalization of rape?[1] What if the idea that sexual assault is just "this thing that happens" is the prevailing social attitude? What if this pervasive message left society at large with the impression that this popular cultural attitude suggested nothing more need be done?[2] The adversarial nature of the existing legal system can be retraumatizing to victims while the defense attorney works to discredit the victim's claims and can significantly negatively impact the victim's mental health, triggering a common form of posttraumatic stress. The court could produce a conviction but also, at the same time, do harm to the victim in the process.

To what degree do these messages bear out in research and lived experience? What role do individual attitudes play in assessing the messaging of rape and sexual violence as "no big deal"? What role do lawyers and judges play in the perpetuation of this minimization of harm? To what degree does the design of the criminal justice system itself perpetuate and minimize the harm of sexual violence?

What might shift this current messaging?

Notes

1. Jeanne Gregory and Sue Lees, *Policing Sexual Assault* (London: Routledge, 1999).

2. Some of these thoughts come in coordination with S. McCarthy-Jones, "Survivors of Sexual Violence Are Let Down by the Criminal Justice System—Here's What Should Happen Next," The Conversation, March 28, 2018, accessed September 25, 2019, https://theconversation.com/survivors-of-sexual-violence-are-let-down-by-the-criminal-justice-system-heres-what-should-happen-next-94138.

KEY TERMS

Combined DNA Index System (CODIS)
Crawford v. Washington
cross complaints
Davis v. Washington
funnel effect
"good victim"
inner circle assaults
International Association of Chiefs of Police (IACP)
Jackson v. Indiana
Jacksoned out
McNaughton test
order for protection
parallel investigation
plea bargain
Police Executive Research Forum (PERF)
polygraph
presentencing investigation

presentencing report
rape kit
second rape
secondary victimization

sexual assault response team (SART)
victim blaming
victim impact statement
victimless prosecution

REVIEW QUESTIONS

1. Overview, briefly, the reputation police departments have achieved at present with regard to their response to sex offenses broadly.

2. What additions to the criminal justice system were made in an effort to better respond to and address the process of sex crimes responses?

3. Explain how the funnel effect can be used to describe the criminal justice system more broadly and the prosecution of sex crimes more specifically.

4. What are some of the dynamics in a court trial that would cause additional pain for victims of crime?

5. What is the role of an advocate in the aftermath of a reported rape?

DISCUSSION QUESTIONS

1. Discuss the issue of rape kits and the number of offices that admittedly have a backlog of evidence that has not been processed. How might this support the idea that police don't care about rape victims?

2. The chapter suggests that rape victims are benefited when police officers do not believe rape myths. What kind of myths are police and the general public likely to believe about rape?

3. What is it about intimate partner violence, initially referred to as domestic violence, when it comes to police officer response? What is it about the dynamic of family violence that makes the police officer response so important and difficult to navigate?

4. Discuss the role of an advocate. Discuss the limitations of that role, the benefits of that role, and the reasons police will sometimes wait for an advocate before talking with the victim.

5. What changes might possibly be brought about to address the issue of the criminal justice system's deficiency in response to sexual violence in terms of providing appropriate police response and prosecutorial care and attention to the case from beginning to end? What is it about the system that will likely never work well in favor of the victims of sexual violence?

NOTES

1. Lynn Langton et al., "Special Report: Victimizations Not Reported to the Police, 2006–2010," US Department of Justice, Office of Justice Programs, Bureau of Justice Statistics, August 1, 2012, accessed September 20, 2019, https://www.bjs.gov/content/pub/pdf/vnrp0610.pdf.

2. Police Executive Research Forum, Critical Issues in Policing Series, "Improving the Police Response to Sexual Assault," March 2012, accessed October 20, 2019, https://www.policeforum.org/assets/docs/Critical_Issues_Series/improving%20the%20police%20response%20to%20sexual%20assault%202012.pdf.

3. Alice Vachss, *Sex Crimes: Ten Years on the Front Lines Prosecuting Rapists and Confronting Their Collaborators* (New York: Henry Holt and Company, 1993), 30.

4. Ibid., xi; "The Response to Rape: Detours on the Road to Equal Justice," May 1993, 2, accessed September 24, 2019, https://www.ncjrs.gov/pdffiles1/Digitization/145360NCJRS.pdf.

5. K. Neumann, *Criminal Justice and Law Enforcement Issues* (Nova Publishers, 2002), 49.

6. David Lisak and Paul M. Miller, "Repeat Rape and Multiple Offending among Undetected Rapists," *Violence and Victims* 17, no. 1 (2002): 73, https://www.wcsap.org/sites/default/files/uploads/webinars/SV%20on%20Campus/Repeat%20Rape.pdf; see also Bonnie S. Fisher, Francis T. Cullen, and Michael G. Turner, "The Sexual Victimization of College Women," National Institute of Justice, December 2000, accessed September 24, 2019, https://www.ncjrs.gov/pdffiles1/nij/182369.pdf; "Criminal Victimization in the United States, 1994," Report No. NCJ-158022, Bureau of Justice Statistics, US Department of Justice, May 1997, accessed September 24, 2019, https://www.bjs.gov/content/pub/pdf/cvius94.pdf.

7. Lucie Ogrodnik, "Spousal Violence and Repeat Police Contact," in *Family Violence in Canada: A Statistical Profile 2006*, ed. L. Ogrodnik (Ottawa: Ministry of Industry, 2006), 11–19, https://www2.unb.ca/observ/Familypercent20Violencepercent20inpercent20Canada_Apercent20Statisticalpercent20Profile_2007_2006/Familypercent20Violencepercent20inpercent20Canada_Apercent20Statisticalpercent20Profile_2006_E.pdf.

8. "Rape in the United States: The Chronic Failure to Report and Investigate Rape Cases," Women's Law Project, https://www.judiciary.senate.gov/meetings/rape-in-the-united-states-the-chronic-failure-to-report-and-investigate-rape-cases.

9. Mark Fazlollah et al., "Women Victimized Twice in Police Game of Numbers," *Philadelphia Inquirer*, October 17, 1999; Mark Fazlollah et al., "How Police Use a New Code When Sex Cases Are Unclear," *Philadelphia Inquirer*, October 18, 1999; Michael Matza and Craig R. McCoy, "Police Used 'Throwaway Categories' Since 1960s," *Philadelphia Inquirer*, October 18, 1999; Mark Fazlollah, Michael Matza, and Craig R. McCoy, "After FBI Questioned One Tactic, Another Was Found," *Philadelphia Inquirer*, October 18, 1999. These articles, as well as those describing Philadelphia's response to the reports and continuing reverberations from this scandal through March 2004, can be found on the *Philadelphia Inquirer*'s website Down With Crime: The Rape Squad Files at http://inquirer.philly.com/packages/crime/html/.

10. "Rape in the United States: The Chronic Failure to Report and Investigate Rape Cases."

11. Callie Marie Rennison, "Rape and Sexual Assault: Reporting to Police and Medical Attention, 1992–2000," US Department of Justice, Office of Justice Programs, Bureau of Justice Statistics, 2002, accessed September 20, 2019, http://bjs.ojp.usdoj.gov/content/pub/pdf/rsarp00.pdf.

12. "Criminal Victimization, 2017," Bureau of Justice Statistics, December 2018, accessed September 20, 2019, https://www.bjs.gov/content/pub/pdf/cv17_sum.pdf.

13. Ibid.

14. Brandon Stahl, Jennifer Bjorhus, Mary Jo Webster, and Hannah Covington, "When Rape Is Reported and Nothing Happens: How Minnesota's Criminal Justice System Has Failed Victims of Sexual Assault," *Minneapolis Star Tribune*, January 25, 2018, accessed October 2019, http://www.startribune.com/denied-justice-series-when-rape-is-reported-and-nothing-happens-minnesota-police-sexual-assault-investigations/487400761/.

15. Ibid.

16. Lee Madigan and Nancy C. Gamble, *The Second Rape: Society's Continued Betrayal of the Victim* (New York: Macmillan, 1991); Jeffrey S. Jones et al., "Why Women Don't Report Sexual Assault to Police: The Influence of Psychosocial Variables and Traumatic Injury," *Journal of Emergency Medicine* 36, no. 4 (2009): 417–24.

17. See Rebecca Campbell et al., "Community Services for Rape Survivors: Enhancing Psychological Well-Being or Increasing Trauma?" *Journal of Consulting and Clinical Psychology* 67, no. 6 (2000): 847–58; Madigan and Gamble, *The Second Rape.*

18. Adam Eley, "Stalking Victim Warns of Legal Loophole," BBC News, April 29, 2015, accessed September 20, 2019, https://www.bbc.com/news/uk-32512132.

19. Jessica Hopper, "Accused Rapist Cross-Examines Alleged Victim during Trial," ABC News, January 12, 2011, accessed September 20, 2019, https://abcnews.go.com/US/accused-rapist-cross-examines-alleged-victim-florida-courtroom/story?id=12600166.

20. L. Lonsway and F. Fitzgerald, "Rape Myths: In Review," *Pschology of Women Quarterly* 18, no. 2 (1994): 133–64, https://doi.org/10.1111/j.1471-6402.1994.tb00448.x.

21. "Fact Sheet: What You Need to Know about Sex Offenders," Center for Sex Offender Management, 2008, accessed October 20, 2019, https://www.csom.org/pubs/needtoknow_fs.pdf; D. Kilpatrick, C. Edmunds, and A. Seymour, "Rape in America: A Report to the Nation," National Victim Center, 1992, http://www.scirp.org/(S(351jmbntvnsjt1aadkposzje))/reference/ReferencesPapers.aspx?ReferenceID=1238870.

22. L. Greenfeld, "Sex Offenses and Offenders: An Analysis of Data on Rape and Sexual Assault," National Institute of Justice/NCJRS, 1997, accessed October 20, 2019, https://www.ncjrs.gov/App/Publications/abstract.aspx?ID=163931.

23. See, for example, David Lisak and Paul M. Miller, "Repeat Rape and Multiple Offending among Undetected Rapists," *Violence and Victims* 17, no. 1 (2002): 73, https://www.wcsap.org/sites/default/files/uploads/webinars/SV%20on%20Campus/Repeat%20Rape.pdf; S. Hambly, "The Path of Helpseeking: Perceptions of Law Enforcement among American Indian Victims of Sexual Assault," *Journal of Prevention and Intervention in the Community"* 36, no. 1-2 (2008): 89–104, https://www.tandfonline.com/doi/full/10.1080/10852350802022340; Heather Murphy, "What Experts Know about Men Who Rape," *New York Times*, October 30, 2017, accessed September 20, 2019, https://www.nytimes.com/2017/10/30/health/men-rape-sexual-assault.html.

24. Koss, M.P., Gidycz, C.J., & Wisniewski, N. (1987). "The Scope of Rape: Incidence and Prevalence of Sexual Aggression and Victimization among a National Sample of Students in Higher education. *Journal of Consulting and Clinical Psychology* 55, 162–70. (Paper that this the subject of the book, *I Never Called It Rape: The Ms. Report on Recognizing, Fighting and Surviving Date and Acquaintance Rape.* Harper Collins, 2018); Cook, S.S., Koss, M.P., Gidycz, C., and Murphy, M. (2011). "Emerging Issues in the Measurement of Rape Victimization. Violence Against Women," 17, 201–18; Swartout, K. M., Thompson, M. P., Koss, M. P., and Su, N. (2015). What Is the Best Way to Analyze Less Frequent Forms of Violence? The Case of Sexual Aggression. Psychology of Violence, 5(3), 305–13; Donde, S. D., Ragsdale, S. K., Koss, M. P., and Zucker, A. N. (2017). If It Wasn't Rape, Was It Sexual Assault? Comparing Rape and Sexual Assault Acknowledgment in College Women Who Have Experienced Rape. Violence Against Women; Thompson, M.P.; Swartout, K. M.; Koss, M.P. (2013) "Trajectories and Predictors of Sexually Aggressive Behaviors during Emerging Adulthood." *Psychology of Violence*, 247–59; Swartout, K. M., Koss, M. P., White, J. W., Thompson, M. P., Abbey, A., and Bellis, A. L. (2015). Trajectory analysis of the campus serial rapist assumption. *JAMA Pediatrics*, 169(12), 1148–54. Scholarly Reviewed: *Journal of Pediatrics* (Current Best Evidence), *New England Journal of Medicine* (Journal Watch – Summary and Comment)

25. Karen Rich and Patrick M. Seffrin, "Police Interviews of Sexual Assault Reporters: Do Attitudes Matter?" *Violence and Victims* 27, no. 2 (2012): 263–79, doi:10.1891/0886-6708.27.2.263.

26. "Enhancing Law Enforcement Response to Victims: 21st Century Strategy," International Association of Chiefs of Police, accessed October 20, 2019, https://www.theiacp.org/resources/document/1-enhancing-law-enforcement-response-to-victims-21st-century-strategy; "Enhancing Law Enforcement Response to Victims: Implementation Guide," International Association of Chiefs of Police. accessed October 20, 2019, https://www.theiacp

.org/resources/document/2-enhancing-law-enforcement-response-to-victims-implementa
tion-guide; "Enhancing Law Enforcement Response to Victims: Resource Toolkit," International Association of Chiefs of Police, accessed October 20, 2019, https://www.theiacp
.org/resources/document/3-enhancing-law-enforcement-response-to-victims-resource-toolkit;
"Enhancing Law Enforcement Response to Victims: Training Supplement," International
Association of Chiefs of Police, https://www.theiacp.org/resources/document/4-enhanc
ing-law-enforcement-response-to-victims-training-supplement.

27. A. Page, "Gateway to Reform?: Policy Implications of Police Officers' Attitudes toward
Rape," *American Journal of Criminal Justice* 33, no. 1 (2008): 44–58, https://link.springer.
com/article/10.1007/s12103-007-9024-9; E. Hickey, *Sex Crimes and Paraphilia* (Prentice
Hall, 2006), 394.

28. C. Furtado, "Perceptions of Rape: Cultural, Gender, and Ethnic Differences," in *Sex
Crimes and Paraphilia*, ed. E. Hickey (Prentice Hall, 2006), 441–66.

29. Ibid.

30. For early studies on police attitudes, see Hubert S. Felid, "Attitudes toward Rape:
A Comparative Analysis of Police, Rapists, Crisis Counselors, and Citizens," *Journal of
Personality and Social Psychology* 36, no. 2 (1978): 156–79; see also Lynda Lytle Holm-
strom and Ann Wolbert Burgess, *The Victim of Rape: Institutional Reactions* (New York:
John Wiley, 1978); Eric R. Galton, "Police Processing of Rape Complaints: A Case Study,"
American Journal of Criminal Law 4, no. 1 (1975): 15–30. Some additional and more con-
temporary studies include Barbara Krahé, "Police Officers' Definition of Rape: A Prototype
Study," *Journal of Community and Applied Social Psychology* 1, no. 3 (1991): 223–44; Jan
Jordan, "Worlds Apart? Women, Rape and the Police Reporting Process," *British Journal of
Criminology* 41, no. 4 (2001): 679–706; Amy Dellinger Page, "Behind the Blue Line: Inves-
tigating Police Officers' Attitudes toward Rape," *Journal of Police and Criminal Psychology*
22, no. 1 (2007): 22–32.

31. Amy Dellinger Page, "Gateway to Reform? Policy Implications of Police Officers' Attitudes toward Rape," *American Journal of Criminal Justice* 33, no. 1 (2008), 44–58.

32. Page, A., Behind the Blue Line: Investigating Police Officer Attitudes about Rape, *Journal of Police and Criminal Psychology* 22, no. 1 (June 2007): 22–23, accessed October 20,
2019, https://link.springer.com/article/10.1007/s11896-007-9002-7.

33. K. Rich and P. Seffrin, "Police Interviews of Sexual Assault Reporters: Do Attitudes
Matter?," *Violence and Victims* 401 (2012), doi:10.1891/0886-6708.27.2.263.

34. Erika Wentz and Carol A. Archbold, "Police Perceptions of Sexual Assault Victims:
Exploring the Intra-Female Gender Hostility Thesis," *Police Quarterly* 15, no. 1 (2012): 25,
doi:10.1177/1098611111432843.

35. Camila Domonoske, "Former OKC Police Officer Sentenced to 263 Years for Sexual
Assaults," NPR, January 21, 2016, accessed September 20, 2019, https://www.npr.org/sec
tions/thetwo-way/2016/01/21/463867164/former-oklahoma-city-police-officer-sentenced-to
-263-years-for-sexual-assaults.

36. Timothy M. Maher, "Police Chiefs' Views on Police Sexual Misconduct," *Police Practice and Research* 9, no. 3 (2008): 239–50, https://doi.org/10.1080/15614260701797504.

37. Neumann, *Criminal Justice and Law Enforcement Issues*, 52.

38. Katharine Bodde and Erika Lorshbough, "There's No Such Thing as 'Consensual Sex'
When a Person Is in Police Custody," ACLU, February 23, 2018, accessed September 20,
2019, https://www.aclu.org/blog/criminal-law-reform/reforming-police-practices/theres-no
-such-thing-consensual-sex-when-person.

39. E. Durkin, "Charges Dropped against ex-NYPD Officers Accused of Raping Woman
in Custody," *The Guardian*, March 7, 2019, https://www.theguardian.com/us-news/2019/
mar/07/ex-nypd-officers-rape-charges-dropped.

40. "Closing the Law Enforcement Consent Loophole Act Would Jail Cops Who Have
Sex with Someone in Their Custody," Govtrack.us, August 30, 2018, accessed September 20,

2019, https://govtrackinsider.com/closing-the-law-enforcement-consent-loophole-act-would-jail-cops-who-have-sex-with-someone-in-their-78b8d11c2804.

41. "Rape, Sexual Assault, and Sexual Harassment Tool Kit," 2008, Incite-National.org, https://incite-national.org/wp-content/uploads/2018/08/toolkitrev-sexualassault.pdf; Craig R. McCoy and Nancy Phillips, "Extorting Sex with a Badge," *Philadelphia Inquirer*, August 13, 2006, A01, https://www.inquirer.com/philly/news/special_packages/inquirer/Extorting_sex_with_a_badge.html.

42. Furtado, "Perceptions of Rape: Cultural, Gender, and Ethnic Differences."

43. Diana E. H. Russell, "The Incidence and Prevalence of Intrafamilial and Extrafamilial Sexual Abuse of Female Children," *Child Abuse & Neglect* 7, no. 2 (1983): 133–46, https://doi.org/10.1016/0145-2134(83)90065-0.

44. Julie E. Tomz and Daniel McGillis, *Serving Crime Victims and Witnesses*, 2nd ed. (Washington, DC: US Department of Justice, 1997).

45. "First Response to Victims of Crime," The National Sheriff's Association Office for Victims of Crime, US Department of Justice, July 2010, accessed October 20, 2019, https://www.ovc.gov/publications/infores/pdftxt/2010FirstResponseGuidebook.pdf.

46. "Case Brief, *Thurman v. City of Torrington*, 595 F. Supp. 1521 (D. Conn. 1985)," http://www.ncdsv.org/images/CaseBrief_ThurmanVCityOfTorrington_1985.pdf.

47. "Rape, Sexual Assault, and Sexual Harassment Took Kit."

48. Ibid.

49. Hambly, "The Path of Helpseeking."

50. Andrew Fulkerson and Shelly L. Patterson, "Victimless Prosecution of Domestic Violence in the Wake of *Crawford v. Washington*," Forum on Public Policy, September 22, 2006, 10, http://forumonpublicpolicy.com/archive06/fulkerson.pdf.

51. Vachss, *Sex Crimes*, 44.

52. K. Seelinger, H. Silverberg, and R. Mejia, "The Investigation and Prosecution of Sexual Violence," Human Rights Center, University of California Berkeley, May 2011, accessed October 20, 2019, https://www.law.berkeley.edu/wp-content/uploads/2015/04/The-Investigation-and-Prosecution-of-Sexual-Violence-SV-Working-Paper.pdf.

53. Vachss, *Sex Crimes*, 44.

54. Ibid., 90; Robin Sax, *It Happens Every Day: Inside the World of a Sex Crimes DA* (New York: Prometheus Books, 2010).

55. Vachss, *Sex Crimes*, 91.

56. Sarina Straus, *Bronx D.A.: True Stories from the Sex Crimes and Domestic Violence Unit* (Fort Lee, NJ: Barricade Books, 2006), 38.

57. For examples, see the cases outlined by Straus, *Bronx D.A.*, beginning on page 61.

58. Vachss, *Sex Crimes*, 241.

59. Straus, *Bronx D.A.*, 61–62.

60. Sax, *It Happens Every Day*, 84.

61. See Straus, *Bronx D.A.*, 77. See also "*Jackson v. Indiana* (1972), United States Supreme Court, No. 70-5009, Argued: November 18, 1971, Decided: June 7, 1972," https://caselaw.findlaw.com/us-supreme-court/406/715.html.

62. Straus, *Bronx D.A.*, 78.

63. Sax, *It Happens Every Day*, 49.

64. Vachss, *Sex Crimes*, 110.

65. Sax, *It Happens Every Day*, 51.

66. Ibid., 90.

67. Ibid., 101.

68. Ibid., Chapter 7.

69. "Improving the Police Response to Sexual Assault," March 2012, 4, accessed October 20, 2019, https://www.policeforum.org/assets/docs/Critical_Issues_Series/improving%20the%20police%20response%20to%20sexual%20assault%202012.pdf.

70. "Critical Issues in Police Series: Improving the Police Response to Sexual Assault," Police Executive Research Forum, March 2012, accessed September 20, 2019, http://police forum.org/library/critical-issues-in-policing-series/SexualAssaulttext_web.pdf.

71. Vachss, *Sex Crimes*, 185; Sax, *It Happens Every Day*.

72. This list of members that are included in a sexual assault team comes from Sax, *It Happens Every Day*, 25–46.

73. Ibid., vi.

74. This list of questions that the prosecutor's office must address comes from Sax, *It Happens Every Day*, 41.

75. Sax, *It Happens Every Day*, 43.

76. Vachss, *Sex Crimes*, 159.

77. Delores D. Stroud, Sonja J. Martens, and Julia Barker, "Criminal Investigation of Child Sexual Abuse: A Comparison of Cases Referred to the Prosecutor to Those Not Referred," *Child Abuse & Neglect* 24, no. 5 (1999): 689–700, https://doi.org/10.1016/S0145 -2134(00)00131-9.

78. "Sexual Assault Incident Reports: Investigative Strategies," International Association of Chiefs of Police, 2005, accessed September 20, 2019, https://www.theiacp.org/sites/default/ files/all/s/SexualAssaultGuidelines.pdf.

79. Delores D. Stroud, Sonja J. Martens, and Julia Barker, "Criminal Investigation of Child Sexual Abuse: A Comparison of Cases Referred to the Prosecutor to Those Not Referred," *Child Abuse & Neglect* 24, no. 5 (1999): 698, https://doi.org/10.1016/S0145-2134(00)00131-9.

80. Straus, *Bronx D.A.*, 129.

81. Ibid., 130.

82. Fulkerson and Patterson, "Victimless Prosecution in the Wake of *Crawford v. Washington*."

83. Straus, *Bronx D.A.*, 203.

12

Correctional Management and Civil Commitment

◆ ◆ ◆

97% of offenders currently serving time for sexual offense will return to our communities. Most offenders spend 2 years in prison and 67% have sentences of 18 months or less, although sentences for sex offenders tend to be longer than the typical sentence for other crimes.

—Washington State Department of Corrections[1]

Every child has the right to live free from violence and sexual abuse. Promoting public safety by holding offenders accountable and by instituting effective crime prevention measures is a core government obligation.

—Human Rights Watch, 2007[2]

THE LAST STAGES OF formally processing an individual through the criminal justice system are the prison sentence itself and, then, for most individuals convicted of a sex offense, the necessary preparations for their eventual return to the community. This chapter focuses attention on the general processing a sex offender is likely to experience throughout their involvement with the criminal justice system postconviction. Utilizing examples as illustrations of the overall experience of a person convicted of committing a sex offense and found guilty, a basic presentation of the process is outlined, followed by information on risk factors and risk assessment strategies for planning transition back into the community postrelease. (A larger conversation about the role of assessments more broadly in the work of sex-offender management and treatment is provided in chapter 13.) Here, the emphasis is placed on a review of the process of reintegration after the individual is released. Programs and techniques for monitoring offenders in the community are introduced briefly for consideration and review. The chapter closes with consideration of the civil commitment program, followed by an overview of information about sex-offender recidivism and the goal of public safety.

GENERAL INTAKE AND PROCESSING: AN OVERVIEW

Before beginning the larger discussion about correctional management of sex offenders, two things need to be highlighted. First, the treatment and management chapters have been separated by chapter boundaries, but the boundary between correctional management (chapter 12) and treatment (chapter 13) is not nearly so neatly drawn in real life. Second, regional and state-level statutory and policy directives for sex-offender management in the community and the related community attitudes that created the processes for sex-offender management will reflect significant differences in different geographic locations. This too will reflect events and priorities in the communities from where they were and are generated.

As both professional and volunteer advocates become more common in the criminal justice system, their work has pushed professionals to increasingly recognize the need to shift the offender-focused nature of sex-offender management processes, which often present as indifferent to the interests of sexual assault victims. The result is a list of goals practitioners follow to advance instead a **victim-centered approach** to the supervision of sex offenders.[3] In 2018, the Center for Effective Public Policy and the National Sexual Violence Resource Center put together a toolkit for practitioners supervising sex offenders in the community. The introduction suggests the following:

> Supervising sex offenders can be particularly challenging and the stakes are high in a number of ways, such as the following:
>
> - The intensely personal and intrusive nature of sexual violence, the complex dynamics involved, and the effects on victims are unlike most other crimes.
> - Responsibility for victim and public safety weighs heavily on officers' shoulders, and high levels of scrutiny can lead to added pressure.
> - Sex offender-specific laws and agency policies have "widened the net," resulting in increased workload demands for officers, usually without additional resources.
> - The potential for burnout and vicarious trauma for officers who work with these cases is heightened.
>
> Professionals who accept these challenges provide a valuable service to survivors and their families, the public, and sex offenders by:
>
> - holding sexual abusers accountable for their behaviors and the harm caused to victims;
> - enhancing victim and public safety through various risk management strategies;
> - using evidence-based strategies to reduce reoffense risk and support lasting behavioral change among perpetrators; and
> - helping ensure that supervision practices are responsive to—and do not run counter to the rights, needs, and interests of sexual assault survivors.
>
> Collectively, these goals and roles reflect what is referred to as a "victim-centered approach" to supervising sex offenders. This approach recognizes that the traditionally offender-focused nature of sex offender management inadvertently can create systems that appear indifferent to the interests of sexual assault victims. In turn, some sexual assault survivors and their families

may feel ignored, invalidated, or further traumatized by the system that is designed to protect and support them.[4]

Exactly how sex-offender management programs are designed and implemented will differ regionally, but this attention and consideration to victims is also an emerging best practice within the field.

A person who is required to register as a sex offender is also under **correctional supervision**, which means they will be in jail or prison or on some form of **community correctional supervision**, where the remainder of the sentence is completed in the community under the supervision of an officer, more traditionally known as a **probation officer** or **corrections agent**. Judges impose different sentences for each offender, depending on the offense, the circumstances around the offense, the offender's prior violations, the specific characteristics of the case, characteristics of harm associated with the incident, age of the victim, and attributes of the state laws.

As discussed in chapter 11, as a proportion of offenses committed, only a small percentage of people identified or arrested for a sex offense will be prosecuted and convicted. When someone is convicted of a sex offense, however, the person convicted will typically be placed under some form of correctional supervision. A standard intake and release process is overviewed in the following text box.

Text Box 12.1.   Standard Correctional Intake and Release Process for a Sex Offender[1]

Once a court issues a conviction, a presentence investigation may be conducted, usually including updates on medical and mental health information.

A psychosexual evaluation may be requested.

The offender is required to turn over all money and personal property not allowed in the facility; for example, offenders may be allowed a wedding band, glasses, and legal papers.

The offender is required to receive a visual body cavity search.

The offender will be thoroughly examined for scars, tattoos, and other identifying marks; in some states, this is done by taking photos of the offender.

Offenders are fingerprinted.

Offenders are photographed front and profile.

Offenders are assigned to a cell.

Offenders are issued personal care items.

Sentence is served; sex offender treatment is an option in some facilities.

The offender is notified of release date.

Additional assessments are conducted.

End-of-confinement review; risk level assigned.

Release to the community; report to police departments (or local protocol) for registration and contact established with community supervision officers and (if required) treatment program.

Note

1. Community Supervision Operations Manual. www.csosa.gov https://www.csosa .gov/wp-content/uploads/bsk-pdf-manager/2018/08/CSS-Operations-Manual.pdf

Some offenders are released into the community directly, without jail time, as the result of a plea agreement, the issuance of a **suspended or stayed sentence**, or a sentence of probation without a jail or prison term. A stayed sentence comes after a conviction, where the court accepts a finding of guilty but elects to delay the imposition of prison time. In some cases, a person will be released with an agreement to accept specific conditions, perhaps attend a sex-offender treatment program, and then be released under **community supervision**. Assuming those stipulations are completed, they will not go to prison. A violation of those terms would return the person to court and likely result in a removal of the stay and an imposition of the original jail or prison sentence. For other cases involving straight release back into the community, a judge could simply order an extended term of probation in lieu of jail or prison.

Examples of offenses where an offender admits guilt and is released from court back into the community are covered in news feeds regularly. For example, a New York case in the spring of 2019 described a bus driver who entered a guilty plea to a third-degree rape charge involving a 14-year-old girl and was sentenced to 10 years on probation.[5] In December 2018, a student accused of raping a woman at a Baylor fraternity party plead no contest (not admitting guilt, but not presenting a defense) to a plea arrangement to a lesser charge of unlawful restraint. He agreed to counseling and to pay court fees but would not spend time in jail or prison or register as a sex offender. If he successfully completes probation will have the charge expunged from his record.[6] As has been discussed in chapter 8 and elsewhere, the impact of court decisions can have a big impact on the individual who was harmed their family and the community.

In spite of the fact that the conditions of any given charge, conviction, and sentencing decision for a sex crime are situationally specific and will vary considerably from state to state and jurisdiction to jurisdiction, the impact of the decisions made by judges and correctional staff are critically important. Decisions made by judges handing down sentencing decisions, practitioners working with individual offenders in a therapeutic environment, and correctional officers managing their situation in the community are informed by various **risk assessments** utilized at various points in an individual's processing. The data collected from conducting assessments is used to inform and at least in part determine actions to be taken at various decision points, including:

- Sentencing or disposition, including prison or probation terms and other court expectations
- Levels and conditions or supervision for offender in the community
- Intensity and targets of treatment
- Release and reentry decisions
- Compliance and progress with respect to supervision and treatment.[7]

While states may have different specifics, a process similar to this one is utilized by each state department of corrections in the management of their sex-offender population. Table 12.1, in the section on Washington state below, provides a fairly thorough overview of that state's process. Two examples of assessments that can be used right away in the court process to assist a judge in making decisions about the best course of action for meeting the offenders' needs and assuring the best efforts are considered for meeting public safety needs are the **presentence investigation (PSI)** and the **psychosexual evaluation**. One popular assessment for people entering the corrections system is a **Level of Service/ Case Management Inventory (LS/CMI)**. This tool measures the risk and need factors for late adolescent and adult offenders to assist professionals in planning the treatment and management protocols for a newly convicted offender. Figure 12.1 illustrates the key areas measured by the LS/CMI assessment: general risk/ need factors, specific risk/need factors, institutional factors, client-specific factors, and special considerations.

A psychosexual evaluation, also referred to as a sex-offender specific evaluation, is often requested in the closing stages of a court process involving a crime of a sexual nature and includes a detailed sexual history of the individual, which includes a review of their exploration of sexual development, attitudes, fantasies, arousal patterns, interests, and preferences.[8] It has been said before, but is important to state again, that the offender population generically lumped together as "sex offenders" is actually a quite diverse population. For this reason, it is important to consider the nuances each offender brings to their confinement and eventually a treatment program. A skilled examiner who includes multiple sources of data can get important information about how best to work with, treat, and manage the individual while in custody and after release.

It is important to be clear that the initial screenings are not related to the court process responsible for finding facts and deciding guilt or innocence, nor are they used to assess someone as being able to be classified or labeled a "sex offender." They are tools used by the court and correctional staff after a conviction and carry considerable weight for determining the next course of action.

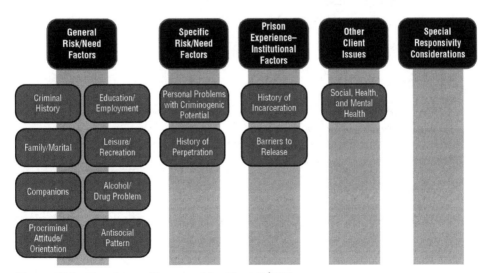

Figure 12.1 Key Areas Measured by the LS/CMI

MHS Assessments. LS/CMI. Key Areas Measured image. https://www.mhs.com/MHS-Publicsafety
?prodname=ls-cmi

Practitioners who administer the assessments must have specialized training to administer these assessments due to the complexity of the instruments and their value in the overall process. By using the best available objective measures to gather information and provide relevant information to the court in preparation for the **disposition**, or judicial decision, all parties rest more easily assured the needs of the convicted offender and the public will be responsibly monitored. (More details on additional assessment tools are presented in chapter 13.)

The few convicted sex offenders who do not return to the community after their sentence has been completed are likely to have been legally deemed a sexually dangerous person, a **sexually violent predator** (SVP), or a sexual psychopath, depending on the statutory, or legal, language in the system governing their detention. These individuals will remain in secure facilities, even after the completion of their criminal sentences and until they meet the legally defined criteria for release. Typically, this means they will be held in state custody, a program referred to as **civil commitment**, until they have been declared by a correctional body to have been rehabilitated. More about the role of civil commitment is presented below.

OFFENDER RELEASE AND COMMUNITY SUPERVISION

By far, the majority of convicted sex offenders will be released from prison to return to the community. In 2016, the Center for Missing and Exploited Children had documented approximately 859,500 registered sex offenders living in communities throughout the United States.[9] The experience of an offender in the world after release can be very different, depending on where they hope to be living.

Chapter 10 overviewed several state and federal policies, such as offender registration, community notification, and residency restrictions. The offender must comply with all of the statutory provisions passed into law in the community where the offender will be located. In addition, a newly released offender will be given a collection of **conditions of supervision**, here, from the state of Colorado, which might include but are not limited to the following:

> Participation in an approved sex offender evaluation and treatment program;
> Registration as a Colorado sex offender;
> Genetic marker testing;
> No use of drugs or alcohol;
> No contact with children (even your own);
> No contact with any victim;
> No dating or marriage of anyone with children under 18 unless approved by the state;
> No possession of porn; and
> No change of residence unless approved by the state of Colorado.[10]

Again, even these general conditions will change from state to state; however, serving the community portion of a sentence is considered a privilege, and violation of any one of these and other conditions can be grounds for sending the offender back to prison to serve out the full sentence.

Because the larger percentage of offenders know the people/person they offended against, community supervisors will work closely with the treatment practitioner to determine the potential impact of the offender's community reintegration plan. Relationships and alliances often develop between community-based corrections/probation staff, treatment practitioners, and support program staff. Increasingly, this collaboration, referred to as the **containment model,** is considered the best practice for providing an overarching management strategy to assure the best possibility for full program participation and offender success.

The **Risk, Need, Responsivity (RNR) Model** takes the assessment of offender risk once it has been identified and works to match the appropriate level of supervision to meet a given individual's particular needs and goals.[11] The general premise of RNR is that the combination of supervision and treatment is most effective when more resources go to the offenders identified as higher risk, while at the same time lower-risk offenders are provided with fewer resources. Research has suggested providing lower-risk offenders with high levels of treatment can result in increased **recidivism,** or the likelihood that an offender will offend again.[12]

Communities are to be notified when a sex offender is released; however, it has been left up to the state to determine how the risk levels will be identified and when and how the community will be notified. Restricted spaces will include schools, parks, churches, and daycares, as examples. If, for example, a bus route moves through an area that is off limits to sex offenders because of a residency restriction, then they would have to find an alternative transportation route to reach their intended destination.[13]

In some communities, landlords or owners of rental properties may take active measures to prevent a person with a sex offense from moving into their neighborhood or building. Offenders must register required information with local police departments. Residency restriction provisions have been resoundingly criticized as ineffectual; however, restrictions for sex offenders are placed on where they can live. If you cannot find a home within the acceptable areas of the city, an offender can be determined to be in violation of their conditions of probation before they are actually released from prison, which can result in an extension of their prison term up to 10 years or longer. Also, residency restriction laws are put in place to limit the places where sex offenders can move freely, which may impact their ability to get a job, find housing, or grocery shop, as examples. Residency restrictions identify within a particular distance 500 feet or 1,000 feet (depending on the statute) locations where children gather, which will be off limits to sex offenders living in the community.

If the offender lived in the same home with the victim or was their neighbor, as examples, the supervising agent will work with other social service providers working with the victim and their family's therapists and/or other professionals involved to monitor that transition on how that happens. In the case of Colorado's restrictions listed above, no contact with children is permitted, even if the children involved are their own. Plans involving a family placement will be carefully considered by all social service providers involved. In some cases, like in Colorado, alternative housing arrangements must be made. Again, this will vary from state to state and will be directed by the supervision agent.

In addition to housing arrangements, another particularly important element of a sex offender's reintegration process is the job search. Sex offenders experience more barriers and hurdles when seeking employment than nonoffenders.[14] Some job applications ask about conviction histories. In short, employers do not always hire sex offenders, and finding a job for which the offender has skills and in an environment free of restrictions can be an obstacle. The 2000 **Campus Sex Crime Prevention Act** requires institutions of higher education to maintain and disseminate information about registered sex offenders.[15]

Compliance could include options such as chemical castration, or an electronic monitoring, or GPS, device used to keep track of more serious offenders' locations at all times; other requirements may include no internet or computer and other digital devices and no drugs or alcohol. The majority of sex-offender treatment programs use mandatory **polygraph testing** as a portion of therapy protocol, and in an effort to be certain offenders were fully accountable for the level of their sex offending and other criminal behaviors. Polygraph testing is considered the most effective means of validating the accuracy of an offender's self-reports.[16] (More about treatment will be presented in chapter 13.) Some of those treatment costs are to be paid by the offender. Once an offender is back in the community, by and large, the onus is on the offender, who will be responsible for checking in with their community supervisor and treatment programs as directed.

It would not be a far stretch to say that some supporters of offenders in the community are concerned about the degree of choice and the level of autonomy offenders are left with when they return to the community. Do these programs, which can be very proscriptive, go too far in leaving very little choice to the individual? If treatment is a choice when you are in the facility, but you don't get out if you don't participate in treatment, is it really voluntary? In some cases programs require very personally invasive testing, which has been challenged by the courts.

Overall, when a person is sentenced to prison, the processes they will experience will likely be quite exacting and will remain so until they have completed the duration of their sentence. After release, the transition back into the community can be difficult. Communities will typically have social service agencies or programs set up to assist offenders with reintegration back into the community. Preliminary research indicates that when all of these resources are poured into individuals who are at the highest risk to reoffend, rearrests for another sex crime are significantly reduced. Individuals interested in learning more about the oversight of offenders in the community can refer to the **Center for Sex Offender Management (CSOM)**, which is a national clearinghouse focused on providing technical assistance for practitioners in state and local jurisdictions, including research and best practice resources on assessment, treatment, supervision, and community reentry. SORNA (Sex Offender Registration and Notification Act) also established the **Office of Sex Offender Sentencing, Monitoring, Apprehending, Registering, and Tracking (SMART)** to assist states with implementation of the SORNA requirements. As of December 2018, 17 states, 134 tribes, and four territories have substantially implemented the SORNA requirements.[17] Finally, individuals interested in learning more about the sex offenders located in their communities or nearby can consult the **Dru Sjodin** (pronounced Drew Shu-deen) **National Sex Offender Public Website** (http://www.nsopw.gov), which includes state-by-state access to sex-offender registry sites. The US Department of Justice established the site to provide a free resource to search for sex offenders registered by state, territories, and tribal communities.[18]

SEX-OFFENDER REGISTRATION AND NOTIFICATION

The Adam Walsh Act of 2006 replaced the notification elements of Megan's Law and replaced the Wetterling Act and its amendments (introduced in chapter 10) put in place for registering sex offenders intended to secure information about every sex offender living in the community, as a means for being able to check on them as needed should a crime happen, or as a means for locating them if they are not in compliance with their conditions of release. Most states share a similar general process, which includes having sex offenders who are released from prison register with local police (or designated agent or agency).

As the offender is released, the departments of corrections are required to establish a scale for use in determining the **level of risk** a sex offender is thought to pose to the community upon their release. A **Tier I** designation for the offender suggests a low level of risk to the community and **Tier II,** a moderate level of risk, and **Tier III** means the offender has been deemed to represent a high level of risk. References are also made to level classifications, referring to offenders as Level 1 (low), Level 2 (moderate), or Level 3 (high) risk, with a Tier III, or Level III, classification assigned to offenders believed most likely to warrant correctional as well as community attention and concerns.

As discussed in chapter 10, federal and state requirements mandating a sex-offender log in their information with the local sex-offender registry will require a person convicted with these stipulations to comply with the designated authorities within a set period of time in the community where they plan to live. Although federal requirements for registration must be followed at the state level, states and tribal governments might also elect to implement specific regulations locally. Alabama's community notification legislation has been identified as perhaps the most restrictive in the United States because everyone convicted of a sex offense, regardless of the nature of the offense, is required to participate in community notification.[19] Another aspect of the Alabama law that makes the restrictions placed on sex offenders more severe is the application of residency restriction provisions, also introduced in chapter 10, which limit offender access to designated locations. Florida has also earned a national reputation for its use of residence restriction ordinances.

The state of Massachusetts, as another example, posts the numbers of Level 2 and Level 3 in each town and directs further inquiries to the local police department or to the Commonwealth of Massachusetts Sex Offender Registry Board.[20] If you would like to do a more detailed search, you must proceed through a screen that requires you to acknowledge that you will not use the information to discriminate or harass an offender and tell the system you are not a robot. Once you proceed through this page, you are taken to a search engine that allows you to research a person by a name, a city, the county where the offender was incarcerated, or postal code.[21]

The state of California has created a **State Authorized Risk Assessment Tool for Sex Offenders (SARATSO)** review committee[22] to consider which risk assessment tool will be used to assess the risk levels for sex offenders in California. Closing their statement with two important points, the Washoe Tribe of Nevada and California include the following statement about the conditions of use on its web page:

> The sex offender registry is NOT intended to replace the Community Notification process—rather, it allows the Washoe Tribe to promote public awareness concerning the potential threat that sex offenders may pose to all citizens. The Registry will empower you to obtain information on some sex offenders within the Tribe's jurisdiction and take the appropriate precautions. Furnishing the public with information regarding convicted sex offenders is a critical step toward encouraging the public to protect themselves from potential future acts. An informed public is a safer public.
>
> Not all sex offenders have been caught and convicted. Most sex offenses are committed by family members, friends, or acquaintances of the victim. For more information, be sure to click on this link: https://www.nsopw.gov/en/SafetyAndEducation.[23]

Dispelling the myths by stating the fact that offenders are often known to their victims and that some offenders have not been caught or convicted and remain outside of the control of the criminal justice system or tribal authorities and therefore would not be listed on the public registries is an important public education message. Text Box 12.2 reviews the list of offenses that require a convicted offender to include their name on the sex-offender registry in the state of Mississippi.

The purpose of sex-offender registration and notification laws was to provide the public with information they could use to better protect themselves and their families from known offenders.[24] Ultimately, the goal of registration and notification was to make sure police and local community members knew where sex offenders were, but a Gallup poll reported that only 23 percent of adults have actually checked the registry.[25] Other indicators that the legislation has not achieved the goals in practice that were intended when they were passed are offered in several studies indicating the data on the registry is notoriously inaccurate.[26] The expectation was that this close regulation of sex offenders in the community would prevent child sexual abuse and rapes; however, the studies that have researched this question have suggested little or no observable influence or slight general deterrence impact but no impact on recidivism.[27] In short, making comparisons across studies can be very difficult because studies might specifically focus on juveniles and other adults, while the subject of the study may also differ significantly, with some studies focusing on a single state or several specified states, but the findings would not accurately reflect outcomes regionally or nationally.

Text Box 12.2. Which Offenses Require Registration in Mississippi?[1]

- 97-3-53 Kidnapping, if the victim was below the age of eighteen (18)
- 97-3-65 Statutory rape
- 97-3-71 Rape and assault with intent to ravish
- 97-3-95 Sexual battery
- 97-5-5 Enticing a child for concealment, prostitution or marriage
- 97-5-23 Touching of a child, or a mentally defective, incapacitated, or physically helpless person for lustful purposes
- 97-5-27 Dissemination of sexually oriented material to children; computer luring of minor to engage in sexual conduct
- 97-5-33 Exploitation of child
- 97-5-41 Carnal knowledge of stepchild, adopted child, or child of a cohabiting partner
- 97-29-59 Unnatural intercourse
- 97-1-7 Attempt to commit any of the above-referenced offenses
- 97-29-3 Adultery or fornication between teacher and pupil
- 43-47-18 Relating to sexual abuse of a vulnerable adult
- 97-3-54.1 (1)(c) Procuring sexual servitude of a minor
- 97-29-63 Filming another without permission where there is an expectation of privacy
- Any offense committed in another jurisdiction, which would be considered one of the above in MS
- Any offense committed in another jurisdiction for which registration is required in that jurisdiction
- Any conviction of conspiracy to commit, accessory to commission, or attempt to commit any offense listed in the statute

Note

1. See MCA Section 45-33-25(g) for the list of registrable crimes, http://state.sor.dps.ms.gov/sor_faqs.html.

A MORE DETAILED OFFERING ON THREE STATES: WASHINGTON, MINNESOTA, AND COLORADO

Much of the information about sex-offender management and practice is included on the relevant web pages used for public notification. Without exception, each state will have a means by which individuals can review the information posted about the state's policy and practice. The degree to which the state pages are updated and monitored for changes will vary. *At a minimum*, however, all registered sex offenders are required to submit the following information to law enforcement:

- Name
- Social security number
- Home, work, and school address
- License plate number
- Vehicle description for all vehicles

- Date of birth
- Email addresses
- Pseudonyms used for instant messaging programs
- Passport numbers
- Phone numbers

Depending on the level of supervision in the community, if an offender travels for more than a specified time, they will need to report to law enforcement, which will notify the destination location. Forensic information will be collected, including a DNA sample, fingerprints, and a palm print. An offender can petition to be removed from the registry, but this is only an option after an offender has served a significant amount of their time.[28]

Several states have earned a reputation for the work being done with sex-offender practice and policy. Three of them will be reviewed briefly here: Washington, Minnesota, and Colorado. As noted above, the intention behind the legislative actions at the federal level often direct the actions taken by the states; however, state implementation and practices vary. Further, gaps between intention and practice can be addressed when the execution of the laws does not always match legislative intent when put in practice. In fact, unexpected implications in the communities in real time and the search for better data to inform public practice have produced data-driven practices coming from within the state departments of corrections, another reason these states were selected to highlight.

Washington

The state of Washington has a long history of working with sex-offender policies and efforts to manage offenders in the community. As has been discussed earlier, state officials made some difficult decisions as a result of some very serious sex offenses and continuing concerns about risk to public safety. Information about the state's sex-offender management process is outlined on its state Department of Corrections website, titled "Sex Offender Treatment and Assessment."[29] Statistics opening the page identify approximately 20 percent of the inmates in Washington state correctional facilities and 18 percent of individuals on community supervision are serving time for sex offenses. Table 12.1 outlines the processing decision points, the party conducting the assessment and the instruments used in the intake and evaluation process. At each of the decision points outlined—sentencing, facility assignment, treatment planning, release, civil commitment, risk level assignment, and postrelease supervision—a risk assessment will be conducted.

The three main goals of the Sex Offender Treatment Program (SOTP) are identified as:

1. help the offender learn to reduce and manage their risk to reoffend,
2. provide information to aid DOC and the community to monitor and manage offenders more effectively,
3. remain accountable to the people of the State of Washington by routinely evaluating and aligning SOTP with evidence-based practices.[30]

Table 12.1 Sex Offender Risk Assessment in Washington State[1]

Decision Points	Party Conducting Assessments	Instrument Employed
Sentencing	Private treatment providers SSOSA/SSODA eligibility	Adults: STATIC-99, SONAR/Stable, and others Juveniles: ERASOR, JSOAP and others
Facility assignment and level of custody in institutions	Department of Corrections Juvenile Rehabilitation Administration	LSI-R ISCA WSSORLCT
Treatment eligibility and planning	Department of Corrections Private Treatment Providers Special Commitment Center	MnSOST-R, RRASOR, STATIC-99, and Stable-2000 Adults: STATIC-99, SONAR/Stable, and others Juvenile: ERASOR, JSOAP and others No set battery
Release from confinement	Indeterminate Sentence Review Board	WSSORLCT, MnSOST-R, LSI-R, STATIC-99
Civil commitment eligibility	End of Sentence Review Committee (ESRC) Juvenile Rehabilitation Administration Joint Forensic Unit Special Commitment Center	WSSORLCT, MnSOST-R, LSI-R, STATIC-99 WSSORLCT STATIC-99, MnSOST-R, and others No set battery
Assignment of risk level for community notification	End of Sentence Review Committee Juvenile Rehabilitation Administration Law Enforcement Agencies	WSSORLCT, MnSOST-R, LSI-R, STATIC-99 WSSORLCT WSSORLCT
Postrelease supervision in the community	Department of Corrections Juvenile Rehabilitation Administration	LSI-R SOSS

SSOSA (Special Sex Offender Sentencing Alternative)
SSODA (Special Sex Offender Disposition Alternative)
SONAR (Sex Offender Need Assessment Rating)
ERASOR (Estimate of Risk of Adolescent Sexual Offense Recidivism)
JSOAP (Juvenile Sex Offender Assessment Protocol)
LSI-R (Level of Service Inventory – Revised)
ISCA (Initial Security Classification Assessment)
WSSORLCT (Washington State Sex Offender Risk Level Classification Tool)
MnSOST-R, (Minnesota Sex Offender Screening Tool – Revised)
RRASOR (Rapid Risk Assessment for Sex Offender Recidivism)
SOSS (Sex Offender Supervision Screen, also known as Intensive Parole Supervision Assessment [IPSA])

1 Tali Klima & Roxanne Lieb. (2008). Risk assessment instruments to predict recidivism of sex offenders: Practices in Washington State. Olympia: Washington State Institute for Public Policy, Document No. 08-06-1101. Retrieved November 26 ,2019. https://www.wsipp.wa.gov/ReportFile/1015/Wsipp_Risk-Assessment-Instruments-to-Predict-Recidivism-of-Sex-Offenders-Practices-in-Washington-State_Full-Report.pdf

Utilizing the Risk, Needs, Responsibility (RNR) principles introduced above, offenders are assessed, and treatment programs are made available to male and female sex offenders at three facilities. All offenders may volunteer to participate in the program; however, because of the lengthy wait period, most people enter treatment when they have only 18 months left on their sentence.

Offenders preparing to leave the facility undergo an assessment and classification process by the End of Sentence Review Committee to determine what level of community notification the offender will be responsible for after release. Anyone involved in the SOTP while in prison is provided continued treatment while being supervised in the community and is expected to continue in treatment for up to three years.[31]

Once back in the community, the individuals must register within 24 hours at the county sheriff's office, report to their community corrections officer (CCO), be available for contact as directed, and remain within specific boundaries. Eighty-six percent of offenders who go back to prison go back for failing to register, which is a felony.[32] Their living arrangements are tightly regulated and must be approved by the CCO. In the state of Washington, sex offenders released into the community *cannot*:

- Own or control personal computers without special permission. If permission is granted, blocks for certain sites must be maintained.
- Have contact with magazines, videos, telephone sites, or anything else with pornographic content.
- Deny their CCO access to any part of their home.
- Purchase, possess, or consume any mind or mood altering substances, including alcohol or drugs not prescribed by a doctor.
- (Typically) have contact with past victims or the victims' families. If the victim is from within their family, any contact will be assessed by the court, and monitored by the CCO.
- Begin a romantic relationship without informing their CCO. Offenders must disclose information about their convictions to potential adult sexual partners before beginning a sexual relationship. Some CCOs may require the offender to disclose abuse to families and friends.
- Patronize any establishment in the sex industry.
- (Felony offenders cannot) own, use, or possess firearms or ammunition.

A closing commentary on the program has to do with the program costs. A 2009 study by Washington State Institute for Public Policy (WSIPP) indicated that for each participant who had treatment in prison and aftercare in the community, there was an estimated $4,064 in victim and taxpayers benefits, and crime was reduced by almost 10 percent. A study conducted by the WSIPP in December 2013 reviewed the costs and benefits of sex-offender treatment and found that treatment saves more money than it costs in both community- and prison-based settings. Costs are typically tabulated in ways that make sense to the state operations, and as a result, it can be hard to make apples-to-apples comparisons between systems.

Minnesota

In Minnesota, information about the community release of sex offenders is discussed in detail at the Department of Corrections web page, under the "Intensive

Supervised Release" (ISR) program. The extended civil commitment program, Minnesota Sex Offender Program (MSOP), is discussed on the Department of Human Services web page, under "Minnesota Sex Offender Program." MSOP serves individuals court ordered to sex-offender treatment.[33] A judge in a civil court proceeding can be tasked with determining whether a person is "a sexual psychopathic personality" or a "sexually dangerous person" as defined by state statute. Should such a determination be made, the individual will be placed in a sex-offender treatment program for an unspecified period of time. As of April 2019, 721 individuals have been admitted into that program, where treatment is provided in two state-run facilities at Moose Lake and St. Peter. The significant controversy about the program centered on the fact that people were not being released from the program. In the years leading up to and immediately following 2015, Minnesota made national news headlines with challenges to the constitutionality of the civil commitment program in the state. Civil commitment will be discussed more broadly at the end of the chapter.

In the state of Minnesota, as of July 1, 2018, there were 9,849 inmates incarcerated in Minnesota correctional facilities. A total of 2,908 (30 percent) of these offenders met the sex-offender definitions used in this report. The majority (58 percent) of the 2,908 sex offenders were classified as a GSO, an inmate whose governing offense was a felony-level criminal sexual conduct. Other sex offenders (OSOs), or individuals who are in prison for another crime but had previously been convicted of a felony-level sex crime in Minnesota (or elsewhere) or are required to register as a predatory offender, accounted for the remaining 42 percent of sex offenders incarcerated in Minnesota correctional facilities.[34] Approximately 1,200 offenders are served quarterly in the Intensive Supervision Program across Minnesota.

Offenders in the state of Minnesota serve two-thirds of the executed sentence in the prison facility and the final one-third of their sentence under community supervision. Minnesota operates under rules of determinate sentencing, with the presumptive sentence lengths based on the severity of the crime (indicated along the left column) and the criminal history score (across the top; see Figure 12.2).[35] Offenders who commit other offenses are subject to a different sentencing guideline.[36]

The gray area on the sex-offender grid indicates the number of months an offender might have their prison term stayed, or temporarily suspended, and placed in the community under supervision, for example. In those cases, failure to follow the imposed guidelines or restrictions will result in the court executing the term of incarceration, and the person will serve out the rest of their sentence in prison.

The DOC FY17 ISR budget was $4.195 million. About 1,200 offenders are served quarterly on ISR across Minnesota. ISR costs about $18 per day, per offender. GPS monitoring costs an additional $6.90–$7.20 per day, per offender. Traditional probation and supervised release costs about $4 per day, per offender. In FY17, $3.869 million was allocated for grants to local entities to provide programming.

Presumptive sentence lengths are in months. Italicized numbers within the grid denote the discretionary range within which a court may sentence without the sentence being deemed a departure. Offenders with stayed felony sentences may be subject to local confinement.

CRIMINAL HISTORY SCORE

SEVERITY LEVEL OF CONVICTION OFFENSE		0	1	2	3	4	5	6 or more
CSC 1st Degree	A	144 *144-172*	156 *144-187*	168 *144-201*	180 *153-216*	234 *199-280*	306 *261-360*	360 *306-360[2]*
CSC 2nd Degree–(c)(d)(e)(f)(h) Prostitution; Sex Trafficking[3] 1st Degree–1(a)	B	90 *90[3]-108*	110 *94-132*	130 *111-156*	150 *128-180*	195 *166-234*	255 *217-300*	300 *255-300[2]*
CSC 3rd Degree–(c)(d)(g)(h)(i)(j) (k)(l)(m)(n)(o) Prostitution; Sex Trafficking 2nd Degree–1(a)	C	48 *41-57*	62 *53-74*	76 *65-91*	90 *77-108*	117 *100-140*	153 *131-180*	180 *153-180[2]*
CSC 2nd Degree–(a)(b)(g) CSC 3rd Degree–(a)(e)(f) or (b) with ref. to subd. 2(1) Dissemination of Child Pornography (Subsequent or by Predatory Offender)	D	36	48	60 *51-72*	70 *60-84*	91 *78-109*	119 *102-142*	140 *119-168*
CSC 4th Degree–(c)(d)(g)(h)(i)(j) (k)(l)(m)(n)(o) Use Minors in Sexual Performance Dissemination of Child Pornography[2]	E	24	36	48	60 *51-72*	76 *67-93*	102 *87-120*	120 *102-120[2]*
CSC 4th Degree–(a)(b)(e)(f) CSC 5th Degree Possession of Child Pornography (Subsequent or by Predatory Offender)	F	18	27	36	45 *39-54*	59 *51-70*	77 *66-92*	84 *72-100*
CSC 3rd Degree–(b) with subd. 2(2) Indecent Exposure Possession of Child Pornography Solicit Child for Sexual Conduct[2]	G	15	20	25	30	39 *34-45*	51 *44-60*	60 *51-60[2]*
Registration of Predatory Offenders	H	12[1] *12[1]-14*	14 *12[1]-16*	16 *14-19*	18 *16-21*	24 *21-28*	30 *26-36*	36 *31-43*

12[1] = One year and one day

☐ Presumptive commitment to state imprisonment. Sex offenses under Minn. Stat. § 609.3455, subd. 2, have mandatory life sentences and are excluded from the Guidelines. See section 2.E, for policies regarding those sentences controlled by law, including conditional release terms for sex offenders.

■ Presumptive stayed sentence, at the discretion of the court, up to one year of confinement and other non-jail sanctions can be imposed as conditions of probation. However, certain offenders in the shaded area of the Grid may qualify for a mandatory life sentence under Minn. Stat. § 609.3455, subd. 4.See sections 2.C and 2.E.

[3]Minn. Stat. § 244.09 requires that the Guidelines provide a range for sentences that are presumptive committment to state imprisonment of 15% lower and 20% higher than the fixed duration displayed, provided that the Minimum sentence is not less than one year and one day and the maximum sentence is not more than the statutory maximum. See section 2C 1-2.

[3]Prostitution; Sex Trafficking is not subject to a 90-month minimum statutory presumptive sentence so the standard range of 15% lower and 20% higher than the fixed duration applies. (The range is 77-108.)

Figure 12.2   MN Sex Offender Grid

http://mn.gov/msgc-stat/documents/NewGuidelines/2018/Guidelines.pdf

Colorado

The state of Colorado provides an "Overview of Sex Offender Management in Colorado" through its Department of Public Safety in the Division of Criminal Justice.[37] The statute defining what constitutes a sex offender opens its page. In Colorado:

16-11.7-102(2)(a) C.R.S. defines a sex offender as anyone who is convicted/adjudicated of the following:

- a sex offense
- any criminal offense if that person had been previously convicted of a sex offense in either Colorado or any other jurisdiction, or if the person has a history of sex offenses
- any criminal offense in Colorado with an underlying factual basis involving a sex offense

The term sex offender also includes a juvenile who has committed a sexual offense.

Sex offense is defined in 16-11.7-102(3)(a) C.R.S. and includes 25 different felony and misdemeanor sex offense crime types including: sexual contact involving minors, use of force/coercion, familial sexual contact, positions of trust, exploitation/trafficking/child prostitution, and use of the internet for a sex crime (luring and child sexual abuse images), among others.

The state overviews the process to follow a plea or conviction to include sex offenses–specific evaluations used to assist in supervision, treatment, and sentencing of the offender. Sentencing options are reviewed, and the role of the Sex Offender Management Board (SOMB) in establishing treatment protocols and the constitution of the board and its function in the process of sex-offender management are outlined. The SOMB is a 25-volunteer collaborative that works together and "develops standards and guidelines for the assessment, evaluation, treatment and behavioral monitoring of adult sex offenders and juveniles who have committed sex offenses."[38] The board works to establish best practices in an effort, legislatively mandated, to provide the "safety of the community and protection of the victims." The SOMB has a collection of working subcommittees continuously reviewing research to ensure current best practices, and their version of containment, or the collaboration of professionals, is called Community Supervision Team (CST) for adults and Multidisciplinary Team (MDT) for juveniles. The teams consist of the supervising officer, treatment provider, victim representative, polygraph examiner, and other professionals as needed.[39] They also accept, review, and determine approval for any agencies seeking to become service providers used by the state.

From the 2019 annual legislative report:

The SOMB will continue to modify the Adult and Juveniles Standards and Guidelines periodically on the basis of new empirical findings. In part, the SOMB stays current on research through the work of its active committees. These committees meet on a regular basis and report back to the SOMB to inform potential modifications to the Adult and Juvenile Standards and Guidelines. The following is a list of the SOMB committees:

1. Adult Community Supervision Standards Revisions Section 5.700 Committee
   1.1. Child Contact Screening Workgroup
2. SOMB Executive Committee
3. Juvenile Standards Revision Committee
4. Best Practices/Treatment Provider Committee
5. Victim Advocacy Committee
6. Application Review Committee
7. Training Committee (in Collaboration with the Domestic Violence Offender Management Board)
8. Family Support and Engagement Committee
9. Sex Offender Registration Legislative Work Group
10. Sex Trafficking Workgroup
11. Community Notification Technical Assistance Team Report Organization

This annual legislative report consists of four sections. The first section provides a summary of the current and relevant literature concerning research and evidence-based practices. The second section highlights relevant policy issues. The third section highlights the 2018 achievements of the SOMB. This section will include priorities identified by the SOMB, which will be addressed in 2019. The fourth and final section provides the future goals and directions of the SOMB.[40]

The general provisions of treatment plans are reviewed, as is the 1998 state Sex Offender Lifetime Supervision Act and the sexually violent predator (SVP) designation. The Sex Offender Lifetime Supervision Act provides various sentencing options to the Court:

- Probation for a minimum of 10 years to a maximum of life for a class 4 felony, and a minimum of 20 years and a maximum of life for a class 2 or 3 felony. Intensive supervision probation (ISP) is required for all lifetime probationers until further order of the court.
- Department of Corrections for at least the minimum of the presumptive range of sentencing to a maximum of life.

The Colorado Department of Corrections oversees the evaluation and treatment of offenders sentenced to the DOC and those on parole. Offenders in the treatment program work toward meeting the release criteria as outlined. The final SVP designation is made by a judge when the following criteria are met:

- Offender must be 18 years old when the offense was committed, or less than 18 years old but tried as an adult;
- The conviction is for sexual assault, unlawful sexual contact, sexual assault on a child, sexual assault on a child by someone in a position of trust (convictions also include attempts, solicitations, and conspiracies to any of the offenses previously outlined);

- The victim must have been a stranger to the offender or a person with whom the offender established or promoted a relationship primarily for the purpose of sexual victimization;
- Meet scoring criteria on the risk assessment instrument, or demonstrate significant psychopathy per testing.

If the person commits a second listed felony, they are automatically recommended to the Court for an SVP designation. The stipulations for registering are directed by the court at sentencing, and if required to register they must contact the law enforcement agency in the jurisdiction where they live, changing the address listed if they move. A non-SVP offender may petition to be removed, depending on their classification, but an offender with an SVP designation must register for the remainder of their life. Juveniles can ask the court to terminate their registration requirements at the conclusion of their supervision.[41]

To close, data from 2016 reported the Colorado Department of Corrections budget included $4,412,697 for assessment, treatment, testing (including polygraphs), program evaluations, and registration coordination for incarcerated sex offenders. According to the 2016 Lifetime Supervision Annual Report, $2,746,871 was spent on approved sex-offender treatment services.[42]

SEX-OFFENDER CIVIL COMMITMENT

Without question, one of the biggest concerns people have about sex offenders is whether they will offend again after they are released from prison. Although most people who go to prison for committing sex crimes will be released back into the community after their time has been served according to the stipulations outlined in the sentencing guidelines, a segment of the sex-offender population has been or will be deemed such a threat to public safety that they will be released from their prison sentence into the custody of a longer-term custodial arrangement referred to as civil commitment. A brief review of information about sex-offender recidivism, and decisions to place someone in the state sex-offender program created for the highest risk offenders is presented below.

History of Civil Commitment

Civil commitment laws date back decades in the United States but are more often known from within the context of psychiatric facilities used for both voluntary and involuntary institutionalization of individuals with mental health problems or concerns. The idea of institutional commitment is linked back to the 1930s, when a national panic erupted about laws working to regulate sexually deviant behavior referred to broadly as sexual psychopathy. People were put under care for what was seen by professionals as a diagnosable, treatable disorder.[43]

Like the legislation of the 1990s, the earlier legislation was passed in response to horrible sex crimes, which motivated people to take action, helping to garner support from the communities for a formal state response. Unlike the assessment advancements utilized today, many decisions about who would be admitted and when they were ready to leave were subjective and not very accurate. State definitions of sexual psychopathy were different, but most states required that there be an imminent threat to safety of the individual or someone else, and this typically meant the individual had a mental illness and/or was thought to be dangerous.[44]

By the 1950s and 1960s, criticisms of the institutionalized care of offenders in government facilities resulted in the development of community programs and a massive deinstitutionalization movement across the country. The number of psychiatric inpatients declined significantly from a high of more than 550,000 in 1950 to 30,000 by 1990.[45] While some states had been decreasing institutional enrollment for decades, others states were coming under different pressures to assure the public that they would be safe from individuals, such as Earl Shriner in Washington (discussed in chapter 10), and the then unknown offender who abducted Jacob Wetterling in 1989. The goal was public safety. The significant legislation discussed in chapter 10 was the result.

States are still working to make decisions about the design of their operations, as illustrated by Texas, which in September of 2011 shifted the civil commitment obligations from the Council on Sex Offender Treatment (CSOT) to a new agency, the Office of Violent Sex Offender Management (OVSOM). Since 1983, the CSOT was established as experts in the field and tasked with organizing the standards of practice for the sex-offender treatment providers in the state.[46]

The issue of community and criminal justice response to sexually violent offenders is also referred to as sexually violent predators (SVP) or sexually dangerous persons, depending on the state statutory definitions. The 1990 Community Protection Act in Washington state (also discussed in chapter 10) became the first attempt to create a means by which to extend custodial control of such offenders. Generally, to be designated a sexually violent predator an offender must:

- Have been convicted or charged with a sexually violent offense
- Suffer from a mental abnormality or personality disorder
- Be determined to be likely to engage in future acts.[47]

As of 2018 numbers, 20 states have implemented civil commitment programs. In 1997, the US Supreme Court heard the case of *Kansas v. Hendricks*, appealed after Leroy Hendricks was identified as a sexually violent predator by a jury in Kansas. With that case, the SCOTUS established that civil commitment could be used for sexually violent predators. The type of mental disorder that may result in an offender's committing a future sex crime has been the subject of debate, but the most common mental disorders used to designate a person as an SVP are paraphilias and personality disorders.[48] A diagnosis of pedophilia, paraphilia not otherwise specified, a psychopathy classification, younger victim age, possible drug and/or alcohol abuse, personality disorder not otherwise specified, or antisocial personality disorder was a finding from research in Florida and Washington likely to warrant classification as an SVP.[49] Particular details on the civil commitment process are left up to the states; however, support for states wanting to add civil commitment programs was included in the Adam Walsh Act, making this a federal initiative.

CONTEMPORARY CRITIQUE OF CIVIL COMMITMENT

Minnesota made national headlines in June 2012, when consideration was given to the release of a known sex offender who had abused several children. From there the courts were taking on the question as to whether the Minnesota statutes governing civil commitment and treatment of sex offenders in the state were unconstitutional.[50] US District Court Judge Donovan Frank in *Karsjens et al. v. Minnesota Department of Human Service et al.* said "the court concludes that Minnesota's civil commitment statutes and sex-offender program do not pass constitutional scrutiny."[51]

The law was connected back to the first Minnesota psychopathic personality law, from 1939. By the early 2000s, concerns were being raised about the number of offenders being held, the costs of the program, the treatment rights of those committed to the program, and the fact that no one had ever been fully released from the program.[52] In his ruling, Judge Frank said the system was a punitive system, which violated the offender's rights to due process. Oral arguments before a three-judge panel of the US Court of Appeals Eighth Circuit were heard in St. Louis, Missouri, on April 12, 2016, and that decision was reversed by the US Court of Appeals Eighth Circuit in January 2017. By May 2017, a petition had been submitted to the US Supreme Court, which declined to hear the case in a statement released October 2, 2017.

Reports are suggesting that the Frank ruling, even though it was overturned, has had an impact in the state's response to some of the offenders' claims. At the time of the Frank ruling, only three people had ever been released. As of the fall of 2018, 26 had been released with certain conditions, and an additional three were released with no conditions, something that had not been done before in the history of the program.[53] A Fall 2018 Minnesota State Supreme Court case ordered the release of an offender, now 63, who committed his first sexual offense in 1975, after which he was in and out of prison for assaulting teenaged girls, often within months of his release. In 1987, the most recent sexual assault resulted in a 20-year sentence, and the offender was committed indefinitely in 1991 as a psychopathic personality. Several of the terms of his discharge require 24-hour surveillance, a GPS device, random searches, and restrictions regarding travel in the community without an MSOP staff person. An extremely controversial release, he was described as a model prisoner who had completed every phase of the program and as a person obsessed with violent sex, known to experience "intrusive and deviant sexual thoughts," but who experts concluded had learned to manage those thoughts.[54]

The state of Minnesota still holds the largest number of sex offenders in state custody, at 732 in Spring of 2019. Critics of the civil commitment programs nationally suggest it violates the offenders' rights to due process and punishes them twice for the same crime by sending them to the secure facility after their prison term has been completed. In addition to the legal and process questions, issues have also been raised about the scientific and ethical basis from which predictive decisions are made using assessment tools shown to accurately indicate the risk of reoffending better than chance[55] but that have been criticized for internal validity[56] and cannot be deemed certain in their valuation.

A final critical reflection has to do with program costs. Estimates of costs vary a great deal partly because states do not always have clear records of civil commitment costs separated from other budget items.[57] A New York story reported taxpayers at $65 million per year to confine the offenders, or $175,000 each, contrasting that with about $9,000 per offender for traditional probation. Another national estimate places the costs for confinement, clinical treatment, and legal assistance for offenders who seek to put their case for release before a judge, and medical coverage, indicating costs of approximately three times that of incarceration.[58]

Making cost comparisons almost impossible, different systems account for different elements of treatment costs within the budget descriptions. Consider the Minnesota Sex Offender Program, outlined in Table 12.2. They attempted to include direct costs, indirect costs, and then per-day costs, based on expense totals and number of inmates in the program. Costs for community programs, in the case of Minnesota that would be the Intensive Supervised Release (discussed above) are in different agencies (the ISR program is assigned to the Department of Corrections, and the MSOP is in the Department of Human Services), and therefore the budgets are also separate. In 2010, the Associated Press published an analysis of costs associated with the 20 programs treating people identified as sexual predators in prison totaling $500 million for a total of just over 5,000 inmates that year. The findings put New York state spending $175,000 per person per year, and California at $173,000 but averaging $96,000 across all of the states with civil commitment programs.[59]

SEX-OFFENDER RECIDIVISM

Researchers, practitioners, and policy makers have had a notoriously difficult time working to find ways to predict sex-offender recidivism. Certainly, the prevention of future crimes is the objective. The focus for sex-offender recidivism, however, is more particularly on the prevention of future sex-related crimes. Knowing which characteristics of an offender make them more likely to offend again would help professionals work to prevent sex crimes and keep the public safe. From what is known, it appears the kinds of factors that predict recidivism for other crimes are not the same factors that predict whether a sex offender will offend again.[60]

Factors found to elevate the chance of failure in the community include:

- Residential instability
- History of drug abuse
- Percentage of time employed in the year prior to arrest
- The number of prior convictions
- Effective informal social controls (e.g., having a committed intimate partner, positive social networks, or full-time employment)[61]

Table 12.2 Program-Wide Per Diem and Fiscal Summary[1]

Minnesota Sex Offender Program (MSOP)		
	FY 2019	
Description	Approp. $$	Per Diem
Direct Costs		
Clinical	$22,048,781	82.86
Healthcare and Medical Services	$6,454,922	24.26
Security	$36,898,512	138.67
Community Preparation Svcs	$4,686,907	17.61
Dietary	$1,512,917	5.69
Physical Plant & Warehouse	$7,248,335	27.24
Program Support	$10,483,724	39.40
Total Direct Costs	$89,334,098	335.73
Operating Per Diem		$336
Indirect Costs		
Statewide Indirect	$147,867	0.56
DHS Indirect	$180,000	0.68
Building Depreciation	$3,969,731	14.92
Bond Interest	$5,359,200	20.14
Capital Asset Depreciation	$101,897	0.38
Total Indirect Costs	$9,758,695	36.68
Total Costs	$99,092,793	372.41
Average Daily Census (ADC)	729	
Published Per Diem Rate		$372

Direct Costs—Costs attributed to providing care and treatment to clients, maintaining facilities and providing general support services to operate the program.
Indirect Costs—Costs not directly attributable to the program but are allocated/assigned as a cost of the overall operations of the program.

NOTE: The program support costs mainly consist of Legal (including Attorney General's Office and the DHS General Counsel's Office), SRB/SCAP, MN.IT and Workers Comp expense. Finance & Staff Development have been transferred to DCT Operations and no longer paid directly from the MSOP budget.

MSOP Per Diem
While there are 21 civil commitment programs (20 state programs and one federal program) in the country, there is no uniform method for calculating the per diem cost of program operations. A survey conducted by MSOP Financial Services revealed that most programs do not include all costs associated with operating and maintaining a program. MSOP uses a comprehensive per diem calculation that includes all direct and indirect costs, including costs incurred by the state for bonding and construction of physical facilities. This all-inclusive per diem for fiscal year 2018 is $372.

1 Minnesota Department of Human Services, "Minnesota Sex Offender Program Annual Performance Report 2017," February 2018, accessed September 26, 2019, https://www.leg.state.mn.us/docs/2018/mandated/180250.pdf.

That work, still evolving, seems to suggest that sex offenders, with the exception of child molesters, reoffend at a rate lower than nonsexual criminals.[62] Research has found that registered sex offenders recidivate at approximately the same rate as offenders who were not required to register (approximately 10 percent).[63] Later research also found no difference in recidivism rates between those asked to register and those who did not register,[64] as was the case with still another study utilizing a specific state focus with a different structural design.[65]

As research continues, some specific work has continued to stress the fact that sex offenders should not be treated the same, and this is reflected in the variation in recidivism findings. In an expansive study including offenders from Canada, the United States, and Great Britain, the findings indicate that most sex offenders did not repeat sex offenses. The study also found that first-time sex offenders were significantly less likely to repeat sex offenses than those with previous convictions for sex offenses, and offenders over the age of 50 were less likely to reoffend than younger offenders. Looking at particular types of offenders, they found:

> Rapists, incest offenders, "girl-victim" child molesters, and "boy-victim" child molesters recidivated at significantly different rates. Recidivism rates were highest for "boy-victim" child molesters and rapists. Generally, the sex offenders that posed the highest risk of recidivism victimized males, had prior sex offenses, and were a younger age.[66]

As indicated in the list above, supervision in the community is often offered in conjunction to **treatment**, which refers to a specialized program focused on helping offenders learn strategies to stop abusive behaviors. Again, protocols will vary from program to program. Chapter 13 more specifically talks about treatment, but for now it is important to note that research largely suggests having a specialized treatment protocol can assist offenders in successfully completing treatment and reducing recidivism.

CHAPTER CONCLUSION

As the offender is introduced into and processed through the criminal justice system, it is not uncommon for treatment practitioners and correctional staff to work together with other service providers to address a collection of offender needs. Information presented throughout the chapter included examples of processes from various states, but it is important to remember elements from the process of defining, identifying, arresting, and prosecuting a sex offender differ in every region of every state.

Each state's system is different, and each county will have established its own formal and informal processes. Therefore, anyone interested in particular information should be sure to consult with professionals in the local area for specific regional information.

A limited number of states are conducting research on their own treatment, reentry, and supervision initiatives. Few studies examine these programs from a cost-benefit perspective.

Will punishment in prison provide the incentive necessary to prevent future offending behaviors once that person gets out of prison? Will punishment in prison or jail combined with mandatory treatment upon release back into the community assure the public's safety when the offender returns to the community?

Text Box 12.3. Media Messages about Community Management and Civil Commitment

News reports often cover stories about offenders who get out of prison and then commit another sex offense. The terrible reality of those cases catches everyone off guard and makes it clear that no one can know whether an offender will commit another offense. It is also certain that someone who has committed a sex crime will leave prison or graduate from a treatment program, move into a community, work to build a life, build trust again with a family or build a relationship moving forward, seek to make a series of connections in the community through their work, faith community, and children's activities and schools, for example. If you learn a sex offender has moved into your community, what do you think your reaction would be? Would you want to learn more? Stop It Now! has a few ideas:

Stop It **NOW**! Tip Sheet: Concerned About Sex Offenders in Your Neighborhood[1]

- Don't panic, respond calmly.
- Create a family safety plan.
- Attend the public community notification meetings.
- Find out if the person convicted of a sexual offense is being supervised.
- Consider joining with another neighbor to meet the offender.
- Notify the police if you see this person in a suspicious situation.
- Do not wait to take action for prevention.
  - Remember 88% of sexual abuse is never reported, so you will not know every person who might commit an offense, just because you have been notified about this one individual.
  - Your safety plan does not change, because awareness is always important.
- Share Prevention Tip Sheets in Your Community.

Given those ideas, what action would you take after learning a sex offender had moved into your community? What would your safety plan look like? What conditions would change your thinking (e.g., if you had young children, if you have teenaged children)? If you or someone living in the same household with you had been a victim of a sexualized harm, how would that influence your collective action? What special conditions might be made for that victim to assure them that they have the support they need?

MEDIA-ting the Middle Ground

Is there a middle ground when it comes to preventing sexual violence?

Deciding Which Messages Moving Forward

If we are not working on solving the problem, is it fair to say we are part of the problem? What does that mean in the circles where children live, where young people hang out together, and as college students exploring the parameters of healthy lifelong relationships? If I am not thinking about my own healthy development, the healthy development of my children, my students, or the young people in my community, how will I respond to those in need of help as a police officer, as a lawyer, as a judge, or as a policy maker? What is it that the community should know about a sex offender? In what ways does the number of men who have been arrested and prosecuted in association with the #MeToo movement illustrate how an offender can go undetected for years? How does the lack of detection invite deeper reflection on unwanted sexual attention? Is it a lack of detection, or is it a lack of reporting and accountability? What is the difference? Why does that difference matter? How do I make sure my understanding of a sexualized conversation is coming from an educated and aware place, rather than perpetuating mystified messages and feeding into what can sometimes become sensationalized media coverage of an issue that skews the public's impression about what research outcomes are finding?

MEDIA MESSAGES: What Can Be Done to Help Prevent Sexual Violence?

Section overview: Section V closes the book with a review of treatment and support options for those harmed by sexual violence but also those who have committed offenses. Offenders harm for various reasons, and even the most well-educated individual cannot completely eliminate the possibility that they could become a victim of sexualized harm. Attention is given to the ways treatment is used to assist offenders in decreasing the likelihood of future offenses. Attention is also given to the ways in which support for people who have been harmed is structured to support the individual but also their family and friends and the community more broadly. The section includes a discussion about the influence of considering sexual violence as a public health issue, and the idea of considering the possibilities for a restorative justice model for addressing a portion of these harms is presented for consideration. The section closes, as we hope any conversation on sexual violence prevention might close, with attention being given to what each of us can do right now to secure the support we might need for ourselves or the people we love and to be mindful of ways to take actions to interrupt or prevent future acts of sexualized violence and harm.

Note

1. Stop It Now. Tip Sheet: Concerned About Sex Offenders In Your Neighborhood. Accessed November 29, 2019. https://www.stopitnow.org/ohc-content/tip-sheet-14

KEY TERMS

Campus Sex Crime Prevention Act
Center for Sex Offender Management (CSOM)
civil commitment
community correctional supervision
community supervision
conditions of supervision
containment model
correctional supervision
corrections agent
disposition
Dru Sjodin National Sex Offender Public Website
level of risk

Level of Service/Case Management
Inventory (LS/CMI)
Office of Sex Offender Sentencing,
Monitoring, Apprehending,
Registering, and Tracking
(SMART)
polygraph testing
presentence investigation
probation officer
psychosexual evaluation
recidivism
risk assessments

Risk, Need, Responsivity (RNR)
Model
sexually violent predator (SVP)
State Authorized Risk Assessment Tool
for Sex Offenders (SARATSO)
suspended or stayed sentence
Tier I
Tier II
Tier III
treatment
victim-centered approach

REVIEW QUESTIONS

1. What does it mean to say that community supervision and treatment programs working with sex offenders in the community adhere to a victim-centered approach? Why is this significant?

2. In the opening of the chapter, reference is made to the increasing effort to integrate services provided to sex offenders in the community in an effort to assure more seamless response to the primary goal of public safety. What is that style of service called?

3. It is possible for a judge to determine a guilty verdict and yet release the individual back into the community with supervision? What is this referred to, and what are the consequences if they do not comply with the conditions outlined by the court?

4. Discuss the model of risk, need, responsivity for offender management.

5. What is the importance of the legal distinction of defining a sexually dangerous or sexually violent predator?

DISCUSSION QUESTIONS

1. Discuss any possible tension that might exist to suggest sex offenders do better when they have support in the community, as compared to the idea that the treatment and management of sex offenders in the community is focused on providing a victim-centered approach.

2. Explore the attitudes you bring to the conversation about sex-offender community treatment and supervision. Are the attitudes of the people in your discussion similar and/or different from each other and from the information presented?

3. Much has been made about the importance of having a resource database for law enforcement and community members when a sex offense is committed. In what ways do the costs become a factor in an important conversation

about ways to assure efforts contribute to public safety? What impact does the information about recidivism have on this conversation?

4. Overviews of three state processes are provided for reflection: Washington, Minnesota, and Colorado. Comparing them, what advantages and disadvantages do you see? Referring to their information online more carefully, how well does their information overview their programs? What questions do you have? Then, how do they compare with state information web pages providing public information on sex-offender management in communities nearby?

5. The challenges to the issue of civil commitment are raised on a variety of grounds. Be prepared to restate those grounds and discuss the advantages and disadvantages each side of the argument is confronting. What resolution do you see for the challenge of weighing individual rights and liberties against the collective desire for public safety? How does learning about the individual stories of the offenders and the victim influence this conversation?

NOTES

1. "Sex Offender Treatment and Assessment," Department of Corrections, Washington State, https://www.doc.wa.gov/corrections/programs/sex-offender-treatment.htm.

2. "No Easy Answers: Sex Offender Laws in the US," *Human Rights Watch* 19, no. 4 (2007): 3, accessed September 20, 2019, https://www.hrw.org/sites/default/files/reports/us0907webwcover.pdf.

3. Kurt Bumby, Karen Baker, and Leileh Gilligan, "Advancing a Victim-Centered Approach to Supervising Sex Offenders: A Toolkit for Practitioners," The Center for Effective Public Policy, 2018, accessed September 21, 2019, https://www.csom.org/pubs/Probation_toolkit_web.pdf.

4. Ibid., II.

5. Kristen Lam, "Judge gives no jail time to former school bus driver who admitted to raping 14-year-old girl," *USA Today*, April 30, 2019, accessed September 21, 2019, https://www.usatoday.com/story/news/nation/2019/04/29/new-york-school-bus-driver-no-jail-time-rape/3622221002/.

6. Richard A. Oppel, Jr., "Court Approves Plea Deal with No Jail Time in Baylor Rape Case," *New York Times*, December 11, 2018, September 21, 2019, https://www.nytimes.com/2018/12/11/us/baylor-rape-plea-probation-jacob-anderson.html.

7. "The Importance of Assessment in Sex Offender Management: An Overview of Key Principles and Practices," Center for Sex Offender Management, July 2007, 1, accessed October 20, 2019, https://www.csom.org/pubs/assessment_brief.pdf.

8. Association for the Treatment of Sexual Abusers (ATSA), "Practice Standards and Guidelines for the Evaluation, Treatment, and Management of Adult Male Sexual Abusers," 2014, http://www.atsa.com/atsa-practice-guidelines.

9. "Map of Registered Sex Offenders in the United States," National Center for Missing and Exploited Children, May 24, 2017, accessed September 21, 2019, https://api.missingkids.org/en_US/documents/Sex_Offenders_Map.pdf.

10. "Standards and Guidelines for the Assessment, Evaluation, Treatment, and Behavioral Monitoring of Adult Sex Offenders," Colorado Department of Public Safety, Division of Criminal Justice Office of Domestic Violence & Sex Offender Management, May 2017, accessed October 20, 2019, https://cdpsdocs.state.co.us/somb/ADULT/OnLine2017Adult StandardsFINAL6.2.2017.pdf.

11. D. A. Andrews and Craig Dowden, "Risk Principle of Case Classification in Correctional Treatment: A Meta-Analytic Investigation," *International Journal of Offender Therapy and Comparative Criminology* 50, no. 1 (2006): 88–100, https://doi.org/10.1177/0306624X05282556; see also D. A. Andrews and Craig Dowden, "The Risk-Need-Responsivity Model of Assessment and Human Service in Prevention and Corrections: Crime-Prevention Jurisprudence," *Canadian Journal of Criminology and Criminal Justice* 49, no. 4 (2007): 439–64.

12. James Bonta and D. A. Andrews, "Risk-Need-Responsivity Model for Offender Assessment and Rehabilitation, 2007–06," Public Safety Canada, 2007, accessed September 21, 2019, https://www.pbpp.pa.gov/Information/Documents/Research/EBP7.pdf.

13. Ibid.

14. Kevin Brown, Jon Spencer, and Jo Deakin, "The Reintegration of Sex Offenders: Barriers and Opportunities for Employment," *Howard Journal of Criminal Justice* 46, no. 1 (2007): 32–42, https://doi.org/10.1111/j.1468-2311.2007.00452.x.

15. "Disclosure of education Records Concerning Registered Sex Offenders," US Department of Education, October 24, 2002, accessed September 21, 2019, https://www2.ed.gov/policy/gen/guid/fpco/hottopics/ht10-24-02.html.

16. Migdalia Baerga-Buffler and James L. Johnson, "Sex Offender Management in the Federal Probation and Pretrial Services System," *Federal Probation* 70, no. 1 (2006), https://www.uscourts.gov/sites/default/files/70_1_2_0.pdf.

17. "Sex Offender Registration and Notification Act (SORNA): State and Territory Implementation Progress Check," Smart.gov, June 10, 2019, https://smart.gov/pdfs/SORNA-progress-check.pdf.

18. "About NSOPW," Dru Sjodin National Sex Offender Public Website (NSOPW), accessed September 21, 2019, https://www.nsopw.gov/About.

19. C. Bennet, "SPLC Sues Alabama Officials for Overly Severe Sex-Offender Law That Punishes Children for Life," September 19, 2019, accessed October 20, 2019, https://www.splcenter.org/news/2019/09/19/splc-sues-alabama-officials-overly-severe-sex-offender-law-punishes-children-life.

20. "Sex Offender Registry Board (SORB)," Mass.gov, 2019, https://www.mass.gov/orgs/sex-offender-registry-board.

21. "Sex Offender Registry Board (SORB) Public Website, Commonwealth of Massachusetts, 2019, https://sorb.chs.state.ma.us/sorbpublic/standardSearchforSexOffenders.action?_p=PXgnGplB8GzncJfy3boIw9w8ylSmYeD6nvdMMRYNNu4.

22. "Guiding Principles of Risk-Based Sex Offender Management," State Authorized Risk Assessment Tools for Sex Offenders, http://www.saratso.org/index.cfm?pid=1354.

23. "Washoe Tribe of Nevada and California Sex Offender Registry," February 13, 2019, accessed October 20, 2019, https://washoetribe.nsopw.gov/ConditionsOfUse.aspx.

24. Jill Levenson, David A. D'Amora, and Andrea L. Hern, "Megan's Law and Its Impact on Community Re-Entry for Sex Offenders," *Behavioral Sciences and the Law* 25, no. 4 (2007): 587–602, https://doi.org/10.1002/bsl.770.

25. Lydia Saad, "Sex Offender Registries Are Underutilized by the Public," June 9, 2005, accessed September 21, 2019, https://news.gallup.com/poll/16705/sex-offender-registries-underutilized-public.aspx; see also "US: Sex Offender Laws May Do More Harm Than Good," Human Rights Watch, September 11, 2007, accessed September 21, 2019, https://www.hrw.org/news/2007/09/11/us-sex-offender-laws-may-do-more-harm-good.

26. See, for example, Richard Tewskbury, "Validity and Utility of the Kentucky Sex Offender Registry," *Federal Probation* 66, no. 1 (2002): 21–26, https://www.uscourts.gov/federal-probation-journal/2002/06/validity-and-utility-kentucky-sex-offender-registry; M. Mulvihill et al., "Monster Next Door: State Losing Track of Sex Offenders," *Boston Herald*, November 2003, p. 1; M. Payne, "Sex Offender Site Criticized," *Southwest Florida News Press*, 2005; Christopher Zoukis, "Sex Offender Registries: Common Sense or Nonsense?" *Criminal Legal News*,

June 2018, https://www.criminallegalnews.org/news/2018/may/15/ex-offender-registries-common-sense-or-nonsense/.

27. Bob Edward Vásquez, Sean Maddan, and Jeffery T. Walker, "The Influence of Sex Offender Registration and Notification Laws in the United States: A Time-Series Analysis," *Crime & Delinquency* 54, no. 2 (2008): 175–92, https://doi.org/10.1177/0011128707311641; E. K. Drake and S. Aos, "Does Sex Offender Registration and Notification Reduce Crime? A Systematic Review of the Research Literature," Washington State Institute for Public Policy, June 2009, accessed September 21, 2019, http://www.wsipp.wa.gov/ReportFile/1043/Wsipp_Does-Sex-Offender-Registration-and-Notification-Reduce-Crime-A-Systematic-Review-of-the-Research-Literature_Full-Report.pdf; see also Elizabeth J. Letourneau et al., "Evaluating the Effectiveness of Sex Offender Registration and Notification Policies for Reducing Sexual Violence against Women," National Institute of Justice, September 2010, September 21, 2019, https://www.ncjrs.gov/pdffiles1/nij/grants/231989.pdf.

28. McPherson, "Practitioner's Guide to the Adam Walsh Act."

29. "Sex Offender Treatment and Assessment," Department of Corrections Washington State.

30. Ibid., "The Three Primary Goals for the Sex Offender Treatment Program."

31. "Sex Offender Treatment and Assessment," Department of Corrections Washington State, 2019, accessed October 20, 2019, https://www.doc.wa.gov/corrections/programs/sex-offender-treatment.htm#prison-treatment.

32. "Sex Offender Treatment and Assessment: Rules in the Community," Department of Corrections Washington State, accessed September 21, 2019, https://www.doc.wa.gov/corrections/programs/sex-offender-treatment.htm#community-rules.

33. "Sex Offender Treatment," Minnesota Department of Human Services, accessed September 21, 2019, https://mn.gov/dhs/people-we-serve/adults/services/sex-offender-treatment/.

34. "Fact Sheet: Sex Offenders in Prison," Minnesota Department of Corrections, May 2019, accessed September 21, 2019, accessed October 20, 2019, https://mn.gov/doc/assets/Sex%20Offenders%20in%20Prison_tcm1089-384033.pdf.

35. "Sex Offender Grid," Minnesota Sentencing Guidelines Commission, August 1, 2019, http://mn.gov/msgc-stat/documents/Guidelines/2019/SexOffenderGrid.pdf.

36. (Minnesota) Minnesota Sentencing Guidelines Commission, 2019 Sentencing Guidelines and Commentary, Sex Offender Grid, August 1, 2019, http://mn.gov/msgc-stat/documents/Guidelines/2019/SexOffenderGrid.pdf.

37. "Overview of Sex Offender Management in Colorado," Colorado Division of Criminal Justice, accessed September 21, 2019, https://www.colorado.gov/pacific/dcj/overview-sex-offender-management-colorado.

38. Ibid.

39. Ibid.

40. Kelly Hume and Chris Lobanov-Rostovsky, "Sex Offender Management Board: Annual Legislative Report: Evidence-Based Practices for the Treatment and Management of Adults and Juveniles Who Have Committed Sexual Offenses," January 2019, accessed September 21, 2019, http://cdpsdocs.state.co.us/dvomb/SOMB/2019Legislative.pdf.

41. "Overview of Sex Offender Management in Colorado."

42. "Lifetime Supervision of Sex Offenders Annual Report," Colorado Department of Corrections, Colorado Department of Public Safety, and State Judicial Department, November 1, 2016, accessed September 21, 2019, https://cdpsdocs.state.co.us/somb/projects/2016Lifetime SupervisionAnnualReport.pdf.

43. Roger N. Lancaster, *Sex Panic and the Punitive State* (Los Angeles: University of California Press, 2011); see also Philip Jenkins, *Moral Panic: Changing Concepts of the Child Molester in Modern America* (New Haven, CT: Yale University Press, 1998).

44. Megan Testa and Sara G. West, "Civil Commitment in the United States," *Psychiatry (Edgmont)* 7, no. 10 (2010): 30–40.

45. Sara West, Susan Hatters Friedman, and John P. Shand, "Civil Commitment," in *Wiley Encyclopedia of Forensic Science—Behavioral Sciences*, ed. Carl N. Edwards (Hoboken, NJ: John Wiley and Sons, Inc., 2012), https://doi.org/10.1002/9780470061589.fsa237.pub2.

46. "Council on Sex Offender Treatment Home Page," Texas Health and Human Services, updated September 19, 2019, accessed September 21, 2019, https://www.dshs.state.tx.us/csot/default.shtm.

47. Karen Terry, *Sexual Offenses and Offenders: Theory, Practice, and Policy* (Belmont, CA: Wadsworth Cengage Learning, 2013), 277.

48. R. Ellwood, "Mental Disorder, Predisposition, Prediction, and Ability to Control: Evaluating Sex Offenders for Civil Commitment," *Sexual Abuse* 21, no. 4 (2009): 395–411, https://doi.org/10.1177/1079063209347723; R. Elwood, D. Doren, and D. Thornton, "Diagnostic and Risk Profiles of Men Detained under Wisconsin's Sexually Violent Person Law," *International Journal of Offender Therapy and Comparative Criminology* 54, no. 2 (2008): 187–96, https://doi.org/10.1177/0306624X08327305.

49. Daniel Montaldi, "A Study of the Efficacy of the Sexually Violent Predator Act in Florida," *William Mitchell Law Review* 41, no. 3, (2015), https://open.mitchellhamline.edu/wmlr/vol41/iss3/4.

50. "Minnesota Sex Offender Program," Minnesota Legislative Reference Library, updated June 2018, accessed September 21, 2019, https://www.leg.state.mn.us/lrl/guides/guides?issue=msop.

51. *Karsjens v. Jesson*, United States District Court District of Minnesota, accessed September 21, 2019, https://www.govinfo.gov/content/pkg/USCOURTS-mnd-0_11-cv-03659/pdf/USCOURTS-mnd-0_11-cv-03659-15.pdf.

52. "Minnesota Sex Offender Program."

53. Chris Serres, "Ending a Long Legal Battle, Minnesota High Court Says Sex Offender Must Be Released from MSOP," *Star Tribune*, September 19, 2018, accessed September 21, 2019, http://www.startribune.com/serial-rapist-cleared-for-release-from-minn-sex-offender-program/493729601/?refresh=true.

54. Ibid.

55. R. Carl Hanson and Kelly Morton-Bourgon, "Predictors of Sexual Recidivism: An Updated Meta-Analysis," Public Safety and Emergency Preparedness Canada, 2004, accessed September 21, 2019, http://static99.org/pdfdocs/hansonandmortonbourgon2004.pdf.

56. Marcus T. Boccaccini et al., "Implications of Static-99 Field Reliability Findings for Score Use and Reporting," *Criminal Justice and Behavior* 39, no. 1 (2012): 42–58, http://sorl.org/wp-content/uploads/2012/09/Criminal-Justice-and-Behavior-2012-Boccaccini-42-58.pdf.

57. David Robinson and Jonathan Bandler, "Civil Commitment: The Cost of Locking Up Sex Offenders," *Poughkeepsie Journal*, May 31, 2017, accessed September 21, 2019, https://www.poughkeepsiejournal.com/story/news/investigations/2017/05/31/civil-commitment-cost-locking-sex-offenders/102339954/.

58. Terry, *Sexual Offenses and Offenders*, 290.

59. "Sex Offender Confinement Costing States Too Much," CBS News, June 22, 2010, accessed September 21, 2019, https://www.cbsnews.com/news/sex-offender-confinement-costing-states-too-much/.

60. R. Karl Hanson and Monique T. Bussière "Predicting Relapse: A Meta-Analysis of Sexual Offender Recidivism Studies," *Journal of Consulting and Clinical Psychology* 66, no. 2 (1998): 348–62, doi:10.1037/0022-006X.66.2.348.

61. Michelle L. Meloy, "The Sex Offender Next Door: An Analysis of Recidivism, Risk Factors, and Deterrence of Sex Offenders on Probation," *Criminal Justice Policy Review* 16, no. 2 (2005): 211–36, https://doi.org/10.1177/0887403404270601.

62. R. Karl Hanson, Richard A. Steffy, and Rene Gauthier, "Long-Term Recidivism of Child Molesters," *Journal of Consulting and Clinical Psychology* 61, no. 4 (1993): 646–52.

480 ◆ Chapter 12: Correctional Management and Civil Commitment

63. S. Maddan, "Sex Offenders as Outsiders." Unpublished PhD dissertation (University of Nebraska at Omaha,. 2005).

64. Kristen Zgoba, Bonita M. Veysey, and Melissa Dalessandro, "An Analysis of the Effectiveness of Community Notification and Registration: Do the Best Intentions Predict the Best Practices?" *Justice Quarterly* 27, no. 5 (2010): 667–91, https://doi.org/10.1080/07418820903357673.

65. Letourneau et al., "Evaluating the Effectiveness of Sex Offender Registration."

66. Andrew J. R. Harris and R. Karl Hanson, "Sex Offender Recidivism: A Simple Question," Public Safety and Community Preparedness Canada, 2004, https://www.publicsafety.gc.ca/cnt/rsrcs/pblctns/sx-ffndr-rcdvsm/sx-ffndr-rcdvsm-eng.pdf.

13

Assessing and Treating Sex Offenders

◆ ◆ ◆

[T]he use of recidivism [as a measure of treatment efficacy] exerts an even more powerful shaping influence because it directs all of our problem-solving energy to the period after a sex crime has been committed. . . . Yet this is a small part of the problem.

—Eric S. Janus, *Failure to Protect*[1]

Do the theories focused on explaining why a sex offender behaves as they do provide the kind of information necessary for creating a treatment response which reduces sex offending behaviors?

—Kirsch and Becker (2006)[2]

THE PROCESS FOR EXPLORING therapeutic and programmatic questions about the efficacy, or effectiveness, of sex-offender treatment remains a bit of a mystery to the general public. As a process it is controversial. The research focused on studying convicted sex offenders typically happens in treatment centers or in prison settings and remains relatively isolated from the mainstream. However, treatment practitioners, scholars, and researchers present a rich body of work targeting this very specific group of offenders.

As introduced in chapter 12, once a determination of guilt has been established, a person convicted of a sex offense will be directed through a series of assessments and screenings in an attempt to identify specific characteristics or better understand that individual. The LS/CMI and the psychosexual evaluation, two assessments used in the criminal justice system process as a pre-sentence inventory, assist the judge with decisions about a final disposition in the case. Assessments are not just used at the beginning of the process, but rather, they offer support for practitioners and treatment professionals all along the way.[3] A central goal for the court is the development of a plan intended to reduce the likelihood of a repeat sexual offense. For correctional personnel this is largely an oversight and accountability objective. For treatment professionals, however, the primary goal is to help work with the offender to establish and set treatment goals and objectives to help avoid reoffending and live healthier lives. Given the heterogeneous or diverse nature of sex offenders and offending behaviors, these assessment strategies help professionals better determine the individual plan for their treatment and supervision needs.

This chapter is focused on exploring the process of treating sex offenders in the United States. After an offender is caught and processed through the criminal justice system, the very serious question remains: Now what? Attention is focused on the sex-offender treatment process as it emerged in the United States and has evolved in response to expanding community and public policy attention being given to sex offenders as a specific population within the criminal justice system. Beginning with the role of risk assessments and describing common assessment tools and the treatment groups they are intended to address, attention is then shifted to outlining characteristics of a more generalized therapeutic process. Remember, treatment programs often use a reduction in recidivism rates as a measure of success. Introduced in chapter 10, recidivism refers to the number of repeat offenses committed by an offender after they complete their assigned prison term or treatment program. The chapter closes with a critical review of treatment efficacy and a report on what research indicates about the recidivism rates for sex offenders and treatment effectiveness.

REMEMBERING SUPPORT FOR VICTIMS

To acknowledge and value the stories of people who have been harmed by sexual violence is critical, particularly in a system that is increasingly adopting victim-centered language and approaches but still maintains laws and processes on the books and in the system that make it hard to hold perpetrators accountable. Chapter 14 is more specifically focused on advocacy in the everyday and an overview of ways communities can not only assist victims with the necessary support for healing but also introduce ongoing efforts to prevent future sexual harms and offenses.

For convicted sex offenders, collective programmatic efforts designed to decrease the number of incidents of sexual violence they might commit after completing their prison sentence includes extensive monitoring, as discussed in chapter 12, but it also increasingly includes assignment to a community treatment program. The information about treatment and transitions back into the community is important because the majority of sex offenders will be released from prison and return to a community. When an offender is released back into the community, the impact on victims, the families of victims, and the community more broadly can be notable. A review of the earlier discussions about the dark figure of crime and the funnel effect within the criminal justice system is timely here. What does it mean to remember victims of sexual violence, when many of those cases do not go to trial and are not sentenced to prison?

Increasingly, attention is given to ways to bring victims and victim service providers into the reentry planning decisions for sex offenders being released.[4]

With support for the victims of sexual violence and sexualized harms in mind, consider the following:

- Over 90 percent of child victims know the person who committed the offense against them.[5]
- Sex offenders are not a homogeneous group of offenders; they are very different, and it is difficult to draw general conclusions about them as a whole.
- Domestic violence—between 14 and 25 percent of women are sexually assaulted by an intimate partner.
- Almost half of perpetrators of child victims are family members.
- Dating violence—35 percent attempted, 22.9 percent threatened, 12.8 percent completed.
- Alcohol is the most common drug used to facilitate sexual assault.[6]
- Cyber and technology-related crimes are expanding, and traditional crimes such as prostitution are being transformed by technology.[7]
- Offenders who were asked if they committed rape said no, but admitted to committing acts that met the definition of rape, raising questions about whether they knew what they did was a sexual assault.[8]

As has been discussed in chapter 6 and elsewhere, statistics about sex crimes are difficult to compile and analyze because so much of what is reported captures only a portion of the lived realities of the people involved. Rates and definitions change over time, and the characteristics of individuals studied may also be different in undetectable ways. Myths about sexual assaults regarding both victims and offenders misdirect popular understandings, and research findings can vary across disciplines and reports.

Given the complex or complicated research nature and the importance of a deep analysis of related findings, coupled with a reliance on limited information, fear of the unknown, and the oppositional attitudes many people carry about sex offenders generally, the result can risk being a short-sighted understanding of the individuals who have committed sex crimes and sexual harms. The degree of social stigma placed on anyone identified as a sex offender can result in offenders carrying a significant social burden for the rest of their lives. Often wielding a "lock them up and throw away the key" attitude toward anyone tagged as a sex offender, many folks in the mainstream have little or no desire to collect additional information or develop a further understanding of what might be of concern to this particular group of offenders. The result can prove to be an extremely one-sided conversation, where anything connected to a person convicted of a sex offense working to return to society, to their communities, and to their families is not elevated or valued in the mainstream.

Having said that, it is important to remember that these offenders are returning to a society, a community, and possibly a family in close proximity to the person they offended against. When a victim of sexual assault, harm, or related trauma is still in need of support themselves, the idea that an offender has been returned to a community contained within a structured support system does not go unnoticed. In fact, this simple reality alone can be seen as just another way the criminal justice system overlooks the very people who have been harmed and for whom it is was allegedly designed to help. The tension between an offender returning to a community where their particular victim lives or works is one thing. It is also true someone harmed similarly, but by another person, could also be impacted by the release of another offender.

Throughout this process, as introduced in chapter 8, victims can feel unheard and not believed and will possibly have feelings about a known offender as they are returning to the community. Victims may not get treatment paid for by the state, as an example. Their family may not be included in treatment programs. And the places where many people might go for support, including faith communities, friends, intimate relationships, and family systems, may no longer feel safe or may also require support in processing the events, the harm, and the movement toward recovery. (Efforts to address some of these systemic gaps between victims and offenders in the community will be presented more fully in chapter 14.) In short, as the focus shifts to providing assistance and help to offenders, it is important to remember victims may also require help and support the existing system is not always set up to provide.

Without question, information, attitudes, and perspectives about sexual health and harm are evolving. Treatment practitioners, probation personnel, and scholars are collaborating, conferencing, and assimilating research findings that may surprise folks in the mainstream who limit their understanding of victims or offenders to what they hear on the nightly news. Initial efforts to study offenders, to make sense of the harm they cause/d and why, and to work to break down the long-standing cultural and social myths about sexual offenders and offending can be confusing and overwhelming. The attention and focus designed to make sure offenders succeed after prison also warrant mindful attention be given to the victims of those harms who traditionally have been left out of any organized systemic response.[9]

SEX-OFFENDER ASSESSMENTS AND TREATMENT

Although this chapter presents a generalized treatment process, it is important to note that treatment processes are designed and redesigned, depending on several things, including the structure of the treatment program, the offense, the offender's history, and the individual's treatment progress. Sometimes, this happens in cooperation among treatment professionals or between treatment practitioners and probation officers or other state departments of corrections officials, referred to as a containment model, introduced in chapter 12. **Treatment programs** (also known as clinical or therapeutic programs) refer to agencies that provide specialized care, which could be a drug rehabilitation program, or a mental health program, or in this case a sex-offender treatment program. Increasingly sex-offender treatment programs are structured to reduce or eliminate inappropriate sexual behaviors and are designed expressly to address the psychological needs or social support needs of people who have committed any range of sexual offenses. By employing various psychological techniques, practitioners work to help individuals target problem areas and return to the community prepared to live offense free. Programs have been built, or designed and applied, and then been refined in an effort to identify the **etiology**, or origin, of sex offending behaviors in an effort to address and resolve those problems moving forward.[10]

Before beginning the larger discussion, three things need to be highlighted. First, the treatment and management of sex offenders has been separated by chapter boundaries and the sections discussing assessment and treatment have been separated by chapter sections, but these separations do not really exist in real life. Second, relationships and alliances that develop between community supervision/probation staff, treatment practitioners, community supervisors, and community advocates working with other services to address offender needs can be seen throughout the system. This intentional effort to address offenders' needs also should be considered within the context of efforts to also address services and support for victims, families, and communities impacted by sexual violence more broadly. Third, this has been repeated several times throughout the text but bears repeating: Sex offenders and the crimes they commit are vastly different, heterogeneous. Chapter 7 introduced the idea that sex offenders do not fit well into groups that share similar characteristics, but rather represent a very diverse collection of personal characteristics. Sex offenders target different types of victims; they differ with regard to their likelihood to commit a future sex crime, their likelihood to respond to treatment and correctional interventions, and their motivation toward treatment involvement.

Because sex offenders are different, have different motivations, efforts are made by correctional and treatment staff to evaluate the specific needs of specific offenders and tailor the system response to that offender. Researchers and treatment practitioners, therefore, have devised several risk assessment tools, or screening instruments, designed to aid professionals in their ability to predict the likelihood of future sexual (or other felony) offenses. The ability to execute the intention of laws and policies to protect the public to some degree come down to the ability of designated professionals to assess the risk of potential harm each offender represents. This is an ongoing and developing field of study and practice.

RISK ASSESSMENT: PRESENTENCE, PRERELEASE, POSTRELEASE

Once a sex offender has been identified and is being processed through the criminal justice system, a fundamental task is attempting to prevent future sexual victimization by the offender. A **risk assessment**, one of several **assessment tools**, is a screening instrument designed to predict the likelihood of future sexual (or other felony) offenses.[11] An assessment tool plays a central role in managing sex offenders, impacting many levels of decision-making.[12] The assessments are used to provide objective, or unbiased, information to professionals throughout the criminal justice process. Past decisions were made by practitioners in the field using their professional judgment. As resources and research expanded, it became clear that those past decisions were seen as potentially subjective and not always trusted by judges and many clinicians.[13] More often, courts base release decisions on progress reports from prison psychologists, relying heavily on their expertise and raising questions about their objectivity. Asking an individual, even a well-respected practitioner, to determine what level of risk an individual poses to a community when there is no definitive way to know for certain is an immense responsibility.[14] The solution has been independent assessments and sometimes collective efforts to conduct oversight and review.

During the decade from 1995 to 2005, risk assessment processes took on a formal, structured quality; researchers found that the use of actuarial risk tables produced a more consistent and accurate prediction of future behavior than unguided professional opinion, based on case files for predicting sexual, violent nonsexual, and general recidivism. **Actuarial testing/risk tables** are best described as indicator patterns that determine risk of an event based on specific characteristics or isolated factors. Similar to actuarial tools used for assessing insurance rates, they seek to evaluate an offender based on a set of standardized scores on a collection of risk factors.

Practitioner research has identified several **risk factors**, or characteristics that indicate the likelihood of reoffending. These include demographic information, history of prior offenses, and a list of psychosocial factors, including personal distress/mood disorders, psychosis, violence used in the index offense, substance abuse, prior violent offense, low intelligence, a juvenile criminal record, a prior adult criminal record, age, negative/criminal companions, antisocial personality disorder/psychopathy, and deviant sexual interests.[15] Risk assessment development has been described as having emerged from within four stages of evolution: (1) unstructured or intuitive professional judgment, (2) structured methods developed in the late 1990s, (3) the use of a combination of static and dynamic risk factors (defined below), and (4) emerging risk–needs instruments that fully integrate assessments with ongoing case planning.[16]

Chapter 7 discussed the ways that sex offenders are not homogeneous, or similar. Because different sex offenders are at different risks to reoffend, higher-risk sex offenders should receive higher-intensity services, and low-risk offenders should receive minimal or no services.[17] Using what are referred to as static and dynamic risk measures, discussed in more detail below, researchers are attempting to develop tools to assist in identifying sex offenders who are more (or less) likely to commit another sex crime.

Static risk factors refer to those features of an individual's social experience that cannot change. Examples of these would include age at first offense, gender of victim, victim–offender relationship, family history, and criminal history. **Dynamic risk factors** include aspects of an offender's life that evolve over time, such as marital status and employment status.

Early studies of risk focused primarily on static factors, but later returned to exploring dynamic risk factors to include subcategories of stable dynamic risk factors, referring to those things expected to remain the same, and acute dynamic risk factors, referring to those things in transition or likely to change rapidly.[18] Also important to note, however, is the rapid increase in numbers of static instruments that have not yet been empirically validated to assure they measure what they were designed to predict.[19] Although there are fewer dynamic instruments compared to static instruments, the dynamic factors have not been tested as sufficiently as many of the static instruments, and their use for recidivism has not yet been satisfactorily established.[20]

The **Association for the Treatment of Sexual Abusers (ATSA)**, a national organization focused on educating practitioners whose clients are sex offenders (www.atsa.org), suggests assessments be used for critical decisions, such as goals of treatment, sex-offender management, criminal sentencing decisions, and probation and community service decisions, in preparation for community notification, civil commitment, or extended treatment of select offenders.[21] It is not uncommon for an offender to be evaluated after the conviction but before the accused is sentenced, again before they are expected to be released back into the community, and again after being released back into the community.[22] **Amenability to treatment**, which refers to both the ability and/or capability to be treated and the motivation to complete treatment, is also identified as a factor to be considered as a marker of risk.[23] More attention is given to each assessment tool and how it is used in Table 13.1.

In 1999, the Minnesota legislature directed the commissioner of corrections to study issues related to the caseloads of probation officers supervising sex offenders.[24] Identified at the time as a relatively new protocol, risk assessments were initially designed to be utilized by the Department of Corrections twice: first, 12 months before release, an assessment was used to determine whether the offenders fit the criteria for commitment as a sexual psychopathic personality or a sexually dangerous person and, second, to determine how those who are newly released will be introduced back into the community. The second use of risk assessment was for the determination of a community notification risk level, assigned by the Minnesota Department of Corrections to each offender released from confinement.

As introduced in chapter 10, federal legislation requires communities to be notified when a sex offender is released, but it has been left up to the state to determine how the risk levels will be identified and when the community will be notified. While different states have different procedures for moving an offender through the system, the process is intended to accomplish the same goal: to process an individual into, through, and then out of the system. Remember Table 12.1 outlined the way the state of Washington outlined the decision points when an assessment would be used. They also identified the party conducting the assessment and the instruments used in the process. At each of the decision points outlined, sentencing, facility assignment, treatment planning, release, civil commitment, risk-level assignment, and postrelease supervision, a risk assessment will be conducted. Another example of the role of risk assessment in the processing of a sex offender's reentry into the community is offered in the example of Arkansas.[25]

Table 13.1 Brief Review of Sex Offender Risk Assessment Tools

Rapid Risk Assessment for Sexual Offense Recidivism (RRASOR)
Created by R. K. Hanson in 1997, the Rapid Risk Assessment for Sexual Offender Recidivism scale was developed to be used by treatment and management professionals to better screen offenders into risk levels by using static measures. The predictive validity of the RRASOR has been replicated.[1] Hanson recommends this instrument be used for correctional placement in conjunction with other information and adjusted by offender action.[2]

STATIC-99, STATIC-99R, and STATIC-2002/R
The Static-99 (2003) and the Static-99R (2012) comprise a collection of tools based on a 10-item actuarial assessment instrument created by R. Karl Hanson and David Thornton for adult male sex offenders at least 18 years of age at the time of their release from prison.[3] Believed to be one of the most widely used sex-offender assessment scales in the world,[4] it does, however, have specific stipulations about what kind of individual classifications of sex offenses are not appropriate for usage, including offenders charged or convicted of only possession or distribution of child pornography (unless the offense involved a real child and the creation of the pornography), female sex offenders, young offenders (under 18), and offenders convicted of prostitution-related offenses with consenting adults.[5]

Ten separate static factors compose the Static-99R.

1. Age at the time of release
2. Ever lived with an intimate partner
3. Index nonsexual violence
4. Prior nonsexual violence
5. Prior sex offenses
6. Prior sentencing dates
7. Any convictions for noncontact sex offenses
8. Any unrelated victims
9. Any stranger victims
10. Any male victims

The revised Static-99R risk categories[6] are scored and assessed as follows:

Level I—Very low risk (Scores of -3 to -2)
Level II—Below average risk (Scores of -1 to 0)
Level III—Average risk (Scores of 1 to 3)
Level IVa—Above average risk (Scores of 4 to 5)
Level IVb—Well above average risk (Scores of 6+)

The Static-2002/R includes five additional items: (1) age, (2) persistence of sex offending, (3) deviant sexual interest, (4) relationships to victims, and (5) general criminality. Further, the updated Static-2002R removed "ever lived with an intimate partner" and "index nonsexual violence" for a total number of 13 items in the inventory.

The revised Static-2002R risk categories[7] are as follows:

Level I—Very low risk (Scores of -2 to -1)
Level II—Below average risk (Scores of 0 to 1)
Level III—Average risk (Scores of 2 to 4)
Level IVa—Above average risk (Scores of 5 to 6)
Level IVb—Well above average risk (Scores of 7+)

Minnesota Sex Offender Screening Tool, MnSOST–R, and MNSOST-3 and 3.1
One of the most widely used actuarial tools in the country, the Minnesota Sex Offender Screening Tool (MnSOST) was updated and revised in 2003 to the MnSOST-R,[8] and then updated again in 2012 to the MnSOST-3, and to MnSOST-3.1 in 2016.[9] The MnSOST was originally an actuarial instrument with 21 items, created in association with the Minnesota Department of Corrections by Epperson, Kaul, and Huot in 1995.[10] Concerns were raised that some of the items did not significantly correlate with recidivism, so the revised edition looked at 12 items outlining historical data and four items focused on institutional information. The most recent iteration of the tool, MnSOST-3.1 was developed in 2016 to provide a modest corrective to theMnSOST-3.[11] Scores on the MnSOST-R ranged from a negative 14 to a positive 30, and offenders could be assigned to one of six risk categories based on their score. The MnSOST-3 included revised coding schemes for certain items, and it used advanced statistical modeling techniques to refine the selection of predictors and to internally validate the items used in the instrument.[12] The final scores reflected the offender's predicted probability for sexual recidivism (with 95 percent confidence interval) and a percentile rank of reoffending risk. The MnSOST-3 and 3.1 are relatively similar, however the Minnesota Department of Corrections started using the MnSOST-3.1 in 2012 because it was determined to be simpler and easier to interpret without raising concerns about predictive accuracy.[13]

Violence Risk Appraisal Guide (VRAG) and Sex Offender Risk Appraisal Guide (SORAG)

The VRAG was developed to assess risk for violent recidivism among males who committed a violent offense. Created by Quinsey, Harris, Rice, and Cormier (2006), the purpose of the SORAG is to predict violent recidivism among sex offenders. The VRAG should be used by those who do not commit a sex crime; however, it is recommended to use both when a sex crime is involved. Unique to the VRAG is its incorporation of mental health issues into its final score.[14] Consdier, for example, the following items included in the VRAG:

1. Did not live with both parents until age 18
2. Elementary school maladjustment
3. History of alcohol problems
4. Marital status
5. Nonviolent offense history
6. Failure on prior conditional release
7. Age at index offense
8. Index victim injury
9. Gender of index victim
10. Whether offender meets the *Diagnostic and Statistical Manual of Mental Disorders–Version Three (DSM-III)* criteria for personality disorder
11. Whether offenders meets the *DSM-III* criteria for schizophrenia
12. Psychopathology Checklist-Revised (PCL-R) diagnoses[15]

Offender scores are used to assign them to one of nine risk categories. The Sex Offender Risk Appraisal Guide (SORAG), developed for predicting violent and sexual recidivism among male offenders, incorporated an additional four sex offense–specific items.[16] The additional items included on the SORAG are:

1. Offender had victims other than girls under the age of 14
2. Offender has failed on prior conditional release
3. Offender was younger at the time of index offense
4. Offender had deviant sexual interests in phallometric testing

1 See Howard E. Barbaree et al., "Evaluating the Predictive Accuracy of Six Risk Assessment Instruments for Adult Sex Offenders," *Criminal Justice and Behavior* 28 (2001): 490–521; Rebecca J. Dempster and Stephen D. Hart, "The Relative Utility of Fixed and Variable Risk Factors in Discriminating Sexual Recidivists and Nonrecidivists," *Sexual Abuse* 14 (2002): 121–38.

2 "Sex Offender Risk Assessment," Institute of Public Policy, University of Missouri—Columbia, June 30, 2006, 3, accessed September 26, 2019, https://www.mosac.mo.gov/file.jsp?id=45355.

3 Static-99 Clearinghouse. Sponsored by Dr. Andrew J. R. Harris, Dr. Amy Phenix, Dr. Karl M. Williams. Accessed November 29, 2019, www.static99.org.

4 "Static-99/Static-99R," National Institute of Corrections, https://nicic.gov/static-99static-99r.

5 Amy Phenix et al., "Static-99R Coding Rules Revised 2016," November 14, 2016, 13, accessed September 26, 2019, http://www.static99.org/pdfdocs/Coding_manual_2016_v2.pdf.

6 Hanson, Babchishin, Helmus, Thornton, & Phenix, 2016. Communicating the results of criterion referenced prediction measures: Risk categories for the Static-99R and Static-2002R sexual offender risk assessment tools. *Psychological Assessment*. Advance online publication. doi:10.1037/pas0000371.

7 Amy Phenix, L. Maaike Helmus, and R. Karl Hanson, "Static-99R and Static-2002R Evaluators' Workbook," October 19, 2016, accessed September 26, 2019, http://www.static99.org/pdfdocs/Evaluators_Workbook_2016-10-19.pdf.

8 Epperson, DL, JD Kaul, S. Huot, R Goldman, Minnesota Sex Offender Screening Tool-Revised (MnSOST-R) scoring guidelines- Updated. 2005. Accessed November 29, 2019 https://mnpals-scs.primo.exlibrisgroup.com/discovery/openurl?institution=01MNPALS_SCS&vid=01MNPALS_SCS:SCS&date=2005http:%2F%2Fwww.psychology.iastate.edu%2F-dle%2FMnSOST-RManual12-22-2005.pdf&aulast=Epperson&iuid=304190&aufirst=D.%20L.&sid=sage

9 Duwe, G., PJ Freske, Using Logistic Regression Modeling to Predict Sexual Recidivism: The Minnesota Sex Offender Screening Tool-3 (MnSOST-3), January 30, 2012, *Sexual Abuse*, https://doi.org/10.1177/1079063211429470; Duwe G., Freske P. (2016) The Minnesota Sex Offender Screening Tool-3.1 (MnSOST-3.1). In: Phenix A., Hoberman H. (eds) Sexual Offending. Springer, New York, NY.

10 Epperson, D.L., J.D. Kaul, S. Huot, R. Goldman, W. Alexander, Minnesota Sex Offender Screening Tool-Revised (MnSOST-R) Technical Paper: Development, Validation, and Recommended Risk Lebvel Cut Scores. Accessed November 29, 2019, https://pdfs.semanticscholar.org/4293/db2c0828e25c338206928fdcc5b6e5c2e58c.pdf

11 Duwe G., Freske P. (2016) The Minnesota Sex Offender Screening Tool-3.1 (MnSOST-3.1). In: Phenix A., Hoberman H. (eds) Sexual Offending. Springer, New York, NY.

12 Duwe, G., PJ Freske, Using Logistic Regression Modeling to Predict Sexual Recidivism: The Minnesota Sex Offender Screening Tool-3 (MnSOST-3) January 30, 2012, *Sexual Abuse*, https://doi.org/10.1177/1079063211429470

13 Minnesota Department of Corrections. 2012. The Minnesota Sex Offender Screening Tool-3.1 (MnSOST-3.1): An Update to the MnSOST-3. Accessed November 29, 2019, http://www.ct.gov/ctsc/lib/ctsc/MnSOST3-1DOCReport.pdf; See also Duwe G., Freske P. (2016) The Minnesota Sex Offender Screening Tool-3.1 (MnSOST-3.1). In: Phenix A., Hoberman H. (eds) Sexual Offending. Springer, New York, NY.

14 Carolin Kroner et al., "Validity of the Violence Risk Appraisal Guide (VRAG) in Predicting Criminal Recidivism," *Criminal Behavior and Mental Health* 17, no. 2 (2007): 89–100.

15 Quinsey, V., G. Harris, M. Rice, C. Cormier, *Violent Offenders: Appraising and Managing Risk*, 2nd ed., APA (2006)

16 Ibid.

Table 13.2 Sex Offender Screening and Risk Assessment (SOSRA)

Arkansas Department of Corrections[1]

Step 1: Examination of the offender's criminal history
Includes investigative reports, judgments, medical information, forensic evaluations, charge and convictions, sexual offenses, and violent offenses. This includes a record check for offenses that might have been sexual in nature, but for which an offender pleaded to a lesser offense. Additional related materials are secured as warranted.

Step 2: Offender interview
Highly trained staff conduct the sex offender interviews.
Number of victims
Age of victims
Sex of victims
The manner in which the offender gained access to the victims
Deviant sexual interests
Age at which offender began sexually offending
Relationship of offender and victims
Level of intrusiveness of sex offending
Whether the victim was physically injured
Whether deadly weapon was used

Step 3: Actuarial Risk Assessments STATIC-99
VASOR (Vermont Assessment of Risk) is the risk factor assessment tool used, which considers both static and dynamic risk factors.

Step 4: Community notification risk level is assigned.

1 The Arkansas sex offender assessment process: doing it right.. (n.d.) >The Free Library. (2014). Retrieved Dec 04 2019 from https://www.thefreelibrary.com/The+Arkansas+sex+offender+assessment+process%3a+doing+it+right.-a0279915390

COMMON ASSESSMENT AND TREATMENT PRACTICES

Sexual abuser–specific assessments are most reliable when they are conducted by a trained expert, incorporate multiple sources of information, use research-supported methodologies, and strive to engage clients in the assessment process fully and with collaborative cooperation.[26] The risk, need, and responsivity framework, introduced in chapter 12, emphasizes the idea that life changes all the time, and as offender risks and needs change, new assessments are required to assure the treatment plan is keeping up with the changes the offender is experiencing in the world. It is essential to meet the offender where they are, intellectually, culturally, learning style, and personality, as examples, building services to meet the client's strengths.[27] In addition, anyone reviewing treatment practitioners is likely to run into the term **evidence-based practice** (EBP). EBP is an approach to clinical or treatment practice utilized since its introduction in 1992 integrating three elements: (1) the best available research, (2) clinical expertise, and (3) client preferences and values. Below are a few additional assessment tools, terms, and considerations that may be involved in treatment plan development.

Psychological Evaluations and Comorbidity

Part of the system of response for individuals accused of committing a sex crime might include a series of psychometric tests, including tests to assess intelligence, personality characteristics, social attitudes, and indicators of psychopathology.

Psychologists use various personality inventories, such as the MMPI (Minnesota Multiphasic Personality Inventory) or, more specifically, a psychosexual evaluation. A **psychosexual evaluation** is a tool developed specifically for measuring traits specific to sexual offending for use by clinicians who evaluate and treat admitting sex offenders. The **Multiphasic Sex Inventory (MSI)** was published in 1984 for adult males. The MSI for adolescent male sex offenders was published in 1986. The MSI II, an improved version of MSI, was made available in 1996. Also important to note is the fact that the more recent versions of the MSI II were developed for adult and adolescent males and adult and adolescent females. Other inventories are not viable beyond adult male populations requiring separate assessments for other offender populations. **Psychosexual Life History (PSL Hx)** is a comprehensive account of an individual's sexual history, which includes efforts to understand subjective feelings and attitudes elicited from the client. The goal is to get the client to talk about their feelings and thoughts in general, but also as they relate to the targeted criminal behaviors.

The MSI II mirrors the diagnostic authority of the *DSM*, which helps clinicians to determine whether their client suffers from a mental disorder. It is not uncommon for an offender to have a designated diagnosis related to sex offending, but then to also suffer from a second condition simultaneously, referred to as **comorbidity**. If a sex offender was diagnosed as having a specific sex offense diagnosis and also diagnosed with depression or anxiety or obsessive compulsive tendencies, this would need to be factored into treatment plans. Further, issues of drug or alcohol abuse must be addressed in coordination with a treatment plan to address sexual offending behaviors.

Polygraph Testing

As a part of the processes moving into treatment, an offender is asked to fill out a form outlining their sexual history. This includes questions about both criminal and noncriminal activities. Offenders in treatment are expected to be completely forthcoming about their sexual fantasies and behaviors, whether legal or illegal, in an effort to better understand what might have connected their sexual behaviors with sexually criminal acts.[28] These claims are measured using a polygraph examination in an effort to determine the degree of accuracy the offender represented, whether there might have been other offenses that were knowingly withheld, and the degree to which the outcomes of this process will be used to inform treatment and management strategies moving forward.[29] Further, the polygraph tests can also be used as an individual is closing out their time in treatment as one final effort to assess whether the individual has been truthful in their efforts to participate in treatment and be accountable to the program, to themselves, and to their team of correctional officers and treatment practitioners.

Penile Plethysmograph and the ABEL Assessment of Sexual Interests

Another treatment protocol or process developed to better assess an offender's sexual arousal patterns is the **plethysmograph**. Designed to detect blood flow to the penis, it is a measure of erotic arousal to various displayed stimuli.

The use of **phallometric tests,** or the procedure to determine sexual interest or preference by measuring the erection response or blood flow to the penis, is logged in association with various pictures or other stimuli. Identified as fairly intrusive measures, treatment professionals may elect to use the **ABEL Assessment of Sexual Interest,** which evaluates sexual interest and arousal using less intrusive measures, having the offender view slides of clothed individuals and measuring the level of attraction to each.

Ongoing Considerations

It is possible a person who has been convicted of a sex crime would also have committed sex crimes for which they had never been caught and therefore would not have a record either in the courts or with police. It can be the case that an offender might hesitate to reveal additional activities as required by the program and assessed via polygraph if the offender believes that disclosure might put them in further jeopardy with the criminal justice system. This is an ongoing reality for treatment programs to address, and as such it is important to make sure to work with judges and correctional officers throughout the process. In many cases, accountability for additional crimes can be addressed within the treatment program under way. Further, it is important for victims to be identified so they can be offered support or services as needed.

It has been said that sexual assaults don't just harm the person who is assaulted. It is important to remember that treatment may involve working within a sexually abusive family facing disclosure, ignorance for some, and the need to create new and healthy ways of interacting. Imagine being the parent of a child who was abused by a partner. The individual parent would need to work with support, in addition to working with the child who is also being treated, in addition to the work being offered to the offender. (More about this is presented in chapter 14.)

Research suggests that around 75 percent of all sex offenders in prison do not receive any treatment while in prison. This suggests that prison-based treatment is limited; however, examples of institutional sex-offender programs do exist, such as the programs introduced in chapter 12. Some practitioners share concerns about whether these offenders will be ready to return to the community without having had any treatment support for their sexually harmful behaviors before they leave prison.[30]

THE TREATMENT OF SEX OFFENDERS

Many people who find themselves in sex-offender treatment programs are indeed convicted sex offenders participating in state-sponsored or state-supported treatment programs as the result of a sex crime conviction in a state or federal criminal court. Treatment programs are offered in some cases as a **diversion program** before a prison sentence is imposed, a presentence alternative to the execution of a prison sentence for those offenders who are identified as appropriate candidates for treatment and who could benefit from a program rather than be subjected to incarceration. For sex offenders, the threat of incarceration is ever present; however, if the individual does not comply with the guidelines outlined in the treatment plan, they risk being sent to prison to serve out their term behind bars. Finally, treatment is often identified as a condition of release once their sentence has been served and they are transitioning back into the community. Almost all treatment programs are either run through state departments of corrections or are supplemented in some way by state funding and therefore subject to the state requirements for sex-offender treatment.

A BRIEF REMINDER OF EARLY TREATMENT

The earliest programs developed for addressing those who offended sexually were designed to treat them as though they were mentally diseased.[31] While the larger social contexts, such as the religious influence on legal definitions outlining sexually appropriate or inappropriate behaviors, were often not considered, the medical arena was typically referenced to provide a treatment or therapy for those who committed sexually offensive behaviors. Chapter 4 highlights some of the early conversations about sexual health in the context of efforts to study, understand, and treat sexual deviance.

Readers may remember John Harvey Kellogg, creator of the popular breakfast cereal corn flakes, who advocated his cereal to reduce one's interest in sex, particularly masturbation. Or the graham cracker, attributed to Presbyterian minister Reverend Sylvester Graham, who advocated a strict vegetarian diet to suppress carnal urges. Both were discussed in chapter 2 when attention was focused on social definitions of sexual deviance and efforts to address those behaviors. The history of treatments for behavior deemed as sexually offending includes a great deal of false starts and complete misses.

Medical practitioners and psychologists among these early pioneers largely based their fledgling assessments and treatments on the **medical model**, the idea that sexual offending indicated a disease in the offender. The disease, having taken hold, created a condition where the actions of the offender were seen to be outside the control of the offender. Remember, at this time not only masturbation was forbidden but also homosexuality, and sex out of marriage (particularly for girls) was identified as a perversion. Under the medical model, such behavior could result in institutionalization to secure the proper medical care.[32] Although the medical responses to sex offending varied from practitioner, to institution, to geographic locale, the search was on to find better ways to treat the "disease" of sex offending and address the perceived public threat. Substantial developments have been made in the study of assessments and treatment of sex offenders over the past 40 to 50 years. Professional standards were developed, and intentional actions were taken to create collaborative professional spaces.

A BRIEF REVIEW OF CONTEMPORARY TYPES OF TREATMENT

Many of the medical options and related psychological and behavioral elements have remained similar in theme since the 1930s and 1940s, while many assessment and treatment processes have advanced in practice. Current understand-ings about the treatment of sex offenders suggest sex offending is a complex mixture of social, psychological, and developmental aspects.[33] As such, it is pos-sible to design coordinated care using both pharmacological responses and **cog-nitive behavioral therapy (CBT)**, for example. Primary themes for contemporary treatment are discussed briefly below.

Medical

Much like today, some of the earliest responses to sexual deviations included medical responses such as psychological assessments, treatment, and medication. The use of prescribed medication, known as a **pharmacological treatment** (also referred to as **biomedical treatment**), can include antiandrogens, antidepressants, antianxiety, antiepileptic, or antipsychotic meds.[34] This practice as a method for addressing sex-offending behaviors continues to date, but was first documented in the *Journal of the American Medical Association* by Charles Dunn (1940) after experimentation with the use of the estrogen stilboestrol.[35] Perhaps two of the most common pharmacological treatments for deviant sexual behav-ior developed in the 1960s are known as CPA (cyproterone acetate) and MPA (medroxyprogesterone acetate) and are still used today for **chemical castration**,[36] to produce a drug-induced reduction in sexual desire. Although controversial, during the 1950s and 1960s **surgical castration** was practiced on offenders who did not respond to treatment.[37]

A second set of drugs used in treating the sex-offender population includes certain classes of antidepressants. These drugs have been found to reduce sexual urges and manage deviant sexual arousal.[38] Traditional usages of these drugs provide support for people with depression or obsessive–compulsive diagnoses. In sex offenders, these medications can offer a reduction in the compulsive ele-ments of their offending behaviors.

Behavioral Therapy

The behavioral programs for treating sex offenders reached their height of popularity in the United States in the 1960s and 1970s. The work of the Ger-man **Hans Eysenck** in the 1950s, who criticized traditional psychotherapy, resulted in a shift toward behavioral therapy as the preferred form of psycho-logical treatment,[39] which remained popular and prominent among treatment professionals and clinicians well into the 1970s.[40] The focus shifted from a psychoanalytic need to understand the origin of the behavior, to a focus on efforts to shift the individual's actions by reinforcing desired behaviors and eliminating undesired behaviors. Several well-known examples of behavioral treatment in practice include operant conditioning (Skinner, 1959), aversion therapy (McGuire and Vallance, 1964), orgasmic reconditioning (Marquis, 1970) and shaping (Bancroft, 1971).[41]

Behavioral therapies were expanded in the 1970s by Gene Abel[42] and his colleagues and William Marshall[43] and his colleagues, to include **multimodal** aspects of their program by expanding the more narrow scope of treating a specific element of deviant behavior to include additional aspects, such as social skills training or relationship development skills.[44] Understanding the influence of flawed thinking, known as **cognitive distortions**, Abel modified behavioral treatment programs to be cognitive behavioral in an attempt to address the cognitive element believed to be driving thoughts and then behaviors.[45] Internationally known Canadian psychologist, researcher, and the director of Rockwood Psychological Services **William L. Marshall** has authored over 300 books and worked in the field of sexual-offender treatment for over 40 years.[46] He suggests that, after the introduction of behavioral therapies in the 1960s, practitioners quickly shifted their focus to include the cognitive elements.

Cognitive Behavioral Therapy

For approximately the past three decades, CBT in a group setting has been the most popular method for treating sex offenders.[47] CBT is focused on making changes in not only how an individual behaves, but also in how they think. A cognitive approach will focus on thinking errors and work to identify the thinking errors related to the offender's crime. Therapy will focus on replacing errors in thought with more functional, healthy thought patterns. The focus on thoughts is combined with a focus on behaviors, helping offenders learn life skills, such as relationship development, healthy family relationships, or parenting classes, skills a significant number of offenders enter treatment needing to develop.

Much has been written as a justification for the CBT treatment protocol, primarily the idea that offenders have to think their way to the commission of a sex crime and therefore need to be trained to process the same information differently. In other words, their actions have to be rationalized by the offender, or they have to justify the action as "no big deal," or think in ways that minimize the impact of their actions in order to follow through with the behavior.[48]

Sex offender–specific treatment programs are likely to share some targeted areas in the treatment protocol. For example, many sex offenders measure a lack of victim empathy, and as such this theme becomes a common objective for individuals in treatment.[49] CBT programs may utilize role-playing, where the offender acts out the role of their victim with either the treatment provider or other offenders taking the role of the offender. To a large degree, sex offenders are working to process through the collection of decisions that led up to their sex offense, and they work to understand how to deconstruct those patterns well before they find themselves in risky situations.

Treatment programs can elect to work within a framework of processes focused on ways to best meet offender needs. At least three examples are of interest: relapse prevention, the Good Lives Model, and a strength-based approach. Adapted for sex offenders in the 1980s, **relapse prevention** is a supportive or adjunctive therapy, originally created as a drug abuse therapy but modified for sex offenders and is based on the idea that an individual can better manage a behavior by avoiding situations, and sometimes people, where offenses may be committed. If an offender avoids these places or situations, then a relapse is much less likely to occur. More recently, contemporary models of treatment that take into account the multiple "pathways" to offending for adults and juveniles are increasingly popular.[50]

The **Good Lives Model** (and the updated Good Lives Model-Comprehensive)[51] was proposed to focus offenders on the goals they want to achieve in developing for themselves well-balanced, "good lives."[52] The program is developed as a means for helping them to use prosocial means for achieving those goals, which might include successful family interactions or fulfilling employment. A **strength-based approach** is another model for sex-offender treatment that identifies a series of steps to help offenders achieve goal-oriented behaviors over time and in various settings by processing through nine steps.[53] Managing emotions is an important treatment outcome for sex offenders. When working with correctional staff in the community and within a treatment protocol, the combination of CBT, relapse prevention, and community supervision has been shown to be quite effective.[54] It is also important to remember the assessment tools and the treatment models are under constant evaluation with an eye toward improvement.

TREATMENT DIFFERENCES BETWEEN JUVENILES, FEMALE, AND ADULT MALE OFFENDERS

Methods used for adult male offenders are not always tested with success in other populations. For this reason, specific albeit brief attention is given to the treatment of both juvenile and female offenders. For young people, early intervention seems to secure effective and positive results, while for women little is known. Relatively small groups have produced research outcomes that sometimes conflict. As a result, caution must be used when reviewing any related research.

Treating Juvenile Sex Offenders

When a young person acts out sexually, parents or family members may not know how to respond. It may be the case that two young people who do not yet meet the legal definition of the age of consent decide to have sex, which offers up one set of concerns, it may be that a family member acts out against another family member in a criminal way, or it may be a completely different dynamic. As such, clarifying the data available for determining the degree to which juvenile sexual offenses are a problem is not easy. As a general rule, a young person can be charged with a criminal offense beginning at approximately age 10 through age 17. It is important to understand that studies examining juvenile sexual offending indicate approximately 41 percent of sexual assaults against children ages 10 to 16 are committed by other children of similar age[55] and up to one-fifth of rapes and one-half of all child molestations each year in the United States are committed by juvenile sex offenders.[56] Research from the FBI, however, using data from 1998–2007 indicated rapes by juveniles have declined more recently; however, it is also clear that juveniles are both the victims and the offenders of sexual assault.

Based on research suggesting juveniles have difficult home lives, histories of abuse and neglect, and suffer forms of social isolation, it is necessary that treatment plans work to address these particular issues. Although research on juvenile sex offenders is limited, the published studies show promising results, particularly if the young person gets early help.[57] Tools that have been used with adult offenders for years, such as evidence-based treatment guidelines and programming (particularly for female juvenile offenders), however, simply have not been fully developed for the younger treatment population.

Like adult offenders, treatment programs are attached to adequate assessments of juvenile offenders. Also like adult offenders, juveniles comprise a heterogeneous population of offenders, and needs specific to each offender must be identified to determine relevance for setting treatment goals. Attention will be given to an overview of two tools used for assessment with juvenile sexual offenders. The first is the Juvenile Sex Offender Assessment Protocol-II (J-SOAP-II), the Estimate of Risk of Adolescent Sexual Offense Recidivism (ERASOR) and the Massachusetts Youth Screening Inventory-2 (MAYSI-2) (see Table 13.3).

Assessments for juveniles are very exacting and detailed and involve multiple interviews with offenders and their parents or family members. Like adult assessment, the primary goal is to identify the risks and needs of the offender and to help them understand the dynamics of their offense.[58] Unlike adult assessments, it is important to contextualize juvenile sexual offending behavior within the context of normal juvenile development. Some characteristics highlighted in the ATSA guide to juvenile treatment and offending include reminders about typical adolescent behavior, which include poor impulse control, susceptibility to peer influence, emotionality, recklessness, lack of responsibility, and limited ability to anticipate and appreciate future consequences.[59] These make for important elements of a treatment plan; however, some differ-

Table 13.3 Juvenile Sex Offender Assessment Tools[1]

ERASOR Overview[2]
Designed for juvenile sex offenders (12–18) who have committed a sex offense.
Measures static and dynamic risk factors.

Evaluators tally scores based on the total number of risk factors exhibited by the offender.
Low-, moderate-, and high-risk levels are tabulated by the evaluator.

J-SOAP-II Overview[3]
Designed for male juvenile sex offenders (12–18) who have committed a sex offense.
Measures static and dynamic risk factors.
Scores include:

Static and dynamic scale scores and an overall score.
No cutoff ratings (ranging from high to low is possible).
Higher scores indicate greater risk for reoffending.

1 This table was modified from tables created by C. Mancini, *Sex Crime Offenders and Society* (Durham, NC: Carolina Academic Press, 2014), 203, 205.
2 Worling, J.R. and T. Curwen, 2001. Estimate of Risk of Adolescent Sexual Offense Recidivism Copyright © 2001 SAFE-T Program, Thistletown Regional Centre, Ontario, Canada, M9V4L8. Accessed November 29, 2019, https://djj.ky.gov/800%20Policy%20Manual/ERASOR%202.0.pdf.
3 Prentky, R. and S. Righthand. 2003. Juvenile Sex Offender Assessment Protocol-II (J-SOAP-II) Manual. NCJ 202316. Accessed November 29, 2019, https://www.ncjrs.gov/pdffiles1/ojjdp/202316.pdf.

ences do exist between adolescents who commit sex offenses and those who commit other crimes, which can be important for treatment practitioners to consider. There are some notable differences between adolescents who commit sexual offenses and those who commit nonsexual crimes that may require specific types of interventions. For example:

- Adolescents who have committed sexual offenses appear more likely to have been sexually victimized and/or exposed to sexual content or pornography at an earlier age than adolescents with nonsexual offenses.
- Youth who have engaged in sexually abusive behavior may be more likely than youth who have committed nonsexual offenses to report higher levels of social isolation, anxiety, and low self-esteem.
- Adolescents who have engaged in sexually abusive behavior may be less likely to have significant criminal histories, associate with antisocial peers, or have substance abuse problems than youth who have committed nonsexual crimes.
- Youth who have offended sexually may be more likely to have sexual interests oriented toward younger children and/or violence than youth who have offended nonsexually.[60]

Like adult male offenders, those who work with juvenile offenders seek to design a treatment plan to target impaired social skills, empathy deficits, cognitive distortions, deviant sexual arousal, problematic management of emotions, impulsive antisocial behaviors, and related issues of child maltreatment.[61] Also like adult male offenders, treatment programs often use a cognitive behavioral approach. Juveniles benefit from early intervention, which also helps with the essential skill building of empathy, an important skill for all people but particularly for people who have experienced neglect and/or isolation as children.[62]

More research is needed for this category of sex offender. This includes an examination of treatment programs to review important content areas. Effective support programs include vocational training, basic living skills, counseling, parent support and perhaps family support groups, greater recognition for mental health issues, and issues related to diversity and cultural values for each juvenile.[63] For juveniles in treatment, moving back into the community can be an important transition, particularly given the important role families play generally, but also in the dynamics of early offending. Also, attention is being paid to the impact of legislation, such as the Adam Walsh Act, discussed in chapter 10, on this offender population. Researchers, advocates, and community activists almost universally agree that the reach of this legislation unduly impacts young offenders.[64]

Treating Female Sex Offenders

Females comprise a much smaller number of sex offenders as compared to males. Estimates suggest approximately 3 to 6 percent of all reported sex offenses are female.[65] As such, little research has focused specifically on the female offender, and this is reflected in the lack of information about treatment and programming for female offenders. As with other offender groups, treatment programs designed for women use a cognitive-based program. One example of a program in Canada includes five components of the program: (1) self-management, (2) deviant arousal, (3) cognitive distortions, (4) intimacy, relationship, and social functioning, and (5) empathy and victim awareness.[66]

As introduced in chapter 7 on offenders, female offenders often get lumped as teacher abusers of underaged students; however, that is a very narrow illustration of a female sex offender. Women may work within sex trafficking networks, or be abusing their own child, or be coerced into offenses by an abusive boyfriend or husband, as examples. The limited number of sex offenders means there is limited data, and researchers are still learning how female offenders and female juvenile offenders differ from adult male offender populations. There are no standard assessment tools that have been developed for women; however, the literature highlights the importance of gender-based responses to meet their needs.[67] Consideration is suggested for the following:

- Dispositional factors or antisocial tendencies
- Historical factors
- Contextual elements regarding the offense, co-offending
- Available support from social networks
- Personal life circumstances, including victimizations and problematic relationships
- Clinical factors, including mental health, substance use, and sexuality[68]

Treating Sex Addiction and Sexually Compulsive Behavior

A brief note on sexually compulsive behavior or sex addiction is warranted. Some of the overlaps between sex offenders and people with sexual addictions are increasingly being explored in treatment programs and by researchers. In some cases, sex offenders are automatically assumed to be sex addicts, which is not necessarily the case.[69] Further, the internet is being identified as the source for an explosion of illegal sexual behavior, committed by otherwise law-abiding citizens.[70] Activities such as viewing child abuse images and soliciting sex with a minor are increasingly common and are easily done from the privacy of a person's own home. As with other addictions, a person with a sex addiction is dominated by sexual thoughts, to the point of having it impact other areas of their lives, such as in their relationships or in work settings. Having an addiction, of course, is not illegal; however, having one may be stigmatized, which prevents individuals from seeking treatment. Questions are being raised about the degree to which a sexual addiction is the driving force of a sex offense and whether standard treatment models for sex offending provide a complete model for addressing addiction and vice versa. Few sex addicts escalate into sexual offending; most do not, and those who do only rarely commit what most people think of as serious sexual offenses. Researchers and professionals are exploring the degree to which the existing actuarial tools are appropriate for sexually addicted offenders.[71] The role of compulsive behaviors and addiction in sexual-offending behaviors will likely be better understood as hidden sexual crimes become more publicly understood.

CONTEMPORARY CONVERSATIONS ON RESEARCH, TREATMENT, AND RECIDIVISM

Many different academic and professional disciplines are involved in the exploration of human sexuality, particularly when the focus is a healing of harm and the target is the prevention of future offenses and harms. Although tremendous progress has been made in the treatment of sex offenders, much of what is being created is also currently underdeveloped as practitioners continue to learn. This may seem obvious in that research and development is a part of the way many other medical and clinical processes work. Academic, clinical, and medical communities collectively reflect on both successful and questionable practices in research publications and at national conferences to provide a forum for evaluating and challenging existing and innovative sex-offender treatment strategies. The focus on sexualized harms, both historically and contemporarily, as discussed throughout the text and as illustrated in the world today, serves as an important reminder of the limits of human understanding and the edges of emerging advancements and growth. Without question, this is a kind of living laboratory with varying and emerging challenges. Coupled with questionable effectiveness of related legislation, blurred lines in a culture caught between sexualizing everything and not talking at all about anything sexual, and persistent myths about both sex offenders and victims of sexual violence, the idea of generating new ideas or innovating collaborative new approaches to sex-offender treatment doesn't secure much purchase for those in the mainstream who just want solutions.

Critical reflection is always necessary throughout any exploration, expansion, and acceptance of new knowledge, but it is especially important at the edges of what is known and what is knowable. This process is very seldom neat and tidy, and in fact can be quite controversial even in assessing what constitutes legitimate treatment. Treatment programs designed to "cure" homosexuality, commonly referred to as "pray-away-the gay" or conversion programs, provide one obvious example of this. Challenged resoundingly from various sectors, the viability of such practices in therapeutic or clinical settings has been resoundingly discredited by the larger scientific and therapeutic communities; however, in spite of rich, layered medical, mental health, psychological and sociological studies, religious and societal attitudes and beliefs, a segment of the population remains unconvinced.[72] The social environment for which these solutions are being developed does not always value the lessons learned in the lab, making it difficult to build a successful community in which to grow that practice.

When the focus is sex offenders, almost without exception, people want to know whether a sex offender can be "cured." Can this individual move forward without being a risk to others in their circle of influence, or are they always going to remain a risk to my family? People, in the main, do not understand that practitioners do not use the language of being "cured." Much like alcoholism, the focus is on behavior and thought management. The better question is "Can sex offenders learn to manage any challenges they might have, avoid committing harmful behaviors, and learn to develop and maintain healthy relationships?" Several future themes on research, treatment, and offender recidivism are presented for review moving forward.

RESEARCH AND TREATMENT

Perhaps it is not surprising that people in the mainstream think sex offenders cannot be successfully treated. In fact, a collection of research in the 1990s suggested as much.[73] But a lot has evolved since that time due in part to advances in research and statistical methods. The quality of research in the area has improved. The evolution of research on sex-offender treatment is relatively new, and recent research on sex-offender treatment has provided some reasons to be optimistic. One of the first studies to get significant attention suggesting that treatment and related research was meeting with notable success came from **R. Karl Hanson**, a leading researcher on sex-offender risk assessment and treatment. Sexual recidivism rates for sex offenders (referencing recidivism rates for sex offenses specifically, rather than offenses of a nonsexual nature) were reported to be relatively low, at about 10 to 15 percent.[74]

Findings from a 2002 meta-analysis of 43 studies, which is considered to be one of the largest and best designed studies in support of treatment effectiveness, suggested those offenders who went to treatment recidivated less than those not treated.[75] A 2004 study indicated that most sex offenders did not repeat sex offenses, first-time sex offenders were significantly less likely to repeat sex offenses than those with previous convictions for sex offenses, and offenders over the age of 50 were less likely to reoffend than younger offenders.[76] In addition, the study found that the longer offenders remained offense free in the community, the less likely they were to reoffend sexually. The data shows that rapists, incest offenders, "girl-victim" child molesters, and "boy-victim" child molesters recidivated at significantly different rates. Recidivism rates were highest for boy-victim child molesters and rapists. Generally, the sex offenders who posed the highest risk of recidivism victimized males, had prior sex offenses, and were a younger age. Given that the level of sexual recidivism was lower than commonly believed, discussions of the risk posed by sex offenders should differentiate between the high public concern about these offenses and the relatively low probability of sexual recidivism. Further, the variation in recidivism rates suggests that not all sex offenders should be treated the same. This requires assessments to determine risk and treatment needs.

In the last decade or so, traditional sex-offender treatment programs have shifted from harsh and confrontational shame-inducing techniques to more positive approaches.[77] The more favored alternative has been referred to as **positive treatment approaches**. Research has established support for positive treatment approaches, demonstrating cases where clinicians who offer encouragement are more likely to facilitate positive treatment gains and outcomes,[78] while the more confrontational approaches have less successful treatment outcomes.[79]

"**Who Works**" is an expanding body of research referencing staff characteristics or therapeutic styles in sex-offender treatment calling for a more empathetic, engaged, and genuine interaction focused on client outcomes and success.[80] The focus here is on the kind of interactions with the individuals in treatment. Traditionally, treatment programs have been linked to a punitive style of punishment and shaming or a combative and punishing boot camp style drill instructor. Research has been done showing not only is this not effective, but it may in fact *decrease* the effectiveness of the treatment experience, and even make recidivism in some individuals *more* likely.[81] The use of a four to one positive reinforcement practice, four positive reinforcements for every one negative, has been recommended as most effective.[82]

The goal of treatment for sex offenders is to reduce **criminogenic**, or crime producing, actions, which in this population, is any crime more broadly, but more specifically it is to prevent sexual recidivism. This includes working on specific personal characteristics and attributes. Treatment research also shows a need to address noncriminogenic client needs, which include basic self-management skills, such as self-esteem, social skills, problem-solving skills, sex education, trauma response and resolution, and victim awareness.[83]

SEX-OFFENDER RECIDIVISM AND REGULATORY CRITIQUE

Attention to research about the effectiveness of sex-offender research requires a commitment and a desire to really understand the larger effort. Consider some research is conducted on victims who are children. Aside of the need to clarify what is statutorily defined as a child, that research is conducted in different states from within different programs. A significant portion of research done on sex offenders is done on adult males. Even when the offender population is comparable, adult males who committed sex offenses, the kind of offense may differ, and the psychological profile of the offender may differ, and these may be impactful in making assessments about what the research can teach the larger body of researchers and treatment practitioners working from within different social, geographic, and clinical settings. The degree to which it is viable to compare female offenders with male offenders or juvenile male or female offenders warrants closer attention. Said differently, various methodological considerations must be factored into any given research comparison. For example:

1. Dependent variable—what is being measured.
2. Sample—who/what group is being studied.
3. Follow-up period—how long after treatment the measurements were taken.
4. Type and location of treatment—what treatment models and measures were used.
5. The type of research design—researchers must incorporate a reliable scientific design, which typically means having a control group and a test group.
6. An objective program evaluator—utilizing someone who is not vested in the evaluation outcome.[84]

In spite of the various orientations of research conducted on sex offenders, the results are producing some information that is noteworthy. Similar to the Hanson studies mentioned above, a meta-analysis including 80 comparisons between treatment and control groups including more than 22,000 individuals globally found a sexual recidivism rate of 11.1 percent for treated sex offenders and a rate of 17.5 percent for nontreated offenders, a reduction of 31 percent.[85]

This lends support to the idea that sex-offender treatment programs utilizing cognitive behavioral treatments are finding some success.

Another way researchers study treatment efficacy is by looking at offender characteristics, including the type of offense they committed, whether the offense was against young boys, or within the family, accessible to the offender through work (as a teacher or faith leader), or the degree to which the offender was invested in the treatment program. Offenders who quit treatment, for example were at an equal or higher risk to reoffend when compared with those who completed treatment.[86]

A few cautions do also exist related to sex-offender treatment and related research efficacy. Because most sex offenders never get caught, are never charged, and do not go to prison, some experts have expressed concern about how information on sex offending is collected and analyzed because the data that the medical and research communities use is based on such a small percentage of offenders (the significantly smaller number of those who *were* caught, charged, and convicted) it is subsequently likely to be highly skewed.[87] Finally, not all studies show positive outcomes for treatment,[88] and in many cases the limitations of research restrictions cannot be fully separated from the research objectives; caution is recommended when drawing conclusions or making inferences about the broader applications.

REVISITING THE DARK FIGURE OF CRIME AND THE FUNNEL EFFECT

Treatment options specifically for sex offenders have advanced significantly in the last 50 years. Professionals in the field are regularly making adjustments based on additional research and treatment innovations. Yet even if the public were to access accurate information about sex offenders more broadly, people are generally skeptical of research findings and can be outright fearful of offender treatment programs if they are perceived to give offenders too much freedom in the community. Few groups have secured more disdain as a collective than individuals who have committed sex offenses, perhaps in large part because most people believe once an individual commits a sex crime they remain a continuous threat to public safety, and for some of the smallest percentage of the worst offenders this seems to be backed by research.

On the surface, this fear makes sense and perhaps may seem to be an obvious if not expected response. People will always want to make efforts to assure the public is safe from such offenders. The news carries stories of people, often children, who are abducted from their beds or chained in a basement for years. Undoubtedly, these are life-altering, horrific crimes that sometimes end in the victim's death. Nothing can capture the trauma or harm or hurt imposed on an individual, their family and friends, or the community in which such an event occurs than when a loved one is harmed in this way. Even when the harm is not fatal, it is intimate and personal and profound.

Yet traditionally sex offenders have been identified as a monolith, a singular type of offender with common characteristics. This could not be further from the truth. Anyone interested in research, research design, and the methods used to determine the implications of the research more broadly will have their work cut out for them as they pull together the information on sex-offender treatment and reoffense rates. Because offenders are heterogeneous coming into the research process, it is not always helpful to generalize study outcomes.

It is likely safe to assume that people who are studying sexual violence and prevention are studying sexual violence in an effort to respond to harm, provide support, and help in healing. Individuals may also be focused on expanding way to prevent sexual assaults from happening. Again, the goal of assessing the effectiveness of the many different programs designed for treating sex offenders is ongoing. The research outcomes are varied, depending on whether attention is given to juvenile offenders, female offenders, child molesters, repeat offenders, or first-time offenders and the myriad of research design features necessary for making comparisons. A small collection of findings was offered here. As attention moves into the idea of a broader awareness of sexual violence prevention and community action, it is also important to remember the number of offenses and offenders who are never reported and therefore never studied. Maybe someone reports to the police, but there is not enough evidence to make an arrest. Many children don't report; nonoffending parents may not know about the abuse. The research being reported is likely the tip of the iceberg when it comes to what is known about sex offenses and offenders.

CHAPTER CONCLUSION

As was discussed in section III, everyone impacted by a sexual offense will go through their own process at their own pace as they address the implications. This is also the case with sex offenders processing through the aftermath of a conviction and treatment. The impacts of a sexual assault are disparate, but research and focused attention illustrate the potential long-range impacts for both the offenders who are convicted and the individuals they harmed. Victims of sexual assault may not ever want to explore and research and discuss facts about sexual violence outside of the reality of their own experience. Other victims may want to explore the various characteristics or consequences of these harms as a means of working through their attack. The lived experience of a sexual assault may not involve the need to take a deep dive into what the statistics say about treatment efficacy.

Further, when the very difficult cases are the ones most people see on the news, or hear about from friends, or talk about at work or school, or in fact experience themselves, it is not hard to understand why a person or even a group of people might carry a "lock them up and throw away the key" attitude toward someone they see as a "sex offender." When a story on the nightly news announces a person who committed a sex crime is getting out of prison, even after serving a lengthy sentence, there is at the same time an unknown number of people who have been impacted or harmed by sexual violence and might find this individual's return to the community somewhere between challenging and infuriating. To accept and acknowledge this reality is important. The idea that this person who was convicted of having committed a very intimate, personal, and hurtful offense is going home to family or going back to the rest of their lives can be a hard reality for crime victims to confront.

The reality of a return to life outside of the prison setting is also uncertain for the convicted offender, as was discussed in more detail in chapter 12. Community attitudes regarding the sex-offender population can become a part of the treatment plan as offenders try to find housing and work and rebuild relationships. As much as the treatment of sex offenders provides resources for convicted sex offenders, many questions remain. Questions about the degree to which sex-offender treatment works are deliberated against an uncertain number of offenses and unidentified offenders who have not been reported or confronted about an act of harm, or the individual who was assessed at a low or no risk but who goes on to commit another offense.

Developing an understanding of the significance of treatment outcomes for sex offenders is undoubtedly important. To expand the reach of prevention efforts, questions of individual character collide with cultural conditions that extend beyond the treatment environment. Advocates, practitioners, and theorists who challenge the exclusive focus on the individual sex offender emphasize the supplemental need to look carefully at the social and cultural conditions outside the therapeutic environment in which these sex offenders live as an additional focus for sexual violence prevention efforts.

Text Box 13.1.   Media Messages about the Treatment of Sex Offenders

The media's coverage of the most extreme cases of sexual violence and harm belie the reality that many sex crimes go unreported, happen in the context of a relationship, and few offenders are caught and prosecuted. In many cases, even when a conviction happens, the media coverage can elevate stories of cases where the conviction and sentencing outcome is insignificant enough—no jail time, probation, or treatment—as to warrant outrage or disgust, which can take the form of a disappointed head shake or a forwarded Facebook post. Coverage of extreme cases, whether that be a reference to the offense or the sentence, can skew the public's understanding of how dangerous a sex offender will be in the future. The history of "sexual psychopath" laws highlights the focus on the extreme end of sex-offending behaviors. More recently, the media profile of a sex offender has been the image of a "predator in plain view." This could be a media tycoon who is called out after years of abusing people he worked with, a wealthy business professional who used lawyers to craft a sweet deal, or a national political operative who gets unexpectedly brought down with no visible indication of their abusive and/or criminal behaviors.

How does the media representation and categorization of people who commit sexual offenses impact the work of treatment professionals and offenders themselves as they are moving their way through prison to treatment and community reintegration?

KEY TERMS

ABEL Assessment of Sexual Interest
actuarial testing/risk tables
amenability to treatment
assessment tools
Association for the Treatment of
 Sexual Abusers (ATSA)
biomedical treatment
chemical castration
cognitive behavioral therapy (CBT)
cognitive distortions
comorbidity
criminogenic
diversion program
dynamic risk factors
etiology
evidence-based practice (EBT)
Good Lives Model
Hans Eysenck
medical model

multimodal
Multiphasic Sex Inventory (MSI)
phallometric tests
pharmacological treatment
plethysmograph
positive treatment approaches
psychological evaluation
psychosexual evaluation
Psychosexual Life History (PSLHx)
R. Karl Hanson
relapse prevention
risk assessment
risk factors
static risk factors
strength-based approach
surgical castration
treatment programs
"Who Works"
William L. Marshall

REVIEW QUESTIONS

1. The chapter begins and ends with references and information about recidivism. Discuss the importance of recidivism in the context of sex-offender assessment and treatment.

2. Describe and explain at least three assessment tools, and include when in the process of the criminal justice system they are used.

3. Early efforts to evaluate sex-offending behaviors were linked with discussions about sexual psychopaths and cereal and graham crackers. Please be prepared to explain this history.

4. Be prepared to define and describe what the actuarial assessments are and how they differ from other kinds of assessments used to treat and manage sex offenders.

5. Describe a medical response to sex-offender behavior and provide two examples.

DISCUSSION QUESTIONS

1. Identify some of the ideas about sex-offender treatment that you brought with you to this discussion before learning anything about sex-offender treatment. How does what you carry with you as an understanding of sex-offender treatment and recidivism impact what you are learning? What

challenges do you see? Where might you go to get additional information to help you resolve those challenges?

2. Consider the idea of sex-offender management from the perspective of a victim. Consider the victim perspective as a victim who has been open about their victimization. Consider the victim perspective as someone who has not told anyone about their victimization. What ideas might be developed to assure a victim of sexual violence is able to receive treatment for any related medical or mental health issues they need addressed?

3. One factor for consideration of sex-offender treatment success is the issue of amenability to treatment. What questions would you have if a friend or family member were entering a treatment facility, and how does the uncertainty of research outcomes influence your concern that the treatment program might not be an effective use of time for your friend or family member? How would you rest assured they would be moving forward in a positive way? Please justify your response.

4. A great deal of information was presented about the assessment tools used in collaboration with programmatic decisions or community management decisions for an offender transitioning back into the community. Which assessments offer a solid sense of understanding in terms of how they related to the process and how they are to be used, and which ones are less clear in terms of the role they play in the treatment and management objectives? Please be prepared to discuss elements of these processes.

5. Repeatedly the research has suggested sex offenders represent a broad range of sex-offending behaviors and personality types. On one end of the cases that are more difficult to see positive outcomes is an offender who measures high on the psychopathy scales. With that, treatment outcomes vary. Ethical concerns were raised about the fact that an assessment tool might not have accurately measured an offender's likelihood to reoffend. How does that information impact your decisions and/or choices about what treatment protocol is appropriate? Be prepared to justify your response.

NOTES

1. E. Janus, *Failure to Protect: America's Sexual Predator Laws and the Rise of the Preventive State* (Cornell University, 2006).

2. L. Kirsch and J. Becker, "Sexual Offending: Theory of Problem, Theory of Change, and Implications for Treatment Effectiveness," *Aggression and Violent Behavior* 11, no. 3 (2006): 208–24, https://doi.org/10.1016/j.avb.2005.08.001.

3. "The Comprehensive Approach to Sex Offender Management, Assessment," Center for Sex Offender Management, accessed October 20, 2019, https://csom.org/tribal-action-guide/assessment-continued.htm.

4. "Bringing Victims and Victim Service Providers into Reentry Planning in New Jersey," The National Center for Victims of Crime, June 2005, accessed September 21, 2019, https://victimsofcrime.org/docs/Reports%20and%20Studies/NJ%20Victims%20Report%20Final.pdf?sfvrsn=0.

5. D. Finkelhor, *Characteristics of Crimes against Juveniles* (Durham, NH: Crimes Against Children Research Center, 2012).

6. Jane Anderson, and Patricia Powers, "Alcohol-Facilitated Sexual Assault: Who Needs Force When You Have Alcohol?: The Prosecutors' Resource on Violence against Women," National Sexual Violence Resource Center, 2016, accessed September 21, 2019, https://www.nsvrc.org/elearning/alcohol-facilitated-sexual-assault-who-needs-force-when-you-have-alcohol-parts-i-ii.

7. T. Sanders, J. Scoular, R. Campbell, J. Pitcher, and S. Cunningham, "Introduction: Technology, Social Change and Commercial Sex Online," in *Internet Sex Work* (Palgrave Macmillan, 2018).

8. David Lisak and Paul M. Miller, "Repeat Rape and Multiple Offending among Undetected Rapists," *Violence and Victims* 17, no. 1 (2002): 73–84, https://www.wcsap.org/sites/default/files/uploads/webinars/SV%20on%20Campus/Repeat%20Rape.pdf.

9. See, for example, "Survivors of sexual Violence Are Let Down by the Criminal Justice System—Here's What Should Happen Next," The Conversation, March 29, 2018, accessed September 21, 2019, http://theconversation.com/survivors-of-sexual-violence-are-let-down-by-the-criminal-justice-system-heres-what-should-happen-next-94138.

10. William L. Marshall et al., eds., *Rehabilitating Sex Offenders: A Strength-Based Approach* (Washington, DC: American Psychological Association, 2011), 10.

11. Tali Klima, and Roxanne Lieb, "Risk Assessment Instruments to Predict Recidivism of Sex Offenders: Practices in Washington State," Washington State Institute for Public Policy, June 2008, accessed September 21, 2019, http://www.wsipp.wa.gov/ReportFile/1015/Wsipp_Risk-Assessment-Instruments-to-Predict-Recidivism-of-Sex-Offenders-Practices-in-Washington-State_Full-Report.pdf.

12. Raymond A. Knight and David Thornton, "Evaluating and Improving Risk Assessment Schemes for Sexual Recidivism: A Long-Term Follow-Up of Convicted Sexual Offenders," National Criminal Justice Reference Service, March 2007, accessed September 21, 2019, https://www.ncjrs.gov/pdffiles1/nij/grants/217618.pdf.

13. Robert A. Prentky, "Introduction: The Assessment and Treatment of Sex Offenders," *Criminal Justice and Behavior* 21, no. 1 (1994): 6–9, https://doi.org/10.1177/0093854894021001002.

14. John Q. La Fond, "Can Therapeutic Jurisprudence Be Normatively Neutral? Sexual Predator Laws: The Impact on Participants and Policy," *Arizona Law Review* 41 (1999): 375.

15. R. K. Hanson, L. Helmus, and D. Thornton, "Predicting Recidivism amongst Sexual Offenders: A Multi-Site Study of Static-2002," *Law of Human Behavior* 34, no. 3 (2010): 198–211, doi:10.1007/s10979-009-9180-1; R. K. Hanson and M. Bussiere, "Predicting Relapse: A Meta-Analysis of Sexual Offender Recidivism Studies," *Journal of Consulting and Clinical Psychology* 66, no. 2 (1998): 348–62, https://psycnet.apa.org/doiLanding?doi=10.1037%2F0022-006X.66.2.348; R. K. Hanson and K. Morton-Bourgon, "The Characteristics of Persistent Sexual Offenders: A Meta-Analysis of Recidivism Studies," *Journal of Consulting in Clinical Psychology* 73, no. 6 (2005): 1154–63, doi:0.1037/0022-006X.73.6.1154; R. Mann, R. K. Hanson, and D. Thornton, "Assessing Risk for Sexual Recidivism: Some Proposals on the Nature of Psychologically Meaningful Risk Factors," *Sex Abuse* 22, no. 2 (2010): 191–217, doi:10.1177/1079063210366039.

16. James Bonta, "Advances in Offender Risk Assessment," *Research Summary* 13, no. 2 (March 2008), Public Safety Canada, http://www.publicsafety.gc.ca/res/cor/sum/cprs200803-eng.aspx.

17. Robert J. McGrath, Michael P. Lasher, and Georgia F. Cumming, "A Model of Static and Dynamic Sex Offender Risk Assessment," National Institute of Justice, US Department of Justice, October 2011, accessed September 21, 2019, https://www.ncjrs.gov/pdffiles1/nij/grants/236217.pdf.

18. See Hanson and Bussiere, "Predicting Relapse"; R. K. Hanson and A. J. R. Harris, "Where Should We Intervene?: Dynamic Predictors of Sex Offense Recidivism," *Criminal Justice and Behavior* 27 (2000): 6–35, http://dx.doi.org/10.1177/0093854800027001002.

19. Howard Barbaree et al., "Evaluating the Predictive Accuracy of Sex Risk Assessment Instruments for Adult Sex Offenders," *Criminal Justice and Behavior* 28, no. 4 (2001): 490–521, https://doi.org/10.1177/009385480102800406.

20. "Sex Offender Risk Assessment," Institute of Public Policy, University of Missouri–Columbia, June 30, 2006, accessed September 21, 2019, https://www.mosac.mo.gov/file.jsp?id=45355.

21. "Risk Assessment," Association for the Treatment of Sex Abusers (ATSA), accessed October 20, 2019, http://www.atsa.com/risk-assessment.

22. "Sex Offender Supervision: 2000 Report to the Legislature," Minnesota Department of Corrections, January 2000, 13, accessed September 21, 2019, https://www.leg.state.mn.us/docs/pre2003/mandated/000243.pdf.

23. Robert J. McGrath, "Sex-Offender Risk Assessment and Disposition Planning: A Review of Empirical and Clinical Findings," *International Journal of Offender Therapy and Comparative Criminology* 35, no. 4 (1991): 328–50, https://doi.org/10.1177/0306624X9103500407.

24. "Sex Offender Supervision."

25. Sherri Flynn, "The Arkansas Sex Offender Assessment Process: Doing It Right," *Corrections Today*, January 1, 2012, accessed October 2019, https://www.thefreelibrary.com/The+Arkansas+sex+offender+assessment+process%3A+doing+it+right.-a0279915390.

26. "ATSA Practice Guidelines for the Assessment, Treatment, and Management of Male Adult Sexual Abusers, 2014," https://www.maine.gov/corrections/adult/2014_ATSA_Practice_Guidelines.pdf.

27. Ibid., 30.

28. Sean Ahlmeyer et al., "The Impact of Polygraph on Admissions of Victims and Offenses in Adult Sexual Offenders," *Sexual Abuse* 12, no. 2 (2000): 123–38, https://doi.org/10.1177/107906320001200204; Don Grubin et al., "A Prospective Study of the Impact of Polygraphy on High-Risk Behavior in Adult Sex Offenders," *Sexual Abuse* 16, no. 3 (2004): 209–222, https://doi.org/10.1023/B:SEBU.0000029133.78168.ab.

29. Grubin et al., "A Prospective Study of the Impact of Polygraphy."

30. See, for example, Anna C. Salter, *Treating Child Sex Offenders and Victims* (Newbury Park, CA: Sage Publications, 1988); Robert E. Freeman-Longo and Fay Honey Knopp, "State-of-the-Art Sex Offender Treatment: Outcome and Issues," *Annals of Sex Research* 5, no. 3 (1992): 141–60, https://doi.org/10.1177/107906329200500301.

31. Laura J. Zilney and Lisa Anne Zilney, *Perverts and Predators: The Makings of Sexual Offending Laws* (Lanham, MD: Rowman & Littlefield, 2009).

32. Michael A. Rembis, *Defining Deviance: Sex, Science, and Delinquent Girls, 1890–1960* (University of Illinois Press, 2013).

33. Karen J. Terry, *Sexual Offenses and Offenders* (Belmont, CA: Wadsworth Cengage Learning, 2013).

34. Eli Coleman and Michael Miner, eds., *Sexual Offender Treatment: Biopsychosocial Perspectives* (Binghamton, NY: The Haworth Press, 2000), 14.

35. C. Dunn, "Stilboestrol-Induced Gynecomastia in the Male," *Journal of the American Medical Association*, 115, no. 26 (1940): 2263–64; see also Robert M. Foote, "Diethylstilbestrol in the Management of Psychopathological States in Males: I. Preliminary Report," *Journal of Nervous and Mental Diseases* 99, no. 6 (1944): 928–29; J. Bierer and G. A. Van Someren, "Stilboestrol in Out-Patient Treatment of Sexual Offenders: A Case Report," *British Medical Journal* 1 (1950): 935–36; Paul Bowden, "Treatment: Use, Abuse and Consent," *Criminal Behaviour and Mental Health* 1, no. (1991): 130–36, https://doi.org/10.1002/cbm.1991.1.2.130.

36. Terry, *Sexual Offenses and Offenders*, 248.

37. Sturup, "Castration: The Total Treatment," *International Psychiatry Clinics* 8 (1971): 175–96.

38. Martin P. Kafka, "Sex Offending and Sexual Appetite: The Clinical and Theoretical Relevance of Hypersexual Desire," *International Journal of Offender Therapy and Comparative Criminology* 47, no. 4 (2003): 439–51, https://doi.org/10.1177/0306624X03253845.

39. William L. Marshall, Dana Anderson, and Yolanda Fernandez, *Cognitive Behavioral Treatment of Sexual Offenders* (Wiley, 1999).

40. William L. Marshall et al., *Treating Sexual Offenders: An Integrated Approach* (New York: Routledge, 2006).

41. Terry, *Sexual Offenses and Offenders*, 249.

42. See, for example, G. Abel, E. Blanchard, and J. Becker, "An Integrated Treatment Program for Rapists," in *Clinical Aspects of the Rapist*, ed. Richard T. Rada (New York: Grune & Stratton, 1978); G. Abel and J. Rouleua, "Sexual Abuses," *Clinical Sexuality* 18 (1995): 139–53, accessed October 20, 2019, https://www.psych.theclinics.com/article/S0193 -953X(18)30076-5/fulltext.

43. W. L. Marshall, D. R. Laws, and H. E. Barbaree, eds., *Handbook of Sexual Assault: Issues, Theories, and Treatment of the Offender* (New York: Plenum, 1990).

44. Terry, *Sexual Offenses and Offenders*, 249.

45. Theresa A. Gannon et al., "Cognitive Distortions in Child Molesters: Theoretical and Research Developments over the Past Two Decades," *Aggression and Violent Behavior* 12, no. 4 (2007): 402–16, doi:10.1016/j.avb.2006.09.005.

46. See, for example, the more recent works describing his program, William L. Marshall et al., *Treating Sexual Offenders: An Integrated Approach*, and the strength-based method, William L. Marshall et al., eds., *Rehabilitating Sex Offenders: A Strength-Based Approach*.

47. W. L. Marshal and D. R. Laws, "A Brief History of Behavioral and Cognitive Behavioral Approaches to Sexual Offenders, Part 2. The Modern Era," *Sexual Abuse* 15, no. 2 (2003): 75–92, https://doi.org/10.1177/107906320301500202.

48. Many authors have written in this area. See, for example, Gene G. Abel et al., "The Measurement of Cognitive Distortions of Child Molesters," *Sexual Abuse* 2, no. 2 (1989): 135–52, https://doi.org/10.1177/107906328900200202; Marshall, Anderson, and Fernandez, *Cognitive Behavioral Treatment of Sexual Offenders*.

49. C. A. Wastell, D. Cairns, and H. Haywood, "Empathy Training, Sex Offenders, and Re-Offending, *Journal of Sexual Aggression* 15, no. 2 (2009): 149–59, doi:10.1080/ 13552600902792599.

50. "Treatment: Overview," Center for Sex Offender Management, accessed September 22, 2019, https://www.csom.org/pubs/cap/4/4_0.htm.

51. W. Marshall, L. E. Marshall, G. A. Serran, and M. D. O'Brien, "Sexual Offender Treatment: A Positive Approach," *Psychiatric Clinics of North America* 31, no. 4 (2008): 681–96, doi:10.1016/j.psc.2008.06.001.

52. T. Ward and C. A. Stewart, "The Treatment of Sex Offenders: Risk Management and Good Lives," *Professional Psychology: Research and Practice* 34, no. 4 (2003): 353–60, http://dx.doi.org/10.1037/0735-7028.34.4.353; T. Ward and T. A. Gannon, "Rehabilitation, Etiology, and Self-Regulation: The Comprehensive Good Lives Model of Treatment for Sexual Offenders," *Aggression and Violent Behavior* 11, no. 1 (2006): 77–94, http://dx.doi .org/10.1016/j.avb.2005.06.001; C. Fortune, T. Ward, and D. Polaschek, "The Good Lives Model and Therapeutic Environments in Forensic Settings," *Therapeutic Communities: The International Journal of Therapeutic Communities* 35, no. 3 (2014): 95–104, https://www .emerald.com/insight/content/doi/10.1108/TC-02-2014-0006/full/html.

53. D. R. Laws and T. Ward, *Desistance from Sex Offending: Alternatives to Throwing Away the Keys* (New York: The Guilford Press, 2011).

54. R. E. Freeman-Longo and F. H. Knopp, "State-of-the-Art Sex Offender Treatment: Outcome and Issues," *Annals of Sex Research* 5, no. 3 (1992): 141–60, http://dx.doi.org/10.1007/BF00849738.

55. T. E. Wind, "The Quandary of Megan's Law: When the Child Sex Offender Is a Child," *John Marshall Law Review* 37 (2003): 73–124, https://heinonline.org/HOL/LandingPage?handle=hein.journals/jmlr37&div=14&id=&page=.

56. "Understanding Juvenile Sexual Offending Behavior," Center for Sex Offender Management, Silver Spring, MD, 1999.

57. J. R. Worling and T. Curwen, "Adolescent Sexual Offender Recidivism: Success of Specialized Treatment and Implications for Risk Prediction," *Child Abuse & Neglect* 24, no. 7 (2000): 965–82, http://dx.doi.org/10.1016/S0145-2134(00)00147-2.

58. J. DiGiorgio-Miller, "Clinical Techniques in the Treatment of Juvenile Sex Offenders," *Journal of Offender Rehabilitation* 21, no. 1-2 (1994): 117–26, http://dx.doi.org/10.1300/J076v21n01_07.

59. "ATSA Practice Guidelines for the Assessment, Treatment, and Intervention with Adolescents Who Have Engaged in Sexually Abusive Behavior," Association for the Treatment of Sexual Abusers, 2017, accessed October 20, 2019, http://www.atsa.com/atsa-practice-guidelines.

60. Ibid., 9.

61. S. Righthand and C. Welch, Juveniles Who Have Sexually Offended: A Review of the Professional Literature," US Department of Justice, Office of Justice Programs, Office of Juvenile Justice and Delinquency Prevention, 2001, 43.

62. G. Ryan, "Treatment of Sexually Abusive Youth," *Journal of Interpersonal Violence* 14, no. 4 (1999): 422–36, doi:10.1177/088626099014004005; W. L. Marshall, S. M. Hudson, R. Jones, and Y. M. Fernandez, "Empathy in Sex Offenders," *Clinical Psychology Review* 15, no. 2 (1995): 99–113, https://doi.org/10.1016/0272-7358(95)00002-7.

63. F. P. Reddington and B. W. Kreisel, *Sexual Assault: The Victims, the Perpetrators, and the Criminal Justice System* (Carolina Academic Press, 2017), 336–37.

64. F. E. Zimring, *An American Travesty: Legal Responses to Adolescent Sexual Offending* (Chicago: University of Chicago Press, 2004), http://dx.doi.org/10.7208/chicago/9780226983592.001.0001.

65. "Reported Cases of Female Sex Offenders," Inside Prison, accessed October 20, 2019, https://www.insideprison.com/all-reported-cases-of-female-sex-offenders.asp; "Female Sex Offenders," Center for Sex Offender Management, A Project of the Office of Justice Programs, US Department of Justice, March 2007, accessed October 20, 2019, https://www.csom.org/pubs/female_sex_offenders_brief.pdf.

66. K. Blanchette and K. N. Taylor, "A Review of Treatment Initiatives for Female Sexual Offenders," in *Female Sexual Offenders*, ed. T. A. Gannon and F. Cortoni, 119–141 (John Wiley and Sons, 2010), doi:10.1002/9780470666715.ch8; *Correctional Services Canada: Women Who Sexually Offend: A Protocol for Assessment and Treatment* (Ottawa, ON: Correctional Services Canada, 2001).

67. B. Bloom, B. Owen, and S. Covington, *Gender-Responsive Strategies: Research, Practice, and Guiding Principles for Women Offenders* (Washington, DC: National Institute of Corrections, 2003).

68. Donna M. Vandiver, Kelly Cheeseman Dial, and Robert M. Worley, "A Qualitative Assessment of Registered Female Sex Offenders: Judicial Processing Experiences and Perceived Effects of a Public Registry," *Crimininal Justice Review* 33, no. 2 (2008): 177–98, https://doi.org/10.1177/0734016808318448; Vandiver et al., 202–203. See also F. Cortoni, R. K. Hanson, and M.-E. Coache, "The Recidivism Rates of Female Sexual Offenders Are Low: A Meta-Analysis," *Sexual Abuse: A Journal of Research and Treatment* 22 (2010): 387–40; L. Craig, K. Browne, and A. Beech, "Assessing Risk in Sex Offenders: A Practitioner's Guide," 2008, 1–249, doi:10.1002/9780470773208.

69. Robert Weiss, "Out of control sexual behavior: addiction or offending?" *PsychCentral* blog, June 9 2015, accessed September 22, 2019, https://blogs.psychcentral.com/sex/2014/09/out-of-control-sexual-behavior-addiction-or-offending/.

70. Samantha Smithstein, "Sex Addiction and Sex Offending: A Growing and Dangerous Relationship," *Psychology Today*, April 6, 2011, accessed September 22, 2019, https://www.psychologytoday.com/us/blog/what-the-wild-things-are/201104/sex-addiction-and-sex-offending-growing-and-dangerous.

71. Dennis M. Donovan and G. Alan Marlatt, *Assessment of Addictive Behaviors*, 2nd ed. (New York: The Guilford Press, 2005).

72. "The Lies and Dangers of Efforts to Change Sexual Orientation or Gender Identity," Human Rights Campaign, accessed September 22, 2019, https://www.hrc.org/resources/the-lies-and-dangers-of-reparative-therapy.

73. G. C. N. Hall, "Sexual Offender Recidivism Revisited: A Meta-Analysis of Recent Treatment Studies," *Journal of Consulting and Clinical Psychology* 63 (1995): 802–9; M. A. Alexander, "Sexual Offender Treatment Efficacy Revisited," *Sexual Abuse: A Journal of Research and Treatment* 11 (1999): 101–16.

74. Hanson and Bussiere, "Predicting Relapse."

75. R. Karl Hanson et al., "First Report of the Collaborative Outcome Data Project on the Effectiveness of Psychological Treatment for Sex Offenders," *Sexual Abuse* 14, no. 2 (2002): 169–94.

76. A. J. R. Harris, and R. K. Hanson, "Sex Offender Recidivism: A Simple Question," Ottawa, ON: Public Safety and Emergency Preparedness Canada, 2004, https://www.ncjrs.gov/App/Publications/abstract.aspx?ID=206023.

77. See, for example, M. Proeve and K. Howells, "Shame and Guilt in Child Sexual Offenders," *International Journal of Offender Therapy and Comparative Criminology* 46, no. 6 (2019): 657–67, doi:10.1177/0306624X02238160; J. Kear-Colwell and P. Pollock, "Motivation or Confrontation: Which Approach to the Child Sex Offender?," *Criminal Justice and Behavior* 24, no. 1 (1997): 20–33, https://doi.org/10.1177/0093854897024001002; W. L. Marshall, "Assessment, Treatment, and Theorizing about Sex Offenders: Developments during the Past Twenty Years and Future Directions," *Criminal Justice and Behavior* 23, no. 1 (1996): 162–99, http://dx.doi.org/10.1177/0093854896023001011.

78. Marshall et al., "Sexual Offender Treatment: A Positive Approach." See also A. R. Beech and C. Hamilton-Giachritsis, "Relationship between Therapeutic Climate and Treatment Outcome in Group-Based Sexual Offender Treatment Programs," *Sex Abuse* 17, no. 2 (2005): 127–40, https://www.ncbi.nlm.nih.gov/pubmed/15974420; W. Marshall, and Geris Serran, "The Role of the Therapist in Offender Treatment," *Psychology Crime and Law* 10, no. 3 (2004): 309–20, doi:10.1080/10683160410001662799.

79. G. Serran, W. Marshal, Y. Fernandez, and L. Marshall, *Sexual Offender Treatment: Controversial Issues* (John Wiley and Sons, 2006).

80. T. McCullough and L. Kelly, "Working with Sex Offenders in Context: Which Way Forward?," *Probation Journal* 54, no. 1 (2007): 7–21, https://doi.org/10.1177/0264550507073324; W. L. Marshall et al., *Treating Sexual Offenders: An Integrated Approach*.

81. T. Ward and S. M. Hudson, "A Model of the Relapse Process in Sexual Offenders, *Journal of Interpersonal Violence* 13 (1998): 700–25; T. Thomas and R. Tuddenham, "The Supervision of Sex Offenders: Policies Influencing the Probation Role," *Probation Journal* 49, no. 1 (2002): 10–18, https://doi.org/10.1177/026455050204900103; Marshall and Serran, "The Role of the Therapist in Offender Treatment."; A. McAlinden, "The Use of Shame in the Reintegration of Sex Offenders," *British Journal of Criminology* 45 (2005): 373–94; Thomas and Tuddenham, "The Supervision of Sex Offenders: Policies Influencing the Probation Role"; Marshall et al., *Treating Sexual Offenders: An Integrated Approach*.

82. P. Gendreau, "Offender Rehabilitation: What We Know and What Needs to Be Done," *Criminal Justice and Behavior* 23, no. 1 (1996): 144–61, http://dx.doi.org/10.1177/0093854 896023001010.

83. This list was taken from the compilation presented here: "Guiding Frameworks and Goals," Center for Sex Offender Management, accessed September 22, 2019, csom.org/pubs/cap/4/4_1.htm. For additional resources, see Marshall et al., *Treating Sexual Offenders: An Integrated Approach*; R. J. McGrath and G. F. Cumming, *Sex Offender Treatment Needs and Progress Scale Manual* (Middlebury, VT: Author, 2003); P. Rich, *Understanding, Assessing, and Rehabilitating Juvenile Sexual Offenders* (Hoboken, NJ: John Wiley & Sons, Inc., 2003); J. R. Worling, "The Estimate of Risk of Adolescent Sexual Offense Recidivism (ERASOR): Preliminary Data," *Sexual Abuse: A Journal of Research and Treatment* 16 (2004): 235–54.

84. Terry, *Sexual Offenses and Offenders*.

85. Friedrich Lösel and Martin Schmucker, "The Effectiveness of Treatment for Sexual Offenders: A Comprehensive Meta-Analysis," *Journal of Experimental Criminology* 1, no. 1 (2005): 117–46.

86. Robert J. McGrath et al., "Outcome of Treatment Program for Adult Sex Offenders: From Prison to Community," *Journal of Interpersonal Violence* 18, no. 1 (2003): 3–17, https://doi.org/10.1177/0886260502238537.

87. Zilney and Zilney, *Perverts and Predators*; Eric S. Janus, *Failure to Protect: America's Sexual Predator Laws and the Rise of the Preventive State* (New York: Cornell University Press, 2006).

88. See, for example, Janice K. Marques et al., "Effects of a Relapse Prevention Program on Sexual Recidivism: Final Results from California's Sex Offender Treatment and Evaluation Project (SOTEP)," *Sexual Abuse* 17, no. 1 (2005): 79–107; Kristen M. Zgoba and Jill Levenson, "Variations in the Recidivism of Treated and Nontreated Sexual Offenders in New Jersey: An Examination of Three Time Frames," *Victims & Offenders* 3, no. 1 (2008): 10–30, https://doi.org/10.1080/15564880701751639.

14

Sexual Violence as a Public Health Issue

Awareness, Advocacy, and Prevention

I thought I understood rape. It happened to me when I was 13 years old. I assumed my job was to model survivorship, and to show readers how to speak up after being abused, molested or attacked. I thought I was supposed to talk to the girls. I had a lot to learn.

—Laurie Halse Anderson, *Speak*[1]

Women raped by men they know—acquaintance rape—is not an aberrant quirk of male-female relations. If you are a woman, your risk of being raped by someone you know is four times greater than your risk of being raped by a stranger.

- 1 in 4 women surveyed were victims of rape or attempted rape.
- 84 percent of those raped knew their attacker.
- 57 percent of the rapes happened on dates.

Those figures make acquaintance rape and date rape more common than left-handedness or heart attacks or alcoholism. These rapes are no recent campus fad or the fantasy of a few jilted females. They are real. And they are happening all around us.

—Robin Warshaw, *I Never Called It Rape*[2]

I once taught students about Rose without ever considering Rufus. For ten years I've been making up for that omission by researching and speaking about sexual violence against enslaved men.

—Thomas A. Foster, *Rethinking Rufus: Sexual Violations of Enslaved Men*[3]

LAURIE HALSE ANDERSON, the best-selling author of several children's and young adult books, wrote her first novel, *Speak*, about a teenage girl's struggles after being raped. For more than two decades, she watched her book garner expanded national attention in high schools and college literature classes, which serves as a springboard for conversations on sexual violence prevention, bullying, and consent. In the time since the book's publication, she has met with community groups, school groups, and faith communities. She has been interviewed by all major media forms and nominated for various awards and continues to intentionally start important dialogues about moving on from and healing after sexual assault.

In early 2019, Anderson wrote an opinion piece for *Time* magazine titled "I've Talked with Teenage Boys about Sexual Assault for 20 Years. This Is What They Still Don't Know." In the article, she writes:

> In schools all over the country, in every demographic group imaginable, for 20 years, teenage boys have told me the same thing about the rape victim in *Speak*: they don't believe that she was actually raped. They argue that she drank beer, she danced with her attacker and, therefore, she wanted sex. They see his violence as a reasonable outcome. Many of them have clearly been in the same situation. They say this openly. They are not ashamed; they are ill-informed. These boys have been raised to believe that a rapist is a bad guy in the bushes with a gun. They aren't that guy, they figure, so they can't be rapists.
>
> This is only made worse by the other question I get most often from these teenage boys in the classroom: Why was the rape victim so upset? They explain, *The sex only took a couple of minutes, but she's depressed for, like, a year.* They don't understand the impact of rape [italics in the original].[4]

Also, in early 2019, an updated edition of journalist Robin Warshaw's 1988 book *I Never Called It Rape* revisited one of the first large-scale studies conducted on rape over 30 years later. At the time, the findings indicated 25 percent of women in college had been victims of rape or attempted rape, 84 percent of those assaulted knew their assailant, and 1 in 12 men admitted to committing acts that met the legal definition of rape.[5] As the title suggests, perhaps one of the most surprising findings was that only 27 percent of the women who had been assaulted identified themselves as a victim of rape. Said differently, 73 percent of the women in the study didn't call it rape.

Finally, also in 2019, Thomas A. Foster published what is considered to be one of the first books ever written about the sexual violations black men endured during slavery. Conversations about the constant access white men granted themselves have been explored, but it is interesting that historical accounts of an era when a black man could be attacked, lynched, castrated, or all of those things for looking at a white woman, the idea of abuse and fear surrounding the myth of the black male sex fiend persist to the present day.[6]

These three frameworks provide a backdrop for considering sexual violence and prevention efforts. One is a fictionalized story reflective of real life, the second is an academic effort intending to measure a section of real life in a scientific way, and the third is a reminder that sometimes an unacknowledged, yet lived reality for someone can be overlooked or ignored even when it has been right in front of us the whole time. Each story, in its own way, centered an unblinking focus on rape, sexual assault, and the idea of awareness and education as an essential part of sexual violence awareness, prevention, and response. Both also talk about the perpetrator of the offense and the person who was offended against in a way that maintains the connectivity of the offense to the social and cultural dynamics of the environmental conditions. Both emphasize gaps in understanding that easily undermine efforts to move prevention efforts forward, framing the information in a uniquely distinct way with the intention of securing and impacting the attention of a larger audience.

These three examples with their decades of reflection and musings about aspects of sexual assault that have changed, remained the same, and/or been ignored completely speak to the multiplicity of struggles that go into efforts to prevent sexual violence and address any related crimes or harms. Certainly, many excellent books explore the deeply nuanced elements of all aspects of a sexual assault, its origins, aftermath, and implications. The individual and collective efforts that have generated ideas and programs to reduce or eliminate this kind of violence and related harms continue to emerge or evolve. Yet, within these discussions in the studies of sexual violence prevention, a large area of uncertainty remains. Strong social movements produce social outcomes only to have those outcomes be reversed or retrenched. Questions remain not only about what the public knows about sexual violence and related prevention options, but also what researchers and practitioners are saying, what actions are being taken, and what practices are being challenged as ineffective by calls for reform. The idea that individuals who might be offenders do not recognize their actions as offenses or realize the extent of the harm their actions cause another human person raises important questions about social and environmental attitudes and behaviors. Treatment options designed for individuals convicted of committing sex offenses discussed in chapter 13 overviewed the important work of individuals and treatment practitioners working to address the harms caused by an individual. Open questions remain, as suggested by the very small sample of quotes at the top of the chapter: How do the collective social attitudes and behaviors held by each individual get forged in community? To what extent are the interpretations of harm or the impact of an assault not immediately clear to the person harmed, and how often do the reverberations of an incident get translated back to a victim in ways that might not come close to capturing or reflecting their own lived experience, or their ability to assess their own needs for help, or their ability to heal? *Are the issues around sexual assault essentially questions of individual offender character, or do they indicate social and cultural influences?*

QUESTIONS OF CHARACTER *AND* CULTURE

As has been discussed in previous chapters, sex crimes are identified as one of the most egregious kinds of offenses a person can commit against another person. It is also true that all sex offenses and offenders are not the same, meaning the harms perpetrated are different, the motivations are different, the willingness to accept responsibility for hurting someone is different, and the desires to change are different. Also, most sex offenders will be released back into the community with all of what that entails for the offender, the victims, and the community. The degree to which the public is made safer by the existing sex offender laws and their enforcement is at best uncertain. Although authentic and positive efforts are under way to address the issue of sexual violence harm and it's prevention, huge gaps exist in the system's response.

As with many examples of risk in the world, the goal is **risk mitigation**, intentionally taking efforts to reduce the likelihood that an incident, in this case an act of sexual violence, might happen. Sadly, no matter how much care a person takes, the chance of reducing the possibility of being impacted by sexual violence and harms cannot be, at least has not yet been, reduced to zero. Different levels of sexual violence and harm across history and across different countries over time, however, offers support for the idea that communities can certainly get better at prevention. The reality of sexual violence in society is a hard truth to accept. The idea that sexual violence is less likely to come from a stranger and more likely to come from someone known to the person harmed is a critical point for consideration because the goal is risk reduction. The fact that the perpetrator of such a harm could in fact be a teacher, a coach, a neighbor, or even a parent or loved one requires a shift in awareness and attention. As a result, intentional, expanded efforts to better understand how broader social attitudes and behaviors impact or can help reduce sexual violence have been building in communities and warrant focused attention.

At the end of the 20-teens—2017, 2018, and 2019—the United States was experiencing an arguably unprecedented period of dynamic social tension, politically and socially. Within that time, gender and sexual violence awareness and prevention took on a prominent focus at the national level. Simultaneously, much like the stories shared above, actions being taken seemed both old and new again, obvious and hidden, active and passive. Large-scale national actions harkened back to historical marches and social activism of decades ago. **#MeToo**, **#SayHerName**, and **#MMIW** elevated long-standing local community actions to national and international prominence. Famous and powerful people were being called out publicly. People in positions of power were being called out and fired for inappropriate sexual behaviors in the workplace, for example. Cities across the country were releasing files of priests who had been credibly accused of sexual abuse. Docuseries, movies, and various media platforms highlighted sexual abuse allegations and sexual violence more broadly. Contemporary efforts seemed to be galvanizing people, generating new programs and resources and bringing generations of disparate groups together to assist in the larger effort to address and prevent sexual harassment, sexual violence, and related harms.

While this contemporary reckoning, of sorts, seemed to be taking place in the public sphere at some of the highest levels, questions were also being raised about what was happening in quieter places. The military released reports of a surge in sexual abuse rates;[7] Georgia became the sixth state to pass a six-week abortion ban (following Ohio, Mississippi, Kentucky, Iowa, and North Dakota), seen by some as a public attack on women;[8] and the Dallas police chief reported the police department's investigative focus on the death of a third black transgender woman in less than a year.[9] These are only a few of the contemporary examples from a recent news cycle. Also interesting, at about this time, historian Thomas A. Foster published a first-of-its-kind book on the sexual abuse of enslaved men, which by its storied content seems to almost beg an entire discipline, followed by society writ large, to be accountable for such a glaring omission from the larger historical record.[10] The example of the victimization of black men at the hands of white overseers is particularly important given the vilification of the black man as a threat to white women historically and culturally and the utilization of those false ideas to perpetrate the related harms, including beatings, lynching, and castration or other mutilations (discussed in chapter 4 on history), that were intentionally activated and also, until more recently, also downplayed in the broader historical narrative. How is it that something so obvious as the sexual abuse of black men during slavery has remained largely hidden or unexplored in the main?

Connecting this all the way back to the introduction of the text, at least some sectors of popular culture are elevating the sounds of what has traditionally been a silence surrounding sexual violence and harm in communities. Although sexual harms typically happen in secret, shrouded in and surrounded by silence, elements of hidden parts of the past seemed to be actively and publicly converging with a larger and more vocal demand for decisive action to address and reduce these harms and then to provide meaningful steps for moving forward. Ultimately, all of the ideas presented in the text up to this point invite a shift, a focus on theory moving into practice. How does anyone take in all of the information presented and find a way to work for a world within a world with a significant reduction in sexual violence and harm? To a degree, these ideas circle back to the beginning of the text where chapter themes started with an introduction to the conflicting and competing ideas of staying quiet and feeling silenced and contrasting that with an intentional movement beyond an exploration of individual character and toward ideas about cultural awareness, community response, and individual action.

Every community across the country has its own history with new or long-standing efforts to address sexual violence and educate toward its prevention and elimination. Although the particular characteristics of sexual violence prevention in local communities will need to be explored in more detail at the community level, efforts are presented here to represent the activism, advocacy, and broad but often unacknowledged efforts to reduce sexualized violence and related harms. The chapter opens with a history of activism and the evolution of advocacy, the early informal groups of individuals in communities who offered aid and assistance especially when the system suggested those harms did not rise to the level of a formal response. The evolution of a more formalized and systemic response to rape and intimate partner violence is offered, followed by a review of some larger social action campaigns focused on public education and sexual violence prevention. These are larger national-level initiatives, and local communities will undoubtedly have programs with a local focus. To address the harm and prevent future harm, victims, family members, advocates, and community members have worked tirelessly with professionals in the field to create solutions.

ACTIVISM, ADVOCACY, AND AGENTS OF CHANGE: HEROES WHO LEAD THE WAY

Although efforts to secure attention and accountability for people who have committed sex crimes can be linked back to other movements for advancing the rights of historically marginalized people, the specific focus to address the lack of attention being given to preventing sexual violence didn't find even partial footing in the United States until the 1940s and 1950s. One of the first recorded incidents when women of color broke the silence around rape in their community happened in 1866 when African American women who were raped by a white mob testified before Congress.[11] Ida B. Wells was well known for her work calling attention to and working to eliminate the issue of lynching in the South in the 1880s and 1890s. Genital mutilations often accompanied lynching as a form of humiliation and torture.

Efforts to find redress were often prompted by incidents of violence. In 1944, Rosa Parks, famous for her work on civil rights, founded the **Committee for Equal Justice for Recy Taylor**. Taylor, who was abducted and raped by six white men as she was walking home from church, never saw justice in the courtroom after two all-white, all-male grand juries refused to indict the perpetrators, even though one confessed to the crime.[12] Although Rosa Parks went on to become a nationally famous civil rights icon, many people like Rosa Parks took direct and decisive action in an attempt to secure a legal accounting for such crimes. In the Jim Crow South, justice for women of color who had been victims of sexual violence seldom reached the courtroom, but people in communities of color all knew about the case and began early efforts to organize in ways committed to judicial and social change.

Additional contemporary reflections on history highlight some of the gaps between communities of color and white women who were directly involved in the women's rights movements at the national level.[13] Much has been written, in this text and in other places, about the lack of support women of color are afforded, particularly around the issue of sexual violence and equal justice and excluded men almost completely.[14]

In the United States, violence against indigenous women has reached unprecedented levels on tribal lands and in Alaska Native villages. More than four in five American Indian and Alaska Native women have experienced violence, and more than one in two have experienced sexual violence. Alaska Native women continue to suffer the highest rate of forcible sexual assault and have reported rates of domestic violence up to 10 times higher than in the rest of the United States. Though available data is limited, the number of missing and murdered American Indian and Alaska Native women and the lack of a diligent and adequate federal response is extremely alarming to indigenous women, tribal governments, and communities. On some reservations, indigenous women are murdered at more than 10 times the national average.[15]

Founded in the 1970s, like many support programs directed at assisting many women victims of sexual violence, **Safe Women, Strong Nations** is a nonprofit law and advocacy program for indigenous women, directing efforts to educate, investigate, prosecute, and punish those who commit violence against Native women, with the goal being a restoration of safety to Native women in their communities.[16] Actions have likely always been taken on behalf of people impacted by sexualized violence and harm yet were clearly happening inside and outside of the mainstream structures of power. The lack of formal acknowledgment of these efforts is also an important aspect of the larger prevention effort moving forward.

Activism defined within the mainstream in the 1970s produced significant writings such as *Sexual Politics* (1970) by Kate Millet, *The Female Eunuch* by Germaine Greer (1970), and Susan Brownmiller's *Against Our Will* (1975), as examples, and the result produced rape crisis centers in larger metropolitan cities. Referred to as the **antirape movement**, the **rape crisis movement**, or the **feminist movement** more broadly, women looking to address issues of sexual violence and harm seemed to be fighting two different battles, based at least in part on racialized experiences. While white women were working the mainstream to bring rape crisis centers into being across the country, organizing in the black community worked to bring national attention to women of color who were assaulted, fought back, killed the perpetrators, and were imprisoned.[17] Efforts to integrate the movements of women of color and white women were trumped by the race dominance of white women during early feminist actions, a reality that has, like so many other factors associated with collective and individual efforts to bring about a response to sexual violence, arguably produced much needed critical reactions and reflections. The degree to which contemporary changes have resulted in an expanded collective awareness remains in a state of evolution.[18]

In the early days, **rape crisis centers** were informal groups, often women survivors seeking to assist other women survivors, and the composition and activities varied from community to community. The more formal centers were created in the early 1970s and in the larger US cities.[19] Other responses to survivors were happening in legal circles, with an emphasis on ending marital rape statutes, a legally supported idea that a husband could not rape his wife, as an example. The contemporary baseline of rape crisis or sexual assault center services is included in the following text box. Collaboration between local service agencies, such as police, child advocacy centers, and service-oriented groups, might also

---

Text Box 14.1.   Early Sexual Assault Center Services[1]

24-hour crisis intervention, hotline, and emergency shelter
Advocacy—hospital accompaniment, victim support, legal and criminal justice assistance
Institutional advocacy/systems change work
Support groups
Counseling and therapy
Prevention and awareness—self-defense classes
Information and referral

Note

1. Kris Bein, "Core Services and Characteristics of Rape Crisis Centers: A Review of State Service Standards," 2nd ed., accessed September 27, 2019, http://www .resourcesharingproject.org/sites/resourcesharingproject.org/files/Core_Services_ and_Characteristics_of_RCCs_0.pdf.

have built interconnectedness between agencies in support of the work, but little support was offered initially. The integrated design would undoubtedly have developed over time and emerged differently in each community.

ADVOCACY: UTILIZING STORIES AND STATISTICS

People in the field of sexual violence prevention often make use of a parable, a story used to illustrate a larger message or moral lesson. Sometimes, the story begins with a fisherman who happens to see someone being swept downstream,[20] and, sometimes, the story starts with a woman sitting on the bank of a river who hears a frantic shout for help.[21] She looks up to see someone struggling and being swept downstream, unable to get to shore. The hero of the story jumps into the water and helps secure the person safely to the riverbank, where, after a moment to gather their composure, the person who was helped ashore shares a great appreciation for the woman's help, and they go on their way. No sooner has our hero said goodbye when she hears another cry for help, then another. This continues all afternoon. She realizes she can't keep this up but is determined to help as much as she can. In some versions of the story, she enlists friends to help her, but they can assist even more of the people perilously flailing away as the river carries them downstream. But soon she realizes, even with great help, the numbers were too great. So many more people needed help ashore. And as she pauses to catch her breath, she realizes she has to go upstream to determine how so many people are being swept into the river in the first place. The moral of the story becomes clear: the more work that can be done upstream, the less emergency rescue work is needed downstream.

In this story, everyone who is illustrated is working in an advocacy role. The history of rape crisis centers and domestic violence centers certainly formalized the process of advocating for victims of sexual assault, bringing fully into the mainstream the idea that victims were falling into the gaps in the criminal justice system and being swept downstream. People who had been victimized were not getting the help they needed at hospitals, or from mental health providers, or with housing or rent or job losses when their injuries prevented them from working. People were being caught in the river's current and couldn't get to shore.

In 2018, *Time* magazine profiled the story of Kelly O'Hara, a young woman on her way to being a college graduate with an eye toward an advertising firm when she was sexually assaulted by a person in the academic program. She did start her professional career in advertising but not without having deeply personal struggles about her assault. She worked a full-time job but volunteered her time as a rape crisis counselor and described her training as guiding people through what was happening but mostly being a friend in support of the victim when they came to the center. Sharing parts of her personal journey, how she went from feeling conflicted about taking time away from her full-time job, to really feeling like she was making a difference in the lives of the people she was helping when she would meet them at the hospital, and eventually to realizing that one of the parts of her job as an advocate that she was really good at was the legal work. Ultimately, she left advertising, and, having learned the importance of the legal elements of the advocacy work, she decided to go to law school to be an advocate full-time.[22] This story illustrates in real life the importance of both the downstream crisis work and other jobs as support "moves upstream."

The immediate support from an advocate can produce positive outcomes for a victim in addressing critical medical needs and preserving evidence necessary should charges be filed. The advocate is trained to assist in making sure the victim is safe and has adequate medical care but also to assure the victim has the full understanding of her options and is providing direction for her own choices.[23] Research suggests that people harmed by acts of sexualized violence and who receive prompt medical care and counseling services are more likely to seek continued medical care, experience less posttraumatic stress, have less difficulty blaming themselves and trusting others, and are more likely to return to work.[24] Beyond the immediate crisis, support is offered for guidance through the legal process, working to prevent what has been referred to by critics of the criminal justice system as the second rape (introduced in chapter 11).

The role of advocacy work has changed dramatically since the early rape crisis centers. The **Minnesota Coalition Against Sexual Assault (MNCASA)**, as an example, has been in operation since 1978 and is a state-level organization started in response for efforts "upstream" to assist the many state sexual assault programs in Minnesota, which were so busy with clients that they could not focus on larger emerging needs such as media coverage, public policy, medical compliance issues, advocacy support, prevention, trafficking, and system change work. MNCASA continues its central mission, to "prevent sexual violence, and improving how advocacy programs, systems and communities respond to it,"[25] connecting people to advocacy positions in the areas of community engagement, legal advocacy, shelter advocacy, Native and Indigenous specific advocacy, and shelter advocacy, as examples.

Advocacy training for volunteer crisis advocates/counselors as outlined by the US Office of Justice Programs (OJP) **Office for Victims of Crime** (OVC) Training and Technical Assistance Center is designed for advocates preparing to respond in crisis situations. The advocate has five primary jobs: (1) provide the victim with information about their options, (2) provide trauma-specific services, (3) work with the victim to develop an action plan, (4) listen to and believe the victim, and (5) be neither investigator nor judge.

Ideally, victims will speak for themselves in response to a critical incident; however, experiencing a traumatic event can have immediate and sometimes debilitative effects, so an advocate will assist as needed. The issue of **trauma-specific services** or trauma-informed response, also referred to as trauma-informed care, is built on establishing five core values: *safety*, *trustworthiness*, *choice*, *collaboration*, and *empowerment* for the person who has been harmed.[26]

The Crisis Prevention Institute (CPI) trains professionals on person-centered, trauma-informed strategies to manage difficult behaviors nonviolently,[27] and defines **trauma** as:

> An event or series of events, an experience or prolonged experiences, and/or a threat or perceived threats to a person's well-being. The individual's daily cop-

ing mechanisms can be negatively impacted by trauma. Subsequent behavioral responses to daily life may be filtered through this perspective.[28]

The trauma-informed responses are relatively new public health approaches for mental health professionals, law enforcement, and other service providers. **Trauma-informed care** is defined as:

> A framework of thinking and interventions that are directed by a thorough understanding of the profound neurological, biological, psychological, and social effects trauma has on an individual—recognizing that person's constant interdependent needs for safety, connections, and ways to manage emotions/impulses.[29]

Those advocating trauma-informed approaches suggest trauma is pervasive, deeply life shaping, and more often impacts people who are more vulnerable in society, and exposure to trauma can affect the way people approach relationships. Further, service agencies have often responded in such a way as to compound existing trauma, rather than work in a way that accounts for and adapts to the longer-term impacts of trauma, and can also be deeply impacted by the stressors that come from working continuously with people operating out of some form of trauma response.[30]

Returning to the broader curriculum offered by the OVC as a model resource for **advocacy training**, the program is designed to be presented in two and a half days and includes 11 modules with supporting materials. The modules include the following:

Module 1: Introductions and Overview
Module 2: What Is Sexual Assault Advocacy/Counseling?
Module 3: Realities of Sexual Assault
Module 4: The Neurobiology of Trauma and Sexual Assault
Module 5: Impact of Sexual Assault
Module 6: Campus Sexual Assault
Module 7: Effects of Sexual Assault on Males
Module 8: Procedures in Common Advocacy Situations
Module 9: Recovery Education and Skills Training
Module 10: Compassion Fatigue and Self-Care
Module 11: Wrap-Up and Evaluation[31]

More contemporary support programs are increasingly professional, meaning they utilize more full-time staff rather than volunteers and have developed or developing networks with local service providers, and training is a part of their design.[32]

This becomes important for advocates because professionals working in highly repetitive situations involving stress and crisis can suffer from **secondary traumatization**, also called **vicarious traumatization**. Advocates themselves can begin to exhibit some of the same kinds of trauma responses seen in the people they are helping. Further, even the people who do this work, day in and day out, are not immune from being harmed, having people they loved harmed and having people they love cause harm to others. A person can know every scenario and statistic and still be in the middle of a situation of domestic or sexual violence. Studying this topic does not make any of us immune to its less than predictable reality. When harmful or violent experiences impact people who work in the field, they can sometimes feel additionally burdened by a false sense that they should have known what to do to prevent the incident from happening, like they should have known how to avoid those situations in the first place.[33] The reality is, of course, that full-on awareness and diligence about the reality of sexual violence does not always protect against the possibility of harm, even for the people who work as professional service providers and educators for others.

Since 1998 when the **Adverse Childhood Experiences (ACES) study**[34] was first conducted, health outcomes associated with ACES research are primarily explained by neurobiological factors that impact early brain development, the immune system, and the endocrine system.

For example, exposure to chronic stress can induce changes in the architecture of different regions of the developing brain (e.g., amygdala, hippocampus), which can impact a range of important functions, such as regulating the stress response, attention, memory, planning, and learning new skills and also contribute to dysregulation of inflammatory response systems that can lead to a chronic "wear and tear" effect on multiple organ systems.[35]

Since the initial research other qualifying characteristics of adversity, like sibling or peer victimization and parental death, have been added as examples of additional life experiences that can act as chronic stressors but were not included in the original study.[36] Links between childhood and young adult experiences impacting adult health and well-being have been repeatedly established.[37] The implications of the expanding body of research as it will be applied to the human services fields are evolving and worthy of continued attention.

The implications of ACES research on treatment interventions particularly in relation to sex offender treatment are also noteworthy. One example of a promising overlap between research on sex offender behaviors and ACES research suggests a large number of sex offenders were raised within a disordered social environment. Compared with males in the general population, sex offenders had three times the odds of child sexual abuse, nearly twice the odds of physical abuse, 13 times the odds of verbal abuse, and approximately four times the abuse of neglect or coming from a family experiencing divorce or other disruptions. Higher ACES scores were seen as associated with higher risk scores and inviting questions about whether better treatment responses will be possible with the trauma-informed interventions.[38] Future research and application of findings in this area could prove quite impactful for both treatment and prevention.

One additional thing about trauma for the discussion here. If an individual is impacted by violence, the statistics about how low the crime rate is in their community, or how much lower violent crime rates are now when compared to 10 years ago, or even how common or uncommon sexual harms are for people in their given age bracket are really just numbers at that point. At the point of trauma, statistics give way to stories that change people's lives. In a very real way, it is the stories of violence and harm that generate a collective desire to act. And although the phrase "hurt people, hurt people" has been used in many ways, it is also very important to remember that "healed people heal people." Some of the strongest voices in the sexual violence prevention movement are people who were harmed and are standing up to say never again.

Police departments, hospitals, social service organizations, and treatment professionals have a role to play in the collaborative efforts put in place to assist victims. Chapter 8 discussed the collaborative that is formed in an effort to immediately respond to an allegation of sexual assault, including SANE nurses, specially trained officers, and support for family and close friends. Similar designs of collaboration and support across disciplines is also the model for advocates beyond medical assistance and police response. Current strategies to make this a community response mean sexual violence prevention is a job for everyone.

ADVOCACY AND OFFENDERS

Unquestionably, sexual harms and crimes are hard to predict and prevent. This fact alone can make people particularly fearful. A person who repeatedly preys on children is distinctly different from a person who engages in a sex act before the children reach the legal age of consent. Under the current system, and depending on the jurisdiction, both incidents could require the individual to be defined as and register as a sex offender. On the other side of that equation, the impacts of harm are also fluid and dynamic for someone who has been injured. Assessing the need for support after someone has been harmed in a sexual way can look very different for each person.

Traditionally, the needs of an offender have been reviewed and considered separate from the needs of a victim. In an adversarial system of justice, there are two sides. When someone is harmed and someone does the harming, it is reasonable to see those as two distinct sides with very different needs. Victim advocates are increasingly supporting a **victim-centered approach**, which suggests that most of the energy should go to the victim and not the offender. This can be illustrated in horrible events where the perpetrator's name is not used and attention and community support go to the individuals harmed in the incident.[39]

The idea of advocacy, that an individual needs support, is, however, a theme these two groups share. The various dynamics of support that have been developed over time also must include support or advocacy for people who have committed sexual harms. At least two themes warrant repeating: first, sex offenders are not all the same and as such require individualized treatment and rehabilitation plans, and, second, most sex offenders know their victims. Undoubtedly, some people who have been harmed will never have or meet any desire to be in contact with the person who hurt them. Others, however, consider a family where domestic violence and related harms have happened may in fact want to find a way to work forward in relationship. The options are varied and must be dictated by the needs of the victim and the situation. It is important, however, to remember that offenders, victims, circumstances, and communities are all different and as such will inevitably produce different results.

Traditional research on sex offenders has focused on the person committing the sex offense, which is a necessary and exacting but particularly narrow focus. Research studying people who have been harmed and the effects of harm, and with intention, focus narrowly on the needs of the person harmed. The degree to which a person who has been harmed might choose to have any relationship with the person who harmed them is completely situational and victim driven. As communities seek to assist in notifications and resource development and as active community and professional efforts bring to the mainstream important public education information about sexual violence and sexual violence prevention, it is possible these two groups may find overlap. Consideration of these issues in the collective, as a community, as a marker of public health, and as a means for providing community-based programming could elicit questions about what an integrated and collaborative model for prevention and response might look like and when such an approach might be warranted.

SEXUAL VIOLENCE AS A PUBLIC HEALTH ISSUE

As treatment practitioners and criminal justice professionals work hard to address the problem of sexual violence as it happens every day, decades old critiques remain. Consider police. Are police officers the best responder to assist with a domestic violence issue, or a rape, or the sexual assault of a child? With time and experience, it has become clear that these professionals are only a small percentage of people who have invested time in the idea that the community can do better in response to sexual violence prevention, situations that deserve formalized and prioritized response and for which rape crisis centers and family violence shelters have been developed. Yet allegations that the system for identifying and responding to sexualized harms is broken[40] or that the criminal justice system fails sexual assault victims spectacularly from the initial police contact all the way through to their mental and emotional health years later, highlight emerging and persistent problems. Response efforts continue to be implemented in an attempt to assure fewer incidents and provide better services to those harmed.

In 1995, the Centers for Disease Control and Prevention (CDC), soon followed by the World Health Assembly in 1996, declared violence prevention a public health priority. Sexual abuse in America was being called out as an epidemic.[41] At approximately the same time, the American Medical Association declared sexual abuse a "silent-violent epidemic." The ACES research, beginning at about the same time, was uncovering research that seemed to link the abuse and/or trauma experienced by children as being associated with long-term behavioral and mental health disorders later in adult life. Researchers, medical practitioners, and government agencies have been working to center the impacts of sexual violence and the need to address related harms.

In May 2011, the executive board of the Association for the Treatment of Sexual Abusers (ATSA), a national organization of treatment practitioners and service providers specializing in the treatment of sexual offenses and offenders, joined a collection of other national organizations and agencies in identifying sexual abuse as a public health problem. They reviewed several studies, including the 1995 report from the American Medical Association that declared sexual abuse a "silent-violent epidemic" (AMA Press Release, 1995). The list went on to explore the rates of sexual abuse in the United States: Black et al. (as reported in National Center for Injury Prevention and Control, 2009), Whitaker et al. (2008), Basile et al. (2007), Jewkes et al. (2002), Tjaden and Thoennes (1998, 2000), and the Fourth National Incidence Study of Child Abuse and Neglect (NIS-4) in 2005 by Sedlak et al. (2010).[42] The conclusion was that the United States *as a society* had a problem.

The difference between a traditional offender–specific approach and a public health approach is partly a shift in focus from an individual offense, or even a collection of offenders and victims, to a focus on the larger social context. Efforts to discuss the ways in which sexual violence is a widespread problem affecting not just the primary victim but also the victim's family and the entire community as secondary victims, as reflected in a tertiary level of impact from abuse and all of the related costs and consequences of a singular event of sexual violence or sexual harm, have demonstrated the need for a collective review of the bigger picture.

In 2004, the CDC raised questions about how sexual abuse affects the health of an entire population. Theoretically, a public health focus on prevention will work to decrease the numbers and incidents of sexual violence and harm before they happen by taking an educational approach with a focus on risk-reduction. The public health model strives to prevent harm through identifying and reducing **risk factors** that may contribute to the perpetration of an offense. It also identifies **protective factors**, those actions that may prevent the development of sexually abusive behaviors and vulnerability to victimization. Identifying issues and modifying them as appropriate may include addressing individual and parental skills deficits, family dysfunction, negative peer influences, adverse community living conditions, and inappropriate social messages.[43] Enhancing protective factors to increase the community's ability to prevent harms may include incorporating information into school curricula, developing interpersonal skills-building training for boys and young men, or launching large-scale public information campaigns that target communities with information about the importance of consent in sexual encounters and the laws regarding sexual assault.[44]

Community partners in a public health model include parents, childcare providers, educators, various local community institutions, nonprofit organizations, law enforcement, and media. Emphasis by the ATSA board was given to an ecological model of victimization (discussed in more detail later in the chapter), which looks at the individual, the relationship, and the social, political, cultural, and environmental factors to see how elements of each of these varying factors have a role to play in changing larger structural supports for the norms in relationships, families, and communities that promote sexual violence and abuse. The five recommendations adopted by ATSA are outlined in Table 14.1.

Support for the idea that sexual violence is a systemic, or system-wide, public health concern involving many agencies, each adding an element toward

Table 14.1   ATSA Recommendations for Supporting Other Agencies Identifying Sexual Violence as a Public Health Problem[1]

1. The Association for the Treatment of Sexual Abusers encourages the recognition of sexual abuse as a public health issue.
Though not universal, the effects of sexual abuse include injuries (Kilpatrick, Edmunds, & Seymour, 1992), sexually transmitted diseases (Lindegren et al., 1998), unwanted pregnancies (Holmes, Resnick, Kilpatrick, & Best, 1996), HIV-risk behavior (Bensley, Van Eenwyk, & Simmons, 2000), depression and subsequent substance abuse (Holmes & Slap, 1999), post-traumatic stress disorder (Cuffe et al., 1998), and suicide attempts (Brener et al., 1999; Bryant & Range, 1995). Family members are also often traumatized when a loved one is victimized by sexual abuse or perpetrates sexual abuse (Newberger, Gremy, Waternaux, & Newberger, 1993; Manion et al., 1996). Given the magnitude of the problem and its physical and mental health impact, ATSA recognizes sexual abuse as an important public health problem.

2. The Association for the Treatment of Sexual Abusers supports the development of a national public health surveillance system for sexual abuse that includes reported, as well as unreported, cases of sexual abuse.
Public health surveillance involves the ongoing, systematic collection, analysis, and interpretation of information on a public health problem that is closely integrated with the timely dissemination of these data to those responsible for preventing or controlling the injury (Thacker & Berkelman, 1988). ATSA supports the development of a national public health surveillance system for sexual abuse that includes officially reported as well as unreported cases of sexual abuse. The inclusion of unreported cases is of critical importance since estimates suggest that only 12% of all cases of child sexual abuse (Hanson et al., 1999) and 16% to 36% of all rapes, including rapes of children, are ever reported to police (Kilpatrick, Edmunds, & Seymour, 1992; U.S. Department of Justice, 1997). Further, research suggests that reported cases of childhood rape are different from unreported cases of childhood rape. Specifically, reported cases are more likely to involve strangers (Hanson et al., 1999) and the perception of life threat or physical injury (Saunders et al., 1999) than are unreported cases. Surveillance data that broadens the view of both victim and perpetrator will have an impact on the shifting of norms that influence policy.

3. The Association for the Treatment of Sexual Abusers encourages researchers to conduct studies and publish data to increase understanding of risk factors and protective factors related to sexual abuse perpetration and victimization, and recommends that such efforts be funded.
ATSA encourages funding for researchers to conduct studies and publish data examining risk factors and protective factors related to sexual abuse perpetration and victimization. Public health scientists believe that ill health or unhealthy behaviors, including violence, are not randomly distributed in the population. These scientists are interested in conducting analyses on risk factors to find the reasons for this nonrandom distribution and the protective factors that might mitigate the expression of violence. Risk factor research focuses on understanding what factors place an individual at higher risk for unhealthy behaviors such as sexual deviance or unhealthy consequences such as sexual victimization. The intent of such research is to find out whether particular situations or behaviors put persons at greater risk for victimization or perpetration.

Identification of a risk factor indicates that developing sexually aggressive behaviors or becoming a victim of sexual abuse is statistically more likely if there is exposure to a particular factor (e.g., attitudes while growing up that support abuse toward women). Identification of a protective factor indicates that developing sexually aggressive behaviors or becoming a victim may be less likely when exposed to a particular factor (e.g., violence and exposure to sexual materials in the home). The presence of any one protective or risk factor does not predict definitively the development of sexually aggressive behaviors or the likelihood of victimization by sexual aggression. Given that sexual abuse is a complex problem, it is likely that risk factors and protective factors are multidimensional in nature and involve a variety of individual, family, community, and societal risk/protective factors (Ryan, 2000; Elliott, 1994; Wurtele, 1999).

(continued)

Table 14.1   Continued

4. The Association for the Treatment of Sexual Abusers supports the development of primary prevention and early intervention programs based on risk and protective factor and related research.

ATSA's position is that primary prevention programs should target modifiable risk factors identified by research. Since it is generally easier to alter developing behaviors than behaviors that are ingrained, ATSA also supports the development of universal and early intervention programs. Points of intervention may focus on the development of appropriate social and emotional skills as well as family, community and cultural factors that may contribute to the development of sexual offending (Whitaker et al., 2008). In developing interventions of this nature, ATSA recognizes that research describing the nuances of the sexual offence process will be particularly relevant (Kaufman, Hilliker, & Daleiden, 1996; Kaufman et al., 1998). Evaluation of prevention programs targeting various segments of society (e.g., sexual abusers, parents, teachers, caregivers) not traditionally targeted as sexual abuse prevention agents is also critical to the eventual success of a public health approach (Chasen-Taber & Tabachnick, 1999).

5. The Association for the Treatment of Sexual Abusers supports the U.S. Centers for Disease Control and Prevention and other federal agencies in the United States in their pursuit of rigorous research to evaluate the effectiveness of programs designed to prevent the perpetration of, and victimization by, sexual abuse, and to ensure that these programs have no iatrogenic effects that may impede the prevention of sexual violence.

Note: **Iatrogenic effects** are unwanted or undesirable effects caused by a treatment or intervention. In some cases the effect of the intervention is worse than the original illness. For example if a person who has high blood pressure is put on medication but one of the effects of the medication is that they cannot sleep, this would be an iatrogenic effect. In the case of sexual violence prevention programs, the goal would be to make sure that the treatment and/or social response does not produce any unintended ill effects on the (primary, secondary, or tertiary) victims affected by sexual violence or on the offenders.

1 ATSA Executive Board of Directors. May 26, 2011. Sexual Abuse as a Public Health Problem. Accessed November 29, 2019. https://www.atsa.com/sexual-abuse-public-health-problem

generating sexual violence as a significant threat to public health, is evidenced in contemporary and historical events where different social systems and sub-systems have been implicated in or used for the purposes of sexual exploitation and/or harm. Although this idea is a complicated one, the focus on social systems is a shift from the initial social theories, including theories of deviance, crime theories, and theories of victimization, that focused more specifically on the individual actor in the act of violence. System theories, such as those needed to look at sexual violence as a public health issue, look more broadly at the society and social conditions in place when this individual learns about and interacts in the social policies and practices governing the larger society. The focus on the individual, referred to as micro theories, and the study of the systems, referred to as macro theories (discussed earlier in chapter 6) are also evident in various specializations of social science study, including history, sociology, social psychology, criminology, political science, economics, and religious studies, as well as other structured mechanisms used for studying society and the people living in these various social systems.

Few places have seen the social aspects of sexualized violence studied in more detail than feminist scholars. Yet feminists are not the only ones talking about the issue of men's violence. Other researchers, referred to as postmodernists or critical theorists ask questions about how society and existing social structures influence individual actions.[45] Sexual violence is often discussed in terms of gender because men are believed to perpetrate more violence than women by overwhelming measures. Increasingly, even if arguably, it is more difficult to refute the system-wide existence of this kind of violence when sexual violence permeates contemporary American culture in so many different areas, in the many other forms of sexual exploitation and/or harm involving sports teams, secondary schools, colleges and universities, churches, nuclear and extended families, groups of peers, or neighborhoods and communities, the idea is that there is no one way that will ever be large enough in scale to address the breadth and depth of the issue. So the goal is to find ways to address the breadth and depth of the problem by involving everyone.

Stories of sexual abuse find expression, whether by way of the news, through stories from friends and family, or as a central theme in a popular TV show. Social scientists, treatment practitioners, and sexual violence prevention educators are all working together to think about ways to create system-wide networks of response. When a person is charged with assault for masturbating on his victim, but then the system settles the case so that the sexual nature of the incident is no longer reflected in the case,[46] or when an 11-year-old Ohio rape victim is challenged by laws that could restrict medical options,[47] or when a woman is drugged and raped by an ex but the way the law is written defines that as legal,[48] it becomes more clear that advocacy is more than what happens on an individual level; it is also representative of the various levels of social systems and structures that play a role in sexual violence prevention and response and highlight what is required for securing laws and policies reflective of the necessary or desired relief, response, or protections when sexual violence does happen.

THE ECOLOGICAL MODEL

While advocates and practitioners were beginning to identify sexual violence as an epidemic and publishing works suggesting the need to address the offenders and related issues in a more holistic fashion, theories were evolving to meet their questions and concerns and the identified social challenges.[49] Modified from Bronfenbrenner's (1995) **ecological model**,[50] designed to assist in the examination of social issues at various levels by illustrating the connectivity and overlap of individuals within their social environment, attention expanded from a more specific focus on the offender, to relationships in the family, between intimate partners, and in the community more broadly. Leaning on reports and outcomes reflecting changes in smoking behaviors or seat belt usage, the CDC attributed the significance of moving from a diagnosis and treatment focus centered on individuals to a collective focus on public health as a much more successful model for shifting public behavior.[51] Figure 14.1 includes the four-level ecological model presented used by the CDC in the public conversation about sexual violence prevention.[52] Illustrating the issue of sexual violence using the ecological model, describing dynamics from the individual to a nuanced review of the

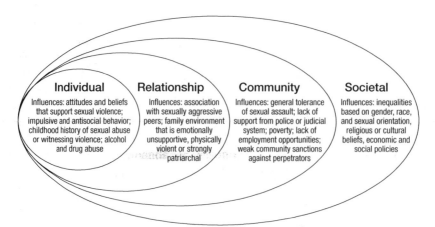

Figure 14.1   The Ecological Model
Centers for Disease Control and Prevention. 2004. Sexual violence prevention: beginning the dialogue. Atlanta, GA: Centers for Disease Control and Prevention.

levels of community and emphasizing the dynamics between individuals in relationships and family groups, as well as in the broader social and environmental contexts, might provide additional information about prevention and assist in efforts to decrease the occurrence of sexual violence and sexualized harms.[53]

RESTORATIVE JUSTICE MODEL

Restorative justice is a framework for addressing and preventing harm steeped in a nonviolent philosophy, working to move beyond punitive punishments, prioritizing instead the need to heal human beings, relationships, and communities (Table 14.2).[54] In the early 1980s, **Howard Zehr** began to ask questions about who was hurt, what they need, whose obligations are the harms, what are the root causes of the harm, how do we engage relevant stakeholders in addressing the harm, and what needs to be done to make things as right as possible, including addressing the root causes of the problem.[55] The modern restorative justice movement has a deep history in connection with indigenous communities, which utilized these processes and prioritized these ideas over contemporary prison and punishments. The focus is more on healing than punishment, rooted in a more holistic, community vision for a healthy life.

A restorative justice model centers attention on what a person needs after they have been harmed, with the idea that true justice is a healing of that harm in part by moving the needs of victims to the forefront. To do that, in the case of sexual abuse, the needs include (1) safety and care; (2) to be believed, absolved, and vindicated or acknowledged; (3) to be given a voice and empowered; (4) to grieve and express as needed; (5) support and education; (6) information and options; and (7) accountability toward healing.[56]

In addition to providing and addressing the needs of those harmed, attention is also offered to the needs of the people who have offended sexually. The challenge is to balance accountability with support by asking what does an offender need to do to take responsibility, and what do they need in order to heal? It is important to be clear about the fact that this is not making excuses or removing accountability from an offender. Prison or other more severe sanctions can be a part of the process; however, when a sex offender is released back into the community, it is a matter of community and public interest to make sure they do not reoffend. The goal is to be open and accountable to many stakeholders, in an effort to increase the likelihood of success.

A final issue that sometimes gets overlooked when discussing restorative justice processes is the importance of the community. Imagine the collective sorrow that a community experiences when a child is abducted or harmed. Imagine the entire community of the Catholic Church as it is managing the ongoing revelations of decades of abuse within the Church. Those harms are felt at the individual church level, state and national levels, and, in this case, international level of that organization. Communities are impacted by sexual violence, and communities also have a responsibility to address the impact of sexual violence when it happens. Educator Cornel West famously said "justice is what love looks like in public." Justice is a community issue.

Table 14.2   Restorative Justice and Sexual Abuse[1]

Key Principles of Restorative Justice for Responding to Sexual Abuse	Key Principles for Restorative Justice for Preventing Sexual Abuse	Key Principles for Restorative Justice Practitioners
1. Believe victims. 2. Establish physical and emotional safety for victims. 3. Create opportunities for victims to heal; empowerment through choice. 4. Offenders are to be held accountable within a context of support, where unaccountable, separation, and incapacitation are options. 5. Offenders are encouraged to acknowledge wrongdoing, identify their sexual offense cycle, and work toward empathy (understanding the impact of sexual abuse) and change. 6. The needs of community members as victims are identified and addressed. 7. The obligations of community members to change contexts that support sexual offending are identified and addressed.	1. Restorative justice undermines the secrecy of sexual abuse by talking about it. 2. Building supportive, accountable, and healthy relationships with victims, offenders, and communities contributes to no further harm. 3. Communities need ownership of conflict and violence resolution.	1. A collaborative approach with other professionals is most effective. These can include criminal justice and therapeutic professionals. 2. Practitioners are better equipped when they can articulate why sexual offending is linked to patriarchy, a system that perpetuates gender-based violence. Men are more likely to be perpetrators. 3. Practitioners are better equipped when they are trauma-informed. 4. Practitioners are better equipped when they understand sexual offending as a cycle. 5. Restorative justice programs are not always the best or most complete option for meeting justice needs. Practitioners need to know their limitations.

1 These justice themes come from Oudshoorn, J. with L. Stutzman Amstutz, M. Jackett. 2015. *The Little Book of Restorative Justice for Sexual Abuse*. (Good Books, NY, NY) pp. 37-38.

Research on the use of restorative justice in the context of sexual assault cases offers outcomes of support for both victims who were less likely to be revictimized and offenders were less likely to reoffend.[57] Remembering the diversity of offenses and offenders, the idea of whether a dialogue between a victim and the offender is appropriate would be situationally specific; however, there are some examples of when a dialogue is appropriate, and with suitable preparation, the outcome can provide the victim a forum where they can be candid in ways that are validating and help them take back some of their personal power.[58] In the current climate of demands for prison reform, professionals argue these processes outperform the outcomes of traditional criminal justice system.[59]

Circles of Support and Accountability (CoSA) is one well-known restorative justice program developed in Canada in 1994 as an alternative means of social support to high-risk sexual offenders released at the end of their sentences without any community supervision. Again, utilizing Indigenous learnings and teaching processes in both Canada and the United States, the tradition was to sit in a circle, face each other as equals, and talk about it. A Mennonite pastor, Harry Nigh, befriended a person with mental disabilities who had spent time in prison for sex offending. CoSA has now spread to multiple countries and is based in a specific set of values, as outlined in Table 14.3.

Research from the Minnesota Department of Corrections suggest that the Minnesota Circles of Support and Accountability (MNCoSA) produced exceptionally impressive results, significantly reducing sexual recidivism, lowering the risk of rearrests for a new sex offense by 88 percent.[60] Another study working with sex offenders from across Canada produced results showing that offenders in CoSA had an 83 percent reduction in sexual recidivism, a 73 percent reduction in all types of violent recidivism, and an overall reduction of 71 percent in all types of recidivism in comparison to the matched offenders.[61] Certainly, the

Table 14.3 Circles of Support and Accountability Goals and Structure

Program Goals
(1) no one is disposable;
(2) no one does this alone;
(3) no more victims;
(4) the community is responsible for its victims and those who offend against them; and
(5) health and safety are among the primary concerns of the community.

Program Structure
Core Member: Person who has been convicted of a sex offense
Volunteer: Local members of the community, often drawn from the faith community
Inner Circle: A collection of one core member and four to six volunteers
Circle Coordinator: A liaison between the inner and outer circles who recruits and organizes volunteers
Outer Circle: Professionals volunteering to support the CoSA project. The members of this outer circle:

- Comprise local, community-based professionals
- Act as a safety net by offering support, guidance, and mentoring to volunteers and core members
- Participate in the steering committee, advisory panels, boards of directors, etc.
- Offer a means of accountability for the local CoSA project

elements of restorative justice suggesting that offenders do better when they feel valued and supported seem to be born out here.

PREVENTION, EDUCATION, AND EXPANDING AWARENESS

The largest national organization focused on treatment of sex offenders, the **Association for the Treatment of Sexual Abusers (ATSA)** (introduced in chapter 7), also places a high priority on sexual violence prevention, defining prevention and the goals of prevention as follows:

> Prevention refers to the efforts intended to stop the perpetration of unhealthy, harmful, dangerous, and illegal behavior and acts as well as victimization and re-victimization by others.
>
> Prevention efforts include developing the attitudes, knowledge, skills, behaviors, and resources necessary to promote individual and community health, safety, and wellbeing. For example, we know that one factor with the potential to contribute to the development of sexually abusive behavior is attitudes regarding women, sexuality, violence and aggression. Therefore, sexual violence prevention efforts might target the development of healthier and less adversarial beliefs. Efforts along these lines in other areas demonstrate that prevention is effective. For example, research shows that public health prevention campaigns targeting tobacco use and drunk drinking have both been very successful at changing the attitudes related to these behaviors.[62]

The particular elements of any programming in a community focused on reducing sexual violence and harm will be linked to the efforts of people, community agencies, faith communities, businesses, and various other community-specific characteristics. Attention is given below to the themes of prevention and basic education programs and the general objective of simply expanding the awareness of people in the community in an effort to assure that fewer sexual offenses happen, but, if they do happen, people in the community will know where to go.

SEXUAL VIOLENCE PREVENTION

Certainly the goal of sex crime prevention is to work toward stopping sex crimes before they happen. The CDC uses a public health model to describe and explain prevention efforts. In the case of sex crimes, this model works at three levels:

1. **Primary prevention**—intervention before the sex crime occurs
2. **Secondary prevention**—efforts to address a sex crime in the earliest stages
3. **Tertiary prevention**—managing offenders after they have been caught in an effort to prevent further harm

Most resources are presented in the primary and secondary levels of prevention and are focused on individuals. The goal in these cases would be to secure information to intervene before the situation occurs, which is **primary prevention.**

Examples of primary education would include healthy sexuality and/or healthy relationships programs and agencies working to educate in an effort to eliminate or reduce the occurrence of sexual violence and related harms (Table 14.4). **Stop It NOW!**, for example, is a program designed to recognize child sexual abuse as a preventable public health problem organized to provide resources for individuals, including potential offenders. Among its range of services, one aspect is the intention to provide information or support to someone prior to an incident.[63] An online help center is available to provide assistance on a variety of themes: to people who are worried about another adult's behavior, about the behavior of an adult with children and youth, working with children, worried about your own thoughts and behaviors, and communities, as examples.

Recently, **Erin's Law** provided a large-scale primary prevention remedy when author, speaker, and activist Erin Merryn developed legislation requiring public schools to teach children personal body safety with the intention of assisting in the prevention and early intervention of child sexual abuse.[64] As of June 2018, 35 states have passed Erin's Law.

Treatment programs and community supervision of sex offenders are an example of **secondary prevention** efforts. A secondary prevention program seeks to address the harm and minimize the impact of that harm as soon as possible after the commission of a sex crime. Victim services and counseling programs offered immediately following a sex crime are also forms of secondary prevention programs. The AMBER Alert program could be described as one of the most successful response programs created to help find children who are missing and at risk. Supported by research suggesting that the first hours after a child goes missing are the most crucial for returning the child, the **AMBER Alert** program is a coordinated, voluntary partnership between law enforcement, transportation agencies, and the communication industries designed to send out an immediate notification when a child goes missing. The program was named for Amber Hagerman, who was 9 years old when she was abducted in Arlington, Texas, in 1996.[65] Although a witness who saw the abduction helped Arlington police respond quickly, tragically, Amber's body was discovered four days later. Her murder remains unsolved over 20 years later.

A local mom, Diana Simone, who had never met Amber, called the local radio station with an idea for broadcasters to alert the public. She reasoned that, if broadcasters could alert the public to severe weather, then maybe they could do the same thing when a child goes missing. The program took off and was replicated in cities around the country.[66] Today the AMBER Alert system is used in all 50 states, the District of Columbia, Indian Country, Puerto Rico, the US Virgin Islands, and 22 other countries.[67]

According to www.amberalert.gov, as of October 2018, the AMBER Alert program has been credited with 934 successful returns of children across the United States.[68] Abductors were reported to have released the child upon hearing an alert had been issued. A coordinated effort that started with an idea from an interested citizen, working with local companies and local law enforcement, produced a powerful resource for responding immediately when harm happens.

Table 14.4 Sampling of Primary Prevention Strategies

Note: There are a variety of primary prevention strategies that may never reach the level of a national audience because those programs live in the communities for which they were created by people who intentionally created a community resource to meet an existing need. These are only a small collection intended to simply provide a few additional examples. Research on the impact of *Safe Dates* and *CBIM* is resourced in the reference.

1. **Safe Dates**[1]
   Safe Dates is an evidence-based dating abuse prevention program directed toward adolescents and used in schools. The program is set up in four parts: (1) develop a school policy, (2) educate about abuse, (3) reinforce student learning, and (4) activate student leaders. The curriculum includes ten 50-minute sessions.

2. **Coaching Boys into Men**[2]
   CBIM is one of many programs from Futures Without Violence that empower individuals and organizations working to end violence against women and children.

Are you a CBIM Advocate?

1. Most men believe violence against women is wrong.
2. Men recognize the role that they can play to address the problem of violence against women and girls.
3. Men are looking for ways to get involved to prevent violence against women, but many don't know how.
4. Men are willing to take the time to get involved in a variety of ways to address the problem of domestic violence and sexual assault.
5. Many men are already taking action to prevent violence against women by talking to young people about healthy, violence-free relationships.

---

3. **One Billion Rising**[3]
   Using the statistic one in three women across the planet will be beaten or raped during her lifetime, totaling more than 1 billion women and girls. Every February, they organize a mass action to end violence against women (cisgender, transgender, and those who hold fluid identities that are subject to gender-based violence).

OBR MANIFESTA 2019
Rise. Resist. Unite.

RISING TO END . . .	RISING TO END . . .
Rape	*Toxic Masculinity*
Battery	*Poverty/ Economic Injustice/ Labor*
Incest	*Exploitation*
Sexual Harassment	*Climate Destruction and Environmental*
Female Genital Mutilation (FGM)	*Plunder*
Sexual Slavery and Trafficking	*Racism, Hate and Discrimination*
Child Marriage	*Religious Fundamentalism*
Femicide	*State and Institutional Violence/*
Sexual, Gender and Reproductive	*Militarization/ War*
Oppression	*Forced Displacement/ Immigrant and*
Violence Towards LGBTQIA+ Communities	*Migrant Abuse*

---

1 Vangie A. Foshee et al., "Assessing the Long-Term Effects of the Safe Dates Program and a Booster in Preventing and Reducing Adolescent Dating Violence Victimization and Perpetration," American Journal of Public *Health 94, no. 4 (2004): 619–24.*

2 M. C. D. Jaime et al., "Using a Domestic and Sexual Violence Prevention Advocate to Implement a Dating Violence Prevention Program with Athletes," Health Education Research *31, no. 6 (2016): 679–96,* http://www.coachescorner.org/wp-content/uploads/2016/12/CBIM-Research-Health-Education-Resources.pdf.

3 Sorcha Pollak, "One Billion Rising: An End to Violence against Women," Time, February 14, 2013, accessed September 28, 2019, http://newsfeed.time.com/2013/02/14/one-billion-rising-an-end-to-violence-against-women/. See also https://www.onebillionrising.org/.

Tertiary prevention strategies work to minimize the likelihood that a sex crime will happen again. As discussed in chapter 10, sex crime laws and policies are an example of this level of prevention response and are under considerable critical review as to their level of effectiveness and whether funds spent here would be better spent on primary responses, such as additional assistance to victims of sexual violence, identify first-time offenders through community- and school-based educational programs, provide counseling to young people with risk factors or tendencies for sexual violence, and fund efforts to research and advocate rational and rehabilitative, evidence-based laws.[69] One size does not fit all.

It is important to note that these kinds of programs are often implemented under the guidelines of prevention programming and are usually linked to an issue identified as important to the founders or participants of that program. That does not necessarily make good or effective programming. In a systemic review of over 140 programs, researchers found a dearth of effective prevention strategies.[70] In fact, little research exists with regard to best determine what the components of an effective primary prevention program might include. Although some themes are recommended, additional research of program efforts in this area is encouraged.[71]

PUBLIC EDUCATION CAMPAIGNS

Public education campaigns take a variety of shapes and come from within diverse community and social organizations at state, local, or national levels. Some programs start as the result of an incident within a community, such as the AMBER Alert system, and others might be implemented by the city government to address a community need. Consider the **It's On Us** campaign, launched in September 2014 following recommendations from the White House Task Force to prevent sexual assault, which prioritized the importance of engaging everyone in the conversation to end sexual violence. From its website:

> It's On Us asks everyone—students, community leaders, parents, organizations, and companies—to step up and realize that the conversation changes with us. It's a rallying cry to be a part of the solution. The campaign combines innovative creative content and grassroots organizing techniques to spark conversation on a national and local level. Over the past two years, almost 300,000 people have taken a stand against sexual violence by taking the It's On Us pledge. The campaign works with 95 partners and students on over 500 campuses. And we're just getting started.[72]

Consider the **Clothesline Project**, a sexual assault awareness program where survivors and significant others can create art using clothes. In the summer of 1990, a coalition of women's groups in Cape Cod, Massachusetts, took a statistic suggesting that 58,000 men had died in Vietnam and compared it to a statistic during that same timeframe that 51,000 women were killed by men who supposedly loved them. They wanted to create something unique that would be provocative but also educational and healing. Each woman would use words or artwork to decorate a shirt that she would then hang on a clothesline. The clothesline was representative of a job that had traditionally been women's work, but the process of creating and leaving and sharing your story was designed to be healing for those who participate and to remind other people who might be suffering in silence to realize they are not alone. The initiative grew from an individual localized effort to an annual, national campaign that has a presence in high schools, college campuses, and community centers across the country. Throughout the month of April, sexual assault awareness month, people are invited to contribute, but it is to be a "silent exhibit and self-expression of the violence that plagues our community."[73]

The Clothesline Project Legend

White is for murder or death as a result of violence.
Yellow, Brown or Beige is for assault or battery.
Pink, Red or Orange is for rape or sexual assault.
Green or Blue is for child sexual assault or incest.
Purple or Lavender is for homophobic violence.
Black is for gang rape.
Jeans are for misconceptions and injustice surrounding rape

Alesha Barlow started **Tell Somebody** as an adult after she didn't want to stay silent any longer. Her mother dropped her off with her grandparents since before she could remember. When she turned seven, she told her that her grandfather had been molesting her. Rather than get support, she was instructed to keep it a secret from the police and her father. By starting her program, she wants to give strength to other survivors and help them understand that they speak up and they can heal.[74]

Green Dot[75] started as a higher education primary prevention program that launched in 2006 at the University of Kentucky with early federal funding, focused primarily on sexual assault, domestic violence, and stalking. In 2009, the program was adapted for local high schools. In 2010, leadership incorporated the program, calling it the Green Dot, etc., Inc., and in 2012, they moved their headquarters to Washington, D.C. Between 2012 and 2016, the program developed pilot initiatives on suicide, workplace violence, and bullying and street harassment and expanded the program and the reach to middle school and K–3. In 2017, the program had a makeover with a larger model and a new name: **ALTERISTIC.** The Green Dot program is still active and available now for K–3, middle school, high school, campus, and the community. The program organizers also host an institute for trainings for those interested in bringing the program back to their own communities.[76]

One of the things important to note about program development is the diversity of programming. In many cases, elements of programs that have worked in other locations get adapted to meet the needs of a different setting. The Green Dot program is a good example of that. As they identified additional needs, they expanded the range of options available to meet those needs. Also, it is important to note that individuals don't have to be affiliated with an organization to learn ways to take action to prevent sexual violence and harms. One of the central elements of the Green Dot program is focused on what is referred to as

bystander intervention. Bystander intervention training teaches people to interrupt situations that might move into potentially high-risk situations. Psychologists John Darley and Bibb Latané formulated and studied the bystander effect in 1968. They believed the presence of people (i.e., bystanders) influenced the likelihood of a person deciding to help someone in need.[77] Bystander education programs such as the Green Dot highlight the importance of proactive behaviors that elevate the importance of nonviolence and actually change the norms and values of a given community or setting.[78]

> When we can heal ourselves, we also heal our ancestors, our grandmothers, our grandfathers, and our children. When we heal ourselves, we heal Mother Earth.
>
> —Rita Pitka Blumenstein, Yup'ik Great Grandmother,
> Indigenous Council of Thirteen Grandmothers

The **Pathway to Hope** was created to provide training and support for ending the silence about child sexual abuse among Native children and to promote healing.[79] The program particularly focuses on addressing **intergenerational trauma**, efforts seeking to understand why the effects of certain adverse life events transmit to subsequent generations. The Alaska Natives believe each community is unique, and as a result, any efforts to address the harm and support healing must be integrated from within the larger social and historical context including the cultural strengths of each community.[80] "Strengths-based solutions built on truth, honesty, compassion and shared responsibility for healing and protecting today's children have been profound and successful."[81] The characteristics of the program are outlined in Table 14.5.

Another area where programs are evolving in support of education and awareness is in the area of computer- and internet-related sexual violence and harms. Consider the information offered at **Zero Abuse Project** (www.zeroabuse-project.org). For children, the guidelines are fairly straightforward. Assuming a healthy parental relationship, children are encouraged to talk to their parents about the internet. Learn together! Sites like netsmartz.org are wonderful places to start. Children are encouraged to be kind and not to post things online that are mean or will hurt other people. Also, children are encouraged not to respond to people using the internet to be mean or rude but instead to talk to a parent or trusted adult about those exchanges. If you see messages or pictures that give you an "uh-oh" feeling, tell a trusted adult right away.[82] For teens the information might also include information on sexting. By far the most advice is offered to parents.

Social Media Tips for Parents:

The internet isn't all bad
    Even though online threats can feel overwhelming, remember that being an involved parent can be a protective factor in helping to keep children safe online.

Table 14.5   Pathway to Hope: Healing Child Sexual Abuse Ending Denial and Silence in Alaska Native Communities

FUNDAMENTAL PRINCIPLES BEHIND THE DEVELOPMENT OF THE PATHWAY TO HOPE: HEALING CHILD *** SEXUAL ABUSE VIDEO AND GUIDEBOOK TOOLS ***

1. Indigenous People/Tribal Communities must take responsibility for the safety and healing of children.
2. Indigenous People/Tribes must have ownership of social problems as well as the development of solutions to those problems.
3. Reclaiming and reviving cultural values, beliefs, practices to heal children and those victimized as children must begin with understanding historical trauma and in multigenerational dialog.
4. Ongoing mentoring and support for "Indigenous couriers of community change" is essential for Tribal communities to achieve long-term change in attitudes and responses toward children who were victims of sexual abuse.

TOPIC AREAS COVERED IN TRAINING TRIBAL COMMUNITY FACILITATORS ON THE PATHWAY TO HOPE *** HEALING CHILD SEXUAL ABUSE VIDEO ***

Applying indigenous learning style and experiential approaches, our faculty guides and instructs participants on issues relating to child sexual abuse dynamics and victimization, healing and wellness for indigenous communities, and community empowerment strategies. In this three (3) day interactive training and dialog, faculty members teach and facilitate participant exploration of the following truths, concepts, and beliefs:

1. Impact of multi-generational and historical trauma on safety of children now
2. Recognizing that there are "protections" that prevent us from:

   • BELIEVING THAT CHILDREN ARE SEXUALLY ABUSED;
   • HOLDING ABUSERS ACCOUNTABLE FOR THEIR BEHAVIOR;
   • ENDING CHILD SEXUAL ABUSE

3. Understanding how children experience sexual abuse:

   • Vulnerability, range of signs/behaviors, emotional impact, short-term/long-term;
   • Perpetrator profiles, vulnerability of children, etc.

4. Evaluating community readiness to end denial about child sexual abuse and begin healing

   • Identify knowledge about child sexual abuse;.
   • Identify resources available to address child sexual abuse;
   • Identify attitude of Tribal and spiritual leaders about child sexual abuse

5. Four (4) ACTION STRATEGIES toward achieving community ownership to end silence about child sexual abuse and establish support for children:

   • Coming together to celebrate and honor our children;
   • Teaching adults and children about personal safety;
   • Setting community standards about children;
   • Healing and support for children when victimized

6. Promoting healing and support for children victimized by sexual abuse

   • Appropriate responses by the criminal justice system;
   • Culturally relevant, supportive services for child and non-offending family member
   • Community, extended family, education system and family support for child's healing in short and long-term

Set expectations

Have an open discussion with your children about social media safety. Work with your child to make a list of expectations for phones and online use. If they are invested and involved in putting the list together, they will feel more ownership in following the rules.

Make telling easier

Most children do not tell an adult if someone is breaking their boundaries or rules online. One of the big reasons we hear from young people is that if they tell, their devices will be taken away. Go through "what if" scenarios before there is a problem. Let them know that you want to know if they were feeling unsafe online and what steps you would take.

Do your homework

In addition to filtering software available to parents, internet and cell phone companies have different resources for parents to help manage accounts. These services can be helpful, but should never be the stand-alone plan for safety. Frequent conversations about your expectations using "what if" scenarios can help make online safety a partnership between you and your child.

Public vs. private

Help your child make the distinction between public and private information. Go through the apps your child is using with them and talk about privacy settings. Go through "what if" scenarios around private information. Remember, privacy isn't just about the school your child attends or their age, it is also being wary when someone starts asking personal or intimate questions.

Digital footprint

Talk to your teen about how their character in the real world should match their character online. The language used and pictures they choose to share should help in building a positive digital footprint that opens doors to future positive opportunities. If your child does make a mistake online that harms their digital footprint, remind them that they don't have to face the situation alone and that they can come to you for help. All online problems have real-world solutions.

Where do they hang out?

Know where your child spends their time online and why. Let them know that you will periodically check their accounts, ask questions about people on friend lists, and check in as to how they are navigating technology. Be aware of hidden apps and multiple accounts that might slide under your radar. Caregivers should be able to approve and remove any of the apps that your children are using. This isn't about spying or creating an adversarial relationship. The more you see that they are using their technology responsibly, the more trust they will receive.

Don't walk away

It can be tempting for parents to feel in over their heads as apps change, online language changes, and technology feels one step ahead. Don't give up! Talking with your young person about your expectations and checking in as to how they are spending their time and why are very important. Know that there are resources to help parents, from classes like ours to online resources like CommonSenseMedia, Netsmartz, and JWRC.

Answer body questions in person

Most people who use the internet do not want to harm your child. The people who do use the internet to cause harm tell us the number one thing they are looking for is young people who want to talk about sex or have questions about sex. Identify with your child healthy ways to get information about their body and people they can go to if they have questions that they are uncomfortable asking you in person.[83]

Be a good example

They are listening to you AND watching your example when it comes to online behavior; from taking time away from screens to not texting while driving. If we tell children to step away from their devices when they are upset or angry, we should do the same.

The examples of programs used to help people in communities across the country better protect themselves and their families and friends from the possibility of sexualized violence and harms are numerous. These are just a few examples. It is also important to remember that these issues are not isolated to the United States and people are impacted globally by sexualized violence and harm. **The Innocence Lost National Initiative (ILNI)** was established in 2003, combining federal and local law enforcement resources to recover child victims and prosecute hose responsible for their exploitation. Nationally, these collaborations have been responsible for recovering or identifying more than 6,600 child victims, and produced more than 2,750 convictions.[84]

Since the ILNI started, key supporters from Innocents at Risk (innocentsat risk.org) have highlighted five critical areas:

1. That these kids are truly victims and the trauma to these kids is significant with no uniform standards that govern their treatment, and inadequate resources;
2. That much of this problem is organized crime syndicates;
3. Offenders are not operating out in the open, but shop online and from the privacy of their homes or hotel rooms;
4. More attention on prevention is essential; and
5. Too little is being done to decrease the demand.[85]

In 2005, the World Health Organization (WHO) implemented a study in collaboration with the London School of Hygiene and Tropical Medicine and PATH, USA (Positive Alternative Therapies in Healthcare; pathusa.org), and includes collaboration with various research institutions and women's organizations from within the 15 sites and 10 countries participating in the study, including Bangladesh, Brazil, Ethiopia, Japan, Peru, Namibia, Samoa, Serbia, Montenegro, Thailand, and the United Republic of Tanzania.[86] Report findings suggested that violence against women is widespread, and they made a connection between "the prevalence of intimate partner violence and its association with women's physical, mental, sexual and reproductive health."[87] Similar to the voices introduced in chapter 6, this report suggests the need for a public health response. The following 15 recommendations were made:

1. Promote gender equality and women's human rights.
2. Establish, implement, and monitor multisectoral action plans to address violence against women.
3. Enlist social, political, religious, and other leaders in speaking out against violence against women.
4. Enhance capacity and establish systems for data collection to monitor violence against women, and the attitudes and beliefs that perpetuate it.
5. Develop, implement, and evaluate programs aimed at primary prevention of intimate-partner violence and sexual violence.
6. Prioritize the prevention of child sexual abuse.
7. Integrate responses to violence against women in existing programs for the prevention of HIV and AIDS, and for the promotion of adolescent health.
8. Make physical environments safer for women.
9. Make schools safe for girls.
10. Develop a comprehensive health sector response to the various impacts of violence against women.
11. Use reproductive health services as entry points for identifying and supporting women in abusive relationships and for delivering referral or support services.
12. Strengthen formal and informal support systems for women living with violence.
13. Sensitize legal and justice systems to the particular needs of women victims of violence.
14. Support research on the causes, consequences, and costs of violence against women and on effective prevention measures.
15. Increase support to programs to reduce and respond to violence against women.

Establishing a better understanding of offenders and of the consequences of immediate and longer-term harms opens a window into the vast range of issues connected to important social conversations and considerations about sex crimes needed to set the stage for considering the appropriate social response. Both formal and informal mechanisms work together to provide appropriate responses to sex-offending behaviors. With this in mind, it is important to be clear: sexual violence is an international issue and warrants attention on an international scale.

FOCUS ON BOTH STOPPING SEXUAL VIOLENCE *AND* STOPPING SEX OFFENDERS

After giving considerable attention to the many different aspects of the subject of sexual violence, including questions about healthy sex, the many forms of abuse and violence, the many victims who do not speak out choosing instead not to report abuse and harm, the many perpetrators who range from those who are fully aware of their actions to those who are arguably unaware of their actions as potentially harmful or criminal, to the persistence of sexual violence as a social phenomenon still more questions remain. Community safety requires effective sex-offender management, as well as professional and public collaboration.[88] How can sexual violence be overlooked while at the same time evoking anger and rage among people when it is discovered?

Consider two questions:

1. Is everyone in the United States affected by some level or form of sexualized violence or harm?
2. If the answer to question 1 is no, then, who remains unaffected by sexualized violence or harm?

If the answer to question 1 is yes, then as a society acknowledging the problem, looking at it squarely will be a required response. If the answer is no and there are those unaffected by sexualized violence, it will be important to look at who they are and how they were able to stay protected against sexual violence, what is by many accounts a pervasive social issue. What social supports or educational resources did they have available to them that provided them the opportunity to learn about and experience sex in a healthy, relaxed way, not forced on them by friends, as a commodity to be traded in search of a relationship, and in their marriages, families, schools, or communities? If, upon further reflection, the answer to question 2 is "sort of" or "no one," then perhaps a better question might be, to what degree and in what ways are people in American society negatively impacted by gender- or sexuality-based violence, sexual harm, or more extreme forms of sexualized violence?

Consider the continuums used at the beginning of the text, in chapter1, when the topic was centered around conversations about healthy sexuality. On a scale of 1 to 10, with 10 being very healthy and 1 being not very healthy, where would you rank society now? Ask yourself and your friends, to what degree are they negatively affected by gender- or sexuality-based violence, sexual harm, or more extreme forms of sexualized violence? Consider questions such as:

- Do you find yourself in social situations where you feel pressure from friends to have sex or be sexual?
- Do you find yourself constantly checking to see whether you are beautiful?
- Do you feel like you have to have sex to be in a couple or to be legitimately dating?
- Do you feel like you have to have sex to prevent your partner from leaving?
- Do you believe young men have been taught how to respect themselves and reflect a healthy understanding of sex and sexuality?
- Do you think young people in high school and middle school use social media in a healthy and age-appropriate way?

Also, consider the fact that the American Psychological Association, one of the premier professional groups focused on mental health and psychological wellness, has just recently (2018) come out with a series of guidelines for professionals working with men and boys that highlights the idea of masculinity as a social construct, addressing issues of violence, healthy relationships, and mental health. From the article:

> Boys and men are diverse with respect to their race, ethnicity, culture, migration status, age, socioeconomic status, ability status, sexual orientation, gender identity, and religious affiliation. Each of these social identities contributes uniquely and in intersecting ways to shape how men experience and perform their masculinities, which in turn contribute to relational, psychological, and behavioral health outcomes in both positive and negative ways (e.g., Arellano-Morales, Liang, Ruiz, & Rios-Oropeza, 2015; Kiselica, Benton-Wright, & Englar-Carlson, 2016). Although boys and men, as a group, tend to hold privilege and power based on gender, they also demonstrate disproportionate rates of receiving harsh discipline (e.g., suspension and expulsion), academic challenges (e.g., dropping out of high school, particularly among African American and Latino boys), mental health issues (e.g., completed suicide), physical health problems (e.g., cardiovascular problems), public health concerns (e.g., violence, substance abuse, incarceration, and early mortality), and a wide variety of other quality-of-life issues (e.g., relational problems, family well-being; for comprehensive reviews, see Levant & Richmond, 2007; Moore & Stuart, 2005; O'Neil, 2015). Additionally, many men do not seek help when they need it, and many report distinctive barriers to receiving gender-sensitive psychological treatment (Mahalik, Good, Tager, Levant, & Mackowiak, 2012).

GUIDELINES:

1. Psychologists strive to recognize that masculinities are constructed based on social, cultural, and contextual norms.
2. Psychologists strive to recognize that boys and men integrate multiple aspects to their social identities across the life span.
3. Psychologists understand the impact of power, privilege, and sexism on the development of boys and men and on their relationships with others.
4. Psychologists strive to develop a comprehensive understanding of the factors that influence the interpersonal relationships of boys and men.
5. Psychologists strive to encourage positive father involvement and healthy family relationships.
6. Psychologists strive to support educational efforts that are responsive to the needs of boys and men.
7. Psychologists strive to reduce the high rates of problems boys and men face and act out in their lives such as aggression, violence, substance abuse, and suicide.
8. Psychologists strive to help boys and men engage in health-related behaviors.
9. Psychologists strive to build and promote gender-sensitive psychological services.
10. Psychologists understand and strive to change institutional, cultural, and systemic problems that affect boys and men through advocacy, prevention, and education.

One of the most deceptive elements of the educational campaign to increase awareness about sexual offenders is the reality, as discussed in greater detail in various places throughout the text, that sex offenders do not meet a specific profile. Remember, as research on sex offenders is broadened and attention to issues of sexual violence is expanded, "those people" who commit sex offenses can look just like the people in our own faith communities, neighborhoods, and school systems who also have committed a sexual offense. A complete understanding of the national and regional nuances of the various cultural, religious, historical, traditional, and economic systems and structures affecting or affected by sexual violence continues to provide nuance for an issue that is critically important, impacts many people, and will require ongoing attention and awareness.

When efforts to understand the offenders in the situation as people who are not well, perhaps uneducated, psychologically unstable, socially inappropriate, and in need of information and treatment resources, this is also something that changes the conversation. As discussed in more detail in chapter 7, although traditional crime theories focus on the individual as the person society holds accountable for crime commission, prevention models also focus on teaching individuals. Linked to the idea that this work involves everyone, the **Spectrum of Prevention** in Figure 14.2 provides a more expansive way to see the work to be done and encourages a focus on more far-reaching change, including laws and policies, a collection of individuals in the sexual violence prevention field coming together in an effort to create networks for long-term change, and a review of organizational practices, service providers, and education for the community and individuals.[89]

One final idea for consideration was developed from the White House Council on Women and Girls in 2010 and reflects on what gets in the way of

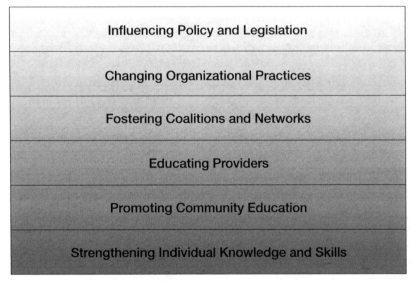

Figure 14.2   The Spectrum of Prevention

"The Spectrum of Prevention." Prevention Institute. https://www.preventioninstitute.org/tools/spectrum-prevention-0.

Text Box 14.2. Barriers to Advancing the Issue of Sexual Violence Prevention[1]

Key barriers:

- The persistence of "rape myths" and misconceptions about sexual violence, which run counter to the majority of victims' experiences, and make it all the more challenging for survivors to disclose their victimization to anyone, from law enforcement and healthcare professionals to family and friends;
- Relentless focus on victim behavior and characteristics—and lack of attention to offenders—which perpetuate victim-blaming attitudes and help offenders evade sanctions;
- Lack of community engagement, which inhibits public discourse on the issue;
- Failure to account for the historical and current contexts of sexual violence as a tool of subjugation and colonization, in particular as this relates to communities of color;
- The discomfort of professionals and the general public with issues of child sexual abuse and incest, which make it even more difficult for survivors to disclose, attain justice, and seek support;
- Victims' reluctance to report their assaults, given that when victims do disclose, they often face skepticism, blame, and further humiliation from professionals, families, and friends, amounting to what many survivors consider a "second victimization";
- Lack of effective training and education on sexual violence, both for first responders and for communities at large; and
- A dearth of relevant research on sexual violence, and the need for better research and data collection to inform the work of practitioners and policy makers.

Note

1. "Sexual Violence in the United States: Summary Roundtable Proceedings," October 27, 2010, p. 6, accessed September 28, 2019, https://www.justice.gov/sites/default/files/pages/attachments/2014/07/24/sexual-violence-report-march.pdf.

advancing and addressing the work of sexual violence prevention. Text Box 14.2 lists the barriers they identified.

Certainly a great deal of information has been provided for consideration, yet a great deal more remains to be more fully explored. How will each person address this important, if not essential, question: When consideration is given to the idea of advocacy in the service of preventing sexual violence and harm, how does each person take action in their daily lives and in their communities to reduce sexual violence in their lives and in the lives of the people they love?

CHAPTER CONCLUSION

Based on the material presented for consideration and reflection, the information researched and compiled throughout this text, it is important to take a moment to think about what options are available to individuals, families, organizations, communities, and even a nation fed up with the seemingly endless string of sexual victimizations of young children, young boys and men, young women, wives, and mothers. If you look at the issue of sexuality, consider educating about healthy sexuality and healthy relationships, discussed in chapter 1; reflect on definitions of sexual deviance and the issue of consent, discussed in chapter 2; and then work your way through the history of this country and the central role sexual violence and sexual assaults have played in chapters 3, 4, 5, and 6. Where does that leave each of us as we reflect on individual, family, school, local community, and national attitudes about relationships and sex? What do you think should be done differently? How can we as a people be sure this will never happen again? What role does each of us play in educating ourselves and breaking the social patterns that keep sexualized violence invisible, unreported, underexamined, and unaddressed?

When attention is given to the conventional thinking about victims of sexual violence, identifying only the impact of the event on a primary victim, as discussed above, the people who are the victims of the sexual assault, it is perhaps easier to see people who are not thought to be impacted by sexual violence. Yet when attention is given to the secondary or tertiary victims, the people who love and care about anyone affected by sexual violence and who want to know how best to help them as they move through the process of healing, it is easier to see how efforts to prevent sexual violence can have a wider, positive impact.

When attention is broadened to consider the effects of sexual harm and victimization beyond just the primary victim, giving specialized attention and educating people about the specific ways people experience and understand appropriate sexual boundaries and practices does not address all forms of sexualized violence, to be sure. In the spectrum of prevention, this is just the beginning. Special attention must be given to the marginalized communities that often get overlooked or mistreated further in the existing criminal justice structure. As has been stated in several places throughout the book, anyone can become a victim at any time. This is a potentially scary social reality. Even if everyone learns and takes advantage of all of the appropriate precautions to reduce the chances of being sexually victimized, victimization is a possibility. When focusing in on the many levels of involvement and the many ways everyone can engage more actively in ongoing efforts to prevent sexualized violence and harm at both the individual and societal level, coordination, communication, and collaboration are key.

> **Text Box 14.3. Media Messages about Sexual Violence as a Public Health Issue**
>
> Allegations of abuse from a pastor or priest within a faith community used to be an unthinkable act. Now archdiocese after archdiocese across the United States and the world has presented information on priests who have committed abuse within the Church going back more than seven decades. What are the tertiary effects on members of the Catholic Church who have watched for decades and, more recently, in the last several months while archdioceses across the United States reveal hundreds of cases of sexual abuse involving priests? Further, what kind of impact does that have on the community of faithful believers and on the larger surrounding community of non-Catholics?[1] How might a public health response differ from the way this issue was handled?
>
> **Note**
>
> 1. Luis Ferré-Sadurní and Mariana Alfaro, "Why They Stay. Why They Can't: New York Catholics Wrestle with Their Faith over Abuse Allegations," *New York Times*, October 23, 2018, accessed September 28, 2019, https://www.nytimes.com/interactive/2018/10/21/nyregion/new-york-city-catholics.html.

KEY TERMS

#MeToo
#MMIW
#SayHerName
Adverse Childhood Experiences (ACES)
advocacy training
ALTERISTIC
AMBER Alert
antirape movement
Association for the Treatment of Sexual Abusers (ATSA)
bystander intervention
Circles of Support and Accountability (CoSA)
Clothesline Project
Committee for Equal Justice for Recy Taylor
ecological model
Erin's Law
feminist movement
Green Dot
Howard Zehr
Innocence Lost National Initiative
intergenerational trauma
It's On Us

Minnesota Coalition Against Sexual Assault (MNCASA)
Office for Victims of Crime (OVC)
Pathway to Hope
primary prevention
protective factors
rape crisis centers
rape crisis movement
restorative justice
risk factors
risk mitigation
Safe Women, Strong Nations
secondary prevention
secondary traumatization
Spectrum of Prevention
Stop It NOW!
Tell Somebody
tertiary prevention
trauma
trauma-informed care
trauma-specific services
vicarious traumatization
victim-centered approach
Zero Abuse Project

REVIEW QUESTIONS

1. Chapter 14 starts with a story about rape and public education efforts by Laurie Halse Anderson. What did she learn in her time talking with people in schools and communities across the country?

2. The chapter talks about the importance of a "both/and" approach to the individual and public education about sexual violence prevention. What does that include, at a minimum? Be prepared to list at least three justifications in support of this idea.

3. What was the Committee for Equal Justice for Recy Taylor? How did it come to be, who was it organized by, and why?

4. How did the history of sexual assault advocacy work in the community overlap with mainstream feminism in the United States? In what ways were early efforts said to fall short of the collective desire to support victims of sexual violence and harm?

5. In what ways does a public health model response to sexual violence and related harms involve victims? Offenders? Others? How is a public health model different from traditional sexual violence prevention efforts?

DISCUSSION QUESTIONS

1. Attention is given to the recent work on the history of the sexual abuse of enslaved black men as an example of a "hidden" element of sexualized violence and harm that happens in plain sight and yet may not be called out as the abusive practice that it is. Why do you think that is? What other examples can be identified that similarly happen openly and are abusive or harmful but don't get called out as problematic behavior?

2. Consider a given news cycle. What elements of the stories have a dimension of sexual violence and/or harm? To what degree do the stories reflect a micro focus on the individual, and to what degree are larger social influencing factors at work? Be prepared to defend your assessments.

3. Be prepared to research and discuss the ways restorative justice is connected to indigenous communities. Why is it important to mention the historical origins of this work as it is referenced in conjunction with sexual violence prevention work? What other organizations prioritize a nonviolent focus?

4. One of the central questions in the book has been whether the issue of sexual assault is a question of individual character or more reflective of cultural attitudes. What happens when the question shifts from either individual or cultural to both individual and cultural? What support would you offer for any given ideology? Individual, cultural, both individual and cultural?

5. Consider the role of men in preventing sexual violence. What significance does this offer the larger sexual violence initiative?

NOTES

1. Laurie Halse Anderson, "I've Talked with Teenage Boys about Sexual Assault for Almost Twenty Years. This Is What They Still Don't Know," *Time*, January 15, 2019, accessed September 22, 2019, http://time.com/5503804/ive-talked-with-teenage-boys-about -sexual-assault-for-20-years-this-is-what-they-still-dont-know/.

2. Robin Warshaw, *I Never Called It Rape* (New York: Harper & Row, 1988).

3. Thomas A. Foster, on Twitter, May 1, 2019; 5:46a.

4. Laurie Halse Anderson, "I've Talked with Teenage Boys about Sexual Assault for Almost Twenty Years. This Is What They Still Don't Know," *Time*, January 15, 2019, accessed September 22, 2019, http://time.com/5503804/ive-talked-with-teenage-boys-about -sexual-assault-for-20-years-this-is-what-they-still-dont-know/.

5. Robin Warshaw, *I Never Called It Rape* (New York: Harper & Row, 1988).

6. Wesley Morris, "Last Taboo: Why Pop Culture Just Can't Deal with Black Male Sexuality," *New York Times Magazine*, October 27, 2016, accessed September 22, 2019, https:// www.nytimes.com/interactive/2016/10/30/magazine/black-male-sexuality-last-taboo.html; see also Stacey Patton, "Who's Afraid of Black Sexuality?" *Chronicle of Higher Education*, December 3, 2012, https://www.chronicle.com/article/Whos-Afraid-of-Black/135960; Sherronda J. Brown, "Erotic Race Pay Reveals How White Supremacy Is a Perversion of Unmatched Proportions," October 2, 2017, http://blackyouthproject.com/white-supremacy -perversion-unmatched/.

7. Jamie Crawford, "Military Sexual Assaults Increase Sharply, Pentagon Report Finds," CNN Politics, May 2, 2019, accessed September 22, 2019, https://www.cnn.com/2019/05/02/ politics/us-military-sexual-assault-report/index.html; see also Dave Philipps, "'This Is Unacceptable.' Military Reports a Surge of Sexual Assaults in the Ranks," *New York Times*, May 2, 2019, accessed September 22, 2019, https://www.nytimes.com/2019/05/02/us/military-sex ual-assault.html.

8. M. Aggeler and A. Arnold, "Which State Will Pass an Extreme Abortion Ban Next?," The Cut, https://www.thecut.com/2019/05/which-states-have-passed-six-week-abortion-bans.html.

9. Janelle Griffith, "'We Are Concerned': Dallas Police Chief Says of Second Transgender Woman's Death in Less than a Month," NBC News, June 4, 2019, accessed September 22, 2019, https://www.nbcnews.com/feature/nbc-out/body-transgender-woman-pulled-white -rock-lake-dallas-n1013361.

10. Thomas A. Foster, *Rethinking Rufus: Sexual Violations of Enslaved Men* (Athens: University of Georgia Press, 2019).

11. Gillian Greensite, "History of the Rape Crisis Movement," *California Coalition Against Sexual Assault* blog, November 1, 2009, http://www.calcasa.org/2009/11/history-of-the-rape -crisis-movement/.

12. Danielle L. McGuire, *At the Dark End of the Street: Black Women, Rape, and Resistance* (New York: Vintage Books, 2011).

13. Cherrie Moraga and Gloria Anzaldua, *This Bridge Called My Back* (New York: SUNY Press, 2015); Patricia Hill Collins, *Black Feminist Thought* (Psychology Press, 2000).

14. Maya Finoh and Jasmine Sankofa, "The Legal System Has Failed Black Girls, Women, and Non-Binary Survivors of Violence," ACLU, January 28, 2019, accessed September 22, 2019, https://www.aclu.org/blog/racial-justice/race-and-criminal-justice/legal-system-has-failed-black -girls-women-and-non; Sandra Park, "How America Systematically Fails Survivors of Sexual Violence," ACLU, October 16, 2018, accessed September 22, 2019, https://www.aclu.org/blog/ womens-rights/violence-against-women/how-america-systematically-fails-survivors-sexual-vi olence; Kanya Bennett, "Say Her Name: Recognizing Police Brutality against Black Women," ACLU, June 14, 2018, accessed September 22, 2019, https://www.aclu.org/blog/criminal-law-re form/reforming-police-practices/say-her-name-recognizing-police-brutality; "Maze of Injustice," Amnesty International, accessed September 22, 2019, https://www.amnestyusa.org/reports/ maze-of-injustice/; Angela Chang, "Ending Sexual Violence against Indigenous Women in the

U.S.," *Amnesty International Human Rights Now* blog, March 10, 2011, accessed September 22, 2019, https://blog.amnestyusa.org/americas/the-fight-to-end-sexual-violence-against-indigenous-women-and-girls-in-the-u-s/.

15. "Ending Violence against Native Women," Indian Law Resource Center, accessed September 22, 2019, https://indianlaw.org/issue/ending-violence-against-native-women.

16. Learn more about the Safe Women, Strong Nations program at the Indian Law Resource Center at https://indianlaw.org/safewomen.

17. Gillian Greensite, "History of the Rape Crisis Movement," *California Coalition Against Sexual Assault* blog, November 1, 2009, http://www.calcasa.org/2009/11/history-of-the-rape-crisis-movement/.

18. "My Chair Is Made of Plastic: Black Women's Seat at the Feminist Table—Part 1," *National Organization for Women* blog, October 26, 2018, accessed September 22, 2019, https://now.org/blog/my-chair-is-made-of-plastic-black-womens-seat-at-the-feminist-table-part-i/.

19. Maria Bevacqua, *Rape on the Public Agenda: Feminism and the Politics of Sexual Assault* (Boston: Northeastern University Press, 2000), 29–30.

20. "Sexual Violence Prevention: Beginning the Dialogue," Centers for Disease Control and Prevention, 2004, accessed September 22, 2019, https://www.cdc.gov/violenceprevention/pdf/svprevention-a.pdf.

21. Corinne Meltzer Graffunder, Rebecca Cline, and Karen Lane, "Chapter 11: Primary Prevention," Ohio Domestic Violence Network, accessed September 22, 2019, http://www.odvn.org/training/Documents/doc-primary-prevention.pdf.

22. Kelly O'Hara, "I Quit My Job to Advocate for Sexual Assault Survivors," *Time*, January 23, 2018, accessed September 22, 2019, http://time.com/5112695/become-sexual-assault-advocate/.

23. "What Is a Victim Advocate?" National Center for Victims of Crime, accessed September 22, 2019, http://victimsofcrime.org/help-for-crime-victims/get-help-bulletins-for-crime-victims/what-is-a-victim-advocate-.

24. See, for example, references in "Sexual Assault Advocacy Programs," Stop Violence Against Women, updated February 10, 2009, accessed October 20, 2019, http://www.stopvaw.org/sexual_assault_advocacy_program.

25. Minnesota Coalition Against Sexual Assault (MNCASA), What We Do tab, accessed October 20, 2019, https://www.mncasa.org/.

26. Roger D. Fallot and Maxine Harris, "Creating Cultures of Trauma-Informed Care (CCTIC): A Self-Assessment and Planning Protocol," April 2009, accessed September 22, 2019, https://traumainformedoregon.org/wp-content/uploads/2014/10/CCTIC-A-Self-Assessment-and-Planning-Protocol.pdf; Maxine Harris and Roger Fallot, eds., *Using Trauma Theory to Design Service Systems: New Directions for Mental Health Services* (San Francisco: Jossey-Bass, 2001).

27. "Trauma-Informed Care Resources Guide-CPI," 14, http://www.esc-cc.org/Downloads/Trauma-Informed%20Care%20Resources%20Guide.pdf.

28. Ibid., 3.

29. Ibid.

30. Fallot and Harris, "Creating Cultures of Trauma-Informed Care (CCTIC)"; Harris and Fallot, eds., *Using Trauma Theory to Design Service Systems*.

31. "Sexual Assault Advocate/Counselor Training: Instructor's Manual," Office for Victims of Crime Training and Technical Assistance Center, 2017, https://www.ovcttac.gov/SAACT/index.cfm.

32. Shana L. Maier, "'We Belong to Them': The Costs of Funding for Rape Crisis Centers," *Violence Against Women*, 17, no. 11 (2011): 1383–1408, https://doi.org/10.1177/1077801211428599.

33. For example, see Reina Gattuso, "Let's Talk about Intimate Partner Violence in Queer Communities," Feministing, accessed September 22, 2019, http://feministing.com/2015/04/28/lets-talk-about-intimate-partner-violence-in-queer-communities/.

34. "Adverse Childhood Experiences (ACEs)," Centers for Disease Control and Prevention, accessed September 22, 2019, https://www.cdc.gov/violenceprevention/acestudy/index.html.

35. Marilyn Metzler et al., "Adverse Childhood Experiences and Life Opportunities: Shifting the Narrative," *Children and Youth Services Review* 72 (2017): 141–49, https://doi.org/10.1016/j.childyouth.2016.10.021; (Shonkoff & Garner, 2012).

36. David Finkelhor, Heather A. Turner, Anne Shattuck, and Sherry L. Hamby, "Violence, Crime, and Abuse Exposure in a National Sample of Children and Youth," *JAMA Pediatrics* 167, no. 7 (2013): 614, https://doi.org/10.1001/jamapediatrics.2013.42.

37. Metzler et al., "Adverse Childhood Experiences and Life Opportunities."

38. Jill S. Levenson, Gwenda M. Willis, David S. Prescott, "Adverse Childhood Experiences in the Lives of Male Sex Offenders: Implications for Trauma-Informed Care," *Sexual Abuse* 28, no. 4 (2016): 340–59, https://doi.org/10.1177/1079063214535819.

39. See, for example, "Excellence in Advocacy: A Victim-Centered Approach," Ohio Family Violence Prevention Center, Ohio Office of Criminal Justice Services, 2008, accessed October 20, 2019, https://www.ocjs.ohio.gov/VictimServicesPublication.pdf; Sekaquaptewa and P. R. Bubar, *A Victim-Centered Approach to Crimes Against American Indian and Alaska Native Children* (Bibliogov, 2013).

40. Rashid Minhas and Julia Shaw, "The System for Reporting Sexual Harassment Is Broken—Here's How to Fix It," Behavioral Scientist, October 9, 2018, accessed September 22, 2019, http://behavioralscientist.org/the-system-for-reporting-sexual-harassment-is-broken-heres-how-to-fix-it/; Linda LeFauve, "Sexual Assault's Broken System of Justice," June 11, 2017, accessed September 22, 2019, https://www.realclearpolitics.com/articles/2017/06/11/sexual_assaults_broken_system_of_justice_134162.html; D. Angiollo, "Risky Sexual Behavior—The 'Broken Windows' of Sexual Assault: A Proposal for Universities to Incorporate Targeted Intervention to Bridge the Gap between Sexual Assault Prevention and Response," *Journal of Gender, Social Policy & The Law* 26, no. 3 (2018): 881–945, https://www.jgspl.org/wp-content/uploads/2018/10/Angiollo_v26n3_881-945-Digital-Commons.pdf.

41. Robert E. Freeman-Longo and Geral T. Blanchard, *Sexual Abuse in America: Epidemic of the 21st Century* (Safer Society Press, 1997).

42. "Sexual Abuse as a Public Health Problem," Association for the Treatment of Sexual Abusers, May 26, 2011, accessed September 22, 2019, https://www.atsa.com/pdfs/Policy/SA_PublicHealthProblem.pdf.

43. Kenneth E. Powell et al., "Prevention of Youth Violence: Rationale and Characteristics of 15 Evaluation Projects," *American Journal of Preventive Medicine* 12, no. 5 (1996): 3–12, https://doi.org/10.1016/s0749-3797(18)30231-9.

44. D. Finkelhor, "The Prevention of Childhood Sexual Abuse," *The Future of Children* 19, no. 2 (2009): 169–94.

45. For more on postmodern feminist or critical theories about sexual violence prevention, see, for example, Rita Felski, *Doing Time: Feminist Theory and Postmodern Culture* (New York: New York University Press, 2000); Moraga and Anzaldua, *This Bridge Called My Back*. For critical theories, see Sarah Jane Brubaker, *Theorizing Gender Violence* (Cognella Academic Publishing, 2018); D. Bell, "Critical Race Theory," in *Critical Race Theory: The Key Writings That Formed the Movement*, ed. Kimberle Crenshaw, N. Gotanda, G. Peller, and K. Thomas (The New Press, 1996), chapter 1.

46. Dan Joling, "No Jail Time in Assault Case Spurs Push to Oust Alaska Judge," *Washington Times*, September 25, 2018, accessed September 22, 2019, https://www.washingtontimes.com/news/2018/sep/25/alaska-judge-targeted-after-giving-no-jail-time-fo/.

47. Eric Zorn, "Should 11-Year-Old Girls Have to Bear Their Rapists' Babies? Ohio Says Yes," *Chicago Tribune*, May 9, 2019, accessed September 22, 2019, https://www.chicagotri-

bune.com/columns/eric-zorn/ct-perspec-zorn-abortion-rape-heartbeat-ohio-child-argentina
-20190509-story.html.

48. Briana Bierschbach, "Woman's Fight for Justice Ends 'Marital Rape' Exception," MPRnews, May 1, 2019, accessed September 22, 2019, https://www.mprnews.org/story/2019/05/01/woman-s-fight-for-justice-ends-marital-rape-exception.

49. Freeman-Longo and Blanchard, *Sexual Abuse in America.*

50. Urie Bronfenbrenner, "Developmental Ecology through Space and Time: A Future Perspective," in *Examining Lives in Context: Perspectives on the Ecology of Human Development*, ed. Phyllis Moen, Glen H. Elder, Jr., and Kurt Lüscher (Washington, DC: American Psychological Association, 1995), 619–47.

51. "Picture of America: Prevention," Centers for Disease Control and Prevention, accessed September 22, 2019, https://www.cdc.gov/pictureofamerica/pdfs/picture_of_america_prevention.pdf.

52. Linda L. Dahlberg, and Etienne G. Krug, "Violence: A Global Public Health Problem," in *World Report on Violence and Health*, ed. Etienne G. Krug et al. (Geneva, Switzerland: World Health Organization, 2002), 1–22, https://apps.who.int/iris/bitstream/handle/10665/42495/9241545615_eng.pdf;jsessionid=9E40111904FA8DC8CE594C52771858D6?sequence=1.

53. Ibid.

54. Judah Oudshoorn with Lorraine Stutzman Amstutz and Michelle Jackett, *The Little Book of Restorative Justice for Sexual Abuse* (New York: Good Books, 2015), 14.

55. Ibid., 25.

56. Ibid., 28.

57. Kathleen Daly, "Restorative Justice and Sexual Assault," *British Journal of Criminology* 46, no. 2 (2006): 334–56, https://doi.org/10.1093/bjc/azi071.

58. Clare McGlynn, Nicole Westmarland, and Nikki Godden, "'I Just Wanted Him to Hear Me': Sexual Violence and the Possibilities of Restorative Justice," *Journal of Law and Society* 39, no. 2 (2012): 213–40, https://doi.org/10.1111/j.1467-6478.2012.00579.x.

59. Tinneke Van Camp and Jo-Anne Wemmers, "Victim Satisfaction with Restorative Justice: More Than Simply Procedural Justice," *International Review of Victimology* 19, no. 2 (2013): 117–43, https://doi.org/10.1177/0269758012472764.

60. Grant Duwe, "Can Circles of Support and Accountability (CoSA) Significantly Reduce Sexual Recidivism? Results from a Randomized Controlled Trial in Minnesota," *Journal of Experimental Criminology* 14, no. 4 (2018): 463–84.

61. Robin J. Wilson, Franca Cortoni, and Andrew J. McWhinnie, "Circles of Support & Accountability: A Canadian National Replication of Outcome Findings," *Sexual Abuse* 21, no. 4 (2009): 412–30, https://doi.org/10.1177/1079063209347724.

62. "What Is Prevention?" Association for the Treatment of Sexual Abusers, accessed September 22, 2019, http://www.atsa.com/what-prevention.

63. "Online Help Center," Stop It Now!, accessed September 22, 2019, https://www.stopitnow.org/help-guidance/online-help-center.

64. www.erinslaw.org

65. S. Crawford and W. Hundley, "15 Years Later, Arlington Police Still Struggling to Solve Amber Hagerman Case," *Dallas Morning News*, January 12, 2011.

66. Jason Sickles, "Who Killed Amber Hagerman? Murder Case That Inspired Amber Alert Remains Unsolved 20 Years Later," Yahoo.news, January 13, 2016, accessed September 22, 2019, https://news.yahoo.com/who-killed-amber-hagerman-murder-case-that-inspired-amber-alerts-unsolved-20-years-later-142605215.html.

67. www.amberalert.gov

68. "How Effective Has It Been?" Amber Alert, https://www.amberalert.gov/faqs.htm#faq3.

69. Kelly K. Bonnar-Kidd, "Sexual Offender Laws and Prevention of Sexual Violence or Recidivism," *American Journal of Public Health* 100, no. 3 (2010): 412–19, https://doi.org/10.2105/AJPH.2008.153254.

70. Sarah DeGue et al., "A Systematic Review of Primary Prevention Strategies for Sexual Violence Perpetration," *Aggression and Violent Behavior* 19, no. 4 (2014): 346–62, https://doi.org/10.1016/j.avb.2014.05.004.

71. Maury Nation et al., "What Works in Prevention: Principles of Effective Prevention Programs," *American Psychologist* 58, no. 6/7 (2003): 449–56, http://www.ncdsv.org/images/AmPsy_WhatWorksInPrevention_6-7-2003.pdf.

72. Itsonus.org.

73. "The Clothesline Project," http://clotheslineproject.info/SAAM-Events-Letters-and-Invitations.

74. "From Hurt to Healer: The 'Tell Somebody' Movement," BlackDoctor.org, accessed September 22, 2019, https://blackdoctor.org/465163/child-molestation-tell-somebody-movement/; Tell Somebody, http://www.tellsomebodytoday.com/index.html.

75. "Green Dot," Alteristic, accessed September 22, 2019, https://alteristic.org/services/green-dot/.

76. Ibid.

77. Jack Cieciura, "A Summary of the Bystander Effect: Historical Development and Relevance in the Digital Age," *Inquiries* 8 no. 11 (2016): 1/1, accessed September 22, 2019, http://www.inquiriesjournal.com/articles/1493/a-summary-of-the-bystander-effect-historical-development-and-relevance-in-the-digital-age.

78. Sarah L. Swan, "Bystander Intervention," *Wisconsin Law Review*, 2015, accessed September 22, 2019, http://wisconsinlawreview.org/wp-content/uploads/2015/12/1-Swan-Final.pdf.

79. "Pathway to Hope: Healing Child Sexual Abuse," accessed September 22, 2019, http://www.tribal-institute.org/2014/E8-HO3.pdf; see also Diane Payne, Kimber Olson, and Jared W. Parrish, "Pathway to Hope: An Indigenous Approach to Healing Child Sexual Abuse," *International Journal of Circumpolar Health* 72, no. 1 (2013), https://doi.org/10.3402/ijch.v72i0.21067.

80. Ibid.

81. Ibid.

82. "Online Safety," Zero Abuse Project, accessed September 22, 2019, https://www.zeroabuseproject.org/victim-assistance/jwrc/keep-kids-safe/online-safety/.

83. Ibid.

84. Special Agenda Amy Meyer. August 6, 2019. Innocence Lost National Initiative and 2019 FBI Denver Operation Independence Day Results in Recovery of Child Victims from Commercial Sex Trafficking. https://www.fbi.gov/contact-us/field-offices/denver/news/press-releases/innocence-lost-national-initiative-and-2019-fbi-denver-operation-independence-day-results-in-recovery-of-child-victims-from-commercial-sex-trafficking, and Operation Independence Day. https://www.fbi.gov/news/stories/operation-independence-day-2019.

85. Awareness is Prevention, Speech to the Innocents at Risk Benefit, September 27, 2011. Washington, DC. http://www.innocentsatrisk.org/wp-content/uploads/Speech-Sept-17-11.pdf.

86. WHO 2005 http://www.who.int/gender/violence/who_multicountry_study/en/

87. Ibid.

88. G. Hover and R. Shilling, "Community Education and Collaboration: Working with the Community on a Complex Problem," in *The Prevention of Sexual Violence: A Practitioner's Sourcebook*, ed. K. Kaufman (Holyoke, MA: NEARI Press, 2010).

89. L. Park, R. Davis, and L. Cohen, "Changing Community Environments to Prevent Sexual Violence: The Spectrum of Prevention," in *The Prevention of Sexual Violence: A Practitioner's Sourcebook*, ed. K. Kaufman (Holyoake, MA: NEARI Press, 2010).

15

Integration and Application
Putting Theory into Practice

Never forget that justice is what love looks like in public.

—Cornel West

People want a silver bullet to protect their children, but there is no silver bullet. There is no simple cure to the very complex problem of sexual violence.

—Patty Wetterling, parent advocate and Jacob Wetterling's mom

ON A MORE PERSONAL NOTE, we close this working collection of information about the people who commit sex offenses and the harm they cause. The text was structured to look at the character of an individual who commits a sex crime, but that was only part of the objective. The text also highlighted the laws, policies, and social practices put in place to clarify appropriate and inappropriate behavior from within that same mix of controversial social actions and practices. If, as community members and coworkers, partners and friends, teachers and neighbors, and genuinely authentic people who walk in the world, we leave the review of this information seeing other people as the parties responsible for addressing "the problem" of sexual assault, then the gap that separates theory from practice becomes another obstacle to overcome. It seems to us that the objective set out for reading and reviewing the information included here or out there in the wider world, for that matter, will not change the current state of sexual violence unless after reading that material you put it into practice. Perhaps you think "I am not a police officer," or a social worker, a lawyer, a judge, or the leader of a strong, healthy, and vibrant faith community, on the front lines and in an "important place" where you might meet someone who is in need of support after having been harmed. Perhaps you think "What can I do?"

Traditional crime theories support research models that isolate the researcher from the subject of their research. More contemporary research models suggest the messiness of our social reality does not always lend itself to such neat separations. Traditional ways of looking at sex offenders suggested that "those people" are violent sexual psychopaths or sexual predators. More contemporary research suggests that there are in fact these types of offenders, and, when we learn about them, we usually see them associated with a lurid story on the nightly news. But those kinds of offenders are a much smaller percentage of the people who commit sex offenses. When we listen to friends or family or hear from the experiences of others, the kinds of sexual harms we learn about are more often committed by someone we know from church, or our domestic partner, or a person in authority whom we thought we could trust. Traditional ways of talking about sex offenders involved old men in raincoats jumping out from behind a bush or misdirected public education programs about keeping kids away from strangers. More contemporary responses to sex offending behaviors are focused on breaking down codes of silence while still working to address existing harm and prevent future harm. In short, we are the bridge that connects theory to practice, built with the materials that come from being educated and aware.

To close, we thought we would briefly review the organization of the text and revisit the questions we started with as we opened this conversation. Then, to conclude, we will leave you with a collection of "Takeaways," which represent best practice based on the collaborative work of researchers and practitioners in the field.

A QUESTION OF CHARACTER AND CULTURE

Efforts to address individual acts of sexual violence must be addressed and perpetrators held accountable. Research and practitioner experience suggests a significantly small number of perpetrators will be caught, arrested, convicted, and sentenced to treatment or prison. To us, and to an increasing number of researchers and practitioners, the objective is to expand the net of influence to address the harms committed as a result of sexual violence—which, for what might be a wide list of reasons, do not get addressed formally in the criminal justice system—so that someone harmed by such violence has the tools they need to heal completely. We suggest the goal of preventing sexual harm begins with a willingness to consider the question raised in section I: *Is it possible to agree about the parameters of healthy, deviant, and criminal sexual behaviors?* In the form of a statement, when people know and respect their own definitions of healthy sexuality, the issues raised about consent, listening, and communication take a central role. Will finding a common definition of "healthy sexuality" solve all our problems? Even if a common definition of healthy sexuality were possible, the answer to that question would probably be no. People have many variations and differences; as such, the question becomes the starting place, not the end.

Section II asked about change over time and the intergenerational factors directing the attitudes of today: *How does history continue to shape modern understandings of sexual harms and sexualized violence?* From the vantage point of today, history can seem both distant and ever present. The number of missing and murdered indigenous women highlights a long-standing issue of conflict and reflects both formal and informal challenges. Similarly, the racialized history of sexualized violence against slaves, both men and women, has a place alongside the efforts to better understand the need to regulate same-sex relationships and the hate crimes that are perpetrated against someone who is believed to be gay. Both changes in contemporary social attitudes and consistencies with these historic attitudes are reflected in attitudes today in the formal process of laws and policies, as well as in individual attitudes and actions.

Section III is the tipping point of the text: *What do researchers and practitioners know about sex offenders and the people they harm?* This is likely a place where you will find a connection, a very individual response to the material. Mary, as an educator, has students who go on to graduate and become treatment professionals working exclusively with sex offenders. Something almost every one of them will say was not really on their radar before they considered these issues more deeply. For others, the research piece might grab your attention and you might wonder how in the world anyone can try to make sense of the kinds of things we are reading about when the world changes so quickly and data points seem to change just as quickly. But data points, research, and a collection of stories and experiences are what we have to go on to better understand both the person who committed the harm and the person who was harmed. The degree of harm and the social conditions that preceded the act of violence can vary, and it is at that point of connectivity where theory meets practice. The potential for influencing the lives of both the people who commit acts of sexual violence and the people who need care and places to heal from an experience of sexual harm is a central point of change, the tipping point. The goal of expanding efforts to prevent sexual harms in the first place is connected to the reality of ongoing evaluations of research, lived experiences, and individual and social responses as well as practitioner and program objectives.

In the case of sexual violence prevention and response, the other side of any tipping point reflective of expanded awareness will likely move forward with a few twists and turns, rather than present a downhill straightaway. People, programs, agencies, justice officials, and the communities in which they work will all be in different places, so there will not likely be a singular, obviously "right" course of action. After reviewing section IV, *In what ways is the justice system addressing the issue of sexual harm?*, a person could be either discouraged or inspired. The justice system does not serve victims well, and that is perhaps one of the most universal agreements among all parties involved in any capacity of work associated with sexual violence response. The critical reflection on laws, both the more contemporary laws enacted within the past 20 years or so and the laws enacted at the turn of the nineteenth century, indicates that having a law doesn't necessarily eliminate the problem; it simply provides a process for what to do with the problem. When that process doesn't seem to have the effect it was intended to create and the issue is socially and politically awkward on one end and panic inducing on the other, the effects can be frustrating for all parties involved.

Section V asks *What can be done to help prevent sexual violence?* We know treatment is showing promising effects for some individuals who have committed a sex crime. We know that advocacy helps people who have been harmed navigate a way forward, whether or not that includes a decision to proceed with a formal prosecution of the offender. Perhaps that question could be clarified further: What can each of us do to help prevent sexual violence? The book includes a lot of information about sexual violence, individual acts of violence, and larger social attitudes and outlines the system's response. As we conclude, we offer a brief collection of what researchers and practitioners recommend we all bring forward in our daily experiences. Armed with information, an expanded awareness, and a focus on what patterns and practices can result in harm, our hope is that sexual violence prevention will become the job of everyone. For those who might go on to work in the field of sexual violence prevention or treatment or in any of several areas of the justice system, thank you for your efforts, now and in the future. For those who go on to do other work in any other field, the world has a place for you too.

TRICKS AND TRAPS FOR BOTH CHILDREN AND ADULTS

The topic of sex crimes appears to be permeating the culture through fictional crime-fighting dramas, documentaries, and news magazine programs. Scathing exposés of corruption and cover-ups are made public through social media conversations, hashtag solidarity, and when a child or young person goes missing all while survivor voices are being elevated in new ways. On one hand, the solutions seem so simple: do no harm; confirm consent; and, if you see something, say something. Yet, on the other hand, the more a person digs into the layers of a given social problem, the more unknowns appear, revealing more complex questions to answer.

- If statistics tell us we all know a survivor of sexual assault, does that mean we all know a perpetrator of sexual assault? If sexual abuse is more likely to be perpetrated by someone we know, how can we hold those people we know, or once cared about, or currently love accountable for their actions while putting the safety of others first?
- If the old adage "hurt people hurt people" is true, then what message does that give to the majority of survivors who do not go on to sexually harm others? How can we provide hope to survivors trying to find a healing way to tell their story without feeling like they are painting themselves into the role of a perceived perpetrator?
- What message do we give to young people and teens about body ownership, consent, and relationships if we never talk about those subjects? What will fill the void in education if we do not seize on opportunities to have these conversations?
- If there truly is a role for each of us to play in prevention, what is my role? How can I use my lived experiences and academic learning to create positive change?

Learning about the effects of sexual violence requires listening. There is a danger, especially as someone who responds to victims, of assuming that all survivors are the same and have the same experiences. If, when working with a survivor of same-gender intimate partner violence and you are surprised that they are responding differently than your college roommate who was sexually assaulted at a college party, your ability to serve them well can be challenged, whether or not you intended to, with the box that you are unable to put them in. Culture, age, social status, gender, sexual orientation, race, immigration status, and language can frame how a survivor of crime is treated and how they are able to access services. For professionals working the front lines of sexual crimes, it is important to remember that each survivor has their own story and, although some themes may align with other stories, there is no one-size-fits-all approach to serving their needs. Be aware that you may also be working with colleagues who have their personal reasons for getting involved in crime advocacy and/or investigation.

Interestingly, historically there has been pushback for professionals to be open about their own lived experiences. Grants and academic projects have recently, within the past 10 years, started highlighting different ways for professionals to tell their own stories. The pendulum has swung between professionals not being able to talk about their own lived experiences for fear that it makes them less professional and the awareness that experience prepares them for the work they do. Start by listening. We learn from our past, especially from those in a place to say, "This happened to me and we need to do better."

Conversations about sexual assaults and rape have been associated with social and cultural questions about dominance and submission. What role does power play in the execution of a sex crime? For the longest time, advocates and researchers have suggested that rape is about power, not about sex.[1] Critics of that thinking suggested that there are many ways to assert power but the decision to use sex as a means by which to assert their power over someone else is a particular aspect of the merging of violence with issues of power, control, *and* sex.

Narcissism, arrogance, and a sense of entitlement have been hypothesized as potentially significant factors in the expression of sexual violence.[2] Sadism and psychopathic traits are also discussed,[3] with innate features such as gender argued to play a role as well as alcohol and date rape drugs. Some rapists are aware of their intention to commit rape, whereas others are willing to admit to the behaviors but not to the use of the term "rape."[4]

Another related idea is that men cannot control their desire for sex after a certain point and therefore should not be held responsible and is argued as being the inevitable outcome of "natural male urges."[5] Now, although this idea may be seen by some as a horrible indictment implicating false limits of male capacity, evidence is offered in popular culture and by legislative and/or justice officials who play into the idea that men "must have sex" and therefore are more driven by an uncontrollable, innate biological desire likely to push the boundaries of social acceptability to find ways to "get" sex. This idea is extremely controversial and unquestionably derogatory toward men in general, but it remains active in conversations about sexual violence perpetration.

The idea that men are hardwired to seek out sex at any cost does not take into account the important truth that most men do not cause sexual harm. This is one more reason why all genders should be at the table when prevention initiatives are discussed and implemented. We need to know what has worked so that it can be replicated. This brings us full circle back to healthy sexuality and healthy relationships; we should study and celebrate what does work as we shine a light on what does not. Instead of always focusing on what to avoid, we should hold up what is working so that our conversations aren't just focused on what is broken but also on how we can move to wholeness going forward.

There is some confusion around why sexual violence is suddenly a problem. The short answer is that it is not. Instead of ignoring it, we are now talking about it. And, to be clear, many individuals, schools, youth-serving organizations, and families are not talking about sexual violence at all. Personally, I was concerned when a friend approached me about concerns she had about one of the coaches in her child's gymnastics program. I asked her to start by following up with the owner of the company to ask what training, monitoring, and screening policies for interaction were already in place. The response from the owner was, "We don't do any training on that because sexual abuse doesn't happen here." This comment came during the same year as the trial of Dr. Nassar when athlete after athlete testified about the abuse they had endured under this man under the guise of sports medicine. Ignoring the problem does not make children safer. Falling back into old stereotypes disproved by clinicians and survivors does not make any of us safer. Child safety should never rest solely on the shoulders of children. It isn't fair nor is it effective. Adults must learn the warning signs and act when they see them.

It is difficult to know whether someone is a child molester, but it is easier to act on behalf of the child when the behavior of concern is more readily identified. Therefore, it is important to focus on the behavior of an individual that pushes a child's boundaries rather than on how the person is known to others or is connected in the community. It is rare that a person will see actual abuse because those making the choice to harm are careful to act in secret. Warning signs, boundary violations, and individuals who continually ignore child safety policies are easier to see than actual abuse.

Two common characteristics of many child molesters are that (1) they rely on their ability to blend in, and (2) they work in secret.[6] Time after time, patterns emerge after the fact about sex offenders who befriended a family with young children and spent time with the family grooming them, a particular child or all the children, and the greater community with the ultimate goal of making a sexual contact with the child or children.

Critically important is the fact that *child abusers are almost always known to the child as a family member or acquaintance*. The relationship allows the offender access to the child. Healthy parents want their children to understand that most people are good and would never hurt them. Yet children and young people should also be taught when it is OK to say no to an adult and that, even if their bodies freeze up and they are unable to say no, it is still not their fault. When offenses are more likely to be committed by people you know, the difficult reality of having to acknowledge a friend is behaving inappropriately is often the social reality of young people. Then, of course, the questions turn to assessing how well sexual deviance, potential sexual harms, or sex crimes have come to reflect social and political attitudes ranging from expanded moral questions to uncontainable moral panics.

If an individual reading about sex offenders believes that the issue of sex offending belongs with the individual who is committing the sex offense, the theories and treatments directly addressing the individual are going to be the theories that make the most sense. If an individual reading about sex offenders believes the issues are within the social system, the structures and institutions in society, then the system theories are going to make the most sense. If an individual believes these issues are a combination of individual and social systems, then the integrated theories are going to be the most relevant in helping to explain the behaviors and actions of the individuals committing these offenses.

Perhaps of equal importance, however, is understanding the fact that the theories used to explain the origins of sex offending behavior are also used to design ways to treat a sex offender or to reduce sexualized violence in society. Whether addressing the issues in society, in the individual, or both, it is important to understand the direction and application of the research. In 2006, Kirsch and Becker introduced a variety of theoretical questions that are essential to explore further because energies put forward continue to focus on creating a reduction in sex offending behaviors. In short, they asked questions about whether the etiological explanations are appropriately placed in creating behavioral change.[7] Do the theories focused on explaining why a sex offender behaves as they do provide the kind of information necessary for creating a treatment response that reduces sex offending behaviors? More on the issue of sex offender treatment is provided in chapter 13; however, as theories of sex offending behavior expand in efforts to explain the causes of criminal behavior, it is essential to understand and clarify the theoretical focus and its application to offenders.

The more researchers and practitioners learn about adverse childhood experiences, and trauma more broadly, the more a collective understanding is emerging about the importance of early intervention and the value associated with opportunities for conversation around lived experiences as a valuable element for people affected by sexualized violence. People are affected by their experiences, but they sometimes reject labels of being defined by those experiences, for example, stating "I am not my trauma." Whether the harm happens to us or to someone we love, no one wants to be seen as a statistic or feel devalued because of a specific incident. We are all much more than our difficult experiences.

For a collection of takeaways, consider the following information.

- How a sex offender behaves:[8]

  ○ Sex offenders describe pursuing a process of victim selection.
  ○ Sex offenders often work within a system that provides access to potential victims.
  ○ Sex offenders will work actively to ingratiate themselves into the community.

- ◦ Most sexual abuse starts with a violation of a boundary.
- ◦ Sex offenders often practice and employ deception.

- Victim selection:

  - ◦ Rapists discriminate; they look for whatever vulnerability in their victim that might insulate them from detection, capture, and punishment.
  - ◦ Children are vulnerable to rapists for a wide variety of reasons, including because we, as a country, tend to doubt the word of a child when they say they have been victimized by an adult.
  - ◦ Rapists trust prejudices to protect them.
  - ◦ Rapists want easy prey; the more defenseless the better.
  - ◦ Some offenders seek out the weak, the lonely, and those unable to defend themselves; however, strong, social individuals from healthy families and social circles can also be targeted as victims. Why? *Because victims make good victims* (emphasis in the original).[9]

- Social conditions that influence behavior include:[10]

  - ◦ Differences in socialization experiences
  - ◦ Beliefs and attitudes about sexuality
  - ◦ Personality
  - ◦ Alcohol or other substance use/abuse
  - ◦ Situational factors play a role; those who commit sexual assault do not do so at every opportunity.
  - ◦ Less acceptance of personal responsibility
  - ◦ Less understanding of social order, rules, and prosocial beliefs
  - ◦ More immaturity
  - ◦ More irresponsibility

- Individual characteristics (for adult male offenders):[11]

  - ◦ There are no *typical* sex offenders.
  - ◦ Likely to be married or in significant relationship
  - ◦ Either well liked and integrated into the community or socially isolated
  - ◦ Likely to be low in empathy
  - ◦ Likely to have peer approval for forced sex
  - ◦ Likely to support rape myths
  - ◦ More motivated to conflate notions of power and sex
  - ◦ Likely to demonstrate high levels of promiscuity
  - ◦ Likely to demonstrate high levels of hostility
  - ◦ Likely to possess multiple paraphilias

Currently, it is safe to say that most researchers and practitioners agree that what many people believe about sex offending behavior is limited if not completely incorrect.

It is our desire that outdated ideas about sexual violence that are not supported by science or lived experience will eventually fade away. Sadly, it seems that, even with national dialogue around sexual assault, consent, and patterns

Text Box 15.1.   Media Messages about Working to Prevent Sexualized Violence and Harm

Don't read the comments. One of the oft-quoted rules for attempting to stay sane while engaging online is to avoid reading comments after news stories. The comments under sexual assault stories can be maddening and hurtful to read because some individuals are often looking to create a reaction, aren't thinking about the impact of the words before clicking send, and/or are perpetuating inaccurate stereotypes. Despite the negative aspects of instant feedback, there are some positive points of reaching out directly to those doing the reporting work. Many news rooms do have someone reading or monitoring the comments and responding to concerns brought up by the public. Public responses in comments sections have been known to change headlines, change story angles, update/correct facts, and influence coverage of upcoming stories.

- Who should be doing the correcting if a story is blaming the victim?
- When, if at all, do you make a choice to make a comment under a news story?
- Do you feel that inaccurate or hurtful words need to be called out online? Does your opinion change if you know the people involved in the story?
- Have you ever been able to change someone's mind via a comment section? Is that an effective use of a person's time, voice, and energy?

MEDIA-ting the Middle Ground

The FrameWorks Institute has done several deep dives around how the media cover child abuse cases and how that coverage impacts prevention. The 2003 study reminds advocates that sensationalized stories with a focus on the results tend to permeate the storytelling narrative. Prevention opportunities, risk factors, and solutions are often ignored, while the episodic story takes center stage. When the focus is on one vivid incident to one child and that child's experience, the details of abuse and injustice are highlighted, and opportunities for community members to support big-picture prevention solutions are not highlighted.

It is helpful for advocates and frontline professionals to have a plan in advance of being approached by the media. The initial ask may be about how abuse was able to continue in this one life, and the professional response can offer programs and resources that are working successfully in the community to help other children at risk. It is often these sensational stories when children are horribly mistreated that pushes a community to do more for its children. The hope is that solutions and coalitions for prevention can exist and have their successes be recognized before there is a rallying cry following one child.

Every child deserves to be safe. One of the reasons the sensational stories get attention is because they capture the hearts of the public. There is a place for these stories to be told because a light shines on the injustice for these cases. It is helpful for agencies doing the work on prevention to have answers to the follow-up questions ready to go: "What can we do to prevent cases like this? What are we already doing that *is* working?" The sensationalism and episodic nature of how child abuse stories are covered tends to demonize the abusers without providing solutions (FrameWorks). Advocates can build relationships with media ahead of time and offer services as a voice for prevention so the public has ideas of ways to channel their justifiable outrage and grief into something positive that is working on behalf of children.[1]

Deciding Which Messages Move Forward

Consider what you can learn about restorative justice. An introduction was provided in chapter 14. Consider the harsh criticisms attached to current issues regarding the way laws related to sex offenders are challenged as being ineffectual when compared to the mission created when these laws were put into place. Which cases of sexual abuse and harm are not at all appropriate for a restorative process? What elements of a restorative practice speak to the future of sex offender treatment and community response? What elements of restorative justice practice would *not* make the kind of seamless fit communities are looking for in the case of sex crimes? How do these themes compare with traditional outcomes in traditional criminal justice system programs and operations? What might an integrated model look like? What questions remain regarding whether the system as it is can ever be "victim centered"? What questions remain about whether the system as it is can be modified to more fully provide a safe prosecutorial experience for victims? What could an entirely new system focused on victim health and offender accountability look like?

Note

1. Axel Aubrun and Joseph Grady, "How the News Frames Child Maltreatment: Unintended Consequences," August 22, 2003, accessed September 25, 2019, http://www.frameworksinstitute.org/toolkits/canp/resources/pdf/HowTheNewsFrames ChildAbuse.pdf.

of behavior, certain myths and incorrect explanations persist in public posts and private discussions. The authors hope that people will be inspired to learn more about the intersectional work and interdisciplinary data that have been gathered to help inform prevention efforts. This one text cannot dive into all of the interconnected issues in our communities, families, and relationships that create and perpetuate the problem of violence, but, hopefully, it will spark interest in continuing to read, listen, and connect around this problem. We need more people gathered around the table to plan prevention. There is room for you; feel free to bring along several of your best friends.

NOTES

1. See, for example, C. Palmer, "Twelve Reasons Why Rape Is Not Sexually Motivated: A Skeptical Examination," *Journal of Sex Research* 25, no. 4 (November 1988).
2. Stinson et al., 6.
3. Ibid., 6–7.

4. Hugo Schwyzer, "The Accidental Rapist," The Good Men Project, September 26, 2011, accessed August 17, 2019, https://goodmenproject.com/featured-content/the-accidental-rapist/; Amanda Hess, "Rapists Who Don't Think They're Rapists," *Washington City Paper*, November 12, 2009, accessed August 17, 2019, http://www.washingtoncitypaper.com/blogs/sexist/2009/11/12/rapists-who-dont-think-theyre-rapists/.

5. Eric S. Janus, *Failure to Protect: America's Sexual Predator Laws and the Rise of the Preventive State* (Ithaca, NY: Cornell University Press, 2006), 90.

6. Anna C. Salter, *Predators: Pedophiles, Rapists, and Other Sex Offenders* (New York: Basic Books), 2003.

7. Laura G. Kirsch and Judith V. Becker, "Sex Offending: Theory of Problem, Theory of Change, and Implications for Treatment Effectiveness," *Aggression and Violent Behavior* 11, no. 3 (May–June 2006): 208–24.

8. Laura A. Ahearn, "How Can I Protect My Child from Sexual Assault?," Crime Victims Center, accessed August 17, 2019, https://www.parentsformeganslaw.org/prevention-child-sexual-abuse/; Michele Elliott, Kevin Browne, and Jennifer Kilcoyne, "Child Sexual Abuse Prevention: What Offenders Tell Us," *Child Abuse & Neglect* 19, no. 5 (1995): 579–94.

9. These are a collection of assessments including A. Vachss, *Sex Crimes: Ten Years on the Front Lines Prosecuting Rapists and Confronting Their Collaborators* (New York: Henry Holt and Company, 1993), 91; Robin Sax, *It Happens Every Day: Inside the World of a Sex Crime DA* (New York: Prometheus Books, 2009), 79.

10. C. Loh, C. Gidycz, and T. Lobo, "A Prospective Analysis of Sexual Assault Perpetration: Risk Factors Related to Perpetrator Characteristics," *Journal of Interpersonal Violence* 20, no. 10 (2005): 1325–48, https://doi.org/10.1177/0886260505278528; A. Abbey, P. McAuslan, and L. T. Ross, "Sexual Assault Perpetration by College Men: The Role of Alcohol, Misperception of Sexual Intent, and Sexual Beliefs and Experiences," *Journal of Social and Clinical Psychology* 17, no. 2 (1998): 167–95, http://dx.doi.org/10.1521/jscp.1998.17.2.167; D. S. Kosson, J. C. Kelly, and J. W. White, "Psychopathy-Related Traits Predict Self-Reported Sexual Aggression among College Men," *Journal of Interpersonal Violence* 12, no. 2 (1997): 241–54, http://dx.doi.org/10.1177/088626097012002006; K. Rapaport and B. R. Burkhart, "Personality and Attitudinal Characteristics of Sexually Coercive College Males," *Journal of Abnormal Psychology* 93, no. 2 (1984): 216–21, http://dx.doi.org/10.1037/0021-843X.93.2.216; D. Laufersweiler-Dwyer and G. Dwyer, "Sex Offenders and Child Molesters," in *Sexual Assault: The Victims, The Perpetrators*, ed. F. Reddington and B. Kriesel (Carolina Academic Press, 2017), Chapter 13.

11. A. Abbey et al., "A Comparison of Men Who Committed Different Types of Sexual Assault in a Community Sample," *Journal of Interpersonal Violence* 22, no. 12 (2007): 1567–80, http://dx.doi.org/10.1177/0886260507306489; Rudy Flora, *How to Work with Sex Offenders: A Handbook for Criminal Justice, Human Service, and Mental Health Professionals* (New York: Routledge, 2001), 117–20; N. M. Malamuth et al., "Using the Confluence Model of Sexual Aggression to Predict Men's Conflict with Women: A 10-Year Follow-Up Study," *Journal of Personality and Social Psychology* 69, no. 2 (1995): 353–69, http://dx.doi.org/10.1037/0022-3514.69.2.353; N. M. Malamuth et al., "Characteristics of Aggressors against Women: Testing a Model Using a National Sample of College Students," *Journal of Consulting and Clinical Psychology* 59, no. 5 (1991): 670–81, https://www.ncbi.nlm.nih.gov/pubmed/1955602; A. Nicholas Groth with H. Jean Birnbaum, *Men Who Rape: The Psychology of the Offender* (Cambridge, MA: Plenum Press, 1979).

Index

About the Authors

◆ ◆ ◆

Mary Clifford has her PhD in Justice Studies from Arizona State University and is a professor in the Department of Criminal Justice Studies at St. Cloud State University in St. Cloud, Minnesota. A founding member of the Community Anti-Racism Education Initiative on the SCSU campus, she has been engaged in researching and writing about various justice issues including approximately 15 years of active involvement in studying sexual deviance, sex crimes, and sex offenders. Editor of the first comprehensive text on environmental crime, titled *Environmental Crime: Law, Policy and Social Responsibility* (1998), and coeditor of the second edition (2011), Dr. Clifford is also the author of *Identifying and Exploring Security Essentials* (2004).

Alison Feigh, MS, is the director of the Jacob Wetterling Resource Center, a program of Zero Abuse Project. In her role as a subject matter expert on child and teen safety, she works with students, parents, youth workers, faith leaders, law enforcement, and the media to help prevent childhood abuse and abductions. Feigh's work also includes writing curriculum for youth serving organizations, training professionals about online challenges kids face and advocating for families of the missing. Feigh has been working in the abuse prevention field for more than 18 years. She is especially drawn to prevention in faith-based communities and youth serving organizations, collaborating with teens regarding technology challenges, and helping empower parents to talk with their kids about personal and online safety.